Money and Banking

Select Research Papers by the Economists of Reserve Bank of India

Dr. A. Vasudevan, currently Honorary Advisor in the Reserve Bank of India, was Executive Director of the Reserve Bank between May 1996 and end-August 2000. As the Executive Director, he was in-charge of research, statistics, monetary policy and information technology departments. He has had vast international experience — Advisor to Executive Director for India at the International Monetary Fund (IMF) between 1984 and 1989; Member of the Indian Delegations to semi-annual IMF/World Bank and G-24 meetings between 1984 and 1989 and again between 1993 and 2000; represented India at the UNDP Conference on financing of sustainable development at Santiago, Chile; Central Bank Deputy at the Group of Two Deputies' meetings; and Member of the Task Force on Implementation of Standards and the Follow-up Group on the Implementation of Standards, appointed by the Financial Stability Forum.

Among the several Committees on which he served, the important ones were: Expert Group on Saving and Capital Formation in India, Government of India, 1996 (Member), the Working Group on Money Supply, Reserve Bank, 1998 (Vice-Chairman), and the Committee on Technology Upgradation in Banking Sector, Reserve Bank of India, 1999 (Chairman).

Apart from the present volume (edited by him), Dr. Vasudevan has recently authored *Central Banking for Emerging Market Economies* (Academic Foundation, 2003). Described as a "path-breaking work" of "encyclopaedic proportions", within a short time-span this publication received extraordinary praise in several reviews across leading newspapers and journals. Having authored/edited a few other books earlier, Dr. Vasudevan has numerous scholarly writings of his own in various professional journals, both Indian and foreign. He also taught M.A. students at the University of Bombay (1966-69) on the theories of money and economic development and central banking.

Currently Dr. Vasudevan is engaged in writing the history of Reserve Bank of India — a task he has been entrusted with by a committee of the central bank, chaired by Dr. C. Rangarajan.

Money and Banking

Select Research Papers by the Economists of Reserve Bank of India

Edited by
A. Vasudevan

Academic Foundation
NEW DELHI

Published in 2003 by
ACADEMIC FOUNDATION
4772-73 / 23 Bharat Ram Road,
(23 Ansari Road), Darya Ganj,
New Delhi - 110 002.

Phones : 23245001, 02, 03, 04.
Fax : +91-11-23245005
e-mail : academic@vsnl.com
www : academicfoundation.com

Money and Banking: Select Research Papers by the Economists of Reserve Bank of india

edited by A. Vasudevan

ISBN 81-7188-318-4

Laser-Typeset at AF's DTP Division.
Printed at Print Perfect, Mayapuri Industrial Area, New Delhi.

A Personal Note

Editing major research articles written by economists of the Reserve Bank during the last twenty-five years of the twentieth century and bringing out in a book form has been one of my very cherished desires. I could not fulfill this wish during my career at the Reserve Bank of India. On retirement, I took up this task cheerfully out of love for the organization that nurtured many of us research workers and treated us with rare kindness. The reach of the articles to the student and teaching community, at home and abroad, has been limited. This book is intended to help reach this community. A book of major research papers in the area of specialization of the Bank, namely money, finance and banking would, I am sure, help readers to appreciate the insights of those who combine analytics with empirics of the problems.

This volume is dedicated to the Governors and Deputy Governors in charge of the research departments, both past and present, for the encouragement and support they have given unhesitatingly to research activities within the Bank. The economists among them had many a time provided value addition to economic research and to some of the contributions selected for publication in this volume.

I thank the authors of the articles whom I contacted for agreeing to inclusion of their articles with editorial changes. I informed the Chairman of the Editorial Committee of the Reserve Bank of India Occasional Papers about the articles being brought together in book-form. I acknowledge with thanks the pre-publication views of this volume provided by Professors Dilip Nachane and R. Radhakrishna. I am grateful to Dr. C Rangarajan for warm encouragement of this endeavour and for the foreword. Last but not the least, the publishers deserve sincere thanks for enthusiastically undertaking the ardous task entailed in the volumes that contain research articles and for imparting excellent quality in publishing this work.

— **A V**

Contents

Foreword by Dr. C Rangarajan 11

Contributors 13

Symbols Used; Sources 17

Editor's Introduction 19

SECTION I *(page 29)*

1. On Testing Some Hypotheses Concerning the Transmission Mechanism of Monetary Policy: The Indian Experience

A Vasudevan and **K A Menon** 33

2. A Short-term Model to Forecast Monetary Aggregates — Interim Results

D C Rao, **T R Venkatachalam** and **A Vasudevan** 43

SECTION II *(page 57)*

3. Reserve Money: Concepts and Policy Implications for India

C Rangarajan and **Anoop Singh** 61

4. Weighted Monetary Aggregates: Rationale and Relevance for India

Narendra Jadhav 73

5. The Dynamics of Money Supply Process in India : An Alternative Empirical Framework
Himanshu Joshi and **Indranil Bhattacharyya** 81

6. Residency in Money Supply
Deba Prasad Rath and **Indranil Sen Gupta** 89

7. Estimating Money Demand Function: A Cointegration Approach
Ashok K Nag and **Ghanshyam Upadhyay** 99

8. The Demand for Money in India : Stability Revisited
Himanshu Joshi and **Mridul Saggar** 107

9. Modelling Buffer Stock of Money : An Indian Experience
B K Bhoi 117

SECTION III *(page 129)*

10. Financial Innovation : Determinants and Implications for Monetary Policy — A Model
N Nagarajan 131

11. Credit Availability and Small Firms : A Probit Analysis of Panel Data
Renu Kohli 141

12. Dynamics of Interaction Between Government Deficit and Domestic Debt in India
C Rangarajan, **Anupam Basu** and **Narendra Jadhav** 151

13. Fiscal Deficit, External Balance and Monetary Growth
C Rangarajan and **M S Mohanty** 169

14. Analytics of Monetary Management
A Vasudevan 195

15. Money, Output and Prices
Y S R Sarma 207

16. Exchange Rate Management in India : An Expirical Evaluation
Michael Debabrata Patra and **Sitikantha Pattanaik** 215

17. REER : The Leading Indicator
Sitikantha Pattanaik 227

SECTION IV *(page 239)*

18. Banks in Financial Intermediation: Performance and Issues
D Ajit and **R D Bangar** 241

19. Scale Economies in Banking — Indian Experience in Deregulated Era
Goutam Chatterjee 265

20. Technical, Allocative and Scale Efficiency of Public Sector Banks in India
Abhiman Das 275

सत्यमेव जयते

Dr. C. RANGARAJAN
CHAIRMAN

बारहवाँ वित्त आयोग
जवाहर व्यापार भवन,
1, टॉलस्टॉय मार्ग, नई दिल्ली-110 001
TWELFTH FINANCE COMMISSION
JAWAHAR VYAPAR BHAWAN,
1, TOLSTOY MARG,
NEW DELHI- 110 001

Foreword

I am happy to write the Foreword to this collection of research papers edited by Dr. A. Vasudevan. "Reserve Bank of India Occasional Papers" acts as a channel for the dissemination of the research work that is undertaken in the Reserve Bank of India. At the same time, it acts as a catalyst of research. Like all central banks, the Reserve Bank of India is also active in several areas of research. The quality of research output very much depends upon the quality of the people working particularly in the research departments. Reserve Bank of India had a galaxy of distinguished economists in the Fifties and Sixties. Thereafter, the stock started depleting. As Dr. Vasudevan has himself pointed out, there was no recruitment of fresh economists from the market for almost two decades between 1965 and 1985. I had a role to play in restarting the process of direct recruitment. The young researchers recruited since that period have blossomed into full economists whose contribution are getting well merited recognition now. As a result, the 'Occasional Papers' has also acquired a new status and commands respect among professional economists. This collection of research papers gives the flavour of the research work that is getting done in the Reserve Bank of India. They reveal both maturity and technical excellence.

I congratulate Dr. Vasudevan in undertaking this effort and choosing a spectrum of articles that is truly representative of the research in the Reserve Bank of India.

CRangarajan.

July 21, 2003

Telephone : 011-23701110, 23701111 Fax : 011-23701110, E-mail : chrtfc@nic.in

Contributors

Names of the authors/co-authors of respective papers included in the present volume are arranged alphabetically (according to last name). The corresponding designations represent current/latest position held.

D Ajit
Director, Department of Economic Analysis & Policy,
Reserve Bank of India, Mumbai
(Now on sabbatical leave)

R D Bangar
Formerly: Assistant Adviser, Department of Economic Analysis & Policy,
Reserve Bank of India, Mumbai

Anupam Basu[+]
Deputy Director, African Department, International Monetary Fund,
Washington D C

Indranil Bhattacharya
Research Officer, Monetary Policy Department,
Reserve Bank of India, Mumbai

B K Bhoi
Director, Department of Economic Analysis & Policy,
Reserve Bank of India, Mumbai

Goutam Chatterjee
Director, Department of Statistical Analysis & Computer Services,
Reserve Bank of India, Kolkata

Abhiman Das
Assistant Adviser, Department of Statistical Analysis & Computer Services,
Reserve Bank of India, Mumbai

Narendra Jadhav
Principal Adviser, Department of Economic Analysis & Policy,
Reserve Bank of India, Mumbai

Himanshu Joshi
Director, Monetary Policy Department, Reserve Bank of India, Mumbai

Renu Kohli
Assistant General Manager, Reserve Bank of India, Kolkata

K A Menon
Formerly: General Manager, Reserve Bank of India, Tiruvananthapuram

M S Mohanty
Economist, Bank for International Settlements, Basle, (Switzerland)

Ashok Nag
Director, Department of Statistical Analysis & Computer Services,
Reserve Bank of India, Mumbai

N Nagarajan
Chief Economist, Indian Banks' Association

Michael Debabrata Patra
Adviser, Department of Economic Analysis & Policy,
Reserve Bank of India, Mumbai

Sitikantha Pattanaik
Assistant Adviser, Department of Economic Analysis & Policy,
Reserve Bank of India, Mumbai

C Rangarajan
Chairman, 12th Finance Commission, Government of India, New Delhi
and Former Governor, Reserve Bank of India, Mumbai

D C Rao +
Formerly: Director, International Finance Department,
World Bank, Washington D C

Deba Prasad Rath
Director, Department of Economic Analysis & Policy,
Reserve Bank of India, Mumbai

Mridul Saggar
Director, Monetary Policy Department,
Reserve Bank of India, Mumbai

Y S R Sarma (Late)
Formerly: Adviser-in-charge, Monetary Policy Department,
Reserve Bank of India, Mumbai

Indranil Sengupta
Assistant Adviser, Department of Economic Analysis & Policy,
Reserve Bank of India, Mumbai

Anoop Singh +
Director, Western Hemisphere Department, International Monetary Fund,
Washington D C

A Vasudevan
Formerly: Executive Director, Reserve Bank of India, Mumbai
(Presently Honorary Adviser, Reserve Bank of India, Mumbai)

T R Venkatachalam
Formerly: Adviser-in-charge, Monetary Policy Department,
Reserve Bank of India, Mumbai

Ghanshyam Upadhyay
Assistant Adviser, Department of Statistical Analysis & Computer Services,
Reserve Bank of India, Mumbai

\+ On secondment from the International Monetary Fund/World Bank to the Reserve Bank of India at the time of the writing of the papers selected for publication here.

Use of Symbols

... Indicates deletion from the original paper.

[ ] Indicates addition to the original (in order to impart continuity to the argument).

( ) Indicates corrections made to the errors (mainly typing) in the paper.

[[ ]] Indicates replacement of the original part: this has been kept to the barest minimum.

Where the deletions of facts– statistical information are major, the editor's note has been specifically added.

Details of the Sources of the Selected Papers

1. On Testing Some Hypotheses Concerning the Transmission Mechanism of Monetary Policy: The Indian Experience, 1956-76, Reserve Bank of India, Recent Developments in Monetary Theory and Policy, Bombay 1978, pp. 138-151.
2. A Short-term Model to Forecast Monetary Aggregates–Interim Results, Reserve Bank of India Occasional Papers, 1981, December, pp. 113-140.
3. Reserve Money: Concepts and Policy Implications for India, RBI Occasional Papers, 1984, June, pp. 1-26.
4. Weighted Monetary Aggregates: Rationale and Relevance for India, RBI Occasional Papers, 1989, March, pp. 39-56.
5. The Dynamics of Money Supply Process in India: An Alternative Empirical Framework, RBI Occasional Papers, 1999, Monsoon, pp. 223-241.
6. Residency in Money Supply, RBI Occasional Papers, 1999, Summer, pp. 1-21.
7. Estimating Money Demand Function: A Co-integration Approach, RBI Occasional Papers, 1993, March, pp. 47-66.
8. The Demand for Money in India: Stability Revisited, RBI Occasional Papers, 1995, June, pp. 79-100.
9. Modelling Buffer Stock of Money: An Indian Experience, RBI Occasional Papers, 1995, March, pp. 27-49.
10. Financial Innovation: Determinants and Implications for Monetary Policy– A Model, RBI Occasional Papers, 1988, December, pp. 329-355.
11. Credit Availability and Small Firms: A Probit Analysis of Panel Data, RBI Occasional Papers, 1997, March, pp. 1-24.

12. Dynamics of Interaction Between Government Deficit and Domestic Debt in India, RBI Occasional Papers, 1989, September, pp. 163-220.
13. Fiscal Deficit, External Balance and Monetary Growth, RBI Occasional Papers, 1997, December, pp. 583-653.
14. Analytics of Monetary Management, RBI Occasional Papers, 1991, September-December, pp. 183-208.
15. Money, Output and Prices, RBI Occasional Papers, 1991, September-December, pp 209-225.
16. Exchange Rate Management in India: An Empirical Evaluation, RBI Occasional Papers, 1998, September, pp. 185-214.
17. REER: The Leading Indicator, RBI Occasional Papers, 1999, Monsoon, pp. 123-151.
18. Banks in Financial Intermediation: Performance and Issues, RBI Occasional Papers, 1997, June and September, pp. 303-349.
19. Scale Economies in Banking–Indian Experience in Deregulated Era, RBI Occasional Papers, 1997, March, pp. 37-59.
20. Technical, Allocative and Scale Efficiency of Public Sector Banks in India, RBI Occasional Papers, 1997, June and September. pp. 279-301.

Introduction

RESEARCH in most central banks of the world centers around issues relating to money, banking, and financial markets. Where financial markets are weak and unorganized, the center of attention would be mainly on money and banking. But many of the internally prepared research pieces in the central banks hardly come out of the closet and when they do, they often appear as articles by individual researchers. These articles often appear in journals published outside the central banking organizations partly because the authors get the satisfaction that their articles are refereed and partly because the articles are likely to be widely read not only by central bankers but also by others including researchers and advanced students in institutions of learning. Notwithstanding such a revealed preference, a number of researchers in the central banks have articles to their credit in the journals of their own organizations. Where central banks have their own research journals, they often prefer to get the articles refereed by experts from outside their organizations in order to quell the criticism of in-breeding and favoritism in the event the articles by staff members were published without being vetted or refereed.

The Reserve Bank of India has promoted research right from the early years of its existence. Economic research was placed on an organized mould with the establishment of a research and statistics department on August 01, 1945. Although some of the researchers who joined the Bank went to academic institutions or to Government or to international organizations quite early in their careers, many stayed back and earned considerable reputation as good research workers. Some of the distinguished names of the past which were on the rolls of the Bank till say 1965 — the first generation of economists in the Reserve Bank, as I would call them — that readily come to one's mind are : J J Anjaria, V V Bhatt, A K Banerjee, A G Chandavarkar, Dharma Kumar, K L Deshpande, A Hasib,

V M Jakhade, K S Krishnaswamy, V B Kadam, D R Khatkhate, B K Madan, S S Madalgi, N A Mujumdar, G Madiman, M Narasimham, P D Ojha, P S N Prasad, V G Pendharkar, P K Pani, K N Raj, V K Ramaswami, N A Sarma, S L N Simha, B R Shenoy, V K Sastry, S S Tarapore, T R Venkatachalam, and T K Velayudham. Of these, five persons had risen in the Reserve Bank to the rank of Deputy Governor, four others had risen to the rank of Executive Director, six others joined international institutions, three others joined the academic field, and one became the Governor of the Bank. The first generation researchers wrote extensively on policy issues and participated as chairpersons/members in various working/study groups of both the Reserve Bank and Government of India. Some of them also represented India at the International Monetary Fund either as Executive Directors or as Alternate Executive Directors. Many of their articles appeared in journals published either in India or outside the country. Unfortunately for the first generation economists in the Bank, they could not articulate their views through an in-house research journal simply because such a journal did not exist.

It was only in 1975 an in-house research journal was started under the name of Reserve Bank Staff Occasional Papers but it did not carry much steam. In fact, the steam was lost by 1978. Many of the first generation economists had either retired or left the Bank and those who were left behind were generally burdened with responsibilities of senior positions within the Bank. As a result, they had very little time left for writing independent pieces. Their burden was further aggravated by the fact that there was very little of recruitment of fresh economists from the market between 1965 and 1985. Realizing the problem, they made an attempt in late 1977 and early 1978 to heighten interest in monetary economics and policy by organizing a seminar on the recent developments in monetary theory and policy. The seminar facilitated the researchers in the Bank to interact with the academics in India but the Bank's initiative turned out to be an isolated effort with no well designed framework of promoting long-term research within the organization. Nonetheless, the initiative underscored the need for encouraging the staff researchers to express themselves and to reach a wider reading public on a continual basis. The Bank, therefore, decided to reaffirm its faith in internal research and encourage the economists to contribute to the in-house research journal. Since there was a break in the publication of the Staff Occasional Papers, it was thought that the journal could well assume a different title, namely, the Reserve Bank of India Occasional Papers, to give an air of a new look.

The new journal would have gone the way of its earlier incarnation had not the researchers persevered with it. But sadly enough, it was not marketed well. Despite its relatively low price, the journal's subscription has been very limited. With the induction of what I would call the third generation of economists since 1985, the journal, however, got some added attention. The shift in the economic policy regime in 1991 also played a part in igniting lively interest among the researchers in monetary, credit and banking policy matters. Besides, the leadership in the research wing of the Bank ensured particularly since about the middle of the 1990s, that articles in the journal are screened and refereed by a panel of outside experts. A number of original articles have appeared in the journal, good many of them being on money and banking. Nonetheless, very few research workers outside the Bank could get hold of them partly because very few libraries subscribe to the journal.

It is against this background the present volume of select 'papers' ('readings', so to say) has been conceived. The objective of the volume is not to include articles in a large number of areas but to include only those that focus on money, monetary policy and banking issues — areas in which the Reserve Bank's expertise is widely recognized. Almost all the selected papers with the exception of one have been taken from the RBI's research journal.

In selecting the papers, I placed maximum emphasis on those papers that emerged from 1991 because of the importance of the year from the point of view of the economic policy regime. The shift in the regime from the dirigiste to relatively market-oriented one has been widely acknowledged as a watershed in the Indian economic development policy. These papers, I believe, are highly relevant even today. However, a few papers relating to the period prior to 1991 are also worthy of a close look because of their criticality to the issues that confront central bankers.

There are in all 20 papers in this volume. The first two papers in the volume stand on their own for their intrinsic value. The first one by the editor in collaboration with Menon on the transmission mechanism of policy was the first one to appear on the subject in the Indian monetary economics literature; it tried to empirically find out the transmission channel for the 20-year period from 1956-57. It was written for the seminar on recent developments in monetary theory and policy essentially to get a feedback from the academics as to what they think would be the transmission channel of monetary policy in India. Those who have background knowledge of the high inflation periods of the 1970s in India would recall that many Indian economists regarded the high inflation rate of 1973-74 and 1974-75 as essentially a monetary phenomenon caused by a large increase in money supply. Was this view based on empirical investigation or was it just contextual to the specific years in the 1970s was the question that haunted the authors of the paper. A longer period analysis, the authors felt, should be attempted to gain insights about the transmission channels of policy. The choice of the initial year was dictated by the consideration that it was from that year the Indian development policy took a turn to regulation and overarching State planning. The conclusion of the paper was eclectic in the sense that no policy action could be expected to achieve the desired outcome with certainty. There could be no single transmission channel for policy makers to bank on. Perhaps this conclusion would be inevitable even when empirical exercises are extended for more recent periods. In fact the problem of finding out an appropriate transmission mechanism has turned out to be intractable even in industrialized economies where the financial markets are much more integrated than in developing or emerging market economies.

The second paper is on the short-term monetary model by a group of authors led by D C Rao (then of the World Bank on a special assignment with the Reserve Bank for a short period of time). It again was the first of its kind in the times it appeared. The paper was written against the background of the well-entrenched thinking of the times that a forecast of the monetary aggregates would have to be an integral part of any financial program. In case economic developments pertaining to national income, the inflation rate, balance of payments, or other macroeconomic variables are not favorable, the authorities will have to take corrective actions including changes in monetary management. Before taking any monetary or credit policy measure, central banks will need some projections of monetary aggregates so that they could compare the likely outcomes with or without the contemplated policy measure. The paper of Rao *et al* signaled the need for forecasting of monetary aggregates in the Indian context. The model was small in size and therefore amenable to control. However, the approach may not be replicated once large quantum of information on economic and monetary / financial variables become available.

The next four papers focus on central bank money (also referred to as reserve money or high-powered money) and the supply of money. The first of these papers is on reserve money concepts authored by C Rangarajan and Anoop Singh. Reserve money as a concept has been made popular in India only since 1977 after the publication of the Second Working Group

Report on money supply. Prior to the publication of this report, the Reserve Bank used to provide yearly data on reserve money but after the publication of the report, the Bank began to publish reserve money data more frequently in its Bulletins. The concept has been in use in the literature on monetary economics but has not been used in India owing to the dominance of thinking in terms of credit planning as an adjunct to the overall economic planning process. The paper throws light on the conceptual issues that arise on account of the changes in cash reserve ratios that were for the first time introduced from May 1973. The paper is useful in that it provides insights on the value of the money multiplier, depending on the measurement of reserve money. The next paper on weighted monetary aggregates by N D Jadhav should be viewed essentially as the song of the skeptic. The criticism that measurement of money supply with the public in terms of currency and deposits (with variations at times in terms of either demand or aggregate deposits) is not satisfactory because of equal weights given for both the currency and deposit components is intellectually appealing but has not been found to be realistic. No central bank in the world could afford to get away from the simple sum approach to the measurement of money supply. An advantage with the simple sum approach is its simplicity : it is easily understood both by laymen and market participants. Assignment of weights for the components is a difficult task in itself and cannot be a priori defended on any well-established theoretical grounds. Empirical work by Jadhav shows that the weighted aggregates have in fact not outperformed the simple sum approach in terms of providing insights on the conduct of monetary policy in India. It appears that the same result would be obtained if empirical testing were to be conducted with the data available for most countries of the world.

Money supply processes often are explained in terms of money demand. In other words, money supply would have to match with the robustly estimated money demand in order to set up monetary equilibrium. But this need not be so. Nor should money supply be only viewed in descriptive terms of what constitutes the transactions use of money or transactions-cum-interest bearing uses of money. In fact the processes could be empirically explained from the point of view of sources of change in money supply, as the paper by Himanshu Joshi and Indranil Bhattacharyya shows. The approach of this paper is largely reminiscent of the approach adopted by the so-called Keynesians in the early 1970s and by the Bank of England under the influence of Charles Goodhart. There is sufficiently useful evidence to show that central banks often make estimations of short-term credit demand and balance of payments outcomes in order to obtain the overall requirements of money supply. Once the required money supply is determined, central banks estimate the likely supply of deposits in the system, and obtain the limits to the residual, namely currency under the uses side. The paper by Deb Prasad Rath and Indranil Sengupta is more contextual : it should be read along with the report of the Working Group on Money Supply: Analytics and Methodology of Compilation published by the Reserve Bank of India in 1998 (not included in this volume). The treatment that one could accord to capital flows in the context of globalization in the compilation of money supply should be based on the residency of the economic units in question. The paper supports the residency criterion used by the Working Group since it tallies with the best international practices, besides providing information efficient outcomes.

Three papers on the demand for money have been included in this volume. On the demand for money in India, the literature is vast. A survey article by the editor that appeared in the Reserve Bank Staff Occasional Papers in 1977 (not included here) showed the enormity of interest of Indian economists in finding out the influences that work on the demand for money beginning with the 1950s. The survey article showed that the influence of real income, whether at the aggregative or at sectoral levels, on the demand for money was predominant. This result should not be baffling when rate variables in the financial markets were regulated and generally inflexible. Besides, the absence of financial innovations indicated that the demand for money was stable. The shift in policy regime should, theoretically speaking, lead to financial innovations and flexible interest rates and bring about instability in the demand for money. If instability exists, then monetary aggregates cannot be viewed as useful targets of monetary policy. Ashok K Nag and Ghanshyam Upadhyay in their paper argue that long term relationships as envisaged in the literature on monetary targeting hold good and estimate the money demand function for India using a cointegration approach. This was perhaps the first time this approach was adopted in the Indian case. Himanshu Joshi and Mridul Saggar in their paper on the subject reported more or less similar results. Their paper appears as the seventh in this volume. On the other hand, B. K. Bhoi questions the stability in the demand for money function in India. Using the buffer stock approach to the demand for money, Bhoi observed that income elasticity has been on the downward drift in the 1980s partly on account of financial innovations.

The next two papers in the volume are somewhat off-beat. Nagarajan's paper on financial innovation published in 1988 was perhaps the earliest to appear on the subject in India. It showed that financial innovation has a self-sustaining tendency and would be accentuated by interest rate spreads, use of modern technology and restrictions imposed by the monetary authorities including monetary targeting. The paper shows that when financial innovation is at work, neither monetary targeting nor interest rate regulation would yield desired or expected results.

The credit view as against the money view has been hotly debated in the literature in the 1990s and the size of the firm often was viewed as a factor in gaining access to bank credit. Small firms often are said to be rationed out by risk-averse lenders but such an outcome may not be helpful from the point of view of the social good. Regulation of financial intermediaries, as argued by Ms Renu Kohli, could be usefully deployed once a determination is made that credit provided to small firms could give rise to social gains that would outweigh the losses that may arise from regulation.

Monetary policy discussions in India have to be conducted in the context of the fiscal policy that is pursued and the expected balance of payments outcome. The latter factor, however, has been insignificant till recently — at any rate till the second half of the 1990s. More often than not, the discussions focused on the unfavorable effects of large fiscal deficits on monetary expansion and on external position of the economy. The impact of the fiscal deficit on money supply depends on the extent of financing of it by the Reserve Bank vis-à-vis others. The paper by C Rangarajan, Anupam Basu and Narendra Jadhav brings out the limitations of domestic debt accumulation by the Government and the dangers of monetary financing of fiscal deficit. Yet another paper on fiscal-monetary nexus and the effects on external balance by C Rangarajan and M S Mohanty contains a model that shows that fiscal deficit in general results in widening of the external current account deficit, depending on the way in which deficit is financed. The model shows that in case the deficit is monetised, the price and income effects would reinforce each other and lead to a further deterioration in external balance. The paper thus leaves a message that deficit financing would often entail costs in terms of loss of control over inflation. Even when the deficit is financed by market borrowing, the paper suggests there would be a need to have prudent limits over it.

Two papers that appeared at the time of the regime shift in 1991 give a flavor of thinking within the Reserve Bank at the beginning of the 1990s. The paper by the editor was forward looking in tone and tenor. It argues for interest rate flexibility, resorting to market based monetary policy procedures such as the use of open market operations, and development of financial markets in order to use monetary policy for optimal domestic debt management. The paper also underscores the need for relaxing rules about portfolio allocation and bringing down reserve ratios. The paper by Y S R Sarma, on the other hand, is much more conventional in its approach. It studies the relationship between money, output and prices and argues that prices are well explained by changes in output and broad money. Holding the output to be constant, the paper observes that the lagged effects of change in broad money on prices were significant for about three years following the change on the basis of the data for the period 1971-72 through 1989-90.

Two papers on exchange rate issues have been included in the volume essentially to convey the message that exchange rate determination being done at the market place would have to be reckoned as a critical indicator of policy and may have to be managed as the economy opens up to the outside world. The paper by Michael Debabrata Patra and Sitikantha Pattanaik gives a historical account of exchange rate management during the 1990s and demonstrates the need for use of indicators of exchange market pressures and interventions as tools for evaluating the exchange rate policy as a part of the overall monetary policy. The paper by Sitikantha Pattanaik on real effective exchange rate as a leading indicator provides a useful insight that market perceptions about the future nominal exchange rates could result in large deviations from the normal capital flows.

The last three papers in the volume are on banking. Ajit and Bangar give an overarching view of the performance of banks in India in financial intermediation and raise issues having a bearing on banking reforms in India since about 1992-93. The banking reforms led to considerable competition in banking and the one way of improving efficiency is through exploitation of scale economies. Goutam Chatterjee's paper studies the experience in this area and reaches positive conclusions. One of the interesting points made by Chatterjee is that small and medium sized banks will gain in terms of cost efficiency provided they expand their business by opening branches. Chatterjee also points to the possibility of small and medium sized banks to merge or regroup in order to reap scale economies.

Abhiman Das gives an account of the various measures of efficiency of banks and observes that while there was some decline in the overall efficiency in the period since 1991-92, the change was not significant. The allocative efficiency on the other hand seemed to have improved during this period. Deregulation, according to Das, was not the only factor affecting the efficiency of a bank and much depends on the bank's risk exposure. The paper gives a hope that the banking sector, once it overcomes technical inefficiency problems, could improve the overall efficiency to a substantial extent.

The papers presented in the volume provide a rich flavor of research in the Bank that could be utilized in gaining useful insights about the conduct of monetary and banking policies in India. Although the empirical evidence cited in the papers end in most cases with the early to mid-1990s, the papers suggest that policy actions in general could be justified by the reported empirical exercises. Obviously, the results would not hold good for all time to come but they may still be good for the near medium term from now, at least surely so long as the financial sector has not fully developed and integrated.

Mumbai **A. Vasudevan**
August 03, 2003 Editor

Section I

THE two papers included in this section should be viewed in the context in which they were written. Till the early 1970s, the Reserve Bank of India had employed very few known monetary policy instruments and that too very sparingly. The ones that were used were : the Bank rate, the statutory liquidity ratio (i.e., the ratio of holdings of government and other approved securities to total deposit liabilities), the net liquidity ratio (the ratio of a bank's cash balances in its vaults and with the RBI, current account deposits with other banks, and investments in government and other approved securities less its borrowings from the RBI and other notified institutions to its total deposit liabilities), the selective credit controls (i.e., controls on advances against commodities in short supply or are subjected to speculative attack), and moral suasion. Refinancing with the above stated ratios in place was frequently used as an important means of liquidity management. Instruments such as the cash reserve ratio (CRR) were hardly wielded. However, from around 1972 onwards, monetary policy was under pressure partly because of the deterioration of the fiscal position and partly because of price increases. The Reserve Bank's credit to Government was not subjected to limits. The Bank also acted as the public debt manager and helped to ensure that the announced market borrowings of the Government sector would be realized. It had to therefore focus its attention essentially to controlling the banking system's credit to the non-pure government sector (known in India as the 'commercial' sector). As a result, monetary policy took the colour of credit policy since the credit of the banking system (including the RBI's) to the pure government sector and net foreign exchange assets of the banking system were exogenously determined. Money supply with the public (M1) was the chief monetary variable, though data on broad money referred to as 'aggregate monetary resources (AMR)' (till 1977) was also provided as part of monetary statistics*. M1 for all good purposes was influenced only to the extent that bank credit to the commercial sector was effectively controlled. Even in the case of bank credit to the commercial sector, the monetary authorities had only constrained freedom in the sense that the public sector banks@ were mandated by the Union Government to provide credit to certain specified sectors — agriculture, food procurement operations, small scale industries, small artisans, and other small borrowers, exports, and public sector undertakings. The public sector banks were required to realize quantitative targets of credit flows in relation to such sectors by specified dates.

Under the circumstances, what would be the channels through which the policy makers could ensure that their actions would transmit their influence throughout the economy ? Would the transmission channels cited in the literature on monetary economics work in the Indian conditions ? There were no academic or official studies till the mid-1970s that addressed these questions with reference to India. All that the policy makers could depend on were informed judgments that both price stability and enhancement of growth would be promoted through 'controlled expansion' of money supply during the 1950s and 1960s and through efforts at credit planning during much of the 1970s. The first article in this volume tried to fill the vacuum in the Indian literature on the subject.

It was in the late 1970s even the one central monetary indicator, namely M1, had become unreliable. Economic units, subjected to high doses of inflation during the first half of the 1970s, felt the need for saving in assets that fetched for them some nominal rates of return. Time deposits with banks provided an important avenue for saving. Time deposits were made up of fixed deposits with definite maturity periods and reasonable interest rates and minimum amounts in saving deposit accounts that attract an interest rate lower than the fixed deposit of short term

* Aggregate monetary resources (AMR) represented narrow money and time deposits with banks. This measure was mentioned right from the days of the first Working Group on money supply published in 1961. But it was not used for policy purposes almost till 1982. In fact till 1977, there was no nomenclature such as M1 and M2 in the Indian monetary economics literature. But what is M2 in the general literature is referred to as M3 in India by the second Working Group on money supply published in 1977. M2 in India reckoned not only M1 but also savings accounts with post offices that often performed the task of collecting deposits and allowing their withdrawals like ordinary banks.

@ Public sector banks are those owned by the Government of India and by the Reserve Bank of India. The State Bank of India, the largest of the Indian commercial banks, was converted into a public sector bank in the middle of the 1950s with predominantly large share holding by the Reserve Bank of India. 14 other major Indian scheduled commercial banks were nationalized in 1969 and 8 more Indian scheduled banks were nationalized in 1980. These banks were subjected to stipulations about what had come to be known as priority sector lending and such loans would have to form a specified ratio of total loans and advances. Such ratios apply to each bank uniformly.

maturity (say of 3-month duration). Commercial banks were required by law to report to the Reserve Bank the demand and time deposits held with them every week. With a view to gaining an appropriate measure of interest-bearing deposits, the Reserve Bank directed the commercial banks in 1978 on the method of apportionment of saving deposits into 'demand' and 'time' liability components. However, not all the banks followed this directive uniformly and on the same date. It took almost three years for all the banks to comply with the spirit of the directive**. In the meantime, there was considerable confusion about the correct measurement of M1 that was used for policy purposes. It had become difficult for researchers as well as policy makers to forecast M1. Without forecasting money supply expansion, it had become difficult to estimate the likely demands on credit that will be made by the Government and commercial sectors. A monetary model for the short term had thus become a necessity. The second article in this volume attempted to provide such a model.

** In August 1978, the Regulation 7 of the RBI Scheduled Banks' Regulations, 1951 was amended. Under the original regulations, the maximum amount that was permitted to be withdrawn from the savings bank account without previous notice was regarded as a demand liability, and the excess over the maximum amount, as a time liability. The regulation required: "Every scheduled bank shall calculate the proportion, as at the close of business on the 30th June and the 31st December of each year, of its demand liabilities to its total liabilities on the above basis and the proportion so calculated shall, until the date of the next calculation, be used for determining the demand and time liabilities for the purpose of these regulations. The amount so calculated shall be included in the total of 'demand liabilities' and 'time liabilities' respectively in the form specified in regulation 6 and shall also be set out separately in the footnote to that form." As the regulation gave freedom to banks to decide on the maximum amounts of withdrawal from savings account, several banks reported all or larger part of their savings deposits as demand liabilities. In October 1977, the Reserve Bank of India suggested that the method followed so far was not realistic. Instead, the average monthly minimum balances arrived at for crediting interest should be treated as 'time liabilities' and the rest of the amounts as 'demand liabilities'. The suggested amendment was made effective from August 16, 1978. But this amendment was carried out by all the banks at different time periods and for the system as a whole, the amounts arrived at as demand deposits or time deposits and as M1 were unrealistic and volatile. Adjustments were made therefore for the demand deposits and time deposits and they were published in the Bank's Bulletin for July 1981 under the title, "M1 Data for the Period March 1978-January 1981." This was done not only to ensure that there is no spuriousness in the M1 data but also to enable the Reserve Bank to forecast M1 which till then was considered the critical monetary magnitude.

1

On Testing Some Hypotheses Concerning the Transmission Mechanism of Monetary Policy

The Indian Experience, 1956-76

A Vasudevan • K A Menon

ONE of the major constraints to optimisation of monetary policy has been the inadequacy of knowledge on the relevant mechanism through which the effects of monetary policy changes are transmitted through the economy. The theoretical literature on the subject, despite being voluminous ...appears to be of little help to policy-makers in developing economies: this is because, in the first instance, there is no unanimity of views on what constitutes the appropriate transmission mechanism, and secondly, the discussions generally pertain to the economic situations as obtained in highly industrialised countries, especially the United States. In the circumstances, therefore, the monetary authorities in developing economies, while formulating their policy-mix, have to exercise considerable judgement in choosing those analytical propositions underlying the transmission mechanism which are validated by the economic experience of the recent past.

The main object of this paper is to test empirically the various hypotheses related to the transmission channels with reference to the Indian data during the twenty-years between 1956-57 and 1975-76. The year 1956-57 has been chosen as the point of origin, since it marks the beginning of conscious and deliberate attempts to raise the rate of growth of the economy with a financing pattern that reposes faith in 'forced savings'. Hypotheses-testing has been conducted mainly by means of regression equations. For reducing the bias of strong common time trends, changes in the variables are employed in the linear equations. Before conducting this empirical analysis which forms part of Section II of this paper, an effort has been made in Section I to formulate a set of hypotheses concerning the transmission mechanism with reference to the economic environment obtained in India, in the process, overviewing briefly through the literature on the subject. Section III draws some inferences from the discussion of the previous two sections.

I

The transmission mechanism is generally viewed in terms of three channels viz., (a) the rate of interest (or the cost-of-capital) channel; (b) the wealth effect channel; and (c) the credit rationing channel. However, in view of the emphasis recently placed by monetarists, on the quantity of money as "a primary determinant of changes in total spending, and should thereby be given a major emphasis in economic stabilisation programmes",[1] it is useful to refer to the money supply channel as distinct from the rest, notwithstanding the fact that elements of both the money supply and rate of interest channels are fused into the portfolio balance approach.

Money Supply Channel

The transmission mechanism in the classical economic thought was essentially in terms of the money supply channel. In the Cambridge equation, the demand for money is made equivalent to K times the money national income (Yn). K represents the pattern of payments and receipts which is determined by custom and social institutions and is amenable to slow changes only. On the other hand, the supply of money is assumed to be exogenously given. In equilibrium, the supply of money would be equal to the demand for it. The direction of causation is determined by the assumption of the exogeneity of money supply, so that income responds to changes in the stock of money.

The views expressed here are the authors' own and are not to be attributed to the organization to which they belong.

Picking up the argument of the classicists and basing on several kinds of empirical evidence,[2] the modern monetarists explain that the exogeneity of money supply arises not because of the erroneous belief that money supply is under the control of monetary authorities, but because of (a) the exogeneity of bank reserves or cash base and (b) the rigid link between bank reserves and money supply. They justify the exogeneity of money supply in terms of the deposit multiplier or bank credit multiplier theory which is given by the formula:[3]

$$MS = RM \frac{(1+C/D)}{(R/D+C/D)}$$

where MS is money supply with the public in its broad connotation (viz., currency with the public, net demand and net time deposits of the banking system), RM is the reserve money or cash base; C/D the ratio of currency to aggregate deposits and R/D the ratio of bank reserves to aggregate deposits. The presence of these two ratios in the formula shows that the credit multiplier theory is essentially behavioural in content in that the portfolio selections by banks and public's references play a major part.

The direction of causality implied in the money supply channel can be simplified and presented pictorially to imply any one of the following:

(a) $MS \longrightarrow Yn$

(b) $AMR \longrightarrow Yn$

(c) (i) $RM \longrightarrow MS \longrightarrow Yn$

(ii) $RM \longrightarrow Yn$ or (iii) $RM \longrightarrow AMR \longrightarrow Yn$

(d) (i) $BR \longrightarrow MS \longrightarrow Yn$

or

(ii) $BR \longrightarrow AMR \longrightarrow Yn$

MS is the money supply with the public; AMR the broader concept of money supply called the "aggregate monetary resources", RM the reserve money, BR the bank reserves (Cash in hand plus reserves with the central bank) and Yn the net national product at current prices.

It is, however, possible to have variants of arrow exhibit (d), given above. As shown by A. James Meigs (1962), it is possible to study the relationship between money stock and 'excess' reserves or 'free' reserves, concepts which are often regarded as reliable measure of banks' potential to create credit and thereby their portfolio behaviour. 'Excess' or 'free' reserves, however, would be more reliable indicators of banks' behaviour than total bank reserves under two conditions, viz., that banks generally maintain excess cash over the statutory limits with the central banks in *large quantities* and/or that banks often borrow *significantly* from the central bank to meet their liquidity requirements. Where these conditions are not fulfilled, total bank reserves could be employed as a useful indicator of the banks' ability to create credit.

Data about the narrow and broad concepts of money supply with the public, their components, the bank reserves, the reserve money, and the nominal national income are available for the Indian economy from the beginning of the 'fifties, and as such straightforward relationships between money stock/reserve money or bank reserves and nominal income could be subject to empirical scrutiny. But such an exercise does not indicate, according to some modern monetarists, as to how the monetary impulses are transmitted to the real economy. The link between the monetary and real sectors can be, as argued by Brunner (1968), established through a relative price process which operates on a vast array of financial and real assets. Thus enters the rate of interest in the monetary policy channels.[4]

The Rate of Interest Channel

The rate of interest channel, as implied in the pure Keynesian analysis is rarely employed as the sole explanation of transmission mechanism. In the familiar income-expenditure models, a variation in the volume of money, given a stable demand for money function, alters the rate of interest so as to equate the demand for money with the supply of money. The change in the rate of interest affects the investment expenditures which in turn affect equilibrium income directly as well as indirectly through the multiplier. The direction of causality in this channel runs thus:

$$r \longrightarrow I \longrightarrow Yn \quad \text{...(e)}$$

where 'r' is the rate of interest and I the investment outlays. The crucial assumptions of the Keynesian analysis consist of relationships between the demand for money and the rate of interest, and between the (investment) expenditure and the rate of interest. In constructing the demand for money function, Keynes considered only substitution between money and bonds. The substitutability between money and other assets — both financial and real — is only an extension of the two — asset world of Keynes. If it is assumed that bonds, equities and private debt are perfect substitutes and if capital markets are competitive and efficient in functioning, the equilibrium rate of interest would represent *simultaneously* the rate of return to lenders, the cost of funds to borrowers, the internal rate of returns on investment and the opportunity cost of holding money.

The versatility of the equilibrium rate of interest to represent diverse elements to diverse people has, of course, been never in doubt. What, however, is in danger of being overemphasized is the element of opportunity cost of holding money as a major determinant of what is held as money stock. By this reasoning, the level of interest rate determines the size of the money stock directly, and through the money supply changes, affects the levels of expenditure in the economy. The causality thus is assumed to proceed from:

$r \longrightarrow MS \longrightarrow Yn$ ...(f)

If this standpoint, however, were to be emphasized alongside the strict Keynesian viewpoint, the transmission mechanism is likely to take the following direction:

$r \longrightarrow I \longrightarrow Yn$; $r \dashrightarrow MS \dashrightarrow Yn$ ...(g)

The impact of changes in the interest rate on the levels of economic activity is seen to be brought about by initial changes in money supply or to adopt the modern monetarists' version, by initial changes in bank reserves (monetary base). The direction of causality may then run in a variety of forms:

$MS \longrightarrow r \longrightarrow Yn$ ....(h)

$\{MS, RM, r\} \longrightarrow Yn$ ....(i)

$\{BR \longrightarrow, r \longrightarrow\}\ M \longrightarrow Yn$ ....(j)

$\{BR \longrightarrow MS, r \longrightarrow\}\ Yn$ ....(k)

$BR \longrightarrow MS \longrightarrow Yn$; $BR \longrightarrow r$; $r \dashrightarrow MS$; $r \dashrightarrow Yn$ ...(l)

$BR \longrightarrow MS \longrightarrow r \longrightarrow Yn$; $BR \longrightarrow r$ ...(m)

$BR \longrightarrow MS \longrightarrow Yn$; $MS \dashrightarrow r$; $r \dashrightarrow MS$; $r \longrightarrow MS$ ....(n)

These transmission processes- (h) to (n) imply that the interest rate is as much important as the money stock/bank reserves in bringing about changes in the levels of economic activity. Actually, there is not much evidence to show that the rate of interest- whether it is long-term or short term-could explain significantly the demand for money in developing economies.[5] There is, besides, the problem of choosing the appropriate rate of interest for both analytical and empirical purposes. The long-term rate of interest in most developing economies is usually fettered and static mainly because of narrow and inactive gilt-edged markets and considerations of servicing burden on public debt. Even in the case of short-term rates of interest, there exist in many developing economies regulations on their movements and positioning. Besides, to the extent that the short-term securities are very close substitutes for money in so far as liquidity and risk of default are concerned, they are, perhaps, not so relevant for analysis. But they yield a positive rate of return and their levels differ considerably from one another depending on the market structure- as for example highlighted by the oft-mentioned dichotomy of money markets into the organized and unorganized – they reflect the different undercurrents of demand for and supply of funds as also the opportunity costs of holding money. The basic problem remains as to which of the short rates should be chosen. There are in India a variety of short-term rates of interest which are available in time series – the equity yield, the bank rate, the call money rate, the rates on indigenous bills (such as the bazaar bill rate and the 'hundi' rate), the short-term deposit rate, and the treasury bill rate. The equity yield which is regarded as the prime indicator of the stance of monetary policy by neo-Keynesians like Tobin (1963a 1963b) and Tobin and Brainard (1968) would be irrelevant in economies where capital markets are small by size of operations and inefficient in functioning. The Bank rate is essentially used to neutralize the conditions of credit in the organised money market, and is probably sensitive to extra-economic situations. Its use as a proxy yielded poor results in that its coefficient was either statistically insignificant or wrongly signed in the demand for money functions in respect of some Asian countries.[6] The call money rate-charged for overnight funds lent by one bank to another- appears to be a better proxy indicator of the money market conditions and is in general market-determined, subject, however, to ceiling limits. The rates charged by the organized banking system on bazaar bills and hundis, provide the links, however limited, forged with the unorganised sector. The short-term deposit rate (on 3 months' deposits) is also subject to regulations concerning its movements and is the cost of funds for only the organized banking system. The treasury bill rate, on the other hand, is largely dictated by considerations of public debt management and is relevant more as a riskless liquidity proposition than as a rate of return for investors who are mostly institutional in character.

While call money rate and treasury bill rate have been employed as proxy variables in some demand for money functions pertaining to India,[7] neither of them recognizes adequately the links that exist between the organized and unorganized money markets and the fact that borrowing is a major means of financing economic activity in most developing economies. To meet these objections, either of the two procedures can be adopted : one is that the interest rates in unorganized money markets may be judged from the degree of credit restraint in the economy as reflected in the reciprocal of the credit multiplier (RM)/(NDC)[8]; alternatively, a harmonic mean of the different short rates may be constructed.[9] But as the former, i.e., the reciprocal of the credit multiplier, would be distorted, in the long run, by variations in the currency to demand deposits ratio and in the ratio of time deposits to demand deposits, a preference is shown for constructing a harmonic mean of short term interest rates in this paper. For empirical purposes, a harmonic mean of four interest rates- the bank rate, the call money rate at Bombay, the bazaar bill rate at Bombay and the SBI hundi rates- representing the organized market and the link to the unorganized market- called the rh was constructed.

The Wealth Effect Channel

Changes in net private wealth are said to bring about changes in expenditures, without necessarily affecting the rate of interest, through the real balances effect. The major assumption in the real balances effect is that monetary base is a component of net private wealth as much as commodities, capital goods, and other financial assets. At the micro level, an individual's excess demand for a commodity depends among others, upon an array of relative prices and on the real value of his initial endowment which includes commodities as well as money (cash). *Ceteris paribus* an increase in net wealth of individuals, of which currency is a part, would raise the level of expenditures in the economy.[10] The wealth effect channels may be visualised to proceed thus:

$$\begin{array}{l} W \longrightarrow C \longrightarrow Y_n \quad ...(o) \\ \uparrow \\ \Delta MS \end{array}$$

The inclusion of only currency and not money supply in the net private wealth is justified on the ground that it is 'outside' money — a money that is backed by foreign securities or government securities or gold or is simply fiat money issued by the government — whereas demand deposit (which is a component of money supply) would form 'inside' money based on private domestic securities. The efforts of Pesek and Saving (1976) to treat demand deposits as part of net wealth of the economy on the ground that they represent capitalized value of a stream of net income, have not been found acceptable. This is because, as pointed out by Yung Chul Park (1972), "any increase in the net worth of the banking sector would, *ceteris paribus,* lead to a corresponding increase in the net worth of the non-banking private sector in the form of an increase in the market value of bank stocks. This means that the value of demand deposits in Pesek and Saving's definition ...... is already included in the market value of equities ...... to the extent that demand deposits (in whole or in part) .... (is) part of net wealth; adding the net worth of the banking sector to the market value of equities amounts to a double counting of the market value of commercial banks stocks."

The empirical studies on the real balance effect or more broadly the wealth effect on consumption expenditures and on the demand for money in respect of the US economy have been many. The few attempts to include wealth as one of the arguments in the demand for money functions for India have shown that the wealth variable is either statistically insignificant or spurious, in the presence of income as a separate argument in the same function.[11] If wealth — say as represented by a series of 'permanent' income-substitutes income as an argument in the function in order to avoid the problem of multicollinearity, it becomes difficult to convincingly justify that changes in the demand for money or in consumption are due to wealth effect rather than income effect. Though this problem can be tackled by introducing a variable representing income from labour — as for example done by Ando and Modigliani (1963) — along with wealth or its proxy variable, permanent income, serious data limitations in preparing time series of wealth and labour income come in the way of our understanding of the role of wealth effect in the transmission mechanism in respect of most developing economies, including India.

The Credit Rationing Channel

The credit rationing channel would affect aggregate demand in the economy whenever the availability of credit is varied by commercial banks on their own or by the monetary authorities, with or without altering simultaneously the cost of funds. The changes in the availability of funds, which alters the degree of credit rationing, can be brought about in a variety of ways — through open market operations, variations in rediscount rates, changes in reserve requirements, direct control of the quantum of commercial bank credit to commercial sector and selective credit controls on lending to select activities and/or regions.

It is a well known proposition that changes in the availability of credit would influence monetary base and *ipso facto* money supply. In other words, the monetary authorities exercise their influence on levels of economic activity not through money stock/high powered money but through one of the major determinants of money supply/reserve money. The direction of causation in this channel runs from the domestic credit expansion (or contraction) to national income via business expenditures. Thus, DC→Yn ..(p). DC here is net domestic credit. But where unorganized money market is large this channel is likely to have not much of an influence on monetary policy since any credit rationing in the organized banking sector would imply a corresponding rise in credit in the unorganized sector.

Empirically, credit rationing cannot be easily measured, since bankers do not often specify or record the non-price terms by which they ration credit, such as changes in down payment terms, requirements for collateral etc. F. de Leeuw and Gramlich (1969) suggested that the ratio of expected deposit flows to actual deposit flows of all financial institutions may be employed as a measure of the degree of credit rationing. But it may be argued that the increase in bank credit may not be entirely reflected in an increase in deposit flows, since credit expansion may be absorbed by balance of payments through an increase in imports. Like-wise, when bank credit is tightened, there may occur a larger demand for credit from the unorganized markets, apart from a substantial reduction in imports. A better measure of credit rationing, as proposed by Jaffee (1971) would be the percentage of total loans of commercial banks that are granted to risk-free customers. But data in this regard for a relatively long period may not be easily available. Besides, the credit ratings themselves may be subject to a bias of subjectivity of bankers.

In respect of the Indian economy, the net domestic credit by the banking system consists of two parts: (a) the net bank credit to the Government sector and (b) the bank credit to the 'commercial' sector. Credit rationing or more correctly, credit planning is relevant more in respect of the credit to the commercial sector, since net bank credit to the Government sector is generally considered to be a given datum, dictated as it is by larger considerations of growth. In regard to the bank credit to the 'commercial' sector too, priorities can be laid down - in terms of sectors for instance - and quantitative regulations can be imposed - from the view point of reconciliation of credit needs with the physical requirements of growth. The quantitative regulations, it may be argued, could take two forms : (a) specification of actual limits to lending by commercial banks for specified sectors or activities, and (b) variation of reserve requirements and conditions of refinance. The former is rarely employed while the latter is recognised as the most frequently used tool of monetary policy. Where reserve requirements vary, *ceteris paribus*, money supply too is affected, as shown, partially, by the channels' arrow-exhibit (j). One may visualise the efforts of banks to reallocate their portfolios and raise time deposit rate with a view to meet atleast partially - the effect of a change in the reserve requirements. Consequently, money supply itself may get influenced owing to a change in the ratio of time deposits to demand deposits. In the alternative, the effect of the change in the time-deposit rate alone or in conjunction with the change in money supply which has been initially disturbed by the change in banks' reserve would be felt on other interest rates having influence on investment expenditures. The channels of transmission thus would take the form of (I) or (m) referred to earlier.

II

The empirical verification attempted in this section pertains to the 20 year period, 1956-57 to 1975-76, with the help of OLS method[12] which would highlight the degree of association between two or more variables in the transmission processes outlined in arrow-exhibits (a) through (p), barring the exhibit (o) and (p) which espouse the wealth effect and credit rationing channels. The wealth effect channel could not be put to test owing to non-availability of data of wealth in a time-series fashion. The credit rationing channel as given by the exhibit (p) gave a poor result and hence has not been reported.[13] The equations fitted are :

(1) Δ Yn f Δ MS (2) Δ Yn f Δ MS-1

(3) Δ Yn f Δ AMR (4) Δ Yn f Δ AMR-1

(5) Δ MS f Δ RM (6) Δ MS f Δ RM-1

(7) Δ AMR f Δ RM (8) Δ AMR f Δ RM-1

(9) Δ Yn f Δ MS Δ BR (10) Δ Yn f Δ AMR, Δ BR

(11) Δ Yn f Δ MS, RH, Δ BR (12) Δ Yn f Δ AMR, RH, Δ BR

(13) Δ Yn f Δ MS, RH (14) Δ Yn f Δ AMR, RH

(15) Δ MS f RH (16) Δ AMR f RH

(17) Δ MS f RH-1 (18) Δ AMR f RH-1

(19) Δ MS f RH, Δ BR (20) Δ AMR f RH, Δ BR

(21) Δ MS f Δ RM, C/D, BR/D (22) Δ AMR f Δ RM, C/D, BR/D

where Δ represents variation, Yn is net national product at current prices, MS is the average stock of money with the public, AMR the average stock of aggregate monetary resources (i.e., MS plus net time deposits of commercial and co-operative banks), RM the average 'reserve' money (i.e., currency with the public plus banks' reserves plus 'other' deposits with the Reserve Bank of India), BR the average bank reserves (as incorporated in the RM calculation), RH the harmonic mean of four weighted average rates of interest, viz., the Bank Rate, call money rate at Bombay, bazaar bill rate at Bombay and SBI hundi rate, C/D the currency to aggregate deposits ratio – the currency and aggregate deposits being averages of month-end figures – and BR/D the ratio of bank reserves to aggregate deposits. The years taken are financial years and the lag-period allowed for is one past year.

The computer estimations of the fitted equations are following:

Equ. No.	*Dependent variable*	*Intercept*	*Coefficients of independent variables*		R^2*(Adj)*
1.	Δ Yn	-317.2982	5.6790	Δ MS	0.7298
	t	(0.417)	(4.760)*		
	El	(-0.1240)	(1.1240)	DW stat. 2.0436	
				SEE 2073.2616	
2.	Δ Yn	189.9470	5.0616	Δ MS-1	0.6284
	t	(0.228)	(3.661)*		
	El	(0.0743)	(0.9257)	DW stat. 2.2630	
				SEE 2359.0515	
3.	Δ Yn	186.1396	2.6653	Δ AMR	0.6505
	t	(0.232)	(3.865)*		
	El	(0.0728)	(0.9272)	DW stat. 2.0868	
				SEE 2303.3817	
4.	Δ Yn	365.8841	2.7805	Δ AMR-1	0.6240
	t	(0.435)	(3.622)*		
	El	(0.1430)	(0.8570)	DW stat. 2.2136	
				SEE 2369.7840	
5.	Δ MS	109.7537	1.3332	Δ RM	0.8634
	t	(1.584)	(7.525)*		
	El	(0.2168)	(0.7832)	DW stat. 1.1963	
				SEE 201.1618	
6.	Δ MS	162.2888	1.1791	Δ RM-1	0.7436
	t	(1.861)	(5.252)*		
	El	(0.3205)	(0.6795)	DW stat. 2.0007	
				SEE 257.3877	

Contd...

...Contd...

Equ. No.	*Dependent variable*	*Intercept*	*Coefficients of independent variables*		R^2*(Adj)*
7.	Δ AMR	196.4875	2.3312	Δ RM	0.7793
	t	(1.188)	(5.512)*		
	El	(0.2208)	(0.7792)	DW stat. 0.8908	
				SEE 480.2233	
8.	Δ AMR	234.8152	2.2454	Δ RM-1	0.7558
	t	(1.381)	(5.130)*		
	El	(0.2639)	(0.7361)	DW stat. 2.0926	
				SEE 501.7431	
9.	Δ Yn	94.5806	3.8246	Δ MS 13.4622 ΔBR	0.7754
	t	(0.129)	(2.669)*	(2.024)*	
	El	(0.0370)	(0.7570)	(0.2060)	
				DW stat. 1.9643	
				SEE 1915.0408	
10.	ΔYn	484.8359	1.5968	Δ AMR 16.6585 ΔBR	0.7461
	t	(0.681)	(2.166)*	(2.533)*	
	El	(0.1895)	(0.5555)	(0.2550)	
				DW stat. 2.0519	
				SEE 2019.4522	
11.	ΔYn	-2528.2958	-0.4310	Δ MS 636.9780 RH 22.4310 ΔBR	0.8045
	t	(1.564)	(0.158)	(1.794) (2.801)*	
	El	(-0.9884)	(-0.0853)	(1.7308) (0.3433)	
				DW stat. 2.3251	
				SEE 1801.2036	
12.	ΔYn	-3952.3822	-1.7482	Δ AMR 1003.1993 RH 27.9731 ΔBR	0.8241
	t	(2.285)	(1.273)	(2.738)* (4.022)*	
	El	(-1.5451)	(-0.6082)	(2.7252) (0.4281)	
				DW stat. 2.4634	
				SEE 1717.7017	
13.	ΔYn	-389.3741	15.8462	RH 5.6039 ΔMS	0.7108
	t	(0.231)	(0.048)	(2.826)*	
	El	(-0.1522)	(0.0430)	(1.1092)	
				DW stat. 2.0488	
				SEE 2133.2227	
14.	ΔYn	-403.5378	127.4845	RH 2.3324 ΔAMR	0.6267
	t	(0.197)	(0.134)	(1.832)	
	El	(-0.1578)	(0.3463)	(0.8114)	
				DW stat. 2.1046	
				SEE 2363.2974	
15.	ΔMS	-397.8082	130.1062	RH	0.7717
	t	(2.244)*	(5.383)*		
	El	(-0.7857)	(1.7857)	DW stat. 0.8349	
				SEE 253.5161	
16.	ΔAMR	-949.6951	264.7280	RH	0.8210
	t	(3.185)*	(6.347)*		
	El	(-1.0672)	(2.0672)	DW stat. 0.8932	
				SEE 437.4921	
17.	ΔMS	-346.0803	130.5030	RH-1	0.6342
	t	(1.444)	(3.713)*		
	El	(-0.6835)	(1.6835)	DW stat. 0.8926	
				SEE 308.2197	
18.	ΔAMR	-977.9490	285.9755	RH-1	0.7344
	t	(2.418)*	(4.822)*		
	El	(-1.0989)	(2.0989)	DW stat. 0.8248	
				SEE 520.0597	
19.	ΔMS	-370.7606	113.1594	RH 2.3172 ΔBR	0.9151
	t	(3.309)*	(7.258)*	(5.305)*	
	El	(-0.7323)	(1.5531)	(0.1792)	
				DW stat. 1.42266	
				SEE 160.0839	

Contd...

...Contd...

Equ. No.	*Dependent variable*	*Intercept*	*Coefficients of independent variables*		*R^2(Adj)*
20.	ΔAMR	-906.0213	237.3639 RH	3.7415 ΔBR	0.9183
	t	(4.267)*	(8.033)*	(4.520)*	
	El	(-1.0181)	(1.8535)	(0.1646)	
				DW stat. 1.2721	
				SEE 303.3927	
21.	ΔMS	1027.7270	-979.4901 C/D	1598.8806 BR/D 0.7626 ΔRM	0.9553
	t	(5.203)*	(5.189)*	(0.501) (4.885)*	
	El	(2.0299)	(-1.7005)	(0.2226) (0.4481)	
				DW stat. 0.9730	
				SEE 117.8916	
22.	ΔAMR	2084.4516	-2746.3769 C/D	14378.3352 BR/D 0.6920 ΔRM	0.9517
	t	(5.289)*	(7.291)*	(2.258)* (2.222)*	
	El	(2.3423)	(-2.7127)	(1.1319) (0.2314)	
				DW stat. 0.8120	
				SEE 235.2228	

* Indicates significance at both 5 per cent and 1 per cent levels.

From the computer results of the fitted equations, it may be seen that all the equations barring those numbering (11) to (14) have coefficients which are statistically significant. The link between money supply and national income in nominal terms seems to have empirical support. This is evident from the simple regression equation results of (1) to (4), in respect of which the estimated regression coefficients are statistically significant. The elasticities of money supply with respect to income ranged from 0.86 to 1.12. The adjusted R^2 bar at 0.73 in respect of equation (1), is the highest of the $\bar{R}^2$s of the first four equations. The results improved when incremental bank reserves were taken as an additional argument in the function: this is reflected in the results of equations (9) and (10) which show that the coefficients of the independent variables are statistically significant and that the $\bar{R}^2$s are 0.78 and 0.75 respectively. The expected connection between money supply and reserve money also has a good empirical support, as evident from the results of the equations (5) to (8). But a degree of auto-correlation may be noticed in equations (5) and (7), in view of the relatively low values of DW statistic.

As the computer results of the equations (15) to (18) indicate, the association between money supply and the rate of interest is found to be positive, a result which is in agreement with the commonly held view and generally obtained results of the demand for money functions. The $\bar{R}^2$s ranged between 0.63 and 0.82 in these equations. The coefficients of the independent variables are all statistically significant. The interest elasticities with respect to money supply are high-ranging between 1.68 to 2.10, as may be seen from equations (15) to (18).

However, the results of the equations (15) to (18) improve when variations in bank reserves are taken as an additional argument in the money supply function. This may be discerned from the results of the equations (19) and (20) wherein the regression coefficients are statistically significant and $\bar{R}^2$s are high at 0.92. Also, their DW statistic are higher than those of equations (15) to (18).

In terms of $\bar{R}^2$s, however, the highest values occur in respect of the multiple regressions (21) and (22), which faithfully put to test the modern monetarists' viewpoint about the money stock determination. However, only in equation (22) are all the regression coefficients statistically significant. Therefore, the fit as postulated by equation (21) cannot be accepted.

On the basis of the results of the equation 22, the variations in AMR can be estimated, and from the estimated AMR, the variations in nominal income could be derived by applying the results of the equation (3). This procedure vindicates the money supply channel and makes the interest rate totally irrelevant from the viewpoint of policy-making. However, this may be rebutted by the argument that both interest rate and variations in bank reserves may be meaningfully associated with the variations in money supply- as implicit from the results of equations (19) and (20)- and therefrom derive nominal income, by using the estimates of equations (1) and (3). This would imply that monetary policy makers can influence the money supply changes through interest rate channel and through changes in bank reserves-policy instruments which are well recognised as important weapons in the armoury of monetary authorities.

III

The empirical analysis attempted in the above section does not offer any definite evidence that money supply alone or the rate of interest is the centre-piece of the transmission process. In fact, it may be argued that all the equations have very high standard mean errors-exceeding 10 per cent – with the result the stability condition is not fulfilled. As a consequence, the estimated coefficients cannot be relied upon. This would imply that the effects of a proposed or likely policy action cannot be expected with certainty and that there is no single-scaled or multiple scaled 'indicator' of monetary policy. Does this then mean that monetary authorities in developing economies should wait for perfect information and tests about the transmission process before they can meaningfully interpret and apply policies?

In reality, there is no unique solution to the problem. Central bankers surely cannot afford the luxury of waiting for perfect information which is, as Brunner (1968) once remarked, not as a banter but in a tone of warning, "the privilege of economists' discourse on policy". The world is much too complicated and the monetary authorities have to depend not only on whatever information available with them but also, to quote Brunner (1968) again, "on mystic insight supplemented by some impressionistic arguments", while doing their exercises on the policy-mix. They recognize the channels but they would rarely emphasize any one of them. The 'guideposts' for action usually are a multiple of arguments, in which money supply or monetary base, the rate of interest, bank reserves and bank credit- on the 'money' side- occupy pride of place. The interactions among these variables are considered by the central bankers-theory has given them enough analytical apparatus for this purpose- and then the 'choice' is made of the policy mix, which implicitly contains some of the important strands of the transmission processes alluded to in the economic literature.

References

1. Adekunle, Joseph O. (1968), "The Demand for Money: Evidence from Developed and Less Developed Economies," *IMF Staff Papers,* Vol. XV, July.
2. Andersen, L.C. and Carlson, K.M. (1970), "A Monetarist Model for Economic Stabilization," *Review,* Federal Reserve Bank of St. Louis, Vol. 52. April.
3. Ando, A. and Modigliani, F. (1963), "The 'Life Cycle' Hypothesis of Saving," *American Economic Review,* March.
4. Balbir Singh (1970), "Price Stability and Money Supply During Fourth Five Year Plan," *Indian Economic Journal,* Vol. XVII, April-June.
5. Brahmananda, P. R. (1977), *Determinants of Real National Income and Price Level in India,* University of Bombay, Bombay.
6. Brunner, Karl (1968), *"The Role of Money and Monetary Policy," Review,* Federal Reserve Bank of St. Louis, Vol. 50, July.
7. Chick, Victoria (1973), *The Theory of Monetary Policy,* Gray-Mills Publishing Ltd., London.
8. de Leeuw F. and Gramlich, E.M., (1969), "The Channels of Monetary Policy," *Federal Reserve Bulletin,* June.
9. Fan, L.S. and Liu, Z.C. (1971), "Demand for Money in Asian Countries: Empirical Evidence," *Indian Economic Journal,* Vol. XVIII, April-June.
10. Friedman, Milton (1969), *The Optimum Quantity of Money and Other Essays,* Macmillan & Co. London.
11. Friedman, M and Meiselman,David (1963), "The Relative Stability of Monetary Velocity and the Investment Multiplier in the US," in Commission of Money and Credit, *Impacts of Monetary Policy,* Prentice Hall, Englewood Cliffs, N.J.
12. Friedman, M, and Schwartz, Anna J (1963), *A Monetary History of the US.,* 1867-1960, National Bureau of Economic Research, New York.
13. Goodhart, C. (1963), "Analysis of the Determinants of the Stock of Money" in M Parkin and A.R. Nobay (eds), *Essays in Modern Economics,* Longmans, London.
14. Gujarati, D. (1968), "Demand for Money in India," *Journal of Development Studies,* Vol. V. October.
15. Gupta G. S. (1973), "A Monetary Policy Model for India," *Sankhya* 'B' Vol. 35, Part 4, December.
16. Gupta K.L. (1970), "Demand for Money in India" *Journal of Development Studies,* Vol. VI, January.
17. Jaffee, D.M. (1971), *Credit Rationing and the Commercial Loan Market,* John Wiley & Sons, New York.
18. Meigs, A.J. (1962), *Free Reserves and the Money Supply,* University of Chicago Press, Chicago.
19. Park, Yung Chul (1972), "Some Current Issues on the Transmission Process of Monetary Policy," *IMF Staff Papers,* Vol. XIV, March.
20. Patinkin, D., (1965), *Money, Interest and Prices,* Harper & Row, New York, 2nd ed.
21. Pesek, Boris & Saving, T.R. (1967), *Money, Wealth and Economic Theory,* Macmillan, New York.
22. Sastry, V.K. (1962), "Demand for and Supply of Money in India," *Indian Economic Journal,* Vol. X. July-September.
23. Tobin, James (1963a), "Commercial Banks as Creators of Money" in D. Carson (ed.), *Banking and Monetary Studies,* Richard D. Irwin Sc., Homewood, Illionis.
24. Tobin, James (1963b), "An Essay on Principles of Debt Management," in Commission on Money and Credit, *Fiscal and Debt Management Policies,* Prentice Hall, Englewood Cliffs, N.J.
25. Tobin, James (1969), "A General Equilibrium Approach to Monetary Theory," *Journal of Money, Credit and Banking,* Vol. 1, February.
26. Tobin, J & Brainard W.C. (1968), "Pitfalls in Financial Model Building," *American Economic Review,* Vol. XIII, May.
27. Vasudevan, A (1977), "Demand for Money in India - A Survey of Literature," Reserve Bank Staff Occasional Papers, Vol.2, June.
28. Venkatachalam, T.R. and Anjaneyulu, D. (1970), "On Estimating the Non-inflationary Level of Money Supply," Paper Read at the All-India Econometrics Conference, Madurai (Mimeographed).

Notes

1. See Andersen LC and Carlson KM (1970), p.7.
2. See Milton Friedman and David Meiselman (1963), Milton Friedman (1969), Milton Friedman and Anna J. Schwartz (1963).
3. The proof of this formula is :

$$MS = Cp + D \quad ....(1)$$

$$C = Cp + C_b \quad ....(2)$$

$$\frac{MS}{C} = \frac{Cp+D}{Cp+C_b} \quad ...(3)$$

$$= \frac{1+D/Cp}{1+Cb/Cp}$$

$$= \frac{(D/Cb)(1+D/Cp)}{D/Cb+D/Cp}$$

$$= \frac{(1/RD)(1+1/CD)}{1/RD+1/CD}$$

$$\therefore MS = C\,\frac{(1+CD)}{RD+CD}$$

where MS = Money Supply in broadest sense, C = Currency; D = Aggregate deposits; Cp = Currency held by the public; C_b = Currency held by banks; RD = Reserves to deposits Ratio; CD = Currency to Deposit Ratio. See for this proof Victoria Chick (1973).

4. The non-monetarists place emphasis on the rate of interest channel, by questioning the validity of the arguments of the monetarists. In Goodhart (1973) and Tobin (1963), the theory of bank behaviour is based on banks' responses and adjustments to private sector portfolio choice, dictated as they are by profit motive. The portfolio adjustment was explained by Tobin (1969) thus: "When the supply of any asset is increased, the structure of rates of return, on this and other assets must change in a way that induces the public to hold the new supply. When the assets' own rate can rise, a large part of the necessary adjustment can occur in this way. But if the rate is fixed, the whole adjustment must take place through reductions in other rates or increase in prices of other assets."

5. A number of Studies on the demand for money in developing economies have appeared in recent years. See Adekunle (1968) Fan and Liu (1971). For a Survey of Literature on the demand for money in India, see Vasudevan (1977).

6. See Fan and Liu (1971).

7. See Venkatachalam and Anjaneyulu (1970) Balbir Singh (1970), Sastry (1962), K.L. Gupta (1970), Gujarati (1968).

8. One of the authors of this paper, A. Vasudevan, has received this idea from Dr. C.H. Wong of the IMF Institute to whom he expresses his thanks.

9. We owe this thought to Brahmananda (1977) who constructed a geometric mean of the interest rates.

10. For an excellent exposition of real balance effect, see Patinkin (1965).

11. For details vide Vasudevan (1977).

12. As an alternative, a simultaneous equation method may be attempted but it would require a specification about the structure of the economic system which is notwithstanding the fine efforts of G.S. Gupta (1973), an area which requires serious attention of economists.

13. The 'r' was only 0.58 when scheduled bank credit was taken an independent variable and nominal national income the dependent variable. The standard mean error was as high as 82 per cent.

2

A Short-Term Model to Forecast Monetary Aggregates

Interim Results

D C Rao • T R Venkatachalam • A Vasudevan

I. Introduction

MONETARY forecasts are required for a variety of purposes. Decisions on monetary policies such as cash reserve ratios and refinance of commercial banks by RBI must clearly be based on an analysis not only of monetary aggregates of the recent past but also of future prospects. The same applies to measures concerning the structure of interest rates and the assessment of commercial banks' credit budgets. Forecasts of growth of bank deposits play an important role in the estimation of resources available for the financing of investment, and particularly of plan outlays in the public sector.

The purpose of the forecast has a bearing on the time horizon over which the forecast is to be made, and, hence on the methodology to be used. For instance, in the estimation of financial resources available for Plan outlays, one of the components is based on a projection of the growth of bank deposits. For this purpose, it is enough to base the projection of deposit growth on an analysis of the demand for deposits, given a projected rate of inflation. This approach is valid because it can be assumed that, in the long run, the supply of bank deposits will have to align itself with its demand, and can be made to do so by the adoption of suitable monetary policy measures from time to time. For short-term analysis related to monetary policy decisions, the problem is that of assessing the imbalance between the forces of demand and supply of money and knowing how to remedy the imbalance in the interests of price stability. Thus, for short run analysis, the role of monetary policy instruments clearly has to be made more explicit.

Short run monetary analysis must, therefore, go beyond analysis based only on the balance-sheet approach or on the assumption of a stable multiplier relationship between reserve money and money supply. In the balance-sheet approach, bank deposits, reserve money and currency are separately estimated and these estimates are not necessarily consistent with each other, except in that they conform to the balance-sheet constraints. In the money multiplier approach it is assumed that the multiplier for each period is stable after making the requisite adjustments for changes in the cash reserve ratio applied by RBI to commercial banks. In fact, the money multiplier is not very stable. ... An algebraic decomposition of the proportionate changes in the marginal multiplier [also] shows that fluctuations in the ratio of currency to deposits rather than changes in the reserve-deposit ratio are responsible for the bulk of the variation in the money multiplier. Thus, for short run analysis relevant to policy making it is necessary to use a consistent forecasting methodology that goes beyond the balance-sheet and multiplier approaches and takes account of the forces of both the demand for and the supply of money and credit. Such an approach must take into account the portfolio behaviour of the public and the commercial banks to the extent possible.

A brief overview of the structure of the present version of the model is given in the following section. Section III discusses the data base and some of the problems encountered in generating a time series for the purposes of econometric estimation of behavioural relationships. Section IV contains a detailed and technical presentation of the model as estimated, and a

The authors wish to acknowledge their great debt to Professor Vikas Chitre of the Gokhale Institute of Politics and Economics who has been very closely associated with the development of this model from the initial stages and whose detailed guidance has been of immense help. Useful comments on an earlier version of the model have been received from Dr. Isher Ahluwalia, Professor C. Rangarajan, Professor S. Chakrabarti and Dr. P.K. Pani. The authors are also grateful to S.S. Tarapore, Director, Credit Planning Cell, for several useful discussions. The assistance of K.S. Namboodiri and S.B. Sapre in programming and computation is gratefully acknowledged.

discussion of the rationale of the structure of the model both in terms of the individual equations and in terms of their interaction to generate model forecasts. The predictive performance of the model both in the sample period and for one year outside the sample period is shown in Section V. The final section discusses the weakness of the present model as perceived by the authors and identifies areas in which further refinements of the model are contemplated.

II. An Overview of the Model

The model's forecasts of monetary aggregates are derived by a simultaneous solution of 4 behavioural equations and 4 identities or statistical relationships. Each of the behavioural equations represents demand or supply relationships for the relevant aggregates and the simultaneous solution procedure ensures that the forecast satisfies both the demand and supply relationships. The individual relationships have been estimated by regression over the period 1970-71 to 1979-80 using annual data for the last Friday of March. The relationships covered by the main equations are as follows:

1. Currency demand, which is estimated as a function of nominal national income, foreign remittances, food procurement credit, an index of prices of sensitive commodities and deposit interest rates.
2. The supply of bank liabilities, which is estimated as a function of bank reserves, the cash reserve ratio, the call money rate and the composition of bank deposit liabilities.
3. National income at current prices, which is estimated as a function of real income, money supply, and the level of national income deflator in the previous year and share of non-agricultural income in national income. This equation may be regarded as a reformulation of the traditional equation for the demand for money.
4. The demand for time and demand deposits, which are estimated mainly as a function of nominal national income, share of non-agricultural income to total income in nominal terms, interest rates and the previous year's inflation rate.

In addition to the above equations, there are definitional and statistical relationships to derive estimates of total bank reserves, deposits and the price level.

In this model, the main exogenous variables, whose values are taken as given are: reserve money, real income, food credit, cash reserve requirements, and interest rates on time deposits. The endogenous variables, whose values are estimated by the model, are: currency with the public, demand deposits, time deposits, total bank liabilities, bank reserves and the implicit deflator for national income.

The basic structure of the model can be grasped by following the process by which the model generates the forecasts of endogenous variables, given the values of exogenous variables. (A flow chart is discussed in greater detail in Section IV). The key exogenous input to the model is the estimated change in reserve money. The first step in the model is to estimate the public's demand for currency. Deducting this currency drain from the previously estimated change in reserve money, the model arrives at an estimate of the reserves available to banks for the expansion of their liabilities. Given the statutory cash reserve ratio and other variables influencing the banks' reserve holdings, the model is then able to estimate the supply of deposits. On the assumption that the supply of currency is identically equal to its demand, this estimate of the supply of money is then faced by an estimate of the demand for money. The essence of the model is that the supply and demand have to be equilibrated, which is done by allowing for changes in nominal income (given an exogenous forecast of real income) which, in turn, affect the estimates of the demand for currency and deposits. The forecasts of money supply are derived by an iterative solution of the entire model, which means that all the relationships specified in the model have to be simultaneously satisfied.

III. Data Base

The data used for this forecasting model are drawn from two basic sources: assets and liabilities of RBI and the commercial banks which are periodically published by RBI using information received in various statutory returns; and time series on national income at current and constant prices, wholesale price indices, inflow of foreign remittances etc. which have been drawn from the relevant official publications, mainly by the Central Statistical Organisation. The scope of the model and the precise specifications of the equations must abide by the limitations imposed by the availability of data, its definition and the timeliness of its publications.

While the data of financial variables are generally available in great detail, reasonably reliable figures pertaining to non-scheduled commercial banks and co-operative banks are received only with considerable delay. Hence, the model's relationships are defined only in respect of scheduled commercial banks, with crude assumptions being made in respect of other banks, where absolutely necessary, to satisfy definitional identities. This restriction in the scope of the model is not a serious drawback because scheduled commercial banks dominate the banking system anyway in terms of both absolute size and growth. As of March, 1980, the end of the sample period of the model, other banks held only about 9 per cent of aggregate deposits of the banking system.

The absence of quarterly or semi-annual national income estimates puts a serious limitation on monetary analysis which is inherently short run in nature. Because real national income is such a crucial variable in the analysis of the demand for money, this model has had to be specified on an annual basis, ignoring the possibility of inter-relationships of shorter duration between the financial and real variables or even among the financial variables alone.

The restriction of the model to annual data imposes an especially severe handicap because the analysis cannot legitimately span too long a period, thereby limiting the number of observations available for the application of statistical estimation procedures. The start of the sample period for the model was set at March 1970 because there is a break in the money supply series due to an enlargement in the coverage of financial institutions.* Further, there has been substantial change in the structure of the economy, and of the banking system in particular, which makes an analysis of earlier decades decidedly less relevant for the purposes of a forecasting model. For instance, the nationalization of the banking system in 1969 led to a number of developments in branch expansion, credit allocation and interest rate policies that have a bearing on monetary analysis. Hence, it was decided to estimate the statistical relationships over the period 1970/71 to 1979/80.

Even during the selected sample period, the financial data are subject to some discontinuities which had to be removed by adjusting the data. The data on the scheduled commercial banks' "liabilities to the banking system" and "liabilities to others" from 1970 to 1975 are different from the data for subsequent years. Similarly the published data of demand and time deposits after January 1978 are not on the same basis as earlier, because banks adopted a revised method of classification of savings deposits into "demand" and "time" liabilities on different dates since January 1978. Using information on individual banks' liabilities, it was necessary to use reconstructed series on demand and time deposits conforming to the new system of classification so that valid forecasts could be generated by the model.

Another area where the financial data proved deficient for the model's purposes was interest rates. Almost all the interest rates on which data are published are regulated in some way and the published time series do not adequately reflect the changing conditions in the financial markets. even moderately reliable time series on interest rates in indigenous money markets and rates paid by non-financial companies to their depositors are not available. Data on interest rates charged by banks on their advances are available only after a considerable delay. On reflection it was decided that only three interest rates were usable for this analysis: the call money rate and the dividend yield on industrial securities, which are practically the only published interest rates that are permitted to fluctuate more or less freely; and the interest rate on fixed deposits which, though fixed by RBI directive, can be expected to have an influence on the demand for time deposits.

Details concerning the precise definitions of the variables included in the model are given in Annexure I.

IV. The Model

The section discusses in detail the equations comprising the forecasting model, along with their underlying rationale, and their inter-relationships. The equations of the present model are given in Annexure II and flow charts depicting the significant interactions in the system are shown in Annexure III. It may be noted that the model only estimates linear equations so as to simplify their simultaneous solution required for simulation.

1. Public's Demand for Currency

The public's demand for currency has a crucial role in monetary analysis for a number of reasons. First, a relatively large share of money is held in the form of currency. The mean value of currency outstanding during the sample period was Rs. 7235 crores, which compares with demand deposits of Rs. 3522 crores and time deposits of Rs. 12110 crores. Thus, for the decade of the seventies, currency amounted to over two-thirds of M1 and nearly one-third of M3. These rates have been declining slowly over the years but they are still much higher than in other countries.

---

* For details, see *Money Supply in India: Concepts, Compilation and Analysis,* Reserve Bank of India, Bombay, 1977.

The second reason for the importance of currency in monetary analysis is its volatility. Not only is it volatile from week to week, reflecting the ebb and flow of payments but the magnitude of annual changes also varies considerably from year to year from a low of Rs. 39 crores in 1974-75 to a high of Rs. 1581 crores in 1978-79. As already noted, the variation in the ratio of currency to deposits is mainly responsible for the fluctuations in the money multiplier. Any monetary forecasting system (whether a formal econometric model or not) that cannot explain these violent swings in currency holdings cannot be very successful in achieving its purpose.

A third feature of the monetary system that reinforces the importance of the public's demand for currency is that the amount of currency in circulation is determined by the demand for it rather than by factors influencing its supply. Deriving from theoretical considerations that currency serves both as a means of payment and a store of value, one may hypothesize that the demand for currency is determined by such factors as the flow of income/ expenditure, its distribution, portfolio considerations etc. Based on these factors, the public expresses a certain demand for holding currency rather than other financial or real assets. Given the arrangements for the issue of currency by the Reserve Bank of India, the public's demand for currency automatically has to be met i.e., the supply of currency is completely elastic in adjusting to its demand. Hence the accurate estimation of the public's demand for currency is vital for monetary forecasting.

Table 1 presents some alternative equations estimating the public's demand for currency, all of which give reasonably good statistical fits despite all but one of them being specified in the form of first differences to eliminate the spurious correlation introduced by common time trends. A comparison of equations 1(a) and 1(b) is instructive. Both the equations have identical specifications except that 1(a) specifies the dependent variable in stock form and 1(b) in first difference form. The second equation has a lower standard error of estimate which is an advantage from the forecasting point of view.

In addition to the income variable, all equations include the rate of interest on time deposits (RLT) which indicates the rate of return on a competing asset. As expected, the income co-efficient is positive and the RLT co-efficent is negative. In two equations the rate of change of wholesale prices ($\overline{WP}$) and the national income deflator ($\overline{NP}$) are also inserted to introduce the asset substitution effect between currency and commodities. But their signs are positive and the co-efficients are not significant.

Another variable that enters all the equations is the credit for food procurement, which serves as a proxy for the actual expenditures incurred in the public procurement of foodgrains. In the first five equations, this is introduced as a ratio to total credit (BCF/BC); in the last equation it is introduced as an annual change in outstanding food credit (ΔBCF). The hypothesis is that the process of procurement puts additional income in the hands of farmers who, traditionally, have a relatively high propensity to hold currency. Hence, in years where food procurement operations are on a larger scale, the public's demand for currency is relatively high. The hypothesis is borne out by the sign and significance of the estimated

TABLE 1

Currency Demand Equations

									$\bar{R}^2$(adj)	D.W.	S.E.E
1 (a)	C	=	3425.2	+ 0.15 Y —	776.1 RLT	+ 4877.9 BCF/BC			0.98	2.64	318.1
				(17.6)	(4.1)	(1.0)					
1 (b)	ΔC	=	2066.0	+ 0.03 Y —	567.6 RLT	+ 9331.6 BCF/BC			0.79	3.32	234.7
				(5.0)	(4.0)	(2.6)					
1 (c)	ΔC	=	2213.9	+ 0.06 Y —	845.3 RLT	+ 19143.6 BCF/BC	+ 699.2 $\overline{WP}$	– 1.5 FR	0.82	3.62	213.5
				(2.8)	(4.1)	(2.6)	(0.4)	(1.5)			
1 (d)	ΔC	=	2091.6	+ 0.05 Y —	791.0 RLT	+ 18053.1 BCF/BC	+ 1057.9 $\overline{NP}$	– 1.4 FR	0.84	3.48	202.4
				(2.6)	(4.3)	(3.4)	(0.8)	(1.3)			
1 (e)	ΔC	=	2036.7	+ 0.06 Y —	803.5 RLT	+ 17377.2 BCF/BC	+ 120.5 $\overline{SCP}$	–1.6 FR	0.82	3.62	216.3
				(3.0)	(4.0)	(3.1)	(0.2)	(1.6)			
1 (f)	ΔC	=	2306.6	+ 0.02 Y —	526.3 RLT	+ 0.9 Δ BCF	+ 851.6 $\overline{SCP}$	+ 1.2 FR	0.71	2.84	274.6
				(1.2)	(2.9)	(2.1)	(0.9)	(1.5)			

Note: Figures in brackets are t-statistics.

co-efficient. On similar reasoning, the inflow of foreign remittances (FR) is also tried. In equations 1 (c), 1 (d) and 1 (e) the co-efficient has the wrong sign but in equation 1 (f) it took on the right sign, albeit only marginally significant. In essence, these variables attempt to capture the effect of changes in the distribution of income on the public's demand for currency.

The positive co-efficient for the price variables in equations 1 (c) and 1 (d) suggests that it is really expressing the transactions demand for currency. Since the specification of income is at current prices, this should itself have fully captured the effect of the price level on the normal transactions demand for currency. This suggests that the additional transactions demand may be for speculative activities. Hence, equations 1 (e) and 1 (f) include the rate of change in the prices of sensitive commodities ($\overline{SCP}$). The co-efficient has the right sign but is not significant.

The final choice for the model lay between equations 1 (e) and 1 (f), the only difference in specification being in food procurement credit. The use of ΔBCF instead of BCF/BC led to a deterioration in the t-statistics (probably because of the introduction of multi-collinearity) and a higher standard error of estimate. Nevertheless, it was felt that for forecasting purposes equation 1 (f) was preferable partly because all the co-efficients had the expected signs. On the basis of the probable scale of procurement operations and announced foodgrain prices, it is possible to make a reasonably good forecast of the increase in food credit (ΔBCF). However, a forecast of BCF/BC also requires an estimate of aggregate bank credit (BC), which cannot be estimated independently of the endogenous monetary aggregates. For the present, the model does not attempt to estimate BC endogenously and, hence, it was decided that the exogenous variable representing food procurement credit should be ΔBCF rather than BCF/BC.

Although the selected equation is not the best equation on statistical criteria, its performance in tracking the highly volatile annual changes in currency is quite commendable. The graph below shows the actual changes and those predicted by the equation. The equation has captured almost all the turning points in the ΔC series during the sample period. (for graph see next page)

2. Supply of Bank Liabilities

Unlike demand, the supply of monetary liabilities can be modelled in a variety of ways. Basically, in a fractional reserve system, the supply of bank liabilities will depend on the availability of reserve assets to the banks and the required ratio of bank reserves to total liabilities. In practice, the banks may wish to hold reserves in excess of the minimum requirement to serve as a cushion against unanticipated reserve losses or spurts in their deposit accretion. Thus, the banks' demand for excess reserves can be estimated as a function of conditions in the money market, volatility of deposits etc. Further refinements are possible by separate estimation of the banks' demand for borrowing from RBI. Alternatively, banks' demand for reserves may be specified as a demand for free reserves (i.e. excess reserves minus borrowed reserves). These refinements were considered and rejected as being unsuitable to the current structure of the Indian banking system for the following reasons. First, the treatment of borrowed reserves as being determined largely by banks' demand at the prevailing Bank Rate is not valid in our economy. The RBI specifies detailed refinance limits in relation to outstanding credit to specified categories (e.g. food, export) and in respect of other forms of refinance, for each bank. Thus, it would be more appropriate to treat RBI's credit to the banks as being a policy variable than to estimate its magnitude on the basis of banks' demand. This is the approach used in this model, where RBI's credit to the banks forms one of the sources of change in reserve money, which is an exogenous input to the model.

Secondly, some of the more refined approaches to the estimation of banks' demand for reserves usually assume that unborrowed reserves are controlled by the monetary authority and set by policy considerations. This assumption may be valid in advanced monetary systems, where open market operations can be used by the monetary authority to influence the level of the banks' unborrowed reserves. In India, open market operations are limited in scale and consist of gradual unloading of RBI's stocks of government securities and switch transactions whereby banks improve their interest earnings through exchanging government securities with RBI. On treasury bills, RBI plays an entirely passive role, selling and rediscounting them at rates that have remained fixed since 1974. Thus, RBI currently does not conceive of open market operations as being a means of influencing the supply of reserves to the banking system.

Thirdly, excess reserves held by scheduled commercial banks consist mainly of cash on hand, the excess balances with RBI being almost negligible in magnitude (See table below). It is possible to treat cash on hand as being mainly a transactions demand, which is determined by administrative considerations (e.g. the spread of branch offices and the location of currency chests.)

CURRENCY WITH THE PUBLIC (INCREMENTAL)

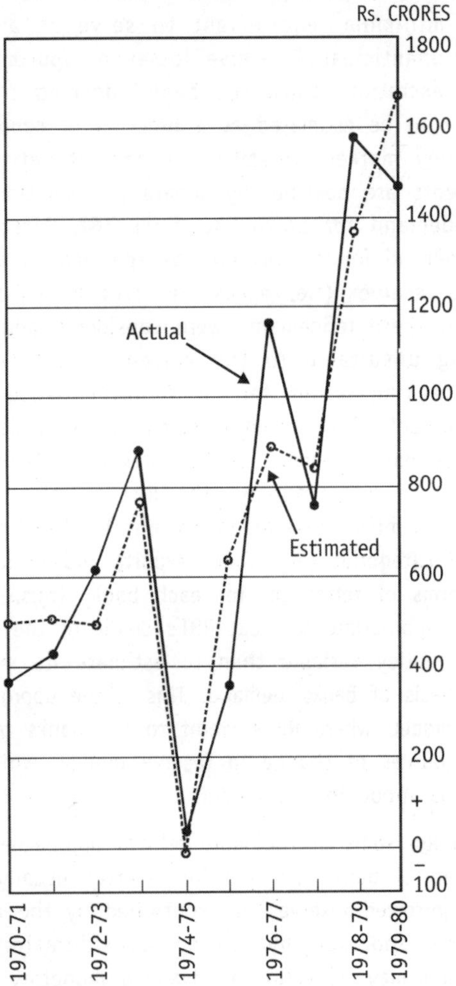

Excess reserves of Scheduled Commercial Banks

(Rs. crores)

(as of last Friday of March)	*Cash on hand*	*Excess of average balances with RBI*	*Excess Reserves*
	(1)	(2)	(1+2)
1971	167	25	192
72	180	37	217
73	221	34	255
74	246	-109	137
75	296	81	377
76	305	41	346
77	354	-122	232
78	469	142	611
79	557	43	600
80 (prov)	616	-	616

Source : Statistical Tables Relating to Banks in India.

Fourthly, the data on excess reserves are subject to measurement error as the data on excess balances with RBI refer to the average of daily balances over the previous week, whereas the data on cash on hand refers to the banks' holdings on a particular Friday. Even small errors in an excess reserves equation can cause severe problems in the overall operation of the model because of the tremendous leverage implicit in translating the demand for excess reserves into a supply of bank liabilities at a given level of aggregate bank reserves.

The present model uses a fairly simple equation relating the supply of bank liabilities to the supply of bank reserves: as noted elsewhere, the amount of bank reserves is determined endogenously (see equation 2 of Annexure II). If it is assumed that banks' excess balance with RBI are always nil and that their cash on hand is a fixed proportion of their liabilities, then liabilities could be determined solely on the basis of the aggregate reserves and the statutory cash reserve ratio. Equation 2(a) in Table 2 uses this approach but the results are unsatisfactory. The standard error of estimate is rather high and the co-efficient of the statutory cash reserve ratio has the wrong sign. These short-comings are remedied by the inclusion of two more variables, the call money interest rate (RC) and the ratio of time deposits to total deposits (TD/D) which may influence the banks' desire to hold excess reserves. For an individual bank, borrowing from the call money market is an alternative to holding excess reserves and can be used to expand its liabilities. Thus, the interest rate on call money borrowing should be negatively related to the expansion of liabilities (given reserves etc.). The same applies to the scheduled commercial banks as a group, since they use the call money market to borrow from co-operative banks and other financial institutions. As expected, the co-efficients of RC in equations 2(b) and 2(c) are negative.

The ratio of time deposits to total deposits (TD/D) expresses the stability of the deposit base as the inflow and outflow of time deposits will be more predictable than that of other deposits. Hence, the higher this ratio, the less the need to hold excess reserves as a precautionary cushion and the greater the expansion of liabilities corresponding to a given supply of reserves. As expected, the co-efficient of TD/D is positive in the estimated equations.

Equations 2(b) and 2(c) differ in the way in which the required reserve ratio is specified. In the former, the statutory cash reserve ratio is specified as an average ratio of reserves to liabilities whereas in the latter equation, the marginal ratio is used. During the sample

TABLE 2

Bank Liability Supply Equations

					$\bar{R}^2$(adj)	D.W.	S.E.E
2 (a) L =	5657.2	+ 6.8 TBR (4.7)	+ 10861.0 S (0.2)		0.95	0.73	2124.5
2 (b) L =	-132160.7	+ 5.9 TBR (12.4)	- 67660.8 S (3.0)	-269.9 RC (2.4) + 190672.6 TD/D (7.4)	0.99	2.24	631.3
2 (c) L =	-139516.7	+ 4.9 TBR (16.8)	- 7132.3 ΔRR/ΔL (3.8)	-440.5 RC (4.0) + 200126.1 TD/D (8.8)	0.99	2.69	540.2

Note: Figures in brackets are t-statistics.

TABLE 3

Nominal Income Equations

						$\bar{R}^2$(adj)	D.W.	S.E.E.
3 (a) Y =	25248.3	- 0.20 YR (0.7)	- 83203.6 YNA/Y (4.0)	+ 88.2 NP_{-1} (1.1)	+ 4.37 (C+DD) (12.7) +3997.0 RLT (3.8)	0.99	2.18	908.1
3 (b) Y =	55142.5	- 0.97 YR (2.4)	- 78935.7 YNA/Y (3.0)	+ 384.6 NP_{-1} (8.4)	+ 1.42 (C+D) (8.7)	0.99	3.03	1494.2

Note: Figures in brackets are t-statistics.

period, RBI has stipulated the cash reserve ratio in both the average and marginal forms. For the present model the marginal form has been used as it is more flexible and can be made to accommodate statutory changes in both the average and marginal requirements for forecasting purposes.

The supply of bank deposits is statistically derived from the supply of liabilities, as deposits account for more than 90 percent of the demand and time liabilities of scheduled commercial banks. The equation used for deriving the supply of bank deposits is as follows:

	$\bar{R}^2$adj	D.W.	S.E.E.
D = 60.9 + 0.94 L (387.7)	0.99	3.16	68.3

where D represents aggregate deposits and L represents aggregate liabilities of scheduled commercial banks. The figure in brackets represent t-statistics.

3. *Nominal Income Determination*

As explained in Section II and elaborated in the discussion of the model's flow chart below, variation in nominal income is the principal mechanism by which monetary equilibrium is brought about. In essence, this approach is derived from the quantity theory of money, which posits that disequilibrium between the supply of and demand for money expresses itself as changes in the aggregate price level. The approach has well known limitations, some of which are touched upon in Section VI which discusses further work on the model. In the present model, however, the equation determining nominal income may be viewed as a reformulation of an equation specifying the demand for money as a function of income, prices and interest rates. Here, the dependent variable is nominal income which is regressed on money stock and other variables influencing the demand for money. Hence, real income and the share of non-agricultural income in total income, which have a positive influence on the demand for money will have a negative influence on nominal income given the supply of money. The lagged national income deflator (NP_{-1}) has been introduced as an indicator of inflationary expectations. The hypothesis is that the higher the expected rate of inflation, the less the inclination to hold money rather than commodities. On this hypothesis, NP_{-1} should have a positive sign in the equation with nominal income as the explained variable.

The difference between the two equations 3(a) and 3(b) of Table 3 lies in the concept of money that is used. Equation 3(a) uses currency plus demand deposits (C+DD), corresponding to a narrow definition of money and 3(b) uses currency plus aggregate deposits (C+D) which is the broader definition of money. The two equations are used in alternative versions of the model.

4. Demand for Deposits

As the demand for deposits is a part of the demand for money and as the latter is already the basis for the specification of the nominal income equation, there is no room in the model for an additional equation, estimating the demand for aggregate deposits. However, in the version of the model that equilibrates around narrow money (currency plus demand deposits), it is necessary to derive an estimate of demand deposits. This can be done directly by a demand deposit equation or indirectly by estimating the demand for time deposits and deriving demand deposits as a residual out of aggregate deposits which are separately determined. There is a conceptual difference between the estimates of demand deposits so derived. In the first case, where a demand deposit equation is used, the estimate is one of demand. In the second case, since the estimate of aggregate deposits is a supply estimate (having been derived from the equation estimating the supply of bank liabilities), the derived estimate of demand deposits should also be interpreted as a supply estimate.

Sets of equations estimating the demand for demand and time deposits are shown in Table 4. The specifications are fairly conventional in form, using income, the share of non-agricultural income in total income and rates of interests as explanatory variables.

Some special features of the equations for time deposits may be noted. A comparison of the income co-efficients in equations 4(a) and 4(b) shows that the inclusion of banks' branch expansion (NB_{-1}) distorts the income effect considerably. Hence, although the expansion of branches may be expected to have contributed to the mobilisation of time deposits, it is concluded that this effect cannot be distinguished from the expansion of time deposits caused by the growth of incomes. The co-efficient of time deposit interest rates (RLT) has remained insignificant and, in many of the equations, has the wrong sign. This may be partly due to the problems in measuring RLT, which is defined as a weighted average of interest rates payable on fixed deposits of different maturities. As the weights change from year to year and the changes in the structure of time deposit rates may sometimes induce shifts among maturities rather than increases or decreases in total time deposits, the sign of this co-efficent may have been affected. Further, as time deposits include the time

TABLE 4

								$\bar{R}^2$(adj)	D.W.	S.E.E
			Time Deposit Demand Equations							
4 (a)	TD =	−20622.4	+ 0.34 Y (20.4)	− 1699.2 RLT (10.1)	+ 44781.6 YNA/Y (7.7)			0.99	1.33	403.9
4 (b)	TD =	−19240.0	+ 0.28 Y (3.1)	− 1540.1 RLT (5.3)	+ 41080.2 YNA/Y (5.1)	+ 0.18 NB_{-1} (0.7)		0.99	1.29	423.0
4 (c)	ΔTD =	−3806.2	+ 0.06 Y (3.5)	− 161.6 RLT (1.0)	+ 6864.2 YNA/Y (1.2)			0.90	1.25	391.0
4 (d)	ΔTD =	−6354.3	+ 0.05 Y (4.1)	− 80.2 RLT (0.6)	+ 6042.6 YNA/Y (1.3)	+ 422.7 RV (1.9)		0.94	1.52	323.1
4 (e)	ΔTD =	−2578.5	+ 0.05 Y (4.3)	+ 42.0 RLT (0.3)	+ 2867.1 YNA/Y (0.6)	− 3537.9 $\overline{WP}_{-1}$ (2.4)		0.94	2.15	289.9
4 (f)	ΔTD =	−4352.8	+ 0.05 Y (4.4)	+ 34.2 RLT (0.2)	+ 3461.3 YNA/Y (0.8)	− 2598.6 $\overline{WP}_{-1}$ (1.5)	+240.3 RV (1.1)	0.94	2.17	286.1
			Demand Deposit Demand Equations							
4 (g)	DD =	−3778.1	+ 0.09 Y (14.2)	+ 9780.1YNA/Y (4.6)	− 457.4 RLT (7.4)			0.99	2.13	148.8
4 (h)	DD =	−2845.5	+ 0.09 Y (13.6)	+ 7965.3YNA/Y (3.3)	− 478.4 RLT (8.0)	− 866.9 $\overline{WP}$ (1.4)		0.99	2.81	139.4

Note: Figures in brackets are t-statistics.

liability component of saving deposits, the relationship between RLT and time deposits is thereby attenuated. A negative co-efficient for RLT may also be the result of the absence of a rate of return on assets competing with time deposits. It is with this in view that the dividend yield on industrial securities (RV) was tried, but without success (possibly because the dividend yield is only an incomplete measure of the return on industrial securities in so far as it ignores capital gains which are the principal motivation for investment in industrial shares). It is only the inclusion of the lagged change in wholesale prices, which may be interpreted as a proxy for inflationary expectations, that resulted in a positive, albeit insignificant, co-efficient for RLT. Thus, it would appear that, given income levels, the aggregate demand for time deposits is only mildly influenced by the interest rates on time deposits and is adversely affected by inflationary expections.

Supply of Bank Reserves

As noted previously, the supply of bank reserves is derived from the reserve money identity. By definition, reserve money consists of currency with the public, bank reserves (including banks' holdings of cash) and other monetary deposits with RBI. This definition can be rewritten as follows to derive total bank reserves (TBR), given reserve money (H), currency with the public (C) and other deposits etc. (X).

TBR = H — C — X

Flow Chart

Following the above discussion of the individual equations, their inter-relationships can be gleaned with reference to the Flow Chart in Annexure III. The basic function of the model is to find values of nominal income and monetary aggregates that are internally consistent, in the sense of satisfying all the equations of the model, given the values of certain exogenous variables such as reserve money, real income, cash reserve ratio etc. Starting from a trial level of nominal income, the model derives a preliminary estimate of the public's demand for currency (using equation 1 of Annexure II) and, therefore, an estimate of the supply of bank reserves (using equation 2 of Annexure II). The same income level is also used to derive an estimate of the demand for time deposits or demand deposits. From the estimate of bank reserves, the model derives the supply of aggregate deposits (using equations 3 and 4 of Annexure II). In one version, the model deducts the estimated time deposits from aggregate deposits to arrive at estimated demand deposits and introduces this estimate (along with the estimated currency) into the nominal income equation. In the other version, where the broader concept of money is used in the nominal income equation, the model introduces the sum of currency and aggregate deposits. Hence a new estimate of nominal income is derived which may be different from the estimate of nominal income with which the series of steps began. If so, a new trial level of nominal income is adopted and fresh estimates of currency and time deposits are made. This leads to all the other magnitudes being re-estimated and, finally, a new estimate of nominal income. The cycle is repeated until the estimates in successive iteration converges and are said to represent the solution of the model for a given year. This process is repeated for each year in the sample period and for the forecast year.

V. Simulation Results

The model has been simulated for the sample period 1970-71 to 1979-80 and the annual predictions generated by the model have been compared with the actual values of the monetary aggregates and the national income deflator for those years. A summary measure of the percentage deviation of the predicted values from the actual values for the period as a whole is provided by the Root Mean Square Percentage Error (RMSPE). The results are presented for two alternative models:

Model A : In this model the equilibration takes place around narrow money i.e. the national income equation used is 7a of Annexure II and demand deposits are derived as a residual by deducting estimated time deposits (equation 5a of Annexure II) from aggregate deposits;

Model B : In this model the equilibration takes place around broad money i.e. the national income equation used is 7b of Annexure II and time deposits are derived as a residual by deducting estimated demand deposits (equation 5b of Annexure II) from aggregate deposits;

For each model, both static and dynamic simulations were made and the results are presented separately. In the static simulation, the previous year's values of each variable are set at their actual levels whereas in the dynamic simulation the values generated within the model continue to be used in successive years, until the end of the sample period. For one period forecasts, the static simulation results are an adequate measure of the model's performance. However, given the delays in obtaining data, it may sometimes be necessary to predict monetary aggregates for the next year without having reasonable data for the current year. In such cases, the dynamic simulation results gain relevance. It may be noted that although the model does not have lagged endogenous variables, it has dynamic properties because of the use of first differences in the estimated equations.

The prediction error for the main variables are shown in the table below:

Prediction Errors in Sample Period Simulations (Root Mean Square Percentage Errors)

	Model A		Model B	
	Static Simulation	*Dynamic Simulation*	*Static Simulation*	*Dynamic Simulation*
Currency	1.67	1.39	2.21	1.96
Aggregate Deposits	5.59	4.59	7.05	6.16
National Income Deflator	4.73	4.15	2.19	2.18
C + DD	4.89	4.46	1.63	1.64
C + D	3.12	2.53	3.85	3.26

The maximum RMSPE for any of the above variables in either model is 7.1 per cent in the estimation of aggregate deposits by model B. The error in the estimation of currency is of the order of 1.4 to 2 per cent and of the national income deflator is of the order of 2 to 5 per cent. The error in estimation of narrow money (C+DD) is much less in model B than in model A because the estimation of demand deposits in model A is as a residual whereas in model B it is direct. In all other respects, however, model A seems to perform better than model B. There is no significant difference between the static and dynamic simulations, and, surprisingly, the dynamic simulation often yields better results. In general, the performance of both the models is satisfactory, although there is clearly scope for improvement in the accuracy of the forecasts of aggregate deposits.

A further test of the model is its performance outside the sample period. Since the model's equations are estimated for the period 1970-71 to 1979-80, the model's predictions for 1980-81 can be compared with the data for 1980-81. Since final data for March 1981 are not yet available, the comparison is made against the partially revised data (as published in the RBI Bulletin April 1981). As far as possible, actual values are used for the exogenous variables such as reserve money etc. In a few cases, actual values are not available and their values had to be assumed. The important assumptions underlying the 1980-81 predictions are that national income in real terms would increase by 6.7 per cent; that the ratio of non-agricultural income to national income at current prices would be 60 per cent (as against 64 per cent in 1979-80); and that foreign remittance inflows would be Rs. 1,000 crores (at the same rate as in 1979-80).

On these assumptions, the model generated predictions of the monetary aggregates for 1980-81 which can be compared against the tentative data for 1980-81. The comparisons are presented in the table below:

Prediction Error for 1980-81 (as of last Friday of March)

		Model A		Model B	
	Actual Value	*Predicted Value*	*Per cent Error*	*Predicted Value*	*Per cent Error*
Currency	13464	13722	-1.9	13888	-3.1
Aggregate Deposits	37847	35540	6.1	34781	8.1
National Income Deflator	212.40	215.4	-1.4	230.8	-8.7
C + DD	21320	19971	6.3	21983	-3.1
C + D	51311	49262	4.0	48669	5.1

Model A which equilibrates around narrow money, has performed better than model B in the accuracy of its predictions of all the major variables presented in the table except for the prediction of narrow money where model B fares better because it uses a direct estimate of demand deposits. The predictions are quite good for all the monetary aggregates, with an error of 2 to 3 per cent in the prediction of currency and of 4 to 5 per cent in the prediction of broad money. The error in model A's prediction of the national income deflator is remarkably low at 1.4 per cent. The errors in the prediction of aggregate deposits are, however, somewhat high.

VI. Further Work

The most striking limitation of the present version of the model is its small size which, from an operational point of view is also a major merit. For repeated policy simulations during the year, it is advisable that the forecasting model be restricted in size, at least in the initial stages. Hence, it was decided to restrict the model to a few monetary equations alone, without attempting detailed modelling of the real sector. In consequence, however, the determination of the national income deflator is extremely rudimentary and, in some circumstances, could even be misleading. Strictly speaking, the forecasting approach adopted in this model requires a more elaborate specification of both the monetary and real sectors of the economy and their interaction. But the limitations of the data, as discussed in Section III, suggest that the estimation of a large short-run model is an enterprise of doubtful utility, at least at this stage. Nevertheless, some improvements of the price determination system must be sought, at least in terms of incorporating some of the non-monetary influences on the price level. In the present version, the model perhaps overemphasises the link between monetary imbalance and the rate of inflation, ignoring such other factors as agricultural output, price level of imports, changes in administered prices, shortages of sensitive commodities etc.

While experimenting with more complex specifications of the interaction between money and prices at the macro level, it should be possible to bring about some improvements even within the present structure of the model. First, the equations could be re-estimated using data averaged over a period rather than only as of the last Friday of March. Data pertaining to a single day are susceptible to substantial random shocks which may affect the quality of the parameter estimates, especially when the number of observations is not large. Secondly, an attempt could be made to estimate the present model on a quarterly or half yearly basis rather than on an annual basis. The main obstacle to this, as noted in Section III, is that national income data are available only on an annual basis. For the purposes of monetary forecasting, however, it may be worth experimenting with some of the unofficial attempts to derive estimates of GDP for six-monthly intervals. If the semi-annual national income series can be used, the model would gain in richness and utility in two major ways. The availability of semi-annual monetary forecasts on a systematic basis would greatly assist the formulation of monetary policy, and, in particular, the monitoring of the results of policy changes in relation to earlier anticipations. A semi-annual model would also permit the exploration of lags in the transmission mechanism between the monetary and real sectors. In the present annual version, the time series is not long enough to permit the use of more flexible lag structures in the estimated equations. Through such improvements in the specifications of the equations, the predictive performance of the model could be considerably improved. With the incorporation of lagged relationships, the model could also be modified to allow temporary disequilibria between the demand and supply of money, whose effects could work themselves through the rest of the model over time. This would add greater realism to the analysis of the interaction between monetary variables and the price level.

The treatment of reserve money as exogenous accords with theory but may not be wholly appropriate in the present context. The composition of reserve money is such that RBI has direct control over only a small part of it and it may be incorrect to assume that by manipulating its lending to banks, RBI will be able to fully offset fluctuations in credit to the government sector or in net foreign assets. Given these limitations, forecasts generated by the present model must be viewed as conditional forecasts of monetary aggregates, conditional on the assumed change in reserve money. The utility of the model would be greatly enhanced if it included an endogenous forecast of the change in reserve money, given only certain exogenous policy variables that may be set at predetermined levels. In the main, this would require the inclusion of a set of fiscal equations to estimate the size of the budgetary deficit. As the rate of inflation may itself have a significant effect on the size of the budget deficit, endogenous estimation of RBI credit to the Government would then bring out the relationship between fiscal and monetary policies.

The assumption that RBI fully controls the quantum of lending to the commercial banks may require some modification in short-run analysis. RBI's lending to commercial banks may, broadly speaking, be divided into two categories: one category consists of refinance schemes under which the bank has an automatic entitlement to refinance based on a prescribed formula in relation to certain categories of advances (e.g. food, or export credit); another category of refinance is wholly discretionary, in that RBI deals with specific applications from banks for temporary accommodation. The extent to which banks actually use their entitlements for refinance under the first category will depend on their liquidity situation. With suitable refinements, these considerations could be incorporated into the forecasting model, making the creation of reserve money endogenous to a greater extent and focussing attention more sharply on the monetary instruments that RBI actually has under its control.

In the same vein, it is also possible to endogenise the estimation of the change in RBI's holdings of dated securities. The statutory liquidity ratio gives the best basis for the estimation of the absorption of government securities by the commercial banks, corresponding to the estimated increase in their demand and time liabilities. Given an estimate of the absorption of government securities by other financial institutions such as LIC and Provident Funds, and the Plan for market borrowing by the government and eligible institutions, the model can estimate the increase in RBI's holdings of dated government securities, which may be one of the important sources of change in reserve money.

It has earlier been noted that the structure of the present model assumes an excess demand for bank credit i.e. that banks are able to find borrowers at prevailing rates of interest for all the funds they wish to advance. While reasonable as an initial approximation, the assumption that banks do not have surplus liquidity is not always correct. There are times when banks find that credit demand has fallen short of expectation (e.g. because of a reduction in food procurement) and they are left with surplus resources to be invested in liquid assets. The model's specification of the bank's supply of liabilities does allow for some flexibility in bank behaviour in this respect but an explicit treatment of the credit market might be preferable. Further, a detailed study of credit demand is needed in order to consider how the estimated increase in bank credit compares with the amount of credit expansion required to support the projected increase in production. It would appear that such an analysis would have to be done first at a somewhat disaggregated level, when the precise relationship between production and credit can be explored in depth. Without such careful analysis, it is doubtful whether aggregative statistical studies will constitute a significant improvement over the present version of the model, in this respect.

ANNEXURE I

List of Variables

*1)	C	–	Currency with the public - (Rs. Crores)
*2)	DD	–	Demand deposits of Scheduled Commercial Banks (Rs. Crore)
*3)	TD	–	Time deposits of Scheduled Commercial Banks (Rs. Crores)
*4)	D	–	Total demand and time deposits of Scheduled Commercial Banks (Rs. Crores)
*5)	L	–	Net demand and time liabilities of Scheduled Commercial Banks (Rs. Crores)
6)	TBR	–	Total reserves of Scheduled Commercial Banks (Rs. Crores)
7)	X	–	Total reserves of banks other than Scheduled Commercial Banks and other Deposits with RBI (Rs. Crores)
*8)	Y	–	Net national product at factor cost at current prices (Rs. Crores)
9)	YR	–	Net national product at factor cost at constant (1970-71) prices (Rs. Crores)
10)	BCF	–	Bank credit for food procurement (Rs. Crores)
#11)	BC	–	Total Bank Credit (Rs. Crores)
12)	RR	–	Required reserves of Scheduled Commercial Banks (Rs. Crores)
13)	RLT	–	Weighted average interest rate on fixed deposits of Scheduled Commercial Banks (percent)
14)	RC	–	Call money rate (percent)
15)	(YNA/Y)	–	Ratio of non-agricultural income to total national income
16)	WP	–	Index number of wholesale prices for all commodities (monthly average with base 1970-71 = 100)
17)	$\overline{WP}$	–	Rate of change in wholesale prices of all commodities.
18)	$\overline{WP}$-1	–	$\overline{WP}$ lagged by one year.
19)	$\overline{SCP}$	–	Rate of change in wholesale prices of sensitive commodities.
20)	H	–	High powered money = [C+TBR +X]
21)	S	–	RR/L
22)	FR	–	Foreign remittances (Rs. Crores)
*23)	NP	–	National income deflator (base 1970-71=100)
24)	TD/D	–	Ratio of time deposits to total deposits.
#25)	RV	–	Yield on industrial securities.

* Indicate endogenous variables in the model.

\# Represents variables figuring only in the alternative equations discussed but not considered in the model.

ANNEXURE II

Monetary Model For the Indian Economy 1970-71 to 1979-80

				$\overline{SCP}$	FR	Δ BCF	Y	RLT	R^2(adj)	D.W.	Mean	S.E.E
1)	Δ C	=	2306.6493	+ 851.6162	+ 1.2259	+ 0.9183	+ 0.0223	-526.3328	0.7084	2.8386	769.20	274.5933
	t			0.945	1.496	2.071	1.234	2.947				
	e			0.098	0.825	0.245	1.734	-4.899				
2)	TBR	=	H	- C	- X							
				RC	TD/D	Δ RR/Δ L	TBR					
3)	L	=	-139516.6667	- 440.4875	+200126.1004	-7132.327	+ 4.8678		0.9966	2.6933	16532.60	540.1636
	t			4.022	8.764	3.763	16.848					
	e			-0.224	9.258	-0.039	0.444					
				L								
4)	D	=	60.9487	+ 0.9420					0.9999	3.1578	15635.40	68.2734
	t			387.653								
	e			0.996								
				YNA/Y	Y	$\overline{WP}_{-1}$	RLT					
5a)	Δ TD	=	-2578.4649	+ 2867.0873	+ 0.0521	-3537.8679	+ 41.9878		0.9485	2.1538	2143.20	289.8477
	t			0.642	4.332	2.433	0.286					
	e			0.735	+ 1.455	- 0.126	0.140					
				RLT	Y	YNA/Y						
5b)	DD	=	-3778.0608	- 457.4288	+ 0.0870	+9780.1080			0.9926	2.1311	3522.10	148.7711
	t			7.395	14.200	4.589						
	e			-0.930	1.477	1.526						
6a)	DD	=	D - TD									
6b)	TD	=	D - DD									
				YR	RLT	NP_{-1}	YNA/Y					
7a)	Y	=	25248.3482	- 0.1960	+3997.0262	+88.2332	-83203.5519		0.9978	2.1814	59795.90	908.0674
	t			0.713	3.779	1.104	5.019					
	e			- 0.128	0.479	0.205	-0.765					
							C+DD					
							+4.3725					
							12.705					
							0.787					
				YR	NP_{-1}	YNA/Y	C+D					
7b)	Y	=	55142.5394	- 0.9703	+384.6295	-78935.6782	+ 1.4199		0.9940	3.0350	59795.90	1494.1660
	t			2.376	8.430	3.016	8.661					
	e			- 0.635	0.895	- 0.725	0.543					
8)	NP	=	(Y/YR) 100									

Note:

1. T & e – indicate t-statistics & elasticities respectively.
2. The sign Δ before a variable denotes that the variable is considered in incremental terms.

ANNEXURE III

Flow Chart of Endogenous Variables

Model – A

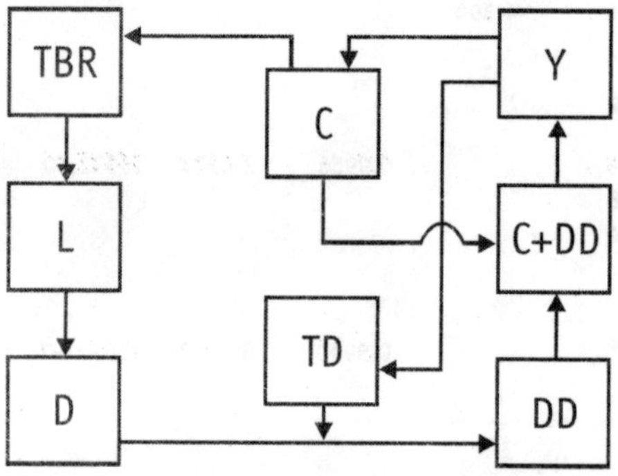

Model – B

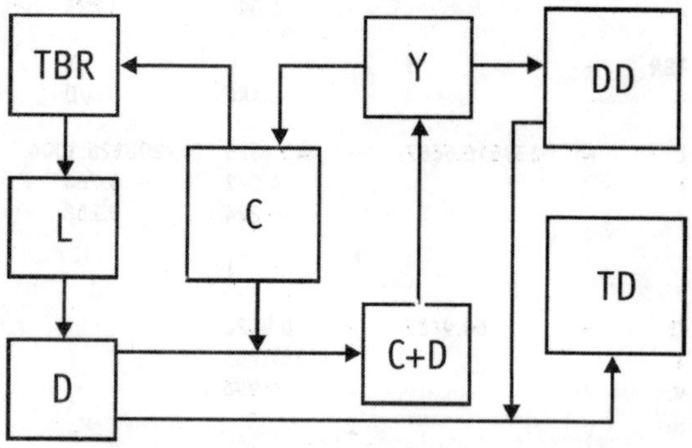

Section II

THIS section has papers that deal mainly with the supply of and demand for money, whichever way money is defined. The papers show the awareness of the Bank's economists of the latest developments in the literature on the subject in question. They attempt to throw light on questions such as these: should reserve money be unadjusted before one could use it for purposes of money supply determination ? Should one accept blindly the conventional measures of money supply and not give weights to the different components of money supply as many academics argue ? Should money supply determination be viewed from the components side say by working out the demands for currency and deposits ? Would it not be useful to work out money supply through exercises that encompass demand for and supply of domestic credit and foreign exchange assets ? When the economy opens up, what kind of liabilities should be considered as part of money supply? Should not residency be the criterion for the purpose ? Should one estimate demand for money conventionally through ordinary least squares method? Can the co-integration techniques be employed for such estimations in order to know whether money demand is stable or not ? Finally, should one study the impact of unanticipated changes in money supply on the demand for money ?

The papers belong to the 1980s and 1990s. The published reserve money data is unadjusted, even though the Reserve Bank had resorted very often to the use of cash reserve ratio as an instrument of policy in the 1970s and 1980s. Why is it that adjustments were not made to bank reserves and thereby to reserve money ? The reasons could be several. One might surmise that even though the Bank economists knew of the concept of reserve money, it probably was not used for policy purposes. In fact the data on reserve money were not regularly (i.e., monthly/weekly/fort-nightly) published till the Second Working Group on money supply came out in 1977 with the series beginning April 1970. The Bank economists' diffidence to use reserve money in monetary analyses during the 1970s was partly because it would be construed as using the money multiplier (MM) approach to money supply determination. It was perhaps because the MM approach was popular with many Indian economists brought up in the Chicago tradition that went by the label of monetarist school of thought (See Suraj B Gupta) and contrary to the Keynesian tradition in which most Bank economists were brought up*. But by 1982, there was some rethinking on this issue within the Bank and the paper of Rangarajan and Anoop Singh included in this volume amply demonstrates such a development.

The emergence of financial assets since about the mid-1980s in India seemed to have given rise to the issue of having an appropriate measure of money stock. The Bank had published series of four money supply measures right from April 1970 but of them, only two, namely the conventional narrow money (M1) and broad money (M3) were in effective use. The measures have been simple sums; they as such did not have weights for their moneyness. There was, however, some academic opinion within India to employ weighted monetary aggregates rather than simple sum aggregates, following the lead given by economists such as Barnett. The Bank, however, was not convinced of the superiority of the weighted aggregates in the operational sense of the term. Jadhav's paper clearly reflects this view. This was the only paper on the subject that was published by the Bank to date.

Money supply process is often viewed in terms of the components of money supply. While this approach has its own merits, it does not give insights about the level of activity underlying the economy that makes use of money irrespective of its components. Besides, most central banks operate on the levels of domestic credit and attempt to influence the

* There was a lively debate on the usefulness of the money multiplier approach in India in the Economic & Political Weekly, a widely read professional journal in 1976. Suraj B Gupta of the Delhi School of Economics was the major proponent of this approach. Some of the Bank economists — in particular N A Mujumdar and S L Shetty — regarded MM approach as mechanistic and irrelevant from the point of view of understanding the behavioral responses of economic units to policy actions. Suraj Gupta's views appeared first in the form of an article, "Factors Affecting Money Supply — Critical Examination of Reserve Bank's Analysis" in *Economic & Political Weekly*, Vol XI, No. 4, January 26, 1976 and subsequently in a theoretical form in his book, *Monetary Planning for India*, Oxford University Press, New Delhi 1979. See for RBI economists' comments, N A Mujumdar, "Money Supply Analysis — Mechanistic and Economic Explanations, *Economic & Political Weekly*, Vol XI, No 9, February 28, 1976, and S L Shetty, V A Avadhani and K A Menon, "Money Supply Analysis: Further Comments", *Economic & Political Weekly*, Vol XI, No. 15, April 10, 1976 and for a sharp rebuttal, Srinivas Madhur, "Money Supply Analysis", *Economic & Political Weekly*, Vol XI, No 23, June 5, 1976. Forecasting of M1 with MM approach was attempted by A Vasudevan, in an article entitled, "An Approach to Money Supply Expansion in India", published in S L Shetty (ed), *Framework For A National Credit Plan*, National Institute of Bank Management, Bombay, 1979.

external position through exchange rate policies. Such an exercise requires central banks to continuously monitor the real developments in the economy and to review their policies in the light of the uncertainties[@]. This approach is sometimes viewed as purely balance sheet oriented as against the money-multiplier approach. In the case of the Reserve Bank of India, credit planning played a major role in influencing the level and direction of credit right from the beginning of the 1970s and as such should have had the advantage of pursuing the balance sheet approach to its logical end. But there were no analytical papers on this subject in the case of India till Himanshu Joshi and Indranil Bhattacharyya attempted it.

As the economy opened up, albeit gradually, in the later part of the 1990s, the need for appropriate criterion for working out the appropriate measure of net foreign exchange assets of the banking system as a source of money stock became urgent especially in the context of non-repatriability of foreign exchange deposits that banks were allowed to collect from non-resident Indians. The best criterion for the purpose is related to residency of the economic unit that influences the monetary magnitudes. The Third Working Group on Money Supply (1998) used this criterion. Deb Prasad Rath and Indranil Sen Gupta explained the rationale of the criterion and considered its appropriateness to the Indian conditions.

The use of monetary targeting on the basis of the stability of money demand is a time-honoured and an established practice with most central banks. For long the Bank economists used the OLS method to test the stability of the demand for real money by using the real income and interest rate as arguments in the function. In fact this approach was widely prevalent in both the official and academic circles in India almost till the mid-1990s. Almost all the studies** showed that the demand for money in India was predominantly income-elastic. Interest rate was said to hold very weak influence partly because most interest rates were administered in any case till the mid-1990s. However, as financial liberalization is attempted and as financial innovations emerged from about the middle of the 1980s, it became necessary to see whether economic units make determination of the anticipated and unanticipated changes in money supply in order to gain insights about the policy effects on output and

---

[@] See Charles Goodhart, *Money, Information, and Uncertainty*, Macmillan, London, 1975.

** See A. Vasudevan, "Demand for Money in India — A Survey of Literature", *Reserve Bank Staff Occasional Papers*, Vol. 2, No.1, June 1977, pp.58-83. Also N D Jadhav, "Monetary Modelling of the Indian Economy: A Survey", *RBI Occasional Papers*, Vol 11, No.2, June 1990, pp. 83-152.

prices. Capturing this mood, B K Bhoi's article, the first authentic one in the case of India, showed concern about the stability of the demand for money in India on the basis of the OLS estimates of the widely used shock absorber model. However, the OLS estimates are not considered useful because they give rise to spurious inferences. By 1990s, the literature had come to accept the co-integration framework as necessary to avoid the pitfalls of time series properties of stationariness. Ashok Nag and Ghanshyam Upadhyay and Himanshu Joshi and Mridul Saggar attempt to reestimate the demand for money using the co-integration and find the demand for money to be fairly stable. Their papers are the early ones to appear using this sophisticated econometric tool in the case of India. While the papers reflect the research abilities of the Bank to move away from the conventional method of estimating the demand for money for purposes of policy, their results cannot be taken as final and incontrovertible, since the financial liberalization process in India tended to move ahead at noticeable speed only from about the second half of the 1990s.

3

Reserve Money: Concepts and Policy Implications for India

A Study of Indian Economy

C Rangarajan • Anoop Singh

I. INTRODUCTION

THIS paper is concerned with specifying the relationship between reserve money and alternative measures of the money stock. In the traditional monetary base/money multiplier framework, the basic relationship may be expressed as :

$$M = m.H$$

where M is a measure of the stock money, H denotes the monetary base, and m is the money multiplier. The discretionary ability of the monetary authority to influence the supply of money is usually reflected in variations in the monetary base. Changes in the multiplier, on the other hand, usually reflect the behavior of the commercial banks, in particular their demand for excess or borrowed reserves; and that of the public, in particular their demand for currency and their preference between time and demand deposits. Shifts in such behavior impart complexity to the relationship between reserve money and money supply. However, such shifts have been observed to occur slowly over a period of time.

In this monetary base/multiplier framework, changes in reserve requirements can be captured either in the multiplier, or in the monetary base. The former procedure is the commonest, and has the additional advantage that the data on the monetary base need no consequential adjustment following changes in the reserve requirement ratio. In this method, the money multiplier tends to rise when the reserve requirement ratio is reduced, indicating the greater multiple expansion of bank liabilities facilitated by the reduced ratio. Alternatively, the impact of changes in the reserve requirement ratio can be reflected in the monetary base by applying an appropriate adjustment. The rationale for making such an adjustment to the monetary base is to capture in it, as completely as possible, elements of the monetary authority's discretionary action, including therefore changes in reserve requirements. Use of a reserve money series adjusted in this manner results in a multiplier that would be relatively more stable than obtained otherwise. In this framework, an increase in the reserve requirement ratio would reduce the adjusted monetary base, consequent to the additional impounding of deposits achieved by the measure.

The objective of this paper is two fold: first, to illustrate the nature of the adjustment that is considered most appropriate to make to the published data for India on reserve money. Application of this methodology results in an adjusted series on reserve money, incorporating the effects of cash reserve requirement (CRR) changes. The CRR instrument has been used actively in India since 1973/74; a new adjusted series on reserve money has been constructed for the period since 1973/74. The second objective of the paper is to use the new adjusted series to examine the lags in the impact of reserve money on various definitions of the money stock. For this purpose, quarterly data have been used for the period 1973/74-1981/82.

Our analysis suggests that the adjustments to reserve money result in a series that shows a systematic and well-defined relationship to the alternative concepts of the money stock.

II. ADJUSTED RESERVE MONEY

1. The relevance of the adjustment

The importance of the monetary base derives from its use as a set of assets that constrain the money supply. It is an aggregate that can be measured quickly and accurately by the monetary authority. As an

---

Work on this paper was initiated when Shri Singh was Special Advisor to the Reserve Bank of India in 1982.

instrument of monetary control, its usefulness depends on the extent to which the monetary authority can determine its expansion and, on the extent to which it bears a systematic relationship with the money stock. The objective of this section is to define the variable most appropriately. Subsequently, its relationship with alternative measures of the money stock is explored.

In its unadjusted form, the impact of changes in cash reserve requirements is captured in the multiplier. However, as discussed above, the impact of reserve money as an instrument of control can be understood easier if the effects of reserve requirement changes are included in the computation of the base. During periods when the legal cash reserve requirement is changed, the growth rate of a monetary base that incorporates the resultant impact would diverge compared with a series unadjusted for such changes. For example, if the reserve requirement is raised, the adjusted monetary base can be expected to grow more slowly compared with its unadjusted counterpart, provided the increased cash reserve requirement is complied with by the system.[1]

The concept of the adjusted monetary base has been applied progressively more frequently in the last decade. Its widest application has been to United States data. The Federal Reserve Bank of St. Louis has published such a series since August 1968 and, in the course of successive articles, has defined and refined the methodology of the Reserve Adjustment Magnitude.[2] Since March 1979, the Board of Governors of the Federal Reserve System have also published a monetary base series incorporating the effects of reserve requirement changes. Both definitions of the adjusted series are similar, differing only in relatively unimportant ways.

In the Indian case, Gupta (1979) has explained the nature of the adjustment, and stressed that the monetary authority can control the adjusted base more effectively through changing reserve requirements. In this manner, the adjusted monetary base can be regarded as being closer to a policy variable in money supply analysis. The same procedure is seen as resulting in the money multiplier being largely an independently determined variable as far as the monetary authority is concerned.

However, not all studies of the subject agree that use of the reserve base adjusted for reserve requirement changes improves the framework for monetary control. Sharpe (1980) concludes that the adjusted concept proves inappropriate as the relevant independent variable in an analysis of money supply influences for Australia. Sharpe's study finds significantly different lag structures for the reserve base variable and the reserve requirement variable in his money supply relationships.

2. The methodology of the adjustment

The methodology of the adjustment factor is designed to keep the money multiplier invariant to changes in the cash reserve requirement. In this method, the difference between the current period CRR and that of a base period is applied to the net demand and time liabilities (DTL) of the current period. The resultant adjustment factor is a measure of the reserves liberated or absorbed by the change in the reserve requirements compared with the base period. This may be expressed as:

$$\text{Adjustment} = (r_t - r_0)\ \text{DTL} \qquad \ldots(1)$$

where r_0 is initial or benchmark CRR;

r_t is the current period CRR; and

DTL comprises the set of bank liabilities (demand and time) relevant to computation of the CRR. In this case, DTL data relate to the penultimate Friday of the month.

This does not complete the computation of the adjustment factor. Consideration has to be given to at least two additional influences. First where incremental reserve requirements are applicable, these need to be incorporated into the adjustment factor to the extent that they did not prevail at the base date. Second, the adjustment factor as derived above assumes compliance with the reserve requirements; to the extent that shortfalls result in some periods they need also to be reflected in the adjustment factor.

Inclusion of the incremental reserve requirements (IR) results in the following:

$$\text{Adjustment} = (r_t - r_0)\ \text{DTL} + \text{IR} \qquad \ldots(2)$$

The adjustment factor thus derived is then subtracted from the unadjusted series of reserve money, to yield what shall here be called the adjusted (1) series.

Finally, any net defaults of commercial banks with respect to the average and incremental reserve requirements need to be incorporated. Shortfalls in the compliance with the reserve requirements release bank reserves in the same manner that an increase in the monetary base would boost bank reserves. Shortfalls are included in the adjustment factor by subtracting the absolute amount of CRR defaults, measured on a net basis for all commercial banks:

$$\text{Adjustment} = (r_t - r_0)\ \text{DTL} + \text{IR} - \text{DF} \qquad \ldots(3)$$

where DF is the net CRR default for all commercial banks. Use of this more comprehensive adjustment factor yields what shall here be called the adjusted (2) series of the monetary base. Both adjusted series have been reconstructed on an end-month basis since April 1973 and are presented in Appendix Table 2.[3] This table also includes a series on adjusted bank reserves obtained by subtracting currency in circulation from the respective adjusted reserve money series. Comparisons between the unadjusted and adjusted series are afforded by Tables 1 and 2.

TABLE 1

Quarterly Average Growth Rates — Reserve Money, Bank Reserves, and Money

(In per cent)

	Reserve Money					Bank Reserves		
	Un-adjusted	Adjusted 1	Adjusted 2	M_1	M_3	Adjusted 1	Adjusted 2	Aggregate Deposits
1973/74								
I	12.9	9.6	9.6	7.9	7.2	10.5	10.5	5.8
II	1.0	-1.2	-1.2	0.1	2.8	13.0	13.0	5.9
III	3.7	1.5	1.6	1.4	3.4	-7.8	-6.4	3.9
IV	4.9	5.0	5.7	5.8	3.8	-9.6	-2.8	3.2
1974/75								
I	5.1	6.3	8.1	7.3	5.6	-0.9	20.2	10.8
II	-5.0	-3.4	-5.7	-1.0	1.0	21.7	-8.1	4.6
III	1.0	-0.5	-0.5	-3.2	1.4	7.2	7.2	2.8
IV	1.9	3.1	3.1	3.6	2.9	7.8	7.8	3.1
1975/76								
I	5.6	5.6	5.6	5.0	5.0	1.4	1.4	4.4
II	-3.5	-3.6	-3.6	-1.2	2.1	0.1	0.1	5.2
III	0.8	0.7	0.7	-0.4	2.7	-1.8	-1.8	3.5
IV	2.1	2.1	2.1	3.3	2.7	5.3	5.3	4.3
1976/77								
I	9.2	9.2	9.2	7.2	7.0	17.2	17.2	6.4
II	0.2	0.1	0.1	0.8	4.2	4.8	4.8	6.2
III	4.6	0.8	1.6	3.6	5.7	-17.6	-10.8	6.7
IV	5.7	4.9	5.5	4.4	3.7	4.0	9.4	3.2
1977/78								
I	8.4	6.8	5.3	6.8	6.7	2.3	-10.2	6.5
II	-0.7	-2.2	-2.2	-1.7	2.6	9.9	9.9	5.1
III	6.0	5.3	5.4	4.4	4.8	16.6	17.6	5.1
IV	2.6	1.3	1.2	4.1	4.2	-5.3	-6.1	5.0
1978/79								
I	10.6	10.1	10.1	7.6	6.3	20.3	20.3	5.4
II	-1.5	-3.0	-3.0	-1.0	2.8	-21.7	-21.7	4.2
III	6.0	4.8	5.0	7.2	5.9	14.7	16.2	6.3
IV	8.7	7.1	7.0	7.0	5.4	11.8	10.4	5.0
1979/80								
I	8.7	8.8	8.8	6.3	5.6	16.9	16.9	4.8
II	1.0	-0.5	-0.5	1.7	4.1	-11.0	-11.0	5.3
III	4.4	4.1	4.1	1.0	3.1	40.4	40.4	4.3
IV	3.8	3.5	3.5	5.3	4.1	-14.2	-14.2	3.3
1980-81								
I	5.0	4.3	11.8	4.7	4.5	-3.0	-3.0	4.2
II	-2.7	-4.3	-10.7	-2.9	1.7	-8.9	-8.9	3.6
III	7.3	7.8	7.8	6.4	5.0	25.4	25.4	4.8
IV	4.8	5.4	5.6	6.8	5.2	5.7	6.8	5.1
1981/82								
I	5.3	6.1	5.9	5.9	5.4	7.0	5.9	5.3
II	0.4	-2.2	-2.2	-1.3	2.5	4.9	4.9	4.3
III	1.0	-0.2	7.2	3.4	3.3	-14.9	-6.5	3.7
IV	1.9	0.7	-3.0	1.4	1.8	-14.9	6.6	1.6

Sources: The Annex and Appendix Table 2.

Tables 1 and 2 present quarterly and six monthly average growth rates for the various reserve money and money supply series. In some periods, the adjusted series on reserve money differ quite significantly from their unadjusted counterpart. During periods when the CRR was raised, the growth rate of the adjusted (1) series is revealed to be significantly less than the growth rate yielded by unadjusted reserve money. Similarly, when the CRR was lowered (1974/75), the adjusted series, appropriately, grew more rapidly particularly when account is taken of the defaults. In summary, the adjustment factors introduced alter not only the magnitude of change in reserve money, but also the direction of change.

TABLE 2

Six Monthly Average Growth Rates - Reserve Money, Bank Reserves, and Money

(In per cent)

	Reserve Money					Bank Reserves		
	Un-adjusted	Adjusted 1	Adjusted 2	M_1	M_3	Adjusted 1	Adjusted 2	Aggregate Deposits
1973/74								
1	-	12.7	12.7			16.7	16.7	
2	6.8	3.4	3.8	4.3	6.7	-7.0	-2.1	5.2
1974/75								
1	4.9	7.1	7.9	9.8	8.1	4.3	13.8	11.5
2	-2.6	-0.7	-2.0	-1.9	3.4	22.3	6.6	6.8
1975/76								
1	4.7	5.2	5.2	6.3	7.6	5.3	5.3	8.7
2	0.1	-0.1	-0.1	0.6	5.6	0.8	0.8	8.4
1976/77								
1	10.4	10.4	10.4	9.4	11.1	23.2	23.2	12.1
2	7.7	3.3	4.4	6.3	9.9	-14.0	-4.5	11.6
1977/78								
1	11.0	8.1	7.0	8.2	10.1	9.5	-1.4	10.9
2	7.0	4.8	4.9	5.6	8.4	18.8	19.3	10.4
1978/79								
1	11.2	9.2	9.1	9.2	10.0	4.3	3.8	10.3
2	9.7	6.9	7.0	10.4	10.2	6.7	7.4	11.2
1979/80								
1	13.8	12.3	12.2	10.9	10.6	16.6	15.9	10.2
2	6.9	5.6	5.6	4.6	7.3	22.8	22.8	8.7
1980/81								
1	5.5	3.9	7.7	5.9	7.5	-14.4	-14.4	7.8
2	8.4	8.3	4.5	8.4	8.6	22.9	23.6	8.6
1981/82								
1	8.0	7.7	7.6	8.7	9.5	12.7	12.0	11.0
2	2.2	-1.0	4.5	3.2	5.4	-19.4	-1.2	6.7

Sources: The Annex and Appendix Table 2.

Further comparison between the alternative series is yielded by Charts 1-3 which contrast the unadjusted monetary base with the adjusted base inclusive of CRR defaults. The adjusted monetary base is demonstrated to grow more slowly, particularly after 1976/77 when successive increases were made in the CRR requirements (chart 1). The resultant multiplier for narrow money is revealed to be considerably more stable than that base on the normally published series on the monetary base (Chart 2). In addition to the stability, the declining trend evident in the multiplier obtained from the unadjusted base is now absent. This highlights the alternative procedures for incorporating the impact of CRR changes in the reserve money multiplier framework of analysis. *Ceteris paribus*, more stringent cash reserve requirements depress the multiplier, based on unadjusted data on the monetary base. Incorporation of the impact of CRR changes in the computation of an adjusted reserve money series demonstrates more clearly the impact of those changes.

Chart 3 compares the quarterly and six monthly growth rates yielded by the two series on reserve money. In 1974/75, when the CRR was lowered the adjusted series grew more rapidly, a result that is different in direction as well as degree from the unadjusted series. After 1976/77, the growth rates of the adjusted series are significantly below those yielded by the unadjusted series, and demonstrate more clearly the trends indicated by Chart 1.

III. MONETARY CONTROL THROUGH THE MONETARY BASE

The importance of the monetary base as a control aggregate to influence variations in the money stock, and in aggregate GNP, has varied, depending on the institutional environment. In some countries, the monetary base has been used directly as the monetary target in the implementation of monetary policy, in place of intermediate targets such as alternative measures of the money stock. In most other cases, the monetary base has been considered, along with measures of money market conditions, as an appropriate policy guide through which to control the money stock. The latter approach leaves open the consequent issue of the transmission mechanism linking the main intermediate monetary aggregate with the changes in aggregate income and activity. Clearly, however, such transmission mechanisms are implicitly assumed in most exercises involving monetary aggregate targeting.

The rationale for using the monetary base as a control aggregate usually derives from the consideration that most monetary authority actions influence, and even determine, the monetary base. Incorporation of the impact of cash reserve requirement changes in the computation of an adjusted monetary base is intended to consolidate further the effects of such actions into a summary aggregate. In countries with developed money market and debt management activities, the major sources of change in the monetary base are the frequent open market operations of the monetary authority. In these countries, such open market transactions are usually the key instrument to offset changes in other sources of reserve money expansion; these transactions have the potential of placing greater control over the monetary base with the monetary authority.

CHART 1

MONETARY BASE 1973-74 TO 1981-82

(QUARTERLY AVERAGES)

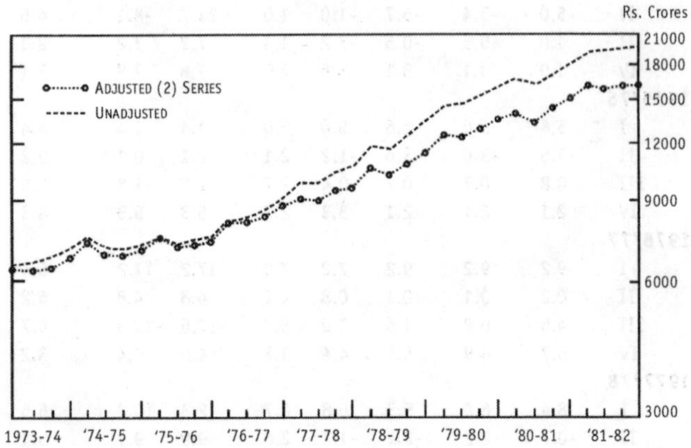

CHART 2

ALTERNATIVE MEASURES OF THE NARROW MONEY MULTIPLIER 1973-74 TO 1981-82

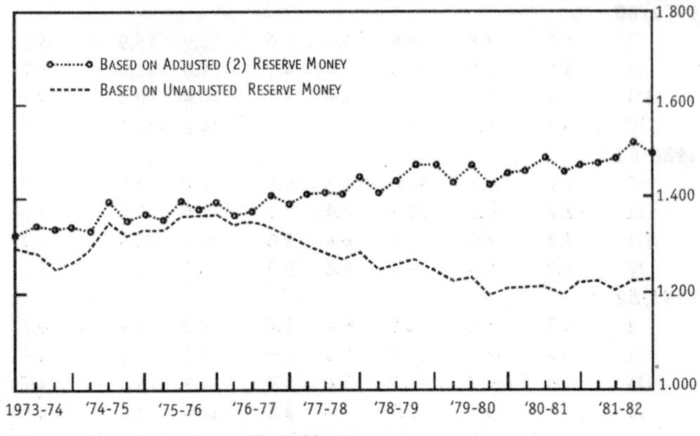

Source : Based on Appendix Table 7.

CHART 3

Growth Rates of Alternative Measures of the Monetary Base 1973-74 to 1981-82

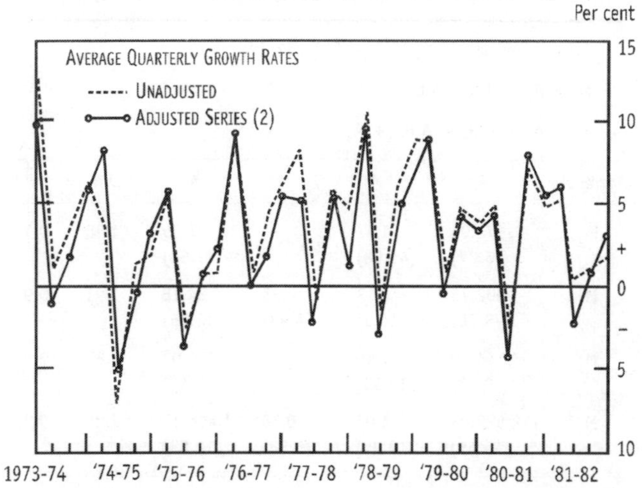

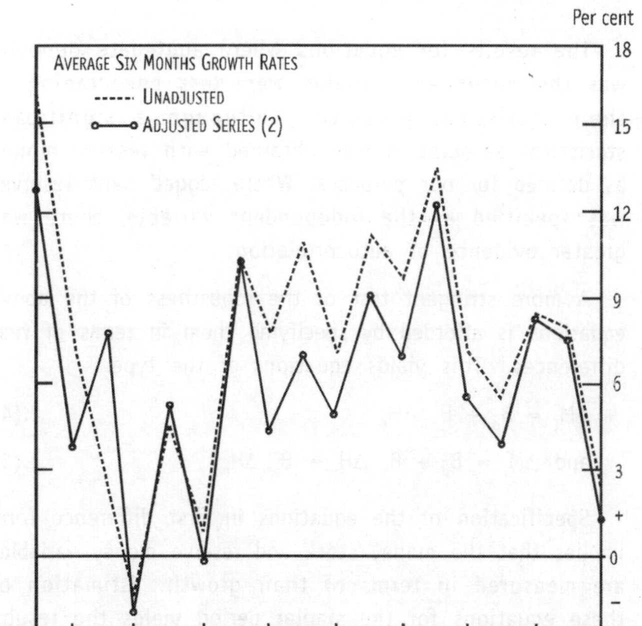

Source : Based on Tables 1 and 2.

In countries with limited open market operations, greater attention needs to be addressed to the other factors influencing the monetary base. The importance of the monetary base, as the set of assets constraining the money supply, remains. In these countries, data on changes in the monetary base are also often available more quickly than other monetary aggregates. However, because of the relatively more important role played by sources of reserve money change not under the direct control of the monetary authority, the use of data on the monetary base requires greater care. In the very short run, there may be erratic movements over which the monetary authority has relatively little control. In these circumstances, a somewhat longer time span of control and analysis may be more appropriate. Systematic relationships may be implicity in the quarterly or six monthly averages that are not yielded readily by weekly or monthly data, because the latter exhibit greater statistical noise. These considerations apply equally, although in different degrees, to monetary authorities in developed and less developed monetary systems; the difference may be reduced to the choice of the appropriate time span for controlling or targeting monetary base developments. It is our judgement that measures for a week or even a month may be of too short a period for inference on underlying trends; data spanning three-month periods may constitute the minimum time perspective for systematic analysis.[4]

The object of this section is to develop the quantitative relationship between the monetary base and alternative measures of the money stock in India. This does not necessarily imply that other indicators of money market conditions, such as total or net borrowed bank reserves, are unimportant. Certainly, bank reserves may be the more appropriate guide to changes in aggregate deposits. However, in India, excess reserves have generally been small. In these circumstances, it may be more appropriate to focus on the monetary base rather than on alternate measures of bank reserves. Certainly, developments in the currency to deposits ratio can significantly alter the relationship between the monetary base and money supply. However, even here, it is important to distinguish between those variations in the currency to deposits ratio that are expected and those that are unexpected.[5]

Our enquiry into the quantitative relationship between the monetary base and money stock is intended to yield conclusions on the usefulness of the monetary base as a control aggregate. As a monetary base, we use the total reserves instead of unborrowed reserves as is the practice in some countries. Borrowings are excluded in some of these countries as these are deemed to be temporary in nature. In India with bulk of the borrowings taking the form of refinance entitlements for food procurement credit and export credit there is no case for netting reserves for borrowings. Consistent with the arguments presented in Section II above, the wider definition of the monetary base is used for the analysis. The reserve money/multiplier identity may be expressed in its simple aggregative form as:

$$M = mH \quad \ldots(1)$$

where M is the money stock;

m is the multiplier consistent with the choice of the money stock measure; and

H is the monetary base defined as the adjusted (2) series.

The multiplier is determined principally by factors outside the control of the monetary authority (e.g., by households), and if it is prone to erratic fluctuations, errors may result in the control of the money supply through changes in the monetary base. However, in most countries, changes in reserve money constitute the main factor determining changes in money supply. The timing of the impact of reserve money changes differs, depending on the institutional environment. The effect of a change in reserve money on a measure of money supply is not necessarily contemporaneous, but may be distributed over a period of time. The quantitative work undertaken here attempts to determine the most dominant lag structure. The various econometric exercises proved to be unexpectedly robust in their results, in the sense that broadly similar or consistent conclusions were yielded from the alternative specifications.

In specifying a simple model based on the identity expressed in (1), the lagged effect of the monetary base needs to be carefully formulated. In particular, the impact of previous period reserve money developments needs to be assessed. This may be incorporated by analyzing alternative equations with different specifications for the termination of the lagged effect. In our case the dominant effects originated from current period and, to a lesser extent, previous period developments in the monetary base. These may be expressed in linear form as:

$$M_t = A_0 + A_1H_t + A_2H_{t-1} + A_3t \quad ...(2)$$

$$\text{and } M_t = A_0 + A_1H_t + A_3t \quad ...(3)$$

In these equations, the variable t has also been included to incorporate the possibility of a time trend in the money multiplier. These equations were estimated using quarterly data for the period 1974/75 I - 1981/82 IV. The statistical results are summarized in Table 3, for alternative concepts of the money stock. The results suggest a high order of statistical significance, with the time trend also being statistically significant. Decomposition of the current period reserve money effect into current and previous quarter variables results in the total effect remaining about the same. This applies to each of the two measures of the money stock and to the aggregate deposits equations. The statistical properties of the equations are good.

TABLE 3

Estimate of Money-Reserve Money Equation: Original Specification

Sample Period: 1974/75 I - 1981/82 IV

$M_t = A_0 + A_1H_t + A_3t$

$M_t = A_0 + A_1H_t + A_2H_{t-1} + A_3t$

Aggregate	A_0	A_1	A_2	A_3	D.W.	$\bar{R}^2$
M_1	-972.06 (-6.27)	1.47 (45.08)	—	27.09 (2.58)	1.98	0.99
M_1	-902.75 (-3.78)	1.13 (16.3)	0.33 (4.93)	34.18 (2.06)	1.91	0.99
M_3	-7,144.60 (-8.69)	3.40 (19.53)	—	309.02 (5.47)	1.87	0.99
M_3	-12,829.03 (-6.45)	1.05 (9.95)	0.38 (3.38)	1,406.13 (12.83)	2.25	0.99

Note: t ratios in parentheses. Corrected for the Cochrane-Orcutt procedure.

The results for equations where aggregate deposits was the dependent variable were less encouraging in their statistical properties, although a significant statistical association was obtained with reserve money as defined for our purposes. Where lagged bank reserves was specified as the independent variable, there was greater evidence of autocorrelation.

A more stringent test of the robustness of the above equations is afforded by specifying them in terms of first differences.[6] This yields equations of the type:

$$\Delta M_t = B_0 + B_1 \Delta H_t \quad ...(4)$$

$$\text{and } \Delta M_t = B_0 + B_1 \Delta H_t + B_2 \Delta H_{t-1} \quad ...(5)$$

Specification of the equations in first difference form implies that the money stock and reserve money variables are measured in terms of their growth. Estimation of these equations for the similar period yields the results presented in Table 4. Again, the associations specified in the equations are statistically significant. The growth in M_1 appears to be relatively more closely influenced by the growth in reserve money, compared with the results for broad money. Acceptable results for the growth in aggregate deposits were again not obtained. While the results for M_3 are slightly less satisfactory than for M_1 the coefficients of the lagged variables remain significant, even at the 1 per cent level.

Finally, the association between the monetary aggregates and the monetary base may be specified within a framework of partial adjustment. In this framework, the actual change in money stock is specified to be some proportion (λ) of the difference between the equilibrium and previous period level of the monetary aggregate. This may be expressed in log-linear terms as:

$$\log M_t = \lambda(\log M_t^* - \log M_{t-1}) \quad ...(6)$$

where λ is the coefficient of adjustment specified to be $0 \leq \lambda \leq 1$ and M_t^* is the equilibrium money stock.

TABLE 4

Estimate of Money - Reserve Money Equation: Specification Based on First Differences

$\Delta M_t = B_0 + B_1 \Delta H_t$

$\Delta M_t = B_0 + B_1 \Delta H_t + B_2 \Delta H_{t-1}$

Aggregate	B_0	B_1	B_2	*D.W.*	$\bar{R}^2$
M_1	94.31 (2.58)	1.24 (13.78)	-	2.17	0.83
M_1	56.62 (1.17)	1.09 (12.36)	0.29 (3.23)	2.09	0.82
M_3	1,185.16 (5.29)	0.78 (8.40)	-	2.50	0.63
M_3	1,011.58 (5.47)	0.98 (8.14)	0.31 (2.40)	2.67	0.68

Note: t ratios in parentheses. Adjusted for the Cochrane-Orcutt procedure.

Combining the equation with an equilibrium condition for M_t^* and M_t results in an equation of the following type:

$$\log M_t^* = C_0 + C_1 \log H_t + C_2 \log M_{t-1} \quad ...(7)$$

The results of this equation, estimated for M_1 and M_3, are reported in Table 5. Again, the equations appear to be fairly well specified; the respective coefficients of determination are very high and the coefficients are all significant at the 1 per cent level. While the Durbin-Watson statistic has been reported in the table, this test for serial correlation is not strictly valid in the presence of lagged dependent variables. However, computation of the alternative Durbin h statistic indicates the absence of serial correlation, most clearly for the M_1 equation, strengthening the acceptability of the results. The long run impact of reserve money on M_1 and M_3 respectively, is indicated by the value of C_3, these tend to confirm the results obtained from the regressions presented in Table 3.[7]

Finally, the equations in Table 5 may be tested further to establish their forecasting ability in dynamic simulations. Within-sample dynamic simulations were conducted for the two equations and the results are reported in Table 6.

TABLE 5

Estimate of Money Reserve Equation: Specifications Based on Lagged Adjustment

Sample Period: 1974/75 I - 1981/82 IV

$\log M_t = C_0 + C_1 \log H_t + C_2 \log M_{t-1}$

Aggregate	C_0	C_1	C_2	λ	C_3	*D.W.*	$\bar{R}^2$
M_1	0.16 (-4.62)	0.85 (13.14)	0.22 (3.58)	0.782	1.09	1.95	0.99
M_3	-0.11 (1.17)	0.42 (9.55)	0.66 (17.00)	0.340	1.22	2.75	0.99

Note: t ratios in parentheses. Adjusted for the Cochrane-Orcutt procedure.

TABLE 6

Dynamic Simulations of M_1 and M_3 Equations Based on Partial Adjustment, 1974-75/1981-82

(In per cent)

Aggregate	*Mean Absolute Error*	*Root Mean Square Error*
M_1	0.11	0.15
M_3	0.48	0.70

The simulations of the two equations perform markedly well. Chart 4 sketches the actual and expected values for M_1 and M_3 obtained from these dynamic simulations. These results strengthen confidence in the equations; in particular, the total impact of reserve money on the respective monetary aggregates is similar to the results obtained by earlier equations. Based on the statistical properties of the equations, it is seen that there is a closed impact of the monetary base on narrow money. This is in part to be expected as currency which is a major component of reserve money constitutes a larger part of narrow money than broad money. In the case of broad money, other influences, omitted from the equations, appear to have been relevant. During 1981-82, the estimated values have remained well above the actual values. Our interest in this paper is not, however, one of specifying a detailed monetary model, but one of exploring the degree to which monetary control can be exercised through acting on a proper definition of the monetary base. In this respect, the results are encouraging.

CHART 4

DYNAMIC SIMULATIONS OF M_1 AND M_3 BASED ON LAGGED ADJUSTMENT 1974-75 I - 1981-82 IV

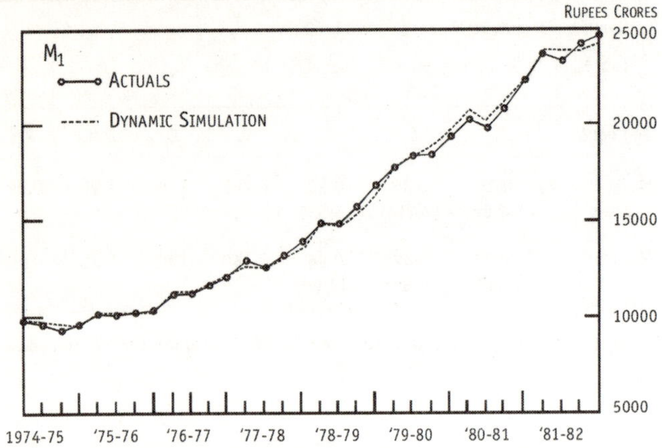

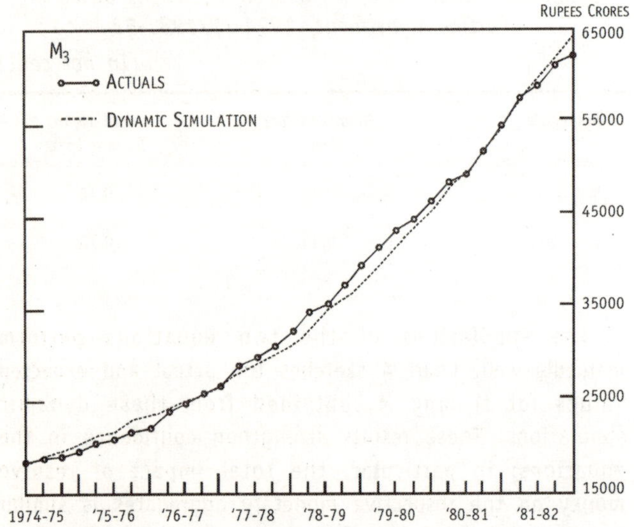

Source : Based on Results Reported in Table 5.

IV. SUMMARY AND CONCLUSIONS

This paper has attempted to examine the relationship between reserve money and alternative measures of the money stock. The lagged response of the money stock to changes in reserve money is one of the many time lags that are experienced between the formulation of monetary policy and its implementation. Certainly, there are other important influences on the supply of money; however, their variability in the short run may be small enough to justify focussing on the monetary base. The behavior of aggregate deposits, on the other hand, may be more dependent on these other influences.

The monetary base may be defined in a variety of ways. In this paper, the published data on the monetary base has been adjusted to incorporate the effect of changes in reserve requirements, and also net deficiencies of commercial banks in complying with the legal reserve requirements. The resultant adjusted monetary base appears to be more appropriate as a guide or control instrument in determining the intermediate money supply aggregates. Compared with the unadjusted data, it performs better in explaining changes in the money stock. The implicit money multiplier derived from the use of the adjusted monetary base displays greater stability compared with that based on the unadjusted series.

Use of the adjusted series enables more systematic quantitative relationships to be estimated between the monetary base and M_1 and M_3. Our results demonstrate that the lag in the impact of reserve money on both measures of money supply is very short. This is particularly so for M_1. In the case of both M_1 and M_3, the current quarter impact is the most dominant. The equations are well estimated with acceptable statistical properties. It is also suggested that quarterly data are the most appropriate for measuring this response. Use of monthly data does not yield useful systematic relationships, a reflection of the statistical noise present in data of such short duration. A preliminary review suggests that the relationships are ... stronger when six monthly data are used. However, more work is necessary for establishing similarly strong relationships with aggregate deposits. The results indicate that in general changes in reserve money are useful and important guides to the behavior of money supply.

Notes

1. Appendix Table 1 lists the CRR changes.
2. From the vast literature published in the *Federal Reserve Bank Quarterly Review*, the following contain the principal developments of the concept and methodology: Anderson and Jordan (1968), Burger (1975), Balbach and Burger (1976), Burger and Rasche (1977), Anderson and Karnosky (1977), Gilbert (1980), and Balbach (1981).
3. Under the present regulations banks are to maintain the required cash reserves as an average of daily balances over a week. Hence the level of balances maintained on a particular day such as Friday does not correspond closely to the level of deposits. However, in the absence of consolidated data on daily balances, we have used the average of the last Friday figures of each month. In fact the fit between reserves and money supply would have considerably improved, had we used the average daily balances.
4. Balbach (1981) suggests that in any event, month-to-month fluctuations in money growth have little impact on economic activity. Over longer periods, controllability of money supply is better assured as multiplier values display greater stability.
5. Further discussion on this issue is contained in Johanne and Rasche (1981).

6. Often, when regressions are estimated with levels, acceptable $\bar{R}^2$ are obtained. However, low values for the Durbin-Watson statistic may still be indicative of misspecification. In these cases, the $\bar{R}^2$ values derived from the regressions estimated in first differences may be a better guide of the association between the variables.

7. While the mean lag in the case of M_1 suggest virtually instaneous adjustment, the results in the case of M_3 are indicative of a longer period for the adjustment to be complete. The latter result needs to be interpreted with caution, particularly because there is some evidence of autocorrelation here.

References

1. Anderson, Leonall C. and Jordan, Jerry L., "The Monetary Base Explanation and Analytical Use", *Federal Reserve Bank of St. Louis Review* (August 1968).

2. Anderson, Leonall C. and Karnosky, Deniss, "Some Considerations in the Use of Monetary Aggregates for the Implementation of Monetary Policy", *Federal Reserve Bank of St. Louis Review* (September 1977).

3. Balbach, Anatol B., "How Controllable is Money Growth", *Federal Reserve Bank of St. Louis Review* (April 1981).

4. Balbach, Anatol B. and Burger, Albert E., "Derivation of the Monetary Base", *Federal Reserve Bank of St. Louis Review* (November 1976).

5. Burger, Albert E., "The Relationship Between Monetary base and Money: How Close?" *Federal Reserve Bank of St. Louis Review* (October 1975).

6. Burger, Albert E., "Alternative Measures of the Monetary Base", *Federal Reserve Bank of St. Louis Review* (June 1979).

7. Burger, Albert E. and Rasche, Robert H., "Revision of the Monetary Base", *Federal Reserve Bank of St. Louis Review* (July 1973).

8. Garvy, George, "Reserve Requirements Abroad", *Federal Reserve Bank of New York Monthly Review* (October 1973).

9. Gilbert, R. Anton, "Revision of the St. Louis Federal Reserve's Adjusted Monetary Base", *Federal Reserve Bank of St. Louis Review* (December 1980).

10. Gupta, Suraj B., *Monetary Planning for India* (Oxford University Press: Delhi, 1979).

11. Johannes, James M., and Rasche, Robert H., "Can the Reserves Approach to Monetary Control Really Work", *Journal of Money, Credit, and Banking* (August 1981).

12. Kaminow, Ira, "Required Reserve Ratios, Policy Instruments and Money Stock Control", *Journal of Monetary Economics* (October 1977).

13. Khatkhate, Deena R. and Villaneuva, Delano P,, "A Behavioural Theory of the Money Multiplier in the United States: An Empirical Test", *IMF Staff Papers* (March 1972).

14. Singh Anoop, Shetty S.L., and Venkatachalam T.R., "Monetary Policy in India: Issues and Evidence", supplement to the *Reserve Bank of India Occasional Papers*, Vol.3, No.1 (June 1982).

APPENDIX

TABLE 1

Changes in Cash Reserve Requirements 1973-74/1981-82

Effective Date	*Change*
May 31, 1973	The cash reserve ratio (CRR) was raised from 3 per cent to 5 per cent of net demand and time liabilities (DTL) of banks.
Sept. 8, 1973	The CRR was raised from 5 per cent to 7 per cent
Sept. 22, 1973	The CRR was raised from 7 per cent to 8 per cent.
June 29, 1974	The CRR was reduced from 8 per cent to 5 per cent
Dec. 4, 1974	The CRR was reduced from 5 per cent to 4.5 per cent.
Dec. 28, 1974	The CRR was reduced from 4.5 per cent to 4 per cent.
Sept. 4, 1976	The ratio was raised from 4 per cent to 5 per cent.
Nov. 13, 1976	The ratio was again raised to 6 per cent.
Jan. 14, 1977	An incremental cash reserve requirement was introduced, which provided that 10 per cent of incremental DTL be also maintained as cash reserves from this date.
Oct. 30, 1980	Banks were exempted from the further application of the incremental cash reserve requirement.
July 31, 1981	CRR raised from 6 per cent to 6.5 per cent.
Aug. 21, 1981	CRR raised from 6.5 per cent to 7 per cent.
Nov. 27, 1981	CRR raised from 7 per cent to 7.25 per cent.
Dec. 25, 1981	CRR again raised from 7.25 per cent to 7.50 per cent.
Jan. 29, 1982	CRR raised to 7.75 per cent.
April 9, 1982	CRR reduced from 7.75 per cent to 7.25 per cent. In respect of the nonresident account schemes, the CRR applicable was reduced to the statutory minimum, 3 per cent.
June 11, 1982	CRR reduced from 7.25 per cent to 7.0 per cent.

APPENDIX

TABLE 2

Reserve Money and Bank Reserves - Adjusted for CRR Changes, 1973-82

(Rs. crores)

	Reserve Money			*Bank Reserves*	
	Unadjusted	*Adjusted 1*	*Adjusted 2*	*Adjusted 1*	*Adjusted 2*
1973/74					
April (last Friday)	6,313	6,313	6,313	573	573
May	6,503	5,312	6,312	444	444
June	6,743	6,546	6,546	717	717
I (average)	6,519	6,390	6,390	578	578
July	6,641	6,438	6,438	668	668
August	6,462	6,255	6,255	683	683
September	6,662	6,244	6,244	609	609
II (average)	6,588	6,312	6,312	653	653
October	6,842	6,422	6,422	619	619
November	6,842	6,416	6,416	628	628
December	6,803	6,377	6,502	560	585
III (average)	6,829	6,405	6,413	602	611
January	7,055	6,620	6,620	599	599
February	7,180	6,746	6,786	567	607
March	7,260	6,820	6,929	467	576
IV (average)	7,165	6,729	6,778	544	594
Annual average	6,775	6,459	6,473	631	646
1974/75					
April (last Friday)	7,417	6,970	7,113	394	537
May	7,592	7,138	7,336	469	667
June	7,584	7,353	7,538	754	939
I (average)	7,531	7,154	7,329	539	714
July	7,363	7,124	7,124	700	700
August	7,096	6,857	6,857	649	649
September	6,994	6,754	6,754	619	619
II (average)	7,151	6,912	6,912	656	656
October	7,101	6,857	6,857	708	708
November	7,094	6,848	6,848	667	667
December	7,044	6,921	6,921	734	734
III (average)	7,080	6,875	6,875	703	703
January	7,013	6,887	6,887	648	648
February	7,242	7,114	7,114	791	791
March	7,387	7,259	7,259	834	834
IV (average)	7,214	7,087	7,087	758	758
Annual average	7,244	7,007	7,051	664	708

Contd...

...Contd...

	Reserve Money			*Bank Reserves*	
	Unadjusted	*Adjusted 1*	*Adjusted 2*	*Adjusted 1*	*Adjusted 2*
1975/76					
April (last Friday)	7,518	7,388	7,388	753	753
May	7,665	7,533	7,533	750	750
June	7,666	7,532	7,532	805	805
I (average)	7,616	7,484	7,484	769	769
July	7,475	7,337	7,337	801	801
August	7,351	7,212	7,212	779	779
September	7,229	7,089	7,089	729	729
II (average)	7,352	7,213	7,213	770	770
October	7,445	7,303	7,303	777	777
November	7,362	7,219	7,219	714	714
December	7,425	7,280	7,280	777	777
III (average)	7,411	7,267	7,267	756	756
January	7,423	7,278	7,278	788	788
February	7,544	7,398	7,398	774	774
March	7,732	7,584	7,584	826	826
IV (average)	7,566	7,420	7,420	796	796
Annual average	7,486	7,346	7,346	773	773
1976/77					
April (last Friday)	8,110	7,957	7,957	931	931
May	8,325	8,169	8,169	952	952
June	8,352	8,194	8,194	913	913
I (average)	8,262	8,107	8,107	933	933
July	8,235	8,071	8,071	949	949
August	8,211	8,045	8,045	936	936
September	8,386	8,218	8,218	1,050	1,050
II (average)	8,277	8,111	8,111	978	978
October	8,609	8,268	8,275	906	913
November	8,701	8,121	8,148	779	806
December	8,676	8,141	8,305	733	897
III (average)	8,662	8,177	8,243	806	872
January	8,872	8,328	8,461	772	905
February	9,042	8,477	8,569	776	868
March	9,544	8,938	9,061	965	1,088
IV (average)	9,153	8,581	8,697	838	954
Annual average	8,588	8,244	8,290	889	934
1977/78					
April (last Friday)	9,779	9,064	9,064	797	797
May	9,992	9,225	9,225	924	924
June	10,001	9,200	9,200	849	849
I (average)	9,924	9,163	9,163	857	857

Contd...

...Contd...

	Reserve Money			Bank Reserves	
	Unadjusted	Adjusted 1	Adjusted 2	Adjusted 1	Adjusted 2
July	9,710	8,848	8,848	806	806
August	9,994	9,097	9,077	1,064	1,064
September	9,867	8,934	8,934	955	955
II (average)	9,857	8,960	8,960	942	942
October	10,212	9,243	9,243	1,131	1,131
November	10,614	9,606	9,606	1,185	1,185
December	10,508	9,457	9,489	977	1,009
III (average)	10,445	9,435	9,446	1,098	1,108
January	10,700	9,565	9,565	1,200	1,200
February	10,523	9,362	9,362	872	872
March	10,941	9,750	9,750	1,049	1,049
IV (average)	10,721	9,559	9,559	1,040	1,040
Annual average	10,237	9,279	9,282	984	987
1978/79					
April (last Friday)	11,643	10,330	10,330	1,233	1,233
May	11,687	10,375	10,375	979	979
June	12,237	10,877	10,877	1,542	1,542
I (average)	11,856	10,527	10,527	1,251	1,251
July	11,521	10,109	10,109	742	742
August	11,792	10,317	10,317	1,140	1,140
September	11,712	10,203	10,203	1,054	1,054
II (average)	11,675	10,210	10,210	979	979
October	12,131	10,555	10,555	1,054	1,054
November	12,310	10,654	10,654	1,049	1,049
December	12,671	10,910	10,956	1,266	1,312
III (average)	12,371	10,706	10,722	1,123	1,138
January	13,185	11,206	11,206	1,133	1,133
February	13,431	11,488	11,488	1,328	1,328
March	13,716	11,722	11,722	1,307	1,307
IV (average)	13,444	11,472	11,472	1,256	1,256
Annual average	12,336	10,729	10,733	1,152	1,156
1979/80					
April (last Friday)	14,257	12,192	12,192	1,430	1,430
May	14,723	12,589	12,589	1,439	1,439
June	14,863	12,673	12,673	1,534	1,534
I (average)	14,614	12,485	12,485	1,468	1,468
July	14,923	12,719	12,719	1,392	1,392
August	14,871	12,499	12,499	1,103	1,103
September	14,479	12,057	12,057	1,422	1,422
II (average)	14,758	12,425	12,425	1,306	1,306
October	15,593	13,151	13,151	1,958	1,958
November	15,315	12,836	12,836	1,827	1,827

Contd...

...Contd...

	Reserve Money			Bank Reserves	
	Unadjusted	Adjusted 1	Adjusted 2	Adjusted 1	Adjusted 2
December	15,323	12,815	12,815	1,713	1,713
III (average)	15,410	12,934	12,934	1,833	1,833
January	15,774	13,188	13,188	1,711	1,711
February	15,730	13,106	13,106	1,250	1,250
March	16,465	13,857	13,857	1,759	1,759
IV (average)	15,990	13,384	13,384	1,573	1,573
Annual average	15,193	12,807	12,807	1,545	1,545
1980/81					
April (last Friday)	16,763	13,969	13,969	1,504	1,504
May	17,062	14,247	14,247	1,689	1,689
June	16,528	13,677	13,677	1,385	1,385
I (average)	16,784	13,964	13,964	1,526	1,526
July	16,499	13,587	13,587	1,421	1,421
August	16,355	13,382	13,382	1,435	1,435
September	16,144	13,141	13,141	1,315	1,315
II (average)	16,333	13,370	13,370	1,390	1,390
October	17,328	14,230	14,230	1,863	1,863
November	17,576	14,467	14,467	1,690	1,690
December	17,655	14,523	14,523	1,676	1,676
III (average)	17,520	14,407	14,407	1,743	1,743
January	17,593	14,427	14,427	1,478	1,478
February	18,055	14,881	14,881	1,657	1,657
March	19,441	16,264	16,324	2,392	2,452
IV (average)	18,363	15,191	15,211	1,842	1,862
Annual average	17,250	14,233	14,238	1,625	1,630
1981/82					
April (last Friday)	19,018	15,814	15,814	1,693	1,693
May	19,303	16,072	16,072	1,861	1,861
June	19,712	16,459	16,459	2,360	2,360
I (average)	19,344	16,115	16,115	1,971	1,971
July	20,271	16,765	16,765	2,498	2,498
August	18,965	15,233	15,233	1,801	1,801
September	19,046	15,289	15,289	1,903	1,903
II (average)	19,427	15,762	15,762	2,067	2,067
October	19,906	16,130	16,257	2,024	2,151
November	19,462	15,556	15,658	1,688	1,780
December	19,507	15,493	15,788	1,568	1,863
III (average)	19,625	15,730	16,901	1,760	1,932
January	19,763	15,600	16,111	1,524	2,035
February	19,766	21,680	15,614	1,288	2,095
March	20,446	16,290	16,659	1,679	2,048
IV (average)	19,992	15,835	16,397	1,497	2,059
Annual average	19,597	15,860	16,044	1,824	2,007

ANNEXURE

Sources and Description of the Data

1. Monetary Data

The data on narrow money (M_1) used for the exercises in this paper differ from the published series. The adjustments that have been made to the published data are intended to ensure greater comparability over time. These adjustments are discussed in the study on Monetary Policy in India contained in the supplement to the RBI Occasional Papers Vol. 3, No. 1 (June 1982). Briefly, savings deposits data after March 1978 were reclassified to reflect the recommendations of the Second Working Group on monetary concepts. Use of the methodology evolved by the Group resulted in about 85 per cent of savings deposits being classified with time deposits; the remainder were treated as being akin to demand deposits. The published data, prior to March 1978, continue to reflect the previous methodology which had resulted in quite the opposite proposition of savings deposits being classified with demand and time deposits. Consistency was sought to be assured by applying to the data prior to March 1978, the assumption that 85 per cent of savings deposits be reclassified as time deposits. Application of the new methodology to three sample periods in the 1960s and 1970s confirmed the appropriateness of extending the assumption, that 85 per cent of savings deposits are more in the nature of time deposits, to the previous period data.

M_1 and M_3 data are both presented in the June 1982 RBI study.

2. Data on CRR deficiencies

In computing the adjustment factor to reserve money, discussed in the text of the paper, one component was the calculation on net bank defaults in relation to the CRR requirement. The data for net bank defaults are presented in the supplement to the June 1982 issue of the RBI Occasional Papers.

4

Weighted Monetary Aggregates

Rationale and Relevance for India

Narendra Jadhav

Introduction

...

MONETARY authorities all over the world present alternate measures of money, leaving the choice to individual researchers and to the dictates of specific situations. The classification of monetary aggregates currently used by most central banks is based either on the functional characteristics of monetary assets or the institutional distinction between banks and non-banks. For example, in India the distinction between M1 and M3 is based on separation of time deposits with banks (which are deemed to be less liquid) from assets like currency and demand deposits with banks (which are highly liquid). Furthermore, the distinction between M1 and M3 on the one hand and M2 and M4 on the other, is based solely on the institutional differentiation between banks and post office saving organisation.

These developments on the operational side have broadly reflected the corresponding evolution of the theory of monetary aggregation. The earliest theoretical work was based on the medium of exchange function of money. Both, currency and demand deposits were deemed to constitute money since demand deposits can be used for transaction purposes. It was Friedman who argued for extending the definition of money to include time deposits on the ground that money serves to bridge the gap between receiving and making of payments. Gurley and Shaw (1960) went a step further and advocated yet another extension that included not only the assets with banks but also those with other financial depositories or intermediaries, which led to even broader monetary aggregates.

...

An important strand of research, initiated by an Indian economist, Chetty, way back in 1969, forcefully argued that each monetary asset has a certain degree of "moneyness" associated with it. The fundamental issue in monetary aggregation is not which assets are to be included in the measure of money stock, but how much of each monetary asset is to be included. A logical approach to monetary aggregation, therefore, is to construct monetary aggregates covering all assets, weighted by their degree of "moneyness".

Since the early 1980s, with changes in financial markets of the industrial countries including the deregulation of financial institutions and innovations in financial instruments, the issue of the appropriate measurement of money has again come into a sharp focus. Building on the earlier work by Chetty (1969) a promising new line of research has emerged at the Federal Reserve Bank of New York led by Barnett, Offenbacher, Spindt and others.

These innovations in the theory and practice of monetary aggregation may have some relevance for developing countries like India. The Indian economy, for example, has witnessed a significant financial deepening and disintermediation in recent years[1]. It is important, therefore, to understand the rationale behind the weighted monetary aggregates, to critically review the alternate approaches to make them operational and to examine their relevance for compilation of monetary aggregates in a developing economy like India. That is precisely the primary objective of this paper.

...

Dr. Narendra Jadhav is grateful to Dr. C. Rangarajan, Dr. Anupam Basu and Dr. S.L. Shetty for comments on the earlier draft. Special assistance by Shri R.K. Das and Sharad Gokhale and computational help from Woizero Nigist (National Bank of Ethiopia) is gratefully acknowledged.

I

RATIONALE FOR WEIGHTED MONETARY AGGREGATES

In devising monetary aggregates, a distinction needs to be maintained between the concept of money and measure of money. Logically, conceptualisation of money must precede its measurement[2].

In a fundamental sense, money stock in any economy can be conceptualised as a quantity aggregate that reflects the source of monetary services that could be generated in the economy. Since monetary services in an economy are rendered by various financial assets like currency, demand deposits, saving deposits, time deposits and the like, it is necessary to combine the potential flows of monetary services by each of these assets into one or more aggregates.

The conventional monetary measures are simple-sum monetary aggregates because they are derived by simple summation over relevant assets. Thus, a measure of narrow money in India, M1, is obtained by simply adding currency with public and demand deposits while a measure of broad money, M3, is obtained by a further addition of time deposits to M1[3].

The unsatisfactory nature of simple-sum monetary aggregates has long been recognised in literature. Hawtrey (1930), Gurley (1960), Friedman and Meiselman (1963) and Kane (1964) have pointed out some limitations of the conventional approach. Indeed, Fisher observed way back in 1922 (in a general context) that the "simple-sum index was the worst index" because it possessed two undesirable properties, i.e., "bias and freakishness".

In the context of monetary aggregation, two shortcomings of the simple-sum aggregates are especially noteworthy:

1) The simple-sum monetary aggregates implicitly assign equal weights to all components, which is inconsistent with economic theory. To give an extreme example, if one wished to obtain measure of transportation vehicles, it is absurd to aggregate over physical units such as cars and bullock carts by simple summation. A meaningful economic measure would be a weighted- sum aggregate, with weights reflecting relevant value-shares. The same principle ought to apply to monetary aggregation.

2) The simple-sum aggregates would be justified in terms of economic theory only if the components included in them were perfect substitues of each other. ... In other words, simple summation of currency and time deposits (as is done for M3 in India) would be justified only if the degree of "moneyness" associated with these two assets is the same. ...

As observed succinctly by Friedman and Schwartz (1970):

> "This (simple summation) procedure is a very special case of the more general approach. In brief, the general approach consists of ... defining the quantity of money as the weighted sum of the aggregated value of all assets, the weights for individual assets varying from zero to unity with a weight of unity assigned to that asset or assets regarded as having the largest quantity of 'moneyness'.... The more general approach has been suggested frequently but experimented with only occasionally. We conjecture that this approach deserves and will get much more attention than it has so far received" (p.151).

...

II

ALTERNATE APPROACHES TO WEIGHTED MONETARY AGGREGATES: AN ANALYTICAL APPRAISAL

Alternate approaches to construction of weighted monetary aggregates can be divided into three broad groups:

a) Substitution Approach
b) User-cost Approach
c) Policy-oriented Statistical Approach

A. Substitution Approach

The basic premise of this approach, based on the pioneering work of Chetty, is that the degree of 'moneyness' associated with any financial asset depends on the elasticity of substitution between that asset and a reference asset that is designated to be the most liquid asset. Thus, "moneyness" of time deposits would depend upon the elasticity of substitution between time deposits and say, currency.

For expository purpose, suppose that narrow money (M) is to be aggregated with time deposits (T). Chetty stipulates a one consumer economy with the consumer's utility over these two assets given by the CES type utility function:

(Eq.1) $u = [\beta_1 M^{-\rho} + \beta_2 T^{-\rho}]^{-1/\rho}$

In this utility function, as is known, the elasticity of substitution between the two assets (σ) is given by

$$\sigma = \left(\frac{1}{1+\rho}\right)$$

Suppose that the consumer has cash holdings of $\overline{M}$ and wishes to allocate them between M and T. If T is the cash value of time deposits in the next period and if R is the interest rate on time deposits of the current period, then the budget constraint of the consumer can be written as

(Eq.2) $\overline{M} = M + \left(\frac{T}{1+R}\right)$

The slope of the budget line is -(1+R), which implies, in the parlance of microeconomic theory, that (1+R) can be considered as the ratio of "prices" of money to time deposits.

The consumer's utility maximisation subject to the budget constraint yields the following marginal conditions:

(Eq.3) $\frac{\partial u}{\partial M} = \lambda$

(Eq.4) $\frac{\partial u}{\partial T} = \frac{\lambda}{1+R}$

where (λ) = Lagrange multiplier.

Dividing (eq.3) by (eq.4), we get,

$$\frac{\left(\frac{\partial u}{\partial M}\right)}{\left(\frac{\partial u}{\partial T}\right)} = \frac{\beta_1}{\beta_2}\left(\frac{M}{T}\right)^{-(1+\rho)} = 1+R$$

Taking logarithms, rearranging terms and adding a disturbance term, we get the following regression model:

(Eq.5) $\log\left(\frac{M}{T}\right) = \left[-\frac{1}{1+\rho}\log\left(\frac{\beta_2}{\beta_1}\right)\right] + \left(\frac{1}{1+\rho}\right)\log\left(\frac{1}{1+R}\right) + \in$

It may be noted from eq.(5) that estimate of the elasticity of substitution[4] between the two assets is directly given by the slope coefficient ($\frac{1}{1+\rho}$). Also the slope coefficient yields estimate of (ρ) which on substitution in the intercept term provides estimate of ($\frac{\beta_2}{\beta_1}$). Chetty assigns the value 1 for (β_1) on the grounds of ordinality of the utility function and thus derives the estimate for (β_2).

Having obtained estimates of the relevant parameters ρ, β_2 (with β_1 assumed to be unity), the "adjusted" measure of broad money stock (M*) is obtained by substituting these values in the utility function. Thus,

$M^* = [M^{-\rho} + \beta_2 T^{-\rho}]^{-1/\rho}$

where M* = "adjusted" money stock

The same method can be readily extended to more than two assets. Subsequent researchers have added further refinements to the approach[5].

The substitution approach is well-grounded in the economic theory and is, therefore, intuitively appealing. On the analytical plane, however, it is beset with some unpleasant features:

1. In Chetty's specification of the relative interest term, it is not clear whether the relevant degree of substitution is measured by elasticity or semi-elasticity.[6]
2. In Chetty's formulation, once the estimates of relevant parameters are obtained, estimates of the "adjusted" money stock are derived by inserting them into the utility function. In this process, the analytical link between the elasticity (or semi-elasticity) of substitution and the degree of "moneyness" of the relevant assets becomes obscure.
3. The original model of the substitution approach applied by Chetty to Indian data for the period 1945 to 1966 yielded unduly large elasticities of substitution. For example, the elasticity of substitution between narrow money (M) and time deposits turned out to be as high as 34.7, which meant that the two were 'very good substitutes' of each other in the Indian context (or equivalently, the "moneyness" of time deposits was as high as the "moneyness" associated with currency or demand deposits).

Subsequent research has shown that this somewhat counter-intuitive result emanated from shortcomings in Chetty's empirical specification. Boughton (1981), for example, has demonstrated that the elasticities of substitution between money and each of the tested substitutes were "much lower than earlier estimates (by Chetty)".

Inspite of the obvious appeal of the substitution approach, it has received, at best, a lukewarm response from monetary authorities[7]. From the operational point of view, the principal shortcoming of the substitution approach is that it involves estimation of model parameters. This parameter sensitivity means that the approach is illequipped to deal with a changing payments mechanism or the spectrum of financial assets, and therefore, has limited operational relevance in the context of developing countries like India.

B. User-Cost Approach

This approach, popularised by the FED economists like Barnett, Offenbacher and Spindt, aims at providing parameter-free money stock measures in accordance with the recent developments in the theory of economic aggregation.

In this approach, conceptually, alternate monetary assets are viewed as durable goods and therefore, their "prices" are represented by the corresponding user costs. The user cost of any real durable good is nothing but its imputed one-period holding cost. Accordingly, user-cost of a durable good is given by its purchase price in current period minus discounted expected resale value of the depreciated good in the next period. The same principle can be applied to a monetary asset in order to derive the relevant user cost.[8]

Each monetary asset, as a durable good, generates monetary services. A unit of monetary services may be defined as that amount of monetary asset in question which buys one unit of a commodity basket in the base period. Suppose a consumer holds X units of the assets and has to pay Xp units of the asset to buy one unit of a commodity basket in the base period, then he holds (X/Xp) units of monetary services.

Unlike the other durable goods where the service flow is expected to be reduced in the next period owing to physical depreciation, for monetary assets there is no depreciation.[9] On the contrary, interest bearing monetary assets appreciate in terms of their ability to generate monetary services. For example, if (r_t) is the nominal interest rate on the asset, then a consumer holding (X/Xp) units of monetary services at t would hold $\left[\frac{X(1+r_t)}{X_p}\right]$ units of monetary services in the next period.

Now, the consumer has to pay (Xp) units of the asset to buy one unit of monetary services in period t (i.e. its purchase price in current period is Xp). The discounted expected resale value in the next period is given by $\left[\frac{(1+r_t)X_p}{1+R_t}\right]$ and hence the user cost of the monetary asset in question is given by

$$\text{(Eq.6)} \qquad \pi = X_p - \left[\frac{(1+r_t)X_p}{1+R_t}\right]$$

where R_t = reference rate of interest used for discounting.

Once the user-costs of alternate monetary assets are obtained, the relevant monetary aggregate can be derived in a straightforward manner:

Suppose that there are (u) monetary assets with balances M1, M2, ... Mn.

Let $\pi_1, \pi_2 \ldots\ldots\ldots \pi_n$ be the corresponding user costs.

Then the "moneyness" associated with the (i^{th}) asset is simply the corresponding user cost evaluated value share in the total. Thus, "moneyness" of (i^{th}) asset

$$\text{(Eq.7)} \qquad Si = \frac{\pi_i M_i}{\sum_{i=1}^{n} \pi_i M_i}$$

and the weighted monetary aggregate is given by

$$\text{(Eq.8)} \quad M^* = \sum_{i=1}^{n} S_i M_i$$

The monetary aggregate thus derived can also be expressed as statistical index numbers. Indeed, the early versions of the approach used the Divisia method to construct the relevant index numbers and hence were also called "Divisia monetary aggregates"

Divisia monetary aggregates (Qt) over n assets with balances M_{1t}, M_{2t}, M_{nt} at time t are defined such that

$$\text{(Eq.9)} \quad (\log Q_t - \log Q_{t-1}) = \sum_{i=1}^{n} S^*_{it} (\log M_{it} - \log M_{it-1})$$

$$\text{where} \quad S^*_{it} = \frac{1}{2}(S_{it} + S_{it-1})$$

In other words, the monetary aggregate based on Divisia index is such that percentage change in the index is equal to the weighted average of percentage changes in individual monetary assets, relevant weights being the user-cost evaluated value shares.

An important advantage of the User-Cost approach to weighted monetary aggregates is that the relevant measures are parameter-free. Unlike the Substitution approach, therefore, this approach is readily adaptable to the changing financial milieu without any cumbersome reestimation requirement. On the other hand, there are some conceptual and practical problems, especially in the context of developing countries:

1. In the User-Cost approach, "money" is regarded as a capital aggregate akin to Friedman's conception presented in his "Restatement of the Quantity Theory of Money" (1956). Accordingly, demand for money by wealth holders is treated as a problem in capital theory. In that sense, a money good is analytically indistinguishable from any other 'capital good'. As pointed out by Spindt (1985), "this conception of money is insufficiently narrow for the analytical and empirical purposes of some monetary economists who ... emphasize the primary significance of money's distinctive role as means of payment" (p.177). In this regard, several other studies have argued that the special role of money goods in the trading process constitutes the fundamental property of money, because it results in an important asymmetry between money goods and other goods as sources of effective demand[10]. The User-Cost approach involves an unduly broad connotation of monetary services, which, apart from the general acceptability as a means of payment, also covers many other things such as liquidity, divisibility, surety of nominal value, etc., and is, therefore, conceptual imprecise.

2. Construction of weighted monetary aggregates or indices in this approach depends critically on measurement of user costs of relevant monetary assets. Typically, in such efforts the user costs of monetary assets are proxied by the following formula:

User cost of (i^{th}) monetary asset during time 't' = $R_t - r_{it}$

Where R_t = the expected maximum available yield on the chosen benchmark asset during time 't';

r_{it} = own rate of return on the (i^{th}) asset during time 't'.

In this regard, Judd and Scadding have rightly observed that such an approach to computing user costs is useful "for a world in which interest rates on monetary assets are unregulated".[11] In developing countries like India where the interest rate structure is an administered one, however, use of this kind of formula can be potentially hazardous. After all, if the primary purpose of constructing weighted monetary aggregates is to eliminate (or atleast alleviate) the potential distortions in the measurement of money stock, it would be ironical if new distortions (such as those involved in computation of user costs) are allowed to creep in. Such distortions may defeat the very purpose of constructing the weighted monetary aggregates, ostensibly in the name of improvement. Thus, with the User-Cost approach, possibility of remedy turning out to be worse than the disease cannot be ruled out, especially in the context of developing countries.

C. Policy-Oriented Statistical Approach

According to this approach, money stock is best measured as that aggregate of financial assets which, when introduced in quantitative relationships among money, output and prices, gives the best results in terms of certain preconceived and predetermined criteria.

Roper - Turnovsky method is a variant of this broad approach that seems to have received the maximum attention in the relevant literature. According to the Roper - Turnovsky method, the optimal monetary aggregate is the one which minimises the forecast variance in nominal income. Thus,

$$M(RT) = \sum_{i=1}^{n} \varnothing it\ Mit$$

where M_{it} = i^{th} monetary asset during time t,

$\varnothing it$ = optimal weight for (i^{th}) asset during time t.

The optimal weights $\varnothing'^{s}_{it}$ are derived by minimising the forecast variance in nominal income using a Vector Autoregressive System (VAR).

This approach is also beset with several conceptual and operational problems:

1. In economic analysis, as in any scientific process, the purpose of empirical work is to test adequacy of concepts and verify theoretical hypotheses. Empirical state, therefore, comes only after the relevant concepts are already defined and hypotheses are rigorously derived from a suitable economic model. The fundamental flaw of this approach is that it is characterised by a logical 'frog-leap'[12]. It aims directly at the measurement of money without its prior conceptualisation. Indeed, the conceptualisation is sought to be done in terms of measurement, rather than the other way round.

2. Even when the lack of theoretical underpinnings is ignored, the Policy-oriented Statistical Approach does not lead to a determinate empirical definition of money. It has been pointed out that there is no generally agreed criterion as a standard for making judgement[13]. Roper - Turnovsky's criterion is only one of the several possible candidates. With different criteria, a whole spectrum of monetary aggregates could be derived and it does not seem possible to claim universal superiority of one measure over all others. Even if it were possible to identify a criterion that is globally optimal, the composition of monetary aggregates may differ widely as between different countries, time periods, functional forms and models. Finally, even when these issues are resolved somehow, the future stability of estimated

empirical regularities cannot be taken for granted. Needless to say, therefore, that the analytical foundations of this approach are weak and rather tenuous.

3. The only redeeming feature of this approach is the excellent forecasting ability of the resultant monetary aggregates. Even this feature is not as attractive as it may appear, prima facie:

(i) Better forecasting ability of these aggregates is hardly surprising because it is embedded in their very construction. Moreover, this attribute applies *exclusively* to the target chosen with which to minimise the forecast variance; it does not necessarily apply to other targets. For example, Roper - Turnovsky method which uses weights that minimise forecast variance in respect of nominal income are not likely to be equally effective in predicting inflation.

(ii) Better forecasting ability may be a necessary condition for optimality of monetary aggregate, but is not a sufficient one. It may be argued that there is another condition which is not only necessary but more vital in a fundamental sense; monetary aggregates must be anchored with sound theoretical base and proper conceptualisation. Often, it is not realised that Roper - Turnovsky aggregate may have better forecasting performance but can actually assign negative "moneyness" to some assets, which defies any sensible economic interpretation!

In recapitulating the analytical appraisal, thus, it may be emphasised that the available approaches for constructing weighted monetary aggregates are riddled with several problems, conceptual, empirical as well as operational. These have to be borne in mind while evaluating any country-specific study.

III

Weighted Monetary Aggregates: A Critical Survey of Studies in the Indian Context

In the Indian context, early studies on the subject seem to have focused on empirically demonstrating the need for differentiating among monetary assets on account of differences in their degrees of "moneyness". Subrahmanyam (1977), Kamaiah and Bhole (1982) or Kamaih and Subrahmanyam (1983) are some noteworthy examples in this regard. Since their basic contention regarding limitations of the simple-sum monetary aggregates is acceptable in entirety, detailed discussion of these studies is unwarranted.

On the more substantive side, Ghose, Madhur and Roy (1984) made a systematic attempt to construct weighted monetary aggregates for India. According to these authors, the traditional monetarist model provides a reasonably good explanation of inflation in the Indian economy between 1960 and 1975 and in the early 1980's. There is, however, a "complete breakdown in the 5-year period between 1975 and 1980 during which the actual inflation rate was 10 per cent per annum lower than the conventional model would have predicted". The authors, among other things, made an effort to examine whether the "missing inflation" could be explained by the weighted monetary aggregates.

The findings of this study were as under.

1. The weights derived using Substitution Approach (i.e., Chetty's model) are "unreasonable and cannot be used in any aggregation".

2. Weighted monetary aggregates in the form of Divisia indices were constructed for M3 covering the relevant period. Analysis of temporal behaviour of these aggregates revealed that the growth rate in Divisia M3 was only marginally lower than the simple-sum M3 which led them to conclude that "replacing simple M3 by a Divisia index in the monetarist model does not explain the inflation puzzle of the late 1970s" (p.54).

More recently, Subrahmanyam and Swami (1989) have come out with an extensive study of weighted monetary aggregates based on the User-Cost approach. They have experimented with three aggregates in the superlative class - Divisia, Diewart linear and Fisher's ideal index as well as one non-superlative one, i.e., geometric index.

Performance of these weighted monetary aggregates was compared with the simple-sum aggregates over the period 1950-51 through 1984-85 in respect of information content, causality and stability. The overall conclusion of this study is quite revealing: "the alleged superiority of the superlative monetary aggregates over their simple-sum counterparts could not be established convincingly. On the contrary, the simple sum aggregates emerge out to be more informative about the goal variable of NDP yielding more plausible and stable patterns of income and interest elasticities" (p.27).

These findings are somewhat discouraging, but not surprising, given the multitude of conceptual, operational and empirical problems that arise in the institutional setting of developing countries like India. Indeed, what is surprising is the fact that there exists at least one study, i.e., Kannan (1989) which finds that on the basis of criteria like stability, predictability and causality, that Roper - Turnovsky method "turns out to be the best weighting method". Since this study stands out in its conclusions, a closer scrutiny is called for.

A critical evaluation of the study reveals several unsatisfactory features:

(i) The empirical analysis is couched in terms of demand and time deposits without explicitly recognising the break in their time series due to a significant structural change introduced in the bifurcation of saving deposits into the two categories of deposits.

In India, saving deposits have both "transaction" as well as "saving" characteristics. It is necessary, therefore, to merge the "transaction" balance with demand deposits and the residual, deemed to be "saving" balance, with time deposits.

In accordance with the recommendations of the Second Working Group on Money Supply (1977), the part of saving deposits which was permitted to be withdrawn without notice was lumped with demand deposits. As a result of this criterion (which was in force from 1961 to 1977), an overwhelmingly large part of saving deposits (about 85 per cent) was clubbed with demand deposits. Effective March 1, 1978, however, the accounting procedure was changed drastically. According to the new procedure (which is applicable to-date), that portion of saving deposits on which interest is actually paid is treated as time deposits, while the residual is deemed to be demand deposits. As a result of this change, the earlier pattern of bifurcation is reversed, in that, nearly 85 per cent of saving deposits are now treated as time deposits.

It is clear, therefore, that the long term time series of demand and time deposits have been subject to major structural shifts in 1978. The study, however, does not show adequate awareness of this phenomenon[14]. As a result, the data series for demand and time deposits as well as econometric results derived from them are questionable.

(ii) As a proxy for interest rate on demand deposits, the study uses "the GDP deflator for the public administration sector". Rationale for this proxy is difficult to understand. Barrow and Santomero and Klein have suggested methods for computing "implicit" rate of return on demand deposits. In the Indian context, Subrahmanyam and Swami (1989) study has used this method. Similar attempt could have been made.

(iii) In computation of relevant user costs, the study does not specify the reference interest rate used for discounting. In the Indian context, this choice would have an important bearing on the final results.

(iv) Even the broad conclusion drawn by the study regarding the Roper Turnovsky method outperforming others does not follow from the tests conducted in the study.

Of the three criteria used, i.e. predictability, stability and causality in the assessment of relative performance of the Roper - Turnovsky method vis-a-vis others, only the latter two are independent. As stated earlier, better predictability is embedded in the derivation of weights in the Roper - Turnovsky method. Using this criterion for the judgement would, therefore, tantamount to a circular reasoning. In respect of causality, the Roper - Turnovsky approach does only marginally better than the simple-sum aggregates, whereas, in respect of stability criterion, the simple-sum aggregate actually outperforms the Roper - Turnovsky method. Under these circumstances, it is difficult to see why the Roper - Turnovsky approach is adjudged to be the "best" one.

The unmistakable conclusion, therefore, is that the case for use of weighted monetary aggregates in India is yet to be established convincingly.

Notes

1. See Jadhav (1988) for discussion on some aspects of recent financial deepening and disintermediation in India.
2. This principle has recently been emphasised by Bhole (1987).
3. 'Other deposits' with RBI which are included in M1 are omitted here for expositional convenience.
4. The relationship between the elasticity of substitution referred to by Chetty and the traditional interest elasticity has, at times, caused needless confusion. For a recent example of misinterpretation, see Bhole (1987), p. 899.

   The conventional interest elasticity is defined as $e = \left(\frac{\partial \log M}{\partial \log R}\right)$ which measures percentage change in M for one percentage change in R, whereas, the elasticity of substitution refers to the Hicks-Allen measure defined as $\sigma = \frac{\partial \log (M/T)}{\partial \log (1/1+R)}$ which measures the percentage change in the ratio of M to T induced by a percentage change in the relative "prices".
5. For example, see Boughton (1981), Husted and Rush (1984).
6. This is because, mathematically, $\left[\log \frac{1}{1+R}\right] \approx -R$. See Husted & Rush (1984) p. 175.
7. C. Rangarajan (1988), (Presidential Address to the 71st Annual Conference of the Indian Economic Association ..., for a recent example.
8. The concept of user cost of money in this form was suggested first by Diewert (1974).

9. For expositional convenience, it is assumed here that there is no change in the general price level. Donovan (1978), however, has shown that price movements do not affect the result.
10. See Spindt (1985), p. 177.
11. Judd & Scadding (1982).
12. Bhole (1987) has also made this point. Generally, this sub-section has drawn on Bhole (1987) to some extent.
13. Ibid.
14. At one point, it is observed in the study that the growth rate in demand deposits for 1981-86 is much lower than that of 1970-80. A dummy variable is used for accommodating the shift; but the dividing line used is 1980 and not 1978 when the shift really occurred.

Selected References

1. Barnett, W.A., "The Optimal Level of Monetary Aggregation, "*Journal of Money, credit and Banking*, Vol.14, November 1982.
2. Barnett, W.A., Offenbacher, E.K., Spindt, P.A., "The New Divisia Monetary Aggregates", *Journal of Political Economy*, Vol. 92, 1984.
3. Bhole, L.M., (1987) "Definition, Measurement and Determination of Money Supply" *Economic & Political Weekly*, Vol. XXII, June 6 and 13.
4. Boughton, J., (1981), "Money and its Substitutes", *Journal of Monetary Economics*, Vol.8.
5. Chetty, V.K., "On Measuring the Neamess of Near-Moneys," *American Economic Review*, Vol.59, June 1969.
6. Diewert, W.E., *"Aggregation Problems in the Measurement of Capital,"* Ed: Usher, D., University of Chicago Press, 1980.
7. Donovan, D.J., (1978), "Modelling the Demand for Liquid Assets: An Application to Canada", *IMF Staff Papers*, Vol. 25, December.
8. Fisher, I., *The Making of Index Numbers: A Study of their Varieties, Tests and Reliability*, Houghton Mifflin, 1922.
9. Friedman, M., *"The Quantity Theory of Money: A Restatement," in Friedman (Ed.), Studies in the Quantity Theory of Money*, the University of Chicago Press 1956.
10. Friedman, M. and Meiselman, D., "The Relative Stability of Monetary Velocity and Investment Multiplier in the U.S., 1897-1958," *in Commission on Money and Credit, Stabilisation Policies*, Eaglewood Cliffs, 1963.
11. Friedman, M. and Schwartz, A.J., *Monetary Trends in the U.S. and the U.K.*, University of Chicago Press, 1982.
12. Friedman, M., and Schwartz, A.J., *Monetary Statistics of the United States: Estimates, Sources and Methods*. NBER Studies - Business, Cycles, No. 20, New York, 1970.
13. Ghose, D., Madhur, S. and Roy, P. (1985), *"Has Monetarism Failed in India? The Case of Missing Inflation," Economic and Social Commission on Asia and Pacific ESCAP*.
14. Gurley, J.G., "Liquidity and Financial Institutions in the Postwar Economy," in the *Study of Employment, Growth and Price Levels*, U.S. Govt. Printing Office, 1960.
15. Hawtrey, R.G., *"Money and Index Numbers", Journal of the Royal Statistical Society*, Vol. 93, 1930.
16. Husted, S. and Rush, M. (1984), "On Measuring the Nearness of Near Moneys: Revisited," *Journal of Monetary Economics*, Vol. 14.
17. Jadhav, Narendra (1988), "Recent Financial Deepening and Disintermediation in India: Incidence, impact and issues", *RBI Occasional Papers*, Vol.9, No. 2, June.
18. Judd and Scadding (1982), "The Search for Stable Demand Function for Money", *Journal of Economic Literature*.
19. Kamaiah, B. and Bhole, L.M. (1982), "An Empirical Definition of Money for India: Some Factor Analytic Evidence", *Malayan Economic Review*, April.
20. Kamaiah, B. and Subrahmanyam, G. (1983), "Some Further Evidence on the Definition of Money Stock for India", *Prajnan*.
21. Kane, E.J., "Money as a Weighted Aggregate," *Zeitschrift fur Nationalokonomie*, Vol.25, September 1964.
22. Kannan, R. (1989), "Monetary Aggregates for India (1970-86)", NIBM Workshop on Monetary System in India.
23. Rangarajan, C. (1988), "Issues in Monetary Management" Presidential Address at the 71st Annual Conference of the Indian Economic Association, December.
24. Reserve Bank of India, *Report of the Committee to Review the Working of the Monetary System* (Chakravarty Committee Report), 1985.
25. Reserve Bank of India, *Report of the Second Working Group on Money Supply, 1977.*
26. Spindt, P. (1985), "Money is what Money Does: Monetary Aggregation and the Equation of Exchange", *Journal of Political Economy*, Vol. 93.
27. Subrahmanyam, G. (1977), "On Nearness of Time Deposits to Money: An Empirical Study", *Indian Economic Journal, Vol.24, 1977.*
28. Subrahmanyam, G. and Swami, S.B. (1989), "Empirical Comparison of Simple Sum and Superlative Monetary Aggregates," NIBM Workshop on Monetary System in India.

5

The Dynamics of Money Supply Process in India

An Alternative Empirical Framework

Himanshu Joshi • Indranil Bhattacharyya

Introduction

FOR the majority of developing countries undertaking liberalisation of hitherto regulated regimes, tracking monetary aggregates becomes difficult. ... Uncertainty surrounding the financial operations of the Government, external capital flows and the induced effects of policy interventions in tune with some underlying reaction function have blurred the customary relationship between money, output, prices and the opportunity cost of holding money. The standard demand for money function appears simplistic for any meaningful analysis of variations in monetary aggregates. An alternative approach of basing monetary forecasting exercises upon a model with the sources of money supply (viz., credit) as explanatory variables has been offered as a practitioner's solution to the problem.

The paper is schematized in three sections. Section I presents a brief review of the 'credit view' of monetary transmission mechanism and its relevance in the context of the present empirical exercise. Section II discusses the empirical framework employed in this paper while Section III presents some concluding observations.

SECTION I

A Review of the 'Credit View' Literature

The dynamics of monetary aggregates and its impact on output has been a hotly debated issue in the economic profession. While a certain consensus has been established on the fact that monetary policy affects economic activity, at least in the short run, there is no agreement on the transmission mechanism through which monetary policy affects output, prices and employment. Economists of Keynesian persuasion argue that the money supply mechanism is essentially endogenous. Their arguments are based on the premise that since deposits are remunerated in most countries, their supply is not independent of interest rates. This is in contrast to the money multiplier framework which assumes exogeneity of money stock, based on the central bank's complete control over the monetary base. While the latter approach explains changes in money supply through processes strictly exogenous to financial market pressures, the former approach views pressures emerging endogenously within the financial markets as the basic determinants of growth in credit availability and money supply. Banks, by extending credit, create deposits which provide scope for further credit creation and look for reserves later. Hence, private initiatives of banks in extending credit and accommodating demand for loans drives the pace of credit creation and consequently monetary expansion. This view is echoed in the 'credit view' of monetary policy transmission. If credit view is, indeed, the correct explanation of the transmission process, then future money stock growth can be forecast with the help of past credit growth, in keeping with the assumed 'endogenous' characteristic of money stock dynamics.

The origins of the credit view can be traced to Irving fisher (1933), who in the first issue of *Econometrica*, argued that the severity of the economic downturn during the Great Depression resulted from the poor performance of financial markets. This viewpoint was later reinforced by the Gurley-Shaw hypothesis (1955) according to which, financial intermediaries play a critical role in facilitating the circulation of loanable funds between savers and borrowers. Also in line with

The authors are grateful to Dr. A. Vasudevan, Executive Director of the Bank who, in the context of Indian economy, suggested the idea of explaining money supply through the sources side and an anonymous referee for constructive comments. The usual disclaimer applies.

this view is the finding by Goldsmith (1958) that a positive co-relation exists between economic growth and the degree of sophistication and development of the financial sector. In this regard, the role of the banking system is crucial as it is the principal agent among financial intermediaries.

The traditional analysis of the monetary policy transmission mechanism is based on IS-LM models (or on aggregate demand and supply frameworks if one assumes price flexibility). Monetary policy interventions by the central bank transmit impulses to economic activity through changes in interest rate in liquid assets first and subsequently, through asset substitution (among the different financial assets) in the long run interest rates. This traditional' approach is founded on the assumption of perfect substitution between the different financial assets and neutrality of firms' financial structure, (Modigliani & Miller, 1958). Following the publication of Friedman and Schwartz's monetary history of the United States (1963b), the idea that money supply is the key financial aggregate gained wide support. They argued that banks did matter in so far as they create money. This is in line with the conclusions of the simple IS/LM models in which the money supply is assumed to be controlled by the central bank – a crucial assumption. In fact, even if the central bank can control the monetary base, other factors influencing money supply adjust to changes in interest rates. As a consequence, the stock of money is, in fact, less important for macroeconomic performance than the *financial capacity* of the economy, defined as the aggregate volume of credit that lenders are ready to grant to borrowers.

The 'credit view' or 'lending view', although not necessarily in conflict with the 'money view', is based on the assumption of imperfect substitution between bank credit and securities and, at least implicitly, between internal and external finance. Credit view models are usually based on the assumption of information asymmetries in financial markets and macro-economic relevance of a firm's financial structure. Banks' assets are assumed to be as relevant as banks' liabilities for transmission of monetary shocks to the real sector of the economy and bank lending is regarded as a 'special asset' that might (in some cases) incorporate monitoring costs and long-run contractual relationships between lenders and borrowers. In such a context, the liquidity preferences and investment decisions of the banking system play a relevant role for the determination of the macroeconomic equilibrium.

... The credit view has been developed through contributions by Bernanke (1983, 1990), Bernanke and Blinder (1988, 1992), Bernanke and Campbell (1988, 1990), Bernanke and Gertler (1989, 1990), B. Friedman and Kuttner (1992, 1993), Gertler and Gilchrist (1993), Kashyap et al. (1993) and others. The 'prologue' to the modern credit view was Bernanke's (1983) empirical analysis, pointing out that the financial distress in 1929 amplified the effects of the Great Depression. Following an earlier study by Mishkin (1978), Bernanke analysed the relative importance of monetary versus financial factors in the Great Depression. The central conclusion was that monetary forces alone were 'quantitatively insufficient' to explain the Depression's depth and persistence, and that the collapse of the financial system, reflected largely in bank failures and stock market crash worldwide, was an important explanatory factor. Bernanke showed that in the period 1930-33 almost half of the existing American banks failed, and the remaining suffered very relevant losses. The stock market crisis of 'Black Friday' (which was the initial event of the crash of 1929) created an enormous increase in the debt burden of the firms. The banks' distress had an effect on real activity by suppressing the financial flows for some categories of firms that did not have direct access to spot financial markets and had to rely on financial intermediaries. In addition, the drastic increase in the debt of industrial companies reduced their ability to obtain finance from intermediaries, who would base their evaluations of the riskiness of customers on indicators of their financial structure. This piece of empirical evidence gave support to the credit view, which argued that financial markets appeared to be imperfect, so the Modigliani – Miller assumptions did not hold and finance did matter. Bernanke refuted the argument of Friedman and Schwartz (op. cit.) to point out that the main role in the propagation of the 1929 crisis would not have been played by perturbations in the banks' liabilities (i.e. in money), but rather in the banks' assets (i.e. credit) – and, in particular, by the elimination (or by the drastic reduction) of the channels through which finance was injected into the real economy. As evidence in support of his thesis, Bernanke showed that the liabilities of the failed banks and the spread between the interest rate on risky and riskless securities significantly increased the explanatory power of the equations determining the level of output. Bernanke (1983) assumed that the 'perceived' riskiness of firms borrowing from the banking system depends on their financial structure. In this way, because of information asymmetries in the credit market, firms' financial structure is not neutral and plays a relevant macro-economic role.

The main feature of the credit view is the 'specialness' of bank credit in the transmission of monetary policy and financial shocks, although a certain attention towards the role of financial intermediaries has occasionally been paid in the past by mainstream macromodels, too. In this context, the most representative theoretical model of the credit view is that of Bernanke and Blinder (1988). It is a modification of the IS/LM framework and contains all the elements that allow for the theoretical definition of imperfect substitution among credit on the one hand, and bonds and securities on the other. Like any other 'credit view' model it explicitly introduces the balance-sheet constraint of the bank, which plays a very important macroeconomic role. They conclude that if money demand shocks are more important than credit demand shocks, then a policy of targeting credit is probably better than a policy of targeting money.

In the 1960s, the 'new view' models (Tobin and Brainard, 1963; Tobin, 1969) relaxed the hypothesis of perfect substitutability between money and other financial assets to describe the behaviour of the financial sector where the credit market can play a specific role in the transmission mechanism of monetary policy. After the 1960s, following Modigliani and Miller's contribution, the view that 'finance is a veil' became widely accepted. If the financial structure of firms is irrelevant, and if financial intermediaries are redundant, then monetary policy can have only a transitory impact on real variables, through unanticipated changes in the money supply. In all the real business cycle models that were developed subsequently, finance does not play any role. The credit view puts a different emphasis on financial market imperfections and rejects the Modigliani-Miller theorem, by assuming non-neutrality of firms' financial structure. However, some similarities with the modelling techniques employed in the 'new view' can be found in the use of aggregate balance-sheet relations and in the formalization of supply functions for some relevant financial assets which allows for imperfect substitutability among different assets. With some additional assumptions that are meant to specify the relevance of the 'credit channel' the 'skeleton' of the 'new view' models could be employed to analyse the macroeconomic implications of imperfect competition in credit markets.

... The implicit assumptions behind the credit view are:

(a) prices do not adjust instantaneously to offset changes in the (nominal) quantity of money.

(b) The central bank can directly influence the volume of credit by adjusting bank reserves.

(c) Loans and securities are imperfect substitutes both for borrowers and for banks.

A survey of the empirical studies in the credit view tend to support to following general statements:

(a) The transmission mechanism of monetary policy (and more generally of monetary disturbances) operates through both banks' assets and banks' liabilities. In particular, a reduction in banks' loans, after a monetary restriction, plays a very important role in reducing the expenditure of those agents that mainly rely on bank credit as an external source of finance.

(b) Not all categories of borrowers have access to security markets and to other sources of external finance alternative to bank credit. This implies that monetary shocks may have different effects on different categories of agents.

Although the credit view highlights the relative importance of credit to that of money in explaining fluctuations in real output, the scope of the present paper is not to test the relative explanatory potential of the credit view. Traditionally, while changes in reserve money or monetary base are analysed by changes in the source of reserve money, analysis of money supply is largely explained by the component side wherein growth in currency and deposits would be indicative of the growth of M_3. The present paper, in trying to break away from the tradition of estimating through components, tries to explain changes in M_3 from the sources side mainly attributable to changes in credit to Government and Commercial Sector. Thus, the assets of the banking system can be a significant and powerful explanatory variable of movements in money supply, in contrast to the money view.

SECTION II

EMPIRICAL METHODOLOGY AND RESULTS

Drawing strength from the main thrust of the credit view, this paper explores the argument that the money supply process is a dynamic process rather than a static *ex post* accounting procedure and a typical multiplier mechanism is central to any exercise that attempts to model the behaviour of monetary aggregates. However, while the traditional multiplier mechanism is based on its proximate determinants viz., currency deposit ratio and reserve deposit ratio, the current study emphasises on the expansionary mechanism of credit creation (cause) in modeling monetary aggregates (effect). A compelling reason for not considering the components of money supply namely, currency and deposits as explanatory arguments for broad money (M_3) originates from our empirical diagnostics for such a specification. Our results indicate the presence of four cointegrating vectors for the system of four variables, i.e., M_3, currency, demand deposits and time deposits indicating that the system was misspecified and not amenable to cointegration. This also implies the absence of a valid EC model and, therefore, of statistical causality.

Typically, in a monetary balance sheet accounting framework, the sources of money supply considered are credit extended to the Government and commercial sector and the net foreign exchange assets of the banking sector. However, as pointed out by Gupta (1979), even though central bank credit and net foreign exchange assets of the banking sector as a whole are also taken as sources for *ex post* accounting of the monetary balance-sheet, it may be recognised that a clubbing of quasi and high powered sources (such as foreign exchange assets and RBI credit to Government with commercial banks credit) appears to bypass the multiplier mechanism which is crucial to the monetarist doctrine. However, in defence of the accounting framework, it may be mentioned that the assets and liabilities need to tally in a balance sheet. Moreover, the accounting framework is representative of both the money issuing sectors viz., the Government, the RBI and other banks and the money holding sectors i.e. the public. While the accounting exercise may be explained as an *ex post* phenomenon, the dynamics of monetary aggregates is not contemporaneous as between the cause and effect of the process. In other words, since both foreign exchange assets and the RBI credit to the Government are high-powered sources, they need to be worked upon through the credit creation mechanism to eventually generate, with a lag, the money stock, its components being currency, time and demand deposits.

Having pointed out this rather strict theoretical dispensation, it may nonetheless be statistically worthwhile to estimate an aggregate money supply (M_3) equation as a function of the lagged values of the outstanding sources of money supply exemplified by credit extended by the banking sector to the Government (CRGOV) and the commercial sectors (CRCOM)[@]. The above specification for explaining money supply can be justified by assuming that the estimated model is indeed a reduced form equation capturing some complex underlying dynamic mechanism. This simple, dynamic model is sufficiently robust for purposes of explaining the evolution of money supply in the Indian economy.

Let,

$$M3_t = f(CRGOV_{t-i}\ ,\ CRCOM_{t-j})$$

where i, j = 1,.....,n.

The first step for modeling the process is to pass the specification through the standard empirical test of cointegration. Accordingly, the system was put through the Johansen's (1988) multivariate cointegration analysis (explained in the Annexure) which suggested that there were two significant cointegrating vectors implying that the relationship is stable in two directions and has a unique long memory component. The time sample in this paper covers a period of almost 6 years from 1993 to 1998 with monthly data on the stocks of relevant aggregates mentioned above. The Phillips-Perron (PP) unit root test statistics based on 12 lags and for testing the order of integration of our series are presented in the Table A below.

TABLE A

Unit Root Test Statistics

Variable	*PP t-Test Statistic*	
Levels	*First*	*Difference*
M3	0.73	-9.92*
CRGOV	-2.45	-8.68*
CRCOM	-1.58	-8.83*

Note to Table A:

(i) Unit Root test statistics for 12 lags and time trend.

(ii) * indicates that the null of unit root is rejected with a confidence of 99%.

Estimated test statistics indicate that all the three series considered in this study are integrated of order one or I(1). Moreover, the first difference series are stationary thus establishing the feasibility of setting up a standard vector error correction model (VECM) with the help of these data in their levels. The test statistics for testing the order of cointegration are presented in Table B below.

@ The non-inclusion of forex assets as one of the explanatory variables in the specification is explained by the fact that these inflows first result in creation of currency and deposits. The portfolio choice of the banking system then determines how much of credit to extend; a mechanism that concurs with the 'credit view'. Dynamically, domestic resource counterpart of forex assets held by the banking sector must eventually get allocated to the asset/credit account in the balance sheet of commercial banks.

TABLE B

The Order of Cointegration

Number of Cointegrating Vectors	Table Value for max-eigen 5%	Estimated value for max-eigen	Table value for Trace 5%	Estimated value for Trace
1	2	3	4	5
R≤2	3.762	1.272	3.762	1.272
R≤1	14.069	17.678*	15.410	18.949*
R=0	20.970	23.661*	29.680	42.610*

Note to Table B:

(i) A star indicates the rejection of null hypothesis of the number of cointegrating vectors as in column 1.

(ii) Table values are from Osterwald Lenum (1990)

(iii) The VECM was estimated with an unrestricted constant because of uniform trends in data and with twelve lags and monthly centered seasonal dummies.

Results in Table B suggest the presence of at least two cointegrating vectors. Thus it can be said that the system follows steady long run equilibrium and is stable in at least two directions.

We also report below some of the relevant diagnostics pertaining to Johansen's VECM estimated in this paper.

TABLE C

Diagnostics for the Residuals obtained from Johansen's VECM

Dependent Variable	J-B Norm	B-P Q(6)	ARCH(6)
ΔM3	2.370	6.558	6.295
ΔCRGOV	0.998	6.655	3.720
ΔCRCOM	0.205	10.857	3.125

Note to Table C:

(i) J-B Norm is the Jarque-Bera test for testing normality

(ii) B-P is Box Pierce Test for testing white noise property.

(iii) ARCH is for testing autoregressive conditional heterocedasticity.

(iv) All of the above statistics follow a central chi-square distribution.

Test statistics in Table C suggest that the residuals are normally distributed and exhibit white noise properties in case of each equation thus implying that the system has been properly defined and conforms to the standard initial conditions necessary for operationalizing Johansen's cointegration procedure.

The short run error correction model augmented with monthly growth in industrial production (IIP) empirically identified in this exercise is as follows:

$$\Delta M3_t = 0.65\ \Delta CRCOM_{t-2} + 0.41\ \Delta CRCOM_{t-3} - 0.58\ \Delta CRGOV_{t-1}$$
$$(3.24) \qquad (2.20) \qquad (-2.71)$$

$$-0.12\ \Delta CRGOV_{t-2} + 0.47\ \Delta CRGOV_{t-3} + 75.99\ \Delta IIP_t - 0.05\ EC_{t-1}$$
$$(-0.58) \qquad (2.04) \qquad (1.24) \qquad (-3.02)$$

$$\bar{R}^2 = 0.20 \quad DW=1.70 \quad SEE=6620.02 \quad Q(21)=20.77$$

where the prefix Δ represents the first differences form of the variable in question.

The long run cointegrating relationship reveal a conspicuously strong effect of Government borrowing on the expansion of money supply as against the much lower impact of borrowing by the commercial sector. The coefficients obtained from the long run relationship imply that a single rupee expansion in Government credit can expand the money supply in the long run by as much as Rupees 1.609 as against barely Rupees 0.90 in case of the commercial sector. The conspicuously large impact of Government borrowing on money supply arises essentially because it includes a relatively higher share of high-powered money in the form of RBI credit. However, the muted effect of commercial borrowing on long run money supply appears theoretically plausible in the Indian context since it is only an intersectoral flow and new money creation is limited to a small amount to the extent of RBI refinance to commercial sector. As pointed out by Mishkin et al, (the main proponents of the structural endogeneity school of money supply), in developing countries where interest rate is the dominant transmission mechanism, this coefficient would be relatively high as additional reserves would be generated within the financial structure itself through innovative liability management practices like borrowing in the call money market and issue of Certificates of Deposits.

The EC model developed in this paper is specified only in terms of *lags* of the first difference form of the explanatory variables thereby capturing the dynamics of money supply expansion. Use can not be made of contemporaneous explanatory variables in view of the criticism that it then becomes merely an *ex post* accounting identity. The short-run EC model throws up some interesting insights. Specifically, the impact of Government borrowing leads to a reduction in money supply in the short run against and increase as in case of commercial borrowing. The short run negative effect of Government borrowing may arise as a consequence of the contractionary effect on the banks ability to create loans due to the transfer of funds from commercial banks to Government accounts in the Reserve Bank of India. Such withdrawal of liquidity from the banking system may reduce the bank's ability to expand credit and hence contract M_3 in the short run.

Finally, though not the least, our tests of causality formulated in terms of the acceptance/rejection of the hypothesis of weak exogeneity reveals that whereas broad money stock is exogenous to the system, both credit aggregates viz., CRGOV and CRCOM are not. This implies that the credit view may be a fair explanation of the evolution of money supply process in the context of the Indian economy. In other words, the causality runs unidirectional from credit to money supply. Table D below presents likelihood ratio (LR) test statistics pertaining to the tests of the hypothesis of weak exogeneity.

TABLE D

Tests of Weak Exogeneity Hypotheses

Equation	*LR Test Statistic*	*p-value*
ΔM3	1.54	0.46
ΔCRGOV	14.31*	0.00
ΔCRCOM	18.54*	0.00

Notes to Table C:

(i) * implies significance below 1% against the null of weak exogeneity.

(ii) The LR test statistic is distributed as a central chi-square distribution.

(iii) The significance if the LR statistic implies that the EC term in that equation is significant thus also showing causality.

Graph I presents a plot of actual and estimated stocks of broad money supply derived from the EC model presented above. The fitness of the estimated model can be gauged by its remarkable ability to follow the actual changes in the stock of M_3 with a root mean square error of just 0.26 per cent.

SECTION III

Concluding Observations

In this paper we demonstrated that composite sectoral credit aggregates could be successfully used to model the dynamic behaviour of money stock variation in the Indian economy. An expansion of credit leads to *pari passu* expansion of broad money stock measure according to our cointegrating equation. The relevance of this result is further justified by the causality test indicating unidirectional causation from credit to money. This implies that the credit view in particular and the concept of endogenous money at least notionally, have some relevance as an analytical framework for the Indian economy.

GRAPH 1

ACTUAL AND ESTIMATED M3 STOCKS FROM EC MODEL

(APRIL 1994 TO OCTOBER 1998)

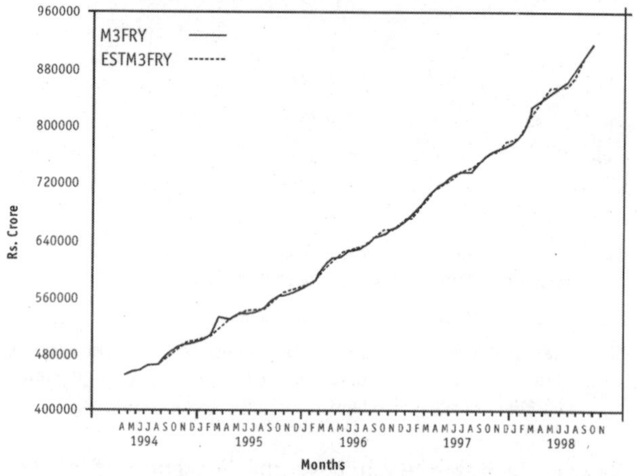

The dynamics of money stock variations can also be studied in terms of their short and long run behaviour. Whereas, the short run effects of Government borrowing upon broad money stock are negative, its long run impact is quite strong. On the contrary, the impact of commercial borrowing is positive both in the short and long run.

References

Bernanke B.S. (1983): 'Non-Monetary Effects of the Financial Crisis in the Propogation of the Real Depression', *American Economic Review*, 73, pp. 257-76.

Bernanke B.S. (1990): 'On the Predictive Power of Interest Rates and Interest Rates Spread' *New England Economic Review* (November/ December), Federal Reserve Bank of Boston, pp. 51-68.

Bernanke B.S. (1993): 'Credit in the Macroeconomy', *Federal Reserve Bank of New York Quarterly Review*, Spring, pp. 50-70.

Bernanke B.S. and A.S. Blinder (1998): 'Is it Money or Credit, or Both, or Neither? – Credit Money and Aggregate Demand', *American Economic Review*, 78, pp. 435-51.

Bernanke B.S. and A.S. Blinder (1992): 'The Federal Funds Rate and the Channels of Monetary Transmission', *American Economic Review*, 82, pp. 901-27.

Bernanke, B.S. and J. Campbell, (1988): 'Is there a Corporate Debt Crisis?', *Brookings Papers on Economic Activity*, 1, pp. 83-125.

Bernanke, B.S. and J. Campbell, (1990): 'US Corporate Leverage Developments in 1987 and 1988', *Brookings Papers on Economic Activity*, 1, pp. 255-78.

Bernanke, B.S. and M. Gertler, (1987): 'Banking and Macroeconomic Equilibrium', in Barnett, W.A. and Singleton, K.J., *New Approaches to Monetary Economics*, New York, Cambridge University Press.

Bernanke, B.S. and M. Gertler, (1989): 'Agency Costs, Net Worth and Business Fluctuations', *American Economic Review*, 79, pp. 14-31.

Bernanke, B.S. and M. Gertler, (1990): 'Financial Fragility and Economic Performance', *Quarterly Journal of Economics* (February), pp. 87-114.

Bernanke, B.S. and M. Gertler, (1995): 'Inside the Black Box: the Credit Channel of Monetary Policy Transmission', *NBER Working Paper*, 5146 (June).

Fisher I (1933): 'The Debt-Deflation Theory of the Great Depression', *Econometrica*, 1 (October), pp. 1-16.

Gupta S.B. (1979): *Monetary Planning for India*

Gurley, J. and E. Shaw, (1955): "Financial Aspects of Economic Development", *American Economic Review*, 45, pp. 515-38.

Friedman B.M. and K.N. Kuttner (1992): 'Money, Income, Prices and Interest Rates', *American Economic Review*, 82, 472-92.

Friedman B.M. and K.N. Kuttner (1993): 'Economic Activity and the Short-Term Credit Markets: An Analysis of Prices and Quantities', *Brookings Papers on Economic Activity*, 2, pp. 193-266.

Friedman, M. and A.J. Schwartz, (1963a): 'Money and Business Cycle', *Review of Economics and Statistics*, 45(1) part 2, Supplement (February), pp. 32-64.

Friedman, M. and A.J. Schwartz, (1963b): *A Monetary History of the United States*, Princeton, Princeton University Press for the National Bureau of Economic Research.

Friedman, M. and A.J. Schwartz, (1982): *Monetary Trends in the United States and the United Kingdom. Their Relation to Income, Prices and Interest Rates, 1867-1975*, Chicago, University of Chicago Press.

Gertler M. and S. Gilchrist (1993): 'The Role of Credit Market Imperfections in the Monetary Transmission Mechanism: Arguments and Evidence', *Scandinavian Journal of Economics*, 95(1), pp. 43-64.

Kashyap, A.K. and J.K. Stein (1993): 'Monetary Policy and Bank Lending', *NBER Working Paper*, 4317.

Kashyap, A.K. and J.K. Stein and Wilcox, D.W. (1993): 'Monetary Policy and Credit Conditions: Evidence from the Composition of External Finance', *American Economic Review*, 83, pp. 78-98.

Modigliani, F. and M.H. Miller (1958): 'The Cost of Capital, Corporation Finance and the Theory of Investment', *American Economic Review*, 48, pp. 261-97.

Tobin J. and W.C. Brainard, (1963): 'Financial Intermediaries and the Effectiveness of Monetary Control', *American Economic Review*, 53, pp. 383-400.

ANNEXURE

For a *p* variable system, the contegration analysis proceeds with the testing of unit roots and setting up of a standard Johansen's (1988) VAR in terms of similarly integrated variables. Let

$$Y_t = \mu + \sum_{i=1}^{k-1} \pi_i Y_{t-i} + \pi_k Y_{t-k} + \varepsilon_t$$

be a VAR (k) with *n* variables in vector Y, a constant *m* and white noise process ε_t. The matrix π_k contains long run information with rank m<n-1 and can be decomposed into two *n' m* matrices α and β such that $\pi_k = \alpha\beta'$

While the matrix β consists of *m* linear cointegrating vectors. α is the matrix of error correction parameters. The maximum likelihood estimate of β is obtained by computing residuals R_{0t} and R_{kt} by regressing δY_t and Y_{t-k} on $\delta Y_{t-1}, \ldots, \delta Y_{t-k+1}$, computing the residual product matrices

$$S_{ij} = T^{-1} \sum_{t-1}^{T} R_{it} R_{jt} \qquad (i, j = o, k)$$

and finally solving the following eigenvalue problem

$$|\lambda S_{kk} - S_{ko} S_{oo}^{-1} S_{ok}| = 0$$

for eigenvalues $\lambda_1 > \ldots > \lambda_k$ and eigenvectors $V = (v_1, \ldots, v_n)$. The estimates of α and β are given by $\alpha = S_{ok}\beta$ and $\beta = (v_1, \ldots, v_m)$, the eigenvectors associated with m largest eigenvalues. The LR test for the presence of at least in cointegrating vectors is given by

$$\text{Trace} = -T \sum_{j=m+1}^{n} \ln (1-\lambda_j)$$

Once the cointegrating relationship is estimated, the long run coefficients are used to generate the error correction term. The error correction term is then fed into a general short term model formulated with stationarised data.

Symbolically,

$$\delta Y_t = \eta_o + \sum_{i=1}^{q} \eta_i \, \delta Y_{t-i} + EC_{t-1}$$

where EC_{t-1} is the vector of stationary error correction terms corresponding to each of the normalized equation in the above representation and *q* is the order of lags in the short run equation chosen on the basis of some optimal lag selection criterion. The short run equation described above is extremely flexible and is usually adapted to provide best out-of-sample forecasts. Note that the estimated short term equation in stationary data is robust and indicates the presence of causality. In this framework, tests of causality are those of the significance/insignificance of error correction terms popularly referred to as weak exogeneity properties. Only if all the explanatory variables are weakly exogenous, it is possible to estimate the model as a single equation. In technical terms, weak exogeneity of a particular variable implies that long run parameters of the model are not important for short run movements in that variable. We shall also provide results of weak exogeneity χ^2 tests to shed light on the interrelationship between the money and the credit markets.

6

Residency in Money Supply

Deba Prasad Rath • Indranil Sen Gupta

Introduction

MONEY supply typically comprises the public's liquid assets such as currency and bank deposits, the variation in the stock of which impacts on aggregate economic activity. The recent globalisation of economies resulting in enhanced cross-border money flows has complicated the treatment of capital inflows in the compilation of money supply. For example, a part of bank deposits, which may be owned by non-residents in foreign currency denominations and in turn invested abroad by banks out of portfolio considerations, would not be directly related to domestic output and money demand. A number of central banks, therefore, compile monetary aggregates on residency basis by not directly including capital flows in money supply.

The claims of both residents and non-residents on the banking sector are presently treated at par in the Indian money supply compilation, which is not compiled on residency basis. Non-resident inflows were typically thought of as remittances and thus considered to be integrated into the national monetary system as the economy had not opened up to capital transactions; notwithstanding recent initiatives to allow banks to retain and even invest a part of their foreign currency funds abroad. In contrast, both the Indian national accounts statistics and the balance of payments (BoP) data are compiled on residency basis. The RBI's recent Working Group on Money Supply: Analytics and Methodology of Compilation (WGMS) (Chairman: Dr. Y.V. Reddy) has, therefore, proposed that the compilation of monetary aggregates be on residency basis by not directly reckoning capital flows in the form of non-resident repatriable foreign currency fixed liabilities with the banking system in India[1] such as the balances under the Foreign Currency Non-Resident Repatriable (Banks) (FCNRB) Scheme.

The present paper attempts to identify the impact of capital flows on money supply in the Indian economy, which has been a matter of recent debate[2]. It is structured as follows: Section I defines the concept of residency. Section II elaborates the accounting of capital flows in the present broad money (M_3) aggregate and evaluates their treatment in terms of the new broad money (NM_3) aggregate recommended by the WGMS. Section III reports the results of our empirical exercises, which suggest that NM_3 is superior in terms of tracking the goal variable of inflation to M_3. Section IV presents our conclusions.

SECTION I
THE CONCEPT OF RESIDENCY

The residency of an economic entity essentially relates to the country in which it has a centre of economic interest. Currency and deposits held by non-residents in the rest of the world (RoW) sector would presumably be related to the balance of payments rather than the use of money in domestic transactions and to the domestic demand for monetary assets and should not, therefore, be directly counted in monetary aggregates (Table 1). The draft Manual on Monetary and Financial Statistics (MFS) of the International Monetary Fund (IMF), which attempts to harmonise monetary data with the System of National Accounts (SNA), 1993 and the BoP statistics, recommends the compilation of money supply on residency basis. The MFS Manual proposes a period-of-stay criterion of one year in order to determine the residency of an economic unit (in line with the BoP Manual, IMF, 1993) but allows countries to define their

The authors are grateful to Dr. R. Kannan for insightful comments and to Shri Deepak Mohanty for the many clarifications on the subject. The usual disclaimer applies.

own criteria in tune with their particular circumstances, especially if their capital flows are characterised by large remittances.

TABLE 1

Residency in Money Supply: An Executive Summary

Banks' Liabilities	Non-government Claims on the Banking Sector: Resident	Non-government Claims on the Banking Sector: Non-resident
Domestic	Reckoned in money supply.	Strictly needs to be excluded from money supply. The US Federal Reserve excludes US dollars held by foreign banks. Included, *inter alia* by India, Malaysia, Taiwan etc.
Foreign Currency	Reckoned in money supply by a number of central banks, e.g., Canada, the Czech Republic, India, Indonesia, Ireland, Malaysia and Sri Lanka. The US Fed includes certain Euro dollar deposits held abroad by residents.	Not reckoned in money supply by most central banks as akin to capital flow. Excluded by the WGMS in the envisaged new monetary aggregates.

Source: Manual on Monetary and Financial Statistics, IMF and the WGMS Report, RBI.

A number of central banks compile money supply on residency basis although country practices vary[3]. Most industrialised countries with high openness ratios exclude overseas residents' foreign currency deposits from monetary aggregates as these relate to capital transactions rather than to domestic money demand. The Bank of England compiles money supply on residency basis and now excludes bank accounts in the Channel Islands and the Isle of Man. The Bank of France restricts the money holding sector to resident non-financial operators in mainland France. The US Federal Reserve, however, includes Euro-dollar deposits held by US residents in the foreign branches of US banks and at all banking offices in the UK and Canada in M_3 but excludes the US dollars held by foreign banks. The Reserve Bank of Australia excludes non-resident deposit flows that followed the abolition of exchange controls in December 1983 from money supply. The Hong Kong Monetary Authority and the Bank of New Zealand compile additional monetary aggregates based on residency. Many central banks in developing countries with large numbers of emigrant workers abroad define the terms of residency in tune with their particular circumstances. The Bango Sentral ng Pilipinas does not reckon banks' foreign currency liabilities in money supply and nets them from banks' foreign currency assets to arrive at net foreign assets. The Bank Negara Malaysia includes residents' foreign currency deposits and non-resident ringitt deposits in quasi-broad money (M_3) but nets non-resident foreign currency liabilities from banks' foreign currency assets to compute their net foreign position. The Central Bank of Sri Lanka includes about half of the non-resident foreign currency (NRFC) accounts in money supply on the assumption that about 50.0 per cent of such deposits are held by 'returnee migrants' and thus constitute foreign currency liabilities to residents while the remaining is treated as foreign currency liabilities to non-residents and adjusted against banks' foreign currency assets to arrive at their net foreign assets. "Dollarised" economies with co-circulation of currencies often compile bi-monetary aggregates. For example, Argentina includes all US dollar deposits in its broader bi-monetary aggregate M_3^*.

The Indian money supply compilation, under the extant procedures, follows the sectorisation of the RBI's First Working Group (FWG) on Money Supply (1961) which did not distinguish between the domestic economy and the rest of the world (RoW) sector in money supply accounts. The FWG divided the economy into three sectors: i) the banking sector, ii) the government sector (constituting the money issuing sector) and iii) the money holding non-government commercial sector comprising a) the rest of the domestic sector (including public sector undertakings) and b) the foreign sector for the purpose of MS compilation. The RBI's Second Working Group (SWG) on Money Supply (1977) included the non-resident rupee balances under the Non-Resident (External) Rupee Accounts, instituted in March 1970 and the non-resident foreign currency balances under the erstwhile Foreign Currency (Non-Resident) Accounts (FCNRA), instituted in November 1975, in money supply. Subsequently, various categories of banks' non-resident foreign currency liabilities such as FCNRB deposits, instituted in May 1993 and more recently Resurgent India Bonds (RIBs), instituted in August 1998, have been included in M_3. Thus, all capital inflows are treated as part of money supply even if funds mobilised are parked abroad as is often the case with FCNRB deposits.

The WGMS proposes to divide the domestic economy into four exclusive sectors, viz., i) households, ii) non-financial commercial sector, iii) general government and iv) financial corporations and introduces the concept of residency by carving out a RoW sector which can transact with any of the domestic sectors (Chart I). The WGMS observes:

CHART I

Sectorisation of Money Supply Accounts

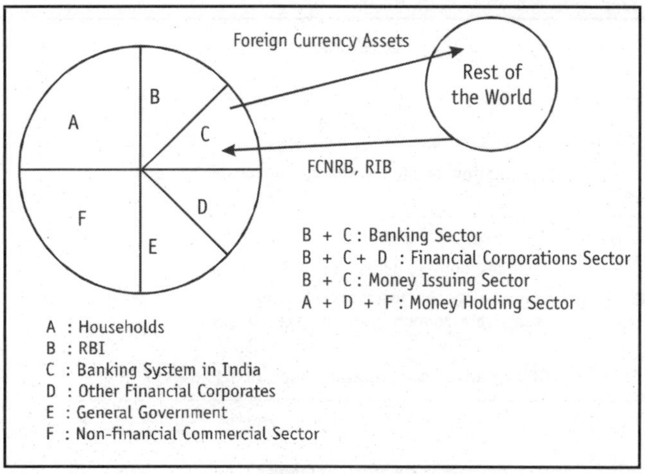

"While there is a need to categorise deposit liabilities by residency, it may not be appropriate to exclude all categories of non-resident deposits from domestic monetary aggregates as non-resident rupee deposits are essentially integrated into the domestic financial system. The Group, therefore, proposes that only non-resident repatriable foreign currency fixed deposits should be treated as non-monetary external liabilities and excluded from the domestic money stock. Accordingly, from among the various categories of non-resident deposits at present only FCNRB deposits may be classified as non-monetary external liabilities... ...Resurgent India Bond(s) denominated in foreign currencies for subscription by non-resident Indians (NRIs) ...could be treated as external liability of the banking sector".

The WGMS has thus recommended the modification of the IMF recommendations in line with the Indian conditions to restrict the claims of the RoW sector in terms of instruments, characterised as banks' non-resident repatriable foreign currency fixed liabilities[4] while its liabilities comprise the banks' foreign currency assets. Money supply, therefore, would now comprise the claims of residents of the domestic non-bank non-government money holding sector on the money issuing sector (Table 2). Capital inflows would be adjusted against banks' foreign assets to arrive at their net foreign assets. As banks' call/term borrowings from non-bank sources are negligible on reporting Fridays, the critical difference between M_3 and NM_3 lies in the treatment of FCNRB deposits and RIBs.

SECTION II

Treatment of Capital Flows in Money Supply

Money supply could be thought to be determined by the central bank, *ceteris paribus*, through its control of the monetary base. Central banks typically modulate the monetary impact of capital inflows by sterilisation. It needs to be noted that the present M_3 compilation, however, is limited by the incongruity that sterilisation of capital flows has no effect on monetary expansion. The need to compile money supply on residency basis is best illustrated by the treatment of FCNRB deposits in i) the present M_3 compilation (Scenario I) and ii) the NM_3 compilation, on residency basis, as recommended by the WGMS (Scenario II) under the assumption of full sterilisation. Scenario III tracks the monetary impact of capital flows in the NM_3 compilation by relaxing the assumption of full sterilisation.

Scenario I: Suppose a bank raises FCNRB deposits worth Rs. 100, swaps Rs. 50 with the RBI and invests the rupee amount in government securities purchased from the RBI. In the present M_3 compilation, in which non-residents are part of the money holding sector, this would increase time deposits and consequently M_3 by Rs. 100 on the components' side (Table 3). On the sources' side, net foreign assets (NFA) of the banking sector would go up by Rs. 100 on account of the accretions to i) other banks' foreign currency holdings by Rs. 50 and ii) the RBI's NFA by Rs. 50 (the swap amount). Further, RBI credit to Government would decline by Rs. 50 while other banks' investments in Government securities would increase by Rs.50. It may be indicated that in this case sterilisation of capital flows has no impact on M_3 expansion. Although there would be no increase in reserve money (M_0) as the increase of Rs. 50 in the RBI's foreign assets is exactly offset by the RBI's divestment of Government paper worth Rs. 50, M_3 would still increase by Rs. 100.

Scenario II: The WGMS proposals may be clearly viewed in the context of our earlier numerical example. In case of the FCNRB deposit of Rs. 100, the components' side of the NM_3 compilation will not be affected, since as per the WGMS recommendations, the RoW sector is no longer considered a part of the money holding sector (Table 4). On the sources' side, the capital inflow of Rs. 100 would now be classified as banks' foreign currency liabilities. Thus, with the bank holding Rs. 50 in foreign currency assets, its net foreign currency assets would work out to Rs. (-)50. Further, with the RBI's foreign assets increasing by the swapped amount of Rs. 50, there would

TABLE 2

Compilation of Broad Money (M_3: Present and Residency Bases)

Second Working Group	*Present Working Group*	*Selected Remarks*
1	*2*	*3*
Broad Money (M_3) (C.1+C.2+C.3 = S.1+S.2+S.3+S.4 -S.5)	Broad Money (NM_3) (C.1+C.2+C.3+C.4 = S.1+S.2+S.3+S.4-S.5-S.6)	Compilation of money supply on residency basis.
Components		
C.1 Currency with the Public	C.1 Currency with the Public	Includes non-residents' rupee & coin holdings.
C.2 Aggregate Deposits with Banks	C.2 Aggregate Deposits of Residents with the Banking System	Computation on residency basis excluding non-residents' repatriable foreign currency fixed deposits.
C.3 'Other' Deposits with the RBI	C.3 'Other' Deposits with the RBI	
	C.4 Call/term Borrowings from Non-Bank Sources	Of negligible magnitude on reporting Fridays.
Sources:		
S.1 Net Bank Credit to the Government	S.1 Net Bank Credit to the Government	
S.2 Bank Credit to the Commercial Sector	S.2 Bank Credit to the Commercial Sector	Includes credit in foreign currency.
S.3 Net Foreign Exchange Assets (NFA) of the Banking Sector (S.3.1+S.3.2)	S.3 NFA of the Banking Sector (S.3.1+S.3.2)	
S.3.1 RBI's NFA	S.3.1 RBI's NFA	
S.3.2 Authorised Dealers' (AD) Balances	S.3.2 Net Foreign Currency Assets of the Banking System (S.3.2.1-S.3.2.2)	AD data discontinued in M_3 compilation.
	S.3.2.1 Foreign Currency Assets	Includes balances held abroad & investments in eligible foreign securities and bonds but excludes bank credit in foreign currency.
	S.3.2.2. Foreign Currency Liabilities	Includes i) banks' non-residents' repatriable foreign currency fixed deposits & ii) overseas borrowings.
S.4 Government's Currency Liabilities to the Public	S.4 Government's Currency Liabilities to the Public	
S.5 Net Non-Monetary Liabilities (NNML) of the Banking Sector	S.5 Capital Account S.6 Other items (net)	NNML includes banks' overseas borrowings as part of other non-bank demand & time liabilities (ODTL).

Source: WGMS Report

TABLE 3

Accounting of Capital Flows in the Present M_3 Compilation: The Case of Full Sterilisation

Component Flow	*Rupees*	*Source Flow*	*Rupees*
1	*2*	*3*	*4*
1. Currency with the Public		1. Net Bank Credit to Government (1.1+1.2)	0
2. Aggregate Deposits (2.1+2.2)	100	1.1 Net RBI Credit to Government	-50
2.1 Demand Deposits		1.2 Other Banks' credit to Government	50
2.2 Time Deposits	100	2. Bank Credit to Commercial Sector	
3. 'Other' Deposits with the RBI		3. Government's Currency Liabilities to the Public	
		4. Net Foreign Assets of Banks (4.1+4.2)	100
		4.1 Net Foreign Assets of the RBI	50
		4.2 Authorised Dealers' Balances	50
		5. Net Non-Monetary Liabilities of Banks	
4. Δ Broad Money (M_3) (1+2+3)	100	6. Δ Broad Money (M_3) (1+2+3+4-5)	100
Memo Item			
Δ Reserve Money (M_0)	0		

Note: Reserve Money (M_0) = Currency in Circulation + Bankers' Deposits with the RBI + 'Other' Deposits with the RBI = Net RBI credit to the Government + RBI's claims on banks + RBI's credit to the commercial sector + RBI's NFA + Government's Currency Liabilities to the Public - RBI's NNML.

be no net effect in the net foreign assets of the banking sector. As before, there would be no net impact on the net bank credit to Government. There would be no increase in NM_3. Thus, capital flows would have no monetary effects in case the amount swapped with the RBI is completely sterilised.

TABLE 4

Accounting of Capital Flows in the New Monetary Aggregates: The Case of Full Sterilisation

Component Flow	*Rupees*	*Source Flow*	*Rupees*
1	*2*	*3*	*4*
1. Currency with the Public		1. Net Bank Credit to Government (1.1+1.2)	0
2. Aggregate Deposits of Residents (2.1+2.2)	0	1.1 Net RBI Credit to Government	-50
2.1 Demand Deposits of Residents		1.2 Other Banks' credit to Government	50
2.2 Time Deposits of Residents	0	2. Bank Credit to Commercial Sector	
3. 'Other' Deposits with the RBI		3. Government's Currency Liabilities to the Public	
4. Call/Term borrowings from non-bank institutions		4. Net Foreign Assets of Banks (4.1+4.2)	0
		4.1 Net Foreign Assets of the RBI	50
		4.2 Net Foreign Currency Assets of Banks (4.2.1-4.2.2)	-50
		4.2.1 Foreign Currency Assets	50
		4.2.2 Foreign Currency Liabilities	100
5. Δ Broad Money (NM_3) (1+2+3+4)		5. Capital Account	
		6. Other Items (net)	
		7. Δ Broad Money (NM_3) (1+2+3+4-5-6)	100
Memo Item			
Δ Reserve Money (M_0)	0		

Note: Reserve Money (M_0) = Currency in Circulation + Bankers' Deposits with the RBI + 'Other' Deposits with the RBI = Net RBI credit to the Government + RBI's claims on banks + RBI's credit to the commercial sector + RBI's NFA + Government's Currency Liabilities to the Public - RBI's capital account - RBI's other items (net).

Scenario III: It is now useful to evaluate the monetary impact of capital flows in case there is no sterilisation. Suppose the bank purchases government paper from the commercial sector in cash with the swapped amount of Rs. 50. In this case, M_0 would increase by Rs. 50 with the accretion to the RBI's foreign assets on the sources' side matched by issuance of currency on the components' side. In the first round, this would also increase NM_3 by Rs. 50 by increasing currency with the public on the components' side and net bank credit to the Government on the sources' side (Table 5). Thereafter, NM_3 would increase in the successive rounds of credit creation depending on the public's preferences for cash and bank deposits and the reserve requirements stipulated by the RBI.

TABLE 5

Accounting of Capital Flows in the New Monetary Aggregates: The General Case

Component Flow	*Rupees*	*Source Flow*	*Rupees*
1	*2*	*3*	*4*
1. Currency with the Public	50	1. Net Bank Credit to Government (1.1+1.2)	50
2. Aggregate Deposits of Residents (2.1+2.2)	0	1.1 Net RBI Credit to Government	
2.1 Demand Deposits of Residents		1.2 Other Banks' credit to Government	50
2.2 Time Deposits of Residents	0	2. Bank Credit to Commercial Sector	
3. 'Other' Deposits with the RBI		3. Government's Currency Liabilities to the Public	
4. Call/Term borrowings from non-bank institutions		4. Net Foreign Assets of Banks (4.1+4.2)	0
		4.1 Net Foreign Assets of the RBI	50
		4.2 Net Foreign Currency Assets of Banks (4.2.1-4.2.2)	-50
		4.2.1 Foreign Currency Assets	50
		4.2.2 Foreign Currency Liabilities	100
5. Δ Broad Money (NM_3) (1+2+3+4)	50	5. Capital Account	
		6. Other Items (net)	
		7. Δ Broad Money (NM_3) (1+2+3+4-5-6)	50
Memo Item			
Δ Reserve Money (M_0)	50		

The theoretical underpinnings of the treatment of capital flows in the M_3 (respectively NM_3) compilation may be explained in terms of the money multiplier approach in the following framework:

$$M_3 = mM_0 \qquad ...(1)$$

where M_3 (respectively NM_3) is broad money, M_0 is reserve money and m is the broad money multiplier;

$m = (1+c)/(c+r)$ ...(2)

where c and r are currency and reserves deposit ratios; and

$M_0 = NDA + NFA$ ...(3)

where NDA and NFA are the RBI's net domestic assets and net foreign assets.

On total differentiation of equations (1), (2) and (3), we obtain.

$dM_3 = m\ dM_0 + M_0\ dm$ ...(4)

$dm = \{(r-1)dc/(c+r)^2\} - \{(1+c)dr/(c+r)^2\}$ ...(5)

$dM_0 = d(NDA) + d(NFA)$ ...(6)

Let us assume, without loss of generality, that i) there is full sterilisation in case of capital inflows, i.e., in (6), $\{(-)\ d\ (NDA) = d(NFA) \Rightarrow dM_0 = 0\}$ and ii) there are no changes in reserve requirements so that dr = 0 in (5). Substituting (5) and (6) in (4), we thus obtain, M_3 growth purely in terms of changes in c,

$dM_3 = \{(r-1)dc/(c+r)^2\}\ M_0$ ...(7)

where $1 \geq c$, $r \geq 0$, so that $0 \geq (r-1)$.

Money supply typically reflects the demand for monetary assets by the money holding sector. Theoretically, c is determined by the transactions costs of liquidity management faced by the money holding sector. In the Indian economy, for example, the spread of the bank branching network following bank nationalisation in 1969, has facilitated the spread of banking habits among the public, leading to a secular decline in c. It may be indicated that as the money holding sector in the extant money supply accounts embraces both residents and non-residents, capital inflows of Rs. 100 to the Indian banking sector count as deposits in Scenario I, reduce c and result in M_3 growth in (7) {i.e., $dM_3 \geq 0$, as $(r-1)dc/(c+r)^2 \geq 0$, if $0 \geq dc$} despite full sterilisation in (6) {i.e., $dM_0 = 0$, (-) d(NDA) = d (NFA)}. However, this implies that c is no longer solely governed by transactions costs of liquidity management within the economy but also influenced by portfolio considerations outside the economy. Once a distinct RoW sector is carved out (as in case of Scenarios II and III), non-residents would be excluded from the money holding sector so that c is insulated from non-resident portfolio decisions. Hence, in case of Scenario II, capital flows would have no monetary impact in (7) {i.e., $dNM_3 = 0$, as $(r-1)dc/(c+r)^2 = 0$, if dc = 0}. In the case of no sterilisation in Scenario III, M_0 would increase by the swapped amount in (6) (i.e., dM_0=dNFA, as dNDA=0) resulting in monetary growth in (4) {i.e., $dNM_3 = m\ dM_0$, as dm = 0 as dr=dc=0 in (5)}. Thus, if m=3 in (1) and dM_0 = Rs. 50 as in case of Scenario III, {$dNM_3 = mdM_0$=Rs. 150} in (4) would measure the true monetary impact of capital flows.

It needs to be emphasised that money supply in the economy should increase only when there is an increase in the monetary base as a result of the swap on account of capital flows as in Scenario III rather than as a result of the mere accounting of the entire amount, *per se*, as deposits on the components' side as in Scenario I. It is in this sense that capital inflows should be thought of as money creating.

SECTION III

EMPIRICAL RESULTS

The strong M_3 growth since 1993-94 (with the exception of 1995-96) was driven largely by capital inflows. However, part of the M_3 increase may be attributed to the fact that FCNRB deposits (and RIBs in 1998-99) were directly reckoned as bank deposits (Table 6 and Chart II). The NM_3 growth rate, on residency basis, was, however, somewhat more moderate. Direct accounting of non-resident deposit flows in money supply led to shifts in the currency-deposit (C/D) ratio (Chart III). The deseasonalised (C/D) series, computed on a residency basis, during 1993-94 to 1998-99 was, therefore, relatively stable (with a coefficient of variation of 5.2 per cent) than that computed on the present basis (with a coefficient of variation of 5.6 per cent).

Price stability has long been the dominant objective of the conduct of the Reserve Bank's monetary policy with broad money as the intermediate target and bank reserves as the principal operating instrument. The compilation of money supply on residency basis would, therefore, be justified only if NM_3 tracks the goal variable of the inflation rate in terms of the Wholesale Price Index (WPI) better than M_3. We, therefore, attempted to empirically test the performance of M_3 and NM_3 *vis-a-vis* WPI in terms of information efficiency during fiscal 1993-94 to 1997-98 in line with the WGMS Report which carried out similar exercises for the new monetary aggregates for fiscal 1993-94 to 1996-97. We found that NM_3 are better correlated with the wholesale price index (WPI) (Table 7). The marginal degree of improvement is to be expected in view of the fact that FCNRB deposits were a negligible proportion of money supply until 1994-95. The results improve once we take the fiscal year growth rates and the average year-on-year growth rates for the 'nineties.

TABLE 6

Annual M_3 Growth: Impact of FCNR(B) Deposits and RIBs

(Per cent)

Year	M_3	NM_3	FCNRB Deposits (Rs. crore)	Resurgent India Bonds (Rs. crore)	(Δ FCNRB Deposits + RIB)/ Δ Deposits of Residents)	Inflation Rate (WPI)
1	2	3	4	5	6	7
1993-94						
March-end	18.4	17.6	3,475		6.6	10.8
Monthly Average	15.9	15.6				8.4
1994-95						
March-end	22.3	21.1	9,648		8.6	10.4
Monthly Average	19.8	18.4				10.9
1995-96						
March-end	13.7	12.10	19,648		22.3	5.0
Monthly Average	15.7	14.4				7.7
1996-97						
March-end	16.2	15.5	26,906		9.4	6.9
Monthly Average	16.3	15.0				6.4
1997-98						
March-end	17.6	17.3	33,445		6.3	5.3
Monthly Average	17.0	16.6				4.8
1998-99						
March-end	17.8	16.0	35,288	17,945	18.9	4.8
Monthly Average	18.9	17.6				6.9
Average						
March-end	17.7	16.6				7.2
Monthly Average	17.2	16.2				7.5

Note: 1. NM_3 refers to the new M_3 aggregate as recommended by WGMS.

2. Monetary data are provisional since September 1997.

3. FCNRB deposits and RIBs are as on the last reporting Friday of the year. The RBI has been publishing data on broad money (M_3) both as presently compiled and that netted for RIBs in the Weekly Statistical Supplement following the RIB inflows in August 1998.

We have followed the WGMS report in testing for the information content of M_3 and NM_3, actuals as well as seasonally adjusted, econometrically by using non-nested hypothesis testing criteria with WPI as the goal variable. The technique of non-nested tests for linear regression models posit that two models (say, M^A and M^B) would be non-nested if the regressors of M^A (respectively M^B) cannot be expressed as an exact linear combination of the regressors of M^B (respectively M^A). The choice criteria, Akaike Information (AIC) and Schwarz Bayesian (SBC) criteria, derived from the maximised log likelihood functions of the models M^A and M^B, state that model M^A would be preferred to M^B if i) AIC (M^A: M^B)>0 and ii) SBC (M^A: M^B)>0, respectively. Otherwise, M^B is to be preferred to M^A.

CHART II

Monetary Growth Rates: Present and Residency Bases

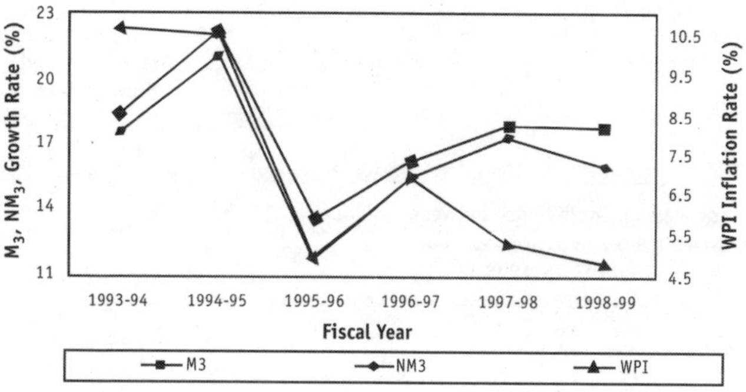

CHART III

Deseasonalised Currency Deposit (C/D) Ratios: The Residency Impact

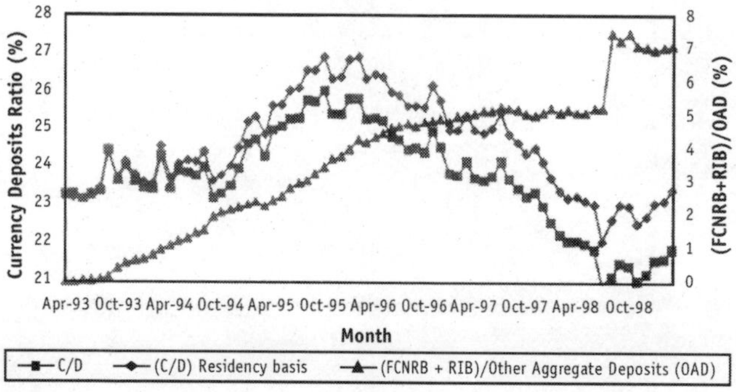

We set out by testing for unit roots for the series used in our exercise. In view of the size-power trade-off, we selected the order of the augmented Dickey-Fuller (ADF) tests using the appropriate model selection criteria of maximising AIC and SBC criteria. All the series used were found to be I(1) (Table 8).

TABLE 7

M_3 and WPI: Cross Correlation Coefficients, 1993-94 to 1998-99

Monetary Variable	*WPI*		*WPIs*	
1	2		3	
M_3	0.9780		-	
M_{3s}	-		0.9782	
NM_3	0.979		-	
NM_{3s}	-		0.980	
Memo Item:				
Measure	Fiscal Year Growth Rate		Average Annual Growth Rate	
	M_3	NM_3	M_3	NM_3
Correlation Coefficients between broad money and Inflation Rate (WPI) (1990-91 to 1998-99)	0.42	0.55	0.28	0.41

Note: Subscript s refers to deseasonalised variable. Monetary (M_{3s} and NM_{3s}) and price (WPIs) data relating to 1993-94 through 1998-99 have been deseasonalised by the X-11 method.

TABLE 8

Unit Root Tests

Variable	*Augmented Dickey-Fuller Test with trend*	*Critical Value 5%*
1	2	3
M_3	-1.02	-3.49
M_{3s}	0.52	-3.49
NM_3	-1.42	-3.49
NM_{3s}	2.0	-3.49
WPI	-2.76	-3.49
WPI_s	-1.78	-3.49
IIP	0.92	-3.49

Note: Data relate to the fiscal years 1993-94 to 1997-98. Subscript s refers to deseasonalised variable.

First, we tested the relative information efficiency of the deseasonalised M_3 (i.e., M_{3s}) and NM_3 (i.e., NM_{3s}) in respect of deseasonalised WPI (i.e., WPIs). We set up two bi-variate vector auto-regression (VAR) models, viz., MM_{3s} and MNM_{3s} on first differences so as to work in a stationary space with dWPIs as the dependent variable and dM_{3s} and dNM_{3s}, respectively, as regressors. Both dM_{3s} and dNM_{3s} were found statistically significant at a month's lag in models MM_{3s} and MNM_{3s}, respectively. We then tested the hypothesis of superiority of the information content of the model MNM_{3s} vis-a-vis the model MM_{3s} with $dWPI_s$ as the goal variable using the non-nested hypothesis testing criteria mentioned above. As both the AIC and SBC were positive, MNM_{3s} was preferred to MM_{3s} in information content in terms of $dWPI_s$. MNM_{3s} was also found to perform better in terms of other model selection criteria (Table 9).

TABLE 9

Models MM_{3s} and MNM_{3s}: Information Efficiency

Test	*MNM_{3s} vs. MM_{3s}*	*MM_{3s} vs. MNM_{3s}*
1	*2*	*3*
Cox's Test	1.497 (0.134)	-1.987 (0.047)
Wald's Test	1.219 (0.223)	-1.406 (0.160)
Fisher and McAleer Test	-1.458 (0.145)	1.753 (0.08)

Note: 1. Parenthetic figures are p values.

2. The test statistics for column no. 2 are not significant at 95% so that the null of model superiority of MNM_{3s} over MM_{3s} cannot be rejected. At the same time, the Cox and Fisher and McAleer test statistics for column no. 3 are significant at 95% and 90% levels, respectively.

3. Both the Akaike Information Criteria (AIC) and Schwarz Bayesian Criteria (SBC) at 0.65 favour MNM_{3s} against MM_{3s}.

Inflation is commonly hypothesised to depend positively on monetary growth on the demand side and negatively on output effects (as measured by the index of industrial production (IIP)) on the supply side. Therefore, in our next exercise, to incorporate the output effect, we again set up two tri-variate vector auto-regression (VAR) models on first differences MM_3 and MNM_3 with dWPI as the dependent variable and dIIP and dNM_3 as regressors in model MNM_3 and dIIP and dM_3 as regressors in model MM_3. From the VAR, we found that M_3 and NM_3 to be statistically significant at a lag of one month in MM_3 and MNM_3, respectively, while IIP appears to be significant in the two models with a lag of three months. The coefficients of the relevant variables carry expected signs at the statistically significant lags. Using the non-nested hypothesis testing criteria as before, we again tested the hypothesis of superiority of information content of the model MNM_3 vis-a-vis the model MM_3 with dWPI as the goal variable. As both the AIC and SBC were positive, MNM_3 was preferred to MM_3 in information content in terms of WPI. MNM_3 was also found to perform better in terms of other model selection criteria (Table 10).

TABLE 10

Models MM_3 and MNM_3: Information Efficiency

Test	MNM_3 vs MM_3	MM_3 vs MNM_3
1	2	3
Cox's Test	-4.882 (0.000)	-19.296 (0.000)
Wald's Test	-0.581 (0.561)	-2.694 (0.007)
Fisher and McAleer Test	0.930 (0.352)	2.693 (0.007)

Note: 1. Parenthetic figures are p values.

2. The test statistics for column no. 2 are not significant at 95% level (except the Cox statistic) so that the null of model superiority of MNM_3 over MM_3 cannot be rejected. At the same time, all the three test statistics for column no. 3 are significant at 95% level.

3. One more result is that both the Akaike Information Criteria (AIC) and Schwarz Bayesian Criteria (SBC) at 6.86 favour MNM_3 against MM_3.

The relevance of compiling monetary aggregates on residency basis has been further underscored by the recent monetary experience of RIBs which raised US $ 4.2 billion (Rs. 17,945 crore) in August 1998, of which US $ 3.2 billion have been swapped with the RBI. As monetary aggregates are presently not compiled on residency basis, the RIB proceeds of Rs. 17,945 crore were straight-away added to banks' time deposits effective August 28, 1998 leading to a jump in the year-on-year M_3 (inclusive of RIBs) growth rate from 17.9 per cent as at end-July 1998 to 20.2 per cent as on August 28, 1998 with the (C/D) ratio dropping from 21.2 per cent as on July 31, 1998 to 20.5 per cent as on August 28, 1998. Netting FCNRB deposits and RIBs from money supply in line with the WGMS recommendations, the year-on-year NM_3 growth rate worked out to 17.8 per cent as at end-July 1998 and 18.0 per cent as on August 28, 1998 respectively. The average NM_3 growth rate, on residency basis, during 1998-99 has been steady at 17.6 per cent and does not show any discernible shift on account of RIB inflows suggesting that RIBs have had only a limited monetary impact (Table 11). The (C/D) ratio, on residency basis, increased to 22.8 per cent as at end-March 1999 from 22.5 per cent driven by the higher cash demand in 1998-99 (January-March, at Rs. 7,839 crore as compared with a mere Rs. 1,509 crore in the comparable quarter of 1997-98). However, the C/D ratio, on present basis, actually declined from 21.5 per cent as at end-March 1998 to 21.3 per cent as at end-March 1999 on account of RIBs which essentially reflected non-resident portfolio considerations rather than domestic liquidity preferences.

TABLE 11

Average Year-on-Year Broad Money Growth Rate (Monthly Basis)

(Per cent)

Period	M_3	NM_3
1	2	3
1998-99	18.9	17.6
1998-99 (up to July)	17.6	17.4
1998-99 (August-March)	19.6	17.6
Memo Item:		
1997-98	17.0	16.6

Note: Data are provisional.

A closer look at the movements in the monetary base between August 14, 1998 and September 25, 1998 which saw the accretion of Rs. 15,505 crore on account of RIB proceeds to the RBI's NFA would tend to support our hypothesis. The RIB inflows from August 21, 1998 onwards pushed up the RBI's net foreign assets by Rs. 7,186 crore (adjusted for revaluation) between August 14 and September 25, 1998, on account of simultaneous net sales to authorised dealers. The resultant liquidity generated market off-take of government paper, reducing the Centre's monetised deficit by Rs. 9,442 crore during this period. Consequently, M_0 expansion was restricted to a mere Rs. 492 crore between August 14 and September 25, 1998[5]. The monetary impact of RIBs was also circumscribed by the one percentage point hike in banks' reserve requirements effective August 29, 1998 (although this has been somewhat mitigated by the spurt in scheduled commercial banks' refinance drawals since late August 1998). This explains why intra-year monetary growth, computed on residency basis, does not exhibit any large-scale shift because of RIB inflows in 1998-99. Thus, the NM_3 growth rate, on residency basis, would be a better guide to the monetary developments in 1998-99.

SECTION IV

CONCLUSIONS

Our findings support the WGMS recommendation of compilation of money supply on residency basis, which reflect the domestic demand for monetary assets more accurately and thus establish a better correlation with inflation. It needs to be emphasised, however, the compilation of money supply on a residency basis does not imply that capital flows in the form of banks' non-resident repatriable foreign currency fixed deposits such as FCNRB deposits and RIBs which are not directly reckoned in monetary aggregates do not have monetary effects. However, the monetary impact of such capital flows would have to be tracked in terms of rounds of money creation as a result of their effect on the monetary base.

Notes

1. The banking sector in India comprises i) the Reserve Bank of India and ii) the banking system in India including a) the State Bank of India and its subsidiaries, b) nationalised banks, c) regional rural banks, d) all other banking companies in private sector (including foreign banks operating in India) - constituting what are commonly known as commercial banks, e) co-operative banks and f) any financial institution notified by the Central Government. Primary dealers so notified are, however, not considered part of the banking sector in money supply compilation.
2. For example, Tarapore (1998) argues that the portion of FCNRB deposits/Resurgent India Bonds (RIBs) swapped into Indian rupees should be directly included in money supply.
3. See the comprehensive 29-country survey of monetary aggregates in the WGMS report. For details consult the websites of member central banks of the Bank for International Settlements at www.bis.org.
4. The WGMS has also recommended that banks' overseas borrowings, which are presently classified under the head of non-monetary liabilities, should be set off against their foreign assets. While past data are not available, their magnitude is believed to be limited.
5. See chapter V on "Monetary and Banking Developments" in the Report on Currency and Finance, 1997-98.

References

International Monetary Fund (1994): *Manual on Monetary and Financial Statistics*, Revised draft, Statistics Department, Washington D.C.

Reserve Bank of India, (1961): *Report of the Working Group on Money Supply*, RBI Bulletin, Bombay (Reprinted in the Second Working Group report).

Reserve Bank of India, (1977): *Report of the Second Working Group on Money Supply*, Bombay.

Reserve Bank of India, (1998): *Report of the Working Group on Money Supply: Analytics and Methodology of Compilation*, Mumbai.

Reserve Bank of India, (1998): *Report on Currency and Finance*, Volume I, Mumbai.

Tarapore, S.S., (1998): "Standstill Monetary Policy", Pistis, *Business Standard*, November 13.

7

Estimating Money Demand Function

A Cointegration Approach

Ashok K Nag • Ghanshyam Upadhyay

Introduction

THE existence of a stable demand function for money is an important building block for many macroeconomic models. In fact, a stable demand function for money "has long been perceived as a prerequisite for the use of monetary aggregates in the conduct of (monetary) policy" (Goldfield, 1990). For an economy undergoing an adjustment program, the existence of a stable money demand function, it is often regarded, gives hope to policy-makers in their search for a target or monetary aggregates consistent with other policy objectives like price stability. In this context one needs to note that the devastating nature of Lucas critique of policy ineffectiveness arises from the fact that the rational agents' forward looking expectations undermine the stability of any relationship between macroeconomic aggregates[1]. According to this view, estimated relationships between such variables based on historical data are of not much use to policy makers because of the impact of policy changes on the relationships themselves. Melnick (1990) specially addressed to this issue while estimating demand for money function for Argentina, and concluded that the instability in the money demand function may be, to a large degree, due to "improper dynamic specification of the short run demand function for money". The money demand functions estimated in the Indian context also generally suffer from this problem of lack of non integration of long-term relationship with proper short term dynamic specification[2].

The parametric regression technique based on ordinary least square (OLS) has so far been the most popular statistical method for establishing relationship among macroeconomic variables, despite the known drawbacks of this method in the case of time-series data. Since most of the macroeconomic time series are nonstationary in their level, OLS regression technique may give misleading results in two respects. Firstly, it may show a significant relationship among variables in term of high R^2 even if no such relationship exists (indication of which may be found in low Durbin-Watson statistic) and secondly the usual t-statistic for individual regression coefficients does not possess even a limiting distribution and is expected to diverge to infinity under the assumption of independence of nonstationary regressors and regressand[3]. Since the publication of Granger and Newbold's oft-quoted paper (Granger and New-bold 1974), there has been enormous growth in literature to deal with such type of problems[4]. The concept of cointegration proposed by Granger and Engle (1987) is an attempt to salvage the regression technique from the problem of non-stationarity and is fast emerging as a potent method in the armoury of applied econometricians. Melnick's empirical exercise shows that the method of cointegration can be a useful empirical technique for estimating long term relationships.

The objectives of this paper are to estimate a money demand function that takes care of some of the shortcomings of the existing exercises on the demand for money in India: to introduce, as an exploratory approach, the cointegration method of viewing the demand for money; and to raise analytical issues emerging from the empirical exercise. The organisation of the paper is as follows: Section I (omitted here-ed) presents a brief description of the concept of cointegration and Johansen's method of identification of the cointegrating space. We present this technical section at the beginning as some of the problems associated with our search for proper specification of money demand function hinges crucially on the time

The authors express their indebtedness to Dr. A. Vasudevan and Shri R.B. Barman for their comments on an earlier draft of this paper, without burdening them with any responsibility for the remaining errors.

series properties of variables to be chosen. It may be noted here that Johansen's method is essentially a multivariate generalisation of Dickey-Fuller's unit root test and is based on likelihood ratio statistic and therefore is likely to possess a better power than the two step Granger-Engle procedure employed by Melnick. In section II, we discuss the specification of money demand function employed in this paper as well as the time series properties of chosen variables. Lastly, the results of exercise are presented in section III.

SECTION II

It is best to begin with Cagan's specification of money demand function developed in the context of hyper-inflationary environment for developing countries[6]. Since no market related interest rates are available in many developing countries, it is believed that a proper opportunity cost of money may be represented by the expected inflation rate-proxy for the rate of return on real goods. However, in the Indian case, we find that inflation rate (measured as first difference of log of Wholesale Price Index (WPI) is an I(0) and not an I(1) variable. Therefore a long term relationship cannot be estimated using expected inflation rate as one of the possible co-variates. In our search for an alternative I(1) variable proxying for a rate of return on an alternative competing asset we experimented with yield on government securities as well as yield on ordinary shares both of which are found to be I(1) variables. On experimentation we settled for yield on ordinary shares (YOS) as the proxy for rate of return on a spectrum of alternative assets. It may be mentioned here that the relation between stock prices and monetary growth has been studied in the context of developed countries like U.S.A. For example, Sprinkel (1964) compared the level of index of stock prices with a moving average rate of changes in the narrow money supply. Although Sprinkel's method of establishing causal direction was found to be statistically deficient, the existence of a relationship between these two variables could not be disputed. Cooper (1974) using a more advanced spectral technique also found a causal link between these variables, although in an opposite direction. Since our interest does not lie in the direction of causality, we may argue that returns in stock market may be taken as one of the determinants of portfolio choice behaviour of households and business in respect of their financial assets. Recently, Brahmanada et al (1992) also explored this relationship and their results suggest that a possible link may exist[7]. Furthermore, during the eighties the growth in share prices was much higher than the general inflation rate. For example, [the] RBI index of prices of ordinary shares at all India level increased from a level of 118.9 (yearly average) for the year 1981-82 to 500.3 in the year 1990-91, indicating [an annual] compound growth rate of around 17.3 per cent. During the same period the wholesale price index rose at an annual rate of 6.9 per cent only. The increasing depth and maturity of stock markets in India also provide at present more liquidity to the stock holdings of individual and therefore reduce the liquidity premium that the demand deposits with banks may command otherwise. The large fluctuation in stock prices on the other hand is expected to generate substantial speculative demand for money, particularly for those with large unaccounted stock of currency. Furthermore, this influence is more likely to show up in respect of narrow money i.e. M_1, than in respect of M_3 as the latter include savings of pure households not given much to speculation in the Indian situation.

As regards the relevant monetary aggregates to be chosen for our exercise, we observe that it is M_1 and not M_3 which exhibit the required time series properties for application of our chosen method. In other words, while M_1 shows the existence of a stochastic trend in it, M_3 shows no such stochastic trend. In fact, a deterministic trend along with a stationary component captures the time series properties of M_3 very well. The relevant results of Augmented Dickey-Fuller (ADF) tests are given in Table 1. It may also be noted that a forecast of M_3 based on trend stationary model outperforms the forecast based on a difference stationary model[8]. The presence of a stochastic trend in M_1 and the absence of it in M_3 ... indicates that a linear combination of M_1 and M_3-M_1 becomes a trend stationary variable although individually both of them are difference stationary variables. This is an interesting observation by itself and requires further study. In so far as this paper is concerned, we have considered M_1 as our monetary aggregate.

As regards the scale variable proxying for the level of economic activities determining the transaction demand for money stock, the only available relevant monthly data is that of Index of Industrial Production (IIP) which is also found to be an I(1) variable. The ADF test in this regard, however, is not as conclusive as in the case of other variables. Ideally, one should use aggregate production data, including agriculture and service sectors but in the absence of reliable data even on a quarterly basis, we are constrained to use IIP, being fully aware of the fact that the share of industrial income in GDP is relatively low. Furthermore, to examine the sensitiveness of our exercise to the use of IIP as a scale variable, we experimented with the quarterly estimates of GDP (at 1980-81 prices) prepared by Burman et al (1983) and found that the broad nature of long term relationships obtained from the monthly IIP series remains invariant even when quarterly GDP and relevant quarterly variables are used. Finally, the other determinant of nominal demand for money is obviously price level, which is clearly an I(1) variable. Since the price homogeniety of money demand function could not be accepted at a desired level of confidence, we settled for estimating a nominal money demand function. It may be pointed out that some of the earlier studies also used nominal money instead of real money as the relevant monetary aggregate in money demand function (or inverted money demand function) [see Rangarajan-Arif (1990)]. Therefore, the specification of long term equilibrium relationship that we are interested in estimating may be written as:

$$\log M_1 = \alpha + \beta_1 \log IIP + \beta_2 \log WPI + \beta_3 YOS$$

where, IIP = Index of Industrial Production

WPI = Wholesale Price Index

YOS = Yield on Ordinary Shares.

SECTION III

The Data

The sample period for our data is April 1982 to March 1991. Although observations on all the variables were available till March 1992 we deliberately omitted them in our main samples so as to test the stability of our results when more observations become available. In cointegration relationship seasonal dummies were used although experiment shows that results do not change in a substantial manner. All variables except yield on ordinary shares (YOS) were used after log transformation.

Empirical Results: The unrestricted model

$H_1 : X_t = A_1X_{t-1} + A_kX_{t-k} + \mu + E_t + D_i's$, (t=1,2, ...T) where E_1 ... E_t are independent and identically distributed (i.i.d.) multivariate normal residuals with mean zero, D_i's are seasonal dummies and X_{-k+1}, ... X_0 are fixed were first fitted for the data. To begin with, the X_t's are four dimensional vectors of $\ln(M_1)$, ln(IIP), ln(WPI) and YOS. Using the F test, we first decided upon the number of lags to be used. The number of lags chosen was 9. To test the correctness of lags so chosen we tested the residuals of the fitted model for normality and autocorrelations. Bera-Jarque test of normality was employed. The results show that residuals pass the tests at reasonable levels. On experimentation, we also observed that residuals obtained from a model with fewer lags could pass the normal i.i.d. assumption about residuals but not the F test for joint non-significance of higher lags (i.e. lags between 5 to 9) with some attendant risk of overfitting. We also took care to see as to what extent our results are sensitive to the proper specification of unknown lags and we observe that our results are sufficiently robust in this respect.

For test of co-integration the reduced model under H_2 : $\pi = \alpha\beta^T$ is fitted and the estimated eigen values d_i's, the normalized eigen vector v for the data set were calculated. The test statistics for cointegration cannot be rejected by the data. The estimated long term relationship given by the normalised eigen vector corresponding to the largest eigen value works out to

$$\text{Ln } (M_1 = 1.80 \text{ Ln(IIP)} - 0.22 \text{ Ln (WPI)} - 0.04 \text{ YOS}$$

The negative sign of the price variable is rather unexpected and led us to search for another long-term relationship that may exist amongst a subset of the four variables. It is observed that if YOS is dropped from the data set and test for co-integration is applied to the 3-dimensional vector process ($\ln M_1$, lnIIP, lnWPI), the test statistic shows that these three variables are not cointegrated. The estimated trace statistic given in Table 5 bring out the point clearly. We also tried to find out whether M_1 and IIP or M_1 and WPI are co-integrated. The results show that the answer is in the negative. However, it is observed that existence of co-integrating relationship between M_1, IIP and YOS can not be rejected at 5 per cent level although the trace statistics is only marginally significant at 1 per cent level. Since the value of trace statistics are dependent upon the number of lags chosen and it is statistically more desirable to use more lags than less, we settled upon 12 lags for the vector auto-regression on the basis of F-tests as stated above. The results of Bera-Jarque test of normality as well as chi-square test of auto-correlations of residuals obtained from this vector auto-regression are reported in Table 2. The estimated eigen values and normalized eigen vector for this three dimensional set is reported in Table 3. The graphs of original data and also of cointegrating relations corresponding to the three eigen values are presented in Figure (1) and Figure (2). The test statistics given in Table 4 indicate that presence of exactly one cointegration vector can not be rejected by the data. Since the power of Johansen's test of non co-integration declines with more lags thrown in than actually required, we experimented with much longer lag structure and it is observed that the value of the trace statistics increases substantially with higher lags, thereby indicating that presence of cointegrating relationship is well validated by the data. The estimated long term relationship, therefore, works out to

$$Ln(M_1) = 1.62 \text{ Ln (IIp)} - .05 \text{ YOS}$$

One heuristic way to examine the stability of the broad features of our estimated relationship is to estimate the cointegrating relationship over different sub-samples, which we tried. The results obtained in this experimentation is quite encouraging and gives confidence in our reported results. When we include more observations from the financial year 1991-92 we find that between April 1991 and September 1991 the results of cointegration become somewhat weak, i.e., the p value of the trace statistics become around 10 to 20 per cent. This is understandable as the unprecedented jump in WPI during the financial year 1991-92, coupled with the steep devaluation in the rupee and simultaneous slow-down in IIP due to stringent monetary policy introduced to douse the inflationary potential to building up in the economy forced the variables under study to move away from the long term relationship so far exhibited by them. Nonetheless, despite the policy intervention, it is ... surprising to note the discernible tendency to revert back to the long term relationship when the effect of unprecedented shocks has run its course. This enables us to claim that the relationship obtained by us is indeed long-term and not merely a statistical artifact.

An error-correction model is then fitted taking the lagged cointegrating relationship as the error. In our error-correction model we also included inflation rate as measured by the first difference in the log of WPI as well as changes in log gold prices as an additional explanatory variable. This was done to examine whether gold prices contain any additional significant information about price movement and thereby having a bearing on the current demand for money. Since gold is an important saving instrument in India and is very often used as a hedge against inflation, it is expected that gold may be looked upon as an alternative asset for those holding idle money for speculative purposes. The chosen error-correction model confirms (the) hypothesis of significant effect of changes in gold prices on movement in money demand. The coefficients of error correction model finally estimated is given in Table 6.

Finally, ... forecasts of M_1 based on error-correction model are compared with univariate Box-Jenkins forecasting model as well as various formulations of partial adjustment model which has been generally tried in the Indian context. The results of this exercise are given in Table 7 and Table 8. It is observed that error-correction model gives a better forecast than the univariate Box-Jenkins forecasting model as well as various formulations of partial adjustment model.

Interpretation of the result

The long term estimated relationship shows that elasticity of narrow money with respect to level of economic activity as measured by IIP is around 1.62. The semi-elasticity of demand for narrow money with respect to yield on ordinary shares, as given by the long term relationship estimated by us, is of the expected sign and the magnitude of the coefficient is quite large as compared to the coefficient of opportunity cost of money variable obtained in the earlier estimated money demand functions in India or in other countries.

Our exercise also throws light on the issue of sources of price rise during the last decade. The fact that the long term movement in M_1 is highly correlated with IIP which is a proxy for level of economic activity and YOS, and much more weakly with WPI and the fact that the given data do not indicate presence of any long term relationships between M_1, WPI or between M_1, WPI and IIP strongly suggest that the growth in narrow money can not be held a causal determinant of growth in prices. In other words a monetarist explanation of Indian inflation is not empirically supported if M_1 is taken as the relevant monetary aggregate.

Conclusion

Johansen's method of estimating co-integrating vector shows the existence of a reasonably stable money demand function for India with yield on ordinary shares emerging as a good proxy for opportunity cost of narrow money. The principal source of change in money stock demanded emanates from the changes in transaction level while a rise in opportunity cost of money, as expected, depresses the demand for money. An error correction model for money demand is identified and it is observed that movements in gold prices do have impact on the level of money demand in the short run. Our exercise also sheds light on the empirical relevance of the validity of the monetarist explanation of Indian inflation during the 'eighties.

TABLE 1

Augmented Dickey Fuller Test

Variable Name	Statistics Used & Their Values	ϕ_3
Ln (M_1)	$\hat{T}\mu$ = -1.5616	4.92
Ln (WPI)	$\hat{T}\mu$ = 2.5046	3.49
Ln (IIP)	$\hat{T}\tau$ = -3.6729	6.79
YOS	$\hat{T}\mu$ = - 1.5616	3.56
Ln (M_3)	$\hat{T}\tau$ = -4.2874	9.57
	$\hat{\beta}\tau$ = 4.266	
INF. RATE	$\hat{T}\mu$ = -8.4104	36.90
Ln (GOLD)	$\hat{T}\mu$ = -1.0301	3.76

Tab. values at 5% : Tμ = -2.89 Tτ = -3.45 ϕ_3 = 6.49

TABLE 2

Bera-Jarque and Box-Pierce Statistics

DEP.VARIABLES	Ln(M_1)	Ln (IIP)	YOS
τ_1 : Chi Sq. (2)	0.04	0.20	2.89
τ_2 : Chi Sq. (12)	4.61	3.82	10.37

Chi-Sq. (2,0.01) = 4.61 τ_1 = Bera-Jarque Statistic

Chi-Sq. (12,0.01) = 18.55 τ_2 = Box-Pierce Statistic

TABLE 3

Sq. Cononical Correlations and Cointegrating Vectors

	(1)	(2)	(3)
SQ.CAN. CORRLNS:	0.001	0.120	0.234
	Co-integrating Vectors (Normalised)		
Ln (M1)	1	1	1
Ln (IIP)	-1.47	-1.85	-1.62
YOS	-0.02	-0.01	0.05

TABLE 4

Test Statistics to Find Dimension of Cointegrating Space (R)

H_0 :	Trace (Calculated)	Trace (Tabulated at 5%)	Trace (Tabulated at 1%)
R < or = 2	00.05	8.08	11.56
R < or = 1	12.31	17.84	21.96
R = 0	37.96	31.26	37.29

TABLE 5

Trace Under the Hypothesis of no Cointegration

Combination of Variables	Trace (Calculated)	Trace (Tabulated) At 5% L.S.	At 1% L.S.
M_1, WPI	9.56	17.84	21.96
M_1, IIP	4.17	17.84	21.96
M_1, WPI, IIP	26.99	31.26	37.29
M_1, WPI, IIP & YGS	44.43	48.42	55.55

TABLE 6

Error Correction Model

Dependent Variable: 1st Difference of LN (M_1)

Explanatory Variables (in 1st DIF)	LAGS	Estimated Coefficients	T-Stats. (Absolute)	Other Statistics
Constant	-	0.0287	0.0110	SEE = 0.0003
LN (IIP)	1	-0.6102	6.1001	
	2	-0.6243	6.1232	R^2 = 0.5936
	3	-0.4807	4.6698	
	6	0.1127	3.1811	
YOS	1	0.0328	3.0795	$\bar{R}^2$ = 0.5381
	3	0.0427	3.6799	
LN (WPI)	3	-0.6238	1.9380	D.W. = 2.2649
LN (GOLD)	1	0.1248	1.6399	
CR*	1	-0.3395	5.5776	
	4	0.2904	5.0737	
	5	0.0323	1.7068	
	6	0.1127	4.1389	

* CR, the cointegration relation corresponding largest eigen value is without any difference.

TABLE 7

Forecast Performance of ECM

No. of Obsns. used	One Step Ahead Forecast Using		ACTUAL	Percentage Error	
	Box-Jenkins	ECM		Box-Jenkins	ECM
100	83495	84045	83088	0.49	1.15
101	84573	84545	86185	-1.88	-1.91
102	87602	85424	86224	1.60	-0.93
103	88139	88977	88704	-0.63	0.31
104	92336	88926	89358	3.33	-0.48
105	88913	89688	90028	-1.24	-0.38
106	90666	91364	92857	-2.36	-1.61
107	95076	95553	92892	2.35	2.87
			MAPE*	1.74	1.21

* Mean Absolute Percentage Error.

TABLE 8

Performance Statistics for Different Models

Model	SEE	MAPE@	MIN#	MAX#
ECM	0.0003	1.21	0.31	2.87
Box-Jenkin's	-	1.74	0.49	3.33
P-Adjustment* Models				
1	0.0005	1.84	0.12	4.02
2	0.0005	2.09	0.75	5.06
3	0.0005	2.10	0.69	5.22

* The three partial adjustment models are:

1. M_1 (t) = f{M_1 (t-1), IIP (t), YOS (t)}
2. M_1 (t) = f{M_1 (t-1), IIP (t), WPI (t)}
3. M_1 (t) = f{M_1 (t-1), IIP (t), YOS (t), WPI (t)}

(All the variables are in logarithm except YOS)

@ Mean Absolute Percentage Errors (MAPE) for one step ahead forecasts (out of sample) are based on 8 repetitions.

\# Minimum and maximum percentage errors (forecast) among 8 repetitions.

FIGURE (1)

Log of M1 (Monthly) From April 1982 to March 1991

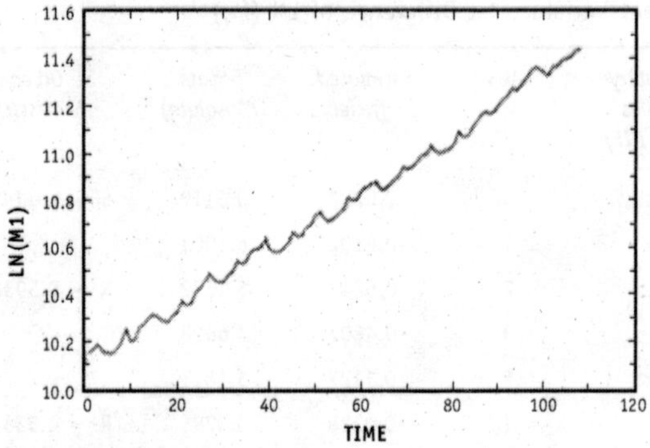

Log of IIP (Monthly) From April 1982 to March 1991

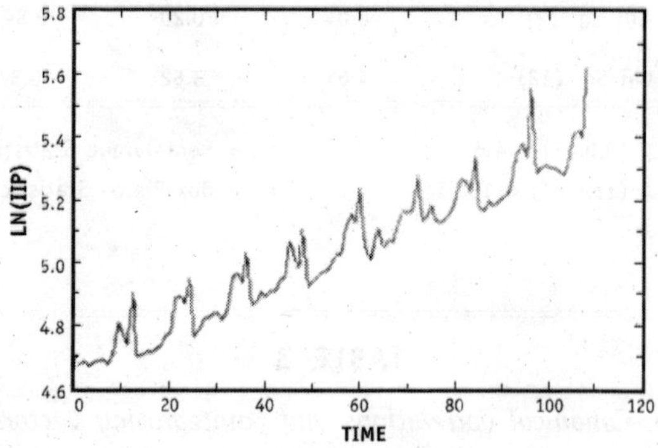

YOS (Monthly) From April 1982 to March 1991

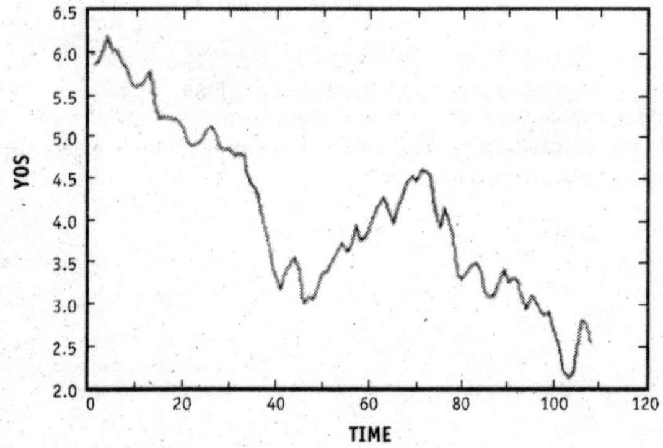

Log of WPI (Monthly) From April 1982 to March 1991

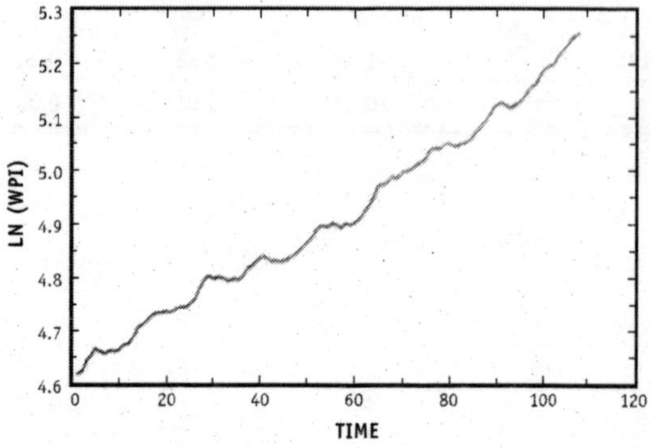

FIGURE (2)

LOG OF GOLD PRICES
APRIL 1982 TO MARCH 1991

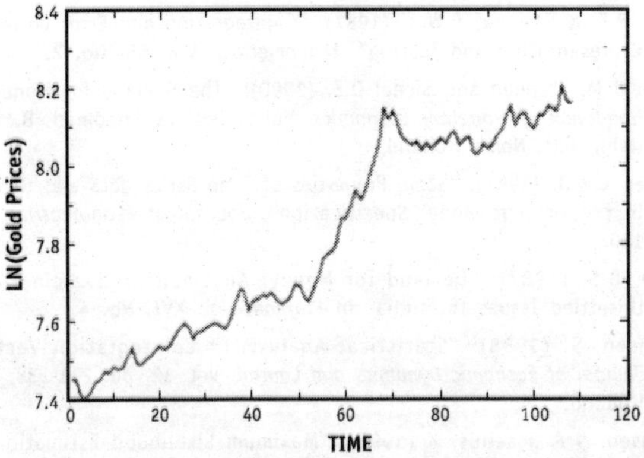

COINTEGRATING RELATION : 1

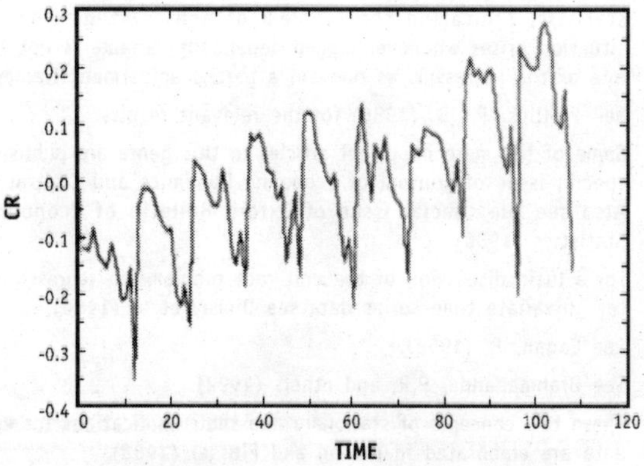

COINTEGRATING RELATION : 2

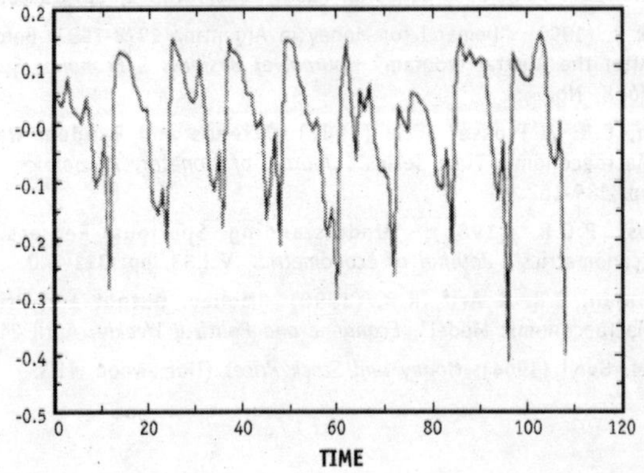

COINTEGRATING RELATION : 3*

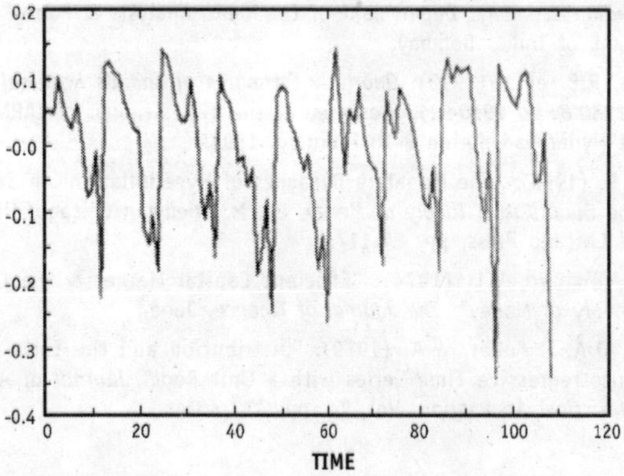

* Corresponding to largest eigen vector (see table 3)

FIGURE 3
M1 (ACTUAL & ESTIMATED)

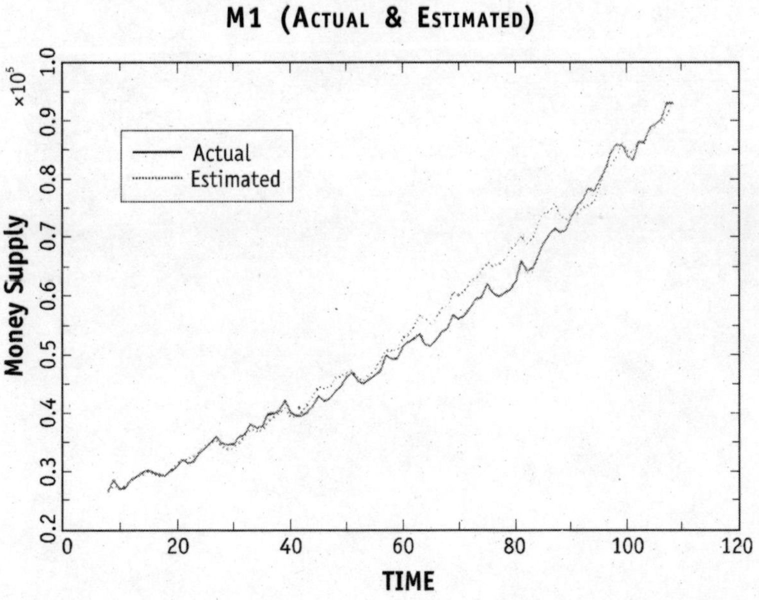

Footnotes

1. See Lucas (1976).
2. For example see Gupta (1987); The results of estimated money demand functions given in the paper show that in many cases the estimated equations are characterised by high R^2 and low D-W statistic, indicating the problem of non-cointegration. Such a situation arises whenever lagged dependent variable is not taken as one of the regressor, as done in a partial adjustment framework.
3. See Phillips, P.C.B. (1986) for the relevant results.
4. Some of the more important articles in this genre are published in a special issue of Journal of Economic Dynamics and Control (1988). Also see the special issue of Oxford Bulletin of Economics and Statistics (1986).
5. For a lucid discussion of the unit root problems in regression set up for univariate time series data see Dickey et al (1986).
6. See Cagan, P. (1956).
7. See Brahmananda, P.R. and others (1992).
8. These two concepts of stationary and their implications for economic data are elaborated in Nelson and Plosser (1982).

References

Brahmananda, P.R. et al (1992): *The Changing Monetary Process in the Indian Economy*, Department of Economic Analysis & Policy, Reserve Bank of India, Bombay.

Burman, R.B. et al (1993): *Quarterly Estimates of India's National Income (1980-81 to 1990-91)*, Presented at the 12th Seminar of IARNIW held at Hyderabad during 8-10 February, 1993.

Cagan, P. (1956): "The Monetary Dynamics of Hyperinflation" in *Studies in the Quantitative Theory of Money*, ed. M. Friedman Chicago: University of Chicago Press, pp. 25-117.

Cooper, Richard, V.L. (1974): "Efficient Capital Market & the Quantity Theory of Money", *The Journal of Finance*, June.

Dickey, D.A. & Fuller, W.A. (1979): "Distribution and the Estimation of Auto-regressive Time Series with a Unit Root" *Journal of American Statistical Association*, Vol. 74, pp. 427-431.

Dickey, D.A. & Fuller, W.A. (1981): "Likelihood Ratio Statistics for Auto-regressive Time Series with a Unit Root", *Econometrica*, Vol. 49, pp. 1057-1072.

Dickey, D.A., W.R. Bell & R.B. Miller (1986): "Unit roots in time series models: Tests and Implications", *The American Statistician*, Vol. 40, pp. 12-16.

Engle, R.F. & Granger, C.W.J. (1987): "Cointegration and Error Correction: Representation and Testing", *Econometrica*, Vol. 55, No. 2.

Goldfield M. Stephen and Sichel D.E. (1990): "The Demand for Money", in *Handbook of Monetary Economics*, Vol.1, (ed) by Friedman, B.M. and Hahn, F.H. North Holland.

Granger, C.W.J. (1981): "Some Properties of Time Series data and their Use in Econometric Model Specification", *Journal of Econometrics*, 121-130.

Gupta, G.S. (1987): "Demand for Money: An Empirical Examination of Unsettled Issues for India" in *Prajnan*, Vol. XVI, No. 4.

Johansen, S. (1988): "Statistical Analysis of Cointegration Vectors", *Journal of Economic Dynamics and Control*, Vol. 12, pp. 231-238, North Holland.

Johansen, S & Juselius, K (1990): "Maximum Likelihood Estimation and Inference on Cointegration - With Application to Demand for Money", *Oxford Bulletin of Economics and Statistics*, Vol. 52, No. 2.

Lucas, R.E. Jr. (1976): "Economic Policy Evaluation: A Critique", *Carnegie Rochester Conference Series on Public Policy*, Vol. 1, pp. 19-46.

Melnick R. (1990): "Demand for Money in Argentina 1978-1987: Before and After the Austral Program", *Journal of Business & Economic Statistics*, Vol.8, No. 4.

Nelson, C.R. & Plosser, C.I. (1982): "Trends and Random Walks of Macroeconomic Time Series", *Journal of Monetary Economics*, Vol.10, pp. 139-162.

Phillips, P.C.B. (1986): "Understanding Spurious Regression in Econometrics", *Journal of Econometrics*, Vol.33, pp. 311-340.

Rangarajan, C.R. & Arif, R.R. (1990): "Money, Output and Prices: A Macroeconomic Model", *Economic and Political Weekly*, April 21.

Sprinkel, Beryl (1964): *Money and Stock Prices* (Homewood, III).

8

The Demand for Money in India

Stability Revisited

Himanshu Joshi • Mridul Saggar

THE link between the demand for money balances and aggregate income is one of the central themes in the theory and practice of monetary economics. Naturally, it is embedded as a recurring issue in the literature on money. The subject, however, has received inadequate attention in recent times in the Indian context. This is somewhat surprising as one would expect the on-going financial innovations and regulatory changes to re-open the question of stability of the money demand function.[1] Secondly, there is a recognition that money demand models of yesteryears, mainly based on the Goldfeld (1973) equation or one of its variants, suffers from the application of the least squares technique to non-stationary variables ignoring their time-series properties but this has hardly been adequately addressed. The least square technique leads to 'spurious inferences' because the usual t-and F-statistics do not have exact limiting distributions (Phillips, 1986). There is, therefore, a need to re-estimate the money demand relation in India by employing a co-integration framework. The efforts made so far in the direction have been limited, with only three studies available, viz, those of Moosa (1992), Nag and Upadhyay (1993) and Parikh (1994). But these fail to relate money balances to aggregate income leaving a number of questions unanswered from the policy-maker's viewpoint.

Our purpose in this paper is to examine if there exists an underlying equilibrium relationship between real money balances and a given set of variables that explain it, including the aggregate real income. We explore this question by studying the long-run monetary relationship and its short-run dynamic adjustments through application of co-integration, error-correction procedures. For this, the recent test procedure of Johansen and Juselius (1990) is preferred to Engle-Granger (1987) and Stock-Watson (1988) methodologies as not only its representation makes all variables endogenous leaving results insensitive to choice of dependent variable, the test statistics have exact limiting distributions as well.[2] Also, the chosen procedure allows for hypothesis testing through restrictions on coefficients in the cointegrating vector as well as on the corresponding weights.

Our work extends on the three previous efforts for the Indian case in three important ways. First, on the specification side, we incorporate aggregate real income instead of trying to proxy real activity through the Index of Industrial Production (IIP). In India, the share of industry in GDP averaged merely 20 per cent over the last three decades. Households engaged in farm and services activities exert a considerable influence over money balances and therefore, industrial production alone cannot be construed to drive the money demand. Besides, from the practioner's viewpoint, the use of IIP restraints policy-maker from obtaining important information content in the form of income-elasticity which provides the basis for monetary targeting. No doubt, the higher frequency of the data on IIP which is monthly compared to annual GDP series enables researchers to have a larger number of observations but the concern for correct specification should override this consideration.

Apart from the activity variable, our specification also differs in that it finds that the opportunity cost variable does not enter the cointegrating vector. We considered the rate of inflation as an opportunity cost variable as the option available to most of economic agents is not between holding of money or placing it in the call market but between money and the cost of holding it.

The authors are grateful to Professor Ashok Parikh fro the discussions they had on various aspects relating to application of the Johansen & Juselius (1990) procedure and to Dr. A. Vasudaven, Prof. Kunal Sen and Shri Madu Mohanty for making a number of helpful suggestions on an earlier draft of this paper. The usual desclaimer applies.

Most of the interest rates, including the call money rate, were regulated in one way or another in the past several years. Therefore, inflation rate becomes more meaningful as an opportunity cost. However, inflation rate, like interest rates, do not satisfy unit root properties.[3] Following Corker (1990) we also include, for the first time for India, a measure of the stock of financial wealth in the model to capture portfolio decisions effected by agents among financial assets and the national product. Secondly, we employ statistical procedures which would increase the credibility of the results even with a small sample as normality in distribution is established. Thirdly, we examine parameter stability through recursive estimation based on CUSUMSQ statistics. Examining the stability of money demand relationship is important as shifts in functional relationship has vital implications for monetary management.

The paper is organized as follows. Section I discusses the literature on money demand function against the backdrop of issues relating to monetary policy and financial liberalisation. Section II gives a description of the experimental design and the empirical results of the specified long run and short run forms. Section III reports on the dynamic tracking and the out-of-sample forecasts generated by our model, together with the conclusions following our exercise. Also, a summary discussion on test procedures related to cointegration and error correction modeling is provided in the technical appendix in the end.

SECTION I

The significance of a stable money demand function for monetary policy with aggregate activity as endogenous variable, lies in the fact that it facilitates the setting out of parameters which are useful for the central bank to control monetary aggregates to stabilise the economy. The test of a stable money demand function which has applied policy utility, to a great extent lies in its predictive power reflected in its out of sample forecasting performance. Under the IS-LM framework, the stable money demand translates into a stable positioning of the LM curve and if IS curve also turns out to be stable, it implies money supply can have a predictable influence on the level of activity. In practice, we live in a stochastic world in which random shocks disturb IS-LM relationship and following Poole's (1970) seminal analysis we know that the efficacy of targeting money supply rests mainly on the stability of money demand function. Friedman (1968) strongly argued that the money supply cannot influence real output in the long-run and given this neutrality proposition, stable money demand functions provide credibility to the quantity theory with a predictable influence on the general price level.

Central banks, all over the world, have long recognised the existence of stable money demand functions as a key to effectiveness of monetary policy. Rangarajan (1989) argued that, "if one were to deny the existence of a reasonably stable demand function for money, there will be very little scope for monetary policy to play role in inflation management." Volcker (1978) acknowledged that evidence of a stable money demand function amidst rising inflation forced the Fed to focus more on control of monetary aggregates in order to check price level.

Evidence on demand for money by and large, supports the hypothesis of a stable relationship between money, output and prices in respect of a large number of countries. In the United States, the stability was considered an established fact following Goldfeld's (1973) examination of quarterly post-war data. The money demand function was found to be more stable based on a narrow definition of money and when current income rather than wealth, and interest rates on short-term instruments (like the treasury bill or commercial paper rates), along with the lagged dependent variable were incorporated as explanatory variables. However, out of sample forecasts from Goldfeld's equation began over-predicting real money balances since 1974 and this led to a veritable explosion of research across the globe to find out whether innovations, liberalisation and institutional changes in financial markets have caused shift(s) in the money demand relationships. Arango and Nadiri (1981) and Boughton (1981) found that with the exception of Canada, narrow money demand remained stable in the case of France, Germany, Japan and United Kingdom. The evidence on instability has been limited to a few periods - episodes - for a few countries. However, Granger and Newbold (1974) asserted that non-stationarity in the log-level or log-difference formulation of economic variables produce spurious regression results, throwing most of the findings on money demand into serious doubt and prompting researchers to revisit the money demand function. Hendry (1980,1985) demonstrated that parameter instability in the case of US and UK money demand functions could be explained by incorrect specification leading to spurious results. Recently, the co-integration and error correction model (ECM) framework has become a standard tool to determine money demand stability. Hafer and Jansen (1991) and Miller (1991) addressed the demand for money in US through such a framework and found that unlike the earlier literature broad money aggregate was more stable than the narrow money - a result which first gained credibility following the results of Hallman, Porter and Small (1989).

The empirical evidence on the demand for money in India also supports the hypothesis of a stable long-run relationship. While reviewing the earlier works, Vasudevan (1977) observed that the literature suggests that money demand in India responds more to income than interest rates and that broader definitions of money yields a more stable demand function. Singh et.al (1982), however, preferred a relationship with narrow money stock though they too found a predictable function of a limited number of explanatory variables using an approximation for activity at quarterly interval. Numerous other studies followed, confirming stable money demand while throwing a mix of evidence on the relative stability from different specifications and different money stock measures. Quite a few of them have continued to employ single-equation OLS model or a traditional simultaneous equation system in which money demand continues to be estimated through least squares. As late as in 1990, studies continued to rely on traditional econometric techniques that do not provide for unit root testing.

However, the money demand relationship is far from settled in the Indian case. The financial structure has undergone a considerable change over the years. The nationalisation of 14 commercial banks in 1969 has made the seventies different from the experience of the sixties. More importantly, the demand side could have been influenced more directly in the eighties with the developments in the capital markets having a profound bearing on the money markets. Portfolio substitutions appear to be pronounced in the eighties. One may cite the example of growing investments of households in shares and debentures. These instruments accounted for merely 3.7 per cent of the gross household saving in financial assets in 1980-81 but increased to 22.2 per cent by 1991-92.[4] Today, a host of mutual funds operate in capital market and provide portfolio management services to households as well as corporates. Also, available on tap are small saving instruments used by the government to finance fiscal deficits. A fledgling market for government debt, a buoyant market for primary issues in stock market, a number of new instruments in both these markets, the introduction of instruments such as Certificates of Deposits and Commercial Papers have brought about new elements in which money demand would have to be studied afresh with an eye on possible shifts in the function. Now that the framework for empirical testing has undergone a radical shift, it is essential to use the cointegration - ECM framework- a discussion on which is presented in the Technical Appendix to this paper.

SECTION II

This study purports to develop and estimate not only a long run equilibrium money demand relationship for the period 1960-61 to 1992-93 but also a shorter term error correction model for India.[5] Real money demand as usual is expected to depend upon a set of proximate variables such as real income or GDP, a representative rate of interest (or opportunity cost), real wealth (proxied by outstanding financial assets held mainly by the household sector) and real exchange rate (to study the effects of exchange rate adjustments carried out either under policy judgments or by the market itself). In keeping with these set of variables we have chosen the following time series for estimating the money demand function: (i) real broad money (M3 deflated with WPI of average basis) and real narrow money (M1 deflated with WPI on average basis) (ii) wholesale price index (WPI), base 1981-82=100 (iii) 36 country trade weighted real effective exchange rate (REER) index published by the RBI (v) real GDP at factor cost (GDPR) at 1980-81 prices as an activity variable and (vi) real financial wealth (FINSVG) proxied by a sum total of outstanding market capitalisation in the capital market and small savings deflated with WPI. We exclude provident and life insurance funds, as amounts collected under this head are mainly involuntary and contractual, and are not amenable to portfolio shifts. As stated earlier in Section I, in this study we consider the rate of inflation (INFL) based upon WPI in preference to the rate of interest as a measure of opportunity cost.[6] It is expected that the demand for both real M1 and M3 should respond negatively to INFL. Our choice of the rate of inflation as a measure of opportunity cost is obvious in view of the existence of regulation on the rate of interest on deposits during the entire sample period chosen for this study. The aim of this paper is to identify pairs of variables that could be cointegrated in the standard function of money demand in order to identify and construct an empirical long term equilibrium relationship among these variables. Discovery of cointegrating vector(s) implies a concomitant existence of an error correction process which could be operationalised to decipher short run variations in money balances in response to changes in explanatory variables. Finally, it is also useful to set up a kalman filter based test to examine the stability of the estimated function(s). It may be noted that kalman filter based recursive residuals are transformed to develop statistics for the CUSUM and CUSUM-Square tests due to Brown et al (1975).

The first step according to the discussion in Section I is empirical testing of unit root for various data series. Among the various tests available, we have employed the Phillips-Perron (PP) test with a constant and time trend. The results are presented in Table I. An examination of test statistics in Table I shows that all data series are integrated of order one, except for the rate of inflation which is justifiably dropped in the rest of the analysis.

TABLE I

Phillips Perron (PP) t-test for Unit Root

Variable	PP-statistic	Integration
REER	-2.43*	I (1)
real M3	0.32*	I (1)
real M1	0.40*	I (1)
real GDP	-0.16*	I (1)
FINSVG	-2.67*	I (1)
INFL(inflation)	-4.27	I (0)

Notes:

a) PP t-tests are based upon having a time trend, an intercept and one lag of the differenced series in the model except for INFL where no trend was employed. The Phillips and Perron (1988) Z_t statistic-a modification of the ADF test statistic was chosen because it carries out non-parametric adjustments for any possible serial correlation or heteroscedasticity in the residual.

b) INFL is inflation rate based upon the WPI.

c) An asterisk indicates that the series are non-stationary. The critical 1 percent value for PP-statistic for the null is -4.38 when a trend is employed and -3.75 when there is no trend. For a series to be stationary the value of PP t-statistic should be less than the critical value.

Models explaining demand for real narrow and broad money balances were set up by selecting appropriate explanatory variables (which include GDPR, REER, and FINSVG). Trace and Maximum eigenvalue tests, a'la Johansen and Juselius (1990), imply that both real narrow and broad money aggregates are cointegrated with real GDP, real effective exchange rate (REER) and real financial wealth. Trace and maximum eigenvalue (Max-E) statistics for all these models are given in Tables II and III against the 95 per cent critical values given for the Johansen and Juselius (1990) procedure.[7] It may be mentioned that while the trace statistic (which is a likelihood ratio) tests the hypothesis of the existence of a rth order rank of the long run impact matrix, the maximum eigenvalue statistic tests the existence of an $(r-1)^{th}$ order rank against an rth order rank of the long run impact matrix. The distributions of these statistics are non-standard and are tabulated in Johansen and Juselius (1990).

TABLE II

Trace and Max-Eigenvalue Statistic for Real M1

Rank	Trace	Trace (0.95)	Max-E	Max-E (0.95)
r < = 3	0.281	3.962	0.281	3.962
r < = 2	9.498	15.197	9.217	14.036
r < = 1	29.439	29.510	19.941	20.778
r < = 0	68.172	47.181	38.732	27.169

Note: 95 percent critical values from Table A1 in Johansen and Juselius (1990) with an unconstrained constant.

TABLE III

Trace and Max-Eigenvalue Statistic for Real M3

Rank	Trace	Trace (0.95)	Max-E	Max-E (0.95)
r < = 3	0.714	3.962	0.714	3.962
r < = 2	13.518	15.197	12.804	14.036
r < = 1	30.486	29.509	16.967	20.778
r < = 0	77.014	47.181	46.528	27.169

Note: Explanation same as in Table II

Trace and maximum eigenvalue tests for the chosen specifications for real M1 and M3 demand functions show that the hypothesis of zero cointegrating vector is rejected. In each case and according to each of the two different tests employed, the existence of cointegrating vector(s) is validated and this characterises stationary long term equilibrium relationship among money, output, effective exchange rate, and financial wealth. However, while the trace test implies the existence of two cointegrating vectors in case of real M3, both the maximum eigenvalue and trace tests infer only one in case of real M1.

Operationalised models are found statistically adequate on the basis of residual diagnostics in M1 and M3 equations in the Jarque-Bera (1980) (J-B) sense. While the J-B test statistics (distributed as chi-square with degrees of freedom 2) turn out to be 3.9 and 3.5 in M1 and M3 specifications, these residuals also show very little skewness and serial independence vide Engle's ARCH test. In view of these properties, efficiency, consistency and unbiasedness of estimates of cointegrating vectors are guaranteed. Deviations from normality are, however, often detected in empirical studies (Johansen and Juselius, 1990 and Parikh, 1994) and arise as a result of the smallness of sample size or production of some large residuals. The real effective exchange rate and financial wealth equations in our case however, show prominent non-normal characteristics which could be due to reasons alluded to earlier[8] As a caveat it must be mentioned that the robustness of the ML cointegration procedure for deviations from normality has not been investigated so far (Johansen and Juselius 1990).

The following cointegrating vectors or equilibrium relationships were obtained for the M1 and M3 models.

Real M1 = [0.005 (GDP), 1.404 (REER), -0.073 (FINSVG)] and

Real M3 = [0.031 (GDP), 6.226 (REER), -1.183 (FINSVG)]

Estimated equilibrium relationships show that all signs are in accordance with theoretical precepts.[9] In the M1 relationship, the coefficient on the income variable is positive. A positive sign on the real exchange rate variable implies that a depreciation of the domestic currency leads to a decrease in narrow cash balances. In terms of the postulates of Branson and Buiter (1983) this could mean that by raising the general price level, the exchange rate depreciation reduces real wealth and the demand for real balance. The effect more than offsets the absorption reducing effect of exchange rate depreciation through a rise in wealth on account of the net debtor position in terms of ownership claims on the rest of the world. Finally, agents reduce cash balances in the face of increasing financial wealth. It is understandable that in an economy characterised with limits on the degree of freedom of financial markets, the growth in financial innovations would lead to dominating substitution effects between money balances and financial assets in keeping with the risk-reward perceptions of the agents. In the M3 relationship, results imply a positive income coefficient. As in the case of real M1, the coefficient of REER in the M3 function turns out positive which implies that a depreciation of domestic currency leads to an decrease in broad cash balances in the long run. This evidence is, however, contrary to the results obtained by Bahmani-Oskooee (1991) for the U.K and Bahamani-Oskooee and Pourheydarian (1990) for the U.S and Canada. However, though indicative of the efficacy of monetary policy in an open economy macro-economic framework, the result of the positive coefficient we obtain on the REER coefficient, needs to be interpreted with caution.

In an extension of this analysis we undertake hypothesis tests of weak exogeneity with respect to each of the variables included in the models. Table IV and V below contain likelihood ratio statistics for testing weak exogeneity for explanatory variables included in our chosen systems.

TABLE IV

Testing Weak Exogeneity in M1 System

Hypothesis	*zero loading on*	*LR(2)-stat*
alfa (1) = 0	GDP	6.98 (0.01)
alfa (2) = 0	REER	1.48 (0.22)
alfa (3) = 0	FINSVG	3.97 (0.05)

Note: Figures in parentheses in the (last) column show p-values or significance levels.

TABLE V

Testing Weak Exogeneity in M3 System

Hypothesis	*zero loading on*	*LR(2)-stat*
alfa (1) = 0	GDP	7.89 (0.00)
alfa (2) = 0	REER	0.47 (0.49)
alfa (3) = 0	FINSVG	5.61 (0.02)

Note: Figures in parentheses in the (last) column show p-values or significance levels.

Results in Tables IV and V imply that the hypothesis of weak exogeneity is upheld for REER in case of both real M1 and M3 functions while it is rejected for GDP and FINSVG. The significant adjustment coefficient associated with the FINSVG equation implies that the speed of adjustment towards its equilibrium state is indeed significant.

General short run dynamic error correction models for real M1 and M3 are constructed once the phenomenon of cointegration among a set of variables is observed. Symbolically, a simple short run model could be expressed as follows.

$$\text{dlog } Y = F(\text{dlog } X1_{t-1}, \text{dlog } X2_{t-1}, \text{dlog } Y_{t-1}, EC_{t-1}, \text{constant}) + u_t$$

where, 'dlog' implies first difference in natural logs and Y and X_i denote dependent and explanatory variables, respectively. The error correction term denoted as EC_{t-1} incorporated in the short term equation is the equilibrium error. A significant presence of this component in error correction equation implies that the system is out of a long term equilibrium and that it has the ability to move towards the equilibrium state. Alternatively, the error correction model could also be specified unconstrained in which case we employ lagged values of all or some level form variables introduced in the long-run equation.

Unconstrained empirical error correction models corresponding to cointegrating systems identified for real M1 and M3 are computed using the OLS through one-step estimation and are presented in Tables VI and VII, respectively. It should be mentioned that these models were obtained through an extended search under general to specific modeling strategy popularised by Hendry and are found to provide good out of sample forecasts in the short run. This approach towards 'hunting' models after a cointegrating relationship is discovered has gained widespread acceptability and is now commonly employed in applied economics (McDonald and Taylor, 1994).

From the unconstrained error correction models presented in Tables VI and VII, it could be observed that these are quite simple in content. In both models lagged level form variables are significant and with expected signs. In case of real M1 the signs on d-GDP and d-REER are positive even though not largely significant. In case of real M3 equation, in the short run, real GDP has a significant and positive impact. The sign observed on FINSVG is consistent even though not clearly significant. As mentioned earlier the choice of these models was predicated upon the desire to have models which perform consistently well in out of sample forecasts. Also, the relative insignificance of some of the important short run variables could occur as a result of serial correlation in the residuals. In this regard, an application of say, Phillips and Hansen (1990) procedure would correct efficiency but in any case is unlikely to significantly alter the numerical estimates of the coefficients arrived without such a correction.

TABLE VI

Unconstrained Error Correction Model for Real M1

Variable	*Coefficient*	*t-statistic*
constant	-101.529	-2.74
d GDPR	0.001	1.16
d REER	0.298	1.25
M1-1	-0.421	-2.98
GDP-1	0.001	3.50
REER-1	0.339	2.00
DW stat = 1.32	Rbarsq = 0.61	

TABLE VII

Unconstrained Error Correction Model for Real M3

Variable	*Coefficient*	*t-statistic*
constant	-132.520	-3.270
d GDPR	0.003	2.940
d FINSVG	-0.003	-0.320
M3-1	-0.259	-2.920
GDPR-1	0.002	3.310
d M3-1	0.507	2.410

p* = 0
Rbarsq = 0.75

Note: p* was found to be significantly not different from zero on the basis of test of autocorrelation with Durbin's alternative formula for cases where in presence of a lagged dependent variable, T, Var (α) is greater than unity, making h-statistics inapplicable.

These short run models possess desirable goodness of fit statistics and have been subsequently subjected to stability and forecasting subroutines.

SECTION III

In this paper a robust demand for money function was estimated by employing Johansen and Juselius (1990) multivariate cointegration procedure. Long term cointegrating relationships for real M1 and M3 functions were identified and finally unconstrained error correcting forms were estimated. Empirical evidence in this study shows that real GDP, trade weighted real effective exchange rate and real financial wealth as a set are cointegrated with real M1 as well as with real M3. LR tests for weak exogeniety show that real effective exchange rate is weakly exogenous in the system. But this, as has been mentioned, is because the real effective exchange rate has been largely managed over almost the predominant part of the sample period under consideration. Also, capital mobility has been low during the same period.

An interesting feature contained in the study is the effect of financial wealth upon the demand for narrow and broad real money balances which are found to be negatively related to the former in the long run. This is a clear reflection of portfolio substitution effects in the models posited here. Short run effects of real GDP are positive for both narrow and broad balances implying that these are important in explaining the short run demand. On the other hand, the short term path of broad balances is negatively affected inter-alia by real financial wealth implying portfolio shifts as real value of financial stocks increases mainly on account of rising share prices.

An investigation of the stability of specified error correction or short run models of demand for both real M1 and M3 for the period 1969-70 to 1992-93 confirm that there exists no significant in-sample instability. This evidence on stability is upheld at a significance level of 1 per cent since the CUSUM Square graph stays within 1 per cent bounds during the period under consideration, except for a brief episode of 1982-84 and that too in case of M3 alone, where CUSUMSQ in any case stay within the 5 per cent bounds. Finally, but not the least, the usefulness of this exercise must be judged against the in-sample dynamic tracking and out of sample forecasts produced by short run models. While tracking is based upon successive estimation and reapplication of dependent variable in the models over time, the out of sample forecasting is the most stringent test of a model's stability and usefulness. In Table VIII below we report tracking beginning 1987-88 to 1992-93.

TABLE VIII

Dynamic Tracking

Year	*M1 model*		*M3 model*	
	Actual	*Forecast*	*Actual*	*Forecast*
1987-88	5.92	5.14	8.14	5.83
1988-89	6.68	6.61	9.60	8.24
1989-90	11.90	9.21	10.68	8.85
1990-91	6.55	6.87	5.74	7.16
1991-92	4.84	5.21	3.08	4.17
1992-93	4.80	4.63	7.51	8.50

Note: Numbers in the Table imply growth rates in real M1 and M3 quantities in corresponding years.

An examination of dynamic forecasts presented in Table VIII suggest that except for the year 1989-90 when these were underestimated, the forecasts for other years are good with the difference between the actuals and forecasted values generally turning out to be less than 1 percentage point in case of M1 model. In case of M3 model also, the turning points are adequately captured in the simulation.

Apart from the dynamic tracking of monetary growth rates reported here we also attempted a two period ahead ex-ante forecast for the years 1991-92 and 1992-93. In conducting this exercise, the sample was truncated at 1990-91 and the entire estimation procedure was replicated. Out of sample forecasts were then produced for the next two years. The forecast for the growth of real M1 for the years 1991-92 and 1992-93 turned out to be 5.37 and 4.72 per cent as compared with the actual figures of 4.84 and 4.80 per cent during the same years, respectively. In case of real M3, for the years 1991-92 and 1992-93, growth rates were estimated at 2.65 and 6.23 per cent as compared with the actuals at 3.07 and 7.51 per cent, respectively. Parsimonious models set up in this study appear to perform well in capturing out of sample turning points, lending credence to the underlying long run and short run representations. While, the method of empirical estimation followed in this paper yield encouraging results, more intensive research effort will be necessary to see if even more accurate forecasts can be generated for the purposes of better policy support. This might necessitate inclusion of new and missing information into models as well as an attempt to control errors of observation and noise which often disturb aggregate data to some extent.

GRAPH A

CUSUMSQ TEST PLOT

DEMAND FOR REAL M1

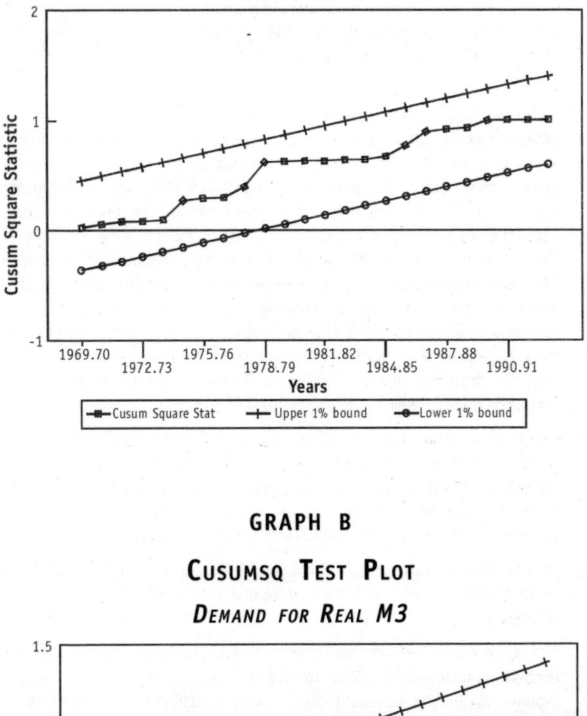

GRAPH B

CUSUMSQ TEST PLOT

DEMAND FOR REAL M3

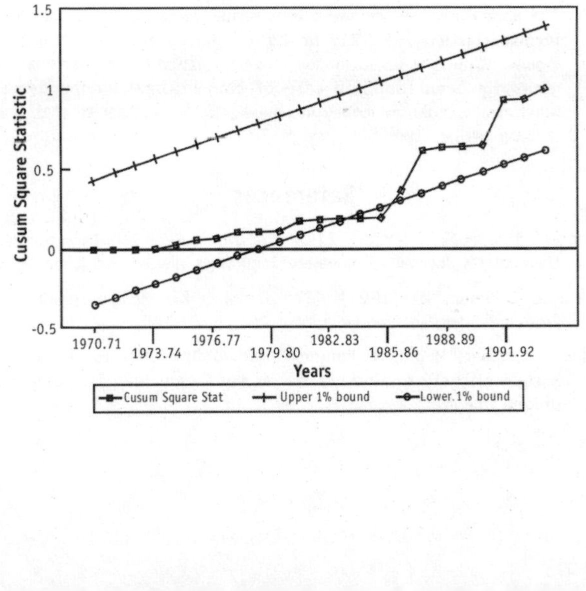

Notes

1) A useful survey of empirical evidence on the impact of financial innovations and regulatory changes on the stability of money demand function in case of U.S. and some other OECD countries is presented in Judd and Scadding (1982). The impact of innovations and regulatory change has, however, not received similar consideration in empirical work on money demand in India.

2) Furthermore, Monte Carlo evidence of Gonzalo (1989) suggests that Johansen's maximum likelihood technique for empirical testing of a cointegration relationship performs better than single equation methods and alternative multivariate methods.

3) The incorporation of inflation rate as an opportunity cost measure when interest rates are regulated has also been underscored in Johansen and Juselius (1990). However, both term deposits and inflation rate fail to enter the cointegrating space in the Indian case.

4) These are inclusive of units of UTI and of other mutual funds.

5) The choice of the period has been dictated by the availability of reliable time-series for variables employed in the study. The time-period taken is smaller than in case of many similar studies for the developed countries, but is in line with the availability of data and past tradition for empirical work for India. The empirical work is based on annual data frequency. In somewhat similar approach Lothian and Taylor (1992) demonstrate that the total length of the sample period, rather than the frequency of observation, should be considered important when examining the long-run properties of time series and that higher frequency observations are unlikely to affect the results significantly. Gonzalo's work with the Johansen and Juselius methodology reinforces this view.

6) Wholesale Price Index (WPI) is widely used in the Indian case to measure the inflation rate in the economy as it has a large coverage of commodities and its computation is based on a well set reporting system. However, as the WPI is affected by changes in administered prices, the choice of Consumer Price Index (CPI) or a GDP deflator may not be discounted altogether, even though we preferred working with the WPI. It is also possible, that expected inflation rate than the inflation rate itself, serves as a better measure of opportunity cost for holding money. Furthermore, it is also possible that with a move towards a market determined interest rate structure, in times to come some benchmark interest rate - short or long, or the entire term-structure of interest rates could be serving as an opportunity cost for holding money balances. These could be useful lines of investigation in future research in this area.

7) The critical values were first presented in Johansen's (1988) paper for VAR without an intercept term. Johansen and Juselius (1990) reported critical values for VAR systems with a constant for systems upto 5 variables. These critical values have been extended by Osterwald-Lenum (1990) for system upto 11 variables.

8) This is hardly surprising as exchange rates are known to be lepokurtik in distribution with a high frequency data displaying strong ARCH effects.

9) The normalized real money cointegrating vector implies a short-run income elasticity of 1.215 for narrow money and 2.274 for broad money. While the broad money income elasticity is higher than has generally been found in case of conventional money demand functions, our narrow money income elasticity is closer to that found in such earlier studies.

References

Arango, S and M.I. Nadiri, (1981), "Demand for Money in Open Economies", Journal of Monetary Economics, Vol. 7, No.1, pp 69-83.

Bahmani-Oskooee, M. (1991), "The Demand for Money in an Open Economy", *Applied Economics*, Vol. 22, pp. 917-25.

Bahmani-Oskooee, M and M. Pourheydarian (1990), "Effects of Exchange Rate Sensitivity of Demand for Money in an Open Economy: The United Kingdom", *Applied Economics*, 22.

Boughton, J.M. (1981), "Recent instability of the Demand for Money: An International Perspective", *Southern Economic Journal*, Vol 43, No.3, pp 579-97.

Branson, W.H. and W.H. Buiter (1983), "Monetary and Fiscal Policy with Flexible Exchange Rates", in J.S. Bhandari and R.H. Putnam ed, *Economic Interdependence and Flexible Exchange Rates*, MIT Press.

Brown, R.L J, Durbin, and M.Evans, (1975), "Techniques for Testing the Constancy of Regression Relationship over Time", *Journal of Royal Statistical Society*, No 2.

Corker, R. (1990), "Wealth, Financial Liberalisation and the Demand for Money in Japan", *IMF Staff Papers*, 37, 418-32.

Engle, R.F. and C.W.J. Granger, (1987), "Cointegration and Error Correction: Representation, Estimation and Testing", *Econometrica*, 55.

Friedman, M. (1968), "The Role of Monetary Policy", *American Economic Review*, vol. 58, ppl-17

Goldfeld, S.M. (1973), "The Demand for Money Revisited", *Brookings Papers of Economic Activity*, No.3, pp 577-638.

Granger, C.W.J and P.Newbold, (1974), "Spurious Regression in Econometrics", *Journal of Econometrics*, 2.

Hallman, J.J., R.D. Porter and D.H.Small (1989), "M2 per unit of Potential GNP as an Anchor for the Price Level", Board of Governors of the Federal Reserve System Staff Study, No. 157, April.

Hafer, R.W. and D.W. Jansen (1991), "The Demand for Money in the United States: Evidence from Cointegration Tests", *Journal of Money, Credit and Banking*, Vol 23, No.2, pp 155-68.

Gonzalo, J. (1989), "Comparison of Five Alternative Methods of Estimating Long-Run, Equilibrium Relationships", Discussion Paper 89-55, University of California at San Diego.

Hendry, D.F. (1980), "Predictive Failure and Econometric Modelling in Macro-Economics: The Transactions Demand for Money", in P.Omerod (ed), *Economic Modeling* pp 217-42, London: Heinemann Educational books.

Hendry, D.F. (1985), "Monetary Economic Myth and Econometric Reality", *Oxford Review of Economic Policy*, 1.

Jarque, C.M. and A.K. Bera (1980), "Efficient Tests for Normality, Homoskedasticity and serial independence of Regression Residuals", *Economic Letters*, Vol.6. pp 225-29.

Johansen (1988), "Statistical Analysis of Cointegrating Vectors", "*Journal of Economic Dynamics and Control*", Vol 12, pp 231-54.

Johansen, S and K.Juselius (1990), "Maximum Likelihood Estimation and Inference on Cointegration - with applications to the Demand for Money", *Oxford Bulletin of Economics and Statistics*, 52, pp 169-210.

Judd J.P. and J.L. Scadding (1982), "The Search for a Stable Money Demand Function: A Survey of the Post-1973 Literature", *Journal of Economic Literature*, Vol XX, pp 993-1023.

Lothian, J.R. and M.P. Taylor (1992), "The Behaviour of the Real Exchange Rate: The Recent Exchange Rate Float from the Perspective of the Past Two Centuries", manuscript, International Monetary Fund, Washington.

Miller, S.M., "Monetary Dynamics: An Application of Cointegration and Error-Correction Modeling", *Journal of Money, Credit and Banking*, Vol 23, No.2, pp 139-154.

Moosa, I.A. (1992), "The Demand for Money in India: A Cointegration Approach", *The Indian Economic Journal*, Vol 40, No.1, pp 101-15.

Nag, A.K. and G. Upadhyay (1993), "Estimation of Money Demand Function: A Cointegration Approach", *Reserve Bank of India Occasional Papers*, Vol 14, No.1, pp 47-66.

Osterwald-Lenum, M. (1990), Recalculated and Extended Tables of the Asymptotic Distribution of Some Important Maximum Likelihood Cointegration Tests, Mimeo, Institute of Economics: University of Copenhagen.

Parikh, A (1994), An Approach to Monetary Targeting in India, Reserve Bank of India, DRG Study No 9

Phillips, P.C.B. (1986), "Understanding Spurious Regression in Econometrics", *Journal of Econometrics*, Vol. 33, pp. 311-40.

Phillips P.C.B and Perron, P. (1988), "Testing for Unit Root in Time Series Regression", *Biometrika*, 75, 335-346.

Phylaktis, K and M.P. Taylor, (1993) "Monetary Demand, The Cagan Model and the Inflation Tax: Some Latin American Evidence", *The Review of Economics and Statistics*.

Podolski, T.M. (1986), "Financial Innovation and the Money Supply," Basil Lackwell Ltd., Oxford.

Poole, W (1970), "Optimal Choice of Monetary Policy Instruments in a Simple Stochastic Macro Model", *Quarterly Journal of Economics*, Vol 84, No. 2, pp. 197-216.

Rangarajan, C (1989), "Issues in Monetary Management", *The Indian Economic Journal*, Vol 36, No.3, ppl-13.

Singh, A., S.L. Shetty and T.R. Venkatachalam (1982), "Monetary Policy in India: Issues and Evidence." *Supplement to Reserve Bank of India Occasional Papers*, Vol 3, No.1.

Stock, J.H. and M.W. Watson (1988), "Testing for Common Trends", *Journal of the American Statistical Association*, December pp 1097-1107.

Vasudevan, A (1977), "Demand for Money in India - A Survey of Literature", *Reserve Bank of India Staff Occasional Papers*, Vol 2,.

Volcker, P.A. (1978), "The Role of Monetary Targets in an Age of Inflation", *Journal of Monetary Economics*, Vol 4, No.2, pp 329-39.

TECHNICAL APPENDIX

From a theoretical standpoint, the theory of cointegration implies the existence of a centre of gravity type linear attractor around which observations of some data series may be found to cluster along time. In other words, while an individual economic variable, viewed as a time series, could wander extensively, yet some series may be expected to move so that they do not drift too far apart. The concept of an attractor is notionally equivalent to a static long run economic equilibrium of variables that are 'cointegrated' in Granger sense. If, therefore, a system of variables is cointegrated, their drifting in relation to the attractor is not permanent and there is a tendency to come back to it. For instance, if money supply and prices are cointegrated then they will move together along the said attractor. A short run shock, however, could disturb either of these variables off the attractor and institute an equilibrium error. However, this disturbance will not be permanent because sooner or later corrections will need to be carried out by forces proposed by economic theory.

In order to concretise these ideas, Granger (1981) and Granger and Weiss (1983) proposed error-correcting models which allow long run components of variables to obey equilibrium constraints while short run components have a flexible dynamic specification. Granger also showed for the first time that a full error correction representation would exist if the variables in the system were 'cointegrable'. Given the cointegrability condition, consistent steady state parameters can be obtained by estimating the static 'cointegration' regression. Engle and Granger (1987) suggest a two step method which allows a robust inference on cointegration. Formally, if each element of a vector of time series first achieves stationarity by differencing, but a linear combination $\alpha' x_t$ is already stationary, the time series x_t are said to be cointegrated with cointegrating vector α. There may be several such cointegrating vectors so that α becomes α matrix. Interpreting $\alpha' x_t = 0$ as a long run equilibrium, cointegration implies that deviations from equilibrium are stationary, with finite variance, even though the series themselves are nonstationary and have infinite variances (Engle and Granger, 1987).

In empirical applications and in keeping with the above exposition, cointegration and error correction modeling involves the following steps. The first involves determining the order of integration of each of the variables under consideration by employing one of the battery of unit root tests. In this paper we employ the widely accepted Phillips-Perron (1988) t-test. The second step involves identification/existence of at least one unique cointegration vector in a multivariate cointegrating relationship as suggested by Johansen and Juselius (1990). Finally, an error correction model is set up. An error-correction model displays long and short run effects of explanatory variables on the dependent variable and throws a good deal of information on the dynamics of the system. This paper follows standard Johansen and Juselius (1990) procedure for estimating multivariate cointegration relationship. Absolving from cumbersome notational algebra, this method could be described as follows: The procedure entails estimating parameters of a traditional first difference VAR (vector autoregression with similarly integrated variables) inclusive of a long run impact matrix that 'contains' information about long-run relationships between the variables in the data vector (Johansen and Juselius, 1990). If the dimension of the impact matrix is less than its rank then it could be expressed as a multiple of two conformably dimensioned matrices, say, 'α' and 'β'. In this case the vectors in matrix 'β' are cointegrating vectors which in linear association with data vectors results in a stationary process. The alfa matrix on the other hand exemplifies coefficients of adjustment that reflect the speed of adjustment towards the equilibrium. In this framework it is desirable to obtain at least one cointegrating vector [so that r (rank) =1] that establishes the model. If for example, r = 2 then one could in principle assume that the system is stable in more than one dimension. Tests of hypothesis for the rank of the impact matrix is conducted using the likelihood ratio (Trace-test) and maximum-eigenvalue test (Lambda-max test).

However, before one begins testing for the rank of the long run matrix, residual diagnostics in the system ought to satisfy the assumptions of normality and serial independence. This is required because the distribution properties of test statistics under Johansen's procedure have not been investigated under departures from normality.

In a further extension of analysis the possibility of weak exogeneity of a single or a group of variables with respect to the long run coefficients α and β is also usually tested within the above framework. A likelihood ratio (LR) test to weak exogeneity tests for the inclusion/exclusion of a variable in the cointegrating space. Specifically, in tests of hypothesis of weak exogeneity, zero restrictions or loadings are placed on the elements of the alfa matrix and LR tests carried out for purposes of inference. If the hypothesis of zero restriction is accepted then the variable is considered to be weakly exogenous and the dimension of the system stands appropriately reduced conditioned on that variable without affecting the estimates of β vector. The Johansen and Juselius (1990) procedure also allows hypothesis tests in case when the β vector is assumed a-priori. This helps in reconfirming or rejecting prevalent notions about parametric estimates such as elasticities obtained through other methods.

Johansen and Juselius (1990) procedure entails estimating a traditional first differenced vector autoregression (VAR) which could be represented as follows

$$\delta X_t = \pi X_{t-1} + T Z_{1t} + \varepsilon \qquad .....(1)$$

where X are a system of fixed vector of variables included in the VAR and the ε are i.i.d Gaussian errors. Z_{1t} is the stacked vector of δX_{t-1}, ..., πX_{t-k}. π and T are coefficients appended to X_{t-1} and Z_{1t} respectively. The system defined in equation (1) is an error correction model and is a transform of the VAR in levels if the series are non-stationary, say I (1), and the rank of matrix $\pi(=\alpha\beta')$ is less than the dimension of the system. As already stated, the reduced rank of the long run matrix π is also the number of cointegrating relationships among the series and β is the cointegrating vector. The solution for β is found by solving the likelihood maximising condition obtained from the likelihood (concentrated on β) corresponding to equation (1). This entails solving the eigenvalues($\varnothing_i$) and vectors for the system

$$1\varnothing\, S_{11} - S_{10}S_{00}{}^{-1}S_{01}\; 1 = 0 \qquad ....(2)$$

where $S_{ij} = (1/T) \sum \hat{R}_{it} \hat{R}'_{jt}$ (for i,j=1,0) with $\hat{R}_{0t}$ and $\hat{R}_{1t}$ as residuals from regressions of δX and X_{t-1} on Z_{1t}. The likelihood ratio test of the null hypothesis of not more than r (the rank of π) cointegrating relationships against the alternative of stationarity of all series is the trace test. On the other hand if the null is posited against the alternative of at most r-1 stationary relationships then the statistic suggested is the maximum eigenvalue. These tests are based upon the significance of eigenvalues and distributions are non-standard and critical percentiles tabulated in Johansen and Juselius (1990) and extended for larger systems in Osterwald-Lenum (1990). Tests of linear restrictions on α and β are conducted by employing the usual LR tests after restricting the free parameters and going back to the solution of restricted equation (2) and the eigenvalue routine. The LR tests are distributed as chi-square with degrees of freedom depending upon the number of restrictions.

9

Modelling Buffer Stock Money

An Indian Experience

B K Bhoi

Introduction

THE consensus about the stability property of the money demand function broke down in the mid-1970s. With the publication of Goldfeld's seminal article, "The Case of Missing Money" (1976), the quest for a stable demand for money was vigorously pursued by economists across countries. Fresh evidence of instability were found by several authors with samples from fairly large number of developed and developing countries as well.[1] The empirical investigations in this area proceeded into several directions. One of the directions of such efforts was towards investigating the plausible reasons for money demand instability. One reason, which is believed to have caused instability in the money demand function is the misspecification. In a search for appropriate specification, supply shock or unanticipated change in money supply was considered by a number of economists as a useful explanation. Before accepting it, one needs to get satisfactory answers to a number of questions. How does the supply shock affect the money demand function? Whether the people immediately change their spending habit or alternatively keep the unanticipated increase in nominal income as a kind of buffer? Whether buffer stock approach to demand for money has resolved the issue of instability in money demand function? These empirical issues are addressed in the literature under 'buffer stock' approach to the demand for money. The basic idea is whether unanticipated change in money supply can be absorbed by economic agents in the short-run. If so, it can be modelled in the money demand function. More precisely, if it turns out to be positive and significant, it can be considered as one of the explanatory variables of the money demand function. Hence, omission of supply shock from the money demand function may be a misspecification leading to instability in the function. The purpose of this study is to examine the evidence of buffer stock money in India and to consider whether the buffer stock approach is an improvement over the partial adjustment model. Furthermore, the study will examine the out-of-sample predictive power and stability property of the money demand function under buffer stock approach.

The paper is divided into five Sections including the introduction. Section II provides a brief review of the micro-theoretic foundations and model specifications of buffer stock approach. Section III adopts appropriate methodology for the investigation of the buffer stock evidence in India and examines the relative superiority of the buffer stock model over the partial adjustment model. Section IV replicates the estimation procedure by breaking the sample at appropriate point of time and studies the out-of-sample predictive power of the buffer stock model. Concluding remarks are presented in Section V.

SECTION II

Micro-Theoretic Foundations

The intuitive idea behind the buffer stock notion could be traced back to the inventory theoretic contributions of Baumol (1952) and Tobin (1956). Even the precautionary motive for holding money balances put forward by Keynes (1936) contains the idea of buffer stock. The terms 'buffer' and 'shock absorbers' are probably due to Friedman and Schwartz (1963)[2]. Friedman's permanent income hypothesis also corroborates the idea of buffer stock. Transitory income affecting asset/liability portfolio of a consumer rather

Shri B.K. Bhoi expresses his gratitude to Dr. A. Vasudevan, Dr. A. Ramanathan, and Dr. T. K. Chakrabarty for their valuable comments on the earlier version of this paper. The author alone is responsible for the errors, if any. The views expressed in this paper are the personal views of the author.

than consumption can well be compared with unanticipated part of his income which serves as a buffer. The methodological improvement and the extension of idea of the buffer stock include discussions by Goodhart (1982, 1984), Judd and Scadding (1982), Laidler (1984, 1987), Bain and McGregor (1985), Cuthbertson (1985), Cuthbertson and Taylor (1987), Milbourne (1988). The major empirical works on the buffer stock concept include, inter alia, Carr and Darby (1981), Khan and Knight (1982), MacKinnon and Milbourne (1984), Carr, Darby and Thornton (1985), Kanniainen and Tarkka (1986), Swamy and Tavlas (1989), Cuthbertson and Taylor (1987), Boughton and Tavlas (1991).

The buffer stock approach provides an appealing framework to understand the behaviour of individuals as well as firms in an uncertain environment. The cost of marginal adjustment in prices, wages, employment and output levels etc., may be very substantial relative to the interest foregone by holding excess money balances. Unanticipated increase in money supply is, in fact, initially willingly held by economic agents, thus providing a buffer of purchasing power, even if it forces the holders to temporarily go off their short-run demand curves. According to Goodhart (1984), the decisions to change plans entail cost viz., the resale price of a durable asset is usually below its purchase price. Thus, in his view "economic agents may rationally and optimally decide to respond to the continuing stream of developments, 'news and shocks', not by a thoroughgoing continuous reconsideration of their full economic dispositions, but by allowing such shocks to impinge initially upon certain assets/liabilities whose characteristics make them suitable to act as buffer." Goodhart concludes "money being the most liquid of all assets, performs the buffer function best." Under buffer stock approach, there is no single-valued demand for money. Rather, there is a band around which money holdings may vary. As soon as holdings of money balances exceed their upper limits, they are slowly used to purchase a broad spectrum of assets - financial as well as real (Jonson, 1976). Goodhart (1984) also observes that "with the passage of time, an individual's reservoir of money balances spills over onto canals of spending on a wide spectrum of assets and goods as real balance effects are set into motion". Thus, the monetary transmission mechanism embedded in buffer stock approach is akin to that advocated by monetarists[3]. Although, micro foundation of this approach seems logically sound, the validity of this approach is an empirical question. "The case for the buffer stock approach ultimately rests on as much upon its empirical content as upon a *priori* reasoning" (Laidler, 1984).

Before we go over to the survey of empirical literature, it will be proper to mention about at least two conceptual issues relating to buffer stock approach. First, people would like to hold not only currency but also deposit money as well as certain 'near money' as buffer. Thus, "buffer assets are likely to consist of a wider set of assets than transaction balances" (Cuthbertson and Taylor, 1987). For the purpose of modelling buffer stock money, holdings of any assets outside money for the purpose of some returns are treated as investment from the anticipated part of one's income although it is extremely difficult to apportion one's income into anticipated and unanticipated parts. With the progress of the transaction technology and information system, it is relatively less costly to effect transfers as between 'money' and 'near money'. Hence, any return from such holdings may be *incidental* but *not planned* as it arises out of unanticipated increase in nominal income. It is important to note that 'buffer money' is willingly held, in the short-run, at the unchanged interest rates. However, the scope of redefining money by including more and more 'near money' from time to time is consistent with buffer stock approach as the adherents were never opposed to this.

Secondly, the idea of holding money as a buffer emanates from the key distinction made between anticipated and unanticipated supply of money which are also made under rational expectation hypothesis advocated by New Classical School. But, the New Classical economists strongly argue for 'market clearing', while buffer stock approach is often termed as 'disequilibrium money'. Nevertheless, certain buffer stock models are not necessarily inconsistent with rational expectation models.

Model Specifications

The partial adjustment model was found inadequate on several grounds and therefore, the buffer stock approach was developed as an alternative paradigm to explain the dynamics of money demand function. To begin with, the typical partial adjustment model specifies the demand for real balance in the following manner:

$$m_t - p_t = b_0 + b_1 y_t + b_2 r_t + b_3 (m-p)_{t-1} + b_4 IR_t + u_t \quad ...(1)$$

where 'm_t' is the logarithm of a measure of money supply, 'P_t' is the logarithm of price index, 'y_t' is the logarithm of a scale variable such as, real income or wealth, 'r_t' is the logarithm of an opportunity cost variable. $(m-p)_{t-1}$ is real money balance lagged by one period. 'IR_t' is inflation rate (i.e., InP_t-InP_{t-1}), 'u_t' is the error term.

Model (1) specified above has been found to be troublesome, among others, on the following grounds : first, short-run elasticities for income and interest rate are very low while the coefficient of lagged dependent variable is close to unity implying higher long-run interest and income elasticities. As the long-run interest elasticity is higher than short-run elasticity, overshooting of interest rate must occur in the short-run [Milbourne (1988), Swamy and Tavlas (1989)]. However, overshooting of interest rate does not seem to be a feature in the real-world money markets (Goodhart, 1984). Secondly, dynamics underlying the move back to long-run equilibrium are complex and unpredictable due to long and variable lags (Boughton and Tavlas, 1990). Thirdly, out-of-sample predictive failure of the partial adjustment model could be attributed to misspecification, arising out of the omission of supply shock as an explanatory variable.

The buffer stock model is designed to effectively deal with each of these problems. Since the role of money is emphasised, *inter alia*, as a shock absorber, it can temporarily smoothen the response of the economy. The innovations in the money supply are specifically modelled by incorporating supply shock as the determinant of money demand. A positive monetary innovation leads to accumulation of cash balances in the short-run, as economic agents move off their short run- demand curves. Therefore, cash balances rather than interest rate adjust in the short run implying that overshooting of interest rate may not occur. The transmission mechanism is complex due to long and variable lags. The lag structure is, however, modelled in the buffer stock approach assuming that they are deterministic rather than variable. Inclusion of supply shock in the money demand function helps reduce the specification bias in the parameter estimation under partial adjustment model.

The literature shows at least four broad approaches to modelling buffer stock money. They are : (A) single equation disequilibrium models, (B) forward looking buffer stock models, (C) complete disequilibrium models, and (D) shock absorber models.

Single Equation Disequilibrium Models

The conventional approach to the demand for money makes the basic assumption that demand for money is always equal to its supply. In other words, it is assumed that supply of money is demand-determined. Alternatively, money supply may be assumed to be independent of demand as long as money markets clear within a time period. In the event, a question arises as to whether the conventional functional form estimates demand function or supply function of money. The impact of the exogenous supply of money is studied in the literature by inverting the conventional money demand function within the framework of a single equation disequilibrium model. Precisely, each of the explanatory variables of the conventional money demand function, such as the price level, output and the interest rate are alternatively considered as dependent variables. The exponents of this approach assume that the chosen dependent variable adjusts slowly to its long-run value. If the supply of money is independent of its demand, agents are temporarily forced off their long-run demand function because of slow adjustment in prices, output and interest rate [Artis and Lewis (1976), and Goodhart (1984)]. Artis and Lewis (1976), by using quarterly data for the U.K. up to 1973, found that money demand functions (both narrow and broad) are more stable than those obtained by taking money as the dependent variable. They also found that there is no overshooting in current period interest rates in response to change in the current period money supply.

There are a number of statistical problems associated with single equation disequilibrium buffer stock models. As is well known, the short run (impact) elasticity with respect to interest rate is b_2 in model (1), while its long-run counterpart is $[b_2/(1-b_3)]$. Empirically, $b_2 \leq [b_2/(1-b_3)]$ with equality established if and only if $b_3=0$, which is rarely found. If the equation inverted with interest rate as dependent variable, then the inequality would be $1/b_2 \geq [(1-b_3)/b_2]$. The latter inequality is referred to as overshooting effect. However, Goodhart (1984) has observed that when interest rates are regressed on movements in money stock. "there is rarely any trace of such apparent overshooting". This, in fact validated the assumption that the arguments in money demand function (interest rate in this case) are subject to slow adjustment. As a natural corollary, it is concluded that excess money supply might have been held as buffer stock.

Inverted equation may not necessarily produce an exact reciprocal coefficient unless the correlation coefficient between money and interest rate is unitary. Therefore, it is statistically incorrect to invert equation (1) and deduce that excess money supply is held as buffer stock as interest rate overshooting was not in evidence. In a single equation framework, one cannot preclude the possibility of price adjusting more rapidly to excess money supply in the event of interest rate adjusting relatively slowly. In order to resolve the inconsistency, Laidler (1982) argued that overshooting refers to models in which interest rate is the dependent variable, while buffer stock theory refers to money demand function which cannot be inverted. Cuthbertson and Taylor (1987) observed that "a major problem with this single equation disequilibrium money approach is that only one argument may be chosen as the dependent variable, whereas on *a priori* grounds one might expect all arguments of the demand function to adjust simultaneously." Therefore, single equation disequilibrium model cannot be fully relied upon for the purpose of investigating the buffer stock evidence in an economy.

Forward-Looking Buffer Stock Model.

The conventional money demand models omit future values of the arguments of the demand for money. Past values of the arguments may not be appropriate proxy for future transactions. The adaptive expectations invoked in partial adjustment models are therefore considered inadequate to capture expectation about the future. The forward-looking buffer stock model tries to resolve this problem. In case of the U.K. economy, Cuthbertson (1984) had estimated a forward looking buffer stock model in the following form:

$$m_t = \lambda m_{t-1} + (1-\lambda)(1-\lambda D)\sum_{0}^{\infty} (\lambda D)^s E_{t-1} m^*_{t+s} \quad ...(2)$$

where 'D' is the discount factor, 'E' is the expectation parameter at time t-1, $E_{t-1}\ m^*_{t+s}$ are the expected values of future long run money balances. The buffer stock arises when the agents make decisions concerning m_t based on information at period t-1. Any surprise increase in nominal income are partly held as buffer money. The long run money demand function would be as follows:

$$m^*_t = a_0 p_t + a_1 y_t - a_2 r_t \quad ...(3)$$

In equation (2), m^*_{t+s} would contain an anticipated part and an unanticipated part. The forward-looking demand for money function is estimated using predictions of the 'forcing variables' y^e_{t+s}, p^e_{t+s}, r^e_{t+s} where the superscript 'e' is the expected value of the respective variables.

This version of the buffer stock approach is consistent with rational expectation hypothesis. However, the forward-looking buffer stock models could exhibit instability because of instability in the process of expectation formation. "Also, long-run equilibrium solutions from such models are, generally invalid under rational expectations" (Cuthbertson 1986). Although forward-looking buffer stock models appear theoretically sound, further research in this area could not proceed on account of limitations associated with expectations formation for future values of money demand argument.

Complete Disequilibrium Models

The single equation money demand functions cannot fully resolve the issue of simultaneity. Therefore, the best way to handle buffer money is to formulate a simultaneous equation model where in the variables included in the money demand function are determined simultaneously within the framework of a disequilibrium approach. Generally, the following type of equations frequently appear in case of complete disequilibrium models:

$$DX_t = f(Z_t) + V(L)\ (M^s_t - M^d_t) \quad ...(4)$$

$$M^d_t = a_0 p_t + a_1 R_t + a_2 Y_t \quad ...(5)$$

where 'DX' may be a set of real or nominal variables in their first difference, 'Z_t' is a vector of predetermined equilibrium variables. 'M^d_t' is the long-run demand for money and M^s_t is the actual supply of money, V(L) is a lag polynomial. As the disequilibrium term appears in a number of equations, the model imposes cross-equation restrictions on the parameters of the long-run demand for money function.

These types of models have performed reasonably well for the US (Laidler and Bentley, 1983), and UK (Davidson, 1984). By and large, these models are estimated by 'system methods' such as, three stage least square, full information maximum likelihood etc. However, these models "have not proved as successful in explaining flexible exchange rate open economies as they have in modelling of closed economies" (Cuthbertson and Taylor, 1987). Moreover, the key problem associated with this approach is that the estimated coefficients in the money demand equation are conditional on the correct specification of the whole model (Cuthbertson, 1988). Particularly, if one is interested to test whether the coefficients are stable over time, the system method is not suitable as it complicates the exercise. However, for macro-modelling, this approach provides opportunity for further research as the various routes of transmission mechanism could be tracked down effectively.

Shock Absorber Models

In modelling buffer stock money, the most widely used approach is perhaps the shock absorber model developed by Carr and Darby (1981). The shock absorber models which have undergone several modifications over time, formulate the demand for money in the following manner.

$$m_t - p_t = b_0 + b_1 y_t + b_2 r_t + b_3 (m-p)_{t-1} + b_4 IR_t + a\ (m_t - m_t^*) + u_t \quad ...(6)$$

$$m_t^* = \hat{g} z_t + e_t \quad ...(7)$$

where 'm_t^*' is the anticipated component of money supply, 'z_t' is vector of variables the agents assume to have systematic influence on the money supply; $\hat{g}$ is a vector of coefficients to be estimated; (m_t - m_t^*) is the difference between actual and anticipated money supply, alternatively called the supply shock, monetary innovations, 'u_t' and 'e_t' are the white noise error terms. *A priori*, the co-efficient of supply shock (i.e., a) is expected to be positive and significant to validate the evidence of buffer stock.

There is no consensus about the process of generating the anticipated money supply series. It can be done through a purely autoregressive process, a distributed lag model, or a combination of the two namely, autoregressive distributed lag model. It can also be generated in a more sophisticated manner through seasonal ARIMA if the frequency of data is either quarterly or monthly, or through polynomial distributed lag model. In all these cases the coefficients of expectations would be constant. But the agents may optimally update the coefficient of their expectations formation process in the light of new information. Therefore, Boughton and Tavlas (1991) have tried a time-varying coefficient of expectation formation by using recursive least square. Carr and Darby (1981) used an unspecified ARIMA model and invoked rational expectation hypothesis to arrive at anticipated money supply; Boughton and Tavlas (1990) have estimated the anticipated part of money supply by regressing the money supply on a polynomial distributed lag (second degree, twelve period) of its past values. It is better to use the best performing alternative to generate the expected money supply.

Carr-Darby hypothesis postulates that anticipated nominal money supply should not affect the real demand for money. This is a testable hypothesis which could be examined under the following specification.

$$m_t - p_t = b_0 + b_1 y_t + b_2 r_t + b_3 (m-p)_{t-1} + b_4 IR_t + a (m_t - m_t^*) + Q m_t^* + u_t \quad ...(8)$$

MacKinnon and Milbourne (1984) pointed out that the OLS estimation of the Carr-Darby model leads to simultaneous equation bias as 'm_t' component of the money supply shock is related with dependent variable. The MM formulation suggested that C-D model may be transformed to remove 'm_t' from the right hand side of the equation (6) which can be generalised as follows:

$$m_t - p_t = b x_t + a (m_t - m_t^*) + Q m_t^* + e_t \quad ...(9)$$

where 'x_t' is the vector of variables which the economic agents consider to have systematic influence on real balance. By transforming equation (9), MM model is set in the following form:

$$m_t - p_t = b^* x_t + a^* (m^*_t - p_t) + Q^* m^*_t + e^*_t \quad ...(10)$$

where $a^* = -a/(1-a)$, $Q^* = Q/(1-a)$, $b^* = b/(1-a)$, $e^*_t = (1/(1-a))e_t$

By using the model (10), MacKinnon and Milbourne rejected the buffer stock evidence for the US economy. Boughton and Tavlas (1991) have, however, indicated serious difficulties with the MM model. While 'm_t' in equation (9) has been removed from the right hand side (RHS) through transformation, it is replaced by 'p_t' which may be correlated with the error term. Moreover, 'm^*_t' and (m^*_t-p_t) may be highly correlated making the test statistics difficult to interpret. Boughton and Tavlas further transformed the equation (10) to eliminate 'p_t' from the RHS which is as follows:

$$m_t = b^* x_t + \hat{Q} m^*_t + \hat{a} p_t + e^*_t \quad ...(11)$$

where $\hat{Q} = (Q-a)/(1-a)$ and $\hat{a} = 1/(1-a)$

SECTION III

Buffer Stock Evidence in India

There is no systematic study on buffer stock approach to demand for money in India with the exception of an early attempt by Paul and Kulkarni (1987)[4]. Their results are neither robust nor free from econometric problems. Even some of their results are quite contrary to the expectation such as negative sign for scale variable. The methodology adopted here would therefore heavily depend on international experience and is akin to that used by Carr and Darby (1981) with appropriate modifications to resolve certain econometric problems pointed out by subsequent critics.

Estimation Procedure

We estimate here the demand for money in India by using partial adjustment model (PAM) and shock absorber model (SAM) and present them together for the purpose of comparison. For PAM, a variant of equation (1) is estimated. Buffer stock demand for money for both M_1 and M_3 is estimated in two stages. In the first stage, the anticipated series on money supply is generated by regressing nominal money supply on GDP, Call Money Rate (CMRT) and Wholesale Price Index (WPI) on their log levels and corrected for auto-correlation through AR(1) process[5]. The supply shock series (InMRES) is derived by deducting InMEST from the actual values of monetary aggregrates (log levels). In the second stage, OLS estimation is made for the real money demand function with respect to both narrow and broad money by estimating a variant of structural equation (6).

Further, the influence of anticipated money supply on real balance is examined by extending the specification under equation (6) to include anticipated money supply term (InMEST). The out-of-sample predictive power of the shock absorber model is studied by repeating the estimation procedure with a break of sample at 1980-81[6].

In the absence of reliable monthly or quarterly data on the scale variable, viz., national income, annual data are used for empirical exercise on buffer stock money in India. The sample period chosen spans over three decades from 1960-61 to 1993-94. Adjusted data on M_1 and M_3 are used for the period from 1960-61 to 1976-77 following definitional changes after the submission of the Second Working Group report on money supply in 1977[7].

Model Comparison

Table 1 reports the OLS estimates of partial adjustment model (PAM) and shock absorber model (SAM). As is evident from Table 1, the inclusion of the monetary shock term in the real money demand function is found to be positive and significant at one per cent level in case of both narrow money and broad money (equations 2 and 5). More than 40 per cent of the supply shock is absorbed by the economic agents in the short-run. In order to know if the anticipated supply of money has any impact on real balances, equations 2 and 5 are extended to include the anticipated money supply term as an argument. The result was found to be mixed. In the case of narrow money (equation 3), anticipated money supply is negative and significant at 5 per cent level which is contrary to the theoretical expectation. In the case of broad money (equation 6), anticipated supply of money is found to have a positive impact on real balance, as the relevant coefficient has a positive sign and significant at 5 per cent level. The hypothesis that the anticipated supply of money does not have any significant impact on real balance is perhaps not valid in the case of India. The current inflation rate is found to be significant and negatively related to the real balance implying the possibility of substitution between money and real assets. Test statistics have improved in terms of R^{-2}, Durbin's 'h' and standard error of regression (S.E.R.) in all cases.

The shock absorber model has seemingly outperformed the partial adjustment model in respect of both narrow money and broad money. The specification bias which seems to have been present in the partial adjustment model, has been reduced considerably as the parameters are now more precise. Moreover, as the test statistics have improved, this shows that the within-sample period predictive power has gone up. Equation 2 and 5 are chosen to study the out-of-sample predictive power of the shock absorber model in the next Section.

SECTION IV

Instability in Money Demand Function

This section examines the stability property of the money demand function under buffer stock approach. The nature of shift in the money demand function, the out-of-sample predictive power and stability property are examined in that order.

Shift in Money Demand and Monetary Control

Unanticipated shift in money demand function generally attenuates the monetary control. This can be illustrated in the following manner. Let 'Mo' be the central bank's 'best guess' of the true money demand function (Diagram 1). There may be random shifts of the hypothetical money demand curve. If the shifts tend to fluctuate in an offsetting fashion around the true function, the central bank can still pursue the policy of monetary targeting under the presumption that the mean of the short-run money demand function would more or less lie on the hypothetical money demand curve. However, if the magnitude of these shifts is high and persists in one direction for a long time, monetary control becomes increasingly difficult. For example, if money demand shifts upward to say 'Mu', controlling money supply at 'Mo' level may result in recession. On the contrary, if the function shifts downward to 'Md', targeting money supply at 'Mo' level may lead to inflation.

The shifts in money demand function may be of two types. It can be a one time permanent shift following definite shocks and remain stable thereafter or there can be general instability after a certain break-point. In case of the former, central bank may commit errors until the shift is identified. In case of the latter, monetary targeting may become difficult.

DIAGRAM 1

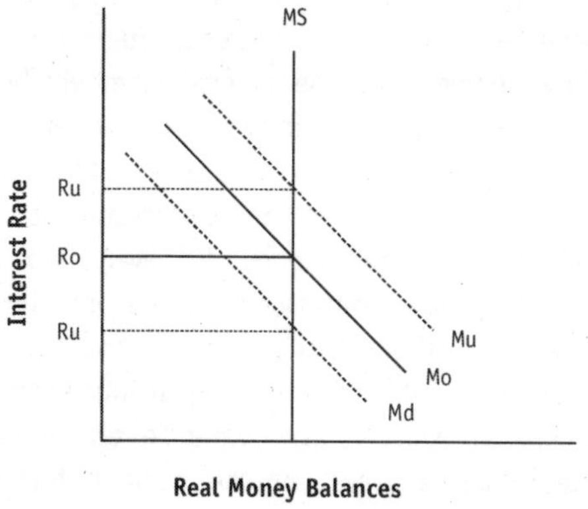

Out of Sample Predictive Power

The preceding section showed that the money demand function estimated under buffer stock approach outperformed that under partial adjustment model. This section examines the out-of-sample predictive power of the buffer stock model. The buffer stock function is re-estimated with the sample truncated at 1980-81. The equation was then simulated to generate *ex post* forecasts for the period 1981-82 to 1993-94. The comparison of the simulated and actual values of real balance is given by the plots in Graphs I and II. While the historical simulation for the period 1960-61 to 1980-81 has turned out to be quite robust, the **ex post** forecasting power of equation is not satisfactory which is evident from the consistent overprediction for the out-of-sample period. The predicted values of 'M_1' and 'M_3' persistently exceeded their respective actual values beyond 1981-82 perhaps reflecting the evidence of 'missing money' in the Indian context. There could be two possible explanations in support of the above findings. First, the money demand itself may have undergone a downward drift in the 1980s. Secondly, the dependent variable might have failed to capture certain types of liquidity in the 1980s following financial innovations. The instability arising out of the first possibility is studied in the next sub-section.

Testing the Stability of Buffer Stock Model

Two types of shifts discussed earlier can be pointed out in a straight forward manner. The existence of a one time shift in 1982 can be tested by using intercept and slope dummies that partitions the data at that point of time. The possibility that frequent random shocks to the real sector might have made the money demand function more unstable in the short-run could be examined by using a unique dummy for each observation after the hypothesised break point. If the coefficient of the individual dummy turns out significant by ordinary 't'

TABLE 1

Estimation of the Demand for Money in India : Partial Adjustment Model and Buffer Stock Model

Sample Period : 1960-61 to 1993-94

Sl. No.	Dependent variable	Explanatory variables							Test Statistics		
		Intercept	lnGDP	lnCMRT	RLM(-1)	lRAT	lnMRES	lnMEST	$\bar{R}^2$	S.E.R.	Durbin's 'h'
1.	RLM1	-1.2531	0.1497** (2.60)	-0.0038 (0.20)	0.9291** (20.32)	-0.7941** (8.37)	-	-	0.997	0.025	1.55
2.	RLM1	-2.2249	0.2958** (7.21)	-0.0254* (2.15)	0.7972** (23.64)	-0.4849** (6.65)	0.4421** (7.02)	-	0.999	0.015	0.85
3.	RLM1	-3.8371	0.4804** (5.31)	-0.0222* (1.99)	0.8176** (24.93)	-0.4363** (6.10)	0.4037** (6.49)	-0.0685* (2.25)	0.999	0.014	1.40
4.	RLM3	-1.6941	0.2011** (2.23)	0.0100 (0.52)	0.9116** (18.19)	-0.8428** (8.36)	-	-	0.998	0.026	2.01
5.	RLM3	-3.9114	0.4765** (5.90)	-0.0189 (1.31)	0.7545** (16.65)	-0.4609** (4.65)	0.4234** (5.53)	-	0.999	0.019	1.52
6.	RLM3	-2.4757	0.3191** (2.97)	-0.0257 (1.84)	0.7187** (15.56)	-0.4911** (5.18)	0.4521** (6.13)	0.0611* (2.08)	0.999	0.017	0.57

Note : lnMRES is the supply shock generated by lnM-lnMEST and lnMEST is the anticipated supply of money worked out from the equation $\ln M = a_0 + a_1 \ln GDP + a_2 \ln CMRT + a_3 \ln WPI + a_4 AR(1)$, (see notes No. 5).
For other variables, see Appendix I.
Figures in parentheses are 't' values.
* Denotes significance at 5 per cent level.
** Denotes significance at 1 per cent level.

statistics, the inference of a structural break at that point may be validated. If the sum of the dummies is significant, the inference would be that the short-run shocks have **not** been offsetting but have had the cumulative effect of shifting the function in one direction. This test is implemented by estimating equations 2 and 5 over the period 1960-61 to 1980-81 and adding each time unique dummy variables for each observation during the subsequent period.

GRAPH 1

PREDICTION OF NARROW MONEY DEMAND

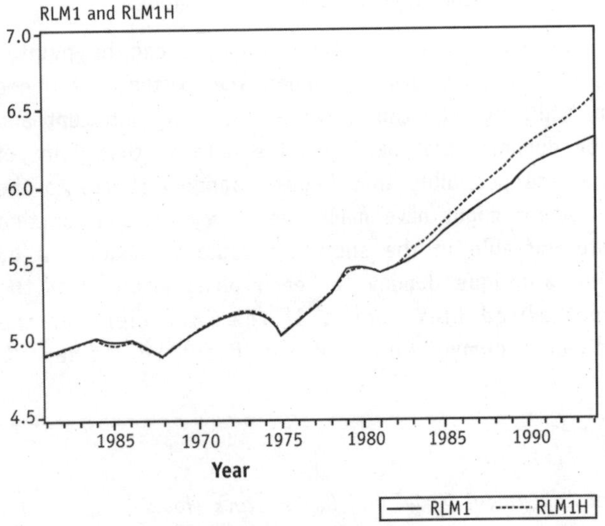

GRAPH 2

PREDICTION OF BROAD MONEY DEMAND

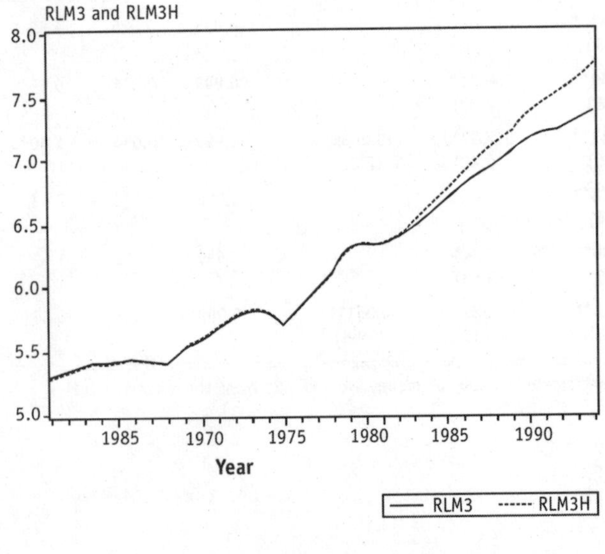

There is a *prima facie* evidence for an upward shift in the money demand function in the 1980s as seen from the positive sign of the intercept dummy (Table 2). But, the slope dummy has the reverse sign which is indicative of the downward shift in the income elasticity of the demand for money. It is also evident that both intercept dummy and slope dummy are significant at one per cent level in case of broad money. However, in case of narrow money, they are insignificant. Therefore, it is necessary to examine further if the sum of the unique dummies used for each observation beginning from 1980-81 is significant so that it will validate our hypothesis of a possible structural break of the demand for both M1 and M3 since early 1980s.

TABLE 2

Short-run Buffer Stock Money Demand Function for India.

Explanatory variables	*RLM1*		*RLM3*	
Intercept	-2.2062		-3.4761	
ln GDP	0.2816**	(5.47)	0.3941**	(5.32)
ln CMRT	-0.0240	(1.92)	-0.0202	(1.65)
RLM (-1)	0.8255**	(13.18)	0.8454**	(17.39)
lRAT	-0.5198**	(5.36)	-0.5910**	(6.13)
ln MRES	0.4248**	(5.91)	0.3297**	(4.64)
DUM 1	0.2680	(0.45)	1.3440**	(3.56)
DUM 2	-0.0233	(0.46)	-0.1155**	(3.59)
	Test Statistic			
$\bar{R}^2$	0.999		0.999	
S.E.R.	0.015		0.016	
Durbin's 'h'	0.74		-0.79	

Notes :
1. Figures in parenthesis are 't' values.
2. * indicates significance at 5 per cent level.
3. ** indicates significance at 1 per cent level.
4. DUM1 is intercept dummy with 'o' up to 1980-81 and '1' thereafter.
5. DUM2 is slope dummy i.e. DUM1 x ln GDP.

Table 3 reports coefficients of intercept and slope dummies of narrow and broad money demand. Intercept dummies used for both M1 and M3 have positive signs in all the years after 1979-80 (except in 1989-90 for M3) signifying possible upward shift. They are significant at one per cent level in two cases (and nearly significant at five per cent level in other two) for M1 and significant in eight cases for M3. While the level of significance has gradually improved for M1, it has moved almost in reverse direction for M3. However, the null hypothesis that 'the sum of the intercept dummies is zero' is rejected at one per cent level in cases of both narrow money and broad money as the 't' values turned out to be significant at

TABLE 3

Buffer Stock Demand for Money in India : Estimates of Short-Run Instability in Post-1980 period

Break Point	Narrow Money (M1)				Broad Money (M3)			
	Coefficient of Intercept Dummy		Coefficient of Slope Dummy		Coefficient of Intercept Dummy		Coefficient of Slope Dummy	
1980-81	0.2680	(0.45)	-0.0233	(0.46)	1.3439**	(3.56)	-0.1155**	(3.59)
1981-82	0.2037	(0.36)	-0.0178	(0.37)	1.2317**	(3.18)	-0.1057**	(3.23)
1982-83	0.2076	(0.37)	-0.0168	(0.36)	1.3113**	(3.05)	-0.1109**	(3.08)
1983-84	0.0233	(0.50)	-0.0233	(0.49)	1.2601**	(2.66)	-0.1065**	(2.71)
1984-85	0.2861	(0.50)	-0.0240	(0.50)	1.3303**	(2.46)	-0.1118**	(2.50)
1985-86	0.4212	(0.66)	-0.0346	(0.66)	1.4085**	(2.15)	-0.1179**	(2.23)
1986-87	0.6738	(0.97)	-0.0624	(0.97)	1.6543**	(2.01)	-0.1377**	(2.04)
1987-88	2.4264**	(2.09)	-0.1979**	(2.08)	2.5486	(1.96)	-0.2102*	(1.98)
1988-89	4.5425**	(2.49)	-0.3703**	(2.50)	2.1891	(1.04)	-0.1809	(1.05)
1989-90	5.8109	(1.93)	-0.4737	(1.94)	-0.2393	(0.06)	0.0166	(0.06)
1990-91	7.5718	(1.94)	-0.6165	(1.95)	0.3458	(0.07)	-0.0305	(0.07)
1991-92	10.5975	(1.46)	-0.8618	(1.45)	9.1920	(0.97)	-0.7470	(0.97)
$\sum_{i=1}^{12} di = 0$		(3.71)		(3.68)		(2.26)		(2.32)

Notes : 1. Figures in brackets are 't' values.
2. * indicates significance at 5 per cent level.
3. ** indicates significance at 1 per cent level.
4. 'd' stands for dummy.

one per cent level. Persistent increase in money supply at a relatively high rate in the 1980s and also in the 1990s so far, irrespective of the level of money demand could be the possible reason for an upward shift in the intercept.

From the policy angle, a central banker is perhaps more interested in the slope of the money demand curve. Unlike intercept dummies, the slope dummies consistently took negative signs for both M1 and M3 (except in 1989-90 for M3) implying a downward adjustment of the money demand function with respect to the growth of real income. The trends with respect to level of significance for M1 and M3 are more or less similar to that of intercept dummy. In case of slope dummies also the null hypothesis that 'the sum of the dummies is zero' is rejected at one per cent level. The stability test shown in Table 3, however, could not justify any unique point of break, rather, it indicated a kind of general instability since 1981-82.

SECTION V

Concluding Observations

Among the variety of buffer stock models, shock absorber model is widely used by researchers to study the impact of unanticipated changes in money supply on the money demand. The empirical findings on shock absorber model presented above indicate an evidence of buffer stock money in India. About 40 per cent of the unanticipated change in money supply is willingly absorbed in the short-run by the spending units. The hypothesis that anticipated change in money supply does not significantly influence money demand could not be maintained due to mixed result. At least for M3, it was positive and significant implying that anticipated money supply does play a role in influencing money demand. The shock absorber model seemed to have outperformed partial adjustment model in many respects and therefore could be used as an alternative paradigm in the study of money demand function in India. However, the out-of-sample predictive power of the shock absorber model was found to be weak perhaps reflecting the 'missing money' aspect in the Indian context. Stability test performed by using intercept and slope dummies for the 1980s showed significant changes in the behaviour of money demand in this period. While the intercept of the money demand function seems to have moved upward, the slope might have drifted downward. The findings were further supported by tests based on unique dummies. The result showed that there has been a tendency towards some downward movement in the slope of money demand function, stemming from a decline in the income elasticity during the 1980s - a phenomenon which could be partly attributed to financial innovations. This has happened side by side with an upward shift of the intercept of the demand for real balances. While these evidence give rise to the concern that the money demand function might have exhibited some degree of instability, further research in this area is needed in terms of time series analysis through co-integration technique. The preliminary evidence presented in this paper make a case for a close relook at the stability aspect of money demand, which will have implications for effective conduct of monetary targeting in India.

Notes

1. For an excellent survey of literature, reference may be made to Judd and Scadding (1982), Akhtar (1983).
2. While discussing portfolio adjustment following monetary innovation, Friedman and Schwartz (1963, P. 63) stated that: "It is this interconnection of stocks and flows that stretches the effects of shocks out in time, produces a diffusion over different economic categories, and gives rise to cyclical reaction mechanisms. The stocks serve as *buffers* or *shock absorbers* of initial changes in rates of flow by expanding or contracting from their normal or natural or desired state and they slowly alter other flows as holders to try to regain that state."
3. Some authors like Bain and McGregor (1985) argue that this approach is an improved version or more precise statement of impact interval analysis of monetarism.
4. Also see Subramanyam (1990) for some comments on buffer stock approach to money demand.
5. The specification assumes rational expectation framework where current values contain all information relevant for expectation formation. The results are:

   lnM_t=-9.0506 + 1.2624lnGDP -0.0307lnCMRT + 0.9568lnWPI
   't'value (5.07) (-0.67) (7.24)

   $\bar{R}^2$ =.99 D.W.=1.88 S.E.R.=0.06.

   lnM_3=-11.9227 + 1.5183 lnGDP -0.0469 lnCMRT + 1.1207 lnWPI
   't'value (5.48) (-0.91) (7.63)

   $\bar{R}^2$ =.099 D.W.=1.86 S.E.R.=0.07.

   The nominal money supply was also regressed on the same variable with one period lag together with lagged dependent variable. The results (not reported) are found to be inferior to those used in contemporaneous model with auto-correlation correction.
6. The conventional Chow test is also performed. As Chow 'F' is not significant, it is not reported. One of the limitations of the Chow test is that it does not perform well in case of gradual change in the function. A possible break in the money demand function was anticipated by the author through the use of dummies in one of his earlier studies [see Bhoi (1992)].
7. Adjusted data used here are from Singh et at. (1982).

APPENDIX I

Definition of Variables Used in the Model

Notation		*Definition of the Variables*
M1	:	Nominal Narrow Money which comprises currency with the public, demand deposits with banks and 'other' deposits with RBI.
P	:	Index Number of Wholesale Prices (WPI): All commodities, (Average of the weeks), Base: 1981-82 = 100.
RLM1	:	Real Narrow Money which is lnM1-lnWPI.
M3	:	Nominal Broad Money which consists of M1 plus time deposits with banks.
RLM3	:	Real Broad Money which in lnM3-lnWPI.
GDP	:	Gross Domestic Product at factor cost at 1980-81 prices.
CMRT	:	Weighted average of Call Money Rate at Bombay (average of the weeks).
IRAT	:	Inflation rate i.e. lnWPI-lnWPI(-1).
In	:	The prefix 'ln' refers to natural log of the respective variables.
DUM1	:	Intercept dummy
DUM2	:	Slope dummy i.e. DUM1 X In GDP.

References

1. Akhtar, M. A., (1983), "Financial Innovations and Their Implications for Monetary Policy: An International Prespective", *BIS Economic Papers,* No.9, December.
2. Artis, M. J., and M. K. Lewis, (1976) "The Demand for Money in the United Kingdom; 1963-1976", *The Manchester School of Economics and Social Studies,* Vol.44, No.21, 147-181.
3. Bain, A. D., and P. G. McGregor (1985), "Buffer stock Monetarism and the Theory of Financial Buffer", *The Manchester School,* Vol. 53, No.4, 385-403.
4. Barro. R. J., (1978). "Unanticipated Money, Output and the Price Level in the United States", *Journal of Political Economy,* Vol. 86, No.4, 549-580.
5. Baumol, W. J. (1952), "The Transactions Demand for Cash - An Inventory Theoretic Approach", *Quarterly Journal of Economics,* Vol. 66, No. 4, 543-551.
6. Bhoi, B. K., (1992), "Issue of Instability in Money Demand Analysis : A Perspective", *RBI Staff Studies,* No. 9.
7. Boughton, J. M., (1981), "Recent Instability of the Demand for Money : An International Prespective", *Southern Economic Journal,* Vol. 47, No.3, 579-97.
8. Boughton, J. M. and George S. Tavlas, (1990), "Modelling Money Demand in Large Industrial countries; Buffer Stock and Error Correction Approaches", *Journal of Policy Modelling,* Vol. 12, 433-461.

9. ———. (1991), "What have We Learned About Estimating the Demand for Money? A Multicountry Evaluation of some New Approaches", *IMF Working Paper (WP/91/16).*

10. Carr, J., and M. Darby (1981), "The Role of Money Supply Shock in the Short-run Demand for Money", *Journal of Monetary Economics,* Vol. 8, No. 2, 183-199.

11. Carr, J., M. Darby and D. Thornton, (1985), "Monetary Anticipations and the Demand for Money : Reply", *Journal of Monetary Economics,* Vol. 16, No. 2.

12. Chow, G. C., (1966), "On the Long-run and Short-run Demand for Money", *Journal of Political Economy,* Vol. 74, 111-131.

13. Cuthbertson, K., (1984), "The Demand for M1 : A Forward-Looking Buffer Stock Model", *National Institute of Economic and Social Research,* Discussion Paper.

14. ———. (1985), *The Supply and Demand for Money,* Oxford, Basil Blackwell.

15. ———. (1986), "Monetary Anticipations and the Demand for Money : Some U.K. Evidence:, *Bulletin of Economic Research,* Vol. 8, No. 3, 257-270.

16. ———. (1988), "The Demand for M1 : A Forward-Looking Buffer Stock Model", *Oxford Economic Papers,* Vol. 40, 110-31.

17. Cuthbertson K. and M. P. Taylor, (1987), "Buffer Stock Money : An appraisal", in C. Goodhart, D. Currie and D. Llewellyn (eds), *The Operation and Regulation of Financial Market,* Macmillan, 125-149.

18. Davidson, J., (1984), "Money Disequilibrium : An Approach to Modelling Monetary Phenomena in the U.K.," *London School of Economics.*

19. Friedman M., and A. J. Schwartz, (1963) "Money and Business Cycle", *Review of Economics and Statistics,* Vol.2., No.2, 32-78.

20. Goldfeld, S. M., (1973), "The Demand for Money Revisited", *Booking Papers on Economic Activity,* No. 3, 577-638.

21. ———. (1976), "The Case of the Missing Money", *Brooking Papers on Economic Activity,* No. 3, 683-730.

22. Goodhart, C. A. E., (1982) "Monetary Trends in the United States and the United Kingdom : A British Review" *Journal of Economic Literature,* Vol. 20 No.4, 1540-51.

23. ———. (1984), "Disequilibrium Money : A Note" in C. Goodhart's *Monetary Theory and Practice: The U.K. Experience,* Macmillan, London, 254-276.

24. Jonson, P. D., (1976), "Money, Prices and Output : An Integrated Essay", *Kredit and Kapital,* Vol.9, No.4, 499-518.

25. Judd J. P. and J. L. Scadding (1982), "The Search for a Stable Money Demand Function: A Review of Post- 1973 Literature", *Journal of Economic Literature,* Vol. 20, No. 3, 994-1023.

26. Kanniainen, V., and T. Tarkka (1986), "On the Shock - Absorption View of Money : International Evidence from the 1960s and 1970s", *Applied Economics,* Vol. 18, No. 10, 1085-1101.

27. Keynes, J. M. (1936), *The General Theory of Employment, Interest and Money,* Macmillan, London.

28. Khan, M. S., and M. D. Knight, (1982), "Unanticipated Money Growth and Inflationary Finance", *Journal of Money, Credit and Banking,* Vol. 14, No.31, 347-364.

29. Laidler, D. E. W., and Bentley, B., (1983), "A Small Macro-model of the Post-war United States", *Manchester School,* Vol. 51.

30. Laidler, D. E. W., (1982) "On the Demand for Money and the Real Balance Effect", in Laidler D., *Monetarist Perspectives.* Cambridge, Massachusetts: Harvard University Press.

31. ———. (1984), "The Buffer Stock Notion in Monetary Economics". *Economic Journal,* Vol. 94, Supplement 17-34.

32. ———. (1987), "Buffer Stock Money and the Transmission Mechanism", *Federal Reserve Bank of Atlanta Economic Review,* March-April, 11-23.

33. MacKinnon, J. G., and R.D. Milbourne (1984), "Monetary Anticipations and Demand for Money", *Journal of Monetary Economics,* Vol. 13, No.2, 263-274.

34. Milbourne, R. (1988), "Disequilibrium Buffer Stock Models : A Survey", *Journal of Economic Survey,* Vol.2, No.3, 187-208.

35. Paul, T., and K. Kulkarni, (1987), "Supply Shock and Demand for Money in India" *The Asian Economic Review,* Vol.29, No.2, 1-16.

36. Singh, A., S. L. Shetty and T. R. Venkatachalam (1982) "Monetary Policy in India : Issues and Evidence" *RBI Occasional Papers,* Vol. 3, No.1, Supplement.

37. Subramnyam, G (1990), "The Demand for Money : A Brief Review of the Historic and Latest Developments", The 18th SEANZA Literature, RBI, Bombay.

38. Swamy, P. A. V. B., and G. S. Tavlas, (1989), "Modelling Buffer Stock Money : An Appraisal", *Journal of Policy Modelling,* Vol.11, 593-612.

39. Tobin, J., (1956), "The Interest Elasticity of Transactions Demand for Cash", *Review of Economics & Statistics,* Vol.84, No.1, 241-247.

Section III

TWO of the eight papers included in this section were written in the 1980s. The growth of financial innovations since about the middle of the 1980s meant the need for a re-look at money supply targeting, assuming that interest rate is market determined. But interest rates were administered in the 1980s. N Nagarajan's model clearly anticipates interest rate flexibility and what is more, emphasizes the role of technology in promoting financial innovations. This paper is in a sense a forerunner of what A Vasudevan has depicted in his 1991 analysis of the issues of monetary management that need to be tackled in economies that make a transition from dirigiste regimes to market-oriented regimes. Interestingly enough, monetary targeting in the dirigiste framework while suggesting a strong hold on prices and a noticeable influence on output, as empirically tested by Y S R Sarma, would not be effective during periods of financial innovations. Sarma's paper, however, could be taken as suggestive of the need for inflation control rather than output expansion through the exercise of money supply channel — a point that is very much in the monetarist tradition. Vasudevan's paper should be read in the context of the reform process that was just introduced in the wake of the balance of payments crisis of 1990/1991. Using the company finances data for the period 1965-78, the typically dirigiste regime, Renu Kohli shows that small firms which according to credit rationing theory would be rationed out of the organized markets, could access bank credit depending on their size, age and the collaterals they could provide. The impression that all small firms had received favourable treatment because small scale industry was placed under the 'priority sector' during the 1970s was not fully vindicated.

Problems of monetary and external sector management intensify often because of inappropriate fiscal position, as standard text books on macroeconomics suggest. The reliance of the government on market borrowings for financing its deficits right from the early 1970s had been well documented in most books on Indian economics. The text book view about the constraining influence of the fiscal position on monetary policy pursuit was predominant in the Indian literature right till the end of the 1980s, whereas the fiscal policy effects on the external sector position were more clearly seen in the 1990s as the exchange restrictions were eased and as exchange rate regime became flexible. These views were tested in the Indian case in two papers by C Rangarajan et al, the first being in the late 1980s and the second being in the second half of the 1990s. The papers point to the dangers of unsustainable debt accumu-lation, and to the quick spread of rigidities in interest rate management, apart from the ill-effects of monetary expansion on prices and of weak external position on exchange rates and a host of other major economic indicators. The unfavourable external effects of weak public finances were quickly brought to light when the Gulf crisis led to oil price flare-up in late 1990 and early 1991, and they could not have been addressed by the traditional means of exchange controls and fixed exchange rate system without incurring very high and often unbearable costs to society. The need for regime shift was necessitated by the economy's vulnerability to internal macro-economic imbalance coinciding with external factors such as the oil price hikes. This was the third time that India was subjected to considerable economic stress — twice in the 1970s at the time of the two oil price hikes followed by the one in 1991.

One of the areas in which policy actions were undertaken to bring about economic liberalization beginning with the mid-1991 relates to exchange rate management as part of macroeconomic policy framework. The fixed exchange rate regime was given up by March 1993 and in its place market-related exchange rate system, a variant of the flexible exchange rate regime, was instituted. This meant that the domestic monetary, and exchange rate policies would need to be pursued consistently along with fiscal prudence in order to install macro-economic balance. The two papers on this subject in this section are highly contextual, as the economy had opened up considerably after 1993 although full capital account converti-bility has not been realized so far. Full capital account liberalization has in fact become passé after the East Asian crisis of 1997. But the Indian authorities recognize that as the economy opens up further, and as the financial sector grows and gets integrated, the exchange rate management would be subjected to influences that have not been hitherto experienced. From all indications, the REER is considered by the Reserve Bank as a valuable indicator of exchange rate policy. As one of the papers argues, it could also be used as a good potential indicator of the financial strength of the country to the extent it is related to capital flows.

10

Financial Innovation: Determinants and Implications for Monetary Policy

A Model

N Nagarajan

1. Introduction

...

IN this paper, an exploratory theoretical attempt is made to assess the determinants of a specific form of financial innovation, viz., interest-bearing-money, substituting non-interest-bearing-money. The model is then articulated to evaluate the likely effects on selected crucial macro-economic variables, viz., rates of interest, interest-bearing-money and non-interest-bearing-money, as also the implications of such innovation for the conduct of monetary policy through the regulation of supply of reserves. The exercise is done within the general framework of portfolio balance approach which is sufficiently flexible to permit a consideration of different types of money. The method adopted is comparative static analysis with equilibrium conditions imposed on all markets.

The desirability of the study stems from two quarters. From a purely academic angle, available literature have accepted financial innovation as a 'shift' or aberration in the conventional demand for money function and a few, which have had focussed attention on innovation, have done so at micro-level. This study, on the other hand, specifies the determinants of financial innovation and then traces its effects. Thus, adequate attention is paid to innovation and its integration with the financial system. Perhaps the importance lies more in its relevance to policy formulation which is the second rationale of this study. Developed countries, especially the USA and Canada, responded to the phenomenon through empirical analysis after its effects were felt; even then, as would be pointed out shortly, they have concentrated on obtaining a stable demand for money function and rarely on the effects of innovation which is more important. In contrast, this study provides a theoretical futuristic perspective which could be used for timely action. This is particularly relevant for India in view of the growing trend towards the rationalisation of administered interest rate structure including gradual withdrawal of rigidities and the large-scale introduction of mechanisation at the banks.

The results indicate that, under given conditions, financial innovation by way of introduction of money-substitute instruments, has a self-sustaining tendency. The trend is accentuated by interest rate spread for the banks, technology and restrictions imposed by the monetary authority including monetary targeting. The consequences of financial innovation are felt on the interest rates as also on interest-bearing and non-interest-bearing monies. While interest rates tend to rise, both types of monies, especially interest-bearing, also expand. Thus, during a period of financial innovation, neither targeting narrow money by way of supply of reserve nor any attempt to regulate interest rates is unlikely to yield expected results.

Following this introductory Section, available major studies are reviewed in Section 2. The basic model is developed in Section 3 and articulated in Section 4. Main findings are summarised, limitations noted and areas for further study identified in the last Section. ... Details of the Model are provided as Appendix I. ...

The study formed a part of the author's work at the Indiana University, Bloomington (USA) to which he was sent by the Reserve Bank of India under its scheme of deputing officers abroad for higher studies.

In the preparation of this study, the author has benefited from valuable comments of many faculty members, particularly Prof. W.E. Witte and Prof. C.J. Waller of the Department of Economics, and Prof. von Hogen of Business School, Indiana University as also officials of the Reserve Bank of India, Bombay, especially, Dr. S.L. Shetty, Shri R. Nagaraja Rao, Shri Y.S.R. Sarma and Dr. N.D. Jadhav. The author is grateful to the Reserve Bank of India for financial and other support. A preliminary draft of this paper was presented at the Seminar in Money at the Indiana University in September 1988.

2. Review of Literature

Recent past witnessed a proliferation of literature on various aspects of financial innovation. The discussions ranged from descriptive international comparisons. [Aktar (1983), BIS (1984), de Cecco (1987) and Suzuki and Yomo (1986)] to theoretical micro-level appraisals (Silber, 1975). Besides, several empirical studies on the effects of financial innovation were attempted. In fact, according to Offenbacker (1982), financial innovation is an empirical issue.

Basically, the empirical studies endeavour to obtain a stable demand for money function. Available literature on this subject is so vast as to invite two surveys. [Jonson and Rankin (1986) and Judd and Scadding (1982)]. The method adopted is either to redefine the dependent variable so as to include a particular money-substitute-financial-asset or re-specify the explanatory variables with the inclusion of dummies to take into account financial innovation. The findings are not unambiguous. Generally, it is accepted that the USA and, to a less extent, Canada has experienced shifts in the demand for money functions. Simpson and Porter (1980) found that, in the USA, the functional relationship between narrow money and real variables was deteriorating. According to Boughton (1981), the money-demand functions in respect of M_1 in the USA and Canada were unstable. Kabir and Mangla (1988) reported that, in Canada, innovation had displaced the money-demand function from its trend in the early 1980s. Similar conclusion was reached by Milbourne and Moore (1986). According to Miller (1986), financial innovation had affected the function in the USA but the effects were gradual. Atkinson et al (1984) maintained that financial innovation had not significantly destabilised the demand for money, especially in the Continent. Chirinko and Colloton (1984) found some instability in the function in the USA but could not attribute the instability to financial innovation. An inescapable conclusion from these studies, especially in view of sophisticated statistical tools employed by Baba et al (1988) and Broemeling and Tsurumi (1987), is that with sufficient treatment, any data could be made to confess to any hypothesis.

As a logical sequence to the search for a stable demand for money function, the implications of shifts in such function for the conduct of monetary policy was examined by Cagan and Schwartch (1975), Hall (1986) and Hester (1981).

At micro level, various hypothesis were advanced to explain financial innovation. Kane (1984) attributed it to 'regulatory dialectics' in which the political process of regulation and the economic process of regulatee-avoidance interact by continuously adapting to each other with the latter always remaining one step ahead of the former. Desai and Low (1987) and Dufey and Giddy (1981) put forward the 'opportunity-gap' theory. This suggested that the financial firms would float new securities to cover the gap, if any, in the maturity pattern of existing securities. Silber (1975) propounded the 'constraint-induced-innovation' hypothesis. According to this, a profit - maximising financial firm would innovate, having regard to the cost of such innovation, when exogenous changes alter its constraints.

On the relationship between innovation and macro-economic activity, Podolski (1986) had presented an excellent perspective on the existing appraisals. Wenninger and Witte made significant contributions to the theoretical relationships. Wenninger (1984), *a priori*, hypothesised that innovation would result in (a) a decline in the interest-elasticity of demand for money since the new instrument would bear market-related interest along with the conventional conveniences of chequing accounts, (b) an increase in the income-elasticity due to the same factors, and (c) an increase in the interest-elasticity of expenditure because loans would be converted/made on floating interest rates. He then tested the effects of innovation within the conventional IS-LM framework. Innovation was equated with shifts in both demand for and supply of money. The static solutions to the system provided complex and ambiguous sets of results. However, he could derive some broad conclusions. First, a shift in the demand for money led to a larger deviation of narrow money from the target, requiring larger compensatory action from the central banking authority if the target was to be achieved. Second, narrow money was found less sensitive to changes in the supply of reserves but income and interest rates became more sensitive. Finally, the effects of innovation on the real sector too, was found ambiguous implying increased uncertainty about the underlying economic relationships. Also, all these relationships were changing simultaneously. For policy, this had two implications: (i) uni-target was inadvisable and (ii) a discretionary rather than a fixed rule monetary policy would be preferable.

On the lines of portfolio approach of Tobin, Witte (1982) developed a model of the financial sector consisting of four assets that included two highly liquid assets, both usable as transaction balances but one of which paid market-determined rate of interest. The model was then used to examine the effects of shifts in demand

and supply, separately, in the interest-bearing-transaction-asset on interest rate and monetary aggregates. The consequent impact on the effectiveness of the conventional monetary policy instruments was analysed and found to be rather ambiguous, especially that of targeting money supply.

Both these studies have treated financial innovation as shocks. This ... is significant since, in the absence of an adequate specification of the phenomenon, its effects cannot reasonably be assessed. Wenninger's attempt suffers from two more drawbacks. First, the IS-LM framework assumes that the LM curve is relatively stable, which, in turn, assumes, *inter alia*, that its composition is unchanged. Since innovation does change this composition, the use of the IS-LM framework would appear inappropriate. Further, 'since modern monetary analysis must take place with reference to the whole financial sector, the conventional LM analysis is inadequate' (Podolski, 1986. p. 227). Second, innovation and deregulation were treated synonymously, which is incorrect (he, however, isolated and omitted the effects of deregulation through a *priori* reasoning).

The foregoing brief review of available major studies reveals that the relationship between financial innovation and the financial system with adequate attention to the former has not been sufficiently explored. The present study is an exploratory theoretical attempt to assess the determinants of financial innovation, to analyse the inter-relationship between financial innovation, and financial sector and to evaluate the effects of selected exogenous variables and policy parameters on critical macro-economic variables.

3. Basic Model*

The model begins with the innovation sector. Financial innovation (I), for the present purpose, is interpreted to mean the availability of an additional financial instrument, whether entirely new or modified version of the existing one, carrying a market-related-interest rate. Conceptually, the participants in the market could be distinguished as the banker who demand innovation and the innovation agency which supplies the innovation (in practice, they correspond to the retail banker and the merchant banker, respectively). Banks demand innovation because it would facilitate them to augment their resources. The demand will increase with the level of interest-bearing-money (IBM). The demand would also depend upon interest rate differentials. The specification of spread instead of absolute levels reflects the present trend of banks to work on margins, particularly after the emergence of liability management techniques. In the present instance, this would imply that the net earnings accruing to banks, i.e., their earnings from the deployment of money obtained *minus* interest payable on the interest-bearing-money, would induce banks to demand innovation. Assuming that the deployment of money is only on the purchase of bonds, this would mean that the spread between interest rate on bonds (r^B) and interest rate on interest-bearing-money (r^{IBM}) would be a determinant in the demand for innovation. Bonds refer to all financial assets except interest-bearing money (IBM) and non-interest-bearing-money (NIBM). Savings account with chequing facility is an example of IBM. Demand deposits are an example of NIBM. The demand function would be positively related to restrictions imposed by the monetary authority (RE) since an important objective of innovation has been to circumvent such restrictions. Advancement in technology (T) would enable the rapid diffusion of innovation and hence a positive relationship is prescribed. 'Technological advances deployed in modern finance have been a common denominator of all major financial innovations. They have had a strong impact on the macro-economic demand for narrowly depicted money, largely by reducing transactions costs' (Podolski, 1986, p.173). These specifications would indicate a positive sloping demand function. This apparently unusual phenomenon is due to the fact that the banks are, in this context, only intermediaries and this function, in reality, refers to the supply of innovation to the public who are the ultimate users. Symbolically,

$$I^d_b = K[\overset{+}{IBM}, \overset{+}{RE}, \overset{+}{T}, \overset{+}{(r^B - r^{IBM})}] \qquad ...(1)$$

As mentioned earlier, I refers to financial innovation. Superscripts on the left hand side variable refer to the type of function - d for demand, for instance, and subscripts to the sector - b for banks, for example. On the right hand side, IBM stands for interest-bearing-money, r for the rate of interest and the superscripts on it for the financial asset to which the respective r relates - r^B for rate of interest on bonds, for example, RE refers to various restrictions, except reserve ratios, imposed by the monetary authority on the banks with regard to the creation of deposits. T stands for technology, i.e., advancement in telecommunication, data processing, data storing and data retrieval. The sign above a variable denotes the hypothesised partial for that variable.

* ***Editor's Note***: Appendix I here was shown as Appendix II in the orginal paper which had Appendix I a note on financial innovation and experience of the USA and Canada. Since this experience was too time-specific, it has been omitted here.

Supply of innovation is assumed to adjust passively to demand. ... Most of the innovative instruments are in effect slightly modified versions of the older ones; only the rapid diffusion, facilitated by technology, has been responsible for the present concern. Further, the requirements of the public (as reflected through the banks) vary necessitating appropriate instrument to suit specific needs. On the other hand, given the resources including technology, innovating new instruments, would be easier. Thus, the supply function is

$$I^{s}_{INN} = I^{d}_{b} \qquad \text{...(2)}$$

Innovation sector will be in equilibrium when supply matches demand. Thus

$$I^{s}_{INN} = I^{d}_{b} = I \qquad \text{...(3)}$$

The formulation of the model relating to the financial system is based on the conventional approach. There are four financial assets. The non-bank (public) holds two assets-non-interest bearing money (NIBM) and interest-bearing money (IBM). Both are bank deposits and hence liabilities of the banks. NIBM is similar to demand deposits and carries no explicit return, but IBM is similar to savings deposits and carries a positive market-determined-return. The *distinguishing feature of NIBM and IBM is thus the latter earns on explicit interest while the former does not.* Hence, the introduction of any new instrument bearing a rate of interest and usable as money will be included in IBM. Both NIBM and IBM are highly liquid. The third asset is bonds (B) which is a financial asset used to finance Government deficits and private investment. Thus, bonds are substitutes for IBM. For the present purpose, bonds on private investment account is taken as zero. Thus, in this model, B stands for bonds of all types issued by the Government. The fourth asset is reserve (R) which is a liability of the central bank and an asset of the banks. Their presence in the banks' portfolio reflects the statutory reserve requirement established by the central bank.

The financial system has three sectors : the non-bank (public), banks and the central bank. In this model, the term 'banks' include all financial institutions. In addition, the innovation sector interacts with the financial sectors. There are five markets - one for innovation and one each for four financial assets.

The public holds non-interest-bearing money, interest-bearing-money and bonds in their portfolios. The respective demand functions are:

$$NIBM^{d}_{p} = N\,(r^{IBM}, \overset{-}{r^{B}}, \overset{-}{I}\ \ \overset{+}{W}) \qquad \text{...(4)}$$

$$IBM^{d}_{p} = M\,(\overset{+}{r^{IBM}}, \overset{+}{r^{INF}}, \overset{+}{I}, \overset{+}{W}) \qquad \text{...(5)}$$

$$B^{d}_{p} = B\,(\overset{-}{r^{IBM}}, \overset{+}{r^{B}}, \overset{-}{I}, \overset{+}{W}) \qquad \text{...(6)}$$

subject to the wealth constraint

$$W = NIBM^{d}_{p} + IBM^{d}_{p} + B^{d}_{p} \qquad \text{...(7)}$$

Four observations on the specification are in order. First, rate of inflation (r^{INF}) is taken as an explanatory variable for IBM^{d}_{p} and the relationship hypothesised is positive. This is because of the observed (in the USA) public's preference to have IBM as a hedge against inflation. Second, in view of imperfect substitution, the effect or r^{B} in the IBM market is likely to be weak. Third, the specification is based on the levels of interest rates because IBM is a substitute mainly for NIBM which bears zero rate of interest. Finally, the effect of I on B^{d}_{p} could be positive in the unlikely event of IBM turning unattractive to the public.

Banks issue two liabilities, NIBM and IBM and hold two assets, reserves (R) and bonds (B). The supply of NIBM by the banks adjusts passively to the demand of the public. This follows from the earlier stipulation, viz., NIBM is non-interest bearing and hence profitable to banks but not so to the public. Banks, therefore, issue all NIBM that the public is willing to hold at the prevailing interest rates structure and would be prepared to issue more. Then,

$$NIBM^{s}_{b} = NIBM^{d}_{p} = NIBM \qquad \text{...(8)}$$

In respect of the other liability of the banks, IBM, one could assume that (a) the banks are profit maximisers and (b) their choice would depend upon the yield differential between the asset of banks, viz., bonds, and interest payable on IBM. Then

$$IBM^{s}_{b} = G\,[(r^{B} \pm r^{IBM}), \overset{+}{I}] \qquad \text{...(9)}$$

Obviously, the spread would have a positive relationship. Innovation would also have a positive relation because the banks would obtain more monies with innovation; also, the new instrument, among other things, would facilitate the banks to economise on cash.

The other asset of the banks is reserves. This includes statutory requirements and excess, if any. One could assume that they would maintain the minimum, both on NIBM and IBM. On NIBM, even if they refer exclusively to currency, it is reasonable to assume that the banks would maintain a specified fixed proportion in cash-either to meet the legal reserve requirement and/or to meet their daily cash drain. Both on NIBM and IBM, the banks are statutorily required to maintain a fixed proportion as reserves. If the statutory ratios on NIBM and IBM are denoted as α and β, respectively, the demand for reserve function is

$$R^{d}_{b} = \alpha NIBM + \beta IBM \qquad \text{...(10)}$$

Similarly, the banks' demand for bonds will depend positively upon the rate on bonds. Thus,

$$B^d_b = C(\overset{+}{r}{}^B) \quad ...(11)$$

The balance sheet constraint of the banks is

$$R^d_b + B^d_b = NIBM^s_b + IBM^s_b \quad ...(12)$$

The central bank is assumed to control the level of reserves by means of open market operations. Then,

$$R^s_c = R^d_b = B_c \quad ...(13)$$

In this framework, the equilibrium conditions are

$$\text{Innovation} = K(.) = I^s_{INN} = I \quad ...(15)$$

Non-interest-bearing-money =

$$N(.) = NIBM^s_b = NIBM \quad ...(16)$$

Interest-bearing-money =

$$M(.) = G(.) \quad ...(17)$$

$$\text{Bonds} = [B(.) + C(.)] = B - B_c \quad ...(18)$$

$$\text{Reserves} = \alpha NIBM + \beta IBM = B_c \quad ...(19)$$

$$\text{where } B^d_p + B^d_b + B_c = \dot{B} \quad ...(14)$$

For simplicity, let the interest rate differential $(r^B - r^{IBM})$ be a.

4. Articulation of the Model

The basic model is articulated in this Section with the twin objective of assessing the relative roles of selected exogenous variables in determining innovation and evaluating the impact of changes in selected exogenous variables and policy variables on the crucial endogenised macro-economic variables. For simplicity, linear relationship is assumed. Technical considerations enable the omission of an equation but keeping in view the number of variables involved, all equations are retained. Of the variables, innovation, interest rates on money and bonds, the size of non-interest-bearing and interest-bearing monies are taken as endogenous. The system is evaluated to obtain comparative static solutions with equilibrium conditions imposed on all the markets.

Determinant of the matrix: The determinant of the coefficient matrix is:

$$\Delta = -m_1 \{\beta(b_2+c_1) + \alpha k_1[n_3(b_2+c_1)+n_2b_3]\} \quad ...(25)$$

The overall effect of the determinant is ... negative [as the US experience shows].

Determinants of Innovation: The numerator for calculating a change in innovation is:

$$\dot{I} = -(k_2R\dot{E}+k_3\dot{T}+k_4\dot{a})\ [\beta m_1\ (b_2+c_1)] + k_1\ ((-m_2i^{INF}+g_1\dot{a})$$
$$\{\alpha[n_1(b_2+c_1)-n_2b_1]\} + (\dot{B}-\dot{B}_c)\ [\alpha m_1n_2] - \dot{B}_c[m_1(b_2+c_1)]) \quad ...(26)$$

The demand response for IBM in innovation market (k_i) plays an extensive role in the determination of changes in innovation. In the process, it affects even the exogenous variables. It accentuates interest rate spread and holdings of bonds by the public and banks: meanwhile, it undermines the rate of inflation and supply of reserves. In view of the complexities involved in respect of others, it is preferable to assess the relative roles of exogenous and policy variables separately.

The contribution of *interest rates spread is*

$$-k_4\beta m_1\ (b_2+c_1) + g_1\ \{\alpha k_1\ [n_1\ (b_2+c_1) - n_2b_1]\}$$

The first term is unambiguously negative. The positive demand response from the public and banks for bonds, together with the product of reserve requirement on IBM and positive demand response of the public for IBM, reacts with the positive demand for innovation from the banks due to interest rate differential; and the term is preceded by a negative sign. The second term also would be negative in the most likely event of $n_2b_1 < n_1\ (b_2+c_1)$ in absolute terms [This was partially seen in the studies on the USA]. In this instance the product of the negative demand response for NIBM in NIBM market due to a change in the rate of interest on bonds (n_2) and the negative demand response for bonds in bond market due to a change in the rate of interest or IBM (b_1) would be less than the product of the negative demand response for NIBM in NIBM market due to a change in the rate of interest on IBM(n_1) and the positive demand responses of banks and the public in the bond market for bonds due to a change in bond rate (b_2+c_1). The net sign of the term is negative and hence the overall effect on innovation is positive.

The share of *technology* is relatively simple:

$$-k_3\beta m_1\ (b_2 + c_1)$$

The term is certainly negative since all the elements are positive but preceded by a negative sign. Since the determinant of the matrix is negative, the result is positive i.e., technological advances lead to greater innovation, through the positive demand response of banks for innovation in innovation market due to a change in technology, reserve requirement on IBM, positive demand response of the public for IBM due to a change in the interest rate on IBM and the combined positive response of the public and banks for bonds due to a change in the bond rate. The total effect on innovation is promotional.

The role of *inflation* is provided by the expression

$$m_2 \alpha [n_1 (b_2 + c_1) - n_2 b_1]$$

This could be negative only in the unlikely event of $n_2 b_1 > n_1(b_2 + c_1)$ in absolute terms and hence it is reasonable to take it as positive. In this context, the earlier condition that $n_2 b_1 < 0$ may also be recalled. This would imply that changes in the rate of inflation tend to depress innovation through public responses in the bond, NIBM and IBM markets, along with the reserve requirement on NIBM. This result is in contrast with the general belief.

Among policy variables, the impact of *supply of reserves or monetary targeting* on innovation is $m_1 (b_2+c_1)$. All the multipliers are positive. However, the policy variable B_c has a negative sign. Thus, the total effect is negative implying a promotional effect on innovation. The extent of the effect is provided by the multipliers viz., the demand response of the public and banks for bonds due to a change in bond rate and the demand response of the public for IBM in the IBM market due to a change in the rate of interest on IBM. Also, restrictions (other than reserve requirements) imposed by the monetary authorities have the following influence:

$$-\beta m_1 (b_2 + c_1)$$

The expression is negative since all the elements are positive and the product is preceded by a negative sign. Reserve requirement on IBM, the public's positive demand response for IBM in IBM market due to a change in the rate of interest on IBM as also the public's and banks' positive demand response for bonds lead to the effect. The impact on innovation is positive.

In short, *change in interest rate spread, an improvement in technology, monetary restraints other than reserve requirements and supply of reserves tend to promote further innovation. Change in the rate of inflation appears to moderate the tendency.*

The effects of selected exogenous and policy variables on the endogenised variables are furnished in the following table.

Changes in interest rate spread: The effect on r^{IBM} is ambiguous. The reserve requirement on IBM is certainly positive resulting in a depressing effect. On the other hand, the reserve requirement on NIBM, the negative demand response for NIBM and bonds in NIBM and bond markets, respectively, due to a change in innovation and the negative demand response for NIBM effect of changes in the rates in NIBM market due to a change in the rate of interest on bonds will positively influence the rate. The precise effect then would depend upon the relative values of these two terms also the values of $n_3(b_2+c_1)$ and $n_2 b_3$.

The effect on r^B is an unambiguous negative. Of the multipliers, b_1, b_3, n_1 and n_3 are negative; g_1, β, α and k_4 are positive. But the interaction leaves the expression negative. The implication is that innovation raises the rates on bonds which is logical since bonds are competitive assets albeit imperfect to IBM.

As for the effects on NIBM, the expression is positive. Multipliers with negative signs such as n_1, n_2, b_1, b_3 are present but in totality the expression is an unambiguous positive. The implication is that, the interest rate spread would depress NIBM, which is in line with the past experience. On the other hand, interest rate spread promotes IBM. Some of the multipliers in the expression such as k_4 m_1, a and (b_2+c_1) are positive but the overall sign is negative. In other words, the interest rate spread increases IBM. This is also in line with the received postulate.

TABLE

Effects of Exogenous and Policy Variables on Endogenous Variables

Exogenous/ Policy Variable	*Effect on* IBM $\dot{r}$	B $\dot{r}$	NIB$\dot{M}$	IB$\dot{M}$
$\dot{a}$	$g_1\{\beta(b_2+c_1) - \alpha k_1\{n_3(b_2+c_1) +n_2b_3]\}$	$g_1[\beta b_1-\alpha[n_3b_1k_1 -b_3n_1]-k_4\beta b_3$	$g_1\{\beta[-n_1(b_2+c_1) +n_2b_1]\}+k_4[\beta \{-n_2(b_2+c_1) +b_3n_2\}]$	$g_1\{-\alpha[n_1(b_2+c_1) +n_2b_1]\}+k_4[m_1 [\alpha\{n_3(b_2+c_1)+ +b_3n_2\}]$
$\dot{T}$	0	$k_3\beta m_1b_3$	$k_3[\beta\{n_3(b_2+c_1) +n_2b_3\}]$	$-k_3[\alpha\{n_3(b_2+c_1) +n_2b_3\}]$
$\dot{B}_c$	0	k_1b_3	$-k_1[-n3(b_2+c_1) -n_2b_3]$	$-m_1(b_2+c_1)$

On the whole, the effects of interest rate spread on the endogenous variables are logically consistent. It raises the interest rates on bonds; promotes IBM; depresses NIBM; and the effect on the interest rate on IBM is uncertain.

Technology: The effects on the endogenous variables are unambiguously negative indicating a promotional overall effect. The effect on r^{IBM} is, however, nil. Technology influences r^B by a factor of reserve requirement on IBM, the public's demand for IBM in IBM market due to a change in r^{IBM} and the public's negative demand response for bonds in bond market due to innovation. These results conform to the generally accepted propositions.

Technology also increases both NIBM and IBM. The extent of the effect depends upon, in addition to those affecting r^{IBM}, the positive demand response of the public and banks for bonds due to a change in r^{B}, the negative demand response of the public for NIBM in NIBM market due to changes in bond rate and innovation as also the positive reserve requirement. These conform the common belief.

Supply of reserves: The impact of this policy parameter or monetary targeting, is an unambiguous increase in r^{B} and expansion in NIBM and IBM. This policy variable has no effect on r^{IBM}. If affects r^{B} by a factor of the positive banks' demand response for innovation due to a change in r^{IBM} and the negative demand response of the public for bonds due to a change in innovation. The impact on NIBM depends, besides these factors, on the public's and the bank's demand response for bonds in bond market due to a change in r^{B} and the public's demand response for bonds and NIBM due to changes in r^{IBM} in bond and NIBM markets, respectively. Pertinently, supply of reserves would increase IBM by a factor of the positive demand response of the public and banks for bonds in bond market due to a change in r^{B} and public's demand response for IBM in IBM market due to a change in r^{IBM}. If the coefficients are lower than unity, this would indicate that this impact would be larger than all others. A reasonable inference then is that during a period of financial innovation, targeting narrow money would result in a substantial increase in IBM. This result conforms the *a priori* proposition of earlier writers such as Tobin and Wenninger. The contribution lies in that this study explains the manner in which the result is obtained and the extent of the effect. In this sense, the present endeavour provides the missing link in the earlier works.

5. Summary and Conclusions

An attempt was made in this exploratory theoretical study to explain financial innovation in terms of selected, commonly accepted contributory factors. The analysis was within the general framework of portfolio balance approach and the method adopted to solve the system was comparative static analysis. The objective was to identify the parameters through which financial innovation is determined as also those through which its effects are transmitted. So far this area had not been sufficiently explored and hence the present study is expected to supplement the existing knowledge on the macro-economic aspects of financial innovation with special reference to its interrelationship with the financial sector. By presenting a futuristic view, this would also enable the policy makers to take necessary anticipatory actions.

The model, when articulated, yielded the following results:

When financial innovation is sought to be explained in terms of technology, interest rate spread, rate of inflation and restrictions imposed by the monetary authorities such as monetary targeting, it is found that technology and restrictions unambiguously tend to promote innovation and, most probably interest rate differential also intensified innovation. On the other hand, rate of inflation appears to have a depressing impact.

The effects of a change in the interest rate spread on r^{IBM}, is relatively uncertain. The effect on r^{B}, and IBM are promotional and, on NIBM, depressing. Technology has no effect on r^{IBM} and positive effect on r^{B}, NIBM and IBM. Supply of reserves also has the same effects as technology. For policy, this would imply that, during periods of financial innovation, adherence to targeting narrow money nor to any set of interest rates may not achieve desirable results.

A major limitation of the study may be noted. Financial innovation has far reaching implications for the solvency of the financial system. The generally held belief is that the system would become more fragile, necessitating extensive use of the lender of last resort function by the central bank. This aspect, though important, is not considered so as to retain the area of enquiry within manageable limits.

Being an exploratory attempt, the present work opens up new areas for investigation, of which two theoretical and one empirical possibilities may be indicated. First, financial innovation sector *per se* may be studied in greater detail. A separate model could be built for this sector. This would supplement the present study in that the specification of the first three equations in this study could be done with greater precision. It may be recalled that, in this paper, a passive supply function is assumed for innovation. The equation on innovation sector contains three exogenous variables (though one is policy and another is implicitly endogenised variable) with accompanying technical limitations. The second probable theoretical study would be to segregate the effects of interest-bearing-money from other interest-bearing-financial assets. In Indian context, this could be of greater use partly because more financial innovations are occuring in this area and partly because for the purpose of monetary policy, the Reserve Bank targets the broad money. At empirical level, the system could be estimated. Such attempt would assess the veracity of the model.

APPENDIX I

The Model

Innovation Sector

Demand for Innovation = $I^d_b = K[\overset{+}{IBM}, \overset{+}{RE}, \overset{+}{T}, (r^B \overset{+}{-} r^{IBM})]$ ...(1)

Supply of Innovation = $I^s_{INN} = I^d_b$ ...(2)

Equilibrium = $I^d_b = I^s_{INN} = I$ ...(3)

Let $(r^B - r^{IBM}) = a$.

Non-banking Sector

Demand for non-interest

bearing money (NIBM) = $NIBM^d_p = N(\overset{-}{r}^{IBM}, \overset{-}{r}^{B}, \overset{-}{I}, \overset{+}{W})$ ...(4)

Demand for Interest-

bearing money (IBM) = $IBM^d_p = M(\overset{+}{r}^{IBM}, \overset{+}{r}^{INF}, \overset{+}{I}, \overset{+}{W})$ ...(5)

Demand for Bonds (B) = $B^d_p = B(\overset{-}{r}^{IBM}, \overset{+}{r}^{B}, \overset{-}{I}, \overset{+}{W})$ ...(6)

Wealth constraint = $W = NIBM^d_p + IBM^d_p + B^d_p$ ...(7)

Banking Sector

Supply of non-interest

bearing money (NIBM) = $NIBM^s_b = NIBM^d_p = NIBM$ ...(8)

Supply of interest-

bearing money (IBM) = $IBM^s_b = G(\overset{+}{a}, \overset{+}{I})$ ...(9)

Demand for reserves = $R^d_b = \alpha NIBM = \beta IBM$ ...(10)

Demand for bonds = $B^d_b = C(\overset{+}{r}^{B})$ ...(11)

Budget constraint = $NIBM^s_b + IBM^s_b = R^d_b + B^d_b$ ...(12)

Central banking sector

Reserves supplied = $R^s_c = R^d_b = B_c$ ...(13)

Bond constraint = $B^d_p + B^d_b + B_c = B$ ...(14)

Equilibrium conditions

$K(.) - I^s_{INN} = I$ ...(15)

$N(.) = NIBM^s_b = NIBM$ ...(16)

$M(.) = G(.)$ ...(17)

$[B(.) + C(.)] = (B - B_c)$ ...(18)

$\alpha NIBMM + \beta IBM = B_c$ ...(19)

Totally differentiated with respect to time, denoting derivatives with, and rearranging the terms

$k_1 \dot{IBM} + k_2\dot{RE} + k_3\dot{T} + k_4\dot{a} - \dot{I} = 0$ ...(20)

$-n_1\dot{r}^{IBM} - n_2\dot{r}^{B} - n_3\dot{I} + n_4\dot{W} - \dot{NIBM} = 0$ ...(21)

$m_1\dot{r}^{IBM} + m_2\dot{r}^{INF} + m_3\dot{I} + m_4\dot{W} - g_1\dot{a} - g_2\dot{I} = 0$ ...(22)

$-b_1\dot{r}^{IBM} + b_2\dot{r}^{B} - b_3\dot{I} + b_4\dot{W} + c_1\dot{r}^{B} - (\dot{B} - \dot{B}_c) = 0$ ...(23)

$\alpha \dot{NIBM} + \beta \dot{IBM} - \dot{B}_c = 0$ ...(24)

Let $m_3\dot{I} = g_2\dot{I}$ and $\dot{W} = 0$

The System in Matrix

$$\begin{bmatrix} -1 & 0 & 0 & 0 & k_1 \\ -n_3 & -n_2 & -n_1 & -1 & 0 \\ 0 & 0 & m_1 & 0 & 0 \\ -b_3 & (b_2+c_1) & -b_1 & 0 & 0 \\ 0 & 0 & 0 & \alpha & \beta \end{bmatrix} \begin{bmatrix} \dot{I} \\ \dot{r}^{B} \\ \dot{r}^{IBM} \\ \dot{NIBM} \\ \dot{IBM} \end{bmatrix} = \begin{bmatrix} -k_2\dot{RE} - K_3\dot{T} - k_4\dot{a} \\ 0 \\ -m_2\dot{r}^{INF} + g_1\dot{a} \\ (\dot{B} - \dot{B}_c) \\ \dot{B}_c \end{bmatrix}$$

The determinant

$\Delta = -m_1 \{\beta(b_2+c_1) + \alpha k_1[n_3(b_2+c_1)+n_2b_3]\}$ ...(25)

Solution for $\dot{I}$

$\Delta\dot{I} = -(k_2\dot{RE} - k_3\dot{T} - k_4\dot{a})\ [\beta m_1 (b_2+c_1)] + k_1\ ((-m_2\dot{r}^{INF} + g_1\dot{a})$

$\{\alpha[n_1(b_2+c_1)-n_2b_1]\} + (\dot{B}-\dot{B}_c)\ [\alpha m_1 n_2] - \dot{B}_c[m_1(b_2+c_1)])$ ...(26)

Effects of $\dot{a}$ on

$\dot{r}^{IBM} = g_1\{\beta(b_2+c_1) - \alpha k_1\{n_3(b_2+c_1) + n_2b_3]\}$ ...(27)

$\dot{r}^{B} = g_1[\beta b_1 - \alpha[n_3b_1k_1 - b_3n_1] - k_4\beta b_3$ ...(28)

$\dot{NIBM} = g_1\{\beta[-n_1(b_2+c_1) + n_2b_1]\} + k_4[\beta\{-n_2(b_2+c_1) + b_3n_2\}]$ ...(29)

$\dot{IBM} = g_1\{-\alpha[n_1(b_2+c_1) + n_2b_1]\} + k_4(m_1[\alpha\{n_3(b_2+c_1)+b_3n_2\}])$ ...(30)

Effects of $\dot{T}$ on

$\dot{r}^{IBM} = 0$ ...(31)

$\dot{r}^{B} = k_3\ \beta m_1 b_3$ ...(32)

$\dot{NIBM} = k_3[\beta\{n_3(b_2+c_1) + n_2b_3\}]$ ...(33)

$\dot{IBM} = -k_3[\alpha\{n_3(b_2+c_1)+n_2b_3\}]$ ...(34)

Effects of $\dot{B}c$ on

$\dot{r}^{IBM} = 0$ ...(35)

$\dot{r}^{B} = k_1\ b_3$ ...(36)

$NIBM = -k_1[-n_3(b_2+c_1) - n_2b_3]$ ...(37)

$\dot{IBM} = -m_1(b_2+c_1)$ ...(38)

References

1. Aktar, M.A. (1983): *Financial Innovation and their implication for Monetary Policy: An International Perspective,* BIS Economic Papers, No.9, Basle
2. Atkinson, P., Blundell-Wignall, A., Rondoni, M. and Ziegelschmidt, H. (1984): The Efficiency of Monetary Targeting: The Stability of Demand for Money in Major OECD Countries, *OECD Economic Studies,* No.3.(Autumn)
3. Baba, Y., Hendry, D.F., and Starr, R.M. (1988): *U.S. Monetary Demand: 1960-1984, Discussion Papers in Economics, No. 27,* Nuffield College, Oxford
4. B.I.S. (1984): *Financial Innovation and Monetary Policy,* Basle
5. Boughton, J.M. (1981): Recent Instability in the Demand for Money: An International Perspective, *Southern Economic Journal,* Vol. 47. No.3. (January)
6. Broemeling, L.D. and Tsurumi, H. (1987): *Econometrics and Structural Change,* Marcel Dekker Inc., New York

7. Cagan, P. and Schwartch. A.J. (1975): Has the Growth of Money Substitutes Hindered Monetary Policy?, *Journal of Money, Banking and Credit,* Vol.7. No. 2 (May)

8. Chirinko, R.S. and Colloton Jr, J.E. (1984) : *Money Demand Instability and Financial Innovation, Working Paper No. 319,* Cornell University (July)

9. de Cecco, M. (ed) (1987): *Changing Money : Financial Innovation in Developed Countries,* Basil Blackwell, New York

10. Desai, M. and Low, W. (1987) : Measuring the Opportunity for Product Innovation, in *Changing Money : Financial Innovation in Developed Countries,* (Edited by Cecco, M.) Basil Blackwell, New York

11. Dufey, G. and Giddy, I.H. (1981): Innovation in the International Financial Markets, *Journal of International Business Studies* (Fall)

12. Hall, R.E. (1986) : Monetary Policy Under Financial Innovation and Deregulation in *Financial Innovation and Monetary Policy : Asia and the West,* (Edited by Suzuki, Y. and Yomo, H.) University of Tokyo Press, Tokyo

13. Hester, D.D. (1981) : Innovation and Monetary Control, *Brookings Papers on Economic Activity : 1*

14. Jonson, P.D. and Rankin, R.W. (1986): On Some Recent Developments in Monetary Economics, *The Economic Record* (September)

15. Judd, J. and Scadding, J. (1982): The Search for a Stable Money Demand Function: A Survey of Post-1973 Literature, *Journal of Economic Literature,* 20

16. Kabir, M. and Mangla, I. (1988): Effects of Financial Innovations on the Money Demand Function: A Canadian Evidence, *Applied Economics,* Vol. 20. No.9. (September)

17. Kane, E. (1984): Microeconomic and Macroeconomic Origins of Financial Innovation in *Financial Innovation,* Federal Reserve Bank of St. Louis, St. Louis

18. Milbourne, R. and Moore, H.A. (1986): Some Statistical Evidence on the Effects of Financial Innovation, *Review of Economics and Statistics* (August)

19. Miller, S.M. (1986): Financial Innovation, Depository-Institution Deregulation and the Demand for Money, *Journal of Macroeconomics* (Summer)

20. Offenbacker, E.K. (1982) : Effects of Substitution Among Assets and Technological Innovation on Money Demand, *Proceeding of the Business and Economic Section of the American Statistical Association*

21. Podolski, T.M. (1986) : *Financial Innovation and the Money Supply,* Basil Blackwell, Oxford.

22. Silber, W. (1975) : Toward a Theory of Financial Innovation in *Financial Innovation,* Silber, W.(ed), Lexington Books, Toronto

23. Simpson, T.D. and Porter, R.D. (1980) : Some Issues Involving the Definition and Interpretation of the Monetary Aggregates, *Federal Reserve Bank of Boston*

24. Suzuki, Y. and Yomo, H. (1986) : *Financial Innovation and Monetary Policy : Asia and the West,* University of Tokyo Press, Tokyo

25. Wenninger, J. (1984): Financial Innovation-A Complex Problem Even in a Simple Framework, *Federal Reserve Bank of New York Quarterly Economic Review* (Summer)

26. Witte, W.E. (1982): A Short-run Analysis of the Effects Of Portfolio Realignments Due to Money Market Innovations, *Journal of Economics and Business,* 34.

11

Credit Availability and Small Firms

A Probit Analysis of Panel Data

Renu Kohli

Introduction

ECONOMIC theory suggests that imperfect credit markets will imply differential access to external finance for different borrower groups. A growing body of literature on the subject also offers evidence that substantiates this viewpoint. In the presence of imperfect information, risk-averse lenders are likely to rely upon observable risk characteristics of potential borrowers to distinguish borrower types. When firm-specific features play a role in credit allocation by financial intermediaries, small firms are more likely to face restrictions in the availability of credit; more specifically, borrower characteristics such as size, age and the availability of collateral are likely to influence credit-allocation as lenders attempt to safeguard themselves against financing a risky borrower. It is the purpose of this paper to examine the role and importance of these risk characteristics in the allocation of credit by banks, using Indian panel data for econometric analysis.

This question has been addressed in the paper by exploiting variations in borrowing features of firms to study the influence of firm size, age and availability of collateral in explaining differences between borrower and non-borrower firms. A probit model fitted on the data confirms that these variables have a significant influence in determining the probability of a firm gaining access to bank finance in the Indian commercial bank credit market. A stratification along these lines between a relatively homogenous category of firms, i.e. small corporate firms, enables us to examine another associated issue, which is whether size within this group matters in access to bank credit. We find that indeed it does. The results have a number of interesting policy implications which are relevant in the Indian context where small firms have been targeted for the selective provision of bank credit.

The paper is organised into five sections: Section II evolves a theoretical framework to motivate the empirical work that follows later. Section III contains a discussion and preliminary examination of the data while Section IV deals with econometric testing of the hypothesis. Section V concludes.

SECTION II

THEORETICAL FRAMEWORK

The modern theory of financial intermediation draws upon Akerlof's idea that the *lemons'* problem may distort economic behaviour between contracting agents.[1] The recognition of informational asymmetries has been extended to the theory of financial markets, notably by Stiglitz and Weiss (1981), who demonstrate that the existence of asymmetric information in debt finance can lead to credit-rationing as an equilibrium outcome. Two broad categories of information problems can be identified in financial markets when either the principal or the agent has an informational advantage: the first is *adverse selection*, where asymmetric information exists between them prior to contracting, such as when particular characteristics of borrowers are unknown to lenders; and second is *moral hazard* - where asymmetries arise after contracting, that is, the possibility that borrowers may be induced to undertake riskier projects, thereby increasing the riskiness of lenders' portfolios.[2]

The problem of adverse selection in financial markets leads to the screening function of intermediaries by which they assess which borrowers and projects are likely to yield them the highest return and accordingly sort

The views expressed in the paper are the author's own and not of the institution to which she belongs. She is grateful to Robert K. Eastwood and Maxwell J. Fry for their comments on an earlier version of this paper. The responsibility for errors, if any, are with the author alone.

out good borrowers from the bad.[3] The objective of the lender here is to minimise adverse selection through a sorting process based upon certain observable characteristics of potential borrowers. He thus evaluates the risk associated with each borrower and decides whether to make a loan or not. In the post-loan stage, he tries to devise the contract in a way so as to ensure maximum recovery of the loan if the borrower defaults. The focus of this paper is on the importance of these risk features in determining the allocation of capital by financial intermediaries, viz. banks.

In the literature associated with Stiglitz and Weiss (1981), the interest rate plays a central role: it is not only the price at which loans are offered, but also a screening device for banks. Borrowers here are observationally indistinguishable *ex ante* and the key unobservable factor is the riskiness of their projects. A rise in the interest rate in this model lowers average borrower quality as the safer projects (borrowers) are the first to drop out; 'bad' borrowers (i.e. those with riskier projects) reveal themselves by remaining in the market.[4] This analysis is further extended by Stiglitz and Weiss to demonstrate a similar effect of collateral conditions.

However, when the interest rate is not determined by market forces, but regulated by monetary authorities, its importance and availability as a sorting device is limited, or even non-existent. Its role in credit-rationing in the Indian credit market until recently was not pertinent as there were interest-rate ceilings on both deposit and loan rates and banks were not free to vary the interest rate either to adjust the supply of funds or to cover the degree of risk that the borrower may pose.[5] We therefore, argue that in the absence of the interest rate as a tool to sort good borrowers from the bad, Indian commercial banks will select borrowers with the least probability of default. The decision to lend therefore, is expected to be based upon the availability of collateral as that is what all banks can expect to recover if the borrower defaults.

For example, borrower's wealth is indicated by the collateral available to secure the loan. From the bank's point of view, this is an observable characteristic of the borrower; risk-averse lenders would consider lending credit to a potential borrower depending on the amount they are able to recover if there is default. Collateral is both a signal to the bank as well as security offered on the loan that it makes. It provides information about the degree of risk associated with each loan. The importance of collateral, or net worth in the allocation of credit in the presence of asymmetric information in the capital market has also been shown by Calomiris and Hubbard (1993) - external finance as a consequence is differentially available to entrepreneurs according to their net worth positions.

Apart from collateral, there are some other features that may play a role in credit allocation by banks. Stiglitz and Weiss's (1981) model also considers the allocation of credit to observationally distinguishable borrower groups, to each of whom the bank is willing to make loans at different optimal interest rates. Given the cost of loanable funds, the banks will lend to those groups for whom the gross return from the loans is highest and the equilibrium interest rates will be such as to equalise the rate of return from loans to each group. This can result in exclusion of some groups from the market altogether since there may be no interest rate at which the bank can lend to them if the cost of funds to the bank is above a critical level.[6,7]

An important implication of the Stiglitz and Weiss analysis is the differential access of distinguishable borrower groups to external finance. In a Modigliani-Miller world, with its assumption of perfect capital markets, all borrowers are able to access external finance at equal terms, the only relevant factor being the cost of capital. This need not necessarily hold in the presence of imperfect information. *Ceteris paribus*, small or new borrowers - perceived as high-risk groups - will face tighter credit constraints than large borrowers or those with a proven performance record. Lenders, in any case, tend to be more knowledgeable about mature firms, since they have had time to assess their performance and record. These firms may also have the advantage of a long-term relationship with the lender, which reduces informational problems through established creditworthiness.[8]

The implication is that since "...the class of large firms consists primarily of mature firms..." and "...there may be an informational economy of scale in lending to large firms, to the extent that lenders may face fixed costs of gathering certain types of critical data about borrowers...financial constraints are likely to have more impact on the real decisions of individual borrowers and small firms than on large firms."[9] This hypothesis has been tested by Hoshi et al (1991) who classify Japanese firms according to the strength of their institutional relationships with banks and find that investment of firms without close banking ties was quite sensitive to liquidity, while it was not so for firms with close bank ties.[10]

These theoretical arguments suggest that size and age of the borrower are relevant factors in the allocation of credit. The importance of requirements of collateral, debt service and other 'non-price' covenants' can also be verified by a common observation of loan contracts. Initial empirical evidence on these dimensions is provided by Fazzari and Athey (1987) who analyse the hypothesis that internal finance and interest expenses, which are observable characteristics of a firm's creditworthiness, are likely to influence its access to credit and thus limit investment; their results were consistent with this hypothesis. Subsequently, Fazzari et al. (1988) find differences across borrowers (US firms) in the structure of loan contracts and in provisions regarding the use of internal finance.[11]

Another factor that might be significant in credit allocation in the Indian credit market is the presence of informal borrowings as a source of funds by the borrower. The hypothesis here is that lenders may view the level and past record of informal borrowings as an indicator of creditworthiness. The possibility of borrowings from informal sources influencing the lender's decision cannot be ruled out, given the findings of several research studies on the subject. For example, the Report of the Banking Commission (GOI, 1972) found in its survey of small-scale industrial units that non-institutional borrowings were high for those firms for which bank-borrowings were also high. It is not known with certainty which way the causality runs though, as Timberg et al (1980: pp. 293), in a survey of urban informal credit markets, find that being a bank borrower facilitates borrowings of informal credit. This fact is usually known to the urban informal intermediary and forms part of borrower screening.

Finally, we cannot ignore demand-related factors such as sales, which indicate the business conditions that a firm faces. We therefore consider sales as a variable representing demand for the firm's products. Given these arguments, we assume that when loans are made with imperfect information on the part of the lender, then the possibility of the borrower getting a bank loan is a function of a set of factors - collateral available to secure the loan, age and size of the firm, informal credit and sales. Thus 'b', defined as the state of success of an applicant firm or otherwise, is a function of

b=f (Size, Age, Collateral, Sales, Informal Credit) ...(1)

Having outlined the theoretical framework, in what follows, we discuss the specification, choice of variables and the estimation method in some detail.

The Specification: In general, at a theoretical level we have assumed success in obtaining a bank loan to be a function of borrower size, age, collateral, sales and informal credit. This sub-section discusses the variables chosen to represent these factors at an empirical level. There are many measures that can be regarded as indices for collateral. Collateral may take the form of current or fixed assets available for pledging, or variables like net worth and profits indicating the standing and debt-servicing capacity of the borrower. Fixed assets and inventories (current assets) are variables that can be used to capture the effects of collateral as they indicate what the bank would acquire if the borrower fails to repay the loan. Fixed assets specifically also act as a proxy variable for size of the firm that is an important factor in accessing external finance. Even though our focus here is exclusively on small firms, we have reason to believe that within this group too, size may matter. For it is likely that banks may prefer to finance the bigger of the small-scale firms to minimise risk.[12]

Net worth indicates the financial health of the borrower. A strong balance-sheet is a positive signal to the lender about the quality of the loan; firms with weak balance-sheets are therefore more likely to be rationed out.[13] Similarly, profits or cash flow[14] are considered by the lender as they contain information about the internal financial position of the firm. A sound internal financial position not only enhances a firm's ability to invest but is also an indicator of its ability to service debt. Internal finance is thus important for firms that need to seek external funding for their operations in markets subject to credit-rationing; it provides a signal because even though lenders may have difficulty predicting the cash flow generated by a new project, the loan will be secure if the firm's existing cash can service the new debt.

The information about age has been incorporated in the model through a binary variable. In doing so we have taken a threshold level of five years; it was not possible to define it with lesser number of years as there were very few firms in the sample that had one or two years of existence. Thus the dummy takes on the value of zero for firms that are less than five years old and one for firms that are more than five years old at a point in time, which has been chosen as 1970, being in the middle of the period. We expect that longer the number of years in existence of a firm, higher would be their probability of gaining access to bank credit for the first time.

The hypothesised model thus takes the following linear form

b=f(Inv/A, NW/A, Cf/A, Sales/A, IC/A, GFA, Age) ...(2)

where b is the probability of a firm being either a bank-borrower or a bank non-borrower. *Inv, NW, Cf, Sales* and *IC* are past year's values of inventories, net worth, cash flow, sales and informal credit, taken as ratios to total assets. All these variables have been scaled by total assets to remove the size effect that they would otherwise represent. GFA has been taken as past year's level of gross fixed assets of the firm to capture the effect of size. *Inv, NW, Cf, Sales, IC* and *GFA* are all assumed to have a positive impact on the lender's decision to make a loan.

Section III that follows describes the data set used, a preliminary examination of the data at the level of descriptive statistics presents some stylised facts that are taken up more formally in Section IV.

SECTION III

The Data and Some Preliminary Observations

The data that we use here is firm-level, balance-sheet data between 1965-78, obtained from the company finance studies of the Reserve Bank of India. The firms are small manufacturing firms engaged in different industrial activities. It was not possible to extend the period later than 1978 for reasons of data availability. It is presumed however, that the results of the study would not be out of context for the present environment as the financing behaviour of small firms would not have changed significantly in the 1980s and the early 1990s. For estimation of the specified model, our sample consists exclusively of small public limited firms engaged in different manufacturing activities.[15] A sub-set of these firms have become bank borrowers at different points in time during the span of the data-period, while another sub-set have been bank borrowers throughout. This distinction between the two sets of firms has been exploited in the research to study the variation in their risk characteristics in determining the firms' probability of being a successful loan applicant firm.

To begin with, we had 219 firms in all with a total of 2001 observations (N*T); the length of the panel varied considerably for each firm, as such, our panel is an unbalanced one. Table 1 below relates bank borrowings to some characteristics of a firm such as size of the firm, collateral as well as another source of external funds - informal credit, to look for evidence of association between the two sets of variables. Note that firms are classified into different ranges by percentage shares of bank finance in their total external borrowings, enabling us to examine any association between the credit worthiness of a firm for bank loans and other variables.[16]

TABLE 1

Bank Borrowings and Some Related Characteristics

Sl. No.	Bank borrowings (% share of total external borrowings)	Class distribution of firms (per cent)	Informal Credit (% share of total external borrowings)[a]	Median Fixed Assets (Levels)	Inventory/ Total Assets	Cash Flow/ total assets	Net worth/ total assets
1	2	3	4	5	6	7	8
1	0	19.9	10	1130	0.95	0.21	0.52
2	1-10	5.0	39	1676	0.54	0.03	0.29
3	11-20	6.3	54	1698	0.73	0.02	0.43
4	21-30	12.5	36	2499	0.76	0.02	0.13
5	31-40	14.4	29	2298	0.89	0.03	0.43
6	41-50	16.0	18	2058	0.93	0.06	0.70
7	51-60	11.1	16	2160	0.98	0.04	0.65
8	61-70	7.7	7	1980	1.00	0.13	0.84
9	71-80	3.7	4	1875	1.10	0.14	0.81
10	80-99	2.7	0	1471	1.53	0.25	1.10
11	100	0.6	0	1403	1.57	0.26	1.38

Note: a= Excludes bank borrowings; Median Values in Cols. 3, 4 & 5.

The dispersion of firms in this classification is fairly spread out: about 20 per cent of the firms have no access to bank credit and 0.6 per cent of them are totally financed by the banks. The rest of the firms are distributed in between, with a majority of them (16 per cent), falling in the 41-50 per cent borrowing category. Thus a majority of the firms are either zero bank-loan borrowers or borrow upto fifty per cent of their total external funds from the banks. 'Informal Credit'[17] has been taken as a share of total external borrowings with bank borrowings excluded to bring out the association if any, between the two variables. Column 4 of the table shows that as firms move up from no bank credit to obtaining upto 20 per cent of external funds from banks, they also have higher shares of informal credit. Thereafter, the extent of informal credit in total external funds declines for firms in the higher range of bank borrowings classification, indicating a substitution rather than complementary relationship between the two variables. This is presumably because bank credit is cheaper and having once gained access to it, the firm's chances of full financing from banks improve.[18]

The association between the size and the extent of bank borrowings in the firms' external financing structure plotted in figure 1 roughly follow an inverted U pattern - the smallest of firms either do not borrow from banks at all or are totally reliant on bank borrowings. This observation substantiates the hypothesis that smaller the firm, the more difficult it is to access bank finance, but once they do, their reliance on it is considerable.

FIGURE 1

SIZE OF THE FIRM AND BANK BORROWINGS

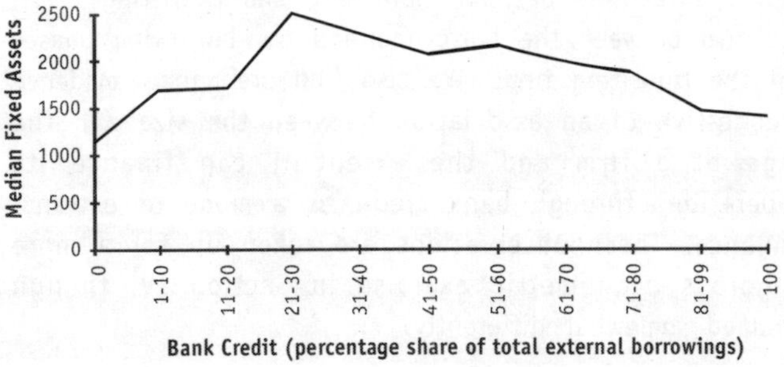

The collateral variables, viz. inventories, cash flow and net worth, suggest a positive association with the extent of bank borrowings, when firms are borrowing from the banks. As firms ascend on a higher class of bank credit in their external finance, collateral goes up too.[19] The positive association between bank credit and collateral might be suggestive of an important role of collateral in obtaining bank finance though it could also indicate an improved performance in the post-debt stage.

Finally we attempted to see what association, if any, existed between the extent that a firm borrowed from the banks, as a share of total external debt, and its age. In Table 2, firms are lumped into average categories according to their age in the middle of the period (1970). It can be seen that a weak inverted-U association exists between age of the firm and the extent that it will rely on bank finance, which is also clear from the plotted values of the two series (Figure 2). Firms which are more than 25 years old and those which are less than 5 years old seem to rely much less on bank borrowings, as a share of total external borrowings, than firms which are in the middle range of the age classification, that is, more than five years and less than 25 years old firms. The latter category of firms obtain about 75 per cent of their external finance from the banks. There is not much difference however between firms in the age-group of 20-25 years and 10-15 years, who seem to finance approximately 75 per cent of their external financing requirements from bank credit.

TABLE 2

Age of the Firm and Bank Finance

Sl.No.	*Age of firm in middle of the period - 1970*	*Bank Borrowings (% share of external borrowings)*
1	*2*	*3*
1	More than 30 years	45
2	25-30 years	42
3	20-25 years	76
4	15-20 years	74
5	10-15 years	77
6	5-10 years	55
7	Less than 5 years	65

This association, in a way supports the idea of a dynamic process, where firms of an intermediate age are most bank-dependent. Further, the cross-section evidence in regard to age as well as size of the firm is very similar, indicating that within the small firms' group too, firms of intermediate size and age have the highest shares of bank finance.

FIGURE 2

AGE OF THE FIRM AND BANK CREDIT

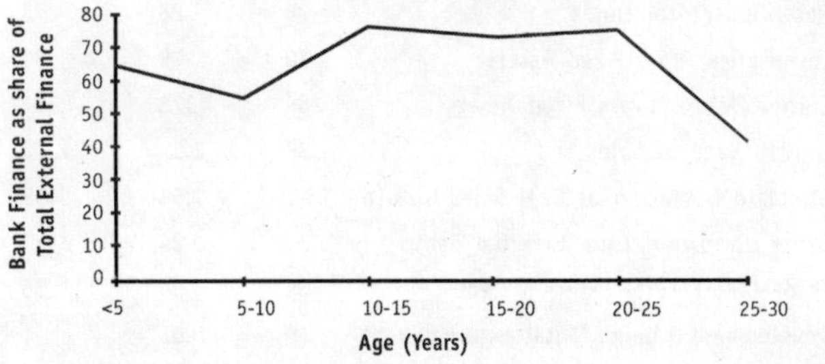

Transition and Borrower Firms: In the next stage, we retained only the borrower and the transition firms in order to look for differences between the two sample classes with respect to some performance and creditworthiness indicators.[20] For this purpose, we had 124 firms that were existing bank borrowers (with 1113 observations) and 47 firms (484 observations) that transited at various points into the bank credit market. Table 3 below presents some features of transiting firms in both phases - as outsiders when not borrowing from the banks and thereafter as bank borrowers after transition, comparing them at the same time with the existing bank borrower firms. Focusing on transition features first, we find that investment, as ratio to total assets (Row 1) shows a rise on transition to bank credit; this ratio is however half that of the existing bank borrower firms.[21] Profits (Row 4) decline on the transition of firms into the bank borrowing phase. When taken as a ratio to total funds, financing from internally generated funds falls steeply on transition to bank finance; moreover, the level of internal funds used for financing operations after transiting is broadly equal to that of the existing borrower firms. This suggests an association between the internal financial position of a firm and its access to bank credit. Collateral variables such as inventories do not show any significant change on transition though current assets as ratio to capital stock show a rise as the firms transit into the bank borrowing stage.

TABLE 3

Summary Features of Transition and Borrower Firms

	Transition firms (%)		
	Pre-Borrowing	*Post-Borrowing*	*Borrower Firms (%)*
1	*2*	*3*	*4*
Investment/Gross Fixed Assets	0.14	1	2
Sales/Gross Fixed Assets	350	260	259
Cash Flow/Gross Fixed Assets	7	5	8.4
Profits/Gross Fixed Assets	3	1.3	3
Retentions/Total Funds	75	28	32
Inventories/Gross Fixed Assets	70	79	80
Current Assets/Gross Fixed Assets	264	313	214
Growth Rate of Sales	1.89	2.32	2.52
Standard Deviation of Real Sales Growth	1.51	1.51	1.59
Other Borrowing/Total External Debt	30	24	7
Trade Credit/Total External Debt	68	34	36
Development finance/Total External Debt	0	0.03	2
Mean Fixed Assets (Rs. '000s)	1030	1250	2053
No. of Observations	182	302	1113

In the external financing structure of the three categories of firms, informal credit shows a slight decline from 30 to 24 per cent for firms transiting into the bank credit market. What is interesting here is the 30 per cent share of informal credit in the external debt of firms that are not borrowing at all and the modest 7 per cent associated with the existing borrower firms. This shows that existing borrower firms borrow much more from banks than do the transiting firms who are relatively new; this is also similar to the evidence from Table 1 above which revealed a higher proportion of financing through informal sources as firms started to borrow from banks. The financing pattern of the transition firms when not borrowing from banks indicates that approximately 72 per cent of these firms were borrowing from informal sources, while 28 per cent of the firms were totally internally financed - these firms did not borrow from any external source at all. After transition, all firms continued to borrow from this source as well as banks.

The preliminary examination of the data thus reveals some differences between borrowing and transiting firms, as also between the borrowing and non-borrowing phases of the transiting firms. We also find preliminary evidence suggestive of an association between the size and the age of a firm and the extent it can finance its operations through bank credit as a mode of external finance. These observations are taken up for a more rigorous econometric exercise in Section IV, though framed somewhat differently.

SECTION IV

ESTIMATION OF THE MODEL

In Section II, the specified model defines the dependent variable 'b' to be the state of being a bank borrower or not. The issue of a firm's probability of being a bank borrower can be appropriately addressed within the framework of an outcome model, which falls into the class of binary choice models.[22] The dependent variable here is a qualitative response or outcome, such as a 'yes' or 'no' decision, representing a choice, which can be given a meaningful value with a zero/one coding. Here 'no' is equated with zero and 'yes' is equated with one, both of which are qualitative choices. The outcome can be seen as the probability that a firm will be a borrower or not, under the assumption that this outcome is a function of a set of factors. The regression model is constructed so as to link the decision or outcome to a set of factors. In our model, the relevant question is to decide whether the borrower firm is a successful applicant (Y=1) or otherwise (Y=0). The probability of a firm being a bank borrower is explained by a set of factors, a vector x, so that

$$\text{Prob } (Y = 1) = F(\beta' x) \qquad \ldots(3)$$
$$(Y=0) = 1 - F(\beta' x)$$

where the set of factors b reflect the impact of changes in x on the probability. A model that will produce predictions consistent with the general framework of probability models, squeezing the estimated probabilities inside the 0-1 interval is the probit model.[23]

Before estimating the probit model, the data was prepared for estimation. The time structure of the panel was collapsed to obtain cross-section values of the variables by averaging the different series for each firm in the following manner. The data on borrower firms was averaged throughout the time-period in order to incorporate all information contained in the data over time about firms having attributes that made them borrowing firms; for the transition firms, only the data prior to transition has been averaged while only one observation for each firm has been included from the post-transition stage. The intuition behind this method has been to capture all the information available in the data about borrowing and non-borrowing firms.

The probit regression was run using the TSP computer program and the results are reported in Table 4 below. The final estimation of the model has been done in semi-logarithmic form as the original hypothesis in ratio form did not perform very well in terms of accepted norms of goodness of fit and some coefficients (notably cash flow) had the wrong sign.[24] Table 4 gives the estimated coefficients and the slopes (derivatives) of the variables.

TABLE 4

Probit estimation for differences in state of borrowing

Explanatory Variables (Dependent Variable=0/1)	*Coefficients*	*Slopes (Marginal Effects)*
1	2	3
Constant	0.055 (0.151)	-
Age	0.187 (1.64**)	0.051
Inventories/Assets	0.326 (2.50***)	0.088
Gross fixed Assets	0.002 (2.27***)	0.00006
Cash Flow/Assets	0.484 (2.54***)	0.131
Sales/Assets	0.017 (0.617)	0.014
Informal Credit/Assets	0.006 (0.220)	0.001
Net worth/Assets	0.363 (2.44***)	0.098

No. of Observations	141	Likelihood Ratio statistic	25.908***
Log Likelihood function (restricted)	-80.8489	Likelihood Ratio Index	0.160
Log Likelihood function (unrestricted)	-67.8946	% correct predictions	75

Note: Figures in parentheses are t-ratios; *, ** and *** indicate significance at 10, 5 and 1 per cent levels respectively. The critical values of the t-distribution for n>100 are 1.96 and 2.32 respectively.

We have reported two measures of goodness of fit. The first is the percentage of correct predictions made which is usually considered a naive predictor.[25] The percentage correct predictions made by the model are seventy five per cent which means that it predicts 105 of 141 observations correctly. The second measure reported is the likelihood ratio statistic calculated from the constrained and unconstrained log-likelihood functions. The likelihood ratio test is highly significant, based on a chi-squared value of 25.90, so the joint hypothesis that the coefficients on all the variables are zero is rejected. The likelihood ratio index, which is analogous to the R^2 in a conventional regression model, is only 0.160.

All the coefficients on the explanatory variables have signs in accordance with our *a priori* expectations. Further, all coefficients except sales/assets and informal credit/assets are statistically significant. The latter result suggests that demand factors, represented by sales/assets are not important in explaining differences across borrower/non-borrower states; further, the hypothesis that informal credit could be a favourable influence on the state of being a bank borrower is also rejected by the data.

The marginal effects of the explanatory variables are given by the partial derivatives of the expression for probability (y=1) with respect to each of the explanatory variables, which are not equal. It is held that the marginal effects generally produce a reasonable approximation to the change in the probability that Y equals one at a point such as the regressor means. The derivatives computed at the means of the explanatory variables are given in Column 3 of the table. The coefficients on the quantitative variables are interpreted as the impact on Y per unit change in x, but the coefficient on age cannot be interpreted as the percentage impact on Y of change in the dummy variable from zero to one status.

Using the normal t test for significance of the coefficients, we see that the t-ratios on all coefficients except that on informal credit and sales are significant. Size of the firm, as proxied by the coefficient on gross fixed assets, has a positive and significant impact on the probability of being a bank borrower indicating that even within the small firms' group, size exerts an important influence upon lender's decision to extend credit to first-time borrowers.[26] The magnitude of the size effect, given by the marginal effect of the coefficient on gross fixed assets is small though, probability values rise by 0.00006 in response to a unit change in the size of the firm.

This result confirms that size is an important constraint on the part of borrower firms, not only as opposed to large firms, but also within the more homogenous group of small firms.[27] It also compares well with the results of the Report of the Banking Commission, 1972, that found the average size of the units in the category of successful loan applicants to be above Rs. 3 lacs (in terms of assets) which was much larger than the mean size of the rejected loan applicants (approximately Rs. 1 lac) and those that did not approach the banks at all (Rs. 95,000). This information brings out the inclination of the commercial banks in financing the larger of the small-scale units.

The coefficients on net worth/assets, cash flow/assets, and inventories/assets, representing the effect of collateral, are highly significant at less than one per cent level. This suggests an extremely important influence of these variables, which essentially represent the effect of collateral on differences in borrower/non-borrower states of small firms. The magnitude of the impact, or the size of the coefficients on these variables is given in Col. 3 of the table - a unit change in net worth/assets, cash flow/assets and inventories/assets changes probabilities of bank borrower or non-borrower state by 0.098, 0.131 and 0.088 respectively. The large size of the coefficient on cash flow/assets indicates that this variable has a particularly important influence on probabilities.

In examining the effect of age upon the probability of a firm being a bank borrower or not, we are primarily examining the effect upon some kind of response - whether the firm will be one or not. This response, or a pattern of it, has been studied in the data with regard to some age threshold which in our specification is five years. The regression results suggest that this categorisation has a significant influence on the probability of a firm being a bank borrower; if a firm is less than five years old then its probability of being a borrower firm is lower than what it would be if it were older. This result has an important policy implication.

SECTION V

CONCLUSION

This paper has focused upon factors such as size, age and collateral as determinants of access to bank credit by small firms. The issue was addressed from a lender's perspective in order to underpin the relative importance of these factors in allocation of credit by Indian commercial banks. An important result of the study was that the collateral effect, represented by net worth, cash flow and inventories was significant in influencing outcomes of borrower/non-borrower states across small firms. Size and age of the firm were again very important though sales were insignificant. This analysis substantiates existing theoretical views on the subject and also adds to the growing body of empirical literature that confirms the significance of these factors in the presence of imperfect information.

The paper attempted to reason out why small firms may be rationed out of organised credit markets. The findings of the paper have a number of policy implications in the Indian context. For instance, the finding that size is a relevant factor in credit-allocation even amongst the small firms deserves attention from the view point of reassessing the merits of the present comprehensive eligibility criteria under the sector-specific lending programme by public sector banks. In relative terms (as for example, small versus large industries) differences in size weighs with risk-averse financial intermediaries which might be affecting credit availability to small borrowers.

Another policy implication emerging from this research relates to the finding of age as a significant determinant of credit allocation. There is a distinction that can be made between the first-time and the existing borrower firms in the light of this evidence. An example here is provided by the Japanese experience: the Japan Development Bank successfully used selective provision of credit to enable new firms to gain access to the bank credit market. Once these firms were well-established, selective funding was withdrawn and re-targeted towards newer firms, thus widening the size of the bank loan market by drawing new borrower firms into it.

The question however still remains whether it is possible to overcome these factors so that small and large firms and young and mature ones could access external finance on equal terms and conditions? Given the nature of finance and financial intermediation itself, clearly lenders safeguard themselves against possible default as far as possible. When size is linked to credit-rationing, it is difficult to arrive at a best policy option in this regard. A reasonable approach under the circumstances could be that such borrower-firms are supported through regulation of financial intermediaries if it were clear that the social gains to be had through special credit dispension arrangements outweighed losses due to regulation.[28]

Notes

1. Akerlof (1970) demonstrates how asymmetric information between buyers and sellers about product quality can cause inefficiencies in market functioning. These are usually referred to as 'principal-agent' problems in the literature.

2. Alternately, one can employ Arrow's (1985) terminology of 'hidden information' and 'hidden action' (Gravelle and Rees, 1992, 2nd ed.).

3. Similarly, the problem of moral hazard arises because some behaviour of the borrower cannot be covered by contract, as for example, the incentive to engage in a riskier project in post-contract stage.

4. The interest rate will not rise beyond a point to equilibriate the market as further increases may lower the lenders' expected return if the adverse selection effect exceeds the direct revenue effect. Excess demand persists in the market where some borrowers are denied credit when the loan demand and supply curves do not intersect.

5. Interest rates on loans have been de-regulated only recently. Throughout the span of our data period, i.e. 1965-78, a regulated interest structure prevailed.

6. Another reason could be that the excluded group has a broader range of available projects - they can invest in all the projects available to the group receiving loans, but can also invest in high-risk projects unavailable to it.

7. There is a welfare consequence of this result: Stiglitz-Weiss point out that this group might precisely be possessing projects, the returns to which could be higher than the group receiving loans. There is therefore no presumption that the market allocation is optimal. This allocative inefficiency in fact leads to an argument for intervention in favour of groups which are rationed out by banks.

8. The existence of a long-term relationship between banks and firms has received importance in another theoretical context by Mayer (1988) who attributes differences in financial systems across countries to the mechanism of commitment between entrepreneurs and financiers. The argument is that firms need stable funding for investing, while banks want to share in their future profits when they extend a long-term loan, thus incurring a risk. The nature of this long-term relationship determines the availability of long-term finance to firms, and this availability explains the differences between financial systems.

9. Gertler (1988: pp. 574).

10. Extending the same work, Hoshi et al (1993) analysed the same firms over a different period when they had loosened their bank ties and moved to the capital market. They found that investment of firms that chose this financing option was much more sensitive to liquidity than that of firms that continued to borrow from banks, confirming the significance of long-term bank-firm relationships.

11. They also find that stronger balance-sheets, that is, greater net worth relative to physical assets, stimulate investment for young and growing firms while such considerations are not important for mature firms active in centralised debt and equity markets. Investment spending and financing are substantially more volatile in the former group.

12. The Report of the Banking Commission (1972) and the Nayak Committee Report (1992) both show the relatively greater flow of credit towards the larger small-scale units.

13. This argument applies mainly to first-time applicants. Where existing borrowers are concerned, it may not be surprising to come across instances of banks lending to financially distressed firms, as they attempt to bail out such firms with a view to having a share in future profits.

14. Defined as retentions after taxation and dividends plus depreciation.

15. The industries (at the 3-digit level of classification) are Foodstuffs, Electrical Machinery, Miscellaneous Machinery, Engineering, Metal products, Medical/Pharmaceuticals, Chemical. Products, Miscellaneous Industries, Sugar and Cotton Textiles.

16. The dependent variable in the empirical model is taken to be the probability that the firm is a bank borrower. This somewhat restricts strict comparison of the observations made here with the empirical results.

17. In the data, the definition of this category of external funds is given under the heading 'non-institutional borrowings' as other borrowings; this variable represents borrowings from friends, relatives etc. Since in any case it is not a formal source of credit, our assumption about its informal nature is valid.

18. Elsewhere (Kohli, 1996) we have found evidence of a weak negative association between the two variables in the post-nationalisation period at the industry level. Both these evidence suggest that as the share of bank credit increases firms reduce their borrowings from the informal sources; the two variables are more often than not substitute modes of finance.

19. The table also reveals that firms that do not borrow from banks do not, by any means, have low levels of collateral. This implied two possibilities: one, that firms that start borrowing from the banks do not need to have a good internal liquidity position or a healthy balance-sheet or that they are distress borrowers; alternatively, that they are simply well-endowed initially and choose not to borrow from banks at all. A closer examination of the data revealed a sub-set of bank non-borrower firms that were well-endowed *ex ante*, this group probably chose not to borrow from banks.

20. All the collateral variables have been taken as ratios to total assets; retentions have also been taken as a ratio to total funds to bring out the extent of self-financing of firms. Finally, the financial variables have been taken as ratios to total external debt to see the extent of financing by each category.

21. This evidence is similar to that found in Kohli (1996) where new firms that entered the bank credit market showed a rise in their investment growth rates.

22. The general framework of these models is : Prob (event j occurs) = Prob (Y = j) = F [relevant effects: parameters].

23. This model specifies a continuous probability distribution like the normal distribution giving rise to Prob $(Y=1)=@\int \beta' x\ \phi(t)dt=\phi(\beta' x)$ where the function $\phi(.)$ is a commonly used notation for the standard normal distribution. The estimation of the probit model is based on maximum likelihood. See Greene (1993: pp. 635-37).

24. Several specifications were tried before choosing the preferred one; these results are available from the author on request. The data was also tested for heteroskedasticity - the likelihood ratio test statistic is 12. The critical χ^2 value at 5% level is 14.07, so the hypothesis that the disturbances in the specification are homoskedastic is accepted. The final estimation in semi-logarthimic form presumably removed whatever heteroskedasticity there was in the data.

25. The usual threshold value is 0.57, under the logic that we predict a 1 if the model says a 1 is more likely than a 0, though it is important not to place too much emphasis upon this measure of goodness of fit. As Greene (1993: pp. 652) points out, in the naive predictor Y=1 if P>0.5 and 0 otherwise (where P is the proportion of ones in the sample), this rule will always predict 100 per cent of the observations, which means that the naive model does not have zero fit.

26. It is also possible that small firms may find costs of borrowing prohibitive and therefore, choose not to borrow. Size of the firm, in that case is a demand rather than supply-side constraint.

27. It's extremely likely that the size effect would be larger were the sample to be more heterogeneous in nature. A Report of the Banking Commission, (GOI, 1972) survey revealed that the maximum percentages of units who approached commercial banks and were successful in obtaining credit from them were in the corporate sector (69 per cent on the average in the case of public and private limited companies, the rest either having been rejected by the bank or not having approached at all, but the figure fell to an average of 36 per cent when the organisational form was a partnership or proprietorship).

28. Research elsewhere by the author (Kohli, 1996) suggests that there can be gains from generation of productive activity in such sectors.

References

Akerlof, G.A. (1970), "The Market For Lemons: Quality Uncertainty and the Market Mechanism" *Quarterly Journal of Economics*, Vol. 84(3), August: 488-500.

Calomiris, C.W. and R.G. Hubbard (1993), "Firm Heterogeneity, Internal Finance, and Credit Rationing" *The Economic Journal*, Vol. 100, March: 90-104.

Eastwood, R.K. and R. Kohli (1996), "Directed credit and investment in small scale industry in India: evidence from firm-level data 1965-78" *University of Sussex Working Paper* (forthcoming).

Fazzari, S.M., and M.J. Athey (1987), "Asymmetric Information, Financing Constraints, and Investment," *Review of Economics and Statistics*, Vol.69(3), August: 481-487.

Fazzari, S.M., R.G. Hubbard, and B.C. Petersen (1988), "Financing Constraints and Corporate Investment," *Brookings Papers on Economic Activity*, No.1: 141-206.

Gertler, M. (1988), "Financial Structure and Aggregate Economic Activity: An Overview" *Journal of Money, Credit and Banking*, Vol. 20(3), August: 559-88.

Government of India (1972), *Report of the Banking Commission* (Chairman, R.G. Saraiya).

Gravelle, H. and R. Rees (1992), *Microeconomics*, 2nd ed., Longman, UK.

Greene, W.H. (1993), *Econometric Analysis*, 2nd ed., Prentice-Hall, Englewood Cliffs NJ.

Hoshi, T., A. Kashyap and D. Scharfstein (1991), "Corporate Structure, Liquidity and Investment: Evidence from Japanese Industrial Groups" *Quarterly Journal of Economic* Vol. 105(1), February: 33-60.

———. (1993), "Bank Monitoring and Investment: Evidence from the Changing Structure of Japanese Corporate Banking Relationships," in R. Glenn Hubbard (ed), *Asymmetric Information, Corporate Finance and Investment*. University of Chicago Press, Chicago Illinois: 105-126.

Kohli, R. (1996), *Replacing Market with Government: The Indian Experience in Credit Allocation*, (Unpublished D Phil thesis), University of Sussex, Brighton, UK.

Mayer, C. (1988), "New Issues in Corporate Finance" *European Economic Review*, Vol. 32: 1167-88.

Reserve Bank of India (1992), *Report of the Committee to Examine the Adequacy of Institutional Credit to the SSI Sector and Related Aspects*, (P.R. Nayak Committee Report), RPCD, RBI, Bombay.

Stiglitz, J.E. and A. Weiss (1981), "Credit Rationing in Markets with Imperfect Information" *American Economic Review*, Vol. 71(2), June: 393-410.

Timberg, T. and Aiyar (1980), "Informal Credit Markets in India," *Economic & Political Weekly* Vol. 15 (5 and 6), Annual No.: 279-302.

World Bank (1993), *The East Asian Miracle: Economic Growth and Public Policy*, World Bank, Washington, DC.

12

Dynamics of Interaction between Government Deficit and Domestic Debt in India

C Rangarajan • Anupam Basu • Narendra Jadhav

Introduction

SEVERAL significant changes have taken place in the dimension as well as the financing pattern of government deficits in India since the early 1980s. Government deficit as a ratio of GDP has increased markedly and the bulk of the deficit is being financed by government's domestic borrowings. Heavy reliance on domestic borrowings has naturally led to a sharp increase in domestic debt of the government held within as well as outside the Reserve Bank of India (RBI). As a result concerns are being voiced about the prudence of large government deficits and sustainability of the growing domestic debt of the government.

Implications of widening government deficits ... in the Indian context have not been adequately and rigorously investigated. Seshan (1987) was probably the first study to draw pointed attention to the possibility of domestic debt in India reaching unacceptably high level in the none too distant future. Subsequently the Report of the Comptroller General of India (1988) also warned against the alarming growth in domestic debt.

These prognoses are being seriously questioned on methodological grounds. For example Rakshit (1989) finds that "the major part of the on-going debate (on the problem of domestic debt is) somewhat heavy going" and that he "could not make much sense of the analytical constructs behind the discussions[1]". Rakshit's skepticism regarding the available predictions is understandable since they are based on simple trend analyses.

As a matter of fact this subject calls for a comprehensive and much deeper analysis. First of all the data-base has to be reconstructed. Available measures of government deficit and domestic debt are accounting measures rather than proper economic aggregates. These need to be replaced by analytical meaningful measures. Secondly in the Indian context widening government deficits have been financed primarily by resorting to net RBI credit to government and by accumulating domestic debt outside the RBI which have different macroeconomic implications and therefore should be treated separately. Finally the methodological basis of the currently available studies also needs to be made more rigorous. Rather than using the simple trend analysis a sound analytical framework must be developed so that the dynamic nexus between government deficits and different modes of financing them can be systematically explored. The present study makes an effort in these directions.

The main text of the study is organised as follows – Section I presents dimensions of fiscal imbalances in India. Alternate estimates of government deficit in India corresponding to different analytical measures suggested in the fiscal literature are presented. The issue of appropriate measurement of domestic debt in the Indian context is also discussed. Trends in these aggregates are examined with a view to providing an assessment of the emerging fiscal situation. Section II provides a brief survey of literature relating to perceived macroeconomic implications of domestic debt accumulation. Section III deals with the "debt-financing scenario"[2] wherein the focus is on the domestic debt held outside the RBI. An analytical framework is developed for projecting the debt-GDP ratio and is applied to the Indian data so as to make appropriate quantitative assessment. Section IV is then devoted to the "monetary financing scenario" wherein the focus is on the net RBI credit to

---

An earlier version of this paper was presented at International Seminar in Public Economics (ISPE) held in New Delhi during January 11-13, 1990, Authors are grateful to the participants especially Dr. Raja Chelliah, Prof. Willem Buiter, Prof Mihir Rakshit, Prof. A Bagchi, Prof. B.B. Bhattacharya, Prof. S.P. Gupta and Ms. Ritu Anand for their comments and to Shri R.K. Patnaik, Shri R.K. Das and Smt. Yasmin Adenwala for assistance.

government. This section presents a suitable analytical framework for capturing quantitative implications of resorting to the RBI financing of government deficits and applies it to the Indian data. Finally, Section V presents conclusions.

At the very outset some caveats and clarifications are in order. Among other things, it is assumed throughout the study that the authorities maintain a constant real GDP growth; also, while developing the debt-financing scenario, inflation rate is assumed to remain unchanged, as though, these were independent of fiscal policy actions. In reality, growing debt-GDP ratio and concomitant debt-service burden may stifle economic growth and aggravate inflation. These feedback effects are ignored in the debt-financing scenario and attention is focussed only on the first round effects in order to keep the analysis uncluttered. Actual outcomes, therefore, are likely to be worse than those predicted in that scenario. On the other hand, in the monetary-financing scenario feedback effects on inflation have been duly incorporated.

Throughout the study attention is focussed on the Central government. Accordingly measurement of government deficits and the different means of financing them as well as the measurement of domestic debt is with reference to the Central Government only.

I. DIMENSIONS OF FISCAL IMBALANCES IN INDIA

Fiscal imbalance in any economy is measured typically by the government deficit. Conceptually government deficit is simply the difference between aggregate disbursements and aggregate receipts. In practice however different measures of government deficit are possible depending upon what items are deemed to comprise aggregate disbursements and aggregate receipts.

(A) Government Deficits: Taxonomy of Concepts and Measures

... The World Development Report (1988) published by the World Bank has emphasised that the "correct" way to measure the government deficit depends on the purpose of analysis. In the present context, therefore, it is necessary to choose the concept which can fully capture the impact of fiscal operations on the indebtedness of the government.

... Exhibit 1 presents a fiscal balance sheet based on terminology used in the Indian budget documents.

EXHIBIT 1

Fiscal Balance Sheet

Receipts		*Disbursements*	
A. Revenue Receipts		A. Revenue Expenditure	
1 Tax Receipts	(R1)	1 Interest Expenditure	(E1)
2 Non-tax Receipts		2 Non-interest Expenditure	(E2)
a) Interest Earning	(R2)		
b) Non-interest Earnings	(R3)		
B. Financing Items		B. Capital Disbursements	
1 Grants	(R4)	1 Capital Expenditure	(E3)
2 Borrowings		2 Net Domestic Lendings	(E4)
i) Foreign Borrowings	(R5)		
ii) Domestic Borrowings			
a) Other than 91-day TBs'	(R6)		
b) 91-day TBs	(R7)		
iii) Change in Cash Balance	(R8)		
Aggregate Receipts (R) = (R1+R2+R3)+(R4)+(R5+R6+R7+R8)		Aggregate Disbursements (E) = (E1+E2+E3+E4)	

* Represent both internal debt liabilities like current market loans, special securities issued to the RBI, 182-day treasury bills as well as other liabilities like small savings, provident funds etc.

Like any other balance sheet, by definition, the fiscal balance sheet must always be in balance. In other words the total resource-gap arising out of government transactions i.e. the difference between aggregate disbursements (revenue expenditure, capital expenditure and net domestic lendings) and revenue receipts must necessarily be matched by the sum total of all financing items. The financing items include grants, foreign borrowings, domestic borrowings (net RBI credit to government, current market loans and other liabilities such as small savings, provident funds etc.) and change in cash balances.

1. Traditional Budget Deficit

In the Indian budgetary practice traditionally while the aggregate disbursements cover revenue expenditure, capital expenditure and net domestic lendings, receipts are *not* confined to revenue receipts alone. Grants, foreign borrowings and domestic borrowings (excluding 91-day treasury bills) are also included in aggregate receipts.

In terms of the fiscal balance sheet presented in Exhibit 1, thus, the traditional deficit.[3]

= (revenue expenditure + capital expenditure + net domestic lendings)

-(revenue receipts + grants + foreign borrowings + domestic borrowings excluding 91-day TBs).

= (E1 + E2 + E3 + E4) - [(R1 + R2 + R3) + (R4 + R5 + R6)]

= (R7 + R8)

In other words, the traditional budget deficit depicts only a part of the resource gap in current fiscal operations that is expected to be financed by (a) issuing 91-day treasury bills and (b) running down on the Government's cash balances with treasuries and the RBI.

This concept of government deficit is extremely narrow. Evidently current fiscal operations lead to increases in several other liabilities of the government. For example, besides foreign borrowings, there are internal debt liabilities like current market loans, special securities issued to the RBI and "other liabilities" such as small savings, provident funds etc. which in recent years have been absorbing significant fractions of resource gap in the government operations. In the budget documents, these are, however, treated in the same way as revenue receipts are and, hence, the traditional budget deficit does not reflect the full magnitude of resource gap and relevant financing or borrowing requirements.

2. Monetary Concept of Government Deficit

Limitations of the traditional budget deficit were also emphasised by the Chakravarty Committee Report (1985). The Report observed that the traditional measure of budget deficit does not reveal the full extent of the government's reliance on Reserve Bank credit. A part of new issues of government securities is taken up by the Reserve Bank when response from the public and financial institutions is inadequate. As a matter of fact, additions to Reserve Bank's holding of government securities contribute to an increase in the reserve money, much the same way as new issues of treasury bills taken over by the Reserve Bank. The exclusion of additions to Reserve Bank's holding of government securities in the traditional measures of budget deficit, therefore may severely understate the monetary impact of fiscal operations. Also, to the extent treasury bills are held outside the Reserve Bank, the traditional budget deficit may overstate the monetary impact. The Report, therefore, argued that "An unambiguous and economically meaningful measure of the monetary impact of fiscal operations is provided by the change in Reserve Bank credit to government"[4].

The monetary concept of government deficit is somewhat broader than the traditional measure but is suitable only for analysing the monetary impact of fiscal operations. In other words, the expanded coverage under the monetary concept of government deficit still falls considerably short of the coverage needed to capture the full impact of current fiscal stance on the overall indebtedness of the government.

3. Fiscal Deficit

As noted before the total resource gap or the overall financing requirement in governments fiscal operations is given by the excess of revenue expenditure, capital expenditure and net domestic lendings over revenue receipts. When grants are deducted from the overall financing requirement, the *residual* which represents the overall borrowing requirement may be called the gross fiscal deficit.

Thus, gross fiscal deficit

= (revenue expenditure + capital expenditure + net domestic lendings)

- (revenue receipts + grants)

which in terms of the fiscal balance sheet

= (R5 + R6 + R7 + R8)

Shortcomings of the traditional measure of budget deficit are evident when it is compared with the gross fiscal deficit. While the gross fiscal deficit captures the *entire* shortfall in government fiscal operations that is expected to be covered by undertaking *all* borrowing operations (domestic and foreign) and/or running down on its cash holdings, the traditional measure is confined besides the deplition of liquidity holdings only to one particular form of domestic borrowings i.e. 91-day treasury bills, thus ignoring other domestic borrowings such as current market loans, small savings, provident funds etc. as well as foreign borrowings.

In the context of developing countries, a sizeable part of central government borrowings is on-lent to other sectors - state and local governments, public sector enterprises and the like. Such lendings are undertaken not to acquire a profitable financial asset but are actuated by motives of public policy such as provision of resources where private capital may not be available. When net domestic lendings (lendings minus repayments) are deducted from the gross fiscal deficit the residual may be called the net fiscal deficit.

Thus, net fiscal deficit

= gross fiscal deficit - net domestic lendings

= (revenue expenditure + capital expenditure)

- (revenue receipts + grants)

When the Central Government is the focal point of analysis as is the case with the present study the net fiscal deficit is, perhaps, more meaningful than the gross fiscal deficit.[5]

4. *Primary Deficit*

One important limitation of the fiscal deficits is that they do not necessarily reflect the extent to which the *current* discretionary fiscal actions improve or worsen the government's net indebtedness. In particular interest payments in the current period are obligatory but reflect *past* budgets.

Corresponding to the two concepts of fiscal deficit, i.e., gross and net, two measures of primary deficits could be constructed. Thus gross primary deficit[6]

= (gross fiscal deficit) - (interest payments - interest earnings)

= (revenue expenditure + capital expenditure + net domestic lendings) - (revenue receipts + grants) - (interest payments - interest earnings)

= (non-interest revenue expenditure + capital expenditure + net domestic lendings) - (non-interest revenue receipts + grants) which in terms of the fiscal balance sheet

= (E2 + E3 + E4) - (R1 + R3 + R4)

And net primary deficit

= (non-interest revenue expenditure + capital expenditure) - (non-interest revenue receipts + grants)

= (E2 + E3) - (R1 + R3 + R4)

Primary deficit concepts, thus defined, indicate the precise extent to which current fiscal actions affect the indebtedness of the Central Government and is therefore most suitable for the present study. Accordingly the analytical framework developed in subsequent sections is based on these measures.

Before proceeding further, it may be worthwhile to apply the measures discussed above to derive different government deficit estimates for India to which we turn next.

(B) Government Deficit in India: Alternate Estimates

Data series relating to various components of the fiscal balance sheet covering the period 1970-71 through 1990-91 are presented in the Statistical Statements (1 to 10) in the data appendix [Editor's Note: not included here]. ... Evolution of the traditional deficit, gross primary deficit and gross fiscal deficit is also illustrated in Exhibits 2 and 3 [Editor's Note: not included here].

Table 1 presents a summary of different government deficit estimates in India for 1970-71 and for the 1980s. For any meaningful analysis, relevant absolute values must be normalised. Following the common practice, relevant magnitudes have also been expressed as ratios of GDP at current market prices. Based on Table 1 several observations can be made.

TABLE 1

Estimates of Government Deficit in India

(Rs. Crores)

Year	*Traditional Deficit*	*Monetary Deficit*	*Gross Fiscal Deficit*	*Net Fiscal Deficit*	*Gross Primary Deficit*	*Net Primary Deficit*
1970-71	285 (0.7)	223 (0.6)	1,409 (3.5)	779 (2.0)	1,378 (3.5)	748 (1.9)
1980-81	2,578 (2.1)	3,551 (2.9)	8,514 (7.0)	5,325 (4.4)	7,613 (6.2)	4,424 (3.6)
1981-82	1,392 (1.0)	3,207 (2.2)	8,348 (5.8)	4,273 (3.0)	7,303 (5.1)	3,228 (2.3)
1982-83	1,657 (1.0)	3,368 (2.1)	10,470 (6.6)	5,817 (3.7)	9,314 (5.9)	4,661 (2.9)
1983-84	1,417 (0.8)	3,949 (2.1)	13,252 (7.1)	8,392 (4.5)	11,052 (5.9)	6,192 (3.3)
1984-85	3,745 (1.8)	6,055 (2.9)	17,390 (8.4)	10,946 (5.3)	15,303 (7.4)	8,859 (4.3)
1985-86	4,937 (2.1)	6,190 (2.6)	21,368 (9.1)	13,054 (5.6)	18,451 (7.9)	10,137 (4.3)
1986-87	8,261 (3.2)	7,090 (2.7)	25,656 (9.9)	16,350 (6.3)	21,759 (8.4)	12,453 (4.8)
1987-88	6,308 (2.1)	6,559 (2.2)	27,044 (9.2)	18,717 (6.4)	21,563 (7.3)	13,236 (4.5)
1988-89	6,242 (1.8)	6,503 (1.9)	30,846 (8.8)	20,777 (6.0)	23,558 (6.8)	13,489 (3.9)
1989-90 (RE)	12,663	14,300	36,274	23,998	27,229	14,953

(Figures in brackets indicate deficit as ratio of GDP at factor cost current prices. 1989-90 GDP figure is CSO's quick estimate)

Editor's note: The source quoted here by the authors refers to data statements which have not been included in this volume.

1. Government deficit in India (as a ratio of GDP) has widened significantly during the 1980s. This fact is brought out uniformly by different measures of government deficit discussed above. As one would expect for each year the traditional budget deficit is generally the smallest whereas the gross fiscal deficit is the largest one in magnitude. The other measures lie in these two extrema.

2. The differences in the relative magnitudes of the traditional deficit and the gross fiscal deficit are quite striking. Indeed, the traditional deficit has generally been placed between one-fifth and one-third of the gross fiscal deficit for the relevant year. It is evident therefore that the traditional budget deficit has been grossly understating the overall borrowing need arising out of the fiscal operations of the Government throughout the 1980s consistently.

3. Ignoring year to year variations, it can be seen that the traditional deficit expanded from 0.7 per cent of GDP in 1970-71 to the average of 1.3 per cent in the first half of the 1980s and to the average of 2.3 per cent in the next four years. During the comparable period the gross primary deficit widened from 3.5 per cent to 6.1 per cent of GDP whereas the gross fiscal deficit worsened from 3.5 per cent to 9.3 per cent of GDP.

4. The gross fiscal deficit in India is large compared to other developing countries. According to the World Development Report (1988) weighted average of fiscal deficits in 1986 for low-income developing countries (excluding India and China) was placed at 5.1 per cent of GNP and for the middle-income developing countries it was estimated to be around 5.8 per cent of GNP as against the comparable figure of about 8.8 per cent in India (in fiscal year 1986-87).

5. The overall borrowing requirement (as reflected in the gross fiscal deficit) can be readily decomposed into analytically meaningful components. In particular, the difference between fiscal and primary deficits gives the interest burden, whereas, the difference between gross and net primary (or fiscal) deficits gives the extent of net domestic lendings. During the four year period ended 1988-89, the gross borrowing requirement (as a ratio of GDP) on an average was 5.8 points percentage higher than in 1970-71. Of this increase, less than one-third was due to the enhanced interest burden and rest due to the increase in *gross* primary deficit. Of the increase in gross primary deficit, little over one-third was on account of rise in net domestic lendings and the balance due to higher *net* primary deficit.

6. As far as the sources of financing are concerned, net RBI credit to government and domestic debt held outside the RBI together cover the bulk of the overall borrowing requirement. In fact, in 1970-71, less than 16 per cent of the overall borrowing need was financed by RBI credit which rose to about one-third on an average during the four year period ended 1988-89. Evidently, thus, proportionate reliance on the net RBI credit for financing government deficits appears to have remained high during the 1980's.

(C) Measurement of Domestic Debt

In the Indian budgetary practice, there are two sets of liabilities which comprise domestic debt.

(A) "Internal debt" which consists of current market loans, treasury bills, special securities issued to RBI and the like, and

(B) "Other liabilities" which consist of small savings, provident funds etc. These liabilities are also classified as the debt because they involve servicing through interest payments and redemption.

The question of the appropriate measure of domestic debt boils down basically to the selection of relevant constituents under these two broad categories of domestic debt.[7]

1. In the category of "internal debt" there is an item entitled, "special floating and other loans" which comprises non-negotiable, non-interest bearing securities issued to international financial institutions like World Bank, IMF etc. These are merely accounting contra entries and, therefore, ought to be excluded.

2. In the traditional method of compiling domestic debt statistics under the heading of the "other liabilities" an item entitled "reserve funds" which comprises depreciation and reserve funds of Railways. Posts and Department of Telecommunication etc. is included as an item of debt. These are, however, intra-governmental liabilities and should therefore be excluded.

3. In the same category, there is an item entitled "deposits" which is included as a debt item in the traditional method. This however, is a grey area. This particular item comprises dozens of diverse items such as civil deposits, judicial deposits, deposits of Local Funds etc. Ideally, one ought to distinguish between "intra governmental" and "non-intra governmental" deposits and only include the latter as a constituent of the domestic debt. Such information, however, is not

available. Prima facie however almost all of them appear to be "intra-governmental" in nature and may, therefore, be excluded.

With these adjustments, an analytical measure of the gross domestic debt (GDD) can be derived. The corresponding net concept i.e. net domestic debt (NDD) can then be obtained in a straightforward manner. For this purpose, debt obligations of others to the Central Government such as Central Governments loans to the States, Union Territories and public enterprises have to be netted out from the gross domestic debt.

Table 2 presents data on the gross and net domestic debt of the Central Government for some benchmark years using the revised method. As a memorandum item, gross domestic debt figures based on the traditional method are also presented. Here again for meaningful comparison absolute values have been normalised using GDP at current market prices. Based on Table 2 several observations can be made.

(i) The domestic debt in India has increased very rapidly in the present decade. Since 1980-81, the gross domestic debt (GDD) has increased nearly two and half times whereas the net domestic debt (NDD) has increased as much as four times. It may be also noted that for any given year, the method proposed here gives a smaller level of debt compared with the traditional method in view of the exclusions discussed above.

TABLE 2

Evolution of Gross and Net Domestic Debt in India

(Rs. Crores)

Year	Gross Domestic Debt (GDD)				Memo Item
	Net RBI Credit (Out standing) to the government	Domestic debt held outside RBI	Gross domestic debt (GDD)	Net Domestic Debt (NDD)	Gross Domestic Debt by the Traditional Method
(1)	(2)	(3)	(4)	(5)	(6)
1970-71	3,843	7,074	10,917	1,664	13,079
% of GDD	(35.2)	(64.8)	(100.0)		
% of GDP	(9.5)	(17.6)	(27.1)	(4.1)	(32.5)
1980-81	15,853	27,174	42,977	13,626	48,151
% of GDD	(36.9)	(63.1)	(100.0)		
% of GDP	(11.7)	(19.9)	(31.6)	(10.0)	(35.5)
1987-88	52,793	94,680	1,47,473	68,638	1,72,038
% of GDD	(35.8)	(64.2)	(100.0)		
% of GDP	(16.0)	(28.6)	(44.6)	(20.8)	(52.1)

(ii) The gross domestic debt to GDP ratio of 44.6 per cent for India in 1987-88 appears to be high in comparison with other developing countries. Indeed, it is broadly in line with the ratios recently estimated for selected industrial countries. Spaventa (1988), for example, has estimated that in 1986, four major industrial countries, viz Germany, France, U.K. and U.S.A. had their debt-GDP ratio in the range 36 per cent (for France) to 54 per cent (for U.K.).

(iii) As far as the distribution of gross domestic debt holdings is concerned about 36 per cent is held by the RBI, all others together accounting for the rest. Indeed, the RBI's share in the gross domestic debt (GDD) has remained remarkably stable around 36 per cent since 1970-71 which suggests that net RBI credit to government has grown in tandem with the enlargement of other domestic borrowings of the government.

(iv) The net outstanding RBI credit to government as a ratio of *net* domestic debt (NDD) in 1987-88 was placed at about 77 per cent. Even when the traditional measure of domestic debt is used, the ratio works out to be around 57 per cent. These relatively large holdings of net domestic debt by the RBI reflect the inadequate development of secondary markets for government securities in India.

II. MACROECONOMIC IMPLICATIONS OF DOMESTIC DEBT

A Review of Literature

"The debate shows little signs of being resolved, although essentially the same arguments have been advanced for two centuries. For those who remain skeptical about the progress of economic science, the debt theory controversy provides ample corroboration".

- James Buchanan (1968)

Macroeconomic implications of domestic debt has been a subject of a long standing controversy in the fiscal literature. In fact, two distinct phases in the controversy are clearly discernible with the changing perceptions regarding the domestic debt. In the old tradition, domestic debts were created during wars or national emergencies and retired during peacetime. Correspondingly, theoretical discussions of domestic debt revolved around a narrow set of well-defined propositions. In the recent past, however, there is a break in this tradition, in that, many industrial countries have experienced a substantial *peacetime* accumulation of domestic debt. Accordingly, with the growing realisation that domestic debt accumulation is not necessarily transitory, theoretical treatments are increasingly becoming wider in their range.

(a) Traditional Controversies

It may be worthwhile to review some propositions from the traditional debate which have contemporary relevance. At least two such propositions can be identified: one relates to the impact of domestic debt and the other one concerns its incidence.

1. Way back in 1817, Ricardo enunciated a theorem which has been called the "Ricardian Equivalence Theorem". The theorem put forth a proposition that domestic debt and a lump sum tax of equivalent amount exert identical effects on the individual.

This theorem, to an extent, has been misinterpreted, partly because the underlying assumptions are not given due consideration. The theorem was derived under the conditions of perfect certainty, perfect capital markets and on the assumption that individuals act 'as if' they will live forever. Within these restrictive premises, the contention of the theorem is simply that for the individual each of the two alternatives (i.e., current taxation and domestic debt issue) impose a burden that in a present value sense is substantially the same. As clarified by Buchanan, "This Ricardian equivalence does not suggest, however, that the objective pattern of cost payments remains the same over the two alternatives. Taxation and debt issue remain different, not similar, financing institutions . . . for the simple reason that taxes require a transfer of resource services from the individual to the fisc during the initial period, whereas debt issue postpones such transfer until later periods."[8]

Recently, Barro and other Rational Expectation theorists have revived the Ricardian Equivalence Theorem. Their contention is that domestic debt does not have any adverse wealth effect on private savings. According to this school, when government accumulates large domestic debt in relation to GDP. "rational" households anticipate higher taxes in the future. Because of this expectation, their "permanent" income is reduced. As a result, the impact of accumulated domestic debt falls on consumption rather than on savings, thereby avoiding the dampening effect on the saving rate.

2. Another widely discussed and recurring proposition in the traditional controversies is: "We owe it to ourselves". The essence of the argument here is that the interest payments arising out of domestic debt represent nothing more than transfers from taxpayers to bondholders and so long as both groups are members of the same polity, no macroeconomic cost is involved. On the basis of this proposition, domestic debt is often dismissed as of no macroeconomic consequence.

The fallacious nature of this proposition is increasingly being realised. As observed by Buchanan (1968): "This conception of national debt contains a fundamental flaw in its failure to translate opportunity cost or burden from aggregative components into something that is meaningful to individual members."[9] According to him "The core of the fallacy lies in equating of the community as a unit, in some aggregated national accounting sense with the individuals-in-the-community, in some political sense as participants direct or indirect in collective decision making."[10] Accordingly, the belief that domestic debt is of no macroeconomic consequence is, therefore, illusory.

In the more recent literature, emphasis has shifted from issues such as whether or not the domestic debt matters towards those relating to how and where does it matter. This change of the focus is symptomatic of the recognition that the domestic debt does really matter. In fact, the fiscal literature which was overwhelmingly oriented towards "micro" aspects is now increasingly dealing with "macro" aspects related mostly to the accumulation of domestic debt. Some of these emerging strands are reviewed next.

(b) Emerging Strands in Debt Literature

1. In the recent fiscal literature considerable research effort is directed towards the so called "sustainability" aspect of domestic debt. It must be emphasised, however, that the underlying notion actually relates to economic "stability" rather than "sustainability". This is evident from the fact that debt-financing of government deficits is deemed to be "sustainable" when the resultant debt-GDP ratio is converging to an asymptotic upper bound and is considered explosive otherwise.

It was Domar who pointed out, way back in 1944 that if the rate of interest is higher than the growth rate of the economy, any primary deficit will lead eventually to an explosive rise in the debt-GDP ratio. Recently, Bispham (1987) and Mason (1987) among others have derived similar results more rigorously, based on intertemporal budget constraint. Basic algebra has been worked out and relevant stability conditions have been derived. Furthermore, formulae have been developed for quantifying the asymptotic upper bound when the debt-GDP ratio is non-explosive. This kind of analytical framework is very useful for deriving rigorous projections of the debt-GDP ratio for any economy.

2. Another important strand in recent fiscal literature relates to the impact of domestic debt on private savings. Boskin (1987) and Bagella (1987) for example

provide detailed analysis of the issue in the context of the US economy, where the saving rate has declined substantially in the recent years.

Of the four avenues by which national fiscal policies can affect private savings (i.e. the structure of taxation, redistribution from rich to poor, differential public and private propensities to consume and the growth of domestic debt) Boskin finds that the growth of implicit and explicit domestic debt may be the major cause of the decline in the US saving rate.

3. Besides the potential impact of domestic debt on the overall saving rate, several specific issues are also being addressed. For example, in the Italian context, impact of domestic debt on financial markets has been explored by Pagano (1988), impact on households demand for monetary assets has been analysed by Bollino and Rossi (1988), and the relationship between debt accumulation and capital controls has been investigated by Giovannini (1988).

4. Implications of rising domestic debt for the conduct of macroeconomic policies has also been attempted. For example, issues relating to monetary and fiscal policy coordination with a high domestic debt have been discussed in the context of Italy by Tabellini (1988). Similarly, issues relevant for supply side policies in the context of the US economy have been examined by Paganetto (1987) and Eltis (1987).

(c) Relevance for Developing Countries

It is evident from the review of fiscal literature presented above that the available theoretical analyses as well as empirical applications have been designed specifically for dealing with debt accumulation in industrial economies. Corresponding literature in the context of developing countries is quite thin. In this regard some broad observations may be made:

1. In developing countries like India, the rational expectation theoretic view that domestic debt accumulation does not affect private savings appears to have little practical relevance. The reasons are not far to seek. As Rakshit has observed, (i) individual economic units can hardly be as rational or have as much information as is presumed ... (ii) the distribution of tax burden is not closely linked with the pattern of holding of public debt..."[11] It follows, therefore, that the possibility of households responding to debt accumulation by anticipating higher taxes in the future and consequently, with the reduced "permanent" income, lowering consumption rather than savings is farfetched in the context of developing economies.

2. In developing countries like India, the potential deleterious impact of "high" domestic debt is likely to emanate from inter-play of a different set of factors. High debt-GDP ratio implies large interest payments which in view of the constraints on raising direct taxes and the limited scope for lowering current outlays may cause current budgetary savings and budgetary capital outlays to be squeezed. On the other hand, recourse to indirect taxes, especially those levied on intermediate inputs would reduce the net value added in production to the extent that the incidence is not passed on to the consumers, thus adversely affecting productive efficiency. In sum, high debt-GDP ratio may result in lowering saving ratio and budgetary capital outlays and/or productive efficiency, thereby impeding economic growth.

In order to analyse diverse ramifications of the domestic debt accumulation, it is necessary as the first step to make rigorous forecasts of the debt-GDP ratio and the resultant interest burden which is taken up in the next section.

III. DEBT-FINANCING SCENARIO

(A) Analytical Framework

A convenient starting point for developing an analytical framework systematically linking government deficit with different modes of financing is provided by simple government budget constraint.

Eq (1) $[(G(t)-T(t)] + iB(t-1) + i^{*}\ RG(t-1) = [B(t)-B(t-1)] + [RG(t) - RG(t-1)]$

where

$G(t)$ = government expenditure in period t (non-interest revenue expenditure plus capital expenditure)

$T(t)$ = government revenue receipts in period t (non-interest revenue receipts plus grants)

$G(t)-T(t)$ = primary deficit in period t

$B(t)$, $B(t-1)$ = gross domestic debt of the government held outside the RBI ("debt-financing") for the periods t and t-1 respectively.

$RG(t)$, $RG(t-1)$ = net outstanding RBI credit to government in period t and t-1 respectively and

i = average interest rate on domestic debt outside the RBI i* = average interest rate on net outstanding RBI credit to government

The budget constraint given in Equation (1) simply states that the government deficit is wholly financed by "debt-financing" or by additional RBI credit to the government. In other words, it is a closed economy government budget constraint in which, additionally, government's lending to other sectors is implicitly assumed to be zero. These simplifying assumptions are relaxed below.

The following additional notations may be introduced here for expositional convenience:

Y(t), Y(t-1) = GDP at current market prices in period t and t-1 respectively

p = inflation rate

n = real GDP growth

k=(n+p) = growth rate of nominal GDP

As elaborated in Technical Appendix with simple manipulations of the budget constraint, it can be shown that:

$$\text{Eq.(2)}\quad \frac{B(t)}{Y(t)} = \left[\frac{G(t)-T(t)}{Y(t)}\right] - \left[\frac{RG(t)-RG(t-1)}{Y(t)}\right] + \left(\frac{i^*}{i+k}\right)\frac{RG(t-1)}{Y(t-1)} + \frac{1+i}{1+k}\left(\frac{B(t-1)}{Y(t-1)}\right)$$

The equation (2) is easy to interpret[12]. The first term on the right hand side of equation (2) suggests that the ratio of "debt financing" to GDP tends to rise when the "primary deficit" increases in relation to GDP. The second term on the right hand side of equation (2) indicates that the ratio of "debt financing" to GDP tends to fall when change in outstanding net RBI credit to government rises as a proportion of GDP. It is essential to note that the secular trend in the "debt-financing" to GDP ratio will be affected directly by these first two terms, namely, the primary deficit as a ratio of GDP and the recourse to RBI financing as a ratio of GDP. The last terms in equation (2) are also important even abstracting from the secular impact of the first two terms, it suggests the conditions under which the "debt-financing" to GDP ratio would grow at a declining rate and converge to a stationary value, as well as the condition under which the growth rate of the ratio would be rising continuously. For convergence, the so called stability condition is that the nominal rate of interest (i) must be less than the growth of nominal GDP (k), that is, $i<k$: this same condition can be stated alternatively as $(i-p)<n$, that is, the real growth rate of GDP should be higher than the real interest rate. If this condition does not hold, equation (2) implies an explosive (or unbounded) growth of the ratio, even if the underlying trend components do not lead to a secular rise.

The exposition so far has not explicitly dealt with official foreign borrowing and *net* domestic lendings and effects of these operations on the government's budget constraint. To deal with these aspects as well as maintain the focus on the problems of domestic debt accumulation, a few simplifying assumptions are made as follows:

(i) The official inflow of foreign resources denoted as [NF(t)-NF(t-1)] is exogenously determined and interest payments constitute a fraction (w) of the outstanding one-year lagged stock of official foreign debt [that is equal to w. NF(t-1)]

(ii) The level of net domestic lendings denoted by (L(t)-L(t-1)) is a proportion (h) of the change in the domestic debt held outside the RBI, (B(t)-B(t-1)), i.e. a fixed proportion of domestic borrowings excluding RBI credit is always on-lent to the non-Central government sectors and

(iii) The interest rate on the outstanding stock of loans advanced by the government is fixed at (e)

With the above assumptions, the government budget constraint (eq. 1) can be reformulated as follows:

Eq. (3) [G(t)-T(t)] + [iB(t-1) + i* RG(t-1) + w. NF(t-1)] + [L(t)-L(t-1) - eL(t-1)] = [B(t)-B(t-1)] + [RG(t)-RG(t-1)] + NF(t)-NF(t-1)

The above equation states that the net primary deficit interest payments on domestic and foreign debt and the government's net lending in excess of interest earnings on its previous lendings must be financed by enlarging the domestic "debt financing" or by additional money creation or else by resorting to foreign borrowings.

Using the notations in assumptions (i) above, the net external resource inflow is defined as follows:

Eq. (4) F(t) = NF(t) - NF(t-1) - w. NF(t-1)

using assumptions (ii) and (iii) it is seen that

Eq. (5) L(t) - L(t-1) = h [B(t)-B(t-1)]

Eq. (6) L(t-1) = h B(t-1)

Substituting eq. (4), (5) and (6) in eq. (3) and on rearrangement of terms, we get

$$\text{Eq. (7)}\quad \frac{B(t)}{Y(t)}=\left(\frac{1}{1-h}\right)\left[\frac{G(t)}{Y(t)}-\frac{T(t)}{Y(t)}-\frac{[RG(t)-RG(t-1)]}{Y(t)}-\frac{F(t)}{Y(t)}\right]$$

$$+\left[\frac{i^*}{(1-h)(1+k)}\right]\frac{RG(t-1)}{Y(t-1)}+\left[\frac{1+\left[\frac{i-eh}{i-h}\right]}{1+k}\right]\frac{B(t-1)}{Y(t-1)}$$

The eq. (7) has the same first order difference equation formulation as the earlier eq. (2)[13]. Moreover, if one assumes h=0, the coefficient of the lagged variable $\frac{B(t-1)}{Y(t-1)}$ in eq. (7)

becomes $\frac{1+i}{1+k}$ which is the same as the coefficient of $\frac{B(t-1)}{Y(t-1)}$ in eq. (2).

The condition for stability of the domestic debt ratio in equation (7) is $\left[1+\frac{i-eh}{(1-h)}\right]<1+k$

which after some manipulation yields the stability condition [he + (1-h) k]>i

The weighted average of the interest rate on domestic lending (e) and the nominal GDP growth rate (k), using the ratio (h) of net lending to the net domestic borrowing as the weight must exceed the interest rate on the government's domestic borrowing. If h=0 one has the already familiar condition k>i. Moreover, the condition has the interpretation that stability of the "debt financing" to GDP ratio can be achieved by appropriately raising the interest rate on domestic lending (e) and/or the nominal GDP growth rate (k) above the nominal cost of "debt financing" (i). It may be noted that artificially lowering the borrowing rate (i) is not a solution to the debt problem because at the limit it implies an unviable financial system. Depressing i would imply raising funds from captive financial institutions at a lower cost and an increasingly lower volume of directly mobilised household savings. In an inflationary environment, the captive financial institutions could not continue to operate profitably with lower interest earnings on government lending without raising their lending rates (or other service charges) to the non-government sectors and/or lowering deposit rates: one would then be either "crowding out" other borrowers or pushing savings out of the financial sectors into inflation hedges.

The equation (7) captures the dynamic relationship between primary deficit (as a ratio of GDP) and different modes of financing it. Accordingly, it forms the basis for projections under the assumed conditions.

The debt-financing scenario developed below addresses the following question: what would be the future time profile of "debt-financing" to GDP ratio if the government deficit is allowed to evolve passively and domestic borrowings (other than those from the RBI) are used for financing it while the other modes of financing such as net RBI credit to government and external financing are maintained at their current ratios of GDP.

In order to conduct this thought experiment the basic dynamic relationship (eq. 7) needs to be suitably modified. As detailed in the Technical Appendix the following form could be derived.

$$\text{Eq. (8)}\quad \frac{B(t)}{Y(t)}=\frac{1}{1-h}\left[\frac{G(t)}{Y(t)}-\frac{T(t)}{Y(t)}-\frac{F(t)}{Y(t)}\right]$$

$$-\left[\frac{k-i^*}{(1-h)(1+k)}\right]\frac{RG(t-1)}{Y(t-1)}+\left[\frac{1+\frac{i-eh}{i-h}}{1+k}\right]\frac{B(t-1)}{Y(t-1)}$$

which forms the basis for the "debt-financing" scenario.

(B) Projections for Debt-GDP Ratio

In order to project the debt-GDP ratio under the "debt-financing scenario", eq. (8) was used with the following numerical values assigned to selected parameters.

n = real GDP growth = 5 per cent

p = inflation rate = 7 per cent

i = nominal interest rate on domestic debt held outside the RBI = 10.2 per cent

i* = nominal interest rate on domestic debt held by the RBI = 5.3 per cent

e = nominal interest rate on government's domestic lending = 7.4 per cent[14]

h = fraction of domestic borrowings on-lent by the government = 0.4

The ratio of net outstanding RBI credit to government to GDP and the ratio of net foreign inflow of official resources were held constant at their 1987-88 levels of 16 per cent and 0.87 per cent respectively. On the other hand, expenditure — GDP ratio and receipts — GDP ratio were allowed to evolve endogenously.

Time profile for government expenditure[15] and receipts[15] and hence the net primary deficit (all expressed as ratio to GDP) were derived using

Eq. (9) $$\frac{G(t)}{Y(t)}=\left[\frac{1+(u1)(n)+(v1)(p)}{1+n+p}\right]\frac{G(t-1)}{Y(t-1)}$$ and

Eq. (10) $$\frac{T(t)}{Y(t)}=\left[\frac{1+(u2)(n)+(v2)(p)}{1+n+p}\right]\frac{T(t-1)}{Y(t-1)}$$

where n = assumed real GDP growth

p = assumed inflation rate

u1 = real income elasticity of nominal expenditure

u2 = real income elasticity of nominal receipts

v1 = price elasticity of nominal expenditure

v2 = price elasticity of nominal receipts

Regression Equations

log (G) = -8.2 + 2.395 log (Y/P) + 0.647 log (P)
(4.57) (6.58) (3.47)

$\bar{R}^2$ = 0.994 DW = 2.21 SEE = 0.0259
(sample period 1970-71 to 1987-88)

log (T) = -14.76 + 2.0730 log (Y/P) + 0.5623 log (P)
(3.04) (5.01) (2.60)

$\bar{R}^2$ = 0.99 DW = 1.60 SEE = 0.0473
(Sample period 1975-76 to 1986-87)

(Figures in brackets indicate respective 't' values)

These regressions which are satisfactory in their statistical properties indicate that the real income elasticity of nominal government expenditure (u1) (i.e., 2.395) exceeds the corresponding elasticity of nominal revenue receipts (U2) (i.e. 2.073). Similarly, price elasticity of nominal expenditure (i.e. v1 = 0.647) exceeds the corresponding elasticity of nominal receipts (i.e. v2=0.562). These phenomena widely observed in developing countries confirm the hypothesis that the primary deficit tends to widen with a passive fiscal policy stance.

Having obtained the elasticity estimates equations (9) and (10) were used for deriving projections of the net primary deficit as a ratio of GDP under the assumed real GDP growth and inflation rate. Given the time profile for the net primary deficit (as a ratio of GDP) and the assumptions regarding the other parameters dynamic evolution of the debt-GDP ratio was derived as detailed in Table 3.

TABLE 3

Projections of Debt-GDP Ratio (1988-89 to 1999-2000)

Year	*Ratios to Y(t)*					
	G(t)	*T(t)*	*F(t)*	*RG(t)*	*B(t)/Y(t)*	*Overall Debt GDP Ratio*
	(1)	*(2)*	*(3)*	*(4)*	*(5)*	*(6)*
1987-88*	17.10	12.60	0.87	16.00	28.60	44.60
1988-89	17.77	12.86	0.87	16.00	33.24	49.24
1989-90	18.47	13.12	0.87	16.00	38.53	54.53
1990-91	19.20	13.39	0.87	16.00	44.50	60.50
1991-92	19.96	13.66	0.87	16.00	51.18	67.18
1992-93	20.75	13.94	0.87	16.00	58.59	74.59
1993-94	21.57	14.22	0.87	16.00	66.78	82.78
1994-95	22.42	14.51	0.87	16.00	75.76	91.76
1995-96	23.30	14.81	0.87	16.00	85.55	101.55
1996-97	24.22	15.11	0.87	16.00	96.20	112.20
1997-98	25.17	15.42	0.87	16.00	107.74	123.74
1998-99	26.16	15.73	0.87	16.00	120.21	136.21
1999-2000	27.19	16.05	0.87	16.00	133.65	149.65

* Actuals

Notes: 1 Col.(1) is based on the formula $\left[\frac{1+(u_1)(n)+(v_1)(p)}{1+n+p}\right]\frac{G(t-1)}{Y(t-1)}$

2 Col.(2) is based on the formula $\left[\frac{1+(u_2)(n)+(v_2)(p)}{1+n+p}\right]\frac{T(t-1)}{Y(t-1)}$

3 Col.(5) = 1.6666 [Col.(1)-Col.(2)-Col.(3)]

$$-0.0997\left[\frac{(RG(t)}{Y(t)}\right]+0.9827\left[\frac{B(t)}{Y(t)}\right]_{-1}$$

4 Col.(6) = Col.(4) + Col.(5)

As indicated in Table 3 a passive fiscal stance is likely to result in enlargement of the net primary deficit to GDP ratio from 4.5 per cent in 1987-88 to as much as 11.1 per cent by the year 1999-2000. The corresponding gross primary deficit could easily be of the order of 19-20 per cent of GDP. Contemporaneously, the "debt-financing" to GDP ratio would increase very rapidly: from 28.6 per cent in 1987-88 to as much as 133.7 per cent and the overall debt-GDP ratio would shoot up from 44.6 per cent in 1987-88 and crossing the 100 per cent mark in 1995-96 would reach nearly 150 per cent by the turn of the century. Such a rapid escalation of debt-GDP ratio naturally raises the question of its sustainability.

(C) Sustainability of Domestic Debt

In the recent fiscal literature, domestic debt accumulation is regarded sustainable as long as the resultant debt-GDP ratio is converging to an asymptotic upper bound and is deemed to be explosive otherwise. This connotation of sustainability appears to be less meaningful for developing countries. In the context of developing countries sustainability ought to be seen in terms of sustaining rapid economic growth. In this regard the pre-emptive impact of mounting interest burden emanating from rising debt-GDP ratio on the revenue receipts assumes crucial importance.

Gross interest burden of domestic debt can simply be defined as the ratio of gross domestic interest payments (GDIP) to governments revenue receipts (T). The level of gross domestic interest payments (GDIP), in turn can be derived as the product of interest rate and the stock of *overall* outstanding domestic debt at the end of the previous year. Thus

Gross Interest Burden (GIB)

$$= \frac{\text{Gross Domestic Interest Payments (GDIP)}}{\text{government receipts (T)}}$$

which can be written as

$$GIB = \frac{r\,D(t-1)}{T(t)}$$

$$= \frac{r\,D(t-1)}{(1+u_2 n+v_2 p)\,T(t-1)}$$

where

D = overall domestic debt

r = average interest rate on overall domestic debt

u_2 = real income elasticity of nominal receipts

v_2 = price elasticity of nominal receipts

$$= \frac{r}{1+u_2 n+v_2 p}\left[\frac{D(t-1)}{T(t-1)}\right] \text{ Thus,}$$

$$\text{Eq. (11) } GIB = \left[\frac{r}{1+u_2 n+v_2 p}\right]\left[\frac{D(t-1)/Y(t-1)}{T(t-1)/Y(t-1)}\right]$$

Since the projections for debt-GDP ratio and receipts-GDP ratio have already been derived, eq. (11) can be readily used for obtaining corresponding projections of the gross interest burden (GIB). It may be noted, however, that for policy purposes what is more relevant is the net interest burden (NIB) rather than the gross burden, i.e., domestic interest receipts arising from the loans and advances of the government should be netted out. A simple way to derive the net interest burden (NIB) is to assume that the ratio of net to gross domestic interest payments remains unchanged at the base year level throughout the projection period. Relevant projections of gross and net interest burden for the period 1988-89 through 1999-2000 are presented in Table 4.

TABLE 4

Interest Burden of Domestic Debt

(Gross & Net)

Year	*Debt-GDP Ratio*	*T(t)/Y(t)*	*Gross Interest Burden GDIP/T*	*Net Interest Burden NDIP/T*
	1	2	3	4
1987-88*	44.60	12.60	26.16	11.43
1988-89	49.24	12.86	28.30	12.36
1989-90	54.53	13.12	30.71	13.42
1990-91	60.50	13.39	33.39	14.59
1991-92	67.18	13.66	36.34	15.88
1992-93	74.59	13.94	39.54	17.28
1993-94	82.78	14.22	43.02	18.80
1994-95	91.76	14.51	46.73	20.42
1995-96	101.55	14.81	50.67	22.14
1996-97	112.20	15.11	54.87	23.97
1997-98	123.74	15.42	59.30	25.91
1998-99	136.21	15.73	63.99	27.96
1999-2000	149.65	16.05	68.90	30.10

* Actuals

Notes: Col (1) = Col (6) of Table 3

Col (2) = Col (2) of Table 3

$\text{Col (3)} = 0.0739\left[\frac{\text{Col (1)}}{\text{Col (2)}}\right]\times 100$

Col (4) = 0.4369 [Col (3)]

It is evident from Table 4 that with the rapid increase in the debt-GDP ratio corresponding net interest burden (NIB) is also likely to go up substantially from about 11.4 per cent of receipts in 1987-88 to as much as 30.1 per cent of projected receipts by the turn of the century.

The enormity of this potential situation can be appreciated with a historical perspective. The net interest burden was actually negative until 1973-74. It was as low as 1 per cent of receipts in 1974-75 and increased to about 5.1 per cent of receipts in 1980-81. With the acceleration of domestic debt accumulation during the 1980's, it rose to about 12 per cent of receipts in 1987-88. And now, if the government receipts and expenditure are allowed to evolve passively while relying on 'debt financing' of the resultant deficits, the net interest burden would shoot up to as much as 30 per cent of projected receipts by the year 1999-2000.

Implications of such a large increase in the net interest burden are fairly obvious. In a developing economy like India raising direct taxes is subject to serious socio-economic constraints. Alternatively, recourse to indirect taxes, especially those levied on intermediate inputs is likely to hurt productive efficiency by reducing the net value added in production (to the extent that the incidence is not passed on to the consumers). On the other hand, on the expenditure side, current outlays tend to be sticky downwards. In such a fiscal environment, higher net interest burden may invariably lead to a squeeze on budgetary capital outlays thereby stifling economic growth.

IV. MONETARY FINANCING SCENARIO

Section III has demonstrated what lies at the end of the rainbow, if the burgeoning government deficit is not arrested in time and "debt-financing" is used for financing the emerging deficit passively while maintaining the other modes of financing at their current ratios to GDP. Given the potential adverse implications of domestic debt accumulation, policy makers may be inclined to rely on some other way of financing the deficit rather than checking its expansion. In the Indian context, resorting to net RBI credit on a larger scale may, especially, be tempting.

This section accordingly develops a monetary financing scenario. The thought experiment here addresses the following question. If government deficit is allowed to evolve passively and is financed by resorting to additional net RBI credit while maintaining the domestic "debt-financing" and foreign financing at their current ratios to GDP. What would be macroeconomic consequences for the economy?

(A) Analytical Framework

As detailed in the Technical Appendix, the dynamic relationship between debt-GDP ratio and different modes of financing government deficit (i.e. eq. 7) can be suitably modified for deriving the monetary financing scenario. The relevant difference equation takes the form

Eq. (12)
$$\left[\frac{RG(t)-RG(t-1)}{Y(t)}\right] = \left[\frac{G(t)}{Y(t)}-\frac{T(t)}{Y(t)}-\frac{F(t)}{Y(t)}\right]+\left(\frac{i^*}{i+k}\right)\frac{RG(t-1)}{Y(t-1)} + \left[\frac{h(k-e)-(k-i)}{1+k}\right]\frac{B(t-1)}{Y(t-1)}$$

This equation forms the basis of our monetary financing scenario.

In order to make eq. (12) operational evolution of each of the terms on the right hand side must be traced. In this regard several adjustments are needed.

1. The inflation rate must be allowed to adjust upwards in response to rising ratio of pure monetary financing to GDP. For this purpose, the following simple formulation is proposed:

Eq. (13) $\Delta P = \beta_0 + \beta_1 (MFR)_{-1} + \beta_2 = (\Delta P)_{-1}$

where $MFR = \left[\frac{RG(t)-RG(t-1)}{Y(t)}\right]$

In this formulation, change in the price level (ΔP) in the current period is posited as a function of the lagged monetary financing ratio to GDP and the own lagged value[16].

Capturing the nexus between monetary financing and inflation, admittedly, requires a more elaborate model with due allowance made for appropriate real sector variables. The emphasis here, however, is on a thought experiment, which is adequately served by this simple specification.

2. When inflation rate is allowed to adjust upwards in response to rising monetary financing ratio, corresponding provision is also needed for revision of nominal interest rate on domestic debt. The indexation of interest rate on domestic debt held outside the RBI is assumed to take the following form:

E. (14) $i_t = p_t + 0.03$

On the other hand, interest rate on domestic debt held by the RBI is expected to take the form:

E. (15) $i^*_t = p_t - 0.02$

In other words, the nominal interest rate on domestic debt held outside the RBI is assumed to be maintained 3 percentage points above the inflation rate whereas the nominal interest rate on debt held by the RBI is assumed to remain 2 percentage points below the inflation. This corresponds roughly to the actual interest rate differentials in the base year.

(B) Application to Indian Data

In order to apply the framework developed above to Indian data, the following numerical values were assigned to relevant parameters:

1. n = real GDP growth rate = 5 per cent per annum[17]

2. h = fraction of domestic borrowings on-lent by the government = 0.5

3. The domestic debt outside the RBI and foreign financing, both as ratios to GDP are maintained at their respective 1986-87 levels.

The relationship between price level and the monetary financing ratio, (i.e. eq. 13) was estimated using Indian data for the period 1970-71 to 1986-87 and the following regression equation was obtained:

$$\Delta P = \underset{(2.59)}{0.075} + \underset{(5.04)}{13.68}\,(MFR)_{-1} - \underset{(-2.81)}{0.7}\,(\Delta P)_{-1}$$

$\bar{R}^2 = 0.71 \quad DW = 2.04$

The price level was measured by the GDP (at factor cost) deflator and the net outstanding RBI credit to government for the period t was measured as the average of the end-period values for periods t-1 and t.

Based on the estimated relationships and the assumed values of relevant parameters, monetary financing scenario was derived recursively as follows:

The monetary financing ratio in the base year (1987-88) using the above mentioned regression equation yields change in the price level and hence the inflation rate (p) in the next year. The inflation rate along with the assumed real GDP growth rate and the relevant estimated elasticities determine expenditure-GDP (G/Y) ratio and receipts - GDP (T/Y) ratio. The inflation rate also determines nominal interest rate (i) on debt held outside the RBI and nominal interest rate (i*) on debt held by the RBI. The values of (p), (i) and (i*) along with other parameters (h), (k) and (e) determine the coefficients for (RG/Y) and (B/Y) in the basic difference equation (eq. 12). Relevant substitutions then yield the pure monetary financing - GDP ratio in that year, which determines inflation rate in the next year and the whole process is repeated again.

Results of this scenario are presented in Table 5. As is evident from the table, resorting to monetary financing is likely to set in motion a vicious circle of large deficit, higher monetary financing, more inflation leading again to a larger deficit and so on. Indeed, reliance on net RBI credit is likely to raise the monetary financing ratio from 2.4 per cent of GDP in the base year to 17.3 per cent of GDP and consequently the inflation rate is likely to shoot up from under 7 per cent in the base year to as much as 20 per cent within five years.

This order of acceleration of inflation emanating from monetary financing alone is very serious given the most favourable conditions assumed. If the real GDP growth falters from the assumed 5 per cent rate say due to supply side shocks such as adverse weather conditions etc, the inflation rate may easily flare up even beyond 20 per cent per annum in a matter of only five years.

Summary and Conclusions

1. Concerns are being voiced about the growing government deficits and the resultant rapid expansion of domestic debt in India and yet relevant issues have not been adequately and rigorously investigated. The subject calls for a comprehensive and much deeper analysis than the treatments presently available. What is needed is a systematic analysis of the dynamic nexus between widening government deficits and different modes of financing them in the framework of inter-temporal budget constraint. This study makes an effort in that direction.

2. For a comprehensive analysis first of all the data base has to be reconstructed. Available measures of government deficit and domestic debt are accounting figures rather than proper economic aggregates. These need to be replaced by analytically meaningful measures.

Alternate government deficit estimates for 1970-71 and for the 1980's have been derived which indicate that government deficit in India as a ratio of GDP has significantly widened during the 1980's. The traditional budget deficit increased from 0.7 per cent of GDP in 1970-71 to the average of 1.3 per cent in the first half of the 1980's and to the average of 2.3 per cent in the next four years ending 1988-89. The traditional budget deficit, however has been grossly underestimating the overall borrowing need arising out of the fiscal operations of the government. Indeed, the traditional budget deficit has been roughly between one-fifth and one-third of relevant gross fiscal deficit, which correctly reflects the overall borrowing need. The gross fiscal deficit expanded from 3.5 per cent of GDP in 1970-71 to the average of 7.0 per cent of GDP in the first half of the 1980's and further to the average of 9.3 per cent in the four year period ended in 1988-89. Contemporaneously the gross primary deficit worsened from 3.5 per cent to GDP to as much as 7.6 per cent of GDP during same period.

An attempt has also been made to derive analytically more meaningful measures of domestic debt. The rapid increase in domestic debt in India is evident from the estimates obtained. According to the method proposed in the study, gross domestic debt expanded from 27.1 per cent of GDP in 1970-71 to 31.6 per cent of GDP in 1980-81 which rose further to as much as 44.6 per cent of GDP in 1987-88.

TABLE 5

Monetary Financing Scenario

Year	P	ΔP	p	$\frac{G(t)}{Y(t)}$	$\frac{T(t)}{Y(t)}$	[Coefficient] $X\left[\frac{RG(t-1)}{Y(t-1)}\right]$	[Coefficient] $X\left[\frac{B(t-1)}{Y(t-1)}\right]$	$\frac{\Delta RG}{Y}$ (=MFR)
	1	2	3	4	5	6	7	8
1986-87	3.62@							
1987-88	3.9282@	0.308@	0.085@	0.171@	0.126@			0.024@
1988-89	4.1162	0.188	0.048	0.182	0.130	0.005	-0.001	0.047
1989-90	4.7022	0.586	0.142	0.193	0.129	0.021	0.010	0.086
1990-91	5.5432	0.841	0.179	0.204	0.126	0.034	0.014	0.117
1991-92	6.6302	1.087	0.196	0.215	0.123	0.047	0.016	0.146
1992-93	7.9422	1.312	0.198	0.227	0.120	0.059	0.016	0.173

@ denotes actuals

3. Starting from the inter-temporal budget constraint, analytical expressions in the form of difference equations were derived so as to establish the dynamic inter-linkages between government deficits and different modes of financing them. This framework was used to conduct two thought experiments:

(a) In "debt-financing scenario", the question addressed is what would be the future time profile of debt-GDP ratio if the government deficit is allowed to evolve passively and domestic borrowings excluding those from the RBI are used for financing it while maintaining the other modes of financing at their current ratios to GDP?

(b) In monetary-financing scenario, the question addressed is what would be the projected impact on inflation if the government deficit is allowed to evolve passively financed by resorting to additional net RBI credit while holding the domestic "debt financing" and foreign financing at their base year ratios to GDP?

4. Under the debt-financing scenario, the overall debt-GDP ratio is projected to increase very rapidly; rising from 44.6 per cent of GDP in 1987-88, the overall debt-GDP ratio would cross the 100 per cent mark in 1995-96 reaching as much as 150 per cent by the year 1999-2000.

With the rapid increase in the *overall* debt-GDP ratio, corresponding net interest burden (i.e., net domestic interest payments as ratio of projected receipts) would also rise substantially. The net interest burden was barely 1 per cent in 1974-75 and rose to about 12 per cent in 1987-88. With the projected acceleration of debt accumulation, it would shoot up to as much as 30 per cent of projected receipts by the turn of the century. Given the limited scope for raising receipts - GDP ratio and the tendency for current outlays to be sticky downwards, the higher net interest burden may invariably lead to a squeeze on budgetary capital outlays, thereby stifling economic growth.

5. Resorting to larger recourse to RBI financing is not a panacea of the problem either. The monetary financing scenario has demonstrated that such an attempt would lead to a vicious circle of large deficit, higher monetary financing, more inflation leading again to a larger deficit and so on. Indeed the inflation rate as measured by GDP deflator, which was under 7 per cent in the base year could by this factor alone, be pushed to unacceptably high level of about 20 per cent within a five year period. If the real GDP growth rate turns out to be less than 5 per cent per annum as assumed say due to adverse weather conditions, the inflation rate may easily flare up even beyond 20 per cent per annum within a short span of time.

Notes

1. Rakshit (1989) p.1.
2. For the sake of brevity domestic borrowings other than net RBI credit to government is referred to as "debt-financing" in this study.
3. All government deficit measures have been so defined here as to have positive values i.e., expenditure minus receipts rather than the other way around.

4. Chakravarty Committee Report (1985), p. 153.
5. The concept of fiscal deficit is widely used by the IMF. No distinction however is made between gross and net deficit in the IMF terminology. The fiscal deficit refers to gross fiscal deficit.
6. Coincides with the IMF's definition of primary deficit
7. It may be noted that in this study, the term "domestic debt" is used rather than "public debt" or "internal debt" or "internal liabilities" presently used in the literature. The term "public" is avoided because it may have a broader connotation covering the entire public sector whereas the focus here is only on the Central Government. The term "internal debt" is discarded because in the Indian budget documents it refers only to a part of the debt not covering small savings, etc. Finally, the term "internal liabilities" is not considered suitable because one rupee coins or notes also constitute an internal liability of the government but it does not qualify for being internal debt.
8. Buchanan (1968), p. 32.
9. Buchanan (1968), p. 4.
10. Buchanan (1968), p. 63.
11. Rakshit (1989), p. 4.
12. Eq. (2) is a first order difference equation of the form Y(t) - a Y(t-1) = f(t) which is linear with constant coefficients. For such equations convergence to a stationary value requires 0<a<1 see RGD Alllen (1973), p. 185.

    This equation is essentially a discrete time version of a differential equation developed by Spaventa (1987).
13. Details of the derivation are in the Technical Appendix
14. As quoted by Seshan (1987) Table 9.
15. G and T are defined as non-interest revenue expenditure plus capital expenditure and non-interest revenue receipts plus grants respectively so that the difference equal the net primary deficit.
16. Equivalently, the equation can also be interpreted as a relationship between price level (P) in the current period on the one hand and the Lagged monetary financing to GDP ratio and the own lagged values for two periods on the other.
17. In terms of the sustainability condition derived in Section II the assumption of five per cent real GDP growth and three per cent real interest rate on domestic debt held outside the RBI implies that explosive evolution of debt-GDP ratio is ruled out by construction. This has been done with a view to demonstrate the potential adverse impact of monetary financing even under a relatively favourable set of circumstances. The outcome could only be worse in less suitable environment.

References

1. Allen R.G.D. (1973), Mathematical Economics, ELBS and Macmillan, Second Edition.
2. Bispham, J.A. (1987), "Rising Public Sector Indebtedness: Some more Unpleasant Arithmetic", *Private Savings and Public Debt*, edited by Boskin, Flemming and Gorini, Basil Blackwell, U.S.A.
3. Blanchard, O.J. (1984), "Current and Anticipated Deficits, Interest Rates and Economic Activity", *European Economic Review*, March.
4. Bollino, A and Rossi N. (1988), Public Debt and Household's Demand for Monetary Assets in Italy: 1970-86 in *High Public Debt: The Italian Experience*, edited by Giavazzi and Spaventa. Cambridge University Press.
5. Boskin, M.J. Flemming, J.S. and Gorini S. (1987) (Eds.) *Private Saving and Public Debt*, Basil Blackwell, U.S.A.
6. Buchanan, J.M, (1968) "Public Debt" in International Encyclopedia of the Social Sciences. The Macmillian, Company and The Free Press.
7. Buiter, W.H., (1983), "A Guide to Public Sector Debt and Deficits", *Economic Policy* 1, November.
8. Comptroller and Auditor Generals Report (1988) (N. 10) Government of India.
9. Dornbusch R. (1978) "Inflation Capital and Deficit Finance" *Journal of Money, Credit and Banking,* February.
10. Dornbusch R (1988) "Discussion of Introduction: Is there a Public Debt Problem in Italy" in *High Public Debt: The Italian Experience*, edited by Giavazzi and Spaventa, Cambridge University Press.
11. Dubashi, J (1989) "Is India Going Bankrupt", A Publication of the Project for Economic Education, Bombay.
12. Eisner R. and Pieper (1986) "Deficits Monetary Policy and Real Economic Activity" Public Debt and Macroeconomics.
13. Giovannini. A (1988), "Capital Controls and Public Finance, The Experience in Italy" in *High Public Debt: The Italian Experience*, edited by Giavazzi and Spaventa. Cambridge University Press.
14. IMF (1986) Manual of Government Finance Statistics.
15. Masson P.R. (1985), "The Sustainability of Fiscal Deficits" *IMF Staff Papers,* Vol. 32, No. 4, December.
16. Pagano. M (1988), "The Management of Public Debt and Financial Markets", *In High Public Debt: The Italian Experience* edited by Giavazzi and Spaventa, Cambridge University Press.
17. Rakshit M (1989), "Internal Debt Trap the Shadow and the Substance" Delivered as S.N. Sen Memorial Lecture, Calcutta.
18. Report of the Committee to Review the working of the Monetary System (1985) Reserve Bank of India, Bombay.
19. Seshan A (1987), "The Burden of Domestic Public Debt in India", *RBI Occasional Papers*, Vol.8, No. 1, June.
20. Spaventa L. (1987), "The Growth of Public Debt Sustainability, Fiscal Rules and Monetary Rules", *Staff papers*, International Monetary Fund, Vol. 34, No. 2, June.
21. Tabellini, G. (1988), "Monetary and Fiscal policy Co-ordination with a High Public Debt" *in High Public Debt: The Italian Experience*, edited by Giavazzi and Spaventa. Cambridge University Press.
22. World Bank (1988), World Development Report.

TECHNICAL APPENDIX

The simple budget constraint is:

$$G(t) - T(t) + iB(t-1) + i^* RG(t-1)$$

$$= [B(t) - B(t-1)] + [RG(t) - RG(t-1)]$$

$$\therefore \quad \frac{B(t)-B(t-1)}{Y(t)} = \frac{G(t)-T(t)+iB(t-1)+i^*RG(t-1)-[RG(t)-RG(t-1)]}{Y(t)}$$

$$\text{Now,} \quad \frac{B(t)}{Y(t)} - \frac{B(t-1)}{Y(t-1)} = \frac{B(t)}{Y(t)} - (1+k)\left[\frac{B(t-1)}{Y(t)}\right]$$

Since Y(t) = (1+k) Y(t-1)

$$\Rightarrow \frac{B(t)}{Y(t)} = \left[\frac{B(t)-B(t-1)}{Y(t)}\right] - k\left[\frac{B(t-1)}{Y(t)}\right] + \left[\frac{B(t-1)}{Y(t-1)}\right]$$

Combining the two results, we get,

$$\frac{B(t)}{Y(t)} = \left[\frac{G(t)-T(t)}{Y(t)}\right] - \left[\frac{RG(t)-RG(t-1)}{Y(t)}\right] + \left[\frac{iB(t-1)}{Y(t)}\right] + \frac{i^*RG(t-1)}{Y(t)}$$

$$-k\frac{B(t-1)}{Y(t)}+\frac{B(t-1)}{Y(t-1)}$$

$$=\left[\frac{G(t)-T(t)}{Y(t)}\right]-\left[\frac{RG(t)-RG(t-1)}{Y(t)}\right]+\frac{i^*RG(t-1)}{Y(t)}$$

$$+(i-k)\left[\frac{B(t-1)}{Y(t)}\right]+\frac{B(t-1)}{Y(t-1)}$$

which using Y(t) = (1+k) Y(t-1) simplifies to

$$\text{(A.1)}\quad \frac{B(t)}{Y(t)}=\left[\frac{G(t)-T(t)}{Y(t)}\right]-\left[\frac{RG(t)-RG(t-1)}{Y(t)}\right]+\frac{i^*}{(1+k)}+\left[\frac{RG(t-1)}{Y(t-1)}\right]$$

$$+\left(\frac{1+i}{1+k}\right)\frac{B(t-1)}{Y(t-1)}$$

which is the equation (2) in the text.

In the general case, the intertemporal budget constraint is:

$$[G(t)-T(t)] + [iB(t-1) + i^*RG(t-1) + w\,NF(t-1)] + [L(t) - L(t-1) - eL(t-1)]$$

$$= [B(t) - B(t-1)] + [RG(t) - RG(t-1)] + [NF(t) - NF(t-1)]$$

In view of the assumptions, we have

$$F(t) = NF(t) - NF(t-1) - w\,NF(t-1)$$

$$L(t) - L(t-1) = h\,[B(t) - B(t-1)]$$

$$L(t-1) = h\,B(t-1)$$

On substitution in the budget constraint, we get

$$[G(t)-T(t)] + [iB(t-1) + i^*RG(t-1)] + h\,[B(t)-B(t-1)] - eh\,B(t-1)$$

$$= [B(t) - B(t-1)] + [RG(t)-RG(t-1)] + F(t)$$

$$\Rightarrow (1-h)\,[B(t) - B(t-1)]$$

$$= [G(t)-T(t)] + [iB(t-1) + i^*RG(t-1)] - eh\,B(t-1) - [RG(t) - RG(t-1)] - F(t)$$

$$\Rightarrow [B(t) - B(t-1)]$$

$$=\left(\frac{1}{1-h}\right)\big[G(t)-T(t) - [RG(t) - RG(t-1)] - F(t)\big]$$

$$+\left[\frac{i^*}{1-h}\right]RG(t-1)+\left[\frac{i-eh}{1-h}\right]B(t-1)$$

$$\Rightarrow B(t)=\left(\frac{1}{1-h}\right)\big[G(t)-T(t) - [RG(t) - RG(t-1)] - F(t)\big]$$

$$+\left(\frac{i^*}{1-h}\right)RG(t-1)+\left[1+\left(\frac{i-eh}{1-h}\right)\right]B(t-1)$$

$$\Rightarrow \frac{B(t)}{Y(t)}=\left(\frac{1}{1-h}\right)\left[\frac{G(t)}{Y(t)}-\frac{T(t)}{Y(t)}-\frac{RG(t)-RG(t-1)}{Y(t)}-\frac{F(t)}{Y(t)}\right]$$

$$+\left(\frac{i^*}{1-h}\right)\frac{RG(t-1)}{Y(t)}+\left[1+\left(\frac{i-eh}{1-h}\right)\right]\frac{B(t-1)}{Y(t)}$$

which using Y(t) = (1+k) Y(t-1) yields

$$\text{(A.2)}\quad \frac{B(t)}{Y(t)}=\left(\frac{1}{1-h}\right)\left[\frac{G(t)}{Y(t)}-\frac{T(t)}{Y(t)}-\frac{RG(t)-RG(t-1)}{Y(t)}-\frac{F(t)}{Y(t)}\right]$$

$$+\left[\frac{i^*}{(1-h)(1+k)}\right]\frac{RG(t-1)}{Y(t-1)}+\left[\frac{1+\left(\frac{i-eh}{i-h}\right)}{1+k}\right]\frac{B(t-1)}{Y(t-1)}$$

which is the basic difference equation [eq. (7)] in the text. If one assumes that there are no domestic lendings (i.e., h=0) and no foreign financing, i.e., F(t)=0, then eq. (A.2) reduces to eq. (A.1) as in the simple case.

(a) Difference Equation for "Debt-financing" Scenario Collecting the terms involving net RBI credit, we have

$$\left[\frac{i^*}{(1-h)(1+k)}\right]\frac{RG(t-1)}{Y(t-1)}-\left(\frac{1}{1-h}\right)\frac{RG(t)}{Y(t)}+\left(\frac{1}{1-h}\right)\frac{RG(t-1)}{Y(t)}$$

$$=\left[\frac{i^*}{(1-h)(1+k)}\right]\frac{RG(t-1)}{Y(t-1)}-\left[\frac{1}{1-h}\right]\frac{RG(t)}{Y(t)}+\left(\frac{1}{(1-h)(1+k)}\right)\frac{RG(t-1)}{Y(t-1)}$$

$$=\left[\frac{1+i^*}{(1-h)(1+k)}\right]\frac{RG(t-1)}{Y(t-1)}-\left[\frac{1}{(1-h)}\right]\frac{RG(t)}{Y(t)}$$

If the net RBI credit to government as a ratio of GDP is kept constant.

$$\frac{RG(t)}{Y(t)}=\frac{RG(t-1)}{Y(t-1)}$$

Accordingly, the expression becomes,

$$\left[\frac{1+i^*}{(1-h)(1+k)}\right]\frac{RG(t-1)}{Y(t-1)}-\left(\frac{1}{1-h}\right)\frac{RG(t-1)}{Y(t-1)}$$

$$=\left[\frac{i^*-k}{(1-h)(1+k)}\right]\frac{RG(t-1)}{Y(t-1)}$$

which on substitution in (A.2) yields

$$(A.3)\quad \frac{B(t)}{Y(t)} = \left(\frac{1}{1-h}\right) - \left[\frac{G(t)}{Y(t)} - \frac{T(t)}{Y(t)} - \frac{F(t)}{Y(t)}\right]$$

$$- \left[\frac{k-i^*}{(1-h)(1+k)}\right]\frac{RG(t-1)}{Y(t-1)} + \left[\frac{1+\left(\frac{i-eh}{i-h}\right)}{1+k}\right]\frac{B(t-1)}{Y(t-1)}$$

which is the eq. (8) in the text, used for the "debt-financing" scenario.

(b) Difference Equation for Monetary Financing Scenario. The last term on the RHS of eq. (A.2) can be simplified to

$$\left(\frac{1}{1+k}\right)\frac{B(t-1)}{Y(t-1)} + \left[\frac{(i-eh)}{(1-h)(1+k)}\right]\frac{B(t-1)}{Y(t-1)}$$

$$= \left(1 - \frac{k}{1+k}\right)\frac{B(t-1)}{Y(t-1)} + \left[\frac{(i-eh)}{(1-h)(1+k)}\right]\frac{B(t-1)}{Y(t-1)}$$

$$= \frac{B(t-1)}{Y(t-1)} - \left(\frac{k}{1+k}\right)\frac{B(t-1)}{Y(t-1)} + \left[\frac{(i-eh)}{(1-h)(1+k)}\right]\frac{B(t-1)}{Y(t-1)}$$

On substitution in eq. (A.2) we get

$$\frac{B(t)}{Y(t)} = \frac{1}{(1-h)}\left[\frac{G(t)}{Y(t)} - \frac{T(t)}{Y(t)} - \frac{RG(t)-RG(t-1)}{Y(t)} - \frac{F(t)}{Y(t)}\right]$$

$$+ \left[\frac{i^*}{(1-h)(1+k)}\right]\frac{RG(t-1)}{Y(t-1)} + \frac{B(t-1)}{Y(t-1)} - \left(\frac{k}{(1+k)}\right)\frac{B(t-1)}{Y(t-1)}$$

$$+ \left[\frac{i-eh}{(1-h)(1+k)}\right]\frac{B(t-1)}{Y(t-1)}$$

If the "debt-financing" to GDP ratio is held at a constant level.

$$\frac{B(t)}{Y(t)} - \frac{B(t-1)}{Y(t-1)} = 0$$

$$\Rightarrow \left(\frac{1}{1-h}\right)\left[\frac{G(t)}{Y(t)} - \frac{T(t)}{Y(t)} - \frac{RG(t)\text{-}RG(t-1)}{Y(t)} - \frac{F(t)}{Y(t)}\right]$$

$$+ \left[\frac{i^*}{(1-h)(1+k)}\right]\frac{RG(t-1)}{Y(t-1)} + \left(\frac{(i-eh)}{(1-h)(1+k)} - \frac{k}{1+k}\right)\frac{B(t-1)}{Y(t-1)}$$

= 0 Thus,

$$(A.4)\quad \left[\frac{RG(t)-RG(t-1)}{Y(t)}\right] = \left[\frac{G(t)}{Y(t)} - \frac{T(t)}{Y(t)} - \frac{F(t)}{Y(t)}\right] + \left(\frac{i^*}{1+k}\right)\frac{RG(t-1)}{Y(t-1)}$$

$$+ \left[\frac{h(k-e)-(k-i)}{1+k}\right]\frac{B(t-1)}{Y(t-1)}$$

which is eq. (12) in the text and forms the basis for the monetary financing scenario.

13

Fiscal Deficit, External Balance and Monetary Growth

A Study of Indian Economy

C Rangarajan • M S Mohanty

Introduction

THE external dimensions of the fiscal deficit have been a concern to the policy makers in developing countries. An endemic deficit in the external current account and a domestic saving-investment gap, or what may be referred to as the twin gap problem, are the typical outcome of development strategies that depend on budget deficits on a continuing basis to promote domestic capital formation and growth. While a moderate government deficit corresponding to a sustainable current account gap may be desirable in building up domestic capital formation, a persistently large fiscal gap however, may turn the external payment situation unsustainable. Persistent high levels of current account deficit poses both a short term risk and a long term problem. To the extent that it generates an unfavourable market sentiment, the adverse effects on interest rate and exchange rate could turn the domestic policy unsustainable. The long term problems manifest through increased debt service payments, erosion in the long run investment prospects and a sustained loss of confidence in the economy. It is in this context that the measures to reduce domestic absorption and improve public saving constitute important policy ingredients of the adjustment towards creating a sustainable balance of payment environment.

The authors are grateful to Dr. K. Krishnamurty for his detailed comments on an earlier version of the paper. They are thankful to Shri S.S. Tarapore, Dr. Vikas Chitre and Dr. M.J. Manohar Rao for very useful discussions on the model developed in the paper. They are thankful to Shri M.D. Patra, Director, Division of International Finance, who provided valuable information and gave his useful suggestions at the various stages of the preparation of the paper. They are also grateful to Smt. Uma Udare for her unstinted help in collection, tabulation and computer processing of the data used in the paper and for her meticulous reading of the manuscript. They acknowledge with thanks the research assistance received from Smt. Nishita Raje, Shri Sunando Roy and Shri M.T. Nagpal and the useful help provided by Shri K.A. Gore in the preparation of the paper. The authors wish to record their special thanks to Shri S.S. Jogle who took painstaking trouble in typing out several versions of the draft. The opinions expressed in the paper are the authors' own personal views.

The interrelationship between the fiscal deficit and external balance is evident from the following national income identity which links domestic saving-investment gap to the current account gap in the balance of payments.

$$(X-M) = Y - (C+I+G) = (S_g - I_g) + (S_p - I_p) \quad \dots (1)$$

The above identity states that the current account deficit (X-M) is the excess of domestic absorption i.e. consumption (C), investment (I) and government expenditure (G) over income (Y); or stated differently, foreign saving equals the sum of the saving and investment gap of the public sector ($S_g - I_g$) and that of the private sector ($S_p - I_p$). It is obvious therefore, that policies that reduce private savings and increase budget deficit lead to a deterioration in current account deficit. While equation (1) is an *ex-post* accounting identity and has to be satisfied for each period, the actual dynamics of the transmission of a fiscal deficit to the external current account needs to be worked out by identifying the routes through which domestic economic variables affect the external sector. The theoretical and empirical literature on transmission mechanism in the open economy context have made considerable progress over the years. Beginning with the basic Keynesian and absorption models, the empirical research in this area has proliferated in many directions to account for the complex behavioural interactions between public and private sectors as also among the various sectors within the economy, both in the static and intertemporal framework [see for example Polak (1957), Crips and Godley (1976) on Cambridge Economic Policy Group (CEPG) model, Khan and Knight (1981), Frenkel and Razin (1987), Haque *et al* (1990), Bartoli (1989) and Mansur (1989)]. The subject has also received a fair amount of attention in India in the context of the on-going stabilisation and structural adjustment programmes [Rakshit (1991), Mohanty and Joshi (1992), Sau (1992),

Bhattacharya *et al* (1994), Rangarajan (1994), Rao and Singh (1995), Krishnamurty and Pandit (1997) and Mohanty (1997)].

This paper outlines an empirical model for the Indian economy to study the dynamic interrelationship between the internal and external balances in the economy. The model covering the period 1971-72 to 1993-94 provides an analytical framework for tracing the income and price routes of adjustment from fiscal deficit to current account deficit in the balance of payments. The main linkages in the model are as follows. Fiscal deficits increase the aggregate demand level in the economy and may influence output (in the absence of supply constraints), disposable income, consumption and investment, thus raising the import demand at each stage of transition. Given the availability of borrowed resources from non-monetary and external sources, a part of the deficit is financed by resorting to borrowing from the Reserve Bank. The stock of money therefore evolves endogenously through the feed-back from reserve money which varies with the changes in fiscal deficit. The money stock along with output determines the price level in the economy, which in turn determines the relative prices of imports and exports. To the extent that the nominal exchange rate deviates from its full purchasing parity level, given the domestic and world price levels, fiscal deficit financed by money creation leads to appreciation of real exchange rate, leading to a rise in imports and decline in the competitiveness of exports. The resulting current account deficit creates a financing need and increases the stock of external debt and interest payment, reinforcing the initial deterioration in the current account balance. A further source of transmission may stem from the changes in the financial balance of the private sector which is behaviourally linked to the government deficit. The prototype model is simulated to conduct certain counter-factual experiments on the policy implications of an increase in fiscal deficit.

The rest of the paper is organised as follows. Section I presents a discussion on the trends in government finances, monetary and real sectors and external balance (This section is omitted here because it is a mere a narration of factual data on some of the major economic indicators - editor). Section II outlines the analytical framework and the major features of the model. Section III presents the empirical estimates of structural parameters, while Section IV outlines the complete model and its simulation performance. The results of policy simulations are discussed in Section V, followed by concluding observations in Section VI.

SECTION II

Framework of the Model

Theoretical literature discusses two major channels of transmission of fiscal impulses to the external sector viz., the income and the price routes of transmission. Fiscal deficits, whatever may be their intended purpose, almost immediately increase the aggregate absorption level in the economy relative to output. The output effect of deficit follows subsequently as government investment outlay raises the capital stock in the economy and as firms respond to domestic demand conditions by utilising the excess capacity already available with them. Therefore, while imports may grow, as a consequence of the increase in absorption, the output effect will generate a chain of secondary impacts on demand for imports through disposable income, private consumption and investment. A further channel of transmission takes place through the relative price changes brought about by the financing side of deficit. When the fiscal deficit is entirely financed by issue of bonds to private sector, the monetary impact of such fiscal operation is limited to the central bank's discretionary policy to ease the pressure on interest rate. Bond financed deficits may however, generate a wealth impact in the private sector financial portfolio and may increase the aggregate demand and price levels in the economy. Different schools of thought, however stand divided on this issue. In the Keynesian framework, bond financed deficits are supposed to generate strong wealth impacts, which is contested by both neoclassical and Ricardian full foresight models [See for example a debate on this issue by Bernheim (1989) and Barro (1989)]. However, when the deficit is financed by borrowing from the central bank the impact on prices is felt more quickly and directly. The inflationary outcome of deficit shifts the relative prices in favour of imports and away from domestic goods and exports resulting in an increase in net imports.

The model [presented here] focuses mainly on the income and price channels of transmission ... Determination of fiscal deficit and its financing constitutes the central feature of the model.

...The relation between fiscal deficit, money and output forms the second important transmission channel in the model. An increase in fiscal deficit leads to monetary expansion, but to the extent that deficit is due to an increase in public investment, the long run impact on prices is expected to be lower than the case when deficit is incurred for current expenditure. Since the output function is augmented with a demand variable, the model recognises the short run expansionary impact of government expenditure on output[1]. Further, the model highlights the link between credit and output by introducing real money stock as an argument in the non-agricultural output function.

The interaction between fiscal deficit, private consump-tion and investment forms the third vital link in the model. A tax-cut or expenditure induced deficit increases the private disposable income, leading to higher consumption in the current period. The model assumes the short-sighted response of private sector to the government deficit, and therefore, rules out the tax discounting hypothesis central to the Ricardian Equivalence proposition. ...

Determination of investment level in the economy forms the fourth major aspect of the model. A single investment function for the entire economy may not accurately account for the behavioural characteristics of investment in different sectors. The model introduces disaggregation at a broad level, viz., agriculture and non-agriculture, in order to capture the determinants of investment in these two sectors. Investment may come from private or public sector, the latter is largely a policy variable and hence treated exogenous in the model. Private non-agricultural investment function is specified through the accelerator framework, augmented with a long run profit variable, interest rate and a variable representing credit availability conditions. Private agriculture investment, on the other hand, is dependent on the income originating from this sector and the government investment in agriculture. Gross investments in these two sectors, along with the depreciation requirement determine the level of capital stock, which in turn determines the output level in the economy.

The import demand is determined by an aggregate demand variable which is defined to include private absorption, government expenditure and exports. This constitutes the fifth important feature of the model. Export demand in the model is a function of export price relative to world price and the level of world income. Export price is expressed as an inverted export supply function which is postulated to depend on domestic cost and demand conditions. The endogenously determined levels of export and import of goods and services together with net external interest payments and international transfers (net) generate the current account balance in the model. An important feature of the model is that the current account balance, apart from being determined endogenously, also influences the stock of external debt and interest payments with a self-generating feed-back effect.

The model, as it emerges, thus combines the features of both the absorption and monetary approach to external adjustment. By bringing out the nexus between money, output and prices it places emphasis on the role of deficit and money in the real economy. The model is estimated using the data for the sample period 1971-72 to 1993-94. ...

SECTION III

Specification of the Model and the Estimated Parameters

1. Fiscal Operations

Given the objectives of the current exercise, government sector constitutes the most important subsector in the model. Consistent with the national income identity, linking fiscal deficit to the current account of balance of payments, the analysis here is based on the consolidated public sector, which in the Indian context comprises general government (Centre, States and Union Territories) and their departmental and non-departmental enterprises. It may be noted that the concept of fiscal deficit used in the budget documents mainly concerns with the measurement of borrowing requirement of the government and may be ill-suited to study the aggregate demand impact of deficit (Blejer and Cheasty, 1991). The budgetary definition of gross fiscal deficit (revenue receipts *minus* total expenditure including net lending) generally overstates the demand impact of deficit. A more meaningful analysis of government expenditure should be based on its economic classification into consumption, transfer payments, and investment, which can be combined with private sector absorption to study the domestic demand impact of fiscal deficit. Similarly, the revenue side of the budget also needs to be redefined to include the savings of the departmental and non-departmental enterprises of the government. Therefore, some adjustment in the published data of fiscal deficit becomes essential to put them to economically more meaningful analysis. In view of this, data on the government sector for the study are drawn from the National Account Statistics which presents the economic and purpose-wise classification of government expenditure. In this paper all nominal variables are denoted by higher case letters and real variables by lower case letters while change between two time points is indicated by the sign Δ.

Following budget constraint of the public sector provides the starting point of the analysis.

$$GXP-TR = \Delta BCG + \Delta RCG + \Delta FICG + DNB + EB + MISCR \quad ...(2)$$

where,

$$TR = DT + DIT + TM + NTX + SE \quad ...(2a)$$

$$GXP = CON + TRP + PCF \quad ...(2b)$$

Equation (2) shows that fiscal deficit, i.e., the excess of public sector expenditure (GXP) over current revenue (TR) is financed by increase in domestic credit to government i.e. by credit from commercial banks (BCG) and from Reserve Bank (RCG); borrowing from other sources, including financial institutions (FICG) and domestic non-banking institutions (DNB); external loans (EB) and miscellaneous capital receipts (MISCR). Total revenue of public sector comprises revenue from direct taxes (DT), domestic indirect taxes (DIT) and import taxes (TM) and non-tax revenue (NTX), consisting of income from property and entrepreneurship and miscellaneous current receipts of administrative departments and the gross savings (SE) of the departmental and non-departmental enterprises in the public sector. Expenditure in the public sector is incurred in the form of government consumption (CON), transfer payments (TRP) including interest payments (IP) and gross public capital formation (PCF).

i. Government Revenues

On the revenue side, tax and non-tax revenue functions are specified through a partial adjustment framework, with the assumption that at any point of time the actual tax revenue partially adjusts to the long run desired level. As revenues are targeted in nominal terms, both tax and non-tax revenue equations are estimated at their current price levels.

Revenue from direct taxes are posited to be a function of real income originating from non-agriculture sector (at factor cost) and domestic price level. Inflation is expected to increase tax revenue, since nominal tax collections should rise at least proportionally with prices. However, if lags in tax collection are long, revenue from direct taxes may not be elastic to inflation and real tax revenue may fall with inflation (Tanzi, 1977). On the other hand, nominal direct tax revenue is expected to rise more than proportionately, if tax brackets are not indexed to inflation. The net effect of inflation on tax revenue will therefore depend on the relative strengths of both the factors. The following equation provides the estimates of relative income and price elasticities of direct taxes in the partial adjustment framework.

$$\underset{}{Ln\ DT} = \underset{(-1.444)}{-2.171} + \underset{(1.042)}{0.316}\ Ln\ ynar + \underset{(2.549)}{0.305}\ Ln\ P + \underset{(4.749)}{0.660}\ Ln\ DT_{(-1)} + \underset{(5.602)}{0.154}\ DDT \quad ...(3)$$

$\bar{R}^2 = 0.99$, $h = 0.12$, SEE = 0.06, Mean = 3.99

Where 'ynar' is real GDP at factor cost originating from non-agricultural sector, 'P' is wholesale price index and 'DDT' is a dummy. The figures in the brackets are the respective 't' values of the regression coefficients. The long run elasticity of direct tax revenue with respect to real non-agricultural income works out to near unity, during the period 1971-72 to 1993-94. The price elasticity of direct tax revenue is about 0.3 in the short run and 0.9 in the long run. The equation was estimated with a dummy to account for the significant changes in tax structure that has taken place since 1991-92 following the introduction of a comprehensive tax reform programme. As is expected, the dummy has a positive sign in the equation.

Indirect taxes are divided into two parts, domestic indirect taxes (DIT) and import taxes (TM). While the former is a function of real income and the price level, the latter is determined by the average import duty rate and the volume of import. The following two equations provide the estimates of domestic and trade taxes.

$$Ln\ DIT = \underset{(-2.427)}{-2.496} + \underset{(2.073)}{0.347}\ Ln\ y + \underset{(2.974)}{0.369}\ Ln\ P + \underset{(6.469)}{0.682}\ Ln\ DIT_{(-1)} - \underset{(-4.08)}{0.065}\ DDIT \quad ...(4)$$

$\bar{R}^2 = 0.99$, $h = -1.33$, SEE = 0.03, Mean = 5.27

$$TM = MR \times (impt \times PIMP) \quad ...(5)$$

Where 'y' is real income at factor cost, 'DDIT' is a dummy, 'MR' is average import duty rate, 'impt' is real imports in Rupees, and PIMP is price of import. The long run elasticity of domestic indirect tax revenue to real income is placed at 1.09. The price elasticity of domestic indirect tax revenue is estimated at 1.16, showing a more than proportional adjustment between inflation rate and the increase in indirect tax revenue. This should be expected, since most of the taxes on goods and services are levied at *ad valorem* rates, making the tax base elastic to inflation. The equation included a dummy to represent the significant changes introduced in the structure of union excise duties in the post-reform period, which had a short term negative effect on revenue. Import tax revenue was specified as an identity linking the revenue to the average import duty rate, the volume of real imports and import prices.

On the non-tax revenue side, government property and entrepreneurial income together with miscellaneous current revenues are related to the level of economic activity, proxied by GDP at current market prices (YM). Gross savings of the departmental and non-departmental public enterprises which represent the net result of their commercial operations are assumed to be determined outside the system. It may be mentioned that the classification and definition of government property income has undergone frequent revisions due to, among others, the changing depreciation norms. In order to smooth out these breaks in data points a shift dummy (DNTX) has been introduced in the non-tax revenue equation. The estimates of the parameters are as follows.

$$NTX = -1.435 + 0.016\ YM - 19.008\ DNTX \quad ...(6)$$
$$(-0.679) \quad (26.449) \quad (-4.109)$$

$\bar{R}^2 = 0.97$, DW = 1.44, SEE = 6.17, Mean = 40.72

ii. Government Expenditure

Of the four major categories of expenditure considered in the model, viz., consumption, interest payment, transfer payments and public investment, the latter two are treated exogenous in the system. Transfer payments consisting of subsidies and pension payments and other current transfers are influenced by a set of social and economic factors. They are frequently used as means to promote certain distributional objectives. In developing countries, public investment outlay subsumes several policy objectives and at times could be a residual item in the budget given the revenue constraints and expenditure commitments in the current account of the budget. It could, however, be argued that in the case where deficit is monetised to a large extent, the financing constraints may not seem to be a binding constraint on the level of investment outlay in the budget.

Real consumption expenditure of the government is related to economic activity which is proxied by the real GDP at market prices. Government consumption function is specified in real terms to underline the fact that government desires to maintain a real level of consumption in each period. The estimated equation in the partial adjustment framework is as follows.

$$Ln\ con = -2.287 + 0.753\ Ln\ ym + 0.489\ Ln\ con_{(-1)} \quad ...(7)$$
$$(-3.984) \quad (4.016) \quad (3.642)$$

$\bar{R}^2 = 0.98$, h = 3.87, SEE = 0.05, Mean = 5.17

The short run and long run income elasticities of government consumption expenditure are placed at 0.71 and 1.47, respectively, during the sample period, which show the fast pace at which government real consumption responds to changes in economic activity. Total interest payment is divided into two parts viz., interest payment on internal debt and that on external debt. Gross internal and external interest payments are related to the respective outstanding debts at the beginning of the year and the average interest rates.

$$IPI = I_d \times IDBT_{(-1)} \quad ...(8)$$
$$IPX^g = I^g_x \times XDBT^g_{(-1)} \quad ...(9)$$

Where 'IPI' and 'IPX^g' are internal and external interest payments of the government, respectively, 'I_d' and 'I^g_x' are average interest rates on internal and external debts, and 'IDBT' and '$XDBT^g$' are the outstanding internal and external government debt.

Total outstanding debt (TDBT) is defined as :

$$TDBT = TDBT_{(-1)} + \Delta TDBT \quad ...(10)$$

The change in outstanding debt (ΔTDBT) in any given year should ideally equal to the fiscal deficit in that year. However, since the published data on incremental debt do not accurately agree with the fiscal deficit (FD), the following functional form was used to estimate the incremental debt.

$$Ln\ \Delta\ TDBT = -0.175 + 1.077\ Ln\ FD - 1.549\ DDBT$$
$$(-0.603) \quad (18.649) \quad (-4.169) \quad ...(11)$$

$\bar{R}^2 = 0.97$, DW = 2.24, SEE = 0.35, Mean = 6.88

Outstanding external debt of the government is determined by the flow of foreign borrowing (EB_g) during the year together with the outstanding debt of the previous year, where EB_g is assumed as a fraction E of the change in total debt. The difference between the total debt and the external debt gives outstanding internal debt. The following identities explain the determination of two different components of government debt.

$$XDBT^g = XDBT^g_{(-1)} + EB^g + VLC \quad ...(12)$$
$$EB^g = E \times \Delta TDBT \quad ...(13)$$
$$IDBT = TDBT - XDBT^g \quad ...(14)$$

iii. Government Borrowing

Financing of fiscal deficit takes place through following major ways :

(1) increase in commercial bank credit to government (ΔBCG);

(2) increase in financial institutions' credit to government (ΔFICG) mainly through their investment in government securities;

(3) borrowing from domestic non-banking sources, namely from households and others in the form of small savings, provident funds and special deposits;

(4) increase in other domestic miscellaneous capital receipts which represents net changes in deposit account, reserve funds, etc.

(5) borrowing from external sources (EB^g); and

(6) increase in net RBI credit to the government, which essentially goes to meet the shortfall between the fiscal deficit and the borrowing from all other sources.

Commercial banks' credit to the government is influenced by two major factors, growth in their aggregate deposits and the statutory liquidity ratio. The following equation was considered for estimating the incremental commercial banks' credit to the government.

$$\text{Ln } \Delta BCG = \underset{(-6.516)}{-3.307} + \underset{(13.924)}{1.331} \text{ Ln } \Delta DEP + \underset{(2.287)}{0.385} \Delta WSLR + \underset{(4.131)}{1.075} DBCG \quad ...(15)$$

$\bar{R}^2 = 0.93$ DW = 2.09, SEE = 0.35, Mean = 3.06

The elasticity of incremental bank credit to the government with respect to incremental deposits (ΔDEP) of commercial banks is estimated to be more than unity. Since the SLR requirements changed frequently even within a financial year, a weighted average rate was used to estimate the sensitivity of banks' investment in government paper to SLR changes. Here, the SLR variable represents the relevant ratio weighted by the number of days it remained in force during a year. The equation was estimated with a dummy (DBCG) to account for sharp variation in bank credit to government in 1975-76 and 1977-78. Incremental deposits of commercial banks was linearly related to increase in M_3.

$$\Delta DEP = \underset{(-0.591)}{-1.118} + \underset{(111.228)}{0.814} \Delta M_3 + \underset{(1.689)}{8.226} DDEP \quad ...(16)$$

$\bar{R}^2 = 0.99$, DW = 2.12, SEE = 9.32, Mean = 252.57

Investment of financial institutions in government securities depends on the growth of their investible resources. Since the regression equation did not show satisfactory statistical relation between the two, this component of borrowing was assumed exogenous in the model. The following equation provided the estimates of domestic non-bank borrowing, which is related to the nominal income (Y) and its own past values. Apart from the level of economic activity, a significant factor explaining a large increase in the government borrowing through small savings and provident funds relates to the tax benefits offered to their investors. Studies have estimated that effective rate of return on some of the small savings instruments after taking into account the tax benefits was as high as 34 per cent in 1990-91 (Bagchi and Nayak, 1993). However, a satisfactory index of effective return on small savings on a time series basis is not available for evaluating the impact of this variable on government borrowing from the household sector.

$$\text{Ln } DNB = \underset{(-14.144)}{-7.151} + \underset{(20.438)}{1.449} \text{ Ln } Y + \underset{(8.860)}{0.498} \text{ Ln } DDNB \quad ...(17)$$

$\bar{R}^2 = 0.97$, DW = 0.53, SEE = 0.21, Mean = 3.66

The estimated income elasticity of small savings and provident fund receipts work out to 1.45, reflecting the combined influence of relatively faster growth of household savings in the 1970s and 1980s and the household's preference for these securities on account of their promise of high post-tax return.

The remaining component of government borrowing, i.e., miscellaneous capital receipt is treated exogenous in the model. This leaves the Reserve Bank credit to the government which is obtained as a residual finance after exhausting the borrowings from all other sources. The following identity links the change in Reserve Bank credit to the government to fiscal deficit and borrowing from other sources.

$$\Delta RCG = FD - \Delta BCG - \Delta FICG - DNB - EB^g - MISCR \quad ...(18)$$

2. Demand for Money and Price Determination

Price equation in the model takes the form of an inverted money demand function. In general form, the demand for real money balances could be postulated to take the following functional specification.

$$\text{Ln } (M/P) = \propto_0 + \propto_1 \text{ Ln } y - \propto_2 i - \propto_3 \pi^e \quad ... (19)$$

where the real money balance is expressed as a function of the real income (y), interest rate (i) and the inflation expectation (π^e). The signs of the coefficients in the equation are consistent with the theoretical expectation regarding the impact of various economic forces on demand for real money balances. The model includes two opportunity cost variables; namely interest rate (i) and inflation rate (π) representing the cost of holding money against other financial assets and goods, respectively. Inverting this function, we get an expression for price as :

$$\text{Ln } P = - \alpha_0 - \alpha_1 \text{ Ln } y + \alpha_2 i + \alpha_3 \pi^e + \text{Ln } M \quad ...(19a)$$

According to the above specification price situation is essentially influenced by the monetary conditions, growth of real income and the peoples' desire to adjust their real money balances in response to changes in interest rate and inflation. Inflation rate in the model should be truly represented by its expected value. Since the price equation is specified in a partial adjustment framework, it is expected that the lagged price level would capture some of the effects of the expected inflation. The empirical version of the price equation is as follows :

$$\text{Ln } P = 2.407 - 0.387 \text{ Ln } y + 0.253 \text{ Ln } M_3 + 0.738 \text{ Ln } P_{(-1)}$$
$$(2.185) \quad (-1.877) \quad (3.524) \quad (7.797)$$
$$+ 0.073 \text{ DP1} + 0.153 \text{ DP2} \qquad \text{...(20)}$$
$$(2.185) \quad (5.892)$$

$\bar{R}^2 = 0.99$, $h = -0.93$, $SEE = 0.03$, $Mean = 4.74$

The general price level (P) refers to the index of wholesale prices. The lagged price variable in the model incorporates the lagged effect of output and money supply on the current year's price level. ... The equation includes two dummies; 'DP1' represents the dummy for high inflation rates in 1973-74 and 1974-75 following the first oil shock and 'DP2' as the dummy for 1980-81 to account for the lag impact of second oil shock. The short run elasticity of price with respect to real income works out to -0.39 and that to 'M_3' to 0.25. As should be expected in the case of an inverted money demand function, long run elasticity of price to money supply works out to near unity (0.97). The corresponding long run elasticity to real income is placed at 1.48. The implicit income elasticity of money demand is placed at 1.53 for the sample period 1971-72 to 1993-94.

3. Interest Rate

Interest rate constitutes an important transmission channel of macro-economic adjustment process, depending on how free and open is the financial market of an economy. In the case of developing countries, with relatively regulated and close financial market this transmission belt is expected to be weak, particularly in relation to the portfolio behaviour of the households which constitutes a major channel of adjustment. Even in the case of these economies, interest rate, while being administered, can have significant influence on the investment decision in the economy and as a result, can influence the level of aggregate demand and output.

In this model, the role of interest rate is addressed in the context of its impact on the cost of credit and the level of aggregate demand in the economy. The objective is to identify the proximate determinants of interest rate and then establish a link between the borrowing and lending rates of commercial bank. While it can be argued that in the Indian context, until recently, interest rate did not play an equilibriating role in the money market, it is also important to recognise that the policy responses by way of interest rate changes in the past were not completely out of place with developments in the money market and domestic price conditions. Keeping in view the current evolving stage of financial markets in India, it is essential to gather some idea about the determinants of interest rate in order to account for its impact on the investment decisions in the economy. In the developing country context interest rate determination has been addressed in a variety of ways, keeping in view the underlying structure and characteristics of the financial economy in question and the extent of its integration with the global financial market. Given the fact that for most of the sample period, Indian economy operated under a relatively high degree of capital control, interest rate was mostly determined by the domestic economic conditions. Accordingly, the theoretical framework considered in the model draws on the money market equilibrium conditions and the Fisher's hypothesis of determination of nominal interest rate. The approach set out below has been extensively discussed in Edwards and Khan (1985).

According to the standard Fisher hypothesis, nominal interest rate (i) is given by

$$i_t = r_t + \pi^e_t \qquad \text{...(21)}$$

where 'r' is real interest rate and 'π^e' is expected inflation rate. The real interest rate in any period is postulated to evolve as a deviation from its long run equilibrium level, this deviation being brought about by the excess or shortage of money supply over money demand.

$$r = \delta - \mu \text{ EMS}_t + w_t \qquad \text{...(22)}$$

Where 'δ' is long run equilibrium real interest rate, 'EMS' represents excess supply of money and 'w_t' is a white noise residual. The excess supply of money is given by the difference between the actual stock of and the demand for real money balances (m)

$$\text{EMS}_t = \text{Ln } m_t - \text{Ln } m^d_t \qquad \text{...(23)}$$

As in equation (19) the money demand function is given by

$$\text{Ln } m^d_t = \propto_0 + \propto_1 \text{ Ln } y_t - \propto_2 (\delta + \pi^e_t) - \propto_3 \pi^e_t \qquad \text{...(24)}$$

which has two opportunity cost variables in $(\delta+\pi^e_t)$ and π^e_t. Assuming a stock adjustment process for real money stock we get,

$$\text{Ln } m_t = \beta(\text{Ln } m^d_t - \text{Ln } m_{t-1}) \qquad \text{...(25)}$$

Where $\Delta\text{Ln } m_t = \text{Ln } m_t - \text{Ln } m_{t-1}$ and β is the coefficient of adjustment such that, $0 \leq \beta \leq 1$. Equation (25) can be simplified as,

$$\text{Ln } m_t = \beta\text{Ln } m^d_t + (1-\beta) \text{ Ln } m_{t-1} \qquad \text{...(26)}$$

Combining (23) and (26) we get,

$$\text{EMS}_t = (1-\beta) (\text{Ln } m_{t-1} - \text{Ln } m^d_t) \qquad \text{...(27)}$$

which together with (21), (22) and (24) yield the following estimatable version of the reduced form equation for nominal interest rate :

$$i_t = \Phi_0 + \Phi_1 \text{ Ln } Y_t + \Phi_2 \text{ Ln } m_{t-1} + \Phi_3 \pi^e_t + w_t \qquad ...(28)$$

Where $\Phi_0 = \delta + \mu (1-\beta) (\propto_0 - \propto_2 \delta)$

$\Phi_1 = \mu (1-\beta) \propto_1$

$\Phi_2 = -\mu (1-\beta)$

$\Phi_0 = [1-\mu (1-\beta) (\propto_2 + \propto_3)]$

Interest rate in the empirical model was represented by the one-to-three year deposit rate of banks (IB) and the variable of expected inflation was substituted by actual inflation. The estimated parameters of equation (28) are presented below :

$$IB = -42.909 + 10.902 \text{ Ln } y \qquad ...(28a)$$
$$(-2.592) \quad (2.546)$$
$$-4.332 \text{ Ln } m_{3(-1)} + 0.068 [(P - P_{(-1)})/ P_{(-1)}] \times 100$$
$$(-1.863) \quad (2.116)$$

$\bar{R}^2 = 0.65$, DW = 1.77, SEE = 0.70, Mean = 8.89

The above equation implies that lagged real money supply exerts a downward influence on the nominal interest rate while real income tends to increase it. Inflation and interest rate are seen to be positively related though not in a very significant way. Given the estimates of deposit rate from equation (28a) the lending rate of commercial banks is estimated by adding to the deposit rate the intermediating cost, which for simplicity is assumed exogenous in the model and is given by the observed difference between the one-to-three year deposit rate and the weighted average lending rate of commercial banks.[2]

WLR = IB + OPC

Where WLR is weighted average lending rate of commercial banks and OPC is intermediating or operating cost of commercial banks.

4. Money Supply Determination

The determination of money supply is a process of determination of the sources of variation in reserve money and the money multiplier. Among the various sources affecting reserve money, the major component *viz.*, the Reserve Bank credit to the government is determined within the model. The objective here is to bring out the nexus between money supply and fiscal deficit as the primary channel of monetary expansion. As mentioned earlier, Reserve Bank credit to the government is endogenously determined in the model from the financing side of deficit. Historically, this was the major source of growth of reserve money during much of the sample period under study. The supply of broad money (M_3) is related to reserve money by the following equation, which gives an estimated parameter for the money multiplier.

$$M_3 = -47.278 + 3.192 \text{ RM}$$
$$(-2.715) \quad (100.985) \qquad ...(29)$$

$\bar{R}^2 = 0.99$, DW = 1.61, SEE = 56.93, Mean = 1239.48

The estimated money multiplier is placed at 3.19 for the sample period 1971-72 to 1993-94. Ideally the money multiplier should be functionally related to behavioural factors, such as ratio of currency to deposits, and a policy variable, i.e. the cash reserve ratio. It has also been contended that money multiplier will depend on demand for credit and hence on output, since the degree at which a given quantum of reserve money will translate into money supply will depend on the credit demand in the economy at that point of time. While this position is theoretically valid, it is to be noted that in the Indian context with an administered structure of interest rate until recently and varying rates of interest for different activities, demand for credit was not a binding constraint. Interest rates charged on some activities were below the market rate and demand for credit at those rates of interest was highly elastic. In fact, the Indian commercial banks do not voluntarily hold any excess reserves and whatever excess reserves they may be holding are involuntary due to inadequate facilities for quick transmission of funds from far flung branches (Rangarajan and Arif, 1990). Further, for a proper estimation of the relationship between money supply and reserve money, at the minimum, it is necessary to adjust the series on reserve money for changes in the cash reserve ratio. In fact, such an adjusted series is found to give a better explanation of changes in money stock particularly when quarterly data are used (Rangarajan and Singh, 1984). However, since we are dealing with annual time series, adjustments have not been made for changes in cash reserve ratio.

5. Private Sector Behaviour

Central to the argument of fiscal dimension of the balance of payments problem is the relation between the fiscal deficit and private spending behaviour. Both in the theoretical and empirical literature, there has been a considerable degree of disagreement on modelling the private sector's response to changes in fiscal deficit and its financing composition. In the conventional Keynesian framework, an increase in government deficit, whether caused by a cut in taxes or by increased expenditure, will boost private spending by increasing disposable income. Since consumers are assumed to be myopic and liquidity constrained, the forward looking behaviour goes out of the Keynesian analysis and what become relevant are the current income and current consumption and thus, current taxation and deficit. The finite horizon models in the typical tradition of life cycle hypothesis state that temporary deficits will have minimum effects on private spending, while deficits brought about by permanent tax cuts will significantly stimulate consumer spending. Both these theories are contradicted by Ricardian equivalence hypothesis, which under the assumptions of infinite planning horizon and perfect capital markets holds that government deficit will be fully neutralised by opposing economic behaviour of the private sector (Barro, 1974). In other words, government deficit by increasing the probability of a future tax rise will result in equivalent reduction of private consumption. Consequently, deficit does not reduce national saving and has no implications for external current account balance.

The mainstream models on fiscal approach to balance of payments follow the Keynesian tradition in modelling private sector response to public deficits, wherein private consumption and investment are lumped together in a single private expenditure function with disposable income as the main explanatory variable (for example, Cambridge Economic Policy Group model, 1976). There are, however, two major limitations of this approach. First, it does not make a distinction between consumption and investment demands of the private sector. These two parts of private absorption may exhibit different behavioural relations with changes in economic activity. Secondly, this approach assumes full exogeneity of private sector in the determination of the current account balance, hence changes in the latter are explained by changes in the public sector financial balances. In reality, however, private consumption apart from being determined by disposable income can be directly influenced by fiscal policy changes, which brings the 'crowding out' phenomenon into the picture.

(i) Private Consumption

In the light of the above discussion the private absorption function considered here draws a distinction between the consumption and investment demand. Private real consumption is a function of its real disposable income. While the Ricardian position with regard to government deficit may not seem to be providing a plausible explanation for the intertemporal consumption behaviour of the private sector in developing countries, it has been, however, argued that government consumption may have direct implications for private consumption [Easterly and Schmidt-Hebbel (1993) and Mohanty (1992)]. In order to account for the possible 'crowding out/in' impact, the private consumption function considered here is augmented with government consumption as an argument. The effect of inflation on consumption has received considerable attention in developing countries. It is expected that in a low income country inflation may lead to reduction in saving levels because of the low resistance of poor consumers to cuts in real consumption. Inflation can also depress savings by encouraging flight from currency and bank deposits to consumer durables (under financial repression). Anticipated inflation is expected to stimulate present consumption while surprise or unanticipated inflation may not have a strong impact on consumption. The empirical evidence in the context of developing countries including India show that real consumption tends to increase with rise in prices, whether anticipated or not (Lahiri 1989). The following equation provides the empirical estimates of various influences on private real consumption expenditure.

$$\text{Ln pc} = \underset{(3.468)}{1.686} + \underset{(5.416)}{0.615}\ \text{Ln pyd} + \underset{(1.855)}{0.107}\ \text{Ln con} + \underset{(1.546)}{0.072}\ \text{Ln P} \quad \ldots(30)$$

$\bar{R}^2 = 0.99$, DW = 1.85, SEE = 0.02, Mean = 7.03

The elasticity of private consumption with respect to disposable income is estimated at 0.62. The coefficient of government consumption is positive though small, indicating that private consumption tends to increase with government consumption. This is probably because government consumption expenditure in certain areas may be crowding in private consumption due to their complementary nature. Price level has a positive impact on the real consumption, although the effect works out to be small.

(ii) Private Investment

Private investment behaviour is modelled in two equations relating to agriculture and non-agriculture investment. The following equation specifies the private real agricultural investment function.

$$\text{Ln piag} = \underset{(-4.133)}{-3.053} + \underset{(8.261)}{0.956}\ \text{Ln yar}_{(-1)} + \underset{(2.109)}{0.210}\ \text{Ln pcfag} - \underset{(-2.603)}{0.167}\ \text{dpiag1} + \underset{(2.714)}{0.165}\ \text{dpiag2} \quad \ldots(31)$$

$\bar{R}^2 = 0.80$, DW = 1.03, SEE = 0.09, Mean = 3.43

Where 'piag' is private gross agricultural investment in real terms, 'yar' is real GDP originating from agriculture, 'pcfag' is real gross public investment in agriculture and 'dpiag1' and 'dpiag2' are two dummies to account for large fluctuations in investment in some years. Private agricultural investment is found to be significantly influenced by the lagged agricultural income, with an elasticity of near unity. Government investment in agriculture has a positive impact on private agricultural investment which reinforces the contention expressed in several studies in this regard [for example, Rath (1989), Shetty (1990), and Krishnamurty et al (1997)]. This should be expected as government provides major infrastructural inputs such as irrigation and research and development in agriculture, which form the critical base for private capital formation.

Real private investment function for the non-agricultural sector is specified through the accelerator framework, where investment is related to the expected increase in demand for output. Following an adaptive expectation framework, the investment equation is expressed in terms of the current year's change in income and the investment level of past one period. In the developing countries, public investment constitutes a key determinant of the private investment. Public investment, especially in infrastructure, increases the long run marginal productivity of private capital and thereby helps promote investment in private sector (Aschauer, 1989). Further, there could be an output linkage where public capital stock raises the demand for private output. On the other hand, public investment may displace private investment in some sectors by depriving the private sector of scarce physical and financial resources. This phenomenon of what is called 'financial crowding out' is generally believed to be strong in developing countries, where the public sector enjoys preferential borrowing treatment over the private sector. Under this situation the actual level of private investment may fall short of its desired level on account of the binding borrowing constraint in the domestic and external credit markets. In the developing country context, including India, several models have recognised this dual and conflicting role of public investment in promoting aggregate capital stock [see Sunderarajan and Thakur (1980), Krishnamurty et al (1985), Blejer and Khan (1984) and Pradhan et al (1988)]. In most of the models, in the Indian context, crowding-out phenomenon has emerged stronger than the complementarity effect. The present model tests for the competitive impact of public investment on private investment in industry and tertiary sector, by including a financial variable in the private non-agricultural investment function, represented by banking sector's credit to commercial sector and net capital inflow from abroad.

$$\text{pinag} = \underset{(1.936)}{30.801} + \underset{(2.621)}{0.253}\,\Delta y + \underset{(1.692)}{0.372}\,(\Delta bcp + capb) - \underset{(-2.168)}{1.420}\,wlr + \underset{(2.107)}{0.486}\,\text{pinag}_{(-1)} \quad ...(32)$$

$\bar{R}^2 = 0.83$, h = -1.035, SEE = 22.03, Mean = 146.57

Where 'pinag' is real investment of private sector in the non-agriculture sector, 'bcp' is real bank credit to private sector, 'capb' is the capital account balance (representing the real capital inflow from abroad) in the balance of payments accounts deflated by wholesale price index and 'wlr' is weighted average real lending rate of commercial banks.[3]

The OLS test statistics show that the equation has good explanatory power and is free from autocorrelation problem. The impact of marginal change in current year's output on private non-agricultural investment is estimated at 0.25 in the short run and 0.49 in the long run. An increase in bank credit to the government for financing its investment is expected to partly 'crowd out' private investment in the same year, the long run impact works out to 0.72. The negative impact of cost of capital on private investment is also confirmed by the coefficient of 'wlr'.

6. Real Output

The output function is specified in two equations viz., agricultural and non-agricultural output in order to bring out the sectoral characteristics of output generation in the economy. Agricultural output is related to rainfall index (RAIN), gross cropped area (AREA) and real net capital stock in agriculture (KAGR).

$$\text{Ln yar} = \underset{(-3.968)}{-7.132} + \underset{(2.139)}{0.169}\,\text{Ln RAIN} + \underset{(3.425)}{0.989}\,\text{Ln AREA} + \underset{(6.421)}{1.231}\,\text{Ln kagr}_{(-1)} \quad ...(33)$$

$\bar{R}^2 = 0.77$, DW = 1.80, SEE = 0.04, Mean = 6.25

Agriculture output is significantly influenced by the initial level of real net capital stock in agriculture. The elasticity of output to capital stock is estimated at 1.25. Output originating from non-agriculture sector is estimated by a production function, featuring an aggregate demand variable (add), real net capital stock in this sector (knagr) and real money stock (m_3). In the short run, output is expected to respond to demand conditions as firms will use up their stock of inventories and utilise their existing capacity more intensively. This impact is intended to be captured by a demand variable, represented by aggregate demand for domestically produced goods (add) and is defined to include government expenditure, private absorption, exports and imports. This variable brings out the interaction between the non-agriculture sector with the rest of the sectors such as agriculture and trade sector. An increase in agricultural output will generate demand for non-agricultural output as also facilitate the supply of essential raw materials for industry [Rangarajan (1982)]. While exports will have a positive impact on the demand for industrial output raising its production, imports will act as a leakage for the domestic output. Non-agricultural output function also includes the stock of real money balance as an explanatory variable to proxy bank credit to real sector.

$$\text{Ln ynar} = \underset{(-12.232)}{-2.098} + \underset{(7.936)}{0.488} \text{ Ln add} + \underset{(12.534)}{0.627} \text{ Ln knagr}_{(-1)} + \underset{(2.058)}{0.045} \text{ Ln } m_3 \quad ...(34)$$

$\bar{R}^2 = 0.99$, DW = 1.93, SEE = 0.001, Mean = 6.82

All variables included in the equation emerged statistically significant. The elasticity of non-agricultural output to demand is estimated at 0.49 and that with respect to lagged capital stock at 0.63. The stock of real money balance has a positive influence on output. This reinforces the credit view argument of money supply in a developing economy.

7. External Sector

External sector in the model is divided into three major blocks *viz;* export and import of goods and services, interest receipts and payments and net international transfers including non-interest investment income. Determination of exports and imports in the model is guided by the consideration that fiscal deficit affects the domestic demand and price conditions, leading to changes in the relative prices in the external sector. Demand for real export of goods and services is postulated as a function of world income and exports price relative to world price. Real exports are positively related to world income and negatively to export price relative to world price. Implicit in this specification is the assumption that as world price of exports goes up world demand would shift in favour of India's exports given her export price. The export demand equation estimated through a partial adjustment process with one dummy to account for unexplained variation in services, which are less price sensitive, is as under.

$$\text{Ln expt\\$} = \underset{(-1.469)}{-1.263} + \underset{(2.417)}{0.574} \text{ Ln wyr} - \underset{(-3.343)}{0.319} \text{ (pexp\\$/wpexp)} + \underset{(4.568)}{0.569} \text{ Ln expt\\$}_{(-1)} + \underset{(5.541)}{0.102} \text{ dexpt\\$} \quad ...(35)$$

$\bar{R}^2 = 0.99$, h = -0.87, SEE = 0.04, Mean = 2.413

Where 'expt$' is export of goods and services at constant dollar price (dollar value of merchandise and services exports deflated by dollar price of exports), 'wyr' is index of world real income, 'pexp$' is index of India's export price (expressed as unit value index of exports (UVIX) deflated by an index of exchange rate) and 'wpexp' is the world export price (unit value index of world exports). The elasticity of export of goods and services to world income is estimated at 0.57 in the short run and 1.33 in the long run and with respect to relative export prices at 0.32 in the short run and 0.74 in the long run.

The unit value index of exports (UVIX) is specified as an inverted export supply function. Theoretically, export supply is related to domestic economic activity proxied by real income, and export price relative to domestic price to measure the impact of relative profitability of export business vis-a-vis domestic sales. Therefore, the export supply function is:

$$\text{Ln expt}^s = \theta_1 + \theta_2 \text{ Ln y} + \theta_3 \text{ Ln (UVIX/P)} \quad ...(36)$$

Equation (35) can be written in terms of export price as :

$$\text{Ln UVIX} = \Psi_1 + \Psi_2 \text{ Ln y} + \Psi_3 \text{ Ln expt}^s + \Psi_4 \text{ Ln P} \quad ...(37)$$

where $\Psi_1 = (-\theta_1/\theta_3), \Psi_2 = (-\theta_2/\theta_3)$

$\Psi_3 = (1/\theta_3)$ and $\Psi_4 = 1$

Equation (37) was estimated in a partial adjustment framework dropping exports to avoid its strong correlation with income. The empirical equation which also included a dummy variable to account for sharp fluctuation in export prices in some years is presented below:

$$\text{Ln UVIX} = \underset{(-3.131)}{-3.467} + \underset{(1.319)}{0.158} \text{ Ln P} + \underset{(2.992)}{0.728} \text{ Ln y} + \underset{(4.958)}{0.482} \text{ Ln UVIX}_{(-1)} + \underset{(6.532)}{0.127} \text{ DUVIX} \quad ...(38)$$

$\bar{R}^2 = 0.99$ h = -1.09, SEE = 0.038, Mean = 4.929

The index of export price is given by pexp$ = (UVIX/IE), where 'IE' is an index of nominal exchange rate (Rupee to US$). Exchange rate in this framework plays the passive role of transforming the Rupee price of exports into dollar. An exchange rate depreciation, *ceteris paribus,* will bring down the export price and stimulate export demand, depending on the value of price elasticity of exports. Therefore, as in the case of pass through framework, the price elasticity of exports in the model determines the degree with which the trade volumes adjust to a change in the exchange rate (Patra and Pattanaik, 1994). Following equation provides the estimates of exchange rate which is related to domestic price level, current account balance (*minus* indicating deficit) and the change in Reserve Banks' foreign assets (ΔRBFA).

$$EXR = \underset{(10.242)}{5.929} + \underset{(3.898)}{0.029}\,P - \underset{(-4.655)}{0.033}\,CAB + \underset{(11.336)}{0.060}\,\Delta RBFA + \underset{(14.050)}{10.936}\,DEXR1 + \underset{(5.596)}{4.691}\,DEXR2 \quad ...(39)$$

$\bar{R}^2 = 0.99$, DW = 2.13, SEE = 0.639, Mean = 12.84

The signs of the coefficients in the equation are consistent with the theoretical expectation about the influence of various economic forces on the exchange rate. An increase in domestic price level and current account deficit causes the exchange rate to depreciate. In the similar manner an increase in RBI's absorption of foreign currency will tend to depreciate the Rupee. The marginal increase in exchange rate (depreciation) due to an increase in wholesale price index and current account deficit in the model are placed at 0.013 and 0.033, respectively. These coefficient values reveal the weak influence of domestic price and current account balance on exchange rate. This goes to explain the relative insulation of exchange rate determination from the economic forces during much of the sample period. The equation includes two Dummies (DEXR1 and DEXR2) to represent the readjustment of the value of the Rupee in 1991-92 and the sharp depreciation in 1992-93, respectively.

Equations 35, 38 and 39 provide the basic building block for the export sector in the model and underline the two way influence of a domestic price change on export price. Domestic price exerts simultaneous impact on unit value index of exports and exchange rate. The unit value index of exports essentially reflects the prevailing domestic cost conditions. Therefore, an increase in domestic price is expected to harden the rupee price of exports and negatively affect the demand for exports. This is true for an economy with passive and fixed exchange rate system. In India, the system of managed float remained in force for a long time, eventually replaced in stages by a market determined exchange rate system. Even within the system of managed float, exchange rate had been responding to domestic price changes, *albeit* at a slow pace. The empirical estimates of price coefficient in the exchange rate equation also reveal the slow rate of adjustment between nominal exchange rate and price. Allowing for this impact, an increase in domestic price is expected to cause a depreciation in nominal exchange rate and partially neutralise the increase in the supply price of exports.

The demand for real imports of goods and services (impt) is posited as a function of the level of economic activity and import prices (PIMP) relative to domestic price. Unlike the conventional specifications that make import demand a function of real income, the specification considered here relates imports to an aggregate demand variable (ad), which is defined as the sum of private sector absorption, government expenditure and exports, all in real terms. Each of these sectors generate demand for imports, so that the actual import reflects a certain portion of the planned import. The equation includes two dummies, representing the import restriction measures put in place during the stabilisation programmes in 1991-92 and the sharp decline in services imports in certain years.

$$Ln\ impt = \underset{(-2.858)}{-2.115} + \underset{(4.206)}{0.641}\,Ln\ ad - \underset{(-10.778)}{0.462}\,Ln\ PIMP + \underset{(8.888)}{0.967}\,Ln\ P - \underset{(-2.411)}{0.111}\,DIMPT1 - \underset{(-8.060)}{0.182}\,DIMPT2 \quad ...(40)$$

$\bar{R}^2 = 0.99$, DW = 1.95, SEE = 0.04, Mean = 5.04

The elasticity of real imports of goods and services with respect to the aggregate real demand is estimated at 0.64 and with respect to import prices at 0.46. The elasticity of imports to domestic price level is placed at 0.97.

Interest Income and Payments

A large part of the interest income from external sources accrues by way of income from investment of foreign assets held by RBI. Therefore, the external interest income in Rupee value (XII) is related to RBI's foreign assets and the world interest rate, proxied by one year LIBOR.

$$XII = \underset{(0.485)}{0.678} + \underset{(5.526)}{0.037}\,RBFA_{(-1)} + \underset{(1.785)}{0.177}\,LBR \quad ...(41)$$

$\bar{R}^2 = 0.87$, DW = 1.62, SEE = 0.91, Mean = 1.116

External interest payment (XIP) has two components, interest payment on government external debt, which is determined in the fiscal sector and that on private external debt. Interest payment on private external debt is related to the average interest rate on private debt (I^p_x) and the beginning of the year outstanding private debt ($XDBT^p_{(-1)}$). Hence,

$$IPX = IPX^g + IPX^p \quad ...(42)$$

$$IPX^p = I^p_x \times XDBT^p_{(-1)} \quad ...(43)$$

$$XDBT = \Delta XDBT + XDBT_{(-1)} \quad ...(44)$$

The stock of private external debt is expressed as;

$$XDBT^p = XDBT - XDBT^g \quad ...(45)$$

The incremental external debt (ΔXDBT) is a function of the current account deficit in the balance of payments and the change in RBI's foreign assets.

$$\Delta XDBT = \underset{(1.304)}{8.575} - \underset{(-13.669)}{1.354}\ CAB + \underset{(7.585)}{0.610}\ \Delta RBFA + \underset{(27.992)}{677.359}\ DXDBT \qquad ...(46)$$

$\bar{R}^2 = 0.98$, DW = 2.35, SEE = 22.54, Mean = 106.91

Where 'DXDBT' is a dummy representing the break in the data series in 1991-92 arising out of the change in the classification of external debt since that year. Short term debts have been excluded from the analysis in order to obtain a comparable data series for the sample period. Ideally, the incremental external debt should equal the current account deficit *minus* the drawals from reserves. Reserves could also be accumulated by borrowing from abroad, in which case it would add to the external debt. The signs of the coefficient of current account balance and the change in RBI's foreign assets show a positive association of both these components with the incremental external debt.

SECTION IV

The Model and its Simulation Performance

The complete model is specified in terms of 26 behavioural equations and 33 identities. There are 49 exogenous variables and 17 lagged endogeneous variables in the model. Applying the order condition it may be seen that the individual equations do not suffer from the over-identification problem. Thus specified, this medium size model attempts to integrate all the major sectors of the economy, with the primary objective to study the monetary, growth and balance of payments implications of the fiscal policy. All the parameter estimates of the individual behavioural equations, barring a few, satisfy the criteria of goodness of fit and have a priori signs and magnitudes. The complete structure of the model including the identities and definition of variables are reported in Table 1.

TABLE 1

Complete Model Structure

			Behavioural Equations	*R^2*	*DW*	*h*	*SEE*	*Mean*
1.	Ln DT	=	-2.17137 + 0.316483 Ln ynar + 0.305434 Ln P (-1.444) (1.042) (2.549) + 0.660085 Ln $DT_{(-1)}$ + 0.153704 $\overline{DDT}$ (4.749) (5.602)	0.994	-	0.121	0.064	3.987
2.	Ln DIT	=	-2.49598 + 0.346666 Ln y + 0.369602 Ln P (-2.427) (2.073) (2.974) + 0.681725 Ln $DIT_{(-1)}$ - 0.065361 $\overline{DDIT}$ (6.469) (-4.08)	0.999	-	-1.334	0.025	5.265
3.	NTX	=	-1.43496 + 0.016150 YM - 19.0084 $\overline{DNTX}$ (-0.679) (26.4495) (-4.109)	0.971	1.441	-	6.172	40.724
4.	Ln con	=	-2.28749 + 0.753424 Ln ym + 0.488608 Ln $con_{(-1)}$ (-3.984) (4.016) (3.642)	0.985	-	3.876	0.054	5.169
5.	Ln ΔTDBT	=	-0.175347 + 1.07725 Ln FD - 1.54867 $\overline{DDBT}$ (-0.603) (18.649) (-4.169)	0.967	2.237	-	0.355	6.882
6.	Ln ΔBCG	=	-3.30739 + 1.33101 Ln ΔDEP + 0.385007 $\overline{\Delta WSLR}$ (-6.516) (13.924) (2.287) + 1.07537 $\overline{DBCG}$ (4.131)	0.930	2.089	-	0.354	3.065
7.	Ln DNB	=	-7.15106 + 1.44915 Ln Y - 0.498085 $\overline{DDNB}$ (-14.144) (20.438) (8.8603)	0.972	0.53	-	0.209	3.662
8.	Ln P	=	2.40682 - 0.386965 Ln y + 0.253435 Ln M_3 (2.185) (-1.877) (3.524) + 0.737810 Ln $P_{(-1)}$ + 0.072752 $\overline{DP1}$ + 0.15342 $\overline{DP2}$ (7.797) (2.185) (5.892)	0.997	-	-0.93	0.030	4.74
9.	PGDP	=	-10.5967 + 1.16519 P (-2.611) (49.526)	0.998	1.617	-	2.538	141.039
10.	PGKE	=	-18.3350 + 1.30327 P - 15.9699 $\overline{DPGKE}$ (-7.880) (76.324) (-4.080)	0.997	1.834	-	5.068	143.939

Contd...

...Contd...

		Behavioural Equations	R^2	*DW*	*h*	*SEE*	*Mean*
11. ΔDEP	=	-1.11842 + 0.813803 ΔM_3 + 8.2263 $\overline{\text{DDEP}}$ (-0.591) (111.228) (1.689)	0.998	2.12	-	9.325	252.569
12. M_3	=	-47.2778 + 3.19291 RM (-2.715) (100.985)	0.998	1.605	-	56.93	1239.48
13. IB	=	-42.9098 + 10.9017 Ln y - 4.3318 Ln $m3_{(-1)}$ (-2.592) (2.546) (-1.863) + 0.0681 $[(P - P_{(-1)}) / P_{(-1)}] \times 100$ (2.116)	0.648	1.77	-	0.70	8.886
14. Ln pc	=	1.68639 + 0.615267 Ln pyd + 0.106510 Ln con (3.468) (5.416) (1.855) + 0.072079 Ln P (1.546)	0.996	1.851	-	0.015	7.03
15. Ln piag	=	-3.05392 + 0.955718 Ln $yar_{(-1)}$ + 0.210001 Ln $\overline{\text{pcfag}}$ (-4.133) (8.261) (2.109) -0.167205 $\overline{\text{dpiag1}}$ + 0.165432 $\overline{\text{dpiag2}}$ (-2.603) (2.714)	0.799	1.031	-	0.095	3.439
16. pinag	=	30.8012 + 0.253447 Δy + 0.372083 (Δbcp + $\overline{\text{capb}}$) (1.936) (2.62106) (1.692) - 1.42006 wlr - 0.485949 $pinag_{(-1)}$ (-2.168) (2.107)	0.832	-	-1.035	22.034	146.573
17. Ln yar	=	-7.13205 + 0.168682 Ln $\overline{\text{RAIN}}$ + 0.988747 Ln $\overline{\text{AREA}}$ (-3.968) (2.139) (3.425) + 1.23067 Ln $kagr_{(-1)}$ (6.421)	0.772	1.799	-	0.036	6.252
18. Ln ynar	=	-2.09781 + 0.487659 Ln add (-12.232) (7.93597) + 0.627139 Ln $knagr_{(-1)}$ + 0.04530 Ln $m3_{(-1)}$ (12.534) (2.058)	0.999	1.930	-	0.001	6.819
19. depag	=	-2.72953 + 0.050066 $kagr_{(-1)}$ (0.380) (4.728)	0.52	1.983	-	4.64	28.64
20. depnag	=	-40.1607 + 0.050198 $knagr_{(-1)}$ (-13.711) (58.510)	0.994	2.05	-	4.18	134.203
21. Ln expt$	=	-1.26315 + 0.573835 Ln wyr (-1.469) (2.417) -0.319581 (PEXP$/WPEXP) + 0.569621 Ln expt$$_{(-1)}$ (-3.343) (4.568) + 0.101755 $\overline{\text{dexpt\\$}}$ (5.541)	0.990	-	-0.869	0.039	2.413
22. Ln UVIX	=	-3.46657 + 0.158920 Ln P + 0.728536 Ln y (-3.131) (1.319) (2.992) + 0.482021 Ln $UVIX_{(-1)}$ + 0.126679 $\overline{\text{DUVIX}}$ (4.95811) (6.5315)	0.996	-	-1.09	0.038	4.929
23. Ln impt	=	-2.11530 + 0.641406 Ln ad - 0.462192 Ln $\overline{\text{PIMP}}$ (-2.858) (4.206) (-10.778) + 0.967421 Ln P - 0.110920 $\overline{\text{dimpt1}}$ - 0.182483 $\overline{\text{dimpt2}}$ (8.888) (-2.411) (-8.060)	0.994	1.959	-	0.036	5.038
24. EXR	=	5.92924 + 0.029026 P - 0.033261 CAB (10.242) (3.897) (-4.655) + 0.059980 $\overline{\Delta\text{RBFA}}$ + 10.9361 $\overline{\text{DEXR1}}$+ 4.69085 $\overline{\text{DEXR2}}$ (11.336) (14.050) (5.596)	0.991	2.126	-	0.639	12.843
25. XII	=	0.678411 + 0.037683 $\overline{\text{RBFA}}_{(-1)}$ + 0.176886 $\overline{\text{LBR}}$ (0.489) (5.526) (1.785)	0.870	1.62	-	0.968	4.692
26. ΔXDBT	=	8.57517 - 1.35405 CAB + 0.610279 $\overline{\Delta\text{RBFA}}$ (1.304) (-13.669) (7.585) + 677.359 $\overline{\text{DXDBT}}$ (27.992)	0.982	2.351	-	22.537	106.908

Note : (1) Exogenous variables are indicated by a line on top of the variable.

(2) Figures in brackets are 't' statistics.

TABLE 1 *(Contd...)*

Complete Model Structure

IDENTITIES

27.	TR	=	$DT + DIT + TM + NTX + \overline{SE}$
28.	TM	=	$\overline{MR} \times [(impt \times \overline{PIMP}) / 100]$
29.	GXP	=	$[(con \times P)/100] + TRP + [(\overline{pcfag} + \overline{pcfnag}) \times PGKE] \times 100$
30.	TRP	=	$IP + \overline{SUBS} + \overline{OCTR}$
31.	IP	=	$IPI + IPX^g$
32.	FD	=	$GXP - TR$
33.	IPI	=	$\bar{I}_d \times IDBT_{(-1)}$
34.	IDBT	=	$TDBT - XDBT^g$
35.	IPX^g	=	$\bar{I}^g_x \times XDBT^g_{(-1)}$
36.	$XDBT^g$	=	$XDBT^g_{(-1)} + EB^g + \overline{VLC}$
37.	TDBT	=	$TD3T_{(-1)} + \Delta TDBT$
38.	RCG	=	$FD - \Delta BCG - \Delta\overline{FICG} - DNB - EB^g - \overline{MISCR} + RCG_{(-1)}$
39.	EB^g	=	$\bar{E} \times \Delta TDBT$
40.	BCG	=	$\Delta BCG + BCG_{(-1)}$
41.	RM	=	$RCG + \overline{RBCS} + \overline{RBFA} + \overline{GCL} - \overline{RNML}$
42.	BCP	=	$M_3 - RCG - BCG - \overline{RBFA} - \overline{OBFA} - \overline{GCL} + \overline{BNML}$
43.	wlr	=	$(IB + \overline{OPC}) - [(P - P_{(-1)})/P_{(-1)}] \times 100$
44.	absp	=	$pc + piag + pinag$
45.	add	=	$absp + con + \overline{pcfag} + \overline{pcfnag} + (expt\$ \times 7.91) - impt$
46.	ad	=	$add + impt$
47.	y	=	$yar + ynar$
48.	Y	=	$(y \times PGDP) / 100$
49.	YM	=	$Y + DIT + TM - \overline{SUBS}$
50.	ym	=	$(YM / PGDP) \times 100$
51.	pyd	=	$ym - [(TR / P) \times 100] + [(TRP / P) \times 100]$
52.	PEXP$	=	$(UVIX \times 7.91) / EXR$
53.	CAB	=	$[(expt\$ \times UVIX \times 7.91) / 100] - [(impt \times PIMP) / 100]$
			$+ (XII - XIP) + \overline{NR}$
54.	IPX	=	$IPX^g + IPX^p$
55.	IPX^p	=	$I^p_x \times XDBT^p_{(-1)}$
56.	XDBT	=	$\Delta XDBT + XDBT_{(-1)}$
57.	$XDBT^p$	=	$XDBT - XDBT^g$
58.	kagr	=	$\overline{pcfag} + piag - depag + kagr_{(-1)}$
59.	knagr	=	$\overline{pcfnag} + pinag + \overline{erom} - depnag + knagr_{(-1)}$

Note : Exogenous variables are indicated by a line on the top of the variable

The model has been solved by running deterministic simulation in both static and dynamic framework for the period 1975-76 to 1993-94. Based on the comparison of predicted and actual values, Table 2 reports three types of simulation error statistics e.g., the Mean Absolute Percentage Error (MAPE), Root Mean Square Percentage Error (RMSPE) and Theil's 'U' statistic for some key endogenous variables. For most of the variables MAPE and RMSPE, both under static and dynamic simulations, stayed within a reasonable range. For example, in the case of some key variables such as government revenue (TR), government expenditure (GXP), money supply (M_3), wholesale price (P), capital stock (kagr and knagr), real output (y), exports (expt$) and imports (impt) the RMSPEs under dynamic simulation are within the range of 1 to 7 per cent. The RMSPE for fiscal deficit is placed at 13.7 per cent under dynamic simulation while for current account balance it is placed at 74.2 per cent. Since these two variables represent the closing identities of the fiscal and external sectors, respectively, the relatively large RMSPE in these two identities reflect the accumulated errors stemming from the individual equation components in these two sectors.

Theil's 'U' coefficient as a measure of robustness of the model shows the extent of inequality between the actual and simulated values. If 'U' is 0, there is perfect agreement between the actual and the simulated series. In our case the 'U' for most of the key endogenous variables is less than 0.1.

Graphs '1 to 4' show the comparison of actual and simulated (reference) values of the key endogenous variables in the dynamic simulation. For most of the variables the turning points are captured by the simulation. For example, in the case of fiscal deficit and current account balance, the two key endogenous variables in the model, the graphs show the close convergence of simulated series with the actual series. This is also true of the variables like money supply, prices and real income. With the limited available data points the model has captured reasonably well the structural changes in the Indian economy since 1991-92.

On the whole, the model performs well in terms of tracking the historical path of the majority of variables. While according to the actual data the average annual rate of inflation and output growth are placed at 8.14 per cent and 4.66 per cent, respectively, during the period 1976-77 to 1993-94, the predicted values of the same variables from the dynamic simulation are placed at 7.90 per cent and 4.64 per cent, respectively. Similarly, the annual average ratios of fiscal deficit to GDP (market price) and current account balance to GDP (market price) are predicted by the simulation at 6.62 per cent and -1.26 per cent, respectively, for 1975-76 to 1990-91 as against the actual ratios of 6.85 per cent and -1.24 per cent.

TABLE 2

Simulation Error Statistics of Some Key Endogenous Variables in the Model

Endogenous Variables	Static Simulation MAPE	Static Simulation RMSPE	Static Simulation Theil's 'U'	Dynamic Simulation MAPE	Dynamic Simulation RMSPE	Dynamic Simulation Theil's 'U'
(1)	(2)	(3)	(4)	(5)	(6)	(7)
Fiscal Sector						
TR	1.39	2.60	0.01	4.12	5.77	0.04
GXP	1.16	1.99	0.01	2.09	4.18	0.02
FD	4.99	12.34	0.06	7.41	13.70	0.07
RCG	2.04	4.71	0.02	4.36	7.90	0.05
Real Sector						
pc	1.17	1.67	0.01	1.35	1.71	0.02
piag	7.77	8.76	0.09	10.14	11.54	0.12
pinag	10.46	12.11	0.13	12.28	15.39	0.15
yar	2.43	3.34	0.03	4.05	4.65	0.04
ynar	0.93	1.12	0.01	1.81	1.98	0.02
y	1.00	1.61	0.01	1.62	2.08	0.02
kagr	0.48	0.59	0.01	0.81	0.97	0.01
Kngar	0.47	0.58	0.01	1.43	1.51	0.02
Monetary Sector						
RM	1.87	3.70	0.02	3.93	6.51	0.05
M_3	2.48	2.92	0.03	4.57	6.56	0.05
P	2.14	2.82	0.02	4.68	5.35	0.05
IB	6.21	6.84	0.07	6.29	6.76	0.08
External Sector						
EXR	3.23	4.61	0.04	3.87	6.10	0.05
expt$	0.40	3.36	0.04	0.51	4.41	0.05
PEXP$	2.70	3.66	0.03	4.00	5.21	0.04
impt	2.74	3.48	0.03	3.87	4.77	0.05
CAB	-23.55	116.02	0.23	-19.89	74.23	0.22
XDBT	3.53	5.85	0.03	4.51	9.79	0.05

MAPE = Mean Absolute Percentage Error.
RMSPE = Root Mean Square Percentage Error.

SECTION V

POLICY SIMULATION

A basic objective of the empirical model presented is to study the economy-wide ramifications of fiscal impulses which could stem from a policy induced change in one of the exogenous fiscal variables. Fiscal deficits pose various trade-offs for the economy. Such trade-offs involve securing growth and price stability, on the one hand, and maintaining internal and external balances, on the other. Fiscal deficit as a means to promote growth has been well recognised in the literature. Its efficacy to do so however, depends on what happens to various intermediate variables such as prices, interest rate, credit, investment and external leakages such as imports, which are influenced by the fiscal deficit. When deficit is financed by money creation the trade-off becomes sharper in terms of higher inflation. Apart from the adverse price impact, fiscal deficit implies higher level of domestic absorption which can trigger an increase in imports and widening of current account deficit in the balance of payments. To be sure, the exact nature of the impact of an increase in fiscal deficit on domestic prices and external deficit would depend on various factors, such as the nature of linkages established in the model, the estimated values of the impact coefficients and the lags in the model which provide feed back effects to the system. The policy simulation exercise conducted in this section is intended to study four types of macro-economic outcomes stemming from changes in the policy variables. In the first exercise public real non-agricultural investment is raised by small magnitudes over its historical values during the sample period (1975-76 to 1993-94) in order to study the implications of this policy change for growth, prices, and balance of payments under the alternative financing scenarios. These financing scenarios fall under three major heads; (a) financing by money creation, (b) financing partly by a rise in public sector saving and partly by money creation, and (c) financing by an increase in commercial bank credit to the government sector. In the second exercise, we study the implications of an increase in government current expenditure, financed by bank credit for the price level, output and balance of payments. In the third exercise, the model is given a pure monetary shock in the form of an increase in the RBI's foreign assets. The impact of this policy change is studied by analysing the changes in paths of the endogenous variables such as money supply, prices, output, exchange rate and the external current account balance. The fourth experiment relates to an increase in world income and its possible implications for exports and the current account deficit in the balance of payments.

In order to evaluate the comparative outcomes, the model is first solved on its dynamic mode by holding all exogenous variables to their historical levels. The simulated path of the variables therefore provide the model generated solutions of the endogenous variables during the sample period. In order to allow for policy induced change to be transmitted throughout the system, a particular exogenous variable is chosen for altering its temporal path during the sample period. The repeated shock arising out of this policy change is allowed to work through the system alongwith the feedback effects to provide the policy solutions for the endogenous variables. The policy solutions are compared with the reference solutions with a view to evaluating the impact of the policy change on some key endogenous variables.

GRAPH 1

MONEY SUPPLY

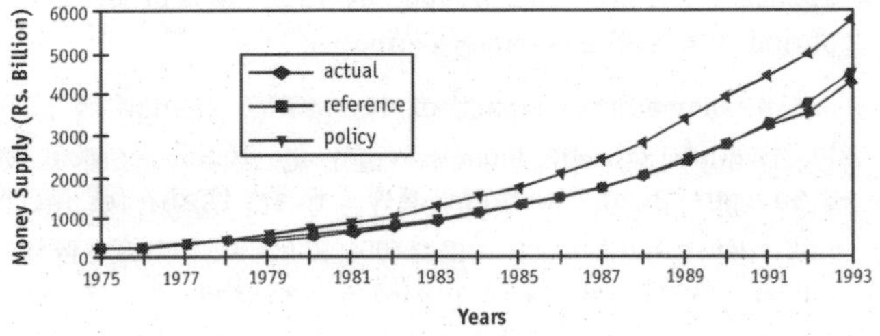

GRAPH 2

PRICE LEVEL

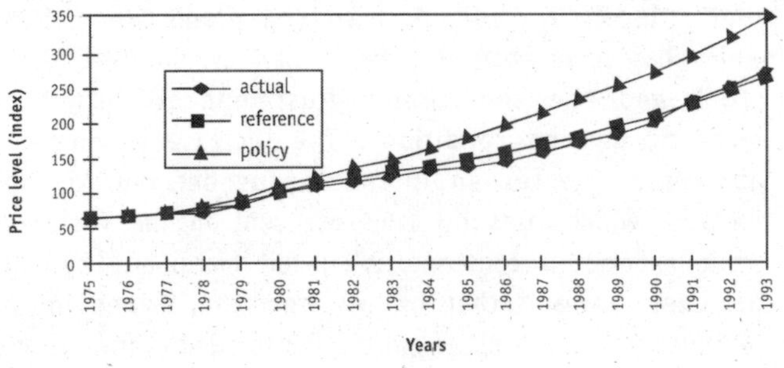

GRAPH 3

REAL INCOME

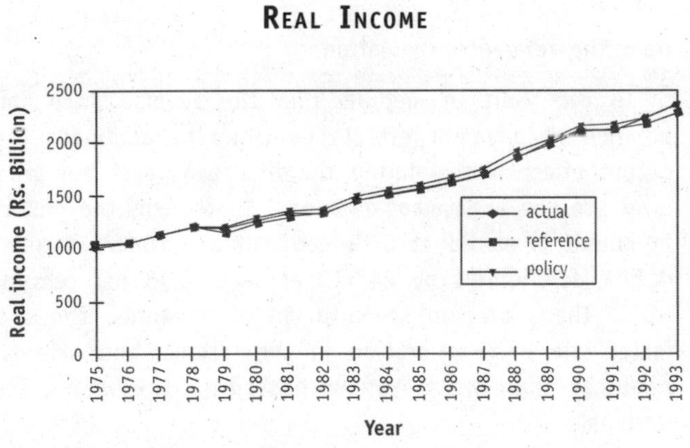

GRAPH 4

CURRENT ACCOUNT BALANCE

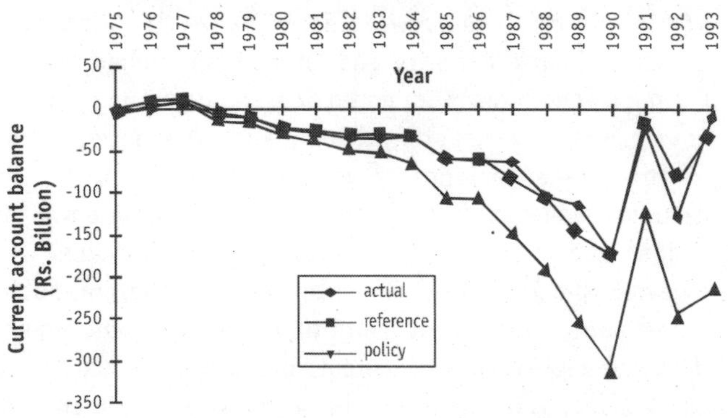

1. Increased Public Investment

Public investment which is an exogenous variable in the model is divided into two broad categories, viz; agriculture and non-agricultural investment. Public investment has a two-fold role in the model. It directly adds to the capital stock and generates output with a lag. In the non-agricultural sector public capital also competes with private capital to the extent that it crowds out the private sector in the credit market.

In the simulation experiment real public investment in the non-agricultural sector is raised by 10 per cent over its historical level in each year of the simulation period. There are three key endogenous variables to which this policy change may be addressed; output, prices and current account deficit in the balance of payment. The impacts of this policy under three different financing scenarios are discussed below.

a) Implications Under the Monetary Financing Scenario

The increased investment expenditure will have an immediate expansionary effect on fiscal deficit, raising the need for net RBI credit to the government. As a result, the reserve money will grow passively with the feedback from RBI credit, leading to expansion in money supply and consequent increase in prices. The ensuing output effect is however, expected to moderate the price rise to some extent. The initial deterioration in the budget balance will feed itself back into the system to the extent that the interest payments will grow in the next period to service the higher level of public debt.[4] The budget balance will also depend on the degree and speed with which government revenues and expenditures adjust to the changes in price and output. On the other hand, the output effect on the budget balance is expected to be favourable given the built-in-elasticity of tax system. On the financing side, while government borrowing from household is structurally related to nominal output, borrowing from banks is related to growth in bank deposits and in turn to money supply. Consequently, domestic non-monetary borrowing of the government will rise to partly finance the deterioration in the budget balance in the subsequent period. The need for monetary financing will, however, grow until the budget deficit returns to a stable equilibrium value. The repeated shock by way of continuous increases in public investment will set in motion a cycle of adjustment involving money, prices, output and budget deficit, until all endogenous variables in the model reach to their new long run equilibrium values.

Another dimension of the higher public investment expenditure relates to its impact on the balance of payments. The output and price effects of public investment outlay are expected to be accompanied by a deterioration in the current account deficit in the balance of payments. This happens as a part of the increase in domestic absorption stemming from the higher government expenditure spills over to the external current account through a rise in imports. Apart from this income effect, the current account deficit will also be influenced by the changes in relative prices in the wake of a change in domestic price. There are two routes in the model through which the domestic price affects the relative price, the direct effect, where the unit value index of exports is positively related to domestic price and the indirect effect, where the dollar price of exports is negatively related to exchange rate. An increase in domestic price will increase the supply price of exports, resulting in a rise in unit value index of exports. The rise in Rupee price of exports will be counteracted to some extent by the depreciation in nominal exchange rate. Consequently, the net impact of the domestic price change on the dollar price of exports, and hence on the export volume, will depend on the relative strength of both the factors. Since imports are positively related to domestic price, an increase in the latter will also cause the former to rise. The domestic price implications of higher public investment spending, therefore, turns out to be a crucial factor for the current account deficit in the balance of payment.

The quantitative impacts of the above policy simulation on key endogenous variables are presented in Table 3. The impact change refers to the immediate change (within the same year) in the endogenous variables in response to a change in the policy variable, the change is worked out as the percentage deviation in the variable over the base line or reference simulation.

$$d = \frac{1}{n}\sum_{i=1}^{n}\frac{(y^s - y^p)}{y^s}$$

Where 'd' is the annual average percentage deviation from the base line simulation, 'n' is number of years in the simulation period, 'y^s'is the value in the reference simulation (dynamic), and 'y^p' is value in the policy simulation. The short run impact refers to the annual average percentage deviation from the base line simulation during the first two years while the long run impact relates to the annual average percentage change during the entire sample period.

The immediate impact of the policy change is a rise in fiscal deficit and money supply by 16.98 per cent and 3.51 per cent, respectively, over their respective reference solutions in the same year of the increase in public investment. The initial price effect is placed at 0.69 per cent. Real net capital stock in non-agriculture sector and real income are higher by 0.60 per cent and 0.47 per cent, respectively, in the first year. Given the one-period lag between capital stock and output, the initial output effect stems from two sources viz; the higher level of credit flow to the production sectors which has come about by the higher level of real money stock and the short run adjustment of output to domestic demand conditions. The increase in domestic absorption creates an instantaneous demand for real imports, which rises by 1.58 per cent in the first year while exports in constant dollar fall marginally by 0.01 per cent, a result that follows from the change in the relative prices against exports. Consequently the current account deficit in the balance of payment shows a deterioration of 17.04 per cent in the first year of the policy change. In terms of ratio to GDP, current account deficit registers an increase of 0.08 percentage point from the reference simulation.

In the short to medium run, the adverse price and balance of payment effects continue to dominate the output effect. While during the first two years the price level rises by an average rate of 1.3 per cent, the growth in output is placed at 0.72 per cent and current account deficit deteriorates by 24.97 per cent (0.13 per cent of GDP). The short run scenario, in other words, shows a faster rate of deterioration in the internal and external balances than what was witnessed in the immediate horizon.

TABLE 3

Policy Simulation 1(a) Impact of Sustained 10 per cent increase in Real Public Investment in Non-agriculture Sector Financed by Money Creation

Endogenous Variables	Annual Average Percentage Deviation from the Base-Line Simulation		
	Impact (first year)	Short run (first two years' average)	Long run (sample period average, 1975-76 to 1993-94)
Fiscal Deficit	16.98	18.13	41.50
Government Revenue	0.60	1.08	16.10
Government Expenditure	4.78	5.46	21.92
Money Supply	3.51	5.34	29.31
Prices	0.69	1.30	18.13
Real Capital Stock in Non-Agriculture Sector	0.60	0.97	4.44
Real Income	0.47	0.72	2.66
Real Exports (US$)	-0.01	-0.06	3.97
Real Imports (Rs.)	1.58	2.39	20.66
Exchange Rate*	0.43	0.68	15.62
Current Account Deficit (Rs.)**	17.04	24.97	161.65
(as % of GDP)	(0.08)	(0.13)	(0.67)
External Debt	0.80	1.42	32.54
Interest Payment on External Debt	0.00	0.001	34.14

* (+) Implies depreciation and (-) appreciation

** (+) Implies increase in deficit and (-) decrease

In the long run, the price and balance of payments situation continue to show sharp deterioration. As the gap between revenue and expenditure increases steadily with inflation and rising stock of public debt, the fiscal deficit rises by an annual average rate of 41.50 per cent, leading to a money supply growth of 29.31 per cent. Prices on an average rise by 18.13 per cent, while real income goes up by an annual average rate of 2.66 per cent. External payments situation records a sharp deterioration with the real import growth averaging 20.66 per cent, and real export in US dollars showing only a small growth of 3.97 per cent, which is primarily caused by the exchange rate depreciation brought about by the combined influence of domestic price increase and the spurt in the current account deficit. The deficit in the current account rises by an average of 161.65 per cent or 0.67 per cent of GDP in the long run. In terms of magnitude, the current account deficit would have increased to 2.08 per cent of GDP in 1993-94, compared to the reference value of 0.36 per cent. Graph 1 to 4 provides the plots of actual, reference simulation and policy outcomes of major endogenous variables.

As may be seen from the graphs while the real output growth in the long run starts to taper off, inflation and balance of payment deficits increase to an unsustainable position, reflecting the relative inefficacy of the policy to achieve sustained output growth through monetary expansion.

(b) Financing Implications Under Increased Public Saving and Money Financing

In this scenario the additional public investment is assumed to be financed partly by an increase in savings of public enterprises while the savings of government administration evolves endogenously with the government revenue and expenditure growth. Historically, the proportion of nominal saving of public enterprises to public investment in the non-agricultural sector varied between 15 to 85 per cent during the sample period 1975-76 to 1993-94. It would seem reasonable to expect that the gross saving of public enterprises rise along with the public investment at a pace which would maintain the above ratios unaltered during the sample period. Implicit in this is the assumption that gap between the incremental investment and saving in each year is financed by money creation.

The quantitative changes recorded in the key endogenous variables under this financing scenario are summarised in Table 4.

The long run impacts on prices and balance of payments under this financing scenario are significantly different from the pure monetary financing scenario. In the long run the annual average increase in fiscal deficit works out to 25.13 per cent, giving a money supply growth of 18.71 per cent over the reference simulation. The price level shows an annual average increase of 11.37 per cent in the long run. It may be noted that the substantial moderation in the price rise compared to the pure monetary financing scenario has come about through a small loss in output growth. The annual average growth in real output over the reference solution is placed at 2.29 per cent under this scenario compared to 2.66 per cent in the pure monetary financing scenario. The ratio of current account deficit to GDP goes up by an annual average rate of 0.46 per cent in the long run. Under this policy exercise, or what may be referred to as restrained monetary expansion scenario, the price and balance of payments impacts remain adverse suggesting that a policy favouring growth in public investment inconsistent with the saving effort would likely to affect the long term prospects of maintaining a sustainable price and balance of payment situation.

TABLE 4

Policy Simulation 1(b) Impact of Sustained 10 per cent increase in Public Real Investment in Non-agriculture Sector Financed by Increased Public Saving and Money Creation

Endogenous Variables	*Annual Average Percentage Deviation from the Base-Line Simulation*		
	Impact (first year)	*Short run (first two years' average)*	*Long run (sample period average, 1975-76 to 1993-94)*
Fiscal Deficit	14.31	14.84	25.13
Government Revenue	1.34	1.86	12.40
Government Expenditure	4.66	5.20	15.34
Money Supply	2.98	4.41	18.71
Prices	0.58	1.07	11.37
Real Capital Stock in Non-Agriculture Sector	0.57	0.91	3.88
Real Income	0.43	0.64	2.29
Real Exports (US$)	-0.01	-0.07	2.11
Real Imports (Rs.)	1.38	2.02	13.24
Exchange Rate*	0.37	0.56	9.74
Current Account Deficit (Rs.)**	14.89	21.05	96.35
(as % of GDP)	(0.07)	(0.07)	(0.46)
External Debt	0.70	1.22	21.88
Interest Payment on External Debt	0.00	0.02	23.22

* (+) Implies depreciation and (-) appreciation

** (+) Implies increase in deficit and (-) decrease

(c) Financing Implications Under Increased Bank Credit to Government

Borrowing from market mainly commercial banks constitutes an alternative source of financing the additional public investment. Under the bond financing scenario, the macro-economic impact of fiscal deficit would depend on several factors such as the impact on interest rate, availability of credit to the private sector and the growth of absorption relative to growth in output. Theoretically, operating under a non-accommodating monetary policy environment, an increase in supply of government bonds is expected to increase the interest rate and adversely affect the economic activity elsewhere. Another consequence of the policy is that the increased flow of bank credit to government could imply reduction of credit for private sector capital formation. These adverse outcomes would have to be evaluated against the monetary stability of the policy which is likely to follow in absence of automatic growth in money supply on account of increase in fiscal deficit.

The policy simulation of above experiment required some change in the framework of the model. Bank credit to government, which was behaviourally determined in the model had to be expressed as an identity while the Reserve Bank credit to government, an endogenous variable earlier, had to be made exogenous. Under this policy experiment commercial bank credit to government is treated as the residual capital receipt to fill the gap between the fiscal deficit and borrowing from all other sources, including the Reserve Bank credit to government. The results of this policy outcome are presented in Table 5.

TABLE 5

Policy Simulation 1(c) Impact of Sustained 10 per cent increase in Public Real Investment in Non-agriculture Sector financed by increase in Commercial Bank Credit to the Government

Endogenous Variables	*Annual Average Percentage Deviation from the Base-Line Simulation*		
	Impact (first year)	*Short run (first two years' average)*	*Long run (sample period average, 1975-76 to 1993-94)*
Fiscal Deficit	15.39	15.11	17.88
Government Revenue	0.10	0.12	-0.12
Government Expenditure	3.93	3.90	4.04
Money Supply	-	-	-
Prices	-0.09	-0.16	-0.74
Commercial Bank Lending Rate	0.84	1.28	0.76
Real Private Investment in Non-Agriculture Sector	-2.55	-2.90	-8.27
Real Capital Stock in Non-Agriculture Sector	0.36	0.51	0.82
Real Income	0.24	0.32	0.57
Real Exports (US$)	-0.04	-0.10	-0.80
Real Imports (Rs.)	0.42	0.37	-6.37
Exchange Rate*	0.05	-0.01	-0.49
Current Account Deficit (Rs.)**	6.15	3.87	-4.79
(as % of GDP)	(0.03)	(0.02)	(-0.03)
External Debt	0.21	0.24	-0.97
Interest Payment on External Debt	-	-0.37	-3.47

* (+) Implies depreciation and (-) appreciation

** (+) Implies increase in deficit and (-) decrease

The outcomes under this policy are perceptibly different from the two other scenarios discussed above. An immediate impact of the policy is that while fiscal deficit rises by about 15.39 per cent in the same year of the increase in public investment, the ensuing output growth (0.24 per cent) and the unchanged level of money stock bring about a marginal decline in prices. Higher credit flow to government crowds out private investment in the non-agriculture sector by 2.55 per cent, although the aggregate capital stock in non-agricultural sector rises by 0.36 per cent. This is reminiscent of partial crowding out situation, implying that a part of the loss of bank credit to private sector is made good by the enterprises through other sources. This method of financing government investment also raises the commercial banks' lending rate by 0.84 per cent and affects private investment. The current account deficit witnesses a deterioration of the order of 6.5 per cent (0.03 percentage points in terms of ratio of GDP) mainly brought out by the growth of 0.42 per cent in real imports and a decline of 0.04 per cent in exports. In the short to medium run, fiscal deficit grows by 15.11 per cent per annum, while the impact on other variables are broadly on the lines of those witnessed in the immediate horizon.

In the long run, real capital stock in non-agricultural sector and output growth are placed at 0.82 per cent and 0.57 per cent, respectively, while private real investment declines at a faster rate of 8.27 per cent, resulting in the loss of much of the potential output. The resource gap of the government shows an annual average increase of 17.88 per cent. As the decline in the price level strengthens in the long run, the real money stock and aggregate demand level falls, and the relative price changes in favour of domestic goods, causing a decline in the real import. This shows up in the perverse effect of some improvement in current account balance. The relative price changes therefore, have a powerful impact on the current account deficit in the balance of payments.

2. Increased Current Expenditure Financed by Bank Credit

A policy induced increase in government current expenditure, financed by borrowing from the credit market is associated with both adverse price and income effects as well as a deterioration in the balance of payment situation. In this policy simulation government nominal current transfers (excluding interest payments) which is an exogenous variable in the model was increased by 10 per cent over its actual value in each year of the sample period. The quantitative outcomes of this policy are presented in Table 6.

It is evident that higher levels of current expenditure imply long run adverse macro-economic outcomes for the economy which stems from reduction in output level, increased pressure on prices and a deterioration in the current account deficit. This is in contrast to the policy outcomes of financing a higher level of public investment through credit from the market. Public investment, despite its adverse 'crowding out' impact on private investment raises the output level in the economy and may not imply severe long run balance of payments effects, if not financed by money creation. Efforts to reduce government expenditure should be therefore targeted at current expenditures, which have potential adverse macro-economic consequences for the economy.

TABLE 6

Policy Simulation 2. Impact of Sustained 10 per cent increase in Government Current Transfers Financed by Bank Credit

Endogenous Variables	Annual Average Percentage Deviation from the Reference Simulation		
	Impact (first year)	Short run (first two years' average)	Long run (sample period average, 1975-76 to 1993-94)
Fiscal Deficit	3.34	3.50	5.82
Money Supply	-	-	-
Real Income	0.02	0.01	-0.34
Prices	-0.01	-0.01	0.35
Real Exports (US$)	-0.003	-0.004	0.36
Real Imports (Rs.)	0.03	0.03	0.19
Exchange Rate*	neg.	neg.	0.23
Current Account Deficit (Rs.)**	0.45	0.29	3.42
(as % of GDP)	neg.	neg.	0.01
External Debt	0.02	0.02	0.28

* (+) Implies depreciation and (-) appreciation.

** (+) Implies increase in deficit and (-) decrease.

Neg.: Negligible.

3. Increased Reserve Bank's Foreign Assets

A pure monetary shock to the model by way of an increase in Reserve Bank's Foreign Assets (RBFA) is expected to work through the system in two ways. First, RBFA constitutes a part of the reserve money, hence there will be an immediate expansionary impact on money supply and prices. Higher real money balances would also go to enhance the credit flow to real sector, leading to some increase in output. The relative prices in the trade sector will however undergo a change with implications for trade flows. Secondly, RBFA has a direct implication for exchange rate, which would tend to depreciate with higher absorption of foreign exchange by RBI from the market. This constitutes a second channel of impact on the external balance. The quantitative dimension of this policy change on the key endogenous variables are reported in Table 7.

TABLE 7

Policy Simulation 3. Impact of Sustained 10 per cent increase in Reserve Bank foreign Assets

Endogenous Variables	*Annual Average Percentage Deviation from the Reference Simulation*		
	Impact (first year)	*Short run (first two years' average)*	*Long run (sample period average, 1975-76 to 1993-94)*
Money Supply	0.73	1.44	1.75
Prices	0.17	0.40	1.41
Fiscal Deficit	0.36	0.80	1.54
Real Income	0.04	0.08	0.02
Real Exports (US$)	0.25	0.36	0.46
Real Imports (Rs.)	0.22	0.50	1.44
Exchange Rate*	0.70	0.92	1.26
Interest Income on External Investment	-	29.28	40.33
Current Account Deficit (Rs.)**	-0.34	-4.63	1.36
External Debt	0.47	0.66	1.37

* (+) Implies depreciation and (-) appreciation

** (+) Implies increase in deficit and (-) decrease

In the first year of the increase in RBFA, money supply increases by 0.73 per cent and price level by 0.17 per cent. The price rise sets in motion an adjustment in government revenues and expenditure and fiscal deficit expands by 0.36 per cent, leading to borrowing from Reserve Bank in the second stage of impact. Real income is higher by 0.04 per cent in the first year. Exchange rate witnesses a depreciation of 0.70 per cent under the combined impact of domestic inflation and Reserve Bank's absorption of foreign exchange from the market. This produces an export growth in dollar terms of 0.25 per cent, while imports in real terms rise by 0.22 per cent. The current account deficit improves by 0.34 per cent over the reference simulation.

In the short to medium run money supply rises at an annual average rate of 1.44 per cent, leading to a price rise of 0.4 per cent. The annual increase in output averages 0.08 per cent. In the long run the balance of payment records a deterioration, as the adverse price effects cause imports to rise at a faster rate, despite an increased rate of depreciation in exchange rate. This shows that containing domestic inflation through other policy measures such as sterilisation has to play a critical role, if the depreciation in exchange rate should have an enduring favourable impact on the current account balance.

4. Growth in World Income

Growth in world income is expected to increase exports of goods and services and improve the current account balance. The economy-wide implications of this change can be studied by solving the model with the repeated favourable shocks during the sample period. The policy experiment conducted in this section is therefore intended to capture the temporal changes in key endogenous variables following one per cent increase in world real income (index) over the observed levels in each year of the sample period. This favourable shock to the external sector is expected to work through the model in the following way.

An increase in world income will have an immediate favourable impact on the current account balance. The decline in current account deficit will reduce the stock of external debt and interest payment, leading to further improvement in external balance. However, some of the gains accruing from this favourable shock will be neutralised by higher imports stemming from the increase in domestic absorption and appreciation of exchange rate following the reduction in current account deficit.

The quantitative dimension of this policy change is given in Table 8.

The immediate impact is an increase in dollar value of real exports of goods and services by 0.53 per cent over the reference simulation. Imports also rise by 0.02 per cent because of the higher level of domestic absorption. The current account deficit declines by 5.90 per cent in the first year implying an improvement of 0.03 percentage point in relation to GDP, which brings down the stock of external debt by 0.28 per cent. The improvement in current account balance and consequent reduction in external debt although brings down the external interest payment in the subsequent years, this also creates the conditions for exchange rate appreciation. In the long run, the annual average rate of decline in the current account deficit is placed at 0.08 percentage point of GDP, over the base-year scenario. The domestic impact of the favourable world output shock is an increase in real income which leads to an improvement in government resource gap and a decline in money supply and price level in the economy.

TABLE 8

Policy Simulation 4. Effects of Sustained 1 per cent increase in World Income (index) Over the Actual Level

Endogenous Variables	*Annual Average Percentage Deviation from the Base-Line Simulation*		
	Impact (first year)	*Short run (first two years' average)*	*Long run (sample period average, 1975-76 to 1993-94)*
Real Exports (US$)	0.53	0.67	0.82
Real Imports (Rs.)	0.02	0.02	-0.06
Exchange Rate*	-0.09	-0.13	-0.59
Current Account Deficit (Rs.)**	-5.90	-8.69	-8.86
(as % of GDP)	(-0.03)	(-0.04)	(-0.08)
External Debt	-0.28	0.50	-2.60
External Interest Payments	-	-0.21	-3.18
Fiscal Deficit	-0.02	-0.03	-0.12
Money Supply	-0.004	-0.01	-0.09
Prices	0.005	-0.01	-0.09
Real Income	0.01	0.02	0.02

* (+) Implies depreciation and (-) appreciation

** (+) Implies increase in deficit and (-) decrease

SECTION VI

CONCLUDING OBSERVATIONS

The major objective of this paper has been to analyse the various inter-relationships among fiscal deficit, prices, output and balance of payments and in this context to evaluate different policy options for maintaining sustainable internal and external balances in the economy. High levels of fiscal deficit pose various problems for the economy, inflation and adverse balance of payments consequences are considered to be the serious concerns of these deficits.

The macro econometric model presented above provides an integrated framework to study the external sector dimension of the fiscal deficit alongwith its monetary and real sector implications. The policy simulation results presented in the paper revealed that fiscal deficit in general results in widening of current account deficit, although this outcome critically depends on how the deficit is financed. In the case of monetary financing scenario, the price and income effects reinforce each other, leading to a rapid deterioration of external balance in the short run as well as in the long run. The external impacts of deficit are, however, less severe when deficit is financed by increased domestic savings. Thus, in any effort to maintain a sustainable balance of payments situation, domestic economic policy aimed at maintaining absorption and price at appropriate levels has an important role to play. This underlines the need for an externally consistent budgetary policy, keeping in view a medium term target of current account deficit in relation to GDP.

It is also important to observe that deficit financing to promote public investment and growth involves costs in terms of loss of control on inflation. The policy simulation results presented in the study show that a sustained increase in fiscal deficit financed by borrowing from the Reserve Bank leads to a spiral impact on prices in the long run although in the short run the adverse impact may look quite moderate. Even when the deficit is financed by borrowing from market, a prudent limit for such borrowing becomes essential. In a system of market determined interest rates, the financing requirement of government from the market should be consistent with the growth in national savings.

The policy simulation results also show that while growth in world income improves the external payments situation, some of the improvements may be lost due to the exchange rate appreciation. While a viable balance of payments strategy would have to be based on the supportive domestic policies to keep absorption and prices at appropriate levels, any temporary disequilibrium in the balance of payments due to adverse relative price movements may necessitate some adjustment of exchange rate.

Notes

1. This impact will not be strong if there are supply constraints or the economy is operating at near full capacity level.
2. The weighted average lending rate refers to the mean lending rates of commercial banks for various ranges of outstanding advances, weighted by the share of the respective outstanding advances to the total.

3. The net capital account transaction in the balance of payments is taken as a proxy for the private capital flows.
4. The increase in interest payment may be, to some extent, offset by higher profit transfers from RBI due to the rising share of RBI's claim on government in the total debt.

References

Aschauer, David A. (1989) : 'Does Public Capital Crowd Out Private Capital?', *Journal of Monetary Economics,* Vol. (24).

Bagchi, Amaresh and Pulin B. Nayak (1994) : 'Public Finance and Planning Process, The Indian Experience : A Survey', in Amaresh Bagchi and Nicholas Stern (eds.) *Tax Policy Planning in Developing Countries,* Oxford University Press.

Barro, Robert J. (1974) : 'Are Government Bonds Net Wealth?', *Journal of Political Economy,* Vol. 82, No. 6 (November-December).

———. (1989) : 'The Ricardian Approach to Budget Deficits', *Journal of Economic Perspectives,*Vol.3, No.2 (Spring).

Bartoli, Gloria (1989) : 'Fiscal Expansion and External Current Account Imbalances', in Mario I. Blejer and Chu Keyoung (eds.) *Fiscal Policy, Stabilisation and Growth in Developing countries,* International Monetary Fund.

Bernheim, Douglas B (1989) : 'A Neoclassical Perspective on Budget Deficits', *Journal of Economic Perspectives,* Vol.3, No.2 (Spring).

Bhattacharya B.B., R.B. Burman and A.K. Nag (1994) : 'Stabilisation Policy Options'; A Macro-econometric Analysis', *Development Research Group Study No.8,* Reserve Bank of India (April).

Blejer, Mario I and Adrienne Cheasty (1991) : 'Measurement of Fiscal Deficits: Analytical and Methodological Issues', *Journal of Economic Literature,* Vol. XXIX, No.4 (December).

Blejer, Mario I and Mohsin S. Khan (1984) : 'Government Policy and Private Investment in Developing Countries', *IMF Staff Papers,* Vol. 31.

Crips, Francis and Wynne Godley (1976) : 'A formal Analysis of the Cambridge Economic Policy Group Model', *Economica,* Vol. 43, No.172 (November).

Easterly, William and Klaus Schmidt - Hebbel (1993) : 'Fiscal Deficits and Macro-economic Performance in Developing Countries', *The World Bank Research Observer,* Vol. 8, No.2 (July).

Edwards, Sebastian and Mohsin S. Khan (1985) : 'Interest Rate Determination in Developing Countries : A Conceptual Framework', *IMF Staff Papers,* 32.

Frenkel, Jacob A and Assaf Razin (1987) : 'The Mundell-Fleming Model A Quarter Century Later : A Unified Exposition', *IMF Staff Papers,* International Monetary Fund, Vol. 34, No. 2 (December).

Haque, Nadeem U, Kajal Lahiri and Peter J. Montiel (1990) : 'A Macro-econometric Model for Developing Countries', *IMF Staff Papers,* Vol. 37, No.3 (September).

Khan, Mohasin S. and Malcolm D. Knight (1981) : 'Stabilisation Programs in Developing Countries : A Formal Framework', *IMF Staff Papers,*Vol. 28, No. 1 (March).

Krishnamurty, K. and V. Pandit (1997) : 'Exchange Rate, Tariff and Trade Flows : Alternative Policy Scenaries for India', *Indian Economic Review,* Vol. XXXI, No. 1.

Krishnamurty, K., V. Pandit, T. Palanivel and P. Saibaba (1997) : 'An Econometric Model for India, 1971-95', (IEG-DSE Research Team), Institute of Economic Growth.

Krishnamurty, K., P. Saibaba and N.A. Kazmi (1985) : 'Inflation and Growth: A Model for India' in K. Krishnamurty and V. Pandit (eds),*Macro-econometric Modeling of the Indian Economy : Studies on Inflation and Growth,* Hindustan Publishing Corporation.

Lahiri, Ashok K. (1989) : 'Dynamics of Asian Savings : The Role of Growth and Age Structure', *IMF Staff Papers,*Vol.36, No. 1 (March).

Mansur, H.A. (1989) : 'Effects of a Budget Deficit on the Current Account Balances : The Case of Philippines', in Mario I. Blejer and Chu Keyoung (eds.), *Fiscal Policy, Stabilisation and Growth in Developing Countries,* International Monetary Fund.

Mohanty, M.S. and Himanshu Joshi (1992) : 'The Dynamic Interrelationship Between Fiscal and Trade Deficits in India : 1970-71 to 1990-91', *Reserve Bank of India Occasional Papers,*Vol. 13, No.3 (September).

Mohanty, M.S. (1996) : 'Budget Deficits and Private Saving in India : Evidence on Ricardian Equivalence', *Reserve Bank of India Occasional* Papers, Vol. 16, No. 1 (March).

———. (1997) : 'Macro-Economic Stability, Growth and Fiscal Reform - The Indian Perspective, *Economic and Political Weekly,* Vol. XXXII, No. 6, February 8.

Patra, Michael D. and Sitikantha Pattanaik (1994) : 'Exchange Rate, Pass Through and the Trade Balance : The Indian Experience', *Reserve Bank of India Occasional Papers,*Vol. 15, No. 4 (December).

Pradhan, B.K., D.K. Ratha and Atul Sarma (1988) : 'Complementarity Between Public and Private Investment in India', *Journal of Development Economics,* Vol.23.

Polak, J.J. (1957) : 'Monetary Analysis of Income Formation and Payments Problems', *IMF Staff Papers,* No.4.

Rakshit, Mihir (1991) : 'The Macro-economic Adjustment Programme, A Critique', *Economic and Political Weekly,* Vol. XVII, No. 34 (August 24).

Rao, M.J.M. and Balwant Singh (1995) : 'Analytical Foundations of Financial Programming and Growth Oriented Adjustment', *Development Research Group Study* No. 10, Reserve Bank of India (January).

Rangarajan, C. (1982) : 'Agricultural Growth and Industrial performance in India', International Food Policy Research Institute, Research Report, 33 (October).

———. (1994) : 'India's Balance of Payments : The Emerging Dimensions', *Sixteenth G.B. Pant Memorial Lecture* (New Delhi).

Rangarajan, C. and Anoop Singh (1984) : 'Reserve Money : Concepts and Policy Implications for India', *Reserve Bank of India Occasional Papers,* June.

Rangarajan, C. and Anupam Basu and Narendra Jadhav (1989) : 'Dynamics of Interaction Between Government Deficit and Domestic Debt in India', *Reserve Bank of India Occasional Papers,* Vol.10, No.3 (September).

Rangarajan, C. and R.R. Arif (1990) : 'Money, Output and Prices : A Macro-econometric Model', *Economic and Political Weekly,* Vol.XXV, No.16 (April 21).

Rath, Nilkantha (1989) 'Agricultural Growth and Investment in India', *Journal of Indian School of Political Economy,* (January-June).

Sau, Ranjit (1992) : 'Making of a Payments Crisis : India 1991', *Economic and Political Weekly,* Vol. XXVII, No. 33 (August).

Shetty, S.L. (1990) : 'Investment in Agriculture : Brief Review of Recent Trends', *Economic and Political Weekly,* February 17.

Sundararajan, V. and Subhash Thakur (1980) : 'Public Investment, Crowding Out, and Growth : A Dynamic Model Applied to India and Korea', *IMF Staff Papers,* Vol. 27 (December).

Tanzi, Vito (1977) : 'Inflation, Lags in Collection, and the Real Value of Tax Revenue', *IMF Staff Papers,* Vol.XXIV, No.1 (March).

APPENDIX 1

Definition of Variables

Endogenous

DT	=	Nominal direct tax revenue of government.
DIT	=	Nominal indirect tax revenue of government.
NTX	=	Nominal non-tax revenue of government administrative departments (includes income from property and entrepreneurship and miscellaneous current receipts).
con	=	Real government consumption expenditure.
ΔTDBT	=	Incremental debt of the government.
ΔBCG	=	Change in commercial bank credit to government (March 31).
DNB	=	Government domestic non-bank borrowing viz., small savings, provident funds and special deposits etc.
P	=	Wholesale Price Index (1980-81 = 100).
PGDP	=	GDP deflator (1980-81 = 100).
PGKE	=	Implicit capital formation deflator in public sector (1980-81 = 100).
ΔDEP	=	Change in aggregate deposit of commercial banks, including co-operative banks (March 31).
M_3	=	Broad money stock (March 31).
IB	=	Interest rate for 1 to 3 year bank deposits.
pc	=	Real private consumption expenditure.
piag	=	Real gross private investment in agriculture sector.
pinag	=	Real gross private investment in non-agriculture sector.
yar	=	Output originating from agriculture (1980-81 prices).
ynar	=	Output originating from non-agricultural sector (1980-81).
depag	=	Depreciation in agricultural sector in real term.
depnag	=	Depreciation in non-agriculture sector in real term.
expt$	=	Exports of goods and services in constant US dollar (includes merchandise and invisible exports, excluding transfers, investment income and miscellaneous current receipts).
UVIX	=	Unit value index of exports (1980-81 = 100).
impt	=	Real imports of goods and services in Rupees (includes merchandise and invisible imports, excluding transfers, investment income and miscellaneous current payments).
EXR	=	Nominal exchange rate (rupee to US dollar).
XII	=	External interest income in nominal term.
ΔXDBT	=	Change in external debt.
TR	=	Nominal current revenue of government.
TM	=	Nominal import tax revenue.
GXP	=	Nominal government expenditure.
TRP	=	Nominal transfer payments of government administration.
IP	=	Total interest payment of government.
FD	=	Public sector fiscal deficit.
IPI	=	Interest payment on internal debt of the government.
IDBT	=	Outstanding internal public debt.
IPX^g	=	Interest payment on external debt of the government.
$XDBT^g$	=	Outstanding external debt of the government.
TDBT	=	Total outstanding public debt of the government.
RCG	=	Outstanding Reserve Bank credit to the government (March 31).
EB^g	=	External borrowing of the government.
BCG	=	Outstanding bank credit to the government (March 31).
RM	=	Outstanding reserve money (March 31).
BCP	=	Outstanding bank credit to private sector (March 31).
wlr	=	Weighted average real lending rate of banks.
absp	=	Real private absorption.
add	=	Real demand for domestically produced goods and services.
ad	=	Real aggregate absorption.
y	=	Real GDP at factor cost.
Y	=	Nominal GDP at factor cost.
YM	=	Nominal GDP at market prices.
ym	=	Real GDP at market prices.
pyd	=	Real private disposable income.
PEXP$	=	Index of dollar price of exports.
CAB	=	Current account balance.
IPX	=	Interest payment on external debt.
IPX^p	=	Interest payment on private external debt.
XDBT	=	Outstanding external debt.
$XDBT^p$	=	Outstanding private external debt.
kagr	=	Real net capital stock in agriculture sector.
knagr	=	Real net capital stock in non-agriculture sector.

Exogenous

DDT	=	Dummy for 1991-92 for the change in the structure of direct taxes.
DDIT	=	Dummy for 1992-93 and 1993-94 for the sharp change in the indirect tax rates.
DNTX	=	Dummy for sharp fluctuations in non-tax revenue in some years.
DDBT	=	Dummy for sharp fluctuation in outstanding debt in 1974-75.
ΔWSLR	=	Weighted average statutory liquidity ratio (SLR weighted by the number of days the ratio was in force).
DBCG	=	Dummy for unusual increase in bank credit to government in 1977-78.
DDNB	=	Dummy for the sharp decline in government non-bank domestic borrowing in 1974-75.
DPI	=	Dummy representing high inflation years in 1973-74 and 1974-75 due to first oil shock.
DP2	=	Dummy for the second oil shock in 1979-80.
DPGKE	=	Dummy for the sharp decline in implicit government capital formation deflator in 1980-81.
DDEP	=	Dummy for large variation in bank deposits in 1985-86 and 1986-87.
pcfag	=	Public sector gross investment in agriculture in real term.
dpiag1	=	Dummy for the sharp decline in public investment in agriculture in certain years.
dpiag2	=	Dummy for sharp increase in public investment in agriculture in certain years.
pcfnag	=	Public sector gross investment in non-agriculture sector in real term.
capb	=	Net capital account in the balance of payments account deflated by wholesale price index.
OPC	=	Intermediating cost of banks.
RAIN	=	Rain fall index (1970-71 = 100).

AREA	=	Index of gross cropped area (1970-71 = 100).
wyr	=	Index of world output (1980-81 = 100).
WPEXP	=	World price of exports (1980-81 = 100).
dexpt$	=	Dummy for unusual large variation in exports of goods and services in some years.
DUVIX	=	Dummy for unusual decline in unit value index of exports in some years.
PIMP	=	Unit value index of imports (1980-81 = 100).
dimpt1	=	Dummy for a large fall in imports following the stabilisation programme in 1991-92.
dimpt2	=	Dummy for sharp variation in imports in certain years.
RBFA	=	Stock of Reserve Bank's foreign asset (March 31).
DEXR1	=	Dummy representing the readjustment of exchange rate of Rupee in 1991-92.
DEXR2	=	Dummy representing a large depreciation of exchange rate of Rupee in 1992-93.
LBR	=	One year London Inter-Bank Offer Rate.
DXDBT	=	Dummy for change in classification of external debt from 1991-92 onwards.
SE	=	Gross savings of departmental and non-departmental enterprises of the government.
MR	=	Average import duty rate.
SUBS	=	Subsidies in nominal term.
OCTR	=	Other current transfers of the government administration representing pension, etc.
I_d	=	Average interest rate on government external debt.
I^g_x	=	Average interest rate on government external debt.
VLC	=	Valuation change in government external debt.
FICG	=	Financial institutions' investment in government securities (outstanding).
E	=	Proportion of external borrowing in the total borrowing of the government.
MISCR	=	Miscellaneous capital receipts of government.
RBCS	=	Outstanding Reserve Bank credit to commercial sector (March 31).
GCL	=	Outstanding government currency liability (March 31).
RNML	=	Outstanding Reserve Bank's net non-monetary liability (March 31).
OBFA	=	Outstanding level of other banks' foreign assets.
BNML	=	Banking sectors' net non-monetary liability.
NR	=	Net external transfers in balance of payments including non-interest investment income and other miscellaneous current receipts.
I^p_x	=	Average interest rate on private external debt.
EROM	=	Errors and omissions in gross capital formation data.

14

Analytics of Monetary Management

A Vasudevan

Introduction

A look at some of the current economic indicators would show that policy makers would have to act swiftly in several areas of policy. There is a potential threat of a *run-away* inflation, triggered *inter alia* by the uncertainties surrounding the recently concluded Gulf War. The 'twin' deficits on the fiscal and balance of payments fronts have been large and may not be easily manageable in the short run. The domestic savings ratio has been generally stable in recent years. Aggregate demand has been buoyant, its rise being considerably high in relation to the modest output expansion.

Against this background, one might like to have a fresh look at the present monetary management with a view to pursuing what might be called "appropriate" monetary policy.

This paper attempts to scan the major issues in the literature on monetary economics with the purpose of gaining analytical insights into the transmission channels at work. One has to recognize that the relevance of analytical literature or theories would have to be empirically tested to be of use for policy-makers. But this would have to be done only when we intuitively feel that the logical reasoning behind a particular theory or theories *could* be valid in the economic circumstances obtaining in India today.

For purposes of convenience, the paper has been divided into three sections. Section I gives a brief view of some of the major analytical ideas that have emerged in monetary economics historically. We had to be selective here, so that we could take up only those ideas that may be of some pertinence to situations generally obtaining in developing countries. Section II provides a snapshot picture of some of the important monetary policy issues faced by transitional economies like India. In the final section, an attempt is made to highlight some of the areas of policy that need to be focussed on.

I

The main proposition that provided the foundation stone for the development of monetary economics is that changes (very often, increases) in money supply tend to bring about changes (increases) in prices. This is the well-known quantity theory of money in its simplest form. This theory, or rather the relationship between money supply and prices, could however be presented in different degrees of sophistication. Whatever version that one may embrace, it is usually taken for granted that the impact runs *uni-directionally* from changes in money supply to changes in prices. There are no feedbacks. In its crude version, the impact is regarded as *direct* and proportionate, if not *instantaneous*. Many text books leave the impression that classical and neo-classical economists,[1] as well as the present day "monetarists" advocated the crudest form of the quantity theory of money. With the exception *perhaps* of Adam Smith,[2] who seemed to have accepted the quantity theory of money without questioning, classical economists did not consider the impact of money supply changes on prices to be direct, and any case, immediate. In fact, David Hume who is often credited as the first or atleast the early, exponent of the quantity theory of money, had argued that "betwixt the acquisition of money and rise in prices .... the increasing quantity of gold and silver is favourable to industry"[3]. It is the favourable effect in this interrugnum – the time-period needed for effects of money supply changes to be felt on prices - that was noted in the writings of many famous writers, such as Henry Thornton[4], David Ricardo,[5] John Stuart Mill,[6] Knut

Prepared in January-February months of 1991, for an internal seminar, this paper is reproduced here with minimum of changes.

Wicksell,[7] and Alfred Marshall[8]. Indeed, it is this favorable effect that provided the sustenance to the concept of 'forced savings' as may be seen in the versatile writings of Dennis Robertson[9] in the 1920s and of John Maynard Keynes[10] in the '30s - a concept which was used as the *raison d'etre* of inflationary financing *in the early stages* of economic development[11].

Barring perhaps John Maynard Keynes, all the writers mentioned above regarded the quantity theory of money to be valid *in the long run*. More importantly, the theory was couched in terms of the *ceteris paribus* clause, from atleast the days of John Stuart Mill. One of the elements of the clause was, and is, the velocity of circulation of money (v), or as Mill had called, the 'rapidity' of circulation of money[12]. Money hoarded, money kept aside to meet contingencies and money in the coffers of the bank are said to have no impact on prices. Fisher[13] explained, while presenting his famous equation of exchange, MV=PT, that both V and T (the index of the physical volume of transactions) are determined by *real* factors and cannot change in the short run. Under this constraint, P, the aggregate price level would respond passively to shifts in M, the money supply.

The equation of exchange however elicited perhaps the largest amount of criticism in the literature. It is dismissed as a truism or mathematical identity. Even the finer Cambridge version attributed to Alfred Marshall[14] and A.C. Pigou[15] (P=kR/M where R stands for total income, and k the proportion of it held in the form of cash balances) was not spared of the criticism that the equations do *not* have "the advantage of separating out those factors through which, in a modern economic system, the causal process actually operates during a period of change"[16]. It has often been said, that V need not be stable even over a period of time, when institutional arrangements and technology are constantly changing. The motives for holding cash balances could be several, and could, it is said, affect k's value. T (or R) too could shift owing to technological changes within a relatively compact time horizon. P, the concept of the general price level, as Hayek contended, would have to be thrown overboard, since "almost any change in the amount of money, ... must *always* influence relative prices."[17]

It was not until Keynes' *The General Theory* appeared in 1936,[18] that the dominance of the quantity theory as a major feature of monetary economics was ever in serious doubt. This has to do, one has good reasons to suspect, with the very logical framework of thinking of the classical and neo-classical economists. Yet, it is often believed, erroneously though, that the effects of changes in money supply are felt entirely in the commodity market, *not* in the loan or bond market. This, however, was not the case with the classical and neo-classical framework. In this world, an increase in money supply is generally brought about through the banking system, thereby resulting in an increased supply of loans. When the supply of loans increase, the rate of interest – the money rate, as against the 'natural' rate of interest on capital - would decline. But this decline was considered to be only temporary. For, in the meantime, prices would have gone up and would have caused an increase in either the volume of borrowing necessary to finance the purchase or the cash holdings. The demand for loans, as a consequence, would increase, as Marshall would have us believe, and cause a return of the money interest to its original level in the long run. In Wicksellian analysis, however, the price increases would generate an internal drain which draws bank reserves down and hence forces banks to raise their rates again. Whatever route-whether Marshallian or Wicksellian - that one takes to find the interest rates to eventually reach equilibrium, the point that one needs to note is that changes in money supply would have symmetrical effects on the demand for and supply of loans and would therefore leave the rate of interest invariant *in the long run*[19].

It would be misleading to suggest that the early discussion in monetary economics, which focussed on the quantity theory of money, could be reduced to common-place impressions that money is *completely neutral* to output, and that the aggregate demand for goods represented by MV is *independent* of the rate of interest. No doubt, one could take a critical stance that the literature on the equation of exchange did not fully exploit the potentialities of arguments regarding the forces at work behind MV and T, and the ways of integrating them. But it must be recognized that the strands of thought that (a) individuals hold cash balances for transactions and precautionary purposes, (b) there could be a possible favourable impact of monetary expansion on productive capital (via forced savings) and (c) the increase in money occuring through the banking system would disturb the initial interest rate position, and thereby would entail decision-taking on the part of investors with reference to cost of borrowing weighed against the rate of return, are some of the important insights on which later day monetary economics and empirical investigations have drawn much support.

Keynes' *The General Theory*, it is commonly recognised, has led to dominance of fiscal policy, and eclipse of monetary economics for a number of years till the emergence of the recent monetarist revolution. But it must be noted that Keynes gave critical importance to the quantity theory of money. Keynes rescued the theory from being seen as totally neutral with respect to output. Treating money as "a subtle device for linking the present to the future", Keynes enunciated: "So long as there is unemployment, *employment* will change in the same proportion as the quantity of money; and when there is full employment, *prices* will change in the same proportion as the quantity of money"[20]. The allusion to employment here, it is well known, is really to output. Keynes referred to a number of factors that would impact on the relation between changes in money and changes in the price level *in the short run*. Some of the important ones Keynes mentioned in Section IV of Chapter 21 of *The General Theory* were: the rate of interest reflecting the liquidity preference, the response of investment to interest rate changes, the investment multiplier, the worker's remuneration relative to their efficiency, the production bottlenecks that impact on supply elasticity, the degree of 'money illusion' in a period of buoyancy in effective demand, and the supply elasticities responding to changes in the money rewards that are effected. The long run relationship between the national income and the quantity of money will depend on liquidity preferences. And price stability in the long run should be viewed with reference to the upward trend of costs and the rate of increase in the productive efficiency.

The quantity of money also plays an important role in the Keynesian theory of rate of interest. Defining the rate of interest at any time as "the reward for parting with liquidity", and the 'price', which "equilibrates the desire to hold wealth in the form of cash with the available quantity of cash", Keynes observed that liquidity preference is a "functional tendency which fixes the quantity of money which the public will hold when the rate of interest is given."[21] Keynes agreed with the 'Cambridge' quantity theorists (and some of the earlier writers) that people hold cash for transaction and precautionary balances. But he added that people hold money to speculate in the bond market. At high interest rate (which implies low bond prices), people will tend to hold bonds rather than money. As the rate of interest falls, bond prices rise, and yields on bonds would decline. Selling bonds would then be attractive because of the rise in bond prices (which permits capital gains). People would choose to hold more of assets in the form of money as rate of interest falls. But there is a minimum rate of interest, say two per cent, where bonds would not at all be attractive and all assets would be held only in money form. Such a situation, called the liquidity trap, would imply that at very low rate of interest, both investment and consumption would remain unaffected, and monetary policy would become helpless. This view was relevant to the economic circumstances that were brought about by the Great Depression of the 1930s, since it implied that it is only through fiscal actions that the economy could be revived out of depression.

The rate of interest is a critical variable in Keynes' *The General Theory*. It affects not only the demand for money, but also-indeed, more importantly - investment spending in the typical Keynesian world. Firms would be induced to invest when the marginal product of capital exceeds the rate of interest, but investment spending as a rule, simple as it may look, would be negatively related to the rate of interest.

The brilliance of Keynes' monetary ideas is best attested by the development of the financial sector that has been taking place as a part of the process of economic development since the end of the Second World War. The growth of financial intermediaries – both bank and non-bank – and markets has given rise to growth in the number of financial instruments. This is a clear signal that money – be it currency or currency plus interest-free bank deposits- alone cannot be the preferred asset of economic units. There are a number of other assets too that could form part of economic agents' holdings, because they have 'moneyness' and could be liquid or readily convertible into cash.[22] Holdings of such assets would imply a certain individual behaviour towards spending with obvious implications for aggregate demand or expenditure. In such a context, demand for money and expenditure functions cannot be regarded as dependent only on income and the rate of interest, as the simple Keynesian framework would suggest. Several other factors come into play. Of these, wealth, as the writings of Patinkin[23] and Leijonhufvud[24] would suggest is the most important one. *Other things being equal*, wealth is positively related to money demand. Wealth also influences income via its effects on consumption spending and thereby on savings.

Much the most of monetary thinking that has emerged since the appearance of *The General Theory*, revolves round the important idea that economic agents attempt to *optimize* their asset portfolios, under the given constraints. Friedman's "restatement" of the quantity theory of money[25] is one of the early approaches to portfolio balance analysis. This analysis, to put it in a most simple way, attempts to postulate the relationship between money and income, and more generally to delineate individual behaviour in the context of the interaction between real and financial markets.

If this is the correct interpretation, it would be misleading to regard Friedman's "restatement" and the subsequent defences of the "restatement" by Friedman,

Brunner, Sargent, Laidler and a number of others who are often identified as "monetarists"[26] as a mere rehash of the old quantity theory of money. In fact, it is not. For, the restatement was formulated as a theory of demand for money and as a theory of stock – money and assets. Monetarists including Friedman do not adhere strictly to neutrality of money. In fact, they acknowledge output effects of shifts in money in the short run. They can also live with a weaker assumption about velocity, which reflects the relationship between money and income rather than money and volume of transactions in the classical and neo-classical literature. The effect of temporary factors on velocity has been duly recognized and the impact that structural aspects could well have to bring about a general downward drift in velocity over secular period has been noted by monetarists.

The portfolio balance of monetarists operates under two critical constraints. Individuals hold cash balances as a proportion of their expenditures, and this ratio has to be constant. Moreover, the ratio of cash balances to other assets holdings of individuals would also be constant.

The transmission mechanism of monetarists could be simplified thus. An injection of money into the system say by deliberate fiscal action would imply that people would hold more money than before. There would thus be an excess of money supply over its demand. This will create additional spending in the commodities and asset markets through the effect upon the rate of interest. The result would be to affect either prices or quantities or both, in the two markets, depending on the elasticity of supply of goods and assets. In any event, there would be a rise in nominal income and asset values. This process would continue till the demand for and supply of money become equal once again. This would be possible when the values of commodities and assets (i.e., incomes) increase as much as the money supply.

The simplified monetarists' transmission process resembles the classical and neo-classical position – only superficially. But there are two differences. Monetarists include the rate of interest and give it a critical role. Moreover, they recognize the impact of money supply shifts on asset market. Because of these two assumptions, the monetarists are able to present a *proportional* relationship between money and income. What if we do not rely on these assumptions?

James Tobin provides an answer to this question by adopting a general equilibrium approach[27]. Under this approach, the individual maximizes his utility by allocating his wealth across a range of assets, including cash. The determination about his asset portfolio – holdings of cash and other assets – would be done *simultaneously* but not for all time to come. Wherever there is an external impetus (such as injection of money), the individual will adjust his asset portfolio, subject of course to budget constraint. This would imply that there is perfect substitutability among assets. In Tobin's framework, housing and equity shares are the two assets which tend to respond closely to monetary policy stances. The effect of monetary policy on the price of these assets would be best reflected in the effect of, what Tobin noted, the valuation ratio on investment. This ratio is a ratio of the market price of an asset to its replacement cost. If the market price exceeds the replacement cost, say, of a house, a potential purchaser of a house may have a house built, rather than buy an existing house. House building would be a form of investment. A rise in the valuation ratio could arise if there is an increase in market value of the asset or a fall in replacement cost.

Tobin's approach that monetary policy has an effect on asset and share prices, would imply that the policy should be employed to bring about a stability in these markets. One way of realising this objective is through a stability of money growth, as monetarists would seek, or through interest rates that have an influence on mortgage rates, as is the case in the United States.

While this approach has no serious limiting assumptions that the monetarists often make, it does not deal with situations where individuals could borrow to optimise their asset portfolios. Credit mechanisms have no role to play in the general equilibrium approach. It is essentially a framework of analysis, and hardly, as Tobin himself admitted in 1989 in his essay on the state of macro-economic theory, a source of specific conclusions about the signs and magnitudes of relationships among economic variables[28].

It is in this context that mention must be made of the reputation of invincibility that an innocent looking downward sloping Phillips curve[29] enjoyed for over a decade since it first appeared in 1958. Phillips' main point was that (money) wage rate (w) increases could be explained by recent values of the unemployment rate (U). Phillips stated: "When the demand for labour is high and there are very few unemployed we should expect employers to bid wage rates up quite rapidly, each firm and each industry being continually tempted to offer a little above the prevailing rates to attract the most suitable labour from other firms and industries."[30] Phillips presented the hypothesis, viz., the percentage rate of increase in wage rates is inversely related to U, by using the data for U.K. for the period 1861-1957.

As inflation rate and increase in the wage rate are highly correlated in steady state situations, say by a given parametric value, λ, one could well regard Phillips' curve as reflecting a trade-off between U and the inflation rate. The curve essentially gives the message that the economy cannot reduce, on a permanent basis, its inflation rate without causing additional unemployment.

Milton Friedman and Edmund Phelps destroyed the invincibility of the logic behind the Phillips curve by substituting the word 'real' in place of 'money' wage rate increase - one of the two macro variables of the Phillips Curve[31]. For, workers are interested in real wages, not in money wages. Hence the real wage rates would rise when demand for labour increases. The wage rate in nominal terms at time 't' would, in such an event, be determined by the unemployment rate in the previous period and the 'expected' inflation rate in period 't' (One has to consider only the expected inflation rate since the actual inflation rate for period 't' cannot be obtained before completing the period). The result is the *expectations - augmented* Phillips Curve. The newly derived curve however, needs to be interpreted with caution since what we would get as the ultimate outcome in respect of the trade-off is entirely different from the one that was obtained under the original Phillips Curve.[32]

The wage rate increase in steady state as mentioned above would be equal to the inflation rate plus the above-mentioned linking parameter, λ. The steady state relationship between inflation and unemployment would be:

$$\Delta P + \lambda = f(U) + \Delta P^e$$

where p is the log of inflation rate, and the superscript 'e' signifies the expectation. In steady state, however, $p=p^e$. Therefore, $\lambda = f(U)$ - a result that clearly demonstrates that steady state unemployment is *not* related to steady state inflation rate but by λ, which is a historically observed parameter. But this reasoning was initially *not* given due credence, because λ was found out to be low at 0.5 in Solow's book[33] which assumed that expectations are formed adaptively. (Friedman - Phelps hypothesis suggested the value to be 1). However, Sargent[34] and McCallum[35] showed that the parameter value (of λ) would be close to 1, if expectations are *rational*.

In addition to the intellectual efforts of Friedman, Phelps and other monetarists, two other aspects worked to negate the validity of the Phillips Curve. The seventies, were characterised by a combination of inflation and stagnation – stagflation – a situation which was unthinkable as per the Phillips Curve's postulate. Besides, Lucas[36] and Barro[37] came out with extra-ordinary contributions to show that Friedman – Phelps position is not a mere critique, but has theoretical underpinnings.

From these developments arose the theory of rational expectations as an approach to the study of expectations. It suggests, in the words of Grossman, that "monetary and fiscal policies may not be able to produce systematic expectational errors, and this implies that the ability of the government to improve the aggregate performance of the economy is.. limited .... Specifically, the idea of rational expectations suggests that it may not be feasible to design monetary and fiscal policies that can actively stabilize aggregate output and employment relative to their natural levels".[38] A critical assumption underlying the theory is that information available to private agents should be perfect and adequate, in the sense that it should enable the agents to have knowledge of the structure of the economy and knowledge of the past and current data, that underlie the economic structure. It is taken for granted that private agents use the information efficiently. Another assumption, critical as it is, is that commodity markets always clear. The theory however sets out to lay labour market micro-foundations, which in effect means that labourers will move voluntarily where the incentives (real wages) are attractive. Labour markets would *over time* attain equilibrium or natural rate of unemployment, but there would be some sectors which would be expanding and some declining. Such a continuous search for equilibrium could, however, be thwarted from occuring if there is monetary policy uncertainty – uncertainty about inflation and relative wages. If monetary policy is certain, then there would be "efficient" equilibrium.

Systematic monetary actions, under the rational expectations theory, would affect nominal variables such as the *level* of prices and inflation *rate*. And *unanticipated* changes in money supply alone, as Barro has informed[39], would affect output. But this result did not last long. Gordon[40] suggested that both anticipated and unanticipated money stock matter. By 1980, it was increasingly getting clear from the econometric evidence that effects of anticipated shifts in money supply would be evident on real side, though in a transitory way[41]. Such effects would work either through fixity of prices or wages so that not all markets clear instantly, or through the expected rate of inflation and thus on real interest rate, so that inventory or fixed capital formation and/or labour supply would be affected[42].

An interesting implication for policy that arises from the rational expectations literature[43] is that the ability of economists to predict responses of economic agents to policies under discretionary policy-making would be limited, since the environments in which the agents believe they are operating in, may not be fully understood. In reality, it would be possible to assess the consequences of only those policies which are guided by fixed, transparent, relatively permanent and predictable policy-rules. For instance, a 4 per cent increase in money supply could be laid down as a rule if this order of expansion is consistent with the observed trends in the rate of growth in output, and with the objective of price stability. Policy rules would not face the problem of "dynamic inconsistency" of optimal policy, under conditions of discretionary policy-making. For, time consistency in respect of monetary policy can be achieved only if a specified growth of nominal prices is maintained. But this effect cannot be achieved by a pre-set path for the quantity of money, because the interaction of fiscal and monetary policy would permit tax policies to alter the effects that a monetary policy may have on prices. Moreover, specific policy rules help to achieve inflation control, and to maintain reputation and credibility of actions.

In spite of the preference of those who advocated the rational expectations approach for policy rules, it is not clear as to how to test the usefulness of rules *vis-a-vis* discretion, and how rules provide better predictions than discretionary policy-making.

The developments in the literature in the eighties are not as heavily weighted in favour of rational expectations as in the seventies. Attempts are being made to represent nominal rigidities in the commodities markets and the absence of market clearance as part of economic life. This approach which attempts to capture the underlying micro and perhaps micro-micro level of relations between individuals and firms, being termed "new Keynesian" economics,[44] is now being increasingly taken up by economists as a new challenge.

The above discussion related implicitly to closed economy situations. Money's role in open economies was for a long time guided by the classical (and neo-classical) idea of price-specie flow mechanism.[45] First enunciated by David Hume, this mechanism may be stated thus: Wealth maximization through continuous trade surplus is a pre-classical (mercantilist) belief, since it entailed gold and silver accumulation. But it ignores the impact that gold and silver inflows would have on money supply, and consequently on the prices of goods including exportables. Foreign countries by paying for their imports in gold and silver would have reduced their money holdings, and experience a fall in prices relative to those in the home country. Foreign countries would therefore buy less goods from the home country. At the same time, domestic consumers in the home country would buy more of foreign goods and turn away from domestically produced goods. Eventually, the trade surplus of the home country would turn into deficit and gold would flow out. This process of inflows and outflows of gold and silver is assumed to occur incessantly in a cyclical fashion.

The burden of adjustment in the case of either a trade surplus or a trade deficit, has as the above description showed, fallen on domestic prices. If however one assumes domestic prices to be sticky, then adjustment would have to take place through exchange rate changes. However, as the experience has shown in the early part of the 20th century, competitive devaluations often take place to deny the trading partner an edge in trade balancing. To avoid uncertainties that arise from a competitive devaluation process, a system of 'fixed' rate was evolved. This was in fact made a part of the post-war international economic plans with the International Monetary Fund charged with the responsibility of having surveillance of exchange rate policies. This implied that all nations would pursue policies for price stability which by definition would have to be the same for the world at large. The fixed rate system too broke down in 1973 when the US delinked itself from the free convertibility of currency into gold and adopted a floating rate system.

The case for a flexible exchange rate system was made by Milton Friedman in 1953 through an influential essay.[46] Friedman assumed that nominal prices would be sticky, so that during a period of payment imbalance, free exchange rates could obviate socially undesirable fluctuations in real income and employment levels. Friedman also made out a case for a permanent system of floating rates in preference to occasional changes in speculative transactions. Floating exchange rates have the added advantage of freeing the monetary authorities from pursuing exchange rate stability as an objective. Now they could focus on price stability with a greater degree of single-minded devotion than would be possible under a fixed rate system.

However, the experience of the floating rate system since 1973 has not been on the expected lines. Exchange rate volatility was high, but this fortunately did not impede trade.[47] But the volatility took place partly because most major nations have in recent years eliminated exchange and capital controls. The movements of capital across national boundaries often in line with changes in interest rates and inflation rates were very large. But in recent years they could be influenced if the major countries concerned pursued both monetary and fiscal policies on predicted lines. The present efforts at international policy coordination among the seven major countries (the USA, the UK, Germany, Japan, France, Canada and Italy) to bring about exchange rate stability within a zone indicate that whether the exchange rate regimes are fixed or floating, the need to pursue appropriate monetary policies cannot be ignored.

This is true in the case of developing countries as well. If capital is immobile, interest rates inflexible, and output inelastic, as is the situation in many developing countries, an increase in domestic money supply would cause a deterioration in the external current account and a depreciation of the domestic currency. The excess money supply would be eliminated by a proportionate rise in the domestic price level. If there is a general proneness to inflation and inflationary expectations, a floating exchange rate could well foster rapid and unstable inflation, which will damage saving, investment and growth. It is for this reason that flexibility in exchange rate management has been generally accepted by many developing countries as one of the objectives of macro-economic policy management.[48]

II

Section I gives an important insight that while monetary policies will have price effects, their output effects cannot be established in a firm manner. Nonetheless, it is important to recognise that policies bearing on the rate of interest could well have impact on the levels of fixed investment or on inventory and thereby the output.

For economies in transition (i.e., those which are diversifying and modernizing activities at relatively high rates by *historical* standards and are pursuing flexible economic policies), there are no well laid down monetary policy strategies that could be considered as appropriate. The issues they face are somewhat different from those of typical developing economies. The Indian case is typically that of a transitional economy.

First looking at the demand side means of monetary management, it is widely accepted that there cannot be one measure of money stock that can be uniquely related with income. Many economies – industrial and developing have adopted *at least* two measures – the 'narrow' money supply (M1), in which currency with the non-bank public and non-interest-bearing bank deposits of the public figure in, and the broad money (M2, and in India M3) which includes narrow money and interest - bearing bank deposits – as indicators to gauge the level and expansion of aggregate demand. The focus in most economies however is more on the broad measure, since the pace of expansion of time deposits is often high, bringing in its wake large potential liquidity effects.[49]

Assuming for the present the currency component to be given, bank deposits which are supposed to grow with income expansion, and at a faster pace than currency with the public, would determine the size of the total monetary stock. In transitional economies, there is a general acceptance among the monetary authorities that interest rates on bank deposits should be attractive, so that resources could flow into the banking system in a regular and predictable manner and in substantial amounts. In reality, however, this principle is not widely applied. Administered interest rates on bank deposits and advances are most commonly seen in many transitional economies. These interest rates are often at low levels, with the result that resources flow out of the banking system, setting in motion what has come to be known as financial disintermediation.

Why does this happen? Is it because there is no standard criterion by which one could test the attractiveness of interest rates?

The general perception is that if nominal interest rates are equal to or higher than the inflation rate derived from some officially recognised price index during a time-period, say of one year, *real* interest rates would be either zero or positive. This, according to the economic literature, is all that is needed to enhance savings. But if the price index is imperfect because of stickiness in the prices of commodities that are included in it,[50] a better method of deriving real interest rates would be to deflate the nominal rates by the inflation rate in the parallel commodity markets, where available, or by the exchange rate changes or by the expected rates of return. In many developing economies where exchange controls exist and capital restrictions are rampant, exchange rates too may not truly reflect the competitiveness of the economies in question. Notwithstanding these limitations, the authorities in transitional economies should set interest rates at such levels that they are perceived by economic units to be positive in real terms. The authorities could judge the economic units' perceptions from the rate at which bank deposits have been growing, the speed and order of expansion of non-bank financial intermediaries (NBFIs), and the rate at which new assets have proliferated.

Essentially this would mean that interest rates should be market-determined. The rates on saving instruments (and on claims created) should reflect such characteristics as their riskiness, maturity, their liquidity and the convenience of their use. Yields should be positively related to their riskiness and negatively related to their liquidity. Longer-term finance for investment would be facilitated if deposits for long-maturity periods offer attractive returns. The spreads between average deposit rates (the cost of loanable funds) and average loan rates should be sufficient to cover costs of intermediation, risks, and 'normal', profits. In many transitional economies, these spreads however, are large. Such spreads reflect high intermediation costs, or large portfolio of non-performing loans or high reserve and liquidity requirements which are inadequately remunerated, or lack of competitiveness in the financial sector.

Interest rate management is crucial for incipient financial liberalisation and for bringing about eventually optimal allocation of resources.[51] But interest rate liberalisation is not all that monetary authorities should aim to achieve. The main issue before them is how to go about freeing the interest rates and *at the same time* take steps to increase competition in the banking system through the strengthening and restructuring of banks. Interest rate liberalization without the accompanying measures to improve the competition could lead to significant distortions in the level and responsiveness of the interest rates.

In many transitional economies, governments attempt to influence interest rates through the mechanism of financing of their budget deficits. This however is an important constraint to the interest rate liberalization strategy, since deficit financing could distort interest rates. To eliminate or soften this constraint, either the governments would have to reduce their budget deficits to levels which could be financed by borrowing directly from the markets or the governments should be required to finance only those expenditures where social rate of return, or at least rate of return on each government project, as suggested by Dasgupta, Sen and Marglin[52], are above the market rates of interest. Governments' efforts to reduce budget deficits or expenditures could be possible only if there is coordination between public domestic debt management and monetary management.

The currency component is often given to central banking authorities since the only overwhelming source of change in reserve money is the net bank credit to Government. Cash holdings of the public, however, could be influenced by interest rates, in the sense that people's proclivity to demand cash would be reduced in an environment of high interest rates on instruments which are relatively liquid and have short maturity periods.

From the supply side means of monetary management, the familiar balance sheet equation, or identity $\Delta M = \Delta NBC^{Gs} + \Delta BC^{CS} + \Delta NFA - \Delta OL$ provides a basis for evolving monetary policy strategies in tune with the overall economic policy framework. OL (other liabilities, which are known in India as non-monetary liabilities of the banking system) may be ignored for the present, since these are not fully accounted for in many developing economies, and are derived as residual thus: $OL = NBC_{Gs} + BC_{CS} + NFA - MS$. NFA (net foreign exchange assets of the banking system) represents the outcome of the external sector performance and could be regarded as 'given' to the authorities of countries which are not "open", notwithstanding the fact that monetary authorities could influence NFA through exchange rate management and freeing of exchange controls and payment restrictions. NBC_{GS} (net bank credit to the government sector) which represents the financing of the government deficit by the banking system, is exogenously given to monetary authorities. BC_{CS} (bank credit to commercial sector which in India includes public sector enterprises as well) is the only variable which is, effectively speaking, amenable to manipulations by central banks.

These manipulations could occur through interest rate changes or/and quantity changes or through the impounding of the resources of banks for meeting legal requirements. Preferential interest rate treatment or/and credit allocation to any class(es) of borrowers, with stipulations about the extent of preferences that need to be provided within a discrete time period, would impose a constraint on banks' ability to optimise their profits. Interventions such as cash reserve ratios and statutory liquidity ratios reduce flexibility of banks in expanding credit and impose budget constraint on efforts of banks in optimizing their loan and investment portfolios. To the extent that the rates of return on the funds placed for fulfilling legal requirements are lower than the market rates of return on comparable claims, banks would find their profits eroding. If, in addition, refinancing from the central banks is made completely discretionary and/or made available generally at penalty rates, banks would be discouraged from taking any actions that could create resources crunch problem for themselves.

The above description is often a good representation of the state of monetary management in many transitional economies. Typically, the situation described requires banks to undertake asset management under severe constraints. Money markets' role would be very exiguous in such an environment, characterised as it is by limited or absence of interest rate flexibility and by portfolio allocation rules. Removal of ceilings on lending rates and provision of some discretion in paying deposit rates on term deposits (or deposits of very short maturity periods) would not be sufficient to give impetus to money markets so long as portfolio allocation rules exist, central banks' refinancing facilities are not subject to definite rules, and cash reserve ratios are relatively high.

Typically, central banks in such situation would have to – there is little choice here – influence prices or nominal incomes by targeting only a quantity variable, simply because rate variables – interest rate or exchange rate – are not free to move. The quantity variables that would be most amenable to targeting would be bank credit or reserves or unborrowed reserves that would influence money supply which, in turn would influence prices and/or economic activity, as the theoretical exposition in Section I has shown. If the target is, on the other hand, bank credit to commercial sector, one would postulate changes in it as dependent on the level of and rate of change in economic activity. The estimated bank credit to commercial sector thus obtained could be added to the exogenously given net bank credit to government and net foreign exchange assets, to obtain the final figure of money stock. In either case, the central bank would not be able to *directly control* money stock. Under the money multiplier approach at least, money stock would, theoretically speaking, depend upon two types of behavioural responses of economic units, viz., holdings of currency *vis-a-vis* deposit holdings, and bank reserves to deposits ratio. If the behavioural ratios are not stable, the outcomes would deviate from the targeted money stock. Monetary authorities therefore watch the movements in these variables and examine the factors that affect them. It is often for these reasons, authorities announce only a range of money stock expansion as a target rather than a pointed single-value increase in money supply as a target.[54]

Besides the money multiplier and additive approaches, one could work out an estimate of increase in money supply, based on a historically given money demand function, on the assumption that money supply (MS) would always be equal to money demand (MD). MD in real terms, as is well known, is positively related to real income, and negatively related to short-term interest rate which represents the opportunity cost of holding cash balances. As interest rates in transitional economies are largely administered, MD would largely reflect the developments in the real sector. From this follows the possible MS increase. If the monetary planner has at the same time information about the fiscal position and external sector performance, she could easily deduce how much the envisaged money stock increase could be sourced to the rise in bank credit to commercial sector. In case the fiscal deficit is large, given the external position, commercial credit would stand crowded out under this approach to money supply determination.

The three approaches are often utilized to get a harmonized or synthetic money supply target or target range. A harmonized target clearly cannot meet the Friedman's rule[55] that money stock expansion should equal output growth rate adjusted for a change in income velocity of money: it will exceed the real output growth rate simply because of the presence of the large fiscal deficit. If the harmonized target is *stabilized*,[56] the liquidity impact it would produce would be reflected in commodity price increases. As interest rates are not adequately flexible, the excess liquidity would not flow back into the banking system in its entirety: it would find itself flowing partly into the curb (financial) market which will serve to meet the credit demands of the commercial sector at a premium. The commercial sector would be tempted to take advantage of the curb market finance if the expected rate of inflation, served favourably by excess liquidity continuously every year, is high.

The stable level of the harmonized money stock target would provide a signal to the markets that money supply change would not show any shift – a signal that keeps alive price expectations. Money stock targets, to have the necessary sobering effect on prices, should, *over time drift towards* the Friedman rule – a 'gradual' prescription favoured by some economists.[57] A medium-term money supply expansion path tending ultimately to the average output growth rate in recent periods, may perhaps be indicated, so that there is an advantage of putting pressure on the fiscal authorities to shift away from dependence on the banking system for financing the deficits. It would also emit signals that the monetary authorities are keen on bringing about flexibility in the financial system through reform measures.

III

Transitional economies have the unenviable task of coping with the challenges posed by partial flexibility in monetary management. The key issue is the uncertainty about domestic debt management. Obviously, no financial reforms and no abatement of price elasticity and expectations would be possible if fiscal deficits are very large and are massively financed by the banking system. Even though informal consultations between the fiscal and monetary authorities take place on the issue of deficit financing by the banking system, it is common to see that the actual outcomes relating to fiscal deficits are much larger than the initially projected figures, even when there are no exogenous random shocks on the fiscal position. The uncertainty in this regard could be obviated if there is a *transparent* and *revealed* agreement about the gradual reduction in government's reliance on the banking system over a *medium term*, irrespective of the actual random influences on the fiscal deficit. To elaborate on this point, a kind of a memorandum of understanding could be prepared, and agreed to both by the Treasury and Central bank. It has to specify, over, say, a 5-year period, the *annual* support to government's short and long term borrowing by the central bank of the country and by commercial and co-operative banks separately. This support should decline year by year, tending ultimately to zero. This exercise is needed for improving resource allocation and thus productivity, and for achieving the objective of price stability which the central banks should single-mindedly pursue. It could also subserve the incipient financial reforms programme.

Consistent with the given medium-term profile of fiscal constraint, central banks in transitional economies would do well to give a medium term money supply growth path as indicated in Section II. In addition, these economies would have to pursue short term policies that are flexible. They have to introduce a greater measure of interest rate flexibility supported by market based procedures for monetary control (e.g., open market operations or discount policy with a view to influencing the level of reserves) and measures for development of money markets. In other words, the medium term monetary policy should be dovetailed with short-term monetary policy. In the short-term, liquidity management would take precedence. To this end, the central bank should essentially discount *only* short-dated government paper, *not* long dated ones in *normal circumstances*. The central bank may on behalf of the government issue treasury bills on a weekly tender basis rather than on tap. These bills could be of different maturities. There could be 6-week (42 day) bills, 3-month (91-day) bills, 17-week (119-day) bills and 6-month (182-days) bills[58]. The central bank could allow dealers in money market to operate without bestowing on them any benefit of special privileges. Commercial banks may be permitted to hold balances for settlement of transactions with the central bank in excess of what is required. The central bank, however, should pay market rate of interest on excess balance held with it by commercial banks.

Management of liquidity would be better facilitated if the rules regarding security holdings or portfolio allocations are relaxed, if not totally eliminated. The relaxation can be undertaken even if fiscal deficit continues to be substantial, requiring financing by the banking system, as a part of the efforts to strengthen the banking system. Unless price stability considerations do not warrant, cash reserve ratio would have to be kept at relatively low levels so that banks' lending rates are more meaningfully related to their deposit rates.

Fostering of money market and enabling banks to involve themselves in liability management need not necessarily lead to price increases. By enabling banks to do business on commercial basis, the central bank encourages banks to meet demands on credit. When credit is utilized to give rise to output, the price situation would be better manageable.

The speed and the extent to which the central banks could go, in introducing full scale financial liberalisation has to be judged with reference to the price situation. If reforms are introduced when price expectations are dormant, there is a greater success of their becoming internalized into the system. To ensure that there are no systemic threats it would be necessary to focus attention on the measures needed to strengthen the financial system before the edifice of liberalization is built. Some of these measures are briefly reported below.

Commercial banks should be re-capitalized and allowed to structure themselves. Improving the capital base is necessary. It would give an opportunity to the existing public sector commercial banks to reduce the ownership share of the government by raising equity capital from the general public. Commercial banks should also be allowed to make larger loan loss provisions, if they felt so necessary. To enable the banks to restructure themselves, it might become necessary to unify and preferably reduce the portfolio allocation rules as well as to bring down the cash reserve requirements.

Secondly, bank supervision systems should be thorough and efficient. Prudential regulations should be clearly laid down, so that the banks do not overextend themselves and face potential losses. Finally, competition among banks should be fostered by allowing new entrants into banking, giving greater autonomy to government – owned managements, and permitting greater transparency of operations, through disclosure of information, and through better risk assessments of the assets held by banks.

The measures to strengthen commercial banks may fruitfully be extended to other financial institutions as well. The question whether these institutions should come under the purview of the central bank is important if their combined operations are significant, and if the central bank's own supervisory system over commercial banks has been fully evolved. The exercise of surveillance by the central bank over the entire financial sector would help boost confidence in the working of the financial system and the banks to re-intermediate.

Notes and References

1. It is difficult to identify the exact periods of dominance of classical and neo-classical economists. However, many text-books on economic thought consider John Stuart Mill as the last of the classical economists, beginning with Adam Smith. After Mill, the neo-classical period may be assumed to have begun, ending with A.C. Pigou. See for difficulties in period-wise identification, Amiya Kumar Dasgupta, *Epochs in Economic Theory*, Basil Blackwell, Oxford, 1985.

2. Adam Smith, *An Enquiry into the Nature and Causes of the Wealth of Nations, 1776*, The Modern Library edition, New York, 1937.

3. See David Hume, "Of Money" in *Political Discourses*, reprinted in Phillip Newman et. al. (eds.) *Source Readings in Economic Thought*, Norton & Co., New York, 1954.

4. Henry Thornton, *An Enquiry into the Nature and Effects of the Paper Credit of Great Britain*, original 1802, George Allen & Unwin, London, 1939.

5. David Ricardo's *the High Price of Bullion, a Proof of the Depreciation of Bank Notes*, published as a pamphlet in 1810 was discussed in Phyllis Deane, *The Evolution of Economic Ideas*, Cambridge University Press, Cambridge, UK, 1978. See also R.S. Sayers, "Ricardo's Views on Monetary Questions", in T.S. Ashton and R.S. Sayers (eds.), *Papers in English Monetary History*, Oxford University Press, London, 1953.

6. John Stuart Mill, *Principles of Political Economy, with Some of their Applications to Social Philosophy*, 1848, University of Toronto Press edition, Toronto, 1965, Book III.

7. Knut Wicksell, *Interest and Prices, A study of the Causes Regulating the Value of Money*, 1898, Macmillan & Co. edition, London, 1936.

8. Alfred Marshall, *Money, Credit & Commerce*, Macmillan & Co. edition, London, 1929 First edition 1923.

9. Dennis Robertson, *Banking Policy and the Price Level*, P.S. King & Sons, London, 1926.

10. John Maynard Keynes, *A Treatise on Money*, Volume I, Macmillan & Co. Ltd., London, first edition 1930, Reprinted 1953.

11. One of the finest articles to appear was in early 'fifties. See Edward M. Bernstein and I.G. Patel, "Inflation in Relation to Economic Development", *International Monetary Fund Staff Papers*, November 1952, reprinted in B. Okun and R.W. Richardson (eds.), *Studies in Economic Development*, Holt, Rinehart & Winston, New York, 1961.

12. John Stuart Mill, *op. cit.*

13. Irving Fisher, *The Purchasing Power of Money: Its Determination and Relation to Credit, Interest and Crisis*, 1911, Macmillan & Co. edition, New York, 1931.

14. Alfred Marshall, *op. cit.*

15. A.C. Pigou, "The Value of Money", *Quarterly Journal of Economics*, Vol. XXXII, November 1917, Reprinted in F.A. Lutz and L.W. Mints (eds.), *Readings in Monetary Theory*, George Allen & Unwin Ltd., London, 1951.

16. John Maynard Keynes, *op. cit.*, p. 133.

17. Friedrich A. Hayek, *Prices and Production*, Routledge & Kegan Paul Ltd., London. First published 1931. Second edition (revised and enlarged) 1935, p.28, italics in the original.

18. John Maynard Keynes, *The General Theory of Employment, Interest and Money*. Macmillan & Co. Ltd., London, First edition, February 1936, Reprinted 1954.

19. The thrust of the reasoning presented in a good part of this paragraph was given originally in D. Patinkin, *Money, Interest and Prices*, First published 1955, Harper International Edition, Second edition, New York, 1965.

20. J.M. Keynes, *The General Theory, op. cit.*, p. 296, italics in the original.

21. *Ibid*, p. 168.

22. One of the early official writings to focus the issue of liquidity as more important than mere conventional money was the Radcliffe Committee in the United Kingdom. See *Report of the Committee on the Working of the Monetary System*, Cmnd 827, HMSO, London, 1959.

23. D. Patinkin, *op. cit.*

24. A Leijonhufvud, *On Keynesian Economics and the Economics of Keynes*, Oxford University Press, London, 1968.

25. Milton Friedman, "The Quantity Theory of Money: A Restatement", originally published in 1956, reprinted in Milton Friedman, *The Optimum Quantity of Money and Other Essays*, Macmillan & Co., London, 1969.

26. The label "monetarist" has perhaps come to be attached to those economists who give importance to monetary factors as the main determinant of nominal GDP in contrast to the fiscal policy actions that seemed to have dominated thinking since Keynes' *The General Theory*.

27. James Tobin, "A General Equilibrium Approach to Monetary Theory", *Journal of Money, Credit and Banking*, Vol.1, No. 1, March 1969.

28. James Tobin's lecture in Werner Sichel (ed.), *The State of Economic Science, Views of Six Nobel Laureates*, W.E. Upjohn Institute for Employment Research, Kalamazoo, Michigan, 1989.

29. A.W. Phillips, "The Relation Between Unemployment and the Rate of Change of Money Wage Rates in the United kingdom 1862-1957", *Economica*, November 1958.

30. *Ibid.*, p. 283.

31. Milton Friedman, "The Role of Monetary Policy", *American Economic Review*, March, 1968; Edmund S. Phelps, "Phillips Curve, Expectations of Inflation, and Optional Unemployment over Time", *Economica*, August 1967.

32. The interpretation of the expectations - augmented Phillips Curve follows the points made in Chapter 9 in Bennett T. McCallum, *Monetary Economics - Theory and Policy*, Macmillan Publishing Co., New York, 1989.

33. Robert M. Solow, *Price Expectations and the Behaviour of the Price Level*, Manchester University Press, Manchester, England, 1969.

34. Thomas J. Sargent, "Rational Expectations, the Real Rate of Interest, and the Natural Rate of Unemployment", *Brookings Papers on Economic Activity*, No. 2, 1973.

35. Bennett T. McCallum, "Rational Expectations and the Natural Rate Hypothesis: Some Consistent Estimates", *Econometrica*, January 1976.

36. Robert E. Lucas, Jr., "Expectations and the Neutrality of Money", *Journal of Economic Theory*, April 1972; also Robert E. Lucas, Jr., "Some International Evidence on output - Inflation Trade-offs", *American Economic Review*, June 1973.

37. Robert J. Barro, "Unanticipated Money Growth and Unemployment in the United States", *American Economic Review*, March 1977.

38. Herschel I. Grossman, "Rational Expectations, Business Cycles, and Government Behaviour" in Stanley Fischer (ed), *Rational Expectations and Economic Policy*, NBER publication, University of Chicago Press, Chicago, 1980, p. 9.

39. Robert J. Barro, "Rational Expectations and the Role of Monetary Policy", *Journal of Monetary Economics*, Vol. 2, January 1976.

40. Robert J. Gordon, "Price Inertia and Policy Ineffectiveness in the United States, 1890-1990", *Journal of Political Economy*, Vol.90, No. 6, December 1982.

41. Stanley Fischer, "Anticipations and the Non-Neutrality of Money", *Journal of Political Economy*, Vol. 87, 1979.

42. Alan Blinder's comment on Robert J. Barro and Mark Rush's article entitled "Unanticipated Money and Economic Activity", in Stanley Fischer (ed.), *Rational Expectations and Economic Policy, op. cit.*

43. There is a large body of literature on rules versus discretion of monetary policy arising from the rational expectations literature. See for example, Robert J. Barro, "Rational Expectations and the Role of Monetary Policy", *Journal of Monetary Economics*, January 1976; Robert J. Barro, "Recent Developments in the Theory of Rules Versus Discretion", *Economic Journal*, 95 supplement, 1985; Robert E. Lucas, Jr., "Rules, Discretion, and the Role of the Economic Advisor", and Stanley Fischer, "On Activist Monetary Policy with Rational Expectations" - both in Stanley Fischer (ed.) *Rational Expectations and Economic Policy, op. cit.*; Finn E. Kydland and Edward C. Prescott, "Rules Rather than Discretion: The Inconsistency of Optimal Plans", *Journal of Political Economy*, June 1977.

44. See Robert J. Gordon, "What is New Keynesian Economics", *Journal of Economic Literature*, September 1990, Lawrence Ball, Gregory Mankiw and David Romer, "The New Keynesian Economics and the Output-Inflation Trade-Off" *Brookings Papers on Economic Activity*, 1, 1988; Jeff Frank, *The New Keynesian Economics, Unemployment, Search and Contracting*, Wheatsheaf Books, Sussex, Great Britain, 1986.

45. International specie-flow mechanism is most appropriately applicable to a pure gold-standard economy. But instead of buying gold to create reserves, central banks could buy bonds to create reserves. One could thus usefully study the relevance of this mechanism even to situations based on paper standard.

46. Milton Friedman, "The Case for Flexible Exchange Rates", in the author's *Essays in Positive Economics*, University of Chicago Press, Chicago, Ilinois, 1953.

47. See, for example, International Monetary Fund, *Exchange Rate Volatility and World Trade*, Occasional Paper No. 28, Washington D.C. 1984.

48. International Monetary Fund, *Issues in the Assessment of the Exchange Rates of Industrial Countries*, Occasional Paper 29, Washington D.C. 1984; International Monetary Fund, *The Exchange Rate System - Lessons of the Past and Options for the Future*, Occasional Paper 28, Washington D.C. 1984.

49. The focus is on the broad measure often because it has become difficult to estimate the demand for cash in the presence of a large number of market instruments that arise out of financial reforms. Besides, the substitutability of assets including deposits has made the distinction between demand and time deposits somewhat irrelevant. In India, M1 has not been employed in any official or academic study during the last 10 years probably for these reasons. More recently, the focus in the literature has shifted on Divisia monetary aggregates. See William A. Barnett, "Developments in Monetary Aggregation Theory" *Journal of Policy Modelling*, Summer 1990, also Barnett W.A. et.al., "The New Divisia Monetary Aggregates", *Journal of Political Economy*, December 1984.

50. The stickiness in prices could be due to market imperfections or preponderance of too many commodities included in the index whose prices are administered.

51. See Sergio Pereira Leite and V. Sundararajan, "Issues in Interest Rate Management and Liberalization", *IMF Staff Papers*. December 1990. Many arguments in this paper are taken note of by us.

52. Dasgupta, Partha, Amartya Sen and Stephen Marglin, *Guidelines for Project Evaluation*, UNIDO, New York, 1972. The argument placed by the authors is that internal rates of return on each project should be estimated, and with experience, evolve an agreement in the Government about the cut-off internal rate of return. It is this agreement on a rate that will make it a socially optimum interest rate.

53. Bennett McCallum proposed that a specific monetary rule could be expressed in terms of a variable that the monetary authority can accurately control. Such a variable could be short-term nominal interest rate or total reserves or unborrowed reserves or monetary base. See Bennett McCallum, *Monetary Economics*, Macmillan Publishing Company, New York, 1989, Chapter 16.

54. The range, of course, has to be limited to not more than 2 to 3 percentage points. The ranges are prescribed for all measures, and *not* for any one measure of money stock.

55. Milton Friedman first proposed automatic variation in the rate of monetary growth, in the author's "A Monetary and Fiscal Framework for Economic Stability", *American Economic Review*, June 1948. The constant money growth rate was developed by Friedman in his *A Program for Monetary Stability*, Fordham University Press, New York 1960. He reiterated this idea later in a number of his writings, most notably in his presidential address to the American Economic Association, "The Role of Monetary Policy", *American Economic Review*, March 1968.

56. If the harmonized target moves within a narrow range of say, 2 percentage points, it is as good as an anticipated target or trend-influenced target.

57. See David Laidler, "The End of Demand Management: Had to Reduce Unemployment in the 1970s" in M. Friedman, *Unemployment Vs. Inflation - An Evaluation of the Phillips Curve with a British Commentary by David Laidler*, Occasional Paper 44, Institute of Economic Affairs, London, 1975, and Michael Parkin and A.R. Nobay (eds), *Current Economic Problems*, Cambridge University Press, Cambridge, 1975. Laidler and Parkin's argument was based on the premise that as money supply determines aggregate demand, it is conceivable that shifts in aggregate supply might cause changes in the level of aggregate demand that could be regarded as optimal.

58. These maturities are available in New Zealand, following the financial reforms in 1984. See Reserve Bank of New Zealand, *Financial policy Reform*, Wellington, New Zealand, 1986.

15

Money, Output and Prices

Y S R Sarma

Introduction

THE interaction between money, output and prices has received considerable attention both in theoretical and empirical analysis. The alternative theories regarding the role of money in economic activity, however, emphasise that variation in money supply is an important cause of the variation in nominal income. The causality or the nature of transmission mechanism between the three macro-economic variables, money, output and prices, has a bearing on the formulation and conduct of monetary and fiscal policies to achieve the goals of economic growth and price stability. Deficit financing by the Government has a significant influence on money supply. Deficit financing or net Reserve Bank Credit to Government is itself determined, among others, by prices as Government receipts and expenditure are influenced by inflation. Thus, the objective of price stability along with stepping up the rate of economic growth assumes importance.

The relationship between money, output and prices is generally summarised in one equation which takes the form of the demand function for real money balances. The real money balances are formulated as function of real income and interest rates, etc. The increase in real income *ceteris paribus* necessitates an increase in the demand for real money balances. So long as money supply expands to this extent, there would be no rise in the price level. The demand for money function can be restated as a price equation as follows:

Prepared for an internal seminar in January-February 1991.

The author wishes to express his sincere thanks to Shri T.R. Venkatachalam for valuable suggestions. Thanks are due to Smt. Sarojini Venkatachalam for valuable assistance in the preparation of the paper.

Price Equation

$P = f(GDPR, M_3, P_{-1})$

Where

P = Price level

GDPR = Real Gross Domestic Product

M_3 = Broad Money (Currency with the public + Deposits with Banks + Other deposits with RBI)

The price equation is a partial adjustment equation. This equation facilitates measurement of the impact of past changes in the explanatory variables (viz., M_3 and GDPR) on the price level. According to the formulation; other factors remaining the same, an increase in real output (GDPR) lowers the price level and an increase in money supply (M_3) raises the price level.

An attempt is made in this paper to explain the behaviour of prices in India during the period 1970-71 to 1989-90.

2. Behaviour of Money, Output and Prices.

Data relating to M_3, GDPR and Prices (Index Number of Wholesale Prices) for the period 1970-71 to 1989-90 are set out in Table 1. The annual compound growth rate of M_3, GDPR and Prices during the [nineteen] seventies and [nineteen] eighties and the whole period were as follows:

Annual compound rate of growth

(per cent)

	M_3	GDPR	P
1970-71 to 1979-80	17.5	2.9	9.0
1980-81 to 1989-90	17.3	5.6	7.4
1970-71 to 1989-90	17.4	4.2	8.2

During the [nineteen] seventies, the annual compound rate of growth of money supply (M_3) was 17.5 per cent while real output (GDPR) rose by 2.9 per cent. This decade witnessed an annual rate of inflation of 9.0 per cent. During the [nineteen] eighties, annual rate of growth of GDPR was higher at 5.6 per cent. The annual rate of growth of money supply was 17.3 per cent. The annual rate of inflation declined to 7.4 per cent. It would, therefore, be observed that a rise in the rate of growth of output accompanied by a moderation in the monetary expansion would contribute to lower price rise.

The movements in M3, GDPR and Prices over the years 1970-71 to 1989-90 are depicted in Chart 1. A broad relationship between money supply and the price level can be noticed.

3. Empirical Price Equation

Two variants of the price equation have been estimated following a partial adjustment mechanism for the period 1971-72 to 1989-90. The equations are specified in double logarithmic form. These are:

$$\text{Log } P = f(\log M_3, \log GDPR, \log P_{-1}) \quad ...(1)$$

$$\text{Log } P = f(\log M_3, \log GDPR, \log DMY, \log P_{-1}) ...(2)$$

Lagged price variable in the above equations represents the influence of past values of output and money supply on the current period price level. A dummy variable (DMY) is included in the second equation to take into consideration the effect of special factors like international oil crisis in 1973-74 and 1974-75 and drought conditions that prevailed in 1979-80 and 1987-88 which had an adverse impact on the price level.

The regression equations are estimated by the method of ordinary least squares. The estimated price equations are presented in Table 2. The adequacy of the equations in explaining price behaviour is judged by the appropriateness of the signs and magnitudes of the regression coefficients, statistical criteria such as the coefficient of multiple determination ($\bar{R}^2$), DW statistic for autocorrelation among residuals as also Durbin's H-statistic, 'T' values of the regression coefficients and the standard error of estimate (SEE) and the ability of the equation in tracking the turning points in price level.

It would be seen from the two price equations that the price behaviour is well explained by money supply (M_3) and output (GDPR) according to a partial adjustment mechanism. The coefficient of multiple determination ($\bar{R}^2$) was about 99 per cent in both the equations, thereby indicating that about 99 per cent of the variation in the price level is explained by money supply and output. The regression coefficients of M_3 and GDPR have the expected positive and negative signs, respectively. The regression equations are free from autocorrelation among the residuals which indicate that no other systematic factor explaining the prices is omitted from the price equations. The regression coefficients are statistically significant. Charts 2a and 2b show the actual and estimated values of the price level during the sample period in respect of both the equations. The movement in the actual price level is well captured by the estimated price equations.

The short-run and the long-run elasticities of price with respect to M_3 and output (GDPR) are estimated as under:

	Short-run elasticity of price with respect to		*Long-run elasticity of price with respect to*		*Implied income elasticity of demand for M_3*
	M_3	*GDPR*	*M_3*	*GDPR*	
Equation (1)	+0.52	-1.03	+0.98	-1.95	1.99
Equation (2)	+0.41	-0.72	+0.88	-1.53	1.74

To test the goodness of fit of the price equation further, annual percentage variations in the actual price level and the estimated price level have been computed. This is a more rigorous test. These are plotted in the charts 3a and 3b in respect of the two equations. It would be observed from these charts that most of the important turning points in the inflation rate have been remarkably captured by the two price equations. Magnitude-wise, there are, however, some differences (sometimes strikingly different) in the actual and estimated values of the inflation rate (column 10 of Table 3a and column 10 of Table 3b). However, there may not be any behavioural equation, be it in relation to consumption or investment, where a closer correspondence between percentage variations in the actual and estimated values can be found.

Commenting on the problem of predictability of percentage changes in prices on a year-to-year basis, Rangarajan observed, in his Presidential Address to the Indian Economic Association in December 1988, that the price relationship holds reasonably well over a period of time. He has shown that averages of price changes over a period of five years can be predicted with reasonable accuracy within a range that would be sufficient as a guide to policy[1]. Following Rangarajan's method, a 5-year moving average of both the actuals and estimates in respect of both price levels and percentage changes in the price level have been computed. These are shown in

Tables 3a and 3b. Charts 4a and 4b show the actual and estimated price levels based on 5 year moving averages for equations 1 and 2 respectively. The corresponding variations are plotted in charts 5a and 5b. A comparison of the actual and estimated values shows that the differences are narrow (columns 7 and 13 of Table 3a and columns 7 and 13 of Table 3b). Thus, price changes can be predicted with reasonable accuracy over a period of, say, five years by the price equation with money supply (M_3) and output (GDPR) as the main explanatory variables.

4. Distributed lag effect on prices of a one unit once-for-all in M_3 and output.

The distributed lag effects on prices of a one per cent once-for-all change in M_3 and output (GDPR) have been worked out from the two price equations. These are shown in Table 4. It is found that the lagged effects of a change in M_3 are significant for about three years following the change and peter out progressively in the subsequent years.

Illustratively, M_3 rose by 18.8 per cent in 1986-87. Other factors remaining constant, the effect of the rise in M_3 would be felt on the price level at least in the next four to five years (Table 5). According to the first equation, it is estimated that the prices would have risen by 9.8 per cent in 1987-88, 4.5 per cent in 1988-89, 2.1 per cent in 1989-90 and 0.9 per cent in 1990-91. According to the second equation, prices would have risen by 7.7 per cent in 1987-88, 4.1 per cent in 1988-89, 2.2 per cent in 1989-90 and 1.1 per cent in 1990-91.

5. Summary

An attempt is made to study the relationship between money, output and prices in India. For this purpose an empirical price equation with wholesale price index as the dependent variable and output (GDP in real terms) and money supply (M_3) as the explanatory variables is estimated for the period 1971-72 to 1989-90. Various tests conducted on the price equation show that the behaviour of prices is well explained by changes in output and M_3. The distributed lag effects of a one percentage once-for-all change in M_3 on prices, holding output constant are examined. It is found that the lagged effects of a change in M_3 on prices are significant for about three years following the change and peter out progressively in the subsequent years.

References

1. C. Rangarajan: "Issues in Monetary Management" Presidential Address at the Conference of the Indian Economic Association, Calcutta, December 1988.

TABLE 1

Money, Output and Prices

Year	Money Stock* M_3 (Rs. Crore)	Output GDPR (Rs. Crore)	Prices P (Index No.)	Annual Growth Rate (g) $M3_g$ (per cent)	$GDPR_g$ (per cent)	P_g (per cent)
1	2	3	4	5	6	7
1970-71	10958	90426	36.2			
1971-72	12690	91339	39.1	15.8	1.0	8.0
1972-73	15033	91048	43.9	18.5	-0.3	12.3
1973-74	17571	95192	57.0	16.9	4.6	29.8
1974-75	19457	96297	62.8	10.7	1.2	10.2
1975-76	22286	104968	58.7	14.5	9.0	-6.5
1976-77	27280	106280	65.7	22.4	1.2	11.9
1977-78	32906	114219	66.0	20.6	7.5	0.5
1978-79	39890	120504	69.0	21.2	5.5	4.5
1979-80	46801	114236	83.7	17.3	-5.2	21.3
1980-81	55358	122226	97.7	18.3	7.0	16.7
1981-82	62426	129600	100.0	12.8	6.0	2.4
1982-83	72868	133469	107.2	16.7	3.0	7.2
1983-84	85899	144310	114.9	17.9	8.1	7.2
1984-85	101957	149966	121.8	18.7	3.9	6.0
1985-86	118338	157348	127.7	16.1	4.9	4.8
1986-87	140633	163924	134.2	18.8	4.2	5.1
1987-88	162660	170716	148.5	15.7	4.1	10.7
1988-89	192085	188481	156.9	18.1	10.4	5.7
1989-90	230352	196962	171.2	19.9	4.5	9.1

* M_3 Outstanding as of last reporting Friday.

GDPR = Gross domestic product at 1980-81 prices.

P = Index number of wholesale prices (base 1981-82=100) as at the end of the year.

CHART 1

Money, Output & Prices

1970-71 to 1989-90

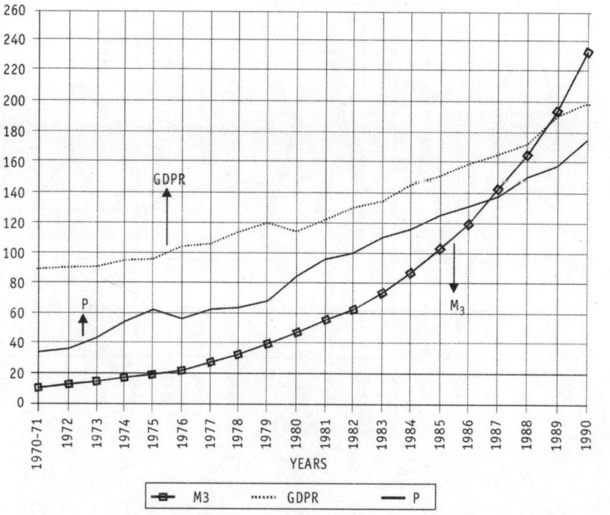

CHART 2A

INDEX NO. OF WHOLESALE PRICES
(ACTUAL & ESTIMATED - LEVELS) - EQUATION 1

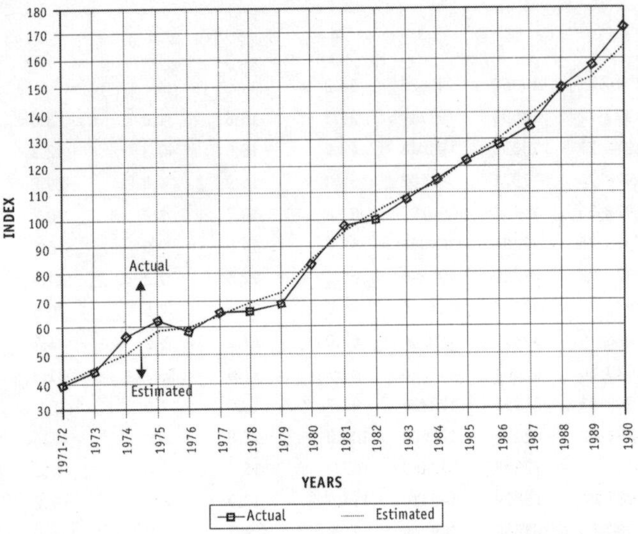

CHART 2B

INDEX NO. OF WHOLESALE PRICES
(ACTUAL & ESTIMATED - LEVELS) - EQUATION 2

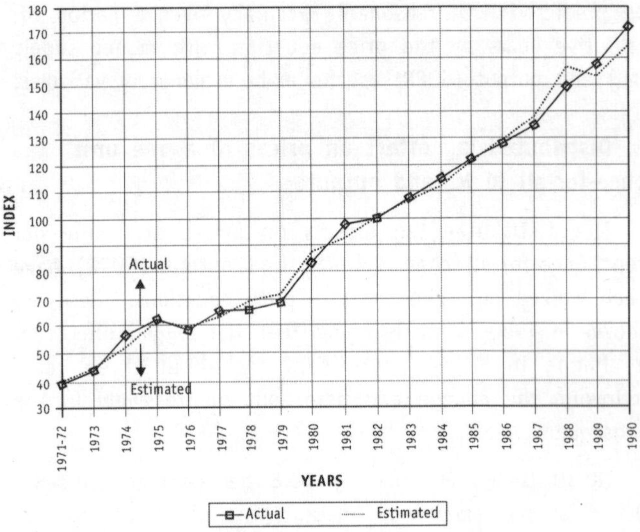

CHART 3A

INDEX NO. OF WHOLESALE PRICES
(ACTUAL & ESTIMATED - % VARIATIONS) - EQUATION 1

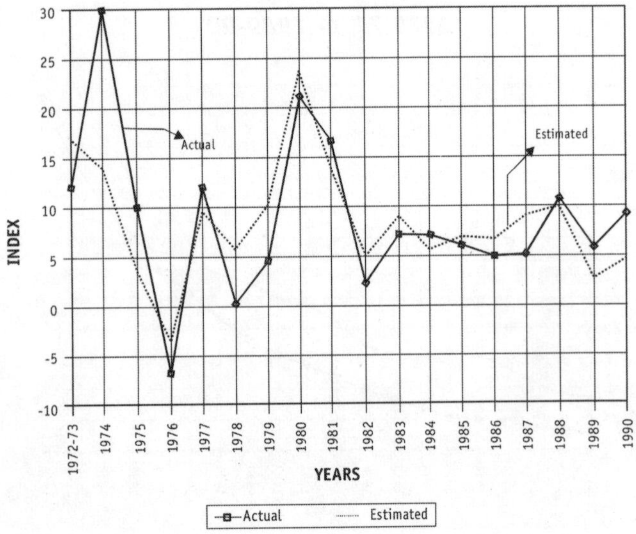

CHART 3B

INDEX NO. OF WHOLESALE PRICES
(ACTUAL & ESTIMATED - % VARIATIONS) - EQUATION 2

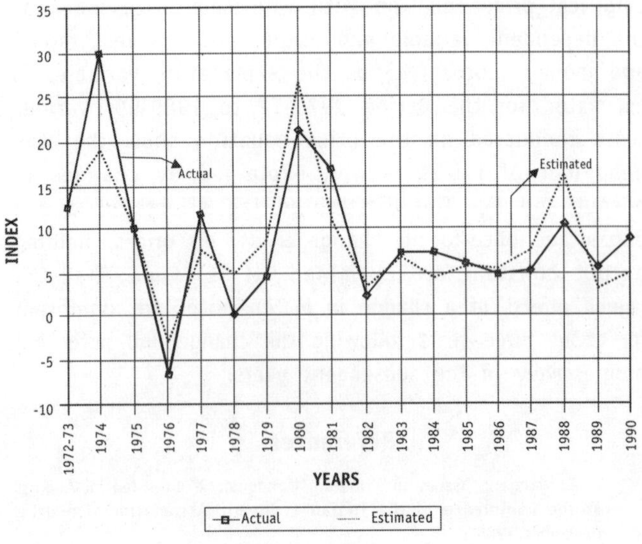

CHART 4A

Index No. of Wholesale Prices

5-yr moving averages (levels) - Equation 1

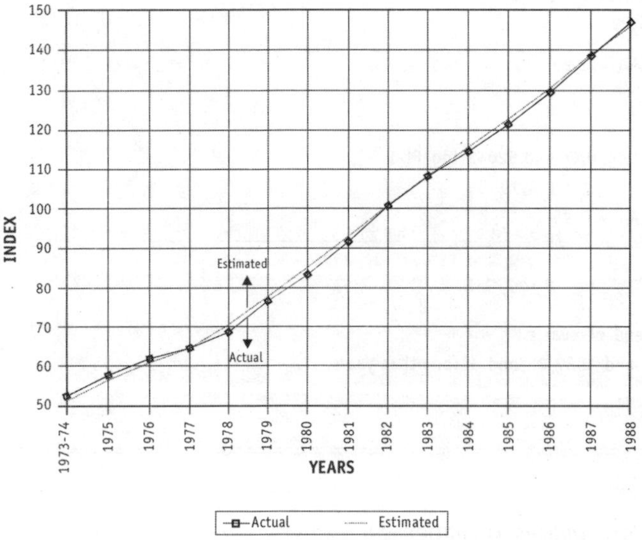

CHART 4B

Index No. of Wholesale Prices

5-yr moving averages (levels) - Equation 2

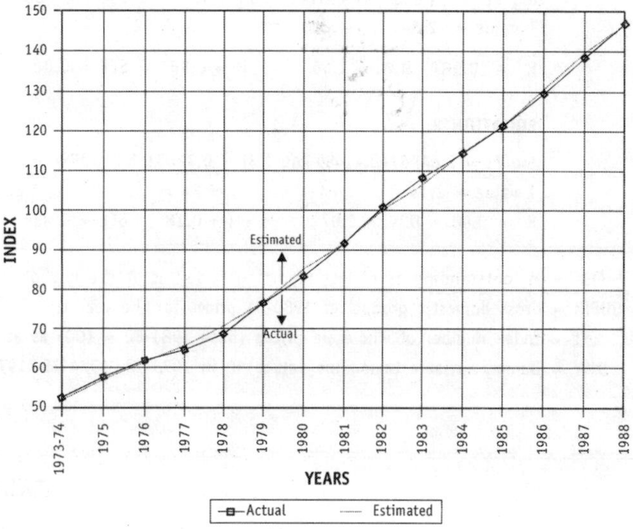

CHART 5A

Index No. of Wholesale Prices

5-yr moving averages (%-Variation) - Equation 1

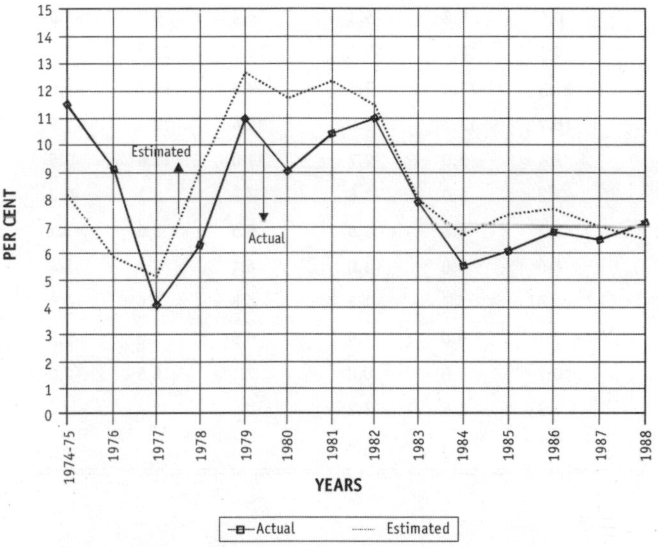

CHART 5B

Index No. of Wholesale Prices

5-yr moving averages (%-Variation) - Equation 2

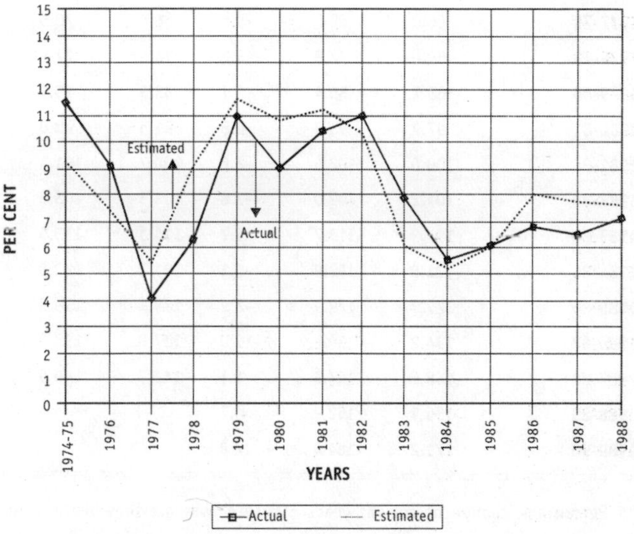

TABLE 2

Relationship Between Money, Output and Prices
Price Equations (1971-72 to 1989-90)

EQUATION 1

log Pt = 3.86357 + 0.51929 log M3t − 1.03330 log GDPRt + 0.47248 log Pt-1
T value = 2.84 4.22 2.92 3.22

$\bar{R}^2$ = 0.987 D.W. = 1.66 H = 0.96 SEE = 0.02 MEAN = 1.95

EQUATION 2

log Pt = 2.64967+0.41489 log M3t − 0.72031 log GDPRt + 0.02985 log DMY + 0.52643 log Pt-1
T value = 2.14 3.73 2.24 2.64 4.19
$\bar{R}^2$ = 0.987 D.W. = 2.07 H = (-) 0.18 SEE = 0.02 MEAN = 1.95

M3t = M_3 outstanding as of last reporting Friday as at the end of the year t
GDPRt = Gross domestic product at 1980-81 prices for the year t.
Pt = Index number of wholesale prices (base 1981-82 = 100) as at the end of year t.
DMY = Dummy variable taking the values 10 in 1973-74, 1974-75, 1979-80 and 1987-88 and 1 for other years.

TABLE 3A

Moving Averages of Estimated Price Indices (Equation 1)

	Levels						Percentage variation over the previous year					
	Wholesale Price Index			5-year moving averages			Wholesale price index			5-year moving averages		
Year	Actual	Estimated	Error	Actual	Estimated	Error	Actual	Estimated*	Error	Actual	Estimated*	Error
1	2	3	4	5	6	7	8	9	10	11	12	13
1971-72	39.1	40.3	-1.2									
1972-73	43.9	45.8	-1.9				12.3	17.1	-4.8			
1973-74	57.0	50.1	6.9	52.3	51.2	1.1	29.8	14.1	15.7			
1974-75	62.8	59.0	3.8	57.6	56.0	1.6	10.2	3.5	6.7	11.5	8.2	3.3
1975-76	58.7	60.6	-1.9	62.0	60.7	1.3	-6.5	-3.5	-3.0	9.2	5.9	3.2
1976-77	65.7	64.4	1.3	64.4	65.3	-0.8	11.9	9.7	2.2	4.1	5.2	-1.0
1977-78	66.0	69.5	-3.5	68.6	70.5	-1.9	0.5	5.8	-5.3	6.3	9.2	-2.9
1978-79	69.0	72.8	-3.8	76.4	77.5	-1.0	4.5	10.3	-5.8	11.0	12.7	-1.7
1979-80	83.7	85.4	-1.7	83.3	85.1	-1.8	21.3	23.8	-2.5	9.1	11.7	-2.6
1980-81	97.7	95.2	2.5	91.5	93.0	-1.5	16.7	13.7	3.0	10.4	12.4	-1.9
1981-82	100.0	102.6	-2.6	100.7	101.1	-0.4	2.4	5.0	-2.7	11.0	11.4	-0.5
1982-83	107.2	109.0	-1.8	108.3	108.6	-0.3	7.2	9.0	-1.8	7.9	8.1	-0.2
1983-84	114.9	113.2	1.7	114.3	115.5	-1.2	7.2	5.6	1.6	5.5	6.6	-1.1
1984-85	121.8	122.9	-1.1	121.2	122.8	-1.7	6.0	7.0	-1.0	6.1	7.4	-1.4
1985-86	127.7	129.9	-2.2	129.4	130.5	-1.1	4.8	6.7	-1.8	6.8	7.6	-0.9
1986-87	134.2	139.2	-5.0	137.8	138.3	-0.5	5.1	9.0	-3.9	6.5	7.0	-0.5
1987-88	148.5	147.4	1.1	147.7	146.5	1.2	10.7	9.8	0.8	7.1	6.5	0.6
1988-89	156.9	152.2	4.7				5.7	2.5	3.2			
1989-90	171.2	164.0	7.2				9.1	4.5	4.6			

* Percentage change of current year's estimate over previous year's actual.

TABLE 3B

Moving Averages of Estimated Price Indices (Equation 2)

	Levels						Percentage variation over the previous year					
	Wholesale Price Index			5-year moving averages			Wholesale price index			5-year moving averages		
Year	Actual	Estimated	Error	Actual	Estimated	Error	Actual	Estimated*	Error	Actual	Estimated*	Error
1	2	3	4	5	6	7	8	9	10	11	12	13
1971-72	39.1	39.8	-0.7									
1972-73	43.9	44.5	-0.6				12.3	13.8	-1.5			
1973-74	57.0	52.4	4.6	52.3	51.9	0.4	29.8	19.4	10.5			
1974-75	62.8	62.2	0.6	57.6	56.6	1.0	10.2	9.1	1.1	11.5	9.4	2.2
1975-76	58.7	60.8	-2.1	62.0	61.5	0.6	-6.5	-3.2	-3.3	9.2	7.5	1.6
1976-77	65.7	63.2	2.5	64.4	65.4	-0.9	11.9	7.7	4.3	4.1	5.5	-1.3
1977-78	66.0	68.8	-2.8	68.6	70.4	-1.8	0.5	4.7	-4.3	6.3	9.0	-2.6
1978-79	69.0	71.9	-2.9	76.4	76.8	-0.3	4.5	8.9	-4.4	11.0	11.7	-0.7
1979-80	83.7	87.5	-3.8	83.3	84.3	-1.0	21.3	26.8	-5.5	9.1	10.8	-1.8
1980-81	97.7	92.4	5.3	91.5	91.9	-0.4	16.7	10.4	6.3	10.4	11.2	-0.8
1981-82	100.0	101.0	-1.0	100.7	99.9	0.8	2.4	3.4	-1.0	11.0	10.4	0.6
1982-83	107.2	106.7	0.5	108.3	106.7	1.6	7.2	6.7	0.5	7.9	6.1	1.8
1983-84	114.9	112.0	2.9	114.3	113.9	0.4	7.2	4.5	2.7	5.5	5.2	0.4
1984-85	121.8	121.4	0.4	121.2	121.2	-0.1	6.0	5.7	0.3	6.1	6.0	0.0
1985-86	127.7	128.6	-0.9	129.4	131.1	-1.7	4.8	5.6	-0.7	6.8	7.9	-1.2
1986-87	134.2	137.5	-3.3	137.8	139.3	-1.5	5.1	7.7	-2.6	6.5	7.7	-1.2
1987-88	148.5	156.0	-7.5	147.7	148.0	-0.3	10.7	16.2	-5.6	7.1	7.5	-0.5
1988-89	156.9	153.2	3.7				5.7	3.2	2.5			
1989-90	171.2	164.8	6.4				9.1	5.0	4.1			

* Percentage change of current year's estimate over previous year's actual.

TABLE 4

Distributed Lag effect on prices of a one per cent once-for-all change in the explanatory variable (per cent)

EQUATION 1

Time Period	For a change in M3, GDPR held constant			For a change in GDPR, M3 held constant		
	Pt/GDPRt = constant	M3t	Pt-1	Pt/M3t= constant	GDPRt	Pt-1
1	2	3	4	5	6	7
0	0	0	0	0	0	0
1	0.52	1	0	-1.03	1	0
2	0.24	0	0.52	-0.48	0	-1.03
3	0.11	0	0.24	-0.23	0	-0.48
4	0.05	0	0.11	-0.11	0	-0.23
5	0.03	0	0.05	-0.03	0	-0.11

EQUATION 2

Time Period	For a change in M3, GDPR held constant			For a change in GDPR, M3 held constant		
	Pt/GDPRt = constant	M3t	Pt-1	Pt/M3t= constant	GDPRt	Pt-1
1	2	3	4	5	6	7
0	0	0	0	0	0	0
1	0.41	1	0	-0.72	1	0
2	0.22	0	0.41	-0.39	0	-0.72
3	0.12	0	0.22	-0.20	0	-0.39
4	0.06	0	0.12	-0.11	0	-0.20
5	0.03	0	0.06	-0.06	0	-0.11

TABLE 5

Illustration of distributed lag effect of the increase of 18.8 per cent in M3 during 1986-87 on the price level in succeeding years with no change in output (per cent)

	Equation 1	Equation 2
1986-87	0	0
1987-88	0.52 x18.8=9.8	0.41x18.8=7.7
1988-89	0.24x18.8=4.5	0.22x18.8 = 4.1
1989-90	0.11x18.8=2.1	0.12x18.8=2.2
1990-91	0.05x18.8=0.9	0.06x18.8=1.1
1991-92	0.03x18.8=0.6	0.03x18.8=0.6

16

Exchange Rate Management in India

An Empirical Evaluation

Michael Debabrata Patra • Sitikantha Pattanaik

SINCE March, 1993 i.e., with the institution of the market based exchange rate system the conduct of exchange rate policy in India has attracted close scrutiny and evaluation. In the period from October 1993 to August 1998, the policy stance of ensuring orderly market conditions and allowing the exchange rate to reflect the macro economic fundamentals has been subjected to alternating phases of exchange market pressure, requiring the Reserve Bank of India (RBI) to 'lean against the wind' against speculative attacks and also to 'lean with the wind' in order to ensure soft landings of the exchange rate in the face of the perceived need for correcting overvaluation. The timing and magnitude of the RBI's intervention in the exchange market has been assessed in various forms, ranging from technical charting to mechanistic interpretations of the drift in the real effective exchange rate (REER). A rigorous empirical evaluation of exchange rate management, drawing from theoretical underpinnings has, in general, been lacking.

With the abandonment of the Bretton Woods parities and the failed tryst with freely floating exchange rates indeed, the first major intervention had occurred by late 1974 and early 1975 to stabilise the US dollar - central banks the world over have chosen to manage exchange rate regimes, the degree of management varying from economy to economy depending on macro economic policy objectives and the state of the development and integration of financial markets. The exchange rate regime in India can best be characterised as 'intermediate' between fully managed and freely floating regimes. Exchange rate policy is generally viewed as subserving the monetary policy stance. Given the evolutionary stage in the development of the foreign exchange market and its fractured linkages with the rest of the market continuum, episodes of exchange market turbulence have essentially been viewed as resulting from developments which do not reflect the underlying fundamentals, amplified by unidirectional expectations in an underdeveloped market. The policy response, however, has generally been crafted in terms of the conventional approach to monetary disequilibrium, reflected in reserve changes, exchange rate adjustments and management of monetary conditions, in general, through the use of instruments of monetary policy. Consequently, an important requirement for the successful conduct of exchange rate policy is a reasonably accurate assessment of pressures in the exchange market and the calibration of policy measures in response to market pressures.

Drawing from a strand in the literature, an attempt is made in this paper to develop objective indicators of exchange market pressure and intervention activity so as to evaluate exchange rate management in the context of the ability to assuage market pressures on the exchange rate of the rupee in the market based exchange rate regime (1993:03 to 1998:03). Although the focus of the paper is on the period 1993-98, analysis is conducted for the period 1990-98 since the institution of the market regime was facilitated through important structural and regime changes in the aftermath of the balance of payments crisis of 1990. An index of Exchange Market Pressure (EMP) and its operational variant, the Monetary Conditions Index (MCI) is proposed for the purpose of policy monitoring. The MCI, which has come to be employed as a monitoring indicator by various central banks who target 'rate' variables (in preference over quantity variables) in the conduct of monetary policy, helps to evaluate the extent to which monetary conditions contribute or run counter to exchange market pressures. As the EMP and the MCI take into the overall developments in the balance of payments reflected in the money account, they are relatively

The authors are grateful to Shri Satyananda Sahoo for valuable help.

efficient alternatives to the conventional REER which is centred on the trade account and yields little insights into balance of payments developments in the face of a mobile capital account. An Indicator of Intervention Activity (IIA) is also constructed to assess the monetary authority's efficacy of managing exchange market pressures reflected in movements of the EMP. These indicators draw upon the inter linkages between monetary policy and exchange rate developments which has been recognised by the authorities in India in the recent period. Thus, the paper provides an empirical framework for evaluating monetary policy in terms of its exchange rate objective. In response to the academic debate on the nature of the exchange rate regime in India, the paper offers a methodology for an ordinal measurement of the degree of 'management' in the exchange rate regime.

In the following Section, a brief review of the select contributions in the literature dealing with the development of the indicators proposed here is presented. In Section II, the theoretical model employed in this paper is described. Section III presents the results of the empirical estimation of the model. In Section IV, an evaluation of India's exchange rate policy in the period since March 1993 to March 1998 is made in terms of the behaviour of the indicators developed in this paper. The final Section contains concluding remarks.

SECTION I
REVIEW OF LITERATURE

With the integration of financial markets globally, massive volumes of turnover [have] endowed markets with such might that national authorities seem diminutive in comparison and cannot realistically hope to impose their will on the market. Yet central banks repeatedly intervene in foreign exchange markets, usually contesting the market view, hoping to nudge the markets in the desired direction. Conventional wisdom embodied in the asset market approach-essentially the flex-price and sticky-price monetary models holds that sterilised intervention, which leaves the volume of money stock unchanged, is largely ineffective in its impact on the exchange rate through monetary channels of transmission although through the expectations channels, even sterilised intervention can alter the current exchange rate by signaling the future course of monetary policy. For this to occur, however, intervention has to be reinforced by monetary policy measures. In portfolio balance models where the assumption of perfect substitutability between domestic and foreign assets is relaxed, sterilised interventions have an impact on the exchange rate; however, the initial change in the exchange rate sets off chain reactions in the current and capital accounts of the balance of payments which, over time, reverse the initial exchange rate change. The effectiveness of unsterilised intervention in affecting the exchange rate is undisputed in the received theories of exchange rate determination. Unsterilised intervention, by causing changes in countries' money supplies, delivers a monetary shock to the exchange rate in much the same manner as monetary policy; in fact, under conditions of perfect substitutability, monetary policy and unsterilised intervention are undistinguishable in their impact on the exchange rate. Unsterilised intervention is to be regarded as an instrument of monetary policy with no independent power over the foreign exchange market. Investigating whether unsterilised intervention to stabilise the exchange rate is compatible with a regime in which monetary aggregates are used as intermediate targets, Genberg and Roth (1979) showed that efforts to moderate movements of the exchange rate in one period by reducing the money supply through unsterilised intervention will be frustrated in the subsequent periods. The commitment to a monetary target and the gradual equalisation of foreign and domestic interest rates will result in a more than average growth in the money supply. Thus, the impact of unsterilised interventions on the exchange rate is not expected to be realised beyond the short run. Since the mid-eighties, however, central bank interventions have caused markets to take note of their visible effects, suggesting the need for a reconsideration of the conventional wisdom.

Girton and Roper (1977) can be regarded as the seminal contribution to the literature on the development of a measure of exchange market pressure. They developed the measure in the framework of the monetary approach to the balance of payments under which money stock disequilibrium (mismatch between demand for and supply of money) is reflected in reserve movements signifying official intervention under a fixed exchange rate regime or in exchange rate changes in a flexible exchange rate regime. In a hybrid regime, money stock disequilibrium is manifested in a combination of official intervention through use of reserves and some amount of exchange rate movements which correspond to the level of the exchange rate considered desirable from the policy point of view. Domestic monetary policy and the extent to which monetary authorities can pursue an independent exchange rate objective within the monetary policy framework are to be assessed against external monetary conditions. They estimated exchange market pressure in a bilateral model comprising Canada and the USA, with the USA representing world monetary conditions. An attempt on the part of the Canadian monetary authorities to increase the growth rate of money supply results in an almost equivalent rate of depreciation in the exchange rate or a loss of reserves at an equivalent rate in relation to a certain base or some combination of the two. Exchange market pressure was found to be impervious to the composition of the authority's intervention i.e., reserve changes and exchange rate adjustments.

Pradhan, Paul and Kulkarni (1989) adapted the Girton and Roper model to Indian conditions over the period 1976 to 1985, using quarterly data to evaluate the relevance of the monetary approach to exchange rate determination. They found reasonably strong evidence for the 'monetarist' hypothesis that increase in money supply leads to reserve losses and exchange rate depreciation. In their view, the monetary authority in India exercises a choice between altering the level of reserves and allowing the exchange rate to adjust to market pressures in response to excess domestic liquidity shocks. Exchange market pressures were, however, reflected more in reserve losses than in exchange rate adjustments giving credence to the view that exchange rate policy in India is conducted with an exchange rate target in perspective rather than a market approach of ensuring orderly rate determination consistent with the underlying monetary conditions.

Weymark (1995) proposed indices of exchange market pressure and intervention in terms of what may be regarded as a generalised version of the Girton and Roper approach in a small open economy model with perfect asset substitutability but without the rigid monetarist assumption of continuous purchasing power parity. While Girton and Roper merely estimated an equation for exchange market pressure in the context of a money demand function in the tradition of the monetary approach, Weymark developed indicators of exchange market pressure which are observable and therefore, useful for policy analysis. Exchange market pressure was defined as the exchange rate change required to relieve excess demand for a currency in the absence of exchange market intervention by the monetary authority. In a managed floating regime, interventions in the form of reserve changes and monetary policy measures in the form of changes in the cost and availability of domestic liquidity are to be translated into exchange rate equivalents and then combined with the observed changes in the exchange rate to yield a composite indicator of exchange market pressure. Despite the fact that sterilisation segregates the money market and the foreign exchange market and can cause a change in the underlying monetary conditions which can obscure exchange market pressure to a certain extent (Pradhan, *et al* pointed out that the absence of sterilisation in framing the EMP model in Girton and Roper is a limitation since the existence of sterilisation can cause simultaneous equation problems), Weymark showed that the market clearing condition necessary to generate the index of exchange market pressure obtains with or without sterilisation. Weymark also proposed an intervention index, developed on the lines of Frenkel's (1980) index of managed float, with the operational advantage of being computable from observable data. Both bilateral and multilateral indices were calculated to evaluate Canada's exchange rate policy over the period 1975 to 1990 using quarterly data. The behaviour of the indices suggested that the pursuit of an exchange rate target was the core objective of the intervention policy in the sample period in Canada.

SECTION II

The Methodology

In the tradition of the asset market approach to exchange rate determination, the exchange rate is viewed as the relative price of national monies, determined by the relative supplies in relation to demand. Thus, while the demand for exports may be formed by a host of underlying real factors, the timing and magnitude of export proceeds flowing into the foreign exchange market responds to interest rate differentials, exchange rate expectations and exchange market conditions, both spot and forward, with little to do with the real factors that caused the export shipment. Similarly, the decision to contract external commercial borrowing may have been provoked by real developments such as the need for capacity expansion, but the timing of bringing in the funds would depend on interest rate differentials and their movements vis-a-vis the forward premia, current and expected exchange rates and the like.

In any economy, irrespective of the wedges between segments of the financial market spectrum created by exchange controls and other barriers, market agents hold a portfolio comprising, inter alia, stocks of domestic and foreign monies. Given the relative rates of return and the degree of substitutability between domestic and foreign assets, they strive to achieve portfolio balance. In the face of a exogenous, domestic monetary shock embodied in an excess supply of money, market agents would reduce domestic money balances and seek to acquire foreign money balances. In a freely floating exchange rate regime, the price of the domestic money would fall i.e., domestic interest rates would decline and the exchange rate would depreciate. Given the relationship between money, interest rates and exchange rates, the decline in interest rates and exchange rates would cause the demand for domestic money balances to rise until monetary equilibrium is restored. On the other hand, in a fixed exchange rate regime, domestic money balances would be exchanged for foreign goods, services, financial assets and money balances until portfolio balance is restored through the monetary authority meeting the resultant increase in demand for foreign money by losing reserves until monetary balance is restored. In the intermediate forms of exchange rate regimes that characterise the real world, a combination of the effects described obtain. Monetary authorities may, in pursuit of a longer term strategy, seek to contest these short run market outcomes. By signaling their stance through various direct policy instruments reflected in changes in the domestic component of base money and in foreign exchange reserves and through indirect instruments such as changes in strategic interest rates, monetary authorities may attempt to induce shifts in the demand for and supply of domestic and foreign money balances, and thereby change or even reinforce the market view on the monetary conditions.

The model developed here draws heavily upon Weymark while taking into account the specific features of the Indian economy. It is drawn up under the assumptions that the demand for money is 'fairly stable', the emerging role of interest rates as an argument in the money demand function-'interest rates too seem to exercise some influence on the decisions to hold money'- the importance of the exchange rate objective of monetary policy in the context of the emerging linkages between money, foreign exchange and capital markets and a loose form of purchasing power parity which links domestic prices to foreign prices in a probabilistic form for an economy with a growing degree of openness (supported by the use of the REER as an information variable for exchange rate policy). The construction of the model draws inspiration from the underscoring of the need for a multiple indicator approach and the perceived utility of a Monetary Conditions Index in a regime where targeting rate variables assumes importance (Annual Reports of the RBI, 1995-96, 1996-97 and 1997-98; Monetary and Credit policy for the Second Half of 1997-98 and for the First Half of 1998-99).

The model is set out as follows:

(1) Mdt = a0 + a1*Pt + a2*Yt - a3*It + ut

(2) Pt = b0 + b1*Pt^ + b2*Et

(3) It = It^ + E*(Et+1 - Et)

(4) Mst = Ms(t-1) + h(ΔNDA + ΔNFA)

(5) ΔNFA = -ut *(ΔEt)

where,

Mdt	=	Demand for money;
Pt	=	Index of wholesale prices (domestic);
Yt	=	Income/output, proxied by industrial production;
It	=	Nominal interest rate represented by the call money rate, monthly averages;
Et	=	Nominal exchange rate expressed in multilateral form i.e., nominal effective exchange rate (NEER) of the rupee, 36 country bilateral weights;
Ft	=	Forward exchange rate;
Mst	=	Supply of money;
NDA	=	Net domestic assets;
NFA	=	Net foreign assets;
^	=	Respective variables for rest of the world;
u	=	Policy authorities response coefficient;
h	=	money multiplier;
Δ	=	changes in stocks or relevant variables;

Equation (1) is the conventional money demand function employed in India augmented to include the interest rate as an argument signifying the opportunity cost of holding money. Output represented by indices of industrial production in the absence of monthly data on GDP is assumed to be exogenous. Equation (2) represents the version of the functional relationship between domestic prices and foreign prices considered in this model: domestic prices are assumed to be responsive to foreign prices in a functional form but purchasing power parity as a rule is not imposed. Equation (2) essentially allows for the estimation of the exchange rate impact on domestic prices. Equation (3) is the uncovered interest rate parity (UCIP) condition which is set out as an underlying assumption relating to the substitutability between domestic and foreign assets rather than a relationship proposed for empirical testing. It is presented as a part of the model specification to allow the model to be identified. Equation (4) describes the standard money supply formation process under the money multiplier approach, implying that any increase in nominal money stock could be on account of the last period's money stock plus the increase in net domestic assets and net foreign assets of the monetary authority accruing to the current period's money stock through the money multiplier. Under the assumption that the money market clears continuously, the equilibrium condition would be reflected in the identity Ms = Md. Equation (5) represents the reaction function of the authorities. Under a freely floating exchange rate, the value of ut=0. The monetary authority does not intervene in the exchange market and hence there is no change in NFA and money supply. When the authorities, on the contrary, peg the exchange rate at a particular level (i.e. ut=∞), there is unlimited intervention and hence proportionate changes in NFA and money supply. (Here, the general assumption is that the authorities intervene only by changing NFA and not by changing NDA; as Weymark (op.cit) has shown, compensating variations in NDA due to sterilisation do not affect the monetary equilibrium condition. Furthermore, in India, variations in domestic credit are not systematically used to influence the exchange rate of the rupee. The value of ut in equation (5) thus gives an idea about the degree to which exchange rate is managed. ut can assume negative values when interventions are used aggressively to obtain an exchange rate change which is contrary to or significantly larger than market expectations.

Following Weymark, the EMP can be derived as

$$EMPt = \Delta Et + n\ \Delta NFA \quad \text{where } n = -1/[b2+a3]$$

and IIA as

$$IIA_t = n\ \Delta NFA/EMP_t$$

The calculation of EMP and IIA thus hinges critically upon the calculation of the elasticity 'n' which, in turn, depends upon estimates of the parameters b2 and a3 i.e., the coefficient of the exchange rate as a determinant of the domestic price level and the interest elasticity of the demand for money respectively. These parameters can be obtained by estimating Equations (1) and (2) of the model.

EMP measures the excess demand/supply for/of foreign exchange associated with the exchange rate policy. It does not measure the actual exchange rate change warranted by conditions of demand and supply but instead the degree of external imbalance and the presence/absence of speculative activity. The critical indicator in the EMP is its sign. Negative values indicate downward pressures on the exchange rate while positive values reflect upward pressures which holds irrespective of the choice of the exchange rate regime. The IIA has a range from -∞ to +∞. Under a freely floating regime, IIA = 0 and under a fixed exchange rate regime, IIA = 1. Under intermediate regimes IIA assumes values between 0 and 1. When the monetary authority leans with the wind, i.e., amplifies the exchange rate pressures generated by the market, the IIA assumes values greater than 1. On the other hand, when the monetary authority contests the market view, the IIA is less than one.

The Monetary Conditions Index (MCI) which has come to be employed as an operating target or more generally, as an indicator of monetary conditions in countries forced to move away from a monetary aggregates approach by the pace of financial innovations, can easily be seen to be a more readily computable version of the EMP. It is a weighted aggregate of the exchange rate and interest rate channels of monetary policy, providing leading information about the monetary conditions since money stock variations impact upon the exchange rate and interest rate with a much reduced lag than upon prices and output. The manner in which monetary policy should be adjusted to offset the deviation of monetary conditions from the desired levels is addressed through targeting the weighted monetary conditions index within a band, the band limits being enforced by, or by the threat of, monetary policy action. The weights assigned to the exchange rate and interest rate generally depend upon their relative influence on output and prices and are usually derived by estimating a money demand function in which the exchange rate and the interest rate are present as explanatory variables. Adjusting money stock to align the MCI with a desirable level would constitute the appropriate stance of policy.

The EMP would indicate the extent of exchange market pressure on account of monetary disequilibria while MCI would directly show the monetary conditions prevailing at any point of time in relation to some base level monetary condition and thereby help the authorities in deciding the degree and timing of monetary policy changes that may be necessary to keep the EMP within manageable limits. A decline in the MCI indicates tightening of monetary conditions whereas an increase in the index reflects easing.

In this paper a standard MCI has been constructed representing a linear combination of the interest rate and exchange rate as follows:

$$MCI = a^* (It - Ib) + b^* (Et - Eb)$$

It and Et represent interest rate and exchange rate at time t and Ib and Eb represent interest rate and exchange rate as at some point which could be considered as equilibrium (and hence base period E and I). a and b represent the weights which are decided on the basis of the respective influence of interest rate and exchange rate on the goal variable.

SECTION III

ESTIMATION OF EMP, IIA AND THE MCI FOR INDIA

For generating estimates of the EMP, the IIA and the MCI under the methodology set out in Section III, the data used are as follows: Month-end nominal money stock (M3), monthly indices of wholesale price indices (WPI) as representative of domestic price movements, monthly indices of industrial production (IIP) as the proxy for scale of economic activities in the absence of monthly data on national income, nominal effective exchange rate (NEER) indices to reflect the movement in the exchange value of the rupee vis-a-vis 36 major trading partners of India, monthly average of inter-bank call money rates (CMR) as representative of the opportunity cost of money, and the weighted average of domestic CPIs of 36 major trading partners of India (WOPI) to reflect the movement of international prices. For countries which do not publish data on intervention purchases and sales, changes in the levels of foreign exchange assets are considered for empirical analysis. In the case of India, however, monthly data on intervention purchases and sales are published regularly by the RBI since June 1995 and for the purpose of estimating and comparing the estimates, both change in reserve levels and net intervention purchases/sales data have been considered.

All the equations for the basic model were estimated in log-linear form. Before estimating the coefficients of the two relevant equations for EMP and IIA, the stationarity properties of the variables were checked by using the Dickey-Fuller (DF) and the Augmented Dickey-Fuller (ADF) tests.

All the variables considered for estimating the two equations turned out be integrated of order one, [i.e. I(1)], indicating that some linear combination of these variables may represent a long run equilibrium relationship. (For the DF and ADF test statistics see Table-1). In order to establish the long run relationship among variables in the money demand and PPP equations, Johansen and Juselius (JJ) type of maximum likelihood tests of multiple cointegration were conducted for the sample period April 1990 to March 1998. The eigen values and trace statistics for both money demand and PPP relationships (presented in Table-2) indicate the presence of two cointegrated vectors as reported below.

Money demand function

(1) LM3 = 4.04 + 0.80 LWPI + 1.00 LIIP - 0.17 LCMR

Purchasing power parity relationship

(2) LWPI = -9.04 + 3.43 LWOPI - 0.51 LNEER

The DF and ADF tests for errors (presented in Table-3) indicate the errors to be stationary.

Relevant coefficients from the above relationships are used to estimate the exchange market pressure and degree of intervention as follows.

$EMPt = \Delta NEERt + u \times \Delta NFA$

Where $u = 1/ -(-0.51-0.17) = 1/0.68 = 1.4705882$

and

$IIAt = u \times \Delta NFA/EMPt$

The estimates of EMP and IIA for the period April 1990 to March 1998 are presented in Table-4. Estimates of EMPs and IIA generated by using the actual interventions data are also shown in Table 5.

For the MCI, the weights for exchange rates and interest rates were estimated from the reduced form of Equations (1) and (2) i.e.,

(6) LM3 = 3.80 + 0.74 LWOPI + 1.38 LIIP - 0.05 LCMR - 0.35 LNEER

The eigen values and trace statistics presented in Table-6 suggest the presence of two cointegrating vectors. The residuals of the two vectors were subjected to normality tests; in view of the relatively higher coefficient of variation of the residuals of the second vector, the first vector was chosen for generating the MCI and is reported above [Equation (6)]. The coefficients of LNEER and LCMR suggest that the weights could be as follows: a = 0.125, b = 0.875; a+b=1. The MCI is presented in Tables 4 and 5 to compare its movements vis-a-vis the EMP and IIA.

SECTION IV

EXCHANGE RATE MANAGEMENT IN INDIA, MARCH 1993 TO MARCH 1998: AN EVALUATION

In the aftermath of the unprecedented payments crisis of 1990, the exchange rate of the rupee was considered to be significantly overvalued in relation to competitor countries (Rangarajan, 1991). A sharp downward adjustment of the exchange rate of about 18 per cent undertaken as an element of a package of structural reform measures in July 1991 set the stage for more fundamental changes in the exchange rate regime recommended by the High Level Committee on Balance of Payments (GOI, 1991). The *de facto* administered regime based on a basket of currencies of important trading partners which had been in place since 1975 was replaced in 1992 by a dual exchange rate system under which one leg of the exchange rate, applicable to 40 per cent of all current receipts, essential imports and debt service payments, was determined by the RBI and the other leg, which applied to all other transactions, was determined by the market. For transactions routed through the market, the dual exchange rate system implied a depreciation in the exchange rate of 11 per cent. In March 1993, the dual exchange rate system gave way to a market based system under which the two legs of the exchange rate were unified and were left to be determined entirely by market forces. The RBI indicated its exchange rate stance as allowing the exchange rate to reflect the macro economic fundamentals.

Over the period April 1990 to June 1991 the EMP recorded negative values indicating that downward pressures on the exchange rate had been building up. The downward movement in the MCI during this period suggests that the pressures on the exchange rate were not on account of monetary conditions which were tight reflecting the stance of monetary policy embodied in high interest rates and reserve requirements, import restrictions and penal provisions for delaying export proceeds. The EMP's movements were due to acute excess demand conditions created by the widening of the current account deficit as the terms of trade shock of the Gulf war and the financing gap in the capital account on account of the waning of the international confidence took a vice like grip on the balance of payments. The average IIA for the period at 0.91 indicated the high degree of management of the exchange rate regime essentially through the use of reserves, supported by monetary policy and exchange restrictions.

In July 1991, i.e., the month in which two step downward adjustment in the exchange rate was carried out, the EMP turned positive and remained so for a prolonged period up to July 1992 showing that the devaluation relieved the accumulated exchange market pressure and in fact, resulted in an over correction. This is borne out by the value of IIA which soared to 2.04 in July 1991 suggesting that the value of the exchange rate would have depreciated by less than the extent of devaluation if market forces alone had been in operation. The MCI plunged in July 1991 and continued to exhibit tight monetary conditions up to August 1992, as monetary policy supported the stabilisation measures. The episodes of easing in October 1991 and May 1992 reflected the turnaround in the balance of payments. Inflows under the Foreign Exchange (Immunities) Scheme and the India Development Bonds in October, 1991 combined with some relaxation of cash margin requirements on imports to yield some respite in stringent monetary conditions. By May 1992, further relaxations in margin requirements for imports, interest rate surcharge on import finance, greater access to export refinance, rolling down of punitive rates on post shipment export credit and reductions in primary and secondary reserve requirements announced in April 1992 were reflected in some easing in the MCI.

From August 1992 to February 1993 the EMP turned negative again indicating the return of downward pressures on the exchange rate. The dual exchange rate imposed an implicit tax on export proceeds and remittances which hindered supplies in the foreign exchange market. Consequently, prior to the abolition of the dual exchange rate system in March 1993, downward pressures had been building up and a regime change was overdue. During this period, the MCI edged upwards and thus, the slackening of monetary conditions contributed to exchange market pressure. Throughout this period the IIA remained above 1 and contrary to the general perception arising from the partial influence of the market on the exchange rate, there seems to have been an increase in the degree of management of the regime in relation to the preceding period.

The unification of the exchange rates and the market based system corrected the misalignment of the exchange rate. The speculative attacks on the exchange rates in the period leading up to the presentation of the Union Budget, 1993-94 ebbed away and a remarkable stability set in. As capital flows built up into a surge, excess supply conditions in the foreign exchange market resulted in a continuous upward pressure on the exchange rate up to March 1995. The EMP remained positive throughout this period except for aberrations in May 1993 and December 1994 when despite purchases from the market by the RBI, the exchange rate appreciated in nominal effective terms. There was also a bunching of debt service payments in December 1994 which in an exception to the general trend of that period, caused a loss of reserves. Throughout the period from March 1993 to March 1995 there were net purchases by the RBI from the market reflecting an effort to prevent nominal appreciation from eroding export competitiveness. The IIA averaged 0.98 during the period, capturing the continuous interventions by the RBI in the market. The MCI eased between June 1993 and April 1994 due to their expansionary effects of capital flows which were only partially sterilised. Although buoyant domestic activity created the conditions for the absorpotion of the capital flows, the monetary aggregates kept well above their targeted trajectories.

By April 1995 the easy money conditions fed through into the foreign exchange market and the EMP turned negative. Excess demand for foreign exchange was met through reserve depletion instead of being allowed to influence the exchange rate. A marginal weakening of the exchange rate was allowed in August 1995, which was also accompanied by large intervention sales by the RBI. Nevertheless, market conditions embodied in an upward drift in the forward premia and widening spread between buying and selling rates in the spot market indicated sentiments which were contrary to the authorities' view. Downward pressures intensified building up into the first major speculative attack on the exchange rate in the post unification period during the period September 1995 to February 1996. The EMP remained negative throughout except for a brief respite in December 1995. The authorities leaned with the wind in September 1995 by halting intervention sales and allowing market forces relative freedom to depreciate the exchange rate. As a consequence, the IIA fell below 1 and even turned negative. The nominal exchange rate plunged in October 1995 as speculation lengthened the normal leads and lags in receipts and payments. Panic demand for cover and cancellations of forward contracts created persistent mismatches of supply and demand both in the spot and forward segments of the market.

Intervention sales were initially supported by a withdrawal of liquidity from the money market and interest rates were raised. The IIA turned positive in October 1995 as the authorities switched to leaning against the wind. The MCI indicated a tightening of monetary conditions since the announcement of the monetary and credit policy for the first half of the year with a strong decline in the MCI in October 1995. Monetary policy attacked speculative sentiment ruling in the exchange market. Although the stance was eased transiently in November 1995 through reductions in cash reserve requirements, the EMP continued to indicate downward pressure in the exchange market and as such, the easing of monetary conditions in November 1995 though unavoidable, was contrary to the requirements of exchange rate management. There was a brief respite in December 1995 as resumption of capital flows absorbed exchange market pressure. The EMP turned positive in that month. The capital flows enabled purchases by the RBI which resulted in an increase in the IIA. Nominal appreciation in the exchange rate suggested a tightening of monetary conditions. In January and February 1996 the EMP turned negative as exchange market pressures flared up and the exchange rate touched a record low. Monetary policy measures were undertaken along with intervention sales. The MCI tightened but the IIA declined as interventions were of a lower order than in the preceding months, being replaced by monetary policy measures.

Normalcy was restored in the foreign exchange market in March 1996. The EMP turned positive and remained so up to August 1997. The MCI showed continued tight monetary conditions and the average IIA for the period March 1996 to July 1997 was at about 0.74 indicating a lower degree of management of the exchange rate than in a comparable period of exchange rate stability during March 1993 to August 1995. In fact in the months of April, May and August 1996 and again in January 1997 the management of the exchange rate was in alignment with the market forces. On the other hand, in June, July, and November 1996 and in February, March, May and June 1997 the RBI contested the market view by effecting large intervention purchases and preventing the exchange rate from appreciating.

Downward exchange market pressures began again in September 1997, captured in the negative sign of the EMP. Exchange market pressures became intense in November and December 1997. Alongside a marginal easing of the MCI in September and October 1997 (reflecting the large interventions rather than any relaxation in the policy stance), the EMP which had turned positive in October 1997 when exchange market pressures had eased, became negative again. In January 1998, monetary policy measures eased the MCI. The EMP turned positive reflecting the ebbing of market pressures. After a long hiatus the RBI purchased foreign currencies from the market in that month. The easing of monetary conditions in January 1998 brought about the return of exchange market pressure on the exchange rate as reflected in the sign of the EMP in February, 1998. By March 1998, however, the easy monetary conditions had been reversed and as a result the EMP eased. In comparison with the previous episode of exchange rate volatility during August 1995 to February 1996 there was a relatively greater degree of management in the exchange rate regime during September 1997 to March 1998 (the average IIAs were 0.72 and 0.91 respectively).

Estimates of EMP and IIA generated by using actual net intervention data corroborate the pattern of movement of these indicators based on changes in foreign currency assets. The IIAs were either less than one but very close to one or were greater than one signifying that not only was the exchange rate regime highly managed but also that the actual exchange rates prevailing in the system (in terms of their movements) were mostly in the opposite direction to what would have prevailed in the absence of intervention. The results of the study indicate that the exchange rate policy in India has been actively supportive of the external sector target in terms of a sustainable level of current account deficit.

SECTION V

CONCLUSION

The paper demonstrates the use of indicators of exchange market pressures, monetary conditions and intervention activity as contemporaneous 'real-time' tools for the evaluation of exchange rate policy as a subset of monetary policy. While interventions have been the principal operating variable they have been reinforced by monetary policy measures when the exchange market has been driven by speculative activity. In this sense interventions have provided leading indications about the future course of monetary policy. A comparison of the two episodes of exchange market pressures in India in the second halves of 1995-96 and 1997-98 shows that the RBI's response to speculative attacks has followed a common pattern. While the exchange rate regime in India can be characterised as highly managed, this needs to be viewed against the transitional phase in the evolution of the regime and the development of the markets. ...

References

Connolly, M. and Silveira J.D.D. (1979): "Exchange Market Pressure in Post War Brazil: An Application of the Girton-Roper Monetary Model", *American Economic Review*, Vol. 69.

Danker, Deborah J. (1987): "Small Empirical Models of Exchange Market Intervention: Applications to Germany, Japan, and Canada," *Journal of Policy modelling*.

Dominguez, K.M. and Frankel J. (1993): *Does Foreign Exchange Intervention Work?* Institute of International Economics, September.

Economics Department (1996): "Summary Indicators of Monetary Conditions", *Reserve Bank of New Zealand Bulletin*, Vol.59, No. 3.

Girton, L. and D. Roper (1977): "A Monetary Model of Exchange Market Pressure Applied to the Postwar Canadian Experience," *American Economic Review*, 67 (4) September.

Government of India (1993): "Report of the High Level Committee on Balance of Payments", April.

Humpage, Owen F. (1989): "On the Effectiveness of Exchange Market Intervention", Federal Reserve Bank of Cleveland, Cleveland.

Kaminisky, G.L. and Lewis K.K. (1993): *Does Foreign Exchange Intervention Signal Future Monetary Policy?* Working Paper No. 4298, National Bureau of Economic Research.

Kenen, Peter B. (1994): "Exchange Rate Management: What Role for Intervention?" *Exchange Rates and Monetary Systems, Selected Essays of Peter B. Kenen*, Edward Elgar Publishing Ltd.

Klein, M.W. and Eric Resengren (1991): "Foreign Exchange Intervention as a Signal of Monetary Policy," *New England Economic Review*, May-June.

Obstfeld, M. (1988): "The Effectiveness of Foreign Exchange Intervention: Recent Experience," *NBER Working Paper Series* No. 2796, Cambridge.

Pradhan, H.K., M. Thomas Paul and Kishore G. Kulkarni (1989): "Exchange Market Pressure in India: An Empirical Test of Monetary Hypothesis", *Prajnan*, Vol. XVIII, No. 1.

Rangarajan, C. (1991): "Exchange Rate Adjustment: Causes and Consequences", *Reserve Bank of India Bulletin*, September.

Reserve Bank of India, *Annual Report*, various issues.

———. (1997): *Monetary and Credit Policy for the Second Half of 1997-98*, October.

———.(1998): *Monetary and Credit Policy for the First Half of 1997-98*, April.

Weymark, Diana N. (1995): "Estimating Exchange Market Pressure and the Degree of Market Intervention for Canada," *Journal of International Economics*, 39 (3-4), November.

Monetary Conditions Index (MCI) for India

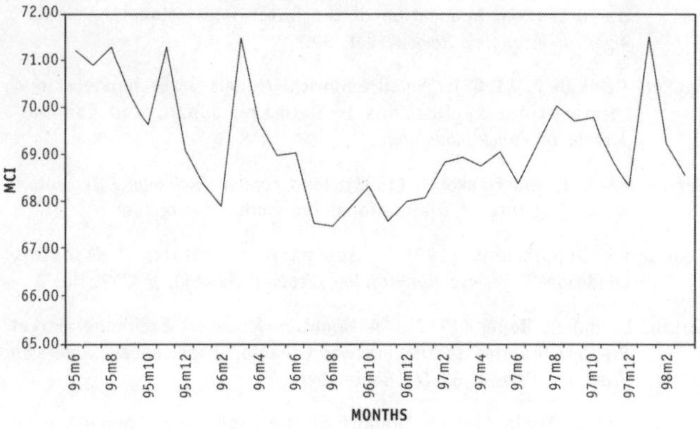

Indicator of Intervention Activity (IIA)

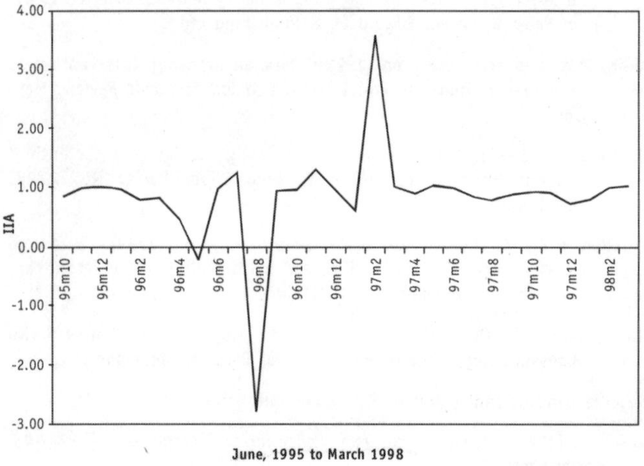

June, 1995 to March 1998

Index of Exchange Market Pressure (EMP)

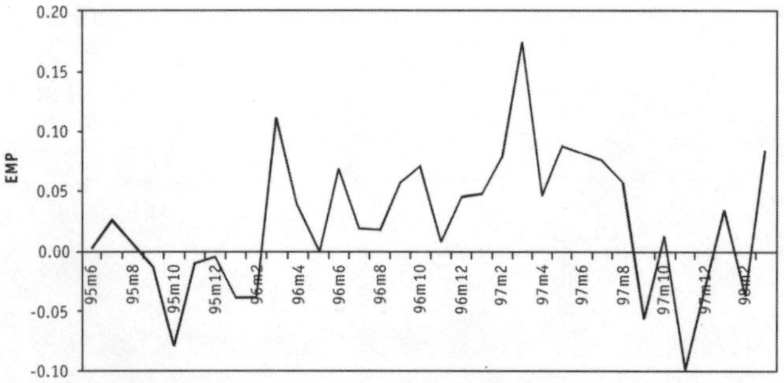

June, 1995 to March 1998

TABLE 1

Unit Root Tests with Trend and a Constant
(Sample period: April 1990 to March 1998)

Variables	*DF*	*ADF*
LM3	-3.84	-2.39
LWPI	-1.32	-1.87
LIIP	-6.16	-2.73
LCMR	-4.64	-2.96
LWOPI	-3.97	-2.41
LNEER	-2.09	-2.17
DLM3	-9.16	-7.38
SLWPI	-6.52	-6.28
DLIIP	-14.87	-9.22
DLCMR	-11.88	-9.72
DLWOPI	-10.06	-9.26
DLNEER	-9.61	-6.98

Note: DF values for LM3, LIIP, LCMR and LWOPI indicate that these variables may be integrated of order zero and can be considered as stationary in their levels. DF equations for these variables, however, do not pass the tests of residual serial correlation (LM statistics) and the heteroscedasticity tests (Engle's ARCH test). Therefore, stationarity properties of the above variables have been tested through ADF test statistics, with appropriate lags for the corresponding ADF equations.

TABLE 2

Cointegration Test Statistics (JJ Method) of Money Demand Function

Null: Alternative Hypothesis	*Trace Statistics*	*5% critical value*	*Null: Alternative Hypothesis*	*Maximum Eigen value Statistics*	*5% critical value*
r=0: r>=1	73.5	53.12	r=0:r=1	32.91	28.14
r<=1:r>=2	40.6	34.91	r<=1:r=2	20.81	22.01
r<=2:r>=3	19.79	19.96	r<=2:r=3	13.46	15.67
r<=3:r=4	6.32	9.24	r<=3:r=4	6.32	9.24
Cointegrated Test Statistics (JJ Method) for the PPP equation					
r=0: r>=1	38.81	34.91	r=0:r=1	25.51	22.01
r<=1:r>=2	13.31	19.96	r<=1:r=2	7.62	15.67
r<=2:r=3	5.68	9.24	r<=2:r=3	5.68	9.24

TABLE 3

DF and ADF tests for errors

	Without trend		*With trend*	
	DF	*ADF*	*DF*	*ADF*
Residuals of Money Demand Relationship	-5.71	-5.33	-5.77	-5.39
Residuals of PPP relationship	-2.15	-3.71	-2.90	-4.03

TABLE 4

EMP, IIA and MCI for India

Year/ Month	*MCI*	*EMP*	*IIA*	*Year/ Month*	*MCI*	*EMP*	*IIA*
90m4	100.00			94m4	73.32	0.00	0.98
90m5	98.25	0.06	1.14	94m5	73.08	0.04	1.10
90m6	97.46	-0.01	0.83	94m6	72.87	0.08	1.05
90m7	95.93	-0.08	0.87	94m7	72.12	0.10	1.08
90m8	94.76	0.08	1.14	94m8	72.12	0.01	0.98
90m9	93.37	-0.30	0.92	94m9	73.05	0.09	1.03
90m10	93.77	-0.26	0.99	94m10	71.76	0.07	1.06
90m11	92.20	-0.26	0.99	94m11	71.96	0.01	0.89
90m12	91.98	-0.44	1.02	94m12	72.55	-0.04	1.14
91m1	91.91	1.63	1.00	95m1	73.03	0.02	1.12
91m2	89.89	-0.15	0.84	95m2	72.56	0.02	1.15
91m3	91.76	-0.05	1.28	95m3	71.32	0.05	1.30
91m4	91.52	-0.64	0.99	95m4	70.58	-0.03	0.85
91m5	91.85	-0.02	-0.15	95m5	71.17	-0.01	1.31
91m6	90.40	-0.17	0.99	95m6	71.21	-0.05	0.98
91m7	80.24	0.10	2.04	95m7	70.88	0.02	0.96
91m8	78.82	-0.17	0.95	95m8	71.30	-0.06	1.11
91m9	77.87	0.74	1.01	95m9	70.25	-0.01	-0.63
91m10	79.07	0.52	1.00	95m10	69.63	-0.12	0.84
91m11	78.45	0.23	1.03	95m11	71.33	-0.04	0.98
91m12	76.22	0.46	1.02	95m12	69.08	0.01	0.99
92m1	76.62	0.08	0.95	96m1	68.39	-0.10	0.95
92m2	76.97	0.16	0.96	96m2	67.89	-0.04	0.78
92m3	72.93	0.47	1.10	96m3	71.51	0.13	0.80
92m4	72.85	-0.06	0.68	96m4	69.72	0.01	0.46
92m5	74.41	0.00	-10.37	96m5	68.99	-0.01	-0.23
92m6	71.64	0.20	1.03	96m6	69.06	0.04	0.98
92m7	71.82	0.06	0.90	96m7	67.53	0.03	1.26
92m8	71.67	-0.03	1.03	96m8	67.49	0.00	-2.81
92m9	72.01	-0.12	1.02	96m9	67.94	0.04	0.95
92m10	72.98	-0.07	1.16	96m10	68.35	0.06	0.95
92m11	74.33	-0.15	1.11	96m11	67.60	0.01	1.32
92m12	73.66	0.18	1.04	96m12	68.03	0.03	0.92
93m1	74.26	-0.06	1.08	97m1	68.11	0.01	0.59
93m2	72.47	-0.02	-0.19	97m2	68.86	0.00	3.61
93m3	74.12	0.35	0.95	97m3	68.98	0.20	0.99
93m4	73.47	0.10	1.10	97m4	68.78	0.02	0.90
93m5	72.90	-0.08	1.00	97m5	69.07	0.09	1.04
93m6	72.93	0.01	0.68	97m6	68.40	0.08	1.01
93m7	73.34	0.05	0.88	97m7	69.26	0.04	0.86
93m8	73.12	0.11	0.01	97m8	70.08	0.03	0.79
93m9	72.64	0.06	1.07	97m9	69.74	-0.005	0.89
93m10	73.03	0.06	0.94	97m10	69.83	0.03	0.95
93m11	73.58	0.06	0.91	97m11	68.91	-0.11	0.91
93m12	73.57	0.29	1.00	97m12	68.35	-0.03	0.73
94m1	74.03	0.10	0.95	98m1	71.57	0.04	0.80
94m2	73.69	0.37	1.01	98m2	69.23	-0.02	1.02
94m3	73.26	0.22	1.02	98m3	68.62	0.11	1.05

Note: EMP and IIA are generated by using variations in levels of foreign currency assets.

TABLE 5

EMP, IIA and MCI for India

Year/ Month	*MCI*	*INTVN ($mn.)*	*EMP*	*IIA*
95m6	71.21	36	0.00	1.62
95m7	70.88	338	0.03	0.97
95m8	7.30	0	0.01	0.00
95m9	70.25	0	-0.01	0.00
95m10	69.63	-785	-0.08	0.76
95m11	71.33	-110	-0.01	0.92
95m12	69.08	-56	0.00	1.02
96m1	68.39	-402	-0.04	0.88
96m2	67.89	-328	-0.04	8.76
96m3	71.51	960	0.11	0.78
96m4	69.72	368	0.04	0.88
96m5	68.99	101	0.00	8.78
96m6	69.06	785	0.07	0.99
96m7	67.53	294	0.02	1.40
96m8	67.49	247	0.02	1.25
96m9	67.94	672	0.06	0.97
96m10	68.35	840	0.07	0.96
96m11	67.60	132	0.01	1.63
96m12	68.03	551	0.04	0.95
97m1	68.11	550	0.05	0.88
97m2	68.86	925	0.08	0.89
97m3	68.98	2329	0.18	0.99
97m4	68.78	641	0.04	0.95
97m5	69.07	1393	0.09	1.04
97m6	68.40	1335	0.08	1.01
97m7	69.26	1185	0.07	0.92
97m8	70.08	872	0.06	0.89
97m9	69.74	-978	-0.06	0.91
97m10	69.83	189	0.01	0.86
97m11	68.91	-1590	-0.10	0.90
97m12	68.35	-407	-0.03	0.72
98m1	71.57	422	0.03	0.78
98m2	69.23	-681	-0.04	1.01
98m3	68.62	1449	0.08	1.07

INTVN: Monthly net interventions by the RBI in the forex market.

EMP and IIA are generated by using intervention sales/purchases of the RBI.

Note:
1. EMP +ve ⇒ Market pressure on the rupee to appreciate
2. EMP -ve ⇒ Market pressure on the rupee to depreciate
3. IIA = 0 ⇒ Free float
4. IIA = 1 ⇒ Completely managed exchange rate.
5. IIA with -ve values ⇒ Authorities actively appreciate/depreciate with respect to the free market value (say an official devaluation)
6. IIA with values greater than one ⇒ Exchange rate moves in the opposite direction to what would have prevailed in the absence of intervention.
7. Declining MCI indicates tighter monetary conditions and rising MCI represents easy monetary condition.

TABLE 6

Cointegration Test Statistics (JJ Method) of Money Demand Function for Estimating MCI

Null	Alternative	Statistic	95% Critical Value	90% Critical Value
Based on Trace Statistics				
r = 0	r = 1	52.0567	34.4000	31.6640
r <= 1	r = 2	33.8465	28.1380	25.5590
r <= 2	r = 3	15.0778	22.0020	19.7660
r <= 3	r = 4	10.9274	15.6720	13.7520
r <= 4	r = 5	8.0874	9.2430	7.5250
Based on Maximum Eigen Value				
r = 0	r = 1	119.9957	76.0690	71.8620
r <= 1	r = 2	67.9390	53.1160	49.6480
r <= 2	r = 3	34.0926	34.9100	32.0030
r <= 3	r = 4	19.0147	19.9640	17.8520
r <= 4	r = 5	8.0874	9.2430	7.5250

17

REER: The Leading Indicator

Sitikantha Pattanaik

Introduction

THE conduct of exchange rate policy in many developing countries has generally been influenced, whether explicitly or implicitly, by consideration of the movements in the Real Effective Exchange Rate (REER). In the nineties, there has been an increasing reference to the REER in the context of leading indicators of future currency attacks. It is perceived that the REER could indicate in advance the likely evolution of the future spot exchange rate. Moreover, there could be a threshold level of REER appreciation beyond which reaction of the market agents may become unidirectional, leading in turn to the collapse of the currency. Goldfajn and Valdes (1996) studied appreciation episodes in 93 countries and found that for real appreciations of above 25 per cent, 90 per cent of the countries experienced currency attacks. The general market perception is that authorities would tolerate real appreciation up to a limit beyond which, as a matter of policy, they would either undertake a large official devaluation or would not resist a market induced orderly correction.

In the aftermath of the Asian currency meltdown, the relevance of the REER as a leading indicator needs a closer scrutiny. Despite the advocacy for greater exchange rate flexibility, on the one hand, and currency board systems/currency unions, on the other, as the preferred alternatives in the choice of the exchange rate regime, majority of the developing countries, however, continue to exhibit a preference for managed flexibility. This is governed by the need to avoid the costs associated with the risks of excessive exchange rate volatility that could accompany free floating and to prevent policy disarmament that a currency board/currency union may entail. The recent Asian experience provides an appropriate benchmark to reassess the role and relevance of the REER in providing leading information for exchange rate management. Section - I presents an assessment of the key perspectives in the literature: the effects of REER misalignments on trade balance, prices and growth, the debate on fundamental determinants of REER, its leading indicator properties and the link between REER and monetary conditions. Section-II contains empirical tests of long-run purchasing power parity (PPP), the "45-degree hypothesis" and causality between the REER and exports. The final section contains some concluding observations.

SECTION I

Key Issues in the REER Debate: A Review of the Literature

REER: The Leading Indicator of Currency Crises

The leading indicator approach offers an alternative, but not necessarily superior method to obtain early indication about the likely future course of the exchange rate. In the exchange rate literature no single approach to exchange rate forecasting has proved superior to others and in general, each method has failed in consistently predicting the exchange rate correctly. In this context Webb and Rowe (1995) observed that "...even the best forecast lacks precision. Macroeconomic forecasts usually have high average errors, but even the average size of errors can change substantially over time. It can, therefore, be difficult to distinguish a good forecasting method from a mediocre one". The poor empirical performance of the major exchange rate models has been extremely well documented in Frankel and Rose (1996), MacDonald and Taylor (1992) and Taylor (1994).

The author is grateful to Shri Muneesh Kapur and one anonymous referee for their useful suggestions on the earlier version of this paper. The usual disclaimer applies.

Meese and Rogoff (1983) compared the out of sample forecasts generated by macro-economic models with those generated through random walk (RW), forward premia (as the predictor of future spot rate), univariate regression of the spot rate and vector auto-regression and concluded (on comparing the root mean square errors) that the RW outperformed all other forecasting techniques. Since then, in empirical research, RW has emerged as a benchmark that every exchange rate forecaster attempts to beat. Rogoff (1996) found that RW models generally outperform structural models over time horizons of less than one year and that the exchange rate reverts to the relative PPP level in floating exchange rate regimes, with half of the adjustment being completed within five years. During this period, however, the factors which determine the equilibrium REER may change and, as a result, it may become extremely difficult to identify the degree of misalignment in terms of the extent of real appreciation that can be considered as close to the threshold level (i.e. the level beyond which currency attacks appear highly probable).

Episodes of currency crises have generally been preceded by appreciating REER. Kaminsky, Lizondo and Reinhert (1997) surveyed 25 studies on currency crisis and found that in 10 out of the 12 studies, the REER turned out to be a statistically significant leading indicator of currency crisis with the longest lead time. Goldfajn and Valdes (1996) regressed expected depreciation (i.e. 3, 6 and 12 months ahead expectations) against 6 measures of overvaluation (i.e. deviation from equilibrium) for 17 developed and 9 developing countries and found that the relevant coefficients were positive for different time horizons - indicating that market agents do consider REER misalignments in forming their expectations. Sachs, Tornell and Velasco (1996) offered two reasons to explain why the market agents also take into account the leading information embodied in the REER: (a) the higher the degree of appreciation of the REER and lower the extent to which tradeables respond to REER depreciations, it is perceived that larger REER adjustment through nominal depreciation may be necessary to restore external balance, and (b) the more vulnerable an economy is to sudden and large demand compression the greater the preference of the authorities for depreciation over recession and such market perceptions often trigger the attack. Kaminsky *et. al.* interpreted currency crises to include both successful attacks (in terms of large currency depreciation) and unsuccessful attacks (in terms of sharp fall in reserves) and constructed an Exchange Market Pressure (EMP) index as a weighted average of monthly percentage changes in exchange rate and reserves. According to their analysis when the EMP deviates from the mean by 3 standard deviations it indicates a condition of crisis. Eichengreen, Rose and Wypolsz (1996) observed that currency attacks could also be averted by raising interest rates and hence, in their construction of the EMP index, along with percentage changes in exchange rate and reserves interest rate changes are also considered. According to Frankel and Rose (1996) a crisis could be interpreted to comprise large devaluation (of about 25 per cent) and larger devaluation than the previous devaluation (by about 10 per cent). Goldfajn and Valdes (1996) interpreted crises differently to include (a) devaluation larger than 1.96 times the standard deviation of the country's rate of change in nominal exchange rate, and (b) 2 per cent plus 1.5 per cent times the devaluation rate of the previous month.

Leading indicator approach involves identifying threshold levels of REER appreciation and when actual behaviour of the REER approximates the threshold level - authorities must receive warning signals and institute policy corrections to avoid a currency attack. Fixing the threshold level is a complex task for the authorities and choice of inappropriate levels may lead to a situation when false signals are regularly picked and right signals are generally missed. Public announcement of the threshold levels could entrench credibility and transparency of policies but achieving levels consistent with the threshold through policy changes may not always be feasible and could even be unnecessary at times. Market agents should, therefore, be left to pick signals from the leading indicators independently and public announcement of the threshold limits should be avoided.

For identifying REER misalignments, both the authorities and the market need to comprehensively assess the alternative macro-economic implications of REER movements. REER indices in their most standard form represent indices of nominal effective exchange rates adjusted for corresponding indices of relative prices. Contrasting views have been expressed relating to (a) choice of a proper price indicator, (b) selection of a base year that would represent an equilibrium condition and against which deviations of REER would represent deviation from PPP, and (c) use of the relevant weighting procedure (Maciejewski, 1983). The effectiveness of the REER as an indicator for the conduct of exchange rate policy would depend on (a) the price elasticities of trade flows, (b) the degree of adjustment of domestic prices and costs to the exchange rate changes, i.e. the price pass-through effects, and (c) the aggregate demand management policies which supplement the exchange rate policies.

Effects on Trade Flows

REER based exchange rate policies which involve nominal depreciations to contain deviation of the exchange rate from the equilibrium PPP assume the efficacy of exchange rate in improving the trade balance position. The underlying assumption in the familiar Marshall-Lerner condition is that export supplies are perfectly elastic and that the full effect of the devaluation/depreciation is passed on in the form of equivalent changes in export/import prices. The value of the pass-through coefficient, therefore, is an important aspect in any analysis of the implications of REER linked exchange rate policies for the external balance position, as also for the transmission of cross border inflation. With wider use of strategic trade policies and increasing recognition of the importance of imperfect competition, industry specific pass-through analyses have also gained prominence. Lack of complete price pass-through at the macro level has been explained in terms of pricing to market behaviour and price discrimination, which are also viewed as the micro foundations of price pass-through effects. Under conditions of price discrimination and pricing to market behaviour, export prices to different destinations from the same country could differ and the law of one price in terms of standard PPP may not hold.

Price and Output Effects

While [some] estimates ... showed a negative impact of real depreciation on growth, Ghura and Hadimichael (1996) found that REER depreciation had positive impact on economic growth. Kalu (1998) also found that in two African regions real devaluations had positive impact on economic growth, both in the short run and in the long run. In the analysis by Razin and Collins (1997) very high real appreciations were seen to be associated with slower growth and moderate to high (not very high) undervaluations depicted significant association with rapid economic growth. REER movements could influence economic growth by (a) affecting domestic and foreign investment and hence capital accumulation, and (b) altering the external competitiveness and affecting levels of exports and imports.

While REER movements could affect growth, the Balassa-Samuelson hypothesis shows that growth as well could lead to deviation of the exchange rate from the PPP. Chinn (1997) estimated that a 1 per cent increase in productivity in the manufacturing sector could cause about 0.5 per cent real appreciation in Indonesia, Korea, Malaysia and the Philippines. Due to non-availability of data on productivity beyond 1991 for these Asian economies, he could not identify statistically the extent of cumulative real overvaluation before the crises. Increase in wages in the tradeable sector, reflecting increase in productivity, may fuel increase in wages in non-tradeable sectors and thereby lead to faster increase in prices than what may be warranted by the overall productivity of the economy. An economy should be better off due to overall increase in productivity, whether in the form of productivity induced lower prices or through productivity related increase in wages and prices that could augment non-inflationary demand. Productivity increases in specific sectors, however, may not necessarily make an economy better off due to higher inflation stemming from demand for wage parity. Many empirical studies find a positive relationship between the ratio of PPP to the exchange rate and the real per capita GDP indicating that faster increases in real incomes contribute to REER appreciation. Koch (1997) found that a 1 per cent increase in real per capita GDP in any of the 25 OECD countries relative to other OECD countries led to 0.59 per cent increase in PPP/ER ratio. Turner and Van't dack (1993) estimated this impact to be about 0.55 per cent. The real income bias of the REER indicates that the excessive emphasis on deviation from PPP at the policy level may not always be correct: [[a real exchange rate (that) appreciates from a low point after (an) initial devaluation may ... reflect good economic policy]]. Assessing the underlying factors that contribute to real appreciation, therefore, is more important than the magnitude of appreciation.

Countries pursuing a REER rule generally devalue to correct for the inflation differentials. Exchange rate depreciation, however, also leads to higher prices through the pass-through effect of higher import prices. In any PPP based analysis inflation rates are generally considered as exogenous and the exchange rate only is endogenised under the assumption that exchange rate changes occur only in response to emergence of inflation differentials. Identifying the feedback effect of exchange rate changes on domestic inflation then becomes crucial at the policy level, given the vicious cycle experience of several Latin American countries in the eighties.

Fundamental Determinants of the REER

There is another strand of literature which decomposes the behaviour of the REER into permanent and temporary components and explains the movements in each of the two components in terms of certain determinants. Such studies try to explain the REER appreciation/depreciation through certain identifiable fundamental determinants and any movement in the REER that remains unexplained by the fundamentals is ascribed to cyclical/temporary shocks (both internal and external) and is interpreted as misalignment. While in some models no significant link is observed between the REER and economic fundamentals, in other models (particularly those dealing with panel data) the past behaviour of the REER is well explained by certain select fundamentals. For the purpose of identifying misalignment some use the various determinants of the exchange rate to model Fundamental Equilibrium Exchange Rate [(FEER) Williamson; Behavioral Equilibrium Exchange Rate [(BEER) Clark and MacDonald; Desirable Equilibrium Exchange Rate [(DEER) Wren-Lewis and Driver; Intermediate-Term Model-Based Equilibrium Exchange Rate [(ITMEER) SB Wadhwani; and Equilibrium Real Exchange Rate [(ERER) Edwards. These model estimates of FEER/BEER/DEER/ITMEER/ERER could be compared with the REER to evaluate the possible extent of misalignment. The impact of any major determinant at any point of time, however, could be ambiguous. For example, changes in the terms of trade could lead to an appreciation or depreciation in the permanent component of the REER depending on the relative importance of the income effect and the substitution effect. Generally, however, inappropriate monetary and fiscal policies affect the determinants of both the permanent and temporary components of the REER and, as has been argued by Edwards (1994), REER misalignments arise mostly on account of inconsistent macro economic policies. Equilibrium level of the REER is not a static concept since it is essentially a function of domestic output growth, demand/absorption and capital flows all of which change over time. In some studies deviation of the REER from PPP is explained in terms of 'nominal' and 'real' factors. Nominal shocks causing misalignment are viewed as temporary and hence the REER must be mean reverting over time. Misalignments resulting on account of real disturbances, however, may be permanent and such misalignments need not be corrected through monetary policy changes.

Monetary Conditions and the REER

Currency crises often result due to pursuance of excessively accommodative monetary policy. Trade deficits and reserve losses resulting from such expansionary monetary policies trigger the attack. Countries which rely excessively on sterilised interventions and neglect fundamental policy corrections, fail to avert an attack despite containing the rate of money growth. MacDonald and Taylor (1994) found strong evidence of close relationship between exchange rates and monetary fundamentals over longer time horizons. While highlighting the strong influence of monetary factors on the exchange rate Mark (1995) observed that over time horizons of three years or more monetary factors could outperform random walk models. Over shorter horizons, however, currency fluctuations may remain inexplicable in terms of monetary fundamentals since during such periods market agents may attach overwhelming importance to technical factors. Williamson (1998), on the other hand, stressed the extremely weak links between the fundamentals and the exchange rate in a floating regime and supported a REER band policy, despite the well known credibility problems associated with such a policy stance and the empirically observed ineffectiveness of central bank interventions in the exchange market. In the Williamson-type band approach certain basic issues have to be addressed which include identifying the equilibrium central level and the limits of the band around the central level within which the REER movement may have to be contained. In the leading indicator approach also identification of the threshold limit of REER appreciation emerges as the critical issue and policies have to be instituted to ensure that the actual REER appreciation at any point of time does not exceed the threshold level of appreciation. The leading indicator approach, however, is free from the credibility problem associated with a band. It also allows for a more flexible exchange rate regime that only requires timely institution of corrective monetary measures by recognising early warning signals from real appreciations. Rising exchange market turbulence in the post Bretton Woods period is often ascribed to the erratically differing national monetary policies. For ensuring a stable exchange rate system national money supplies may have to be stabilised by picking the relevant information about monetary conditions embodied in the REER.

The exchange rate, as the relative price of two national monies, is largely determined by the national money supplies in relation to relative money demands. The REER captures two of the critical monetary variables underlying this relationship directly (i.e. prices and nominal exchange rate) and also gets affected indirectly by the movements in the third critical monetary factor, i.e. the interest rate. When the monetary management is prudent, in a market determined exchange rate system the nominal exchange rate would evolve on its own in response to developments in price and interest rates. Temporary jumps in the exchange rate due to noise factors operating in the market may be smoothened through sterilised interventions, with sustained exchange rate pressures being countered through tighter monetary policy. Use of interest rate to stabilise exchange rate, however, may often conflict with price and output goals of monetary policy. In defense of the higher interest rate response recommended by the IMF to the crisis-ridden economies of Asia, the IMF offered the following arguments: (a) to make domestic currency more attractive to hold, (b) to raise the cost of shorting domestic currency for the speculators, (c) to reduce the adverse impact on corporates with large external liabilities - i.e. corporates with large external liabilities may suffer more from a currency depreciation than a temporary increase in the interest rate, and (d) to encourage corporate restructuring involving more equity in relation to debt (Fischer, 1998). Some others argue that higher interest rates may have adverse output implications and higher rates, if persist longer, could aggravate the recessionary conditions, leading to further fall in the exchange rate.

The recent literature cites the possible existence of some sort of "exchange rate interest rate Laffer curve" - indicating that lower interest rates could strengthen the currency and the economy. While Jeffrey Sachs and Stiglitz endorse such assessments Krugman completely discards the argument (Goldfajn and Baig, 1998). At the policy level, however, the interest rate response needs to be assessed by taking into consideration the relative exposure of an economy to "exchange rate shocks" *vis-a-vis* "interest rate shocks". For Indonesia, given its large external debt, a high exchange rate depreciation could significantly expose the economy to the adverse effects of "exchange rate shocks". On the other hand, in Korea, most of the corporates have high debt/equity ratios and relatively low external debt, indicating thereby to its greater vulnerability to "interest rate shocks" than "exchange rate shocks". Furthermore, during a crisis the risk premium required by the investors may increase considerably, and the increase in interest rate must exceed the increase in these risk premia to stem speculation and capital outflows.

Countries which maintain capital controls and do not allow speculative positions may succeed in stabilising the exchange rate by resorting to high interest rates. But in an open financial system a temporary increase in interest rate, at times, may lack the force to effectively lean against the wind. Some authorities even consider high interest rate stance in the face of currency attacks as a credible signaling device - indicating the determination of the monetary authority towards exchange rate stability. In the face of weak fundamentals, such signaling erodes credibility of the central bank since the market agents know that the high interest rate policies can not be sustained and must have to be reversed. In a study focusing on the effectiveness of tight monetary policy in stabilising exchange rates, Goldfajn and Gupta (1999) concluded that higher interest rate policy helps in reversing excessive undervaluation (as experienced in the affected Asian economies after the currency turmoil) through nominal appreciation rather than leaving the correction to be achieved through higher inflation feeding into the system in the form of higher import prices. Monetary tightening in the face of large real undervaluations could, therefore, restore equilibrium in terms of PPP by containing inflation as well as by forcing nominal appreciation. In the face of financial/ banking crises, however, a higher interest rate policy to restore PPP may prove ineffective. As a result, the equilibrium would be mostly attained through domestic price increases; but such an equilibrium will accompany both higher inflation and a depreciated exchange rate.

SECTION II

Analysis of Empirical Findings

Standard Approaches to Empirical Tests of PPP

The simplest version of the PPP hypothesis would suggest that $E = \lambda\ (P/P^*)$, where E is the nominal exchange rate (units of domestic currencies per unit of foreign currency), P and P* are the respective domestic and foreign price indices, and λ is a constant that reflects all those factors which prevent absolute PPP to hold. Under the assumptions of *symmetry* between domestic and foreign prices and *proportionality* between relative prices and exchange rate, the simplest approach to test PPP is just a test of stationarity of the $REER=E\ (P^*/P)$. Standard unit-root tests are then applied to determine if the null hypothesis of a unit root in the REER can be rejected. Rejection of the null indicates evidence in favour of the long-run PPP; i.e. deviations from the PPP could be temporary and over time REER must be mean reverting.

Since the early 1980s there has been a growing recognition that exchange rates and prices are generally non-stationary and, therefore, a necessary condition for obtaining PPP is that E, P, and P* must be co-integrated. In other words, the REER could be represented as : $q = e - p + P^*$, where q, e, p and p^* are the logarithms of REER, E, P and P*. Under the assumptions of symmetry and proportionality, the cointegrating vector becomes (1,-1, 1) and the test of co-integration reduces to a test of unit-root in the real exchange rate itself. If the unit-root tests fail to establish PPP, an alternative approach to test it is through establishing cointegration between a combination of (e+p*) and p. For this purpose, generally foreign prices P* are converted into domestic prices at E (say F, or f in log form), and the linear combination that is tested for the cointegrating relationship boils down to:

$$f_t = \beta_0 + \beta_1 p_t + \varepsilon_t \qquad \ldots(1)$$

so that ε_t is stationary and the cointegrating vector is such that β_0=0 and β_1=1. Stationarity of ε_t would indicate that deviations from a linear combination of f_t and p_t will be mean reverting and, therefore, f_t and p_t are tied together in the long run. β_0=0 and β_1=1 represent the assumption of proportionality, which may however differ from 0 and 1 respectively in empirical estimates. The first step Engle-Granger regression (1) could be followed by second step error correction representations of the following type:

$$\Delta f_t = \alpha_0 + \alpha_1 \varepsilon_{t-1} + \alpha_2 \Delta f_{t-1} + \alpha_3 \Delta p_{t-1} \qquad \ldots(2a)$$

and

$$\Delta p_t = \mu_0 + \mu_1 \varepsilon_{t-1} + \mu_2 \Delta f_{t-1} + \mu_3 \Delta p_{t-1} \qquad \ldots(2b)$$

More lags of Δf_{t-1} and Δp_{t-1} could be used and even Δf_{t-1} and Δp_{t-1} terms could be completely dropped from the error-correction equations depending on the lag-length tests. Estimating error-correction equations would be important in order to identify the speed of adjustment, i.e. to know the extent by which any deviation from the PPP would be corrected per unit of time and hence, the total units of time over which the misalignment would disappear. Of the two error-correction equations, the first one would show whether the misalignment is corrected through adjustments in nominal exchange rates and the second equation would indicate whether it is domestic price adjustments over the long run that restores equilibrium in the exchange rate. α_1 and μ_1, the respective speed of adjustment coefficients, therefore represent two crucial parameters for the policy makers.

Most of the studies in the 1990s use system estimation techniques of Johansen and Stock-Watson (instead of the Engle-Granger single equation cointegration and error-correction techniques) to examine PPP. The optimality of Johansen estimates have been highlighted by Phillips in terms of symmetry, unbiasedness and efficiency properties. Gonzalo's Monte Carlo study also supports the superior properties of Johansen technique.

Data and Empirical Results

Monthly REER data for the five affected Asian economies (Thailand, Korea, Indonesia, Malaysia, and Philippines) as well as India are taken from the JP Morgan (Economic Research Home page) which has the most consistent data on REER for all these economies for the longest time horizon (i.e. January 1970 to June 1999). Quarterly data on prices (WPI indices) and exchange rates (quarterly average) for the above six countries and CPI indices for the US are taken from the International Financial Statistics, IMF.

ADF stationarity test statistics reported in Table-1 show that only in the case of Philippines PPP (as defined earlier) holds. Once a trend is included in the ADF equation, PPP holds for Korea also.

TABLE 1

Stationarity Test Statistics for REER (1970:01 to 1999:06)

	ADF with constant REER	ADF with constant Log (REER)	ADF with trend and constant REER	ADF with trend and constant Log (REER)
India	-0.8391	-0.5755	-1.9350	-2.0788
Indonesia	-1.2268	-1.4889	-2.9364	-2.9281
Korea	-2.0769	-1.7736	-4.2814*	-3.1908*
Malaysia	-0.9258	-0.5850	-2.2363	-1.9523
Philippines	-3.4817*	-2.6072	-3.8249*	-3.2440*
Thailand	-1.7652	-1.9077	-2.2391	-2.4378

All reported ADF results relate to optimal lags selected through AIC criterion. For India the respective lags are 4, 4, 10, 3.

In view of the symmetry and proportionality assumptions underlying the tests based on stationarity of the REER and the possible resultant rejection of PPP, cointegrating vectors among the relevant variables are also estimated, both in the Engle-Granger and Johansen framework. For this purpose F_t series for each country is generated by converting CPI of the US into domestic currencies at respective exchange rates. Both F_t and P_t series for each country should be of the same order of integration for testing PPP through Engle-Granger and Johansen techniques.

Table-2 presents the stationarity test statistics for these two variables for all the six countries. These tests are conducted over 1973-98 (the post Bretton Woods period) using quarterly data. For all six countries both the series turn out to be I(1). ADF test statistics for errors of Equation-1 (Engle-Granger step-1 regression) and Johansen trace statistics are reported in Table-3 and Table-4, respectively. Excluding Indonesia, Korea and Thailand, long-run PPP relationship is validated for the other three countries (i.e. India, Malaysia and the Philippines) by both Engle-Granger and Johansen techniques.

TABLE 2

Stationarity (ADF) Test Statistics for F_t and P_t of Eq. 1 (1973:1 - 1998:4)

	Log (F_t)	ΔLog (F_t)	Log (P_t)	ΔLog (P_t)
India	0.4195	-5.2066*	-0.5145	-4.5155*
Indonesia	0.2933	-4.5633*	0.4854	-3.0018*
Korea	-1.5748	-3.2654*	-1.6445	-3.5832*
Malaysia	0.0866	-4.5489*	-2.6571	-3.4879*
Philippines	-1.2070	-4.5365*	-1.6446	-4.6027*
Thailand	-1.1084	-5.4899*	-1.9833	-4.8717*

All reported ADF results relate to optimal lags selected through AIC criterion. For India the respective lags are 4, 3, 2, 2.

TABLE 3

Stationarity Tests for the Errors in Equation-1 (1973:1 to 1998:4)

India	Indonesia	Malaysia	Philippines	Korea	Thailand
-3.4058*	-0.9122	-2.9436**	-3.3136*	-1.1254	-2.5042

All reported ADF results relate to optimal lags selected through AIC criterion. For India the optimal lag was 4. * significant at 5 per cent; ** significant at 10 per cent.

Any deviation from the PPP could be corrected over time through adjustments in nominal exchange rates, domestic prices, and foreign prices (or any combination of the three). Results of the error correction representations (Equation 2a and 2b) reported in Table-5 show the speed and degree of adjustment that is achieved in each country through price and exchange rate adjustments. The error-correction parameters α_1 and μ_1 must turn out to be statistically significant, the α_1 coefficient should be negative and the μ_1 coefficient should be positive (Enders, 1997). For India, α_1=-0.077 and μ_1=0.06 indicate that a one unit positive deviation from PPP (signifying undervaluation or over-depreciation) would be corrected by nominal exchange rate appreciation or fall in foreign prices by 7.7 per cent per quarter and through increase in domestic prices by 6 per cent per quarter. Similarly, for one unit negative deviation from the PPP (implying overvaluation) the misalignment would be corrected by about 7.7 per cent of the misalignment per quarter through exchange rate depreciation or increase in foreign prices and through 6 per cent per quarter fall in domestic prices. These estimates suggest that if any misalignment from the PPP is to be corrected through nominal exchange rate changes, then it would take about 8.7 quarters (two years and two months) for removing 50 per cent of the misalignment. If no adjustment through foreign price corrections is assumed, then the adjustment period could exceed 8.7 quarters by few more quarters. Greater speed of adjustment for India than those obtained for developed countries could be ascribed to the high degree of exchange rate management and to the use of REER as a reference point in this management strategy in the medium to long run.

TABLE 4

Johansen Trace Statistics (1973:1 to 1998:4)

Eigenvalue	Likelihood Ratio	5 per cent Critical Value	1 per cent Critical Value	Hypothesized No. of CE(s)
INDIA				
0.184043	20.57978	15.41	20.04	None**
0.000366	0.036988	3.76	6.65	At most 1
MALAYSIA				
0.192620	24.65017	15.41	20.04	None **
0.022796	2.398261	3.76	6.65	At most 1
PHILIPPINES				
0.226086	29.34722	15.41	20.04	None**
0.025558	2.692548	3.76	6.65	At most 1
INDONESIA				
0.063571	6.442235	15.41	20.04	None
5.58E-05	0.005470	3.76	6.65	At most 1
KOREA				
0.057642	9.975474	19.96	24.60	None
0.040547	4.097830	9.24	12.97	At most 1
THAILAND				
0.144706	19.50689	19.96	24.60	None
0.039911	4.032228	9.24	12.97	At most 1

Constant in both VAR and cointegration and each with four lags.

For more open economies a considerable degree of adjustment could also be achieved through domestic price changes. Overvalued REER could be countered to a certain extent through favourable price impact emanating from lower import prices. Similarly, undervalued REER may be automatically corrected partly through the adverse effects on domestic prices stemming from higher import prices. Despite low order of integration with the rest of the world, 6 per cent quarterly correction of misalignment through domestic price changes indicate that exchange rate developments have considerable implications for domestic prices in India. At the policy level, therefore, the inflation anchor role of exchange rate must also be evaluated against the efficacy of depreciated exchange rate in fostering external competitiveness. One of the two error-correction terms turns out to be statistically insignificant for Malaysia and Philippines. While in Malaysia about 12 per cent of the misalignment is corrected through nominal exchange rate/foreign price changes every quarter, in Philippines, about 9 per cent quarterly correction in domestic prices is seen to restore equilibrium.

TABLE 5

Error-correction equations 2a and 2b (1973:1 to 1998:4)

INDIA

$$\Delta f_t = \underset{(4.38)^*}{0.002} - \underset{(-2.36)^*}{0.077\varepsilon_{t-1}} + \underset{(2.69)^*}{0.260\Delta f_{t-1}} - \underset{(-0.23)}{0.034\Delta p_{t-1}}$$

$$\Delta p_t = \underset{(4.11)^*}{0.014} + \underset{(2.87)^*}{0.061\varepsilon_{t-1}} - \underset{(-0.52)}{0.032\Delta f_{t-1}} + \underset{(4.08)^*}{0.378\Delta p_{t-1}}$$

MALAYSIA

$$\Delta f_t = \underset{(2.65)^*}{0.012} - \underset{(-3.24)^*}{0.117\varepsilon_{t-1}} + \underset{(4.62)^*}{0.418\Delta f_{t-1}} - \underset{(-1.07)}{0.259\Delta p_{t-1}}$$

$$\Delta p_t = \underset{(4.17)^*}{0.008} + \underset{(1.40)}{0.020\varepsilon_{t-1}} + \underset{(1.46)}{0.053\Delta f_{t-1}} + \underset{(2.14)^*}{0.209\Delta p_{t-1}}$$

PHILIPPINES

$$\Delta f_t = \underset{(3.00)^*}{0.017} - \underset{(-1.42)}{0.064\varepsilon_{t-1}} + \underset{(3.98)^*}{0.429\Delta f_{t-1}} - \underset{(0.04)}{0.005\Delta p_{t-1}}$$

$$\Delta p_t = \underset{(2.81)^*}{0.011} + \underset{(2.85)^*}{0.089\varepsilon_{t-1}} + \underset{(0.84)}{0.063\Delta f_{t-1}} + \underset{(7.08)}{0.574\Delta p_{t-1}}$$

As could be seen from Chart-1, during 1990 to June 1997 (i.e. the pre crisis period) the REER appreciation was moderate at 6.2 per cent for Indonesia and 7.7 per cent for Thailand and somewhat high at 16.6 per cent in Philippines and 16.9 per cent in Malaysia. (During this period the REER depreciated in both India and Korea.) As a result of large currency depreciations experienced by these countries beginning July 1997, there has been considerable over-correction. As per the PPP mechanism, which essentially is a theory of exchange rate determination under flexible regimes, the present misalignment could be corrected through nominal appreciation as well as increase in domestic prices. At the moment, the latter seems to have dominated the former. Our finding that 9 per cent of the misalignment is corrected every quarter through domestic price adjustments in Philippines is amply demonstrated in Chart-1. While for all other five countries the REER remains depreciated in the range of 10 to 25 per cent compared with their respective 1990 levels, for Philippines it keeps appreciating and at more than 16 per cent real appreciation in relation to its level in 1990 it is again back at the same level as it was in the pre crisis period. Possible correction of misalignment through 6 per cent quarterly domestic price adjustment in India suggests, therefore, that undue exchange rate depreciation to enhance external competitiveness could be counter productive in the long run as higher resultant inflation would erode the induced competitive advantage over several quarters. Identifying a threshold level at which the probability of currency attacks may be large is difficult because Thailand and Indonesia had appreciation levels of about just 6 to 7 per cent and Korea's REER even did not show any appreciation. More than identifying the threshold level of REER appreciation, creating conditions to ensure natural realignment with long run PPP becomes rather more important. The emphasis should be placed, therefore, on more flexible exchange rate regimes supplemented by trade and structural reforms to facilitate greater wage price flexibility and cross-border price convergence. If one takes in to consideration the ongoing debate relating to the "exchange rate regime neutrality of the REER", greater exchange rate flexibility alone may not always lead to automatic gradual convergence with the long run PPP. Both greater exchange rate flexibility and wage price flexibility are crucial to avoid persistent misalignments.

REER and Exports

It is often argued that exchange rate could be a useful instrument to gain external competitiveness. But the PPP argument shows that a policy of real undervaluation attained through competitive depreciation may not work in the long run as the misalignment would be corrected automatically over time, though the speed of correction through domestic price adjustments would depend upon the degree of openness of an economy. To identify the causal relationships between REER depreciation and export performance, Granger causality tests were conducted which are reported in Table-6 (for quarterly exports in dollars) and Table-7 (for annual volume exports). Of the six countries considered, the null hypothesis of "REER does not cause exports" is rejected only for India, Malaysia and the Philippines when exports in US dollar are considered. On the other hand, causality holds only for India and Thailand when quantum index of exports are considered. Excluding India, causality tests indicate that the behaviour of REER may not be an important determining factor for exports.

TABLE 6

Granger Causality Tests
(1970 to 1998-quarterly data on dollar exports)

India	Indonesia	Korea	Malaysia	Philippines	Thailand
4.77*	1.72	1.69	4.40*	5.77*	1.33

*F-statistics significant at 5 per cent. (lag of two years in each Granger equation)

TABLE 7

Granger Causality Tests
(1970 to 1997-Annual data on quantum index)

India	Indonesia	Korea	Malaysia	Philippines	Thailand
4.06*	0.94	1.02	0.30	0.58	4.32*

*F-statistics significant at 5 per cent. (lag of two years in each Granger equation)

Causality results indicate that there may be a host of factors other than the exchange rate which could explain the strong export performance of the Asian economies. In a search for identifying such factors, one could test for the relevance of the "45 degree hypothesis" which suggests that there may be a one-to-one relationship between "estimated demand elasticity of export" and "average annual domestic growth". This relationship is more of an empirically observed pattern than any established causal link. (Several reasons are identified to justify this pattern in Krugman, 1989 and Ito et.al., 1996.) Demand elasticities of exports are estimated for the six countries with quantum index of exports as the dependent variable and world GDP at constant price and respective country's REER as the two explanatory variables (all in log forms). Estimated elasticities and the respective annual average growth rates are presented in Table-8 and Graph-1. It could be seen that the "45-degree hypothesis" is somewhat validated, indicting the importance of domestic GDP growth for export performance. Higher domestic growth may lead to higher levels of imports, but due to the "45-degree" relationship, export levels may also increase simultaneously and, therefore, trend changes in real exchange rates may become unnecessary.

At times, it is argued that the high estimated demand elasticities could be on account of favourable supply-side effects represented in the form of higher domestic output growth and, therefore, supply terms must also be included in export volume equations to test for the "45-degree" rule (Ito et. al, 1996). We estimate the export supply equations for the six countries with log of quantum index of exports as the endogenous variable and log of domestic GDP at constant price and log of REER as the independent variables. All three variables turn out to be I(1) and the errors of the respective OLS equations for each of the three countries also appear stationary. (See table-9) Annual data are used due to non-availability of quarterly GDP figures for these countries. The time period for estimation covers 1970 (since consistent REER data are not available for previous years) to 1997 (1998 is not included since most of the Asian economies experienced negative GDP growth this year). The estimated equations presented below show that (a) domestic GDP growth is a more important factor than the REER for sustaining any export drive in five of the six countries, and (b) REER appears to be a statistically significant determinant of exports for four of the six countries. For India, (as also for Thailand) estimated elasticities indicate that the impact of domestic GDP growth on exports could be about four times higher than that of a depreciation in the REER. These results corroborate the "45-degree rule" that there may exist a one-to-one relationship between "demand elasticities for exports" and "growth in domestic output". They also signify the importance of both REER and domestic economic activity for export performance. In the face of an appreciating REER, therefore, deceleration in both GDP and export growth could signal considerable risk to exchange market uncertainties. Due to unidirectional market perceptions, such a situation may lead to sudden attacks. In a high-growth high-export scenario, however, REER appreciation of a moderate level alone is unlikely to trigger an attack.

Export Supply Equations

India:

Log(exports) = -1.90 + 0.98 Log(GDP) - 0.28 Log (REER)
(-1.22) (8.06)* (-2.24)* $\bar{R}^2$ = 0.95

Philippines:

Log(exports) = -6.04 + 2.07 Log(GDP) - 0.84 Log (REER)
(-7.40)* (13.80)* (-3.23)* $\bar{R}^2$ = 0.92

Malaysia:

Log(exports) = -3.08 +1.11 Log(GDP) - 1.17 Log (REER)
(-1.41) (9.65)* (-5.14)* $\bar{R}^2$ = 0.93

Thailand:

Log(exports) = -6.42 + 1.63 Log(GDP) - 0.31 Log (REER)
(-10.59)* (62.02)* (-2.86)* $\bar{R}^2$ = 0.99

Indonesia:

Log(exports) = -3.89 + 0.73 Log(GDP) - 0.05 Log (REER)
(-2.24)* (7.92)* (-0.29) $\bar{R}^2$ = 0.85

Korea:

Log(exports) = -14.99 + 1.64 Log(GDP) -0.03 Log (REER)

(-3.57)* (11.89)* (-0.05) $\bar{R}^2 = 0.93$

GRAPH 1

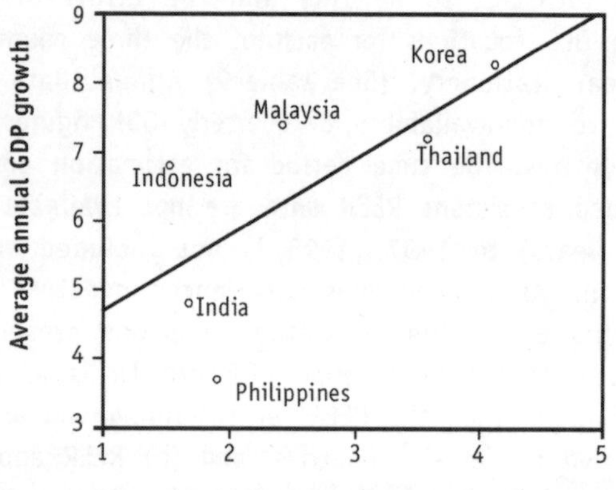

TABLE 8

Estimated Demand Elasticity and Average Annual GDP Growth (1970-97)

	India	Indonesia	Korea	Malaysia	Philippines	Thailand
Estimated elasticities	1.66	1.50	4.11	2.40	1.89	3.56
Avg. GDP growth	4.8	6.8	8.3	7.4	3.7	7.2

SECTION III
CONCLUSIONS

Real overvaluations – representing deviation from the equilibrium PPP – could provide early indication about the likely evolution of the future nominal exchange rate and when such misalignments are large, unidirectional market perceptions could trigger an attack. When ideal conditions are created to ensure automatic convergence of the exchange rate to PPP in the medium to long run, currency attacks could be avoided. These ideal conditions comprise greater exchange rate flexibility and trade/structural reforms to ensure greater wage price flexibility and convergence of cross-border prices. Deviations from PPP could result from both nominal and real shocks. The ideal conditions would only help in removing the temporary deviations caused by nominal/ monetary shocks. Deviations from PPP caused by real shocks, however, could become permanent. Real overvaluations stemming from positive real shocks need not be corrected. In such situations, estimation of misalignment may have to be done against a more recent base which appropriately internalises the possible increase in purchasing power stemming from the positive real shocks.

For India, Malaysia and the Philippines both Engle-Granger and Johansen techniques suggest that PPP holds in the long run. Error correction results indicate that any REER misalignment in India gets corrected by 7.7 per cent every quarter through nominal exchange rate adjustments and by 6 per cent in the form of domestic price adjustments. At this speed of adjustment it could take about 8.6 quarters for removing 50 per cent of the misalignment through nominal exchange rate adjustments. In the face of adverse foreign price developments, however, the adjustment phase could exceed by several more quarters. 6 per cent quarterly correction of the misalignment through domestic price adjustments shows the importance of exchange rate developments for domestic prices. It could be interpreted that any policy to use exchange rate as an instrument to gain external competitiveness may prove ineffective in the long-run. Real undervaluation achieved through nominal depreciations would be inflationary and gradual REER appreciation resulting from such inflation would ensure convergence with the long run PPP.

While large real appreciation needs to get corrected through nominal depreciations in a market determined exchange rate system, ensuring orderly market conditions during such corrections in the market emerges as a critical task for the authorities. With a view to preventing disruptive corrections, the authorities often resort to tighter monetary policy measures. If the market could read the leading information embodied in the REER and chart the course of the nominal exchange rate in a manner that smoothens the correction, the need for assigning monetary policy to the exchange rate objective to that extent could be limited. In such a scenario, monetary policy could focus on its primary goal of low and stable inflation, which in turn would be the first best way to avoid real overvaluation.

Nominal exchange rates were almost unchanged in the affected five Asian economies throughout the nineties before the crisis; however, low orders of cumulative real appreciations experienced in these countries indicate that a part of the misalignment was getting corrected through domestic price adjustments. Evidence against long run PPP for Korea, Thailand and Indonesia could also be ascribed to the operation of Balassa-Samuelson

TABLE 9

Stationarity (ADF) Tests (1970 to 1997, annual data)

	L(GDP)	ΔL(GDP)	L(Export)	ΔL(Export)	L(REER)	ΔL(REER)	Errors@
India	1.3586	-3.8287*	0.8009	-2.6528**	-0.0239	-3.2007*	-1.6819**
Malaysia	-0.0001	-3.1561*	1.6189	-3.7970*	-0.7899	-2.9416**	-2.2132*
Philippines	-1.3579	-2.9137*	-0.4526	-3.8509*	-2.4694	-4.1226*	-1.9202**
Korea	-0.7713	-3.4206*	-1.7282	-3.5053*	-0.1279	-3.3089*	-3.1323*
Thailand	0.3293	-2.8983**	0.9803	-3.6728*	-2.5430	-2.7811**	-3.4122*
Indonesia	-1.2034	-3.4643*	-0.0635	-2.8269**	-0.1990	-3.2510*	-1.9126**

@ Errors of the respective export equations (no constant in ADF equations). One year lag and a constant in all other ADF equations. To get all variables with same order of integration for each country, the period for India and Thailand relate to 1970-94 and 1970-96, respectively.

* significant at 5 per cent; ** significant at 10 per cent.

type real factors which, unlike monetary factors, could lead to permanent deviations from the long run PPP. The general argument that high Asian growth was not propelled by productivity growth does not contradict the possibility of some productivity growth in the "tradeable sector". Greater wage-price flexibility in the overall economy, sectoral wage and price developments that are guided by productivity considerations rather than by demand for parity across sectors, and exchange rate flexibility constitute the key for avoiding persistent misalignments from the long run equilibrium PPP.

Empirical validation of the "45 degree rule" for the six countries considered in the paper highlights the importance of domestic GDP growth as a key export determinant. In the face of deteriorating fundamentals, particularly deceleration in domestic growth and exports, REER appreciation could assume greater importance as a leading indicator of currency crisis. Market forces, therefore, should strive to ensure the necessary correction during periods of above trend performance in GDP and export growth. During normal conditions, surges in capital flows may largely influence the course of the exchange rate. But in the inter-temporal sense, most of the capital flows in a developing country with capital restrictions represent current account flows in the long run. The REER, therefore, embodies crucial leading information that both the market forces and the authorities must use efficiently in designing their medium to long-run strategies.

CHART 1

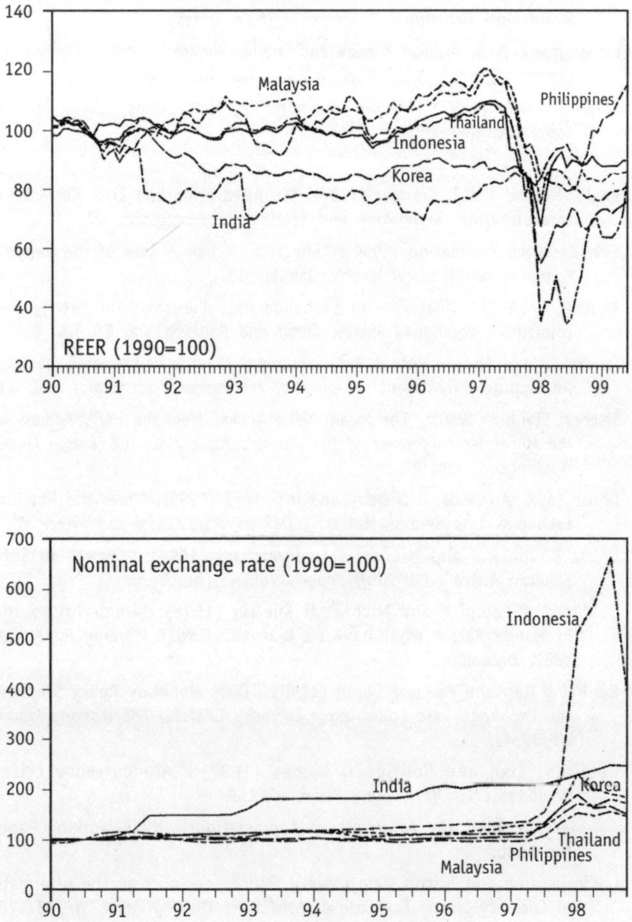

References

[edited version]

Agenor, Pierre Richard (1991): "Credibility and Exchange Rate Management in Developing Countries", *IMF WP/91/87,* September.

Agheveli, Bijan B., Mohsin S Khan and Peter J Montiel (1991): "Exchange Rate Policy in Developing Countries: Some Analytical Issues", *IMF Occasional Papers No. 78,* March.

Calvo, Guillermo A., Carmen M. Reinhart and Carls A. Vegh (1994): "Targeting the Real Exchange Rate: Theory and Evidence", *IMF WP/94/22,* February.

Chinn, Menzie David (1997): "The Usual Suspects? Productivity and Demand Shocks and Asia Pacific Real Exchange Rates", *NBER Working Paper No. 6108,* July.

Chinn, Menzie David and Louis Johnston (1996): "Real Exchange Rate Levels, Productivity and Demand Shocks: Evidence from a Panel of 14 Countries", *NBER Working Paper No. 5709,* August.

...

Dennis, Richard (1997): "A Measure of Monetary Conditions", *Reserve Bank of New Zealand Discussion Paper Series,* G97/1, January.

Edwards, S (1988): "Real and Monetary Determinants of Real Exchange Rate Behaviour: Theory and Evidence from Developing Countries", *Journal of Development Economics,* Vol. 29, November.

———. (1994): "Exchange Rate Management in Developing Countries", *World Bank Occasional Paper No. 2* (New Series).

Eichengreen, Bary, Andrew K Rose and Charles Wyplosz (1996): "Contagious Currency Crises", *NBER Working Paper No. 5681,* July.

Enders, Walter (1997): "Applied Econometric Time Series", *John Wiley & Sons,* Inc, New York.

...

Engle, RF and C.W.J. Granger (1987): "Co-integration and Error Correction: Interpretation, Estimation and Testing", *Econometrica, 49.*

EPW Research Foundation (1994): "Effective Exchange Rate of the Rupee", *Economic and Political Weekly,* January 15.

Frenkel, J (1994): "Patterns in Exchange Rate Forecasts for twenty five countries", *Journal of Money, Credit and Banking,* Vol. 26, No. 4.

Frenkel, J and Andrew Rose (1996): "Currency Crashes in Emerging Markets: An Empirical Treatment", *Journal of International Economics,* Vol. 41.

Fischer, Stanley (1988): "The Asian crisis: A View from the IMF", *Address at the Midwinter Conference of the Banker's Association for Foreign Trade,* Washington, Jan. 22.

Ghosh, A R, A. Gulde, J D Ostry and H.C. Wolf (1995): "Does the Nominal Exchange Rate Regime Matter?", *IMF WP/95/121.*

Ghura Dhaneswar and Michael T Hadjimichael (1996): "Growth in Sub-Saharan Africa", *IMF Staff Papers,* Vol. 43, No. 3.

Goldberg, Pinelopi K and Michael M Knetter (1996): "Goods Prices and Exchange Rates: What have we learned?, *"NBER Working Paper No. 5862,* December.

Goldfajn, Ilan and Poonam Gupta (1999): "Does Monetary Policy Stabilise the Exchange Rate Following a Currency Crisis?", *IMF Working Paper,* WP/99/42.

Goldfajn, Ilan and Rodrigo O Valdes (1997): "Are Currency Crises Predictable?", *IMF Working Paper, 97/159.*

———. (1996): "The Aftermath of Appreciations", NBER Working Paper No. 5680.

Goldfajn, Ilan and Taimur Baig (1988): "Monetary Policy in the Aftermath of Currency Crises: The Case of Asia", *IMF Working Paper,* WP/98/170.

...

Ito, Taktoshi, Peter Isard, Steven Symansky, and Tamim Bayoumi (1996): "Exchange Rate Movements and their Impact on Trade and Investment in the APEC Region", *IMF Occasional Paper No. 145,* December.

Isard, Peter and Steven Symansky (1996): "Long run Movements in Real Exchange Rates", Chapter-2, *IMF Occasional Paper No. 145,* December.

Johansen, S (1995): "Likelihood Based Inference on Co-integration in the Vector Autoregressive Model", *Oxford University Press.*

Kalu, Marc (1998): "Exchange Rate Regimes and Inflation and Output in Sub-Saharan Countries", *BIS Working Paper No. 53,* March.

Kamin Steven B (1997): "Some Multi Currency Evidence on the Effects of Real Exchange Rates on Output", *BIS Working Paper No. 45,* August.

Kamin Steven B and Marc Kalu (1997): "Output and Real Exchange Rate in Developing Countries: An Application to Mexico", *Investment Finance Discussion Paper No. 580,* Board of Governors of Federal Reserve System, Washington DC.

Kaminsky GL, S Lizondo and C.M. Reinhert (1997): "Leading Indicators of Currency Crises", *IMF WP/97/79.*

Koch, Elmar B (1997): "Exchange Rates and Monetary Policy in Central Europe: A Survey of Some Issues", *Oesterreichische Nationalbank, Working Paper No. 24,* September.

Krueger Anne O (1978) : "Liberalisation Attempts and Consequences", *NBER,* New York.

Krugman, Paul R (1991): "Target Zones and Exchange Rate Dynamics", *Quarterly Journal of Economics,* August.

———. (1989): "Differences in Income Elasticities and Trends in Real Exchange Rates", *European Economic Review, 33.*

MacDonald, R and Mark P. Taylor (1992): "Monetary Approach to Exchange Rate: Rational Expectations, Long-run Equilibrium and Forecasting", *IMF Working Paper* WP/92/34 May.

Krugman, Paul R and Lance Taylor (1978): "Contractionary Effects of Devaluation", *Journal of International Economics,* Vol. 8, August.

Maciejewski Edouard B (1983): "Real Effective Exchange Rate Indices", *IMF Staff Papers,* Vol. 30, September.

Meese, Richard A and Kenneth Rogoff (1983): "Empirical Exchange Rate Models of the Seventies: Do they fit Out of Sample?, *"Journal of International Economics,* 14.

Montiel Peter J and Jonathan Ostry (1993): "Real Exchange Rate Targeting in Developing Countries", *IMF PPAA/93/2.*

Moreno, Ramon (1999): "Did a Boom in Money and Credit Precede East Asia's Recent Currency Crisis?", *FRBSF Economic Review,* Number-1.

Patra, M.D. and Sitikantha Pattanaik (1998): "Exchange Rate Management in India: An Empirical Evaluation", *Reserve Bank of India Occasional Papers,* Vol. 19, No. 3, September.

Pattanaik, Sitikantha (1997): "Target and Instruments for the External Sector with an Open Capital Account", *Economic and Political Weekly,* October 4.

———. (1996): "Management of Official Reserves: The Perspectives and the Indian Experience", *Reserve Bank of India Occasional Papers,* Vol. 17, No. 2, June.

Razin Ofair and Susan M Collins (1997): "Real Exchange Rate Misalignments and Growth", *NBER Working Paper No. 6174,* September.

Rogoff Kenneth (1996): "The Purchasing Power Parity Puzzle", *Journal of Economic Literature,* Vol. 34, June.

Sachs J, Tornell and A. Velasco (1996): "Financial Crises in Emerging Markets: The Lessons from 1995", *Brookings Papers on Economic Activity 1.*

...

Svensson, Lars E.O. (1994): "Why Exchange Rate Bands", *Journal of Monetary Economics,* 33, North Holland.

Taylor, Mark P (1994): "The Monetary Model of the Exchange Rate: Long-run Relationships, Short-term dynamics, and How to Beat a Random Walk", *Journal of International Money and Finance,* Vol. 13.

Turner, Philip and Jozef Van't dack (1993): "Measuring International Price and Cost Competitiveness", *BIS Economic Papers No. 39,* November.

Webb, Roy H and Tazewell S. Rowe (1995): "An Index of Leading Indicators for Inflation", *Federal Reserve Bank of Richmond, Economic Quarterly,* Vol. 81/2 Spring.

Williamson John (1998): "Crawling Bands or Monitoring Bands: How to Manage Exchange Rate in a World of Capital Mobility", *World Bank.*

Section IV

THIS section has papers on commercial banking which gained in importance ever since the onset of the financial sector reforms, and in particular banking sector reforms from 1992. The Narasimham Committee* report of 1992 gave a bird's eye view of what the reforms entail. Discussions on prudential norms, and regulations and supervision as also issues of scale and scope along with efficiency considerations came to the fore. On each of these themes, the Reserve Bank of India acted fairly quickly — within a period of hardly five years from the beginnings of the discussion on financial sector reforms. Ajit and Bangar's paper is a comprehensive analytical survey of developments in banking as a financial intermediary right from the 1950s and in a more comprehensive way from the time public sector banks were carved out in 1969. Gautam Chatterjee as well as Abhiman Das discuss issues of scale economies and efficiency issues relating to public sector banks. Essentially, the papers are centered on issues that came up in the 1990s as urgently in need of focused attention of policy makers at the Reserve Bank of India and the Government of India.

* Government of India (1992), The Committee on Financial System (Chairman: M. Narasimham).

18

Banks in Financial Intermediation

Performance and Issues

D Ajit • R D Bangar

THE relationship between financial development and economic growth is a complex phenomenon. The early works of Gurley and Shaw (1955), Patrick (1966), Goldsmith (1969) and McKinnon (1973) document a positive association between income levels and measures of financial development, and show that finance contributes to economic growth in that it increases the volume of investment and improves resource allocation. Recent contributions in 'new' growth theory [Romer, P (1986) and Lucas (1988)] and the literature on endogenous financial intermediation [Leland and Pyle (1977), Diamond and Dybvig (1983), Diamond (1984), Bernanke and Gertler (1985) and Williamson (1986)] have developed models which show that the emergence of a large number of financial markets is the outcome of capital market imperfections.

Banks are the dominant financial intermediaries in developing countries: bank deposits form the preponderant portion of the financial savings of the household sector, and bank credit is the most important source of external finance. Banks can be distinguished from other financial intermediaries in terms of the 'franchisc value of banks' i.e., the special power conferred by the banking charter to issue liabilities that are accepted as a means of payment. They take unsecured deposits from the public, which are usually immediately accessible to the depositors and hence have become the principal means of making payments. Even when corporates or government approach households directly with new financial instruments, the associated payments are cleared through the banking system. Given the increasing role of financial markets and the emergence of intermediaries which perform functions similar to banks in India (like NBFCs), the role of banks in financial intermediation still remains highly significant, drawing considerable interest of both academics and practitioners of policy. This paper mainly analyses the role of banks in financial intermediation in India and discusses some of the issues confronting banking system. The scheme of the paper is as follows: Section I examines the role of banks in financial intermediation in India. Section II examines the performance of banks in India. Section III provides a discussion of the issues confronting banking industry in India in the context of the ongoing financial sector reforms.

SECTION I

THE ROLE OF BANKS IN FINANCIAL INTERMEDIATION

Theoretical Considerations

One of the major debates in financial economics pertains to the role of banks in the financial intermediation process. In an ideal world of complete and perfect capital markets with full and symmetric information, there is no role for banks and financial intermediaries [Fama (1980)]. Hence, one has to answer first the question as to why economic agents prefer an intermediated outcome to an unintermediated one.[1] Two ways by which financial intermediaries can improve on unintermediated markets is by reducing *search costs and transaction costs.* Without intermediation, savers will have to search for suitable investors and similarly investors will have to look for suitable sources of funding. By engaging an intermediary, agents can cut across costs of duplicating searches and can reap economies gained by financial intermediaries which specialise in such search activity. Similarly, financial intermediaries can also reduce transaction costs by reducing the number of transactions required and by offering standardised products.

Financial intermediaries can also help to reduce monitoring costs. There are certain assets whose value can be realised by investing a certain amount of time and effort for monitoring their performance. The existence of monitoring costs gives another reason why an intermediary can improve on the outcome of an unintermediated market. It has also been argued that intermediaries can also reduce verification costs. The value of an asset to its owner depends on how he invests his time and effort into monitoring and verifying its performance. A financial intermediary is often better placed to ensure verification of value of asset without much duplication. Thus, individuals instead of spending time and money to verify the value of assets, can entrust this job to an intermediary which possesses economies in undertaking such tasks. Financial intermediaries also provide instruments that allow for diversification and hedging of risks, thereby allowing economic agents to utilise resources efficiently. The basic economic function of bank intermediation can be summarised as follows (Rangarajan 1997):

1. "Liability-Asset transformation i.e., accepting deposits as a liability and converting them into assets such as loans;
2. Size transformation i.e., providing large loans on the basis of numerous small deposits;
3. Maturity transformation i.e., offering savers alternate forms of deposits according to their liquidity preferences while providing borrowers with loans of desired maturities; and
4. Risk transformation i.e., distributing risk through diversification which substantially reduces risk for savers which would prevail while lending directly in the absence of financial transformation".

Financial intermediaries like banks are unique and specialise in performing functions such as (a) mobilising savings and channelling them to most productive uses, and (b) acting as efficient conduit for payments. Regarding the role of banks, there are divergent views in the literature. According to the 'old' view, commercial banks are 'unique' among financial institutions. This is in contrast to the views of the 'new' school which considers commercial banks as 'pure' or passive intermediaries i.e., they act like brokers rather than creators of loanable funds.[2] In other words, according to 'pure' view, banks are not independent source of net addition to aggregate spending.[3] There is a growing body of literature regarding the credit view of the monetary transmission process, which attributes to financial intermediaries like banks, a key role in the transmission mechanism of monetary policy.[4] In recent years, the issue of how monetary policy affects the level of financial intermediation or the credit channel has attracted a great deal of attention. This key role in monetary transmission process emanates from banks' position as an interface between monetary authorities and the non-bank private sector. According to Fama (1985), borrowers will have to pay a higher rate (return) for unintermediated debt than intermediated debt, as for some borrowers bank credit is 'special' i.e., they are not perfectly substitutable for bonds. The main argument of Fama (1985) for bank intermediated debt (credit) is that banks have comparative advantage in gathering information about borrowers. In view of the importance given to banks in the theoretical literature, it would be appropriate to analyse the role of banks in the Indian context.

Structure of Banking System in India

India's financial system, as of now, is large with a variety of banks, financial institutions, capital market institutions, non-banks and a number of indigenous banking and financial institutions, going beyond the dichotomy prevalent in the pre-independence period of organised and unorganised financial sectors. The organised sector traditionally meant the Imperial Bank of India (now State Bank of India), the exchange banks and the Indian joint stock banks. The unorganised sector consisted of indigenous bankers, moneylenders, chit funds, nidhis, etc. The indigenous bankers were known by names such as Shroff, Kothiwal, Mahajan, Chettiar, etc[5]. As regards the origin of indigenous banking in India, Bagchi (1987) says:

> "At the time the British began establishing their political supremacy over the whole subcontinent, *there was an extensive network of Indian banking houses connecting all cities and towns which were commercially important. Inland bills of exchange or hundis were the major staples of transaction between these Indian bankers and transregional connections.* They lent money to other bankers, landlords and princes; they financed the movement of commodities and, in times of war, the movement of whole armies, very often sharing in the spoils of the conquest and acting as revenue farmers..." (p.31) (emphasis ours)

In fact, the share of unorganised or non-institutional (informal sector) source of finance in the rural sector was far higher than in urban areas. At the time of independence, the share of unorganised (non-institutional) sources in debt of rural households was as high as 92.8 per cent (Table 1).

TABLE 1

Debt Owed to Different Credit Agencies by Rural Households

(per cent)

Credit Agency	1951	1961	1971	1981
1	2	3	4	5
1. Institutional	**7.2**	**17.3**	**29.2**	**61.2**
1.1 Government	3.7	6.6	6.7	4.0
1.2 Co-operative societies/Banks	3.5	10.4	20.1	28.6
1.3 Commercial Banks	-	0.3	2.2	28.0
1.4 Insurance	-	-	0.1	0.3
1.5 Provident Fund	-	-	0.1	0.3
2. Non-Institutional	**92.8**	**82.7**	**70.8**	**38.8**
2.1 Landlords	3.5	1.1	8.6	4.0
2.2 Agriculturist money lenders	25.2	47.0	23.1	8.6
2.3 Professional money lenders	46.4	13.8	13.8	8.3
2.4 Traders	5.1	7.5	8.7	3.4
2.5 Relatives/Friends	11.5	5.8	13.8	9.0
2.6 Others	1.1	7.5	2.8	5.5
3. Total (1+2)	**100.0**	**100.0**	**100.0**	**100.0**

Source: All India Debt and Investment Survey (Various Issues).

At the time of independence, India had a relatively weak economic base and financial infrastructure. Saving and investment were relatively low and only two-thirds of the economy was monetised. Given the fact that the role of foreign saving was negligible, the contribution of the public and private corporate sectors to mobilisation of saving was also not commensurate with the investment in these sectors. Hence, the burden of raising the required rate of saving fell on the household sector; the gross saving rate of household sector increased from 10.4 per cent of Gross Domestic Product (GDP) in 1950-51 to 15.7 per cent in 1970-71 and further to 25.6 per cent by 1995-96. The bulk of the saving of the household sector was in the form of financial assets, of which saving in terms of bank deposits was high and critical. This was especially so since the nationalisation of major commercial banks in 1969. Bank loans, which constituted the most important source of external finance for companies in India, formed, in the late 1970s, nearly 63 per cent of total borrowings of the private corporate sector in India [Table 2(A) and (B)]. Over a period of time, this share has come down to 32 per cent by 1992-93.

The dependence on banks for external finance, however, could vary according to size of the companies. In fact, the recent literature on 'differential impact of monetary policy' has shown that small firms are bank-dependent i.e., bank credit is special and not substitutable [Gertler and Gilchrist (1993a, 1993b and 1994), Olinear and Rudebusch (1995)]. The small-sized companies which constitute a dominant segment of manufacturing sector, have increased their dependence on banks for external finance; in fact the share of bank loans in total borrowing of small firms increased from 40.5 per cent in 1968-69 to 60 per cent by 1990-91; this is partly explained by the fact that they have virtually no access to capital markets. The limited access of small firms to capital markets has attracted the attention of the MacMillian Committee in U.K. so much so that the gap has come to be known as the 'MacMillian Gap'. On the other hand, medium and large (ML) firms in private corporate sector have reduced their dependence on banks: the share of banks in total borrowing of ML firms declined from 53.3 per cent in 1968-69 to 32 per cent in 1992-93 [Table 2(B)].[6] Their access to capital market funds increased from 4.0 per cent in 1968-69 to 20.8 per cent by 1992-93. A major reason for the lack of access of small firms to bank finance is that much of the information on small firms is private and hence banks have to incur higher agency costs (than for large firms) to gain access to these private information. Besides, small firms are usually not in a position to meet the regulation in the capital market. Hence for small firms, banks are the most and perhaps the only economic source of debt financing.

TABLE 2(A)

Components of Total Borrowing of Private Corporate Sector in India: 1968-69 to 1992-93

(per cent)

Year	Capital Market Funds*	Loans and Advances	Of which: from Banks	Other Financial Institutions	Foreign Institutional Sources	Others	Total Borrowing
1	2	3	4	5	6	7	8 (2+3+7)
1968-69	3.5	79.3**	62.7	N.A.	N.A	17.2	100.0
1984-85	11.4	63.4	39.1	23.0	1.3	25.2	100.0
1990-91	20.4	70.4	34.5	25.9	1.6	9.2	100.0
1991-92	21.2	70.7	32.1	28.4	1.4	8.1	100.0
1992-93	20.8	72.4	32.0	30.0	1.6	6.7	100.0

* Capital Market Funds comprise of funds mobilised through debentures.

** Derived.

Source Reserve Bank of India, Studies on Public Limited Companies, RBI Bulletin (Various Issues)

TABLE 2(B)

Components of Total Borrowing of Private Corporate Sector-Size Wise: 1968-69 to 1992-93*

(per cent)

Year	Small Companies		Medium and Large Companies	
	Share of		Share of	
	Banks	Capital Market Funds	Banks	Capital Market Funds
1	2	3	4	5
1968-69	40.5	Nil	53.3	4.0
1984-85	59.1	Nil	46.1	7.5
1990-91	60.0	Nil	34.5	20.4
1991-92	50.0	Nil	32.1	21.2
1992-93	42.9	Nil	32.0	20.8

* The size of companies was determined on the basis of paid-up capital (PUC); Small Companies (less than Rs. 5 lakhs PUC), Medium and Large Companies (more than Rs. 5 lakhs PUC).

Source: As in Table 2(A)

Among the financial institutions in India, banks are the predominant financial intermediaries and in fact financial intermediation was largely synonymous with banking. Chart 1 reports the share of banks and other financial institutions in the aggregate financial assets. The share of banks in total financial assets comes to around two-third in the 1990s although this share has marginally declined over the period. On the other hand, the share of investment institutions like UTI, LIC, GIC and its subsidiaries etc., has shown a marked increase in the 1980s and 1990s.

CHART 1

SHARE OF BANKS AND FINANCIAL INSTITUTIONS IN TOTAL FINANCIAL ASSETS IN INDIA : 1980-81 TO 1995-96

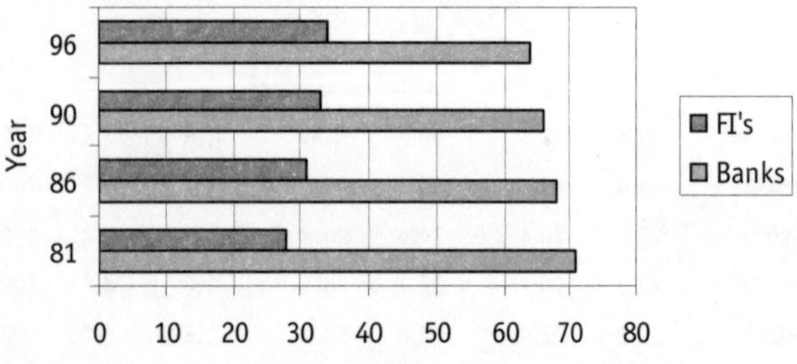

The banking system in India consists of commercial banks and co-operative banks. Commercial banks, which include foreign banks, are the predominant segment. Co-operative banks, which are organised on the 'unit' banking principle, are mainly rural-based, although there are urban co-operative banks operating in urban areas. Additionally, government-owned post offices mobilise deposits but they do not undertake any lending activity. Besides, there is an extensive network of all-India and State-level development banks catering to agriculture, industry, housing and exports. Also, there exist several financial institutions such as the UTI, LIC, GIC and its subsidiaries, mutual funds, investment and loan companies, and equipment leasing and hire purchase companies, all engaged in mobilising resources and providing financial services as well as in medium- and long-term investment. In addition, the National Bank of Agriculture and Rural Development (NABARD), the Industrial Development Bank of India (IDBI), Export Import Bank of India (Exim Bank) and the National Housing Bank (NHB) have been established to serve as apex banks in their specified areas of responsibility and concern. The three important term lending institutions, namely, IDBI, Industrial Credit and Investment Corporation of India (ICICI) and Industrial Finance Corporation of India (IFCI) dominate the term lending market and provide medium and long term financial assistance to corporate sector.

Scheduled commercial banks constitute the major segment of the banking system. They possessed about 97 per cent of the total deposits of the banking system in March 1951; this proportion was marginally lower at 94 per cent by March 1996. Table 3 provides an overview of the progress of commercial banking in India. Between 1956 and 1996, the total number of commercial bank branches rose from 4,067 to 63,092 thereby reducing the average population served per bank office from 98,000 in 1956 to 15,000 in 1996. As a ratio of GDP at current prices, bank deposits increased from 12 per cent in 1955-56 to 43 per cent in 1995-96, indicating the growing importance of banks in the mobilisation of saving in the country.

As regards the structure of banking in India, it was dominated by public sector banks, after the bank nationalisation in 1969. In 1970, nearly 85 per cent of bank deposits and credit of scheduled commercial banks was accounted for by public sector banks and this proportion has increased in 1980, accounting for over 90 per cent of bank deposits in the country [Table 4(A)]. In terms of branches, public sector banks accounted for nearly 80 per cent in 1969 and this proportion declined to 70 per cent by end-June 1996 [Table 4(B)]. Nearly one-fourth of total bank branches of public sector banks in 1969 were in rural areas and this proportion increased to 44 per cent by June 1996.

TABLE 3

Progress of Commercial Banking at a Glance : 1951 to 1996

	1951*	1956*	1961*	1969	1980	1990@	1996
1	2	3	4	5	6	7	8
1. Number of Commercial Banks (a+b)	566	423	292	89	80	78	94
(a) Scheduled Commercial Banks	92	89	82	73	75	74	91
(b) Non-Scheduled Commercial Banks	474	334	210	16	5	4	3
(c) Reg. Rural Banks	-	-	-	-	73	196	196
2. No. of Offices in India	4,151	4,067	5,012	8,262	32,419	59,756	63,092
3. Population per office (in '000s)	87	98	88	64	21	14	15
4. Bank Deposits as a % of GDP at current prices	10.5	11.9	13.2	13.7	32.6	42.5	43.2

* Position at end-December. @ Position at end-March.

Note: The data relate to end-June

Source: Reserve Bank of India (1) Statistical Tables Relating to Banks in India (Various Issues), and (2) Banking Statistics (Various Issues).

Foreign banks have virtually no presence in rural areas in India. Public sector banks have a wide-spread network of 44,145 branches; this fact enables them to dominate not only the deposit and credit markets but also allows them to play important role in money and capital markets. With the introduction of financial sector reforms in 1991, new private sector banks have been allowed. As at end-March 1996, they account for 1.6 per cent of total deposits and 6.0 per cent of incremental deposits of scheduled commercial banks in India in 1995-96.

TABLE 4(A)

Structure of Banking Industry in India: 1969-70 to 1995-96

(per cent)

Year	Share of Public Sector Banks: Deposits	Public Sector Banks: Credit	Private Sector Banks: Deposits	Private Sector Banks: Credit	of which: Foreign Banks: Deposits	of which: Foreign Banks: Credit
1	2	3	4	5	6	7
1970	84.7	84.6	15.3	15.4	8.9	9.8
1975	84.8	86.0	15.2	14.0	5.7	5.7
1980	91.9	92.1	8.1	7.9	2.9	3.3
1985	92.5	92.3	7.5	7.7	2.9	3.5
1989	92.0	92.0	8.0	8.0	3.8	4.2
1990	91.7	92.1	8.3	7.9	4.4	4.5
1996	85.4	82.2	14.6	17.8	6.7	8.9

Source: 1. Report on Currency and Finance, Reserve Bank of India, (Various Issues).
2. Statistical Tables Relating to Banks in India (Various Issues).

TABLE 4(B)

Structure of Distribution of Commercial Bank Branches in India: 1969-1996

	End-June 1969: Total	End-June 1969: Of which rural branches (in %)	No. of Banks [end June 1996]	Last Friday of June 96: Total	Last Friday of June 96: Of which rural branches (in %)
1	2	3	4	5	6
1. State Bank of India (SBI)	1,569 (19.0)	29.4	1	8,852 (14.0)	46.7
2. Associate Banks of SBI	893 (10.8)	40.0	7	4,116 (6.5)	33.4
3. Nationalised Banks	4,134 (50.0)	16.6	19	31,177 (49.4)	44.7
4. Public Sector Banks (1+2+3)	6,596 (79.8)	22.8	27	44,145 (70.0)	44.0
5. Indian Private Sector Banks	1,319 (16.0)	20.1	34	4,266 (6.8)	26.7
6. Foreign Banks	130 (1.6)	0.8	30	156 (0.2)	-
7. Private Sector Banks (5+6)	1,449 (17.6)	18.4	64	4,422 (7.0)	25.8
8. Non-Scheduled Banks	217 (2.6)	28.1	3	8 (-)	37.5
9. Regional Rural Banks	-	-	196	14,517 (23.0)	86.0
10. Total (4+7+8+9)	8,262 (100.0)	22.2	290	63,092 (100.0)	52.4

Note: Figures in brackets indicate percentage to total number of branches.

Source: Same as in Table 4 (A)

TABLE 5

Balance Sheet of Scheduled Commercial Banks: 1950-51 to 1995-96 (As at the end of March)

(Rs. crore)

Liabilities	*1951*	*1969*	*1981*	*1991*	*1996*	*Assets*	*1951*	*1969*	*1981*	*1991*	*1996*
1	2	3	4	5	6	7	8	9	10	11	12
1. Deposits (i+ii)	859	4,079	37,988	1,92,542	4,33,819	1. Investments in Govt. Securities	304	1,051	13,186	75,065	1,64,782
(i) Demand Deposits	283		7,798	33,193	80,614	2. Reserves[b]	95	248	4,858	25,665	53,780
(ii) Time Deposits	576		30,190	1,59,349	3,53,205	3. Bank Credit	547	3,107	25,371	1,16,301	2,54,015
2. Others[a]	87	327	5,427	24,489	38,758						
Total	946	4,406	43,415	2,17,031	4,72,577	Total	946	4,406	43,415	2,17,031	4,72,577
						Memorandum Items:					
						1. Reserves/Deposits Ratio	11.0	6.1	12.8	13.3	12.4
						2. Investment/Deposit Ratio	35.4	25.8	34.7	39.0	38.0
						3. Credit/Deposit Ratio	63.7	76.2	66.8	60.4	58.6

a : includes mainly inter-bank borrowing and borrowings from the Reserve Bank

b : relate to cash in hand and balance with RBI.

Source : Same as in Table 5.

A banking firm and the nature of its output are difficult to define. Some have viewed banks as producing loans from inputs of deposits while some others have considered them as creating deposits from loans. Often, a bank is specified in terms of its assets and liabilities. Table 5 presents summary balance sheet of scheduled commercial banks for selected years during the period 1950-51 to 1995-96. The main source of funds for scheduled commercial banks during 1950s through 1990s was deposits while the share of non-deposit sources has gained relative prominence in the 1990s (accounting for 5-10 per cent of total liabilities). Deposits were mainly raised from interest-bearing time deposits; its share in total bank deposits increased from 67 per cent in 1950-51 to 81.4 per cent by 1995-96 although evidence of interest sensitivity of bank deposits in India is found to be weak [Ajit (1997)]. Within term deposits, deposits with maturity of more than one year increased from 40.7 per cent in 1969 to 71.7 per cent by 1994 (Table 6). An interesting development is the emergence of short-term money market (45 to 90 days) since 1985; term deposits under maturity of 45 to 90 days now accounts for 13.3 per cent of term deposit market. This was mainly due to the shortening of the minimum period of short term deposit market over the years and at present the shortest period of term deposit market is 30 days[7].

On the assets side, nearly 35 per cent was accounted by investments in government securities at end-March 1996; on the eve of bank nationalisation this figure was only about 24 per cent. Statutory cash reserves accounted for 11.4 per cent at end-March 1996 and the remaining 53.8 per cent was accounted by loans. Cash reserve maintenance can be used for prudential as well as for monetary policy purposes. Maintenance of statutory liquidity ratio (SLR) (investment in government securities) is essentially for prudential purposes. But in India, the SLR has often been used to give support to Government borrowing programme, even though prudential considerations would have entailed the ratio to be placed at a much lower level than what was the case. Together with the interest rates administered on both sides of the balance sheet, the banking scene during 1970s and early 1980s represented what has come to be known as 'financial repression' in the literature.[8] The ability of the market-based banking system to foster economic development was, in other words, not appreciated, *nay* recognised.

A major argument in favour of the interventionist approach at that time was the high concentration of banking activities in urban and metropolitan areas and the skewed distribution of credit in favour of large industry and trading sectors, which entailed failure to support some of the crucial segments of the economy

TABLE 6

Scheduled Commercial Banks-Maturity Pattern of Term Deposits: 1969 to 1994
(As at the end of March)

(Rs. crore)

Period of Maturity	1969		1980		1986		1991		1994	
1	2	3	4	5	6	7	8	9	10	11
	Amount	% to total	Amount	% to total	Amount	% to total	Amount	% to total	Amount	% to total
1) Upto 90 days	456	20.2	810	4.7	2,670	5.5	9,217	8.1	25,737	13.3
2) 91 days and above but less than six months							5,897	5.2	13,772	7.1
3) More than 6 months but upto 1 year	882	39.1	478	2.8	1,861	3.9	7,003	6.1	15,056	7.8
4) More than 1 year but upto 2 years	198	8.8	3,074	17.9	5,225	10.9	16,312	14.3	49,195	25.4
5) More than 2 years but upto 3 years	118	5.3			3,298	6.9	30,927	27.1	26,975	13.9
6) More than 3 years but upto 5 years	461	20.4	2,194	12.8	11,500	23.9	23,492	20.6	38,031	19.6
7) 5 years and above	140	6.2	10,616	61.8	23,503	48.9	21,234	18.6	24,855	12.8
Total (1 to 7)	**2,255**	**100.0**	**17,172**	**100.0**	**48,057**	**100.0**	**1,14,082**	**100.0**	**1,93,621**	**100.0**

Note : The figures reported here may not tally with those given in Table 5 due to differences in data sources.

Source : Banking Statistics (Various Issues), Reserve Bank of India.

like agriculture, small-scale industries, and other socially neglected sections of the society. This argument was found empirically correct. The 'security-cum-guarantee lending system' in the pre-nationalisation period was skewed in favour of industry and trade sectors. Thus at the commencement of Five Year Plans in India i.e., at end-March 1951, industry and trade sectors accounted for 83 per cent of bank credit; this proportion increased to 90 per cent by March 1968. The Dehejia Committee (1969) and the Tandon Committee (1975) had drawn attention to the excessive reliance by the industrial sector, especially the medium and large industries on banks for financing their activities. This was mainly due to the urban orientation of the banking system and the low capital base of commercial banks, which was controlled by a few persons through interlocking of directorships and corporate borrowers [Ghosh, (1988)]. This phenomenon was sought to be corrected by nationalisation of major banks first in 1969 and then again in 1980. As part of the measures to increase credit to socially neglected sectors, banks were advised to designate a certain proportion of credit to priority sectors[9] (like agriculture, small-scale industries, road transport operators, etc.). The post-nationalisation period saw the emergence of policies based on development potential rather than security. The underlying aim of credit policies since the early seventies was to extend the reach of bank credit both geographically and functionally.

Progress of Banks in the Post-Bank Nationalisation Period

Market Intervention and Social Banking Phase (1969 to 1996)

The post-nationalisation period saw the emergence of 'social or mass banking' and was essentially supply-oriented [Tyagarajan (1975), Shetty (1978), Mujumdar (1982)]. Geographically the thrust was to cover the underbanked hinterland and functionally to extend credit to agriculture, small-scale industries, *et al*. The pre-emption of bank credit for 'priority sectors' like agriculture with concessionality, was the notable feature of banking development in the post-bank nationalisation period till 1990. It was only after September 1990, with rationalisation of lending rates on the basis of size of loans, the element of concessionality was contained. Commercial banks were subject to a number of restrictions: high cash reserve requirements, and high mandatory holding of government securities (statutory liquidity ratio) till 1992. The norms regarding credit delivery existed till 1996.

One of the main issues often addressed by researchers on Indian banking is the rationale of official intervention at both macro and micro levels. As the objective function of such intervention is *not* specified, maximisation of economic welfare implied by bank actions following the interventionist policies, is also not measurable. The only litmus test for judging the success of intervention is the extent of increase in output/ exports of the concerned sectors of activity. But even here, the approach often adopted by most writers is to weigh aggregate output against aggregate credit, rather than to examine the sectoral output effects of credit deployment.

Agricultural Credit - Market Failure and Intervention

Intervention in credit markets, especially with regard to rural credit markets, is a common feature in developing countries and India is no exception [World Bank (1989, 1993)]. In India, the agricultural sector supports nearly two-third of the labour force and contributes nearly one-half of national income (Table 7).[10] However in 1951, the share of agriculture in bank credit was only 2 per cent and this proportion marginally increased to 2.2 per cent by end-March 1968.

TABLE 7

Share of Agriculture and Industrial Sector in Output and Bank Credit: 1950-51 to 1995-96

Year	*Share of Agriculture in*		*Share of Industry in*	
(End-March)	*Output*	*Bank Credit*	*Output*	*Bank Credit*
1	*2*	*3*	*4*	*5*
1951	55.8	2.0	12.4	31.5
1960	47.7	0.6	15.5	52.5
1968	47.9	2.2	15.3	67.5
1975	43.4	10.5	19.0	65.0
1980	36.2	13.0	22.1	51.3
1985	34.5	16.0	22.4	47.0
1990	31.1	17.4	23.5	56.6
1996	27.9	11.8	24.3	54.7

Notes: Col.2 and 4 - Share of Agriculture in GDP at current market prices. Col.3 and 5 - Share of Agriculture in Total Bank Credit.

Source: (a) Reserve Bank of India
(i) Supplement to Banking and Monetary Statistics in India - Part I
(ii) Report on Currency and Finance (Various Issues)
(iii) Annual Report (Various issues)
(b) Government of India, National Accounts Statistics, Central Statistical Organisation (Various Issues).

The Report of the Committee on All-India Rural Credit Survey (1954) observed that rural credit in India was grossly inadequate and recommended an integrated scheme of rural credit based on co-operatives. In the Committee's view, the chief merit of the co-operative banking structure was its ability to operate the credit delivery system at the very door steps of farmers. The Committee, however, advocated a well defined role for commercial banks in providing credit for agriculture in specialised areas such as marketing, processing, storage and warehousing. After nationalisation of major commercial banks in 1969, opening of rural branches in large numbers helped to broaden the points of rural credit delivery. By the middle of the seventies, it was felt that the task of providing agricultural credit on the requisite scale cannot be met by commercial banks unless they acquire specialised knowledge of rural setting. It is against this background, the Narasimham Working Group (1975) recommended the setting up of Regional Rural Banks (RRBs). Consequently, by the end of 1975, three separate institutional arrangements (Commercial Banks, Co-operative Banks and Regional Rural Banks) known as the Multi-agency approach for providing credit in the rural areas emerged.[11] By end-March 1996, the share of agriculture in bank credit increased to 11.8 per cent from 2.2 per cent in 1968 and 10.5 per cent in 1975. The actual outcome is short of the sub-target for agriculture at 18 per cent of net credit specified under priority sector lending.

In the pre-bank nationalisation period (1951 to 1969), the progress of banking was very slow. The average population per bank office declined from 1,32,700 in 1950 to 64,000 in 1969, recording an average decline of 4.5 per cent per annum. In the post-bank nationalisation period, this was drastically reduced: it was a mere 15,000 by June 1996. At the time of bank nationalisation (i.e. in 1969), rural branches constituted only 3 per cent of deposits and 1.5 per cent of bank credit of scheduled commercial banks. By June 1996, the share of rural branches in deposits and credit increased to 15.4 per cent and 12.4 per cent, respectively (Chart 2). The distribution of credit also underwent a structural transformation in the post-bank nationalisation period. The share of priority sector in total bank credit, which was a meagre 11 per cent at end-March 1968, increased to 33.1 per cent at end-March 1996 (Table 8). On the other hand, the share of medium and large industries declined from 62.8 per cent at end-March 1968 to 42.0 per cent by end-March 1996 which according to Mujumdar (1982) was a 'correction of a historical distortion'. Similar decline occurred in credit to trade sector during this period (1968-96). Although the priority credit scheme had succeeded in altering credit allocation, its impact on the viability and stability of the banking system and economic growth was not clear-cut and definitive.

TABLE 8

Purpose-Wise Distribution of Bank Credit (Outstanding) by Scheduled Commercial Banks: 1968-96

(Rs. crore)

Sectors	March 1968		March 1980		March 1996	
	Amount	in %	Amount	in %	Amount	in %
1	2	3	4	5	6	7
1. Gross Bank Credit	3,064		21,235		2,31,697	
2. Food Procurement Credit	109		2,100		9,791	
3. Non-Food Gross Bank Credit (1-2)	2,955	100.0	19,135	100.0	2,21,906	100.0
of which:						
3.1. Priority Sectors	325	11.0	6,730	35.2	73,391	33.1
3.2 Industry (Medium and Large)	1,857	62.8	8,269	43.2	93,108	42.0
3.3 Wholesale Trade	432	14.6	1,915	10.0	11,993	5.4
3.4 Others	341	11.5	2,221	11.6	43,414	19.5
Memorandum Items:						
(A) Industrial Credit (Small, Medium and Large)	2,068	70.0	10,904	57.0	1,24,992	56.3
(B) Priority Sector Credit as a Proportion of Net Bank Credit		10.7		30.6		32.1

Source: Annual Report (Various Issues), Reserve Bank of India

CHART 2

SHARE OF RURAL BRANCHES IN TOTAL DEPOSITS AND CREDIT OF SCHEDULED COMMERCIAL BANK IN INDIA: 1969-96

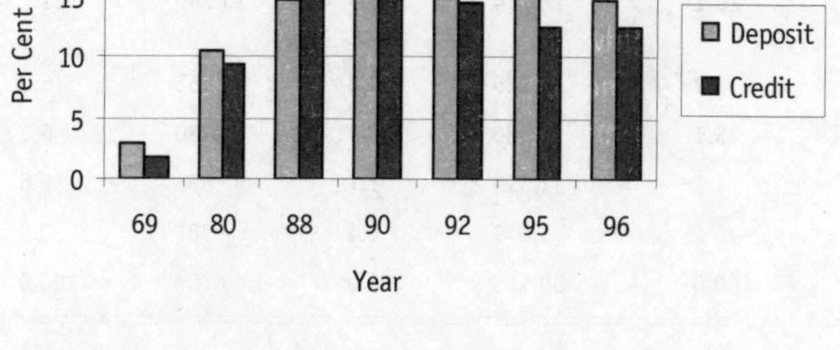

One of the major weaknesses of banking was the low recovery of loans. Recovery of IRDP loans was low at 30 per cent[12] at end-March 1996 and that of direct agricultural advances was at 60 per cent at end-June 1995. On the other hand, nearly 14-15 per cent of total industrial credit was tied up in sick units in the early 1990s. In the case of small-scale industries, this figure has shown a decline from 20.9 per cent at end-June 1988 to 16.3 per cent by end-March 1994 [Table 9(A)]. The problem of overdues was more acute in the rural areas than in urban/metropolitan areas: overdues constituted 29.2 per cent of outstanding credit as at end-March 1993 [Table 9(b)].

TABLE 9(A)

Trends in Bank Credit in Sick Industrial Units in India: 1980-94

(Rs. crore)

Year (End-June)	Small-Scale Units Amt. Outstanding		Medium and Large (ML) Units. Amt. Outstanding		Total Amount Outstanding	
	Bank Credit to Sick SSIs	Total Bank Credit to SSIs	Bank Credit to Sick ML Industries	Total Bank Credit to ML Industries	Bank Credit to Sick Industries	Total Industrial Credit
1	2	3	4	5	6 (2+4)	7 (3+5)
1980	295	3,068	1,221	21,807	1,516	24,875
1985	955	6,629	2,655	43,366	3,610	49,995
1988	1,980	9,493	3,026	61,792	5,006	71,285
1992 March	3,101	18,150	5,787	47,090	8,888	65,240
1993 March	3,443	20,026	7,901	58,636	11,344	78,622
1994 March	3,680	22,617	8,152	57,860	11,832	80,477
Proportions to Bank Credit						
1980	9.6		5.6		6.1	
1985	14.4		6.1		7.2	
1988	20.9		4.9		7.0	
1992 March	17.1		12.3		13.6	
1993 March	17.2		13.5		14.4	
1994 March	16.3		14.1		14.7	

Source: Report on Currency and Finance, Vol. 1 (Various Issues), Reserve Bank of India.

TABLE 9(B)

Region-wise Distribution of Overdues of Scheduled Commercial Banks in India: End-March 1993

Regions:	*Outstanding Credit (Rs. crore)*	*Overdues (Rs. crore)*	*Overdues as a proportion of Outstanding Credit (%)*
1	*2*	*3*	*4*
1. Rural	14,728	4,304	29.2
2. Semi-Urban	17,104	3,996	23.4
3. Urban/Metropolitan	55,910	10,510	18.8
Total	87,742	18,810	21.4

Source: Banking Statistics - March 1993, Reserve Bank of India.

Credit Delivery System in India

The operations of banks would be best judged from their credit delivery. In India, the credit system has for long been characterised by cash credit reflecting the legacy of the Scottish bankers. Nearly 50 per cent of total bank credit extended by scheduled commercial banks was in the form of cash credit in early 1970s and this proportion has marginally come down to 40 per cent by end-March 1994 (Table 10). Only about 8 per cent of bank credit was in the form of overdrafts. The share of bills in total bank credit was low, having declined from 17.3 per cent in December 1972 to 11.7 per cent in end-March 1994. The major weakness of the cash credit system is that the burden of credit management falls on banks. In fact in India, nearly one-third of credit limits were unutilised in the 1970s, 1980s and 1990s. For this reason, the first move to shift to loan system was made in April 1995. The Reserve Bank stipulated that for borrowers with assessed maximum permissible bank finance (MPBF) of Rs. 20 crore and above, the proportions of cash credit and loans should be 75 per cent and 25 per cent, respectively, before July 21, 1995 or at the next quarterly review of the borrowal account whichever is earlier.

Credit appraisal system of banks was largely dictated by considerations of working capital needs. Following the inflationary years of 1973 and 1974, a study group appointed by the RBI (popularly known as the Tandon Committee) came up with guidelines for assessing the credit requirements of industry. The Committee proposed specific norms for inventory and receivables for 15 major industries (designated in terms of months' holdings). The guidelines related to the extent of financing to be undertaken by banks of the 'net working capital gap', defined as the difference between current assets and current liabilities excluding the portion represented by short term borrowing from banks.[13] The rationale behind fixing inventory and receivable norms was to prevent banks from financing flabby[14] and profit making inventories - those held with the idea of profiteering.

TABLE 10

Distribution of Outstanding Credit of Scheduled Commercial Banks by Type of Account

(Rs. crore)

Category	*Dec. 1972*	*% to total*	*Dec. 1980*	*% to total*	*March 1990*	*% to total*	*March 1994*	*% to total*
1	*2*	*3*	*4*	*5*	*6*	*7*	*8*	*9*
1. Cash Credit	2,544	50.4	8,578	42.4	29,054	36.2	57,319	39.9
2. Overdrafts	480	9.5	1,345	6.7	5,879	7.3	11,114	7.7
3. Demand Loans	331	6.6	981	4.9	2,913	3.6	9,219	6.4
4. Term Loans	601	11.9	4,492	22.2	24,643	30.7	40,887	28.5
5. Packing Credit	210	4.1	755	3.7	3,973	5.0	7,592	5.3
6. Bills purchased and discounted of which:	874	17.3	4,070	20.1	12,624	15.8	16,790	11.7
(i) Exports Bills	212	4.2	796	3.9	3,025	3.8	7,155	5.0
(ii) Import Bills	632	12.5	3,057	15.1	8,280	10.3	8,780	6.1
(iii) Advance against import bills	30	0.6	217	1.1	1,319	1.7	855	0.6
7. Others	11	0.2	-	-	1,079	1.4	782	0.5
Total Bank Credit (1 to 7)	5,051	100.0	20,221	100.0	80,165	100.0	1,43,703	100.0

Source: Banking Statistics (Various Issues), Reserve Bank of India

The concept of Maximum Permissible Bank Finance (MPBF) emerged out of the recommendations of Tandon Committee (1975) and has been the cornerstone of the credit delivery system in India. It was a way of rationing and allocation of scarce financial resources among large number of the claimants and formed part of the micro level regulation. MPBF also became the basis of consortium arrangement which had come into existence in 1972. As per the MPBF concept, any borrower enjoying working capital limit of Rs. 1 crore and above, has to be assessed as given below, using the Second Method of Lending.

(i)	Current Assets (as assessed by financing bank/banks/consortium/syndicate)	A
(ii)	Current Liabilities other than short term bank borrowing (as assessed by the financing bank/banks/consortium/syndicate)	B
(iii)	Working Capital Gap	A-B=C
(iv)	Minimum Net Working Capital (NWC) (25 per cent of current assets i.e., A)	D
(v)	Actual/Projected Net Working Capital (NWC)	E
	Maximum Permissible Bank Finance (MPBF)	(C-D) or (C-E) whichever is less

As a result of the implementation of the inventory-receivable norms of the Tandon Committee, the inventory management of private corporate sector improved considerably. The inventory to sales ratio of private corporate sector in India declined from 34 in 1965-66 to 26 by 1992-93. Bank borrowings covered nearly two-third of inventories and this ratio has shown a mixed trend; it declined during the 1970s but showed an upward trend in the late 1980s.

The system of credit appraisal and credit delivery based on the concept of MPBF is perceived to have two major limitations: (i) rigidity, and (ii) delay in the availability of funds. The pre-sanction scrutiny by the RBI of large borrowers was withdrawn in October 1988, and recently (in April 1997) banks were given the freedom to do away with the concept of MPBF and evolve their own method of lending.[15] The alternatives suggested include (a) turnover-based credit, (b) cash budgeting, and (c) credit based on borrowers' rating. Banks, however, could retain MPBF as their method of lending, if they so desire.

Administered Interest Rate Regime and Cross-Subsidisation

Administered interest rate regime could be traced from October 1, 1958 when interest rates on bank deposits were fixed on the basis of the Inter-Bank Agreement. Since 1964, there was an increasing degree of official intervention by the Reserve Bank in the money and credit markets. The intervention was essentially in the form of (a) prescription of certain ceiling rates on deposits and minimum rates for long-term deposits, and (b) a ceiling rate on advances.

After the nationalisation of banks in 1969, the administered interest rate regime in India was characterised by cross-subsidisation: credit to priority sectors was accorded interest rate concessions and this was compensated by high interest rates on advances to non-priority sectors. The regulation of lending rates led to regulation of the deposit rates. Over a period of time, the administered lending rates became unduly complex and was characterised by detailed prescriptions on the lending as well as on the deposit side. The structure of interest rates on bank advances, taking into account all stipulations (sector-specific, programme-specific and region-specific), resulted in a plethora (estimated at around 1,000) of interest rates. The rationalisation of interest rates effected in September 1990, was based on size of loans, replacing the interest rate structure hitherto in existence, based on type of loan activity, location viz., class and efficiency of borrowers. Further rationalisation of lending rates since September 1990 resulted in the prescriptions of only two loan rates: a lending rate for loans upto Rs. 25,000 and a lending rate for loans above Rs. 25,000 and upto Rs. 2 lakh. Loans for over Rs. 2 lakh could be charged at different interest rates, these being determined between the banks and the borrowers. As a result of these changes in loan rate structure, nearly 70 per cent of the advances were freed from 'interest rate' controls (see Table 11). The rationalisation of the structure of interest rates culminated in the Reserve Bank abolishing the minimum lending rate in October 1994 and leaving banks to determine their own prime lending rates (PLR). Chart 3 presents the weighted lending rates of scheduled commercial banks for the economy, industrial sector (including SSI) and agriculture.[16] After the rationalisation of interest rates, the bank lending rates have generally moved upwards, rising from 14.1 per cent in 1988 to 16.6 per cent in 1994. In the case of agricultural credit, the bank lending rate rose from 12.3 per cent to 15.6 per cent in the corresponding period. The upward movement in bank lending rates, which is normally seen as a consequence of financial liberalisation, has led to concerns about their effects on production.

TABLE 11

Distribution of Outstanding Credit of Scheduled Commercial Banks According to Size of Credit Limit: End-March 1990 and 1994.

	Credit Limit Range	*End-March 1990*			*End-March 1994*		
		Amount Outstanding (Rs. crore)	*% to Total*	*Cumulative Total*	*Amount Outstanding (Rs. crore)*	*% to Total*	*Cumulative Total*
	1	*2*	*3*	*4*	*5*	*6*	*7*
1.	Less than Rs. 25,000	24,147.24	23.1	23.1	32,187.98	18.3	18.3
2.	Above Rs. 25,000 to Rs. 50,000	3,016.04	2.9	26.0	4,683.55	2.7	21.0
3.	Above Rs. 50,000 to Rs. 1 lakh	5,711.20	5.5	31.5	6,564.22	3.7	24.7
4.	Above Rs. 1 lakh to Rs. 2 lakh	5,623.54	5.4	36.9	10,298.78	5.9	30.6
5.	Above Rs. 2 lakh to Rs. 5 lakh	5,985.05	5.7	42.6	8,769.80	5.0	35.6
6.	Above Rs. 5 lakh to Rs. 10 lakh	4,499.13	4.3	46.9	6,360.39	3.6	39.2
7.	Above Rs. 10 lakh to Rs. 25 lakh	6,579.24	6.3	53.2	9,092.67	5.2	44.4
8.	Above Rs. 25 lakh to Rs. 50 lakh	6,985.79	6.7	59.9	9,242.57	5.3	49.7
9.	Above Rs. 50 lakh to Rs. 1 crore	7,396.55	7.1	67.0	10,798.39	6.1	55.8
10.	Above Rs. 1 crore to Rs. 4 crore	15,544.22	14.9	81.9	25,769.59	14.7	70.5
11.	Above Rs. 4 crore to Rs. 6 crore	4,881.11	4.7	86.6	8,250.26	4.7	75.2
12.	Above Rs. 6 crore to Rs. 10 crore	4,536.59	4.3	90.9	8,183.54	4.6	79.8
13.	Above Rs. 10 crore	9,406.23	9.1	100.0	35,689.52	20.2	100.0
	Total (1 to 13)	**1,04,311.93**	**100.0**		**1,75,891.27**	**100.0**	

Source: Banking Statistics, Reserve Bank of India.

CHART 3

WEIGHTED BANKS LENDING RATES IN INDIA: 1972-94

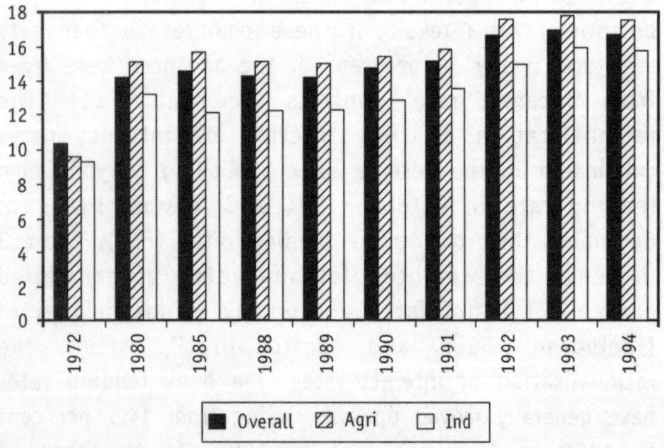

SECTION II

PERFORMANCE OF SCHEDULED COMMERCIAL BANKS IN INDIA

In this section, the performance of scheduled commercial banks in India is examined. The period covered for the exercise is the same as in Section I namely, 1951 to 1996. The analysis is carried out at the aggregate level.

Profits and Efficiency of the Banking System in India

Although the progress made by the banking system in India in terms of functional and geographical coverage is generally laudable, the question that arises is how efficient has been the banking system in India. The term efficiency has various meanings. In terms of operational efficiency and viability of the banking system, the performance of the Indian banks and that of public sector banks in particular, has been far from impressive (Chart 4). The gross operating profit as a proportion of total assets of scheduled commercial banks in India was a meagre 0.8 per cent in 1970s, 0.91 per cent in 1980s and 1.5 per cent in the early 1990s. Similarly, net profit of scheduled commercial banks was a meagre 0.12 per cent in the 1970s, 0.11 in the 1980s and a negative of (-)0.07 in the early 1990s. The profitability figures of Indian banks have to be read with caution. Prior to the introduction of prudential accounting norms, the balance sheets and profit and loss accounts of banks did not disclose their actual financial health. Banks were notionally applying interest on loans which had gone bad and treating as income and paying tax on such unrealised income. It was only after 1991 when banks implemented, in a phased manner, disclosure norms by way of income recognition, asset classification and provisioning for bad and doubtful debts that balance sheets became more transparent.

CHART 4

PROFITABILITY OF SCHEDULED COMMERCIAL BANKS IN INDIA: 1969-70 TO 1995-96

(AS A PROPORTION TO TOTAL ASSETS)

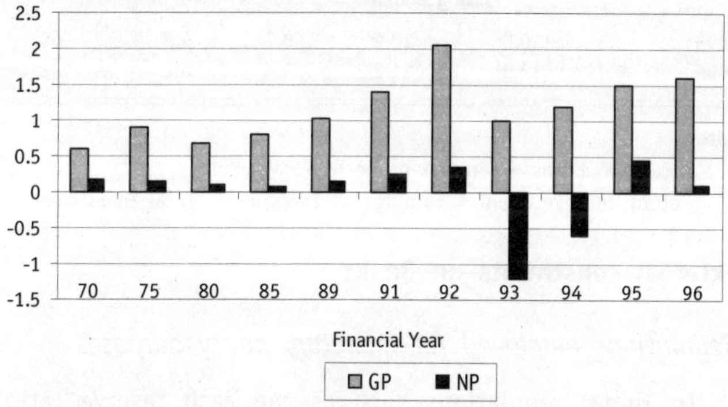

In order to understand the various factors influencing the (low) profitability of banks in India, it would be appropriate to examine the structure of earnings and expenses of scheduled commercial banks in India. An analysis of earnings shows that the share of interest earnings amounted to 80 per cent of total earnings in 1951; it rose to 84.5 per cent in 1969 and 90.4 per cent by 1989 but subsequently declined to 86.3 per cent by 1995-96 (Table 12).

Among the expenses, interest expenses constituted 32.3 per cent of the total expenses in 1951; this proportion increased to 50.1 per cent by 1969 and further to 58.1 per cent by 1995-96 (Table 13). The upward movement of expenses under this head could be attributed to the rise in deposit rates since 1980 and this proportion reached a figure of 69.1 per cent by 1989. Since 1991, this proportion has declined reflecting the downward movement of deposit rates especially of lower maturities. On the other hand, operating expenses have shown an increasing trend in the reform period partly reflecting the automatic indexation of wages and salaries of bank employees and the expenses on account of fresh wage agreement in 1995.

TABLE 12

Earnings of Scheduled Commercial Banks in India: 1951 to 1996

Year	Interest Earnings		Earnings from Other Sources		Total Earnings	
	Rs. crore	% to total	Rs. crore	% to total	Rs. crore	% to total
1	2	3	4	5	6	7
Ending December						
1951	36	80.0	9	20.0	45	100.0
1960	93	84.5	17	15.5	110	100.0
1969	361	84.5	66	15.5	427	100.0
1975	1,354	86.2	216	13.8	1,570	100.0
1980	3,754	88.7	478	11.3	4,232	100.0
1985	9,647	91.4	905	8.6	10,552	100.0
1989	20,602	90.4	2,182	9.6	22,784	100.0
Ending March						
1991	27,521	90.5	2,883	9.5	30,404	100.0
1992	34,959	88.2	4,689	11.8	39,648	100.0
1993	37,488	89.3	4,489	10.7	41,977	100.0
1994	37,848	86.5	5,889	13.5	43,737	100.0
1995	44,567	87.4	6,397	12.6	50,964	100.0
1996	56,181	86.3	8,931	13.7	65,112	100.0

Source: (1) Statistical Tables Relating to Banks in India (Various Issues), and

(2) Report on Trend and Progress of Banking in India, (Various Issues), Reserve Bank of India.

The profitability of banks depends on a number of factors such as cost of funds, return on assets, level of non-performing assets, subsidised lending, etc. The cost of mobilising deposits of scheduled commercial banks in India amounted to 0.9 per cent in 1951 and 3.4 per cent in 1970; this more than doubled to 8.0 per cent by 1989 (Table 14). At the same time, the return on investments increased from 2.6 per cent in 1951 to 3.5 per cent in 1970 and to 4.2 per cent by 1989 reflecting the low yields on government securities. Return on loans, on the other hand, increased from 4.5 per cent in 1951 to 7.2 per cent in 1970 and to 12.8 per cent by 1989. The return on loans has to be viewed with caution as it is not based on realised basis. Consequently, the interest margin (net interest income) which is nothing but the difference between the interest cost of funds and the return (interest) on the total assets of scheduled commercial banks was a meagre 2.1 per cent in 1951, 2.7 per cent in 1970, and 2.9 per cent in 1989. During the financial sector reform period (1991-96), the net interest income improved marginally to above 3 per cent. This spread was generally lower as compared with some developed and developing countries, but was far better than countries such as France, Switzerland, etc. (see also Annexure I).

TABLE 13

Expenses of Scheduled Commercial Banks in India: 1951 to 1996

Year	Interest Expenses		Establishment Expenses		Other Expenses		Total Expenses	
	Rs. crore	% to total	Rs. crore	% to total	Rs. crore	% to total	Rs. crore	% to total
1	2	3	4	5	6	7	8	9
Ending December								
1951	10	32.3	15	48.4	6	19.3	31	100.0
1960	44	50.0	33	37.5	11	12.5	88	100.0
1969	190	50.1	141	37.2	48	12.7	379	100.0
1975	853	55.4	501	32.6	185	12.0	1,539	100.0
1980	2,717	65.0	1,027	24.6	435	10.4	4,179	100.0
1985	6,935	66.5	2,427	23.3	1,069	10.2	10,431	100.0
1989	15,410	69.1	4,622	20.7	2,261	10.1	22,293	100.0
Ending March								
1991	18,968	64.0	7,596	25.6	3,097	10.4	29,661	100.0
1992	23,677	61.6	8,878	23.1	5,888	15.3	38,443	100.0
1993	27,836	60.4	10,248	22.2	8,043	17.4	46,127	100.0
1994	26,800	56.6	11,485	24.2	9.077	19.2	47,362	100.0
1995	29,041	59.5	14,229	29.1	5,540	11.4	48,810	100.0
1996	37,316	58.1	17,591	27.4	9,293	14.5	64,200	100.0

Source:

1. Reserve Bank of India:
   (i) Statistical Tables Relating to Banks in India (Various Issues).
   (ii) Report on Trend and Progress of Banking in India (Various Issues).
2. Indian Banks' Association, Financial Analysis of Banks.

SECTION III

FINANCIAL SECTOR REFORMS AND ISSUES CONFRONTING BANKING SECTOR IN INDIA

One of the objectives of bank nationalisation was to extend banking services to all geographical regions and to extend credit to 'socially' important segments of the economy like agriculture, small-scale industries, etc. To some extent, these objectives were met. But the system lacked the degree of flexibility required for interest rates to act as price signals for allocation of scarce resources. There were a number of banking regulations which had a crucial bearing on the performance of banks in India. These issues are addressed hereafter.

TABLE 14

Return on Assets of Scheduled Commercial Banks in India

Year	Cost of Deposits	Return on Loans	Return on Investments	Interest Income/ Total Assets	Interest Expended/ Total Assets	Net interest Income/ Total Assets
1	2	3	4	5	6	7
Ending December						
1951	0.9	4.5	2.6	2.9	0.8	2.1
1960	2.1	5.5	3.4	3.6	1.7	1.9
1970	3.4	7.2	3.5	5.4	2.7	2.7
1975	5.2	11.9	4.7	7.5	4.3	3.2
1980	5.7	11.4	4.5	7.0	4.8	2.2
1985	6.1	12.1	3.7	7.0	4.5	2.5
1989	8.0	12.8	4.2	9.0	6.1	2.9
Ending March						
1995	6.3	10.5	10.9	8.7	5.6	3.1
1996	6.9	12.3	11.2	9.4	6.2	3.2

Notes:

Return on Loans = Earnings on Loans/Total Loans

Return on Investment = Earnings on Investments/Total Investments.

External constraints on Banks

Regulations employed for monetary policy purposes

In India, regulations such as the cash reserve ratio (CRR) and the statutory liquidity ratio (SLR) were often pitched high, to subserve policy objectives. This was particularly so after the oil price shock of 1973, and in the process, the credit expansion of banks had been severely constrained. In 1991, the statutory pre-emptions under CRR and SLR, on an incremental basis, reached a level of 63.5 per cent and on the balance of 36.5 per cent, there were pre-emptions under the priority sector of 40 per cent, export credit and food credit and other formal or informal pre-emptions.

Other direct controls

Besides the CRR and SLR, there were other monetary control measures; these include administrative interest rate regime on both sides of the balance sheet, controls on foreign exchange, selective credit controls against sensitive agricultural commodities, credit delivery system based on Maximum Permissible Bank Finance (MPBF), etc.

Regulations employed for 'safety and soundness' reasons

A number of measures were also taken to promote financial soundness and avoid instability in the banking system in India. Theoretically, the first formal attempt to model banking instability and rationalise government intervention was given by Diamond and Dybvig (DD) (1983). DD model suggests that banking instability arises because of depositors' liquidity demands and because the value of uncertain bank assets is often less than the bank liabilities. It suggests that banking instability is harmful because it destroys the risk-sharing agreement and damages production and therefore provides argument for government intervention in the form of deposit insurance. In India, deposits upto Rs. 1 lakh are insured by the Deposit Insurance and Credit Guarantee Corporation (DICGC) - a fully owned subsidiary of the Reserve Bank of India which was set up in 1971. DICGC also provides credit guarantee for small loans especially those from priority sectors. Other measures include ceiling on credit expansion like a ceiling on non-food credit-deposit ratio (imposed in 1988-89).

Deposit insurance is not necessarily the appropriate response to avoidance of instability. The main criticism against it is that it encourages excessive risk-taking. Besides, it has been argued that since depositors are protected by insurance coverage, they have little or no incentive to monitor their banks' activities or to demand risk premium on deposit interest rates. There is a moral hazard inherent in deposit insurance, especially if the insurance is provided officially with implicit guarantees.

Where there are no prudential norms and assets are not classified according to their quality, the possibilities of banks accumulating large non-performing assets (NPAs) would increase, exacerbating the prevalence of deposit insurance.

Regulations regarding Entry and Exit in Banking Industry

The entry to banking industry was restricted till the onset of financial sector reforms. The policy about expansion of branches was also to achieve certain social goals. Given the negative externalities associated with bank failures and the consequential potential systemic effects, the policy preference in most countries is not to allow banks to fail. In India, this perception prevailed: ever since the failure of Palai Central Bank in 1960, weak banks have not been allowed to exit.

Financial Sector Reforms in India

The first attempt at reforming the financial sector was visible from the recommendations of the Committee to Review the Working of the Monetary System (1985) (referred to as the Chakravarty Committee Report). The Committee advocated the necessity of moving away from quantitative controls which, it felt, led to distortions in the credit market and resulted in curbing the growth of the economy. As regards administered interest rates, the Committee felt that they had become unduly complex and the concessional interest rates allowed projects of doubtful viability to be undertaken. The Committee recommended a more liberal approach to interest rates which included a selective approach to concessional interest rates and a hike in coupon rates on government borrowing.[17] But the impetus to reforms in the financial sector was given by the Report of the Committee on the Financial System (1991) (Chairman: M. Narasimham) popularly referred to as 'the Narasimham Committee'.

The Narasimham Committee was appointed in the background of the balance of payments crisis in 1991 and the macro-imbalance. India took the opportunity of addressing the crisis through a comprehensive set of stabilisation and structural measures. The financial sector reforms was a crucial element of overall structural reforms, encompassing industrial, external, fiscal and public enterprises. The Narasimham Committee recommended wide ranging reforms which included the reduction in pre-emptions of banks' resources (in the form of SLR and CRR) and in the proportion of directed credit. It also recommended deregulation of interest rates so as to reflect market conditions and abolition of branch licensing policy which regulated entry into banking. As regards SLR, the Commitee was of the view that it should be used as a prudential requirement and not as an instrument for financing public sector deficit and recommended that the SLR be brought down to 25 per cent over a period of five years and CRR be gradually reduced and recommended improvements in the interest rate on the resources pre-empted under reserve requirements. The Committee also recommended various remedial measures to strengthen the viability of the banking system and these included, *inter alia*, capital adequacy norms and other prudential norms such as income recognition, assets classification and provisioning for bad debts.

As a follow-up of Chakravarty and Narasimham Committees' recommendations, various measures have been taken by the Reserve Bank of India to move away from direct monetary policy instruments to indirect monetary control. The level and structure of interest rates have been rationalised in a phased manner and letting the banks to determine their own prime lending rates. In 1995, all controls on deposits rates above one year maturity have been removed.[18] Steps were initiated for bringing down the CRR and SLR. Prudential norms and regulations were introduced to ensure the safety and soundness of the financial system and at the same time to encourage markets to play increasing role.[19]

Prudential Regulations

A major element of the financial sector reforms has been the application of prudential norms and regulations aimed at ensuring the safety and soundness of the financial system and at the same time encouraging markets to play increasing role. This is in contrast to the earlier comprehensive system of controls – administered interest rates, credit controls, etc.

Prudential norms serve two primary purposes - first, they reveal the true position of the bank's loan portfolio and secondly, they help to arrest its deterioration [Rangarajan (1994)]. Prudential reforms introduced in India relate to income recognition, asset classification, provisioning for bad and doubtful debts and capital adequacy (see Table 15). The capital adequacy measure can be viewed as an orientation towards incentive based regulation for well capitalised and efficient banks to compete while costs are imposed on undercapitalised and poorly managed banks. The standards also permit banks that are more efficient at controlling their risks to hold less capital than the inefficient banks. In India, most of the banks have achieved the minimum stipulated capital adequacy ratio. By end of March 1996, 19 out of the 27 public sector banks (as against 13 in the preceding year) have attained the bench-mark of 8 per cent capital adequacy, with the help, in many cases, of the Government's recapitalisation programme (see Annexure 2). In recent times, a number of public sector banks have gone into the capital market to augment their capital base. Non-performing assets of public sector banks in India have been on the decline; but at 19.5 per cent of total advances in 1994-95, these are considerably higher than in many other developing countries [Sheng, (1996)]. In 1993-94, 18 out of the 27 public sector banks had NPAs exceeding 20 per cent; by 1995-96 this number came down to 10. Overall NPAs came down to about 17.3 per cent of total advances in 1995-96.

Annexure 3 provides bank-wise information of major financial indictors of scheduled commercial banks during the financial sector reform period i.e., 1991-92 to 1995-96. Net profit of most of the public sector banks (PSBs) have declined during this period, while that of private sector banks, including foreign banks, have shown improvement. This was mainly due to higher provisioning by PSBs on account of their relatively higher bad and doubtful debts as well as higher provisioning on account of their larger investment portfolio which was increasingly made mark-to-market over the years. Spread as a proportion of working funds has generally shown

TABLE 15

Changes in the Bank Regulatory Framework in India: 1992-97

	Norms	1992-93	1993-94	1994-95	1995-96	1996-97
	1	2	3	4	5	6
(A)	**Capital adequacy requirements** (per cent of risk-weighted assets)					
	Other domestic banks	4	4	4	8	8
	Indian banks with international operations	4	8	8	8	8
	Foreign banks	8	8	8	8	8
(B)	**Non-performing assets:** Past due period (No. of quarters)	4	3	2	2	2
(C)	**Provisioning rquirements** (Per cent)					
	Small loans[1]	2.5	5.0	7.5	10.0	15.0
	Large loans:					
	Sub-Standard Assets	10.0	10.0	10.0	10.0	10.0
	Doubtful Assets : Secured portion	20-50	20-50	20-50	20-50	20-50
	: Unsecured portion	100	100	100	100	100
	Loss Assets	100	100	100	100	100
(D)	**Mark-to-market requirements**					
	Government and approved securities (per cent)	30	30	30	40	50

Source : Same as Table 3.

1 : Loans less than Rs. 25,000.

decline in all banking groups during this period. A notable development is the increase in spread of 10 out of 27 public sector banks although public sector banks as a group has shown a decline in the spread [Annexure 3 (A)]. On the contrary, only 3 out of 25 Indian private sector banks and 7 out of 29 foreign banks showed increase in spread during the financial sector reforms period.

A major achievement of financial sector reforms in India is the avoidance of financial instability during the reform period. This was mainly due to proper sequencing of reforms and at the same time putting in place a sound supervision system. Being a late starter in the reform process, India had the benefit of knowledge of the experiences of other reformers, including developing countries like Malaysia and Indonesia. This is best reflected in the fact that deposit rates deregulation was undertaken at the end of the reform process after India had achieved reasonable price stability. The reforms in the financial sector in India have removed the external constraints on the banks' functioning and have instilled greater degree of competition. The interest rate deregulation has also given greater degree of flexibility to banks to charge risk-premium and reduce credit rationing. In a deregulated regime, the ability and efficiency of banks to screen and monitor projects have significant implications for the efficiency of the system.

Theoretically, financial liberalisation should remove the liquidity constraints of corporates and households. But the recent experience shows that notwithstanding the substantial freeing of resources from statutory pre-emptions, credit offtake has been subdued and prime lending rates (PLR) are sticky downwards. Banks have generally found investments in government securities worthwhile. Perhaps, a solution to this situation could be found in the reduction of NPAs of banks, which implies a more careful credit appraisal and regular follow-up. It must be recognised that the purpose of banks is to take risk through the extension of credit to business and households. This is so vital to the growth and stability of the economy.

One of the current issues relates to the convergence in the liability and asset matrix of banks, NBFCs and FIs. Initially, banks faced competition on the liability side of their balance sheets from NBFCs, mutual funds, financial institutions (FIs). In the past- at any rate till the nineties, FIs had a distinct resource base: they were dependent on the soft window of Long Term Operations (LTO) Funds from the Reserve Bank for their long-term funding. Banks were also funding FIs through subscription to SLR bonds. NBFCs, on the other hand, were also dependent on their respective business group resources. But today, FIs are accessing more and more retail funds through bonds; NBFCs are also competing in the same markets. More recently, similar developments have occurred in the asset side of the balance sheet with banks competing with NBFCs and FIs. Traditionally, FIs were funding only term lending and banks were funding working capital. Now, especially with RBI allowing banks to sanction term finance, banks have been meeting term finance needs in a relatively significant way. FIs, on their part, have also been found to be sanctioning short-dated loans. Banks have also entered into the traditional NBFCs' business like hire purchase, consumer finance, stock market finance, etc.

The convergence in liability and asset side of banks and NBFCs raises an important regulatory issue. The competition between banks and non-banks are not level-playing: banks have to bear higher regulatory costs in the form of higher CRR on their deposit liabilities compared with non-banks. A major advantage banks have in financial intermediation is the relatively low cost of funds as they have the gains out of economies of scale. Even with disintermediation and competition, the entire payments and settlement will have to be done through banks. The large and geographically spread branch network has been the mainstay and strength of banks in the financial intermediation process. With liberalisation of the financial sector, non-banking financial institutions will still have to depend on banks for their survival and growth rather than displace them in the financial intermediation process.

Other issue which needs to be attended to speedily, is the quality and speed of the payments and settlements system in India. As statutory pre-emptions decline, the importance of payment system is enhanced. In India, the speed and technology of the payment and settlement system has not kept pace with the developments in the financial sector, notwithstanding the significant moves made in the form of Delivery Versus Payment (DVP) system for SGL transactions, Electronic Clearing Services for MICR cheques, etc. There are a number of areas where the systems need to be inbred with latest information technology applications - electronic funds transfer, electronic debits and credits and securities settlements. With increasing openness and liberalisation of the economy, the volume of payment and settlement is likely to expand substantially in near future and it is very essential that the risks associated with payment and settlement are eliminated so that the stability of the banks and financial intermediaries are maintained.

ANNEXURE 1

Structure of Income of Banks in India and Some Industrialised Countries: 1985 and 1994

Countries	*Interest Income*		*Non-Interest Income*		*Net Interest Income (Spread)*	
	As a percentage to Gross Income				*As % to Total Assets*	
	1985	*1994*	*1985*	*1994*	*1985*	*1994*
1	2	3	4	5	6	7
i) India	91.4	86.5	8.6	13.5	2.5	2.5
Industrialised Countries						
ii) United States	73.3	65.7	26.7	34.4	3.5	3.8
iii) United Kingdom	65.5	56.8	34.5	43.2	3.1	2.3
iv) Australia	61.0*	58.7	39.0	41.3	2.9*	2.6
v) France	81.6**	55.5	18.4	44.6	2.1**	0.9
vi) Germany	70.0	74.5	30.1	25.5	2.4	2.2
vii) Switzerland	52.6	45.3	47.4	54.7	1.4	1.4
Developing Countries						
viii) Mexico	64.2	78.4	35.8	21.7	N.A.	5.1
ix) Portugal	76.0	72.7	24.1	27.3	2.4	2.8
x) Turkey	49.3	140.7	50.7	-40.7	1.9	12.4
xi) Spain	81.7	74.8	18.3	25.2	3.6	2.6

N.A. : Not Available
* : For the year 1986.
** : For the year 1988

Source : OECD (1996)

ANNEXURE 2

Level of Net Non-Performing Assets and Capital Adequacy of Public Sector Banks in India: 1995-96

Sl. No.	*Public Sector Banks*	*Net NPAs as a % of Net Advances 1995-96*	*Capital Adequacy Ratio 1995-96*
1	*2*	*3*	*4*
1.	State Bank of India	6.33	11.60
2.	State Bank of Patiala	6.60	9.51
3.	State Bank of Hyderabad	9.94	9.90
4.	State Bank of Travancore	N.A.	9.40
5.	State Bank of Bikaner & Jaipur	6.11	9.59
6.	State Bank of Mysore	8.59	8.81
7.	State Bank of Saurashtra	N.A.	12.40
8.	State Bank of Indore	N.A.	8.80
9.	Bank of Baroda	6.40	11.20
10.	Bank of India	7.00	8.44
11.	Punjab National Bank	N.A.	8.23
12.	Canara Bank	7.45	10.38
13.	Central Bank of India	N.A.	2.63
14.	Union Bank of India	6.70	9.50
15.	Indian Overseas Bank	N.A.	5.95
16.	Indian Bank	N.A.	Negative
17.	Syndicate Bank	8.39	8.39
18.	UCO Bank	N.A.	7.83
19.	Allahabad Bank	16.12	9.68
20.	United Bank of India	N.A.	3.50
21.	Oriental Bank of Commerce	3.70	16.99
22.	Dena Bank	7.00	8.27
23.	Vijaya Bank	12.60	N.A.
24.	Bank of Maharashtra	N.A.	8.49
25.	Andhra Bank	N.A.	5.07
26.	Punjab & Sind Bank	N.A.	5.50
27.	Corporation Bank	2.30	11.30

Source: Balance Sheets of the respective banks for the year 1996-97.

ANNEXURE 3(A)

Financial Ratios of Public Sector Banks (PSBs) in India: 1991-92 to 1995-96

Sl. No.	Public Sector Banks	Net Profit/Loss as % to Working Funds			Establishment Expenses as % to Total Expenses			Spread as % to Working Funds		
		91-92	94-95	95-96	91-92	94-95	95-96	91-92	94-95	95-96
1	2	3	4	5	6	7	8	9	10	11
I.	State Bank of India (SBI)	0.18	0.59	0.58	14.19	22.08	22.52	3.63	3.25	3.28
	II. Associates of SBI									
2.	State Bank of Patiala	0.79	0.50	0.63	14.19	18.17	17.90	5.93	3.64	3.48
3.	State Bank of Hyderabad	0.32	0.62	0.61	16.37	17.45	19.37	4.62	3.40	3.72
4.	State Bank of Travancore	0.15	0.35	0.39	17.53	16.30	16.06	3.29	2.63	3.29
5.	State Bank of Bikaner & Jaipur	0.30	0.15	0.39	20.43	24.15	25.86	4.95	2.85	3.50
6.	State Bank of Mysore	0.16	0.07	0.54	23.06	19.85	23.68	3.87	3.30	3.88
7.	State Bank of Saurashtra	0.34	0.44	-4.94	17.88	21.44	15.26	4.88	4.08	3.30
8.	State Bank of Indore	0.19	0.34	0.39	18.62	21.49	22.27	4.48	3.90	4.10
	Total of 7 SBI Associates (II)	**0.35**	**0.38**	**-0.09**	**17.93**	**19.38**	**19.55**	**4.61**	**3.32**	**3.57**
	III. Nationalised Banks									
9.	Bank of Baroda	0.44	0.56	0.59	13.32	15.49	14.49	2.92	3.59	3.72
10.	Bank of India	0.24	0.17	0.83	32.22	22.36	21.67	2.25	2.59	2.87
11.	Punjab National Bank	0.58	0.30	-0.30	16.62	21.53	21.18	3.42	2.85	3.43
12.	Canara Bank	0.95	0.77	0.81	15.48	18.73	18.57	4.42	3.60	3.44
13.	Central Bank of India	0.21	-0.41	-0.32	19.66	24.25	24.95	2.80	2.46	3.15
14.	Union Bank of India	0.34	0.62	0.39	19.98	17.97	18.49	3.81	3.32	3.40
15.	Indian Overseas Bank	0.10	0.06	0.02	17.52	18.79	21.62	1.73	1.79	2.12
16.	Indian Bank	0.33	0.09	-7.51	12.09	15.50	11.97	1.99	1.73	0.52
17.	Syndicate Bank	0.05	-0.64	0.13	24.58	28.33	28.15	3.02	2.74	3.20
18.	UCO Bank	-0.18	-0.63	-1.53	18.68	24.07	26.80	1.93	2.19	2.17
19.	Allahabad Bank	0.36	-0.68	0.05	14.75	17.21	20.68	2.09	1.99	2.67
20.	United Bank of India	0.10	-2.04	-2.17	20.53	21.91	22.97	2.33	0.94	1.62
21.	Oriental Bank of Commerce	0.67	1.38	1.64	14.39	14.34	14.87	4.29	3.81	3.80
22.	Dena Bank	0.22	0.41	0.63	23.64	25.27	21.43	3.24	3.23	3.64
23.	Vijaya Bank	0.06	0.47	-3.47	19.26	22.51	17.99	3.19	2.61	2.53
24.	Bank of Maharashtra	0.10	-0.59	0.16	22.54	25.06	29.30	3.04	2.65	3.59
25.	Andhra Bank	0.19	-0.69	0.16	19.20	21.97	22.65	2.50	2.53	3.03
26.	Punjab & Sind Bank	0.02	-0.12	-1.83	21.71	18.72	18.97	2.67	2.54	2.15
27.	Corporation Bank	0.19	1.02	1.52	17.25	16.67	14.06	3.47	2.96	3.74
	Total of 19 National Banks (III)	**0.33**	**0.10**	**-0.36**	**16.84**	**20.28**	**19.93**	**2.86**	**2.73**	**2.95**
	Total of 27 PSBs (I+II+II)	**0.28**	**0.25**	**-0.07**	**16.22**	**20.71**	**20.61**	**3.22**	**2.92**	**3.10**

Source: Indian Banks' Association Bulletin, March 1997.

ANNEXURE 3(B)

Financial Ratios of Indian Private Sector Banks in India: 1991-92 to 1995-96

Sl. No.	Indian Private Sector Banks	Net Profit/Loss as % to Working Funds			Establishment Expenses as % to Total Expenses			Spread as % to Working Funds		
		91-92	94-95	95-96	91-92	94-95	95-96	91-92	94-95	95-96
1	2	3	4	5	6	7	8	9	10	11
	IV. INDIAN PRIVATE SECTOR BANKS									
1.	The Vysya Bank Ltd.	0.68	1.64	2.01	17.21	9.46	10.87	3.21	1.90	2.18
2.	The Federal Bank Ltd.	0.37	1.30	1.04	20.35	15.25	14.41	3.22	3.28	2.44
3.	The Jammu & Kashmir Bank Ltd.	0.17	0.58	0.53	13.21	18.65	14.32	5.66	4.43	4.05
4.	Bank of Rajasthan Ltd.	0.97	2.04	1.50	22.37	20.44	16.70	3.97	3.69	2.90
5.	Karnataka Bank Ltd.	0.76	0.80	1.11	21.31	20.14	18.09	3.74	3.64	3.41
6.	The South Indian Bank Ltd.	0.62	0.85	0.22	26.32	19.23	18.32	3.72	3.02	3.73
7.	The United Western Bank Ltd.	0.34	0.63	0.75	23.70	16.72	16.92	3.54	3.07	3.13
8.	Bank of Madura Ltd.	0.74	2.08	0.55	24.60	20.52	16.84	4.60	2.91	2.61
9.	The Catholic Syrian Bank Ltd.	0.51	0.35	0.02	23.35	19.72	18.23	3.87	2.94	3.04
10.	The Karur Vysya Bank Ltd.	1.39	1.53	2.11	22.56	15.06	14.67	3.98	2.83	3.35
11.	Tamilnadu Mercantile Bank Ltd.	1.03	1.35	1.68	17.41	14.14	13.16	5.16	3.71	4.33
12.	The Lakshmi Vilas Bank Ltd.	0.84	1.56	0.90	23.29	15.40	16.66	4.13	2.94	3.34
13.	The Sangli Bank Ltd.	0.46	0.18	0.36	23.62	23.33	28.31	4.30	3.23	3.80
14.	The Dhanalakshmi Bank Ltd.	0.18	0.84	0.57	36.03	17.87	16.93	3.94	3.32	3.09
15.	Development Credit Bank Ltd.			2.34			15.72			5.00
16.	Bharat Overseas Bank Ltd.	0.74	0.79	1.17	12.07	14.29	15.11	4.02	3.80	3.90
17.	City Union Bank Ltd.	0.66	1.07	1.32	21.07	15.34	13.63	4.32	3.26	3.38
18.	The Benares State Bank Ltd.	0.01	-1.87	-3.21	23.96	22.61	19.37	2.82	1.26	2.48
19.	The Nedungadi Bank Ltd.	0.60	0.42	0.36	31.09	26.61	27.13	4.01	3.57	4.05
20.	Lord Krishna Bank Ltd.	-1.17	1.42	1.54	40.78	16.40	12.02	2.00	3.76	3.72
21.	Bareilly Corporation Bank Ltd.	0.02	-0.22	-0.82	29.52	29.46	28.96	2.72	3.10	3.59
22.	Nainital Bank Ltd.	0.60	0.25	0.28	22.43	26.41	27.73	4.65	3.36	4.19
23.	The Ratnakar Bank Ltd.	0.53	0.56	0.58	23.17	19.82	22.70	4.21	3.42	3.55
24.	The Ganesh Bank of Kurundwad Ltd.	0.97	0.29	0.20	23.24	15.42	14.50	4.73	4.22	2.74
25.	The Punjab Co-operative Bank Ltd.	0.07	0.59	0.65	32.45	23.05	17.50	..	2.73	2.83
	Total 25 Pvt. Banks (IV)	**0.57**	**1.16**	**1.03**	**20.80**	**16.86**	**15.96**	**4.01**	**3.07**	**3.17**
	V. NEW PRIVATE SECTOR BANKS									
26.	IndusInd Bank Ltd.			2.42			1.23			3.02
27.	Global Trust Bank Ltd.			1.82			1.98			1.58
28.	UTI Bank Ltd.			0.92			3.02			2.28
29.	ICICI Banking Corporation Ltd.			1.43			3.76			2.70
30.	HDFC Bank Ltd.			2.04			4.30			4.51
31.	Times Bank Ltd.			1.23			6.24			2.52
32.	Bank of Punjab Ltd.			2.86			8.01			4.51
33.	Centurion Bank Ltd.			2.71			3.55			4.82
34.	IDBI Bank Ltd.			0.72			5.84			6.05
	Total of 9 New Private Banks (V)			**1.83**			**2.97**			**2.85**
	VI. NON-SCHEDULED BANK									
35.	Bari Doab Bank Ltd.	1.72	3.09	3.47	20.00	13.87	16.14	..	3.86	5.15
	Total of 35 Pvt. Banks (IV+V+VI)	**0.57**	**1.16**	**1.19**	**20.80**	**16.86**	**13.70**	**4.01**	**3.07**	**3.10**

Source: Same as in Annexure 3(A)

ANNEXURE 3(C)

Financial Ratios of Foreign Banks in India: 1991-92 to 1995-96

VII. FOREIGN BANKS IN INDIA

Sl. No.	*Foreign Banks*	*Net Profit/Loss as % to Working Funds*			*Establishment Expenses as % to Total Expenses*			*Spread as % to Working Funds*		
		91-92	*94-95*	*95-96*	*91-92*	*94-95*	*95-96*	*91-92*	*94-95*	*95-96*
1	*2*	*3*	*4*	*5*	*6*	*7*	*8*	*9*	*10*	*11*
1.	Citibank N.A.	2.11	2.09	2.02	3.29	4.95	5.00	3.25	4.72	4.06
2.	ANZ Grindlays Bank	1.88	1.17	0.77	8.90	14.76	13.52	3.99	3.07	3.03
3.	Hong Kong Bank	1.64	1.11	1.74	9.48	9.25	9.24	3.99	4.20	4.40
4.	Standard Chartered Bank	-5.92	0.34	2.43	5.29	17.03	23.38	3.44	2.45	5.54
5.	American Express Bank	2.75	3.16	1.17	4.68	7.68	7.95	5.43	5.16	3.76
6.	Bank of America NT&SA	7.39	1.95	1.38	4.54	5.67	5.47	2.45	4.97	3.53
7.	Deutsche Bank AG	2.74	0.75	1.19	4.27	5.92	6.18	6.56	4.60	4.91
8.	The Bank of Tokyo-Mitsubishi	1.55	3.62	2.21	4.90	5.92	3.96	4.69	6.51	4.99
9.	The British Bank of the Middle East	1.16	2.35	1.44	3.08	3.26	3.84	3.04	3.53	2.87
10.	Banque Indosuez	2.99	2.08	1.20	1.77	3.52	3.10	3.83	3.14	1.17
11.	Credit Lyonnais	2.17	2.16	1.04	2.21	3.01	2.87	5.82	6.28	1.75
12.	Societe Generale	1.52	1.30	0.56	2.71	1.92	2.24	4.67	4.08	1.98
13.	ABN-AMRO Bank N.V.	3.21	1.77	1.43	5.70	6.77	5.08	5.09	3.71	2.32
14.	Banque Nationale De Paris	2.86	2.84	1.39	9.85	6.48	11.07	6.86	8.45	4.63
15.	Mashreq Bank Psc	0.87	3.28	1.32	2.47	3.11	4.26	5.84	4.90	3.97
16.	The Sakura Bank Ltd.	3.18	2.37	2.43	5.13	2.74	2.81	7.55	5.76	5.71
17.	Abu Dhabi Commercial Bank Ltd.	1.04	1.59	1.05	4.85	3.47	2.77	3.99	2.80	2.57
18.	Bank of Bahrain and Kuwait BSC	1.66	2.03	1.60	2.20	3.27	3.70	5.77	5.63	5.77
19.	Oman International Bank SAOG	1.49	0.55	1.32	1.73	2.50	2.56	5.93	5.90	4.60
20.	The Bank of Nova Scotia	0.82	0.57	0.51	2.30	6.19	2.96	2.50	3.32	1.02
21.	Barclays Bank PLC	2.50	0.98	2.02	2.85	6.41	6.14	6.78	4.83	4.16
22.	The Sanwa Bank Ltd.	2.61	1.31	0.16	3.64	2.92	2.71	5.37	4.41	3.78
23.	Dresdner Bank AG			-4.64			17.03			0.99
24.	Sonali Bank	2.12	2.67	5.58	27.48	24.83	16.35	6.21	6.37	7.99
25.	ING Bank		-9.00	-1.07		31.14	11.90		2.14	-0.31
26.	The Development Bank of Singapore			0.77			12.62			2.57
27.	State Bank of Mauritius Ltd.		-0.68	5.21		21.08	10.30		1.78	9.85
28.	Chase Manhattan Bank N.A.		-15.01	-8.10		35.65	33.65		1.83	6.09
29.	Commerzbank AG			-4.39			23.75			1.57
	Total of 29 Foreign Banks (VII)	**1.57**	**1.66**	**1.45**	**5.56**	**8.39**	**8.63**	**3.89**	**4.25**	**3.76**
	Total 91 Banks (I to VII)	**0.39**	**0.41**	**0.14**	**15.46**	**19.48**	**19.09**	**3.31**	**3.03**	**3.15**

Source: Same as in Annexure 3(A).

Notes

1. For the literature on why financial intermediaries exist, see Diamond (1984), Dowd (1996).
2. The 'new' view is articulated in the writings of Gramley and Chase (1965), Black (1970), Fama (1980), *et al.*
3. For an overview of the debate on old and new views on the role of banks, see Selgin, G. (1996).
4. Useful surveys on this topic include Romer and Romer (1993), Kashyap, Stein and Wilcox (1993), Kashyap and Stein (1995).
5. The term Shroff meant those bankers who exchanged one kind of money for another. Kothiwal meant bankers who owned offices/ establishments; Mahajan was referred generally to bankers but was also used to refer to guilds (organisation of bankers). For details, see Chatterjee, K (1993).
6. Regarding the role of capital market funds, there are broadly two schools of thoughts. According to one view, capital (financial) market has a greater stimulating effect on economic growth than financial intermediation as this is conducive to venture capital and technical progress than the banks. On the other hand, another school of thought stresses the negative impact of the stock market on economic development. According to this school, the failing of stock market in the (a) pricing process, and (b) takeover mechanism, has led to short-termism.
7. Even with the reduction in the period for the shortest term deposits, there still exists a gap in the yield structure for the period 14 to 30 days.
8. The role of banking sector controls in the process of economic development is actively debated in the literature, see Galbis (1977), Courakis (1984), Fry (1988), World Bank (1989), Demetrigades and Lunintel (1996), Gibson and Tsakalotos (1994).
9. Initially, the policy guidelines issued in 1974 stipulated that public sector banks extend one-third of their credit outstanding by March 1979; private sector banks (excluding foreign banks) were also included and the target to be achieved by March 1985 was enhanced to 40 per cent. In August 1988, foreign banks were also brought under this purview. But as foreign banks did not have rural branches, they were exempt from making advances to agriculture under the priority sector lending requirement. These banks, however, were required to extend also export credit to the extent of 10 per cent of their net credit. Together with the export credit stipulation, foreign banks were required to provide for 32 per cent of their net credit under priority sector since April 1993. Subsequently, in October 1996, export credit target for all the scheduled commercial banks has been increased to 12 per cent to be achieved by March 1997.
10. The share of institutional credit to rural households was as low as 29.2 per cent in 1971. By 1981 this proportion increased to 61.2 per cent but still falls short of the contribution of rural sector.
11. The All-India Rural Credit Review Committee (1969) made a comprehensive review of the agricultural credit system and recommended that the requirements of the agricultural sector was so large and diverse that commercial and co-operative banks can play a mutually complementary role without getting into conflict with each other.
12. Reserve Bank of India, Report on Trend and Progress of Banking in India 1995-96, p. 37.
13. The Tandon Committee proposed three methods of lending whereby the borrower's contribution to working capital steadily increases as the borrower graduates to business stability. The three methods are: Method I-25 per cent of the working capital gap i.e., difference between current assets and current liabilities excluding bank finance to be funded from long term resources. Minimum current ratio of 1:1; Method II-25 per cent of current assets to be funded from long term resources. Balance 75 per cent of current assets less current liabilities to be funded by bank finance. Minimum current ratio of 1.33:1; Method III-25 per cent of current assets less core current assets being funded from long term resources. Current ratio greater than 1.33.
14. The Tandon Committee Report (1975) had identified four types of inventories namely (i) normal inventory (ii) safety inventory (iii) profit making inventory, and (iv) flabby inventory. The Committee defined flabby inventory as comprising finished goods, raw materials and stores held because of poor working capital management and inefficient distribution.
15. Under the cash credit system which prevailed in India, the burden of credit management was solely on the banks. Borrowers who obtain the credit limit from the banks could draw upto the credit limit any time without incurring any commitment fee for the utilised/ sanctioned limit. Under the modified scheme, borrowers will have to fully draw the cash credit limit first before using the demand loan component. Once the demand loan component is used, it is again subject to fresh credit appraisal.
16. The weights being the corresponding amounts outstandings.
17. Some of the other important recommendations of the Report included a shift in emphasis from the traditional concept of budget deficit to Net Reserve Bank Credit to Government and a system of monetary targeting with a feedback.
18. In September 1990, the interest rate structure was reduced to two; (a) a concessional rate of lending for small borrowers (upto Rs. 2 lakh) and (b) a maximum deposit rate. In September 1995, the deposit rates above 2 years have been totally freed. Now, deposit rates for 30 days to 1 year have been fixed at not exceeding 10 per cent (since revised to 9 per cent).
19. Indian banks having foreign branches were asked to achieve a capital to risk weighted assets ratio of 8 per cent by March 31, 1995. Foreign banks operating in India have already achieved this norm as on March 31, 1993. Other banks were to achieve the 8 per cent norm by March 31, 1996.

References

Ajit, D (1992): 'The Determinants of Money Multiplier in India – 1960-61 to 1989-90', *Prajnan* 21, 287-307.

———. (1997): 'Interest Sensitivity of Bank Deposits in India: An Empirical Analysis' (mimeo).

Bagchi, A.K. (1987): *The Evolution of the State Bank of India: The Roots, 1806-1876*, Bombay: Oxford University Press.

Bank for International Settlements, *Annual Report (Various Issues)*.

Bernanke, B.S. and Gertler, M. (1985): '*Banking in General Equilibrium*', NBER Working Paper No. 1647.

Black, F. (1970): 'Banking and Interest Rates in a World Without Money: The Effects of Uncontrolled Banking', *Journal of Bank Research*, Autumn, 9-20.

Chatterjee, K. (1993): 'Collaboration and Conflict: Bankers and Early Colonial Rule in India: 1757-1813', *The Indian Economic and Social History Review*, 30, 284-310.

Courakis, A.S. (1984): 'Constraints on Bank Choices and Financial Repression in Less Developed Countries', *Oxford Bulletin of Economics and Statistics*, 46, 341-70.

Demetrigades, P.O. and Lunintel, K.B. (1996): 'Financial Development, Economic Growth and Banking Sector Controls: Evidence from India', *Economic Journal*, 106, 359-74.

Diamond, D. (1984): 'Financial Intermediation as Delegated Monitoring', *Review of Economic Studies*, 51, 393-414.

Diamond, D. and Dybvig, P. (1983): 'Bank Runs, Deposit Insurance and Liquidity', *Journal of Political Economy*, 91, 401-19.

Dowd, K. (1992): 'Models of Banking Instability: A Partial Review of the Literature' *Journal of Economic Surveys*, 6, 107-132.

———. (1996): *Competition and Finance: A Reinterpretation of Financial and Monetary Economics*, London: MacMillan.

Fama, E.F. (1980): 'Banking in a Theory of Finance', *Journal of Monetary Economics*, 6, 39-57.

———. (1985): 'What is Different About Banks', *Journal of Monetary Economics*, 11, 39-57.

Fry, M.J. (1988): *Money, Interest and Banking in Economic Development*, Baltimore: The John Hopkins University Press.

Galbis, V. (1977): 'Financial Intermediation and Economic Growth in Less Developed Countries: A Theoretical Approach', *Journal of Development Studies*, 13, 58-91.

Gertler, M. and Gilchrist, S. (1993a): *'Monetary Policy, Business Cycles and the Behaviour of Small Manufacturing Firms'* Finance and Economics Discussion Series 93-4, Washington: Division of Research and Statistics, Division of Monetary Affairs, Federal Reserve Board, February.

———. (1993b): 'The Role of Credit Market Imperfections in the Monetary Transmission Mechanism: Arguments and Evidence', *Scandinavian Journal of Economics*, 95, 43-64.

———. (1994): 'Monetary Policy, Business Cycles and the Behaviour of Small Manufacturing Firms', *Quarterly Journal of Economics*, 109, 309-40.

Ghosh, D.N. (1988): 'Banking: Lessons from Indian Experience', *State Bank of India Monthly Review*, 28, 531-43.

Gibson, H. and Tsakalotos, E. (1994): 'The Scope and Limits of Financial Liberalisation in Developing Countries: A Critical Survey', *Journal of Development Studies*, 30, 578-628.

Goldsmith, R. (1969): *Financial Structure and Development*, Yale University Press, New Heaven.

Government of India (1975): *'Report of the Working Group on Rural Banks'* (Chairman: M. Narasimham).

Gramley, L. and Chase (Jr.), S.B. (1965): 'Time Deposits and Monetary Analysis', *Federal Reserve Bulletin*, 1380-1904.

Gurley, J.G. and Shaw, E.S. (1955): 'Financial Aspects of Economic Development', *American Economic Review*, 45, 515-38.

Jadhav, N.D. and Ajit, D. (1997), 'The Role of Banks in Economic Development of India', *Prajnan*, 25, 309-21.

Kashyap, A.K., Stein, J.C. and Wilcox, D.W. (1993): 'Monetary Policy and Credit Conditions: Evidence from the Composition of External Finance', *American Economic Review*, 83, 78-98.

Kashyap, A.K. and Stein, J.C. (1995): 'The Impact of Monetary Policy on Bank Balance Sheets', *Carnegie - Rochester Series on Public Policy*, 42, 151-195.

Leland, H.E. and Pyle, D.H. (1977): 'Informational Asymmetries, Financial Structure and Financial Intermediation', *Journal of Finance*, 32, 371-87.

Lucas, R. (1988): 'On the Mechanics of Economic Development', *Journal of Monetary Economics*, 22, 3-42.

McKinnon, R. (1973): *Money and Capital in Economic Development*, Washington D.C., Brookings Institution.

Mujumdar, N.A. (1982): 'Structural Transformation in the Development of Credit: Some Implications', *RBI Occassional Papers*, 3, 97-113.

———. (1996): 'Financial Sector Reforms: An Exercise in Introspection', *Economic and Political Weekly*, 31, March 23, 727-30.

OECD (1996): *Bank Profitability - Financial Statements of Banks - 1985-1994*, Paris.

Olinear, R.F. and Rudebusch, G.D. (1995): 'Is There a Bank Credit Channel for Monetary Policy', *Economic Review*, Federal Reserve Bank of San Francisco, 2, 3-20.

Patrick, H. (1966): 'Financial Development and Economic Growth in Underdeveloped Countries', *Economic Development and Cultural Change*, 14, 174-89.

Rangarajan, C. (1984): 'Financial Infrastructure and Economic Development', *RBI Bulletin*, 71-79.

———. (1988): 'Issues in Monetary Management', Presidential Address at the 71st Conference of the Indian Economic Association, Calcutta, December.

———. (1994): 'Monetary Policy Revisited', *RBI Bulletin*, 737-43.

———. (1994): 'Indian Financial System: The Emerging Horizon', *RBI Bulletin*, 747-58.

———. (1997) 'Banking Sector Reforms: Rationale and Relevance', RBI Bulletin, 41-51.

Reserve Bank of India (1954) *All-India Rural Credit Survey*.

———. (1969) *Report of the All India Rural Credit Review Committee*.

———. (1970) *History of the Reserve Bank of India 1935-51*.

———. (1975) *Report of the Study Group to Frame Guidelines for Follow-Up of Bank Credit* (Chairman: P.L. Tandon), Bombay.

———. (1985) *Report of the Committee to Review the Working of the Monetary System* (Chairman: Sukhamoy Chakravarty), Bombay.

———. (1991) *Report of the Committee on the Financial System* (Chairman: M. Narasimham), Bombay.

———. *Annual Report* (Bombay), (Various Issues).

———. *Report on Currency and Finance*, (Bombay), (Various Issues).

———. *Report on Trend and Progress of Banking in India*, (Bombay), (Various Issues).

———. *Banking Statistics: Basic Statistical Returns* (Bombay), (Various issues).

———. *All India Debt and Investment Survey* (Various Issues).

Romer, C.D. and Romer, D.H. (1993): 'New Evidence on the Transmission Mechanism', *Brookings Papers on Economic Activity*, 1,149-213.

Romer, P. (1986): 'Increasing Returns and Long-Run Growth', *Journal of Political Economy*, 98, S71-S102.

Selgin, G. (1996): 'Commercial Banks as Pure Intermediaries', in Selgin, G. (1996) *Bank Deregulation and Monetary Order*, London: Routledge, 119-28.

Shetty, S.L. (1978): 'Performance of Commercial Banks Since Nationalisation of Major Banks: Promise and Reality', *Economic and Political Weekly*, 13, Special Number, 1407-51.

Sheng, A. (1996) *Bank Restructuring, Washington, D.C.*: The World Bank.

Stiglitz, J.E. and Weiss, A. (1981): 'Credit Rationing in Markets with Imperfect Information', *American Economic Review*, 71, 393-410.

Tarapore, S.S. (1996): *'Financial Sector Reforms: Retrospect and Prospect'*, RBI Bulletin, 299-306.

Tyagarajan, M. (1975): 'Expansion of Commercial Banking - An Assessment', *Economic and Political Weekly*, 10, 1819-24.

———. (1975): 'Impact of Expansion of Bank Earnings, Expenses and Profits', *Economic and Political Weekly*, 10, 1841-47.

Williamson, S.D. (1986): 'Costly Monitoring, Financial intermediation and Equilibrium Credit Rationing', *Journal of Monetary Economics*, 18, 159-179.

World Bank (1989): *World Development Report 1989: Financial Systems and Development*, New York: Oxford University Press.

———. (1993): *The East Asian Miracle*, New York: Oxford University Press.

19

Scale Economies in Banking

Indian Experience in Deregulated Era

Goutam Chatterjee

Introduction

TILL the 'seventies, bankers all over the world operated in beneficially regulated markets and as cartels, restricting competition. Since then, several developments such as the deregulation of the banking sector, the improvement in the banking technology and the growth of non-bank financial intermediaries like mutual funds have taken place, changing the financial environment drastically. The banking industry has come to be characterised with intense competition, declining margins on traditional banking business, increased cost pressures and greater risk. As a fall out, instances of bank failures and mergers have increased. While banks have ventured into new lines of business, increased competition has brought in its wake increased reliance on cost minimisation and improvement in efficiency.

The Indian banking scenario too has undergone a change in the recent past. The financial sector liberalisation attempted since 1991, has allowed more operational flexibility and functional autonomy to banks than hitherto with a view to enhancing their efficiency, productivity and profitability. The broad direction of the policy reform has been towards rationalisation of the administered interest rate structure followed by deregulation of most of the deposit and lending rates, reduction in the governmental pre-emption of banks' funds in the form of CRR and SLR and relative freedom in branch licensing. Simultaneously, the supervisory mechanism has been strengthened and prudential norms relating to capital adequacy, income recognition, asset classification and provisioning have been put in place. Operational flexibility has infused a great deal of competition among the Indian banks which has been further heightened by introduction of new players in the market. New domestic banks have been allowed entry in the private sector and foreign banks have been permitted to open offices in India, subject to fulfilment of specified eligibility criteria. Establishment of mutual funds both in the public and private sector as also the growing influence of non-bank financial companies have increased the competition from outside the banking system. In such a milieu, the banking industry has to sustain itself by reaching new heights of efficiency.

Several types of efficiencies are associated with a production process. One such is the scale efficiency which relates the firm size to its production/cost curve. At present there exists a wide variation in the size of the banks operating in India. Thus a question arises: will all the banks of varying sizes be equally efficient under competitive environment? The paper makes an attempt to study the scale economy aspect of banks in India following the cost function approach and using accounting data for the year 1994-95 of all scheduled commercial banks (excluding the Regional Rural banks). The remaining part of the paper is organised as follows: Section II presents a few stylized facts of Indian banking industry. Section III reviews a number of studies on scale and scope economies in banking, mostly covering the experience of the U.S.A. and raises some conceptual issues. Section IV outlines the methodology of the present study while Section V presents the econometric evidence on scale economies. Section VI provides the broad conclusions and policy issues emanating from the study.

The author is grateful to Dr. T.V. Sethuraman, Professor, Indian Institute of Technology, Mumbai and Dr. A.K. Nag, Director, DESACS for their guidance in preparing this paper. The author acknowledges the help received from Sarvashri V.S. Damodar, A.L. Antony and T.V. Sreenivas of Computer Cell of D.B.O.D., in extracting the required data from their data base. The author is thankful to Shri Partho Ray of the Department of Economic Analysis and Policy for his comments on an earlier draft of this paper. The author is also indebted to an anonymous referee, for his valuable comments. The errors and omissions remaining, if any, is the author's responsibility.

SECTION II

Indian Banking System: A Size-wise Profile

As at the end of March 1995, Indian banking system comprised 27 Public sector banks, 29 Private sector banks (including 6 newly opened banks), 27 foreign banks (including 4 banks which opened their maiden branch in India during 1993-94/1994-95), 2 non-scheduled banks and 196 Regional Rural Banks besides the Co-operative banks. Our analysis was restricted to the Scheduled Commercial banks (excluding the Regional Rural Banks) for similarity of their operations and their predominant position in the banking industry. Further, the newly opened 6 Indian Private sector banks and 4 foreign banks were also excluded for lack of sufficient data. Thus, the study was based on the operation of 73 commercial banks during the year 1994-95. The data for the study were collected from the published Balance Sheets and Profit & Loss Accounts of these banks.

The inter-se size difference of the Indian banking system, based on the sample banks, can be gauged from the following Table.

TABLE 1

Variability in the Basic Parameters of the Indian Banks - As of March 1995

(Amount in Rs. Crore)

	Deposits	Total Assets or Liabilities	Invest-ments	Advances	Number of Employees	Number of Branches
Average	5526	6944	2355	2835	13187	677
Minimum	23	27	5	4	31	1
Maximum	85122	121814	41673	48530	232086	8878

The 73 banks included in the study can be grouped into the following classes based on their size of deposits.

TABLE 2

Distribution of Banks in India according to Deposit Size

Deposit Size (Rs. crore)	Number of Banks	Broad Constituents
1. Upto 500	19	Small Private Sector Banks
2. 501 - 2000	17	Medium Private Sector Banks
3. 2001 - 4000	10	Large Private Sector Banks + Small Public Sector Banks
4. 4001 - 7000	14	Medium Public Sector Banks
5. More than 7000	13	Large Public Sector Banks

These size classes have been used for further analysis in the study. Variations in some of the operational parameters of the banks in each of the above size classes are brought out in the following Table.

TABLE 3

Deposit Size-wise Variation in the Operational Parameters of Banks in India

Parameter/size-class (Rs. crore)	1 Upto 500	2 501-2000	3 2001-4000	4 4001-7000	5 More than 7000
1. Liability Mix					
Deposits	0.74	0.82	0.80	0.81	0.79
Borrowings	0.12	0.08	0.06	0.05	0.05
2. Deposit Mix					
Current Deposits	0.15	0.15	0.17	0.16	0.18
Savings Deposits	0.16	0.14	0.17	0.21	0.24
Term Deposits	0.69	0.71	0.66	0.63	0.58
3. Asset Mix					
Advances	0.48	0.48	0.44	0.39	0.40
Investments	0.30	0.30	0.32	0.34	0.34
4. Credit Mix					
Cash Credit etc.	0.63	0.58	0.66	0.59	0.62
Term Loan	0.18	0.24	0.21	0.28	0.25
Bills Discounted etc.	0.20	0.18	0.13	0.13	0.14
5. Interest Income in Total Income	0.89	0.85	0.84	0.86	0.88
6. Interest Expense in Total Expense	0.58	0.60	0.55	0.59	0.60
7. Operating Expense in Total Expense	0.22	0.24	0.29	0.29	0.30
8. Average Cost per unit of Asset (in Rs.)	0.0805	0.0752	0.0772	0.0771	0.08

The following broad trends are discernible from the above Table:

(i) The share of borrowings was relatively high in the two smallest size classes.

(ii) The share of term deposits was higher in the smaller banks than the larger ones.

(iii) The share of investments in total assets was higher for large sized banks than for the small sized banks

(iv) Credit-mix of the smaller banks was more concentrated in favour of short-term loans (i.e. cash credit, bills etc.).

(v) Operating expense as a share of total expense was found to be high for the large sized banks.

(vi) The average cost per unit of asset was U-shaped and reached the minimum in the second size-class i.e., for banks with deposits between Rs. 501-2000 crore.

SECTION III

Scale Economies in Banking : Some Conceptual Issues and A Select Resume

A number of studies have been conducted to measure scale and scope economies in banking/financial institutions largely based on the experiences of U.S.A. The broad approach followed in these studies has been to specify a suitable production/cost function[1] for banking activity, estimate parameters of the cost function using accounting data of sample banks/financial institutions and finally arrive at measures of scale and/or scope economies at the sample mean and/or for different output ranges. However, these studies differed in their approaches in defining banks' output, selecting the functional form of the production/cost function, the range of bank sizes included in the sample and the measures of scale and scope economies used.

What Do the Banks Produce?

A fundamental issue in studying the production economies of a banking firm is: what constitutes a bank's output? While there is a wide consensus on the multi-product nature of a bank, views differ on the conceptual issue of the appropriate definition of outputs and inputs in the banking industry and consequently the banking costs. The two most commonly used approaches are the 'intermediation approach' and the 'production approach'. Under the intermediation approach, financial institutions are viewed as intermediaries which transform and transfer financial resources from units in surplus to units in deficit. In this approach, deposits are treated as input alongwith capital and labour and earning assets are taken as measures of output. Also, consistent with this approach, costs are defined to include both interest expenses and other operating expenses.

The production approach, on the other hand, views financial institutions as producers of services associated with individual loan and deposit accounts using capital and labour. Under this approach, it follows that number of accounts of each type form the appropriate definitions of output. Interest expenses are excluded in measuring the cost.

Murray and White (1983), H.Y. Kim (1986), Noulas, Ray and Miller (1990), Glass and Mckillop (1992) among others adopted intermediation approach to define banks' output while Gilligan and Smirlock (1984), Gilligan, Smirlock and Marshall (1984) based their analysis on production approach. Benston, Hanweck and Humphrey (1982) also adopted production approach but they combined number of deposit and loan accounts in several ways to obtain composite indices of bank output. Berger, Hanweck and Humphrey (1987) measured bank output and costs using both production and intermediation approach and observed that the scale economy measures are qualitatively comparable under both the methods. Berger and Humphrey (1991) followed a variation of intermediation approach where costs included both operating and interest expenses and output was measured on the basis of 'value added' approach. Banking functions which are associated with a substantial labour or physical capital expenditure were identified as the major outputs. As consensus on what should constitute an output measure of a bank has eluded economists, it would be ideal to define banks' output adopting both 'intermediation' and 'production' approaches and test the sensitivity of the scale economy measures.

Form of the Cost Function for the Banking Industry

A number of studies prior to the 1980s, assumed production function of the Cobb-Douglas or CES type, which were not capable of generating a U-shaped average cost curve, implying that returns to scale would remain constant across all output levels. Consequently, an optimum size of a bank could not be determined. In order to correct this shortcoming, most of the studies since 1980s have selected Translog (TL) function to represent banks' cost structure which allows multiple outputs to enter as separate variables and can generate U-shaped average cost curve. Thus scale economies can vary according to the size of the bank. However, one important limitation of the TL function is its inability to admit zero output which is required for estimation of scope economy and/or product specific scale economy. This led to the use of more flexible cost functions in recent studies. Glass & Mckillop (1992) used a hybrid TL function while Hunter, Timme and Yang (1990) used minflex Laurent approximation to estimate the scale and scope economy. McAllister & McManus (1992) observed that TL cost function may behave poorly if the global behaviour of the approximated function differs from its local behaviour and used nonparametric techniques which are designed to estimate a function uniformly well over some region.

Choice of the Sample

Previous studies on scale economies in banking can be grouped in two classes based on the choice of sample banks included in the study. Most of the studies included a cross section of banks of all sizes and typically found scale economies among small banks —

usually banks with less than $100 million in total assets — and scale diseconomies among larger banks. Some authors, however, restricted their study only to large banks (above $1 billion in total assets) and found evidence of scale economies for relatively large banks ($2 billion to $10 billion of total assets). McAllister and McManus (1992) demonstrated that such results could be due to trying to fit a single TL function over a population of banks that varied widely in terms of size and output mix which systematically misrepresented costs for certain types of banks leading to specification bias.

Measures of Scale Economies

Conventionally, scale economies are measured through elasticity of cost with respect to output keeping product mix unchanged. Further, as the number of branches enter as an independent variable in most of the cost function specifications, in this measure, this variable is also assumed to remain constant as output expansion takes place.[2] Arguing that banks expand primarily by opening new offices (which attract new accounts) rather than by adding accounts to existing offices, Benston, Hanweck and Humphrey (1982) defined an augmented scale economy measure which takes into account both the sources of banks' output expansion.[3] Noulas, Ray and Miller (1990) measured the 'plant' level scale economy through inclusion of branch variable in the cost function and 'firm' level scale economy by excluding the same from the cost equation. Berger *et al.* (1987) developed a new measure of scale economy called Expansion Path Scale Economy (EPSCE) which captures the impact of changing scale and product mix simultaneously by choosing the mean output levels of representative banks in successive size classes as expansion path.

The studies discussed so far assumed that all sample banks are technically efficient and the observed cost represents the frontier. Berger & Humphrey (1991) observed that economies or diseconomies found in such studies were relatively small despite the fact that bank costs revealed a striking degree of dispersion. The authors estimated a 'thick frontier' cost function and showed that inefficiency residuals completely dominated scale and product mix effects. Review of other studies which fitted frontier cost/production function and estimated scale efficiency therefrom, has not been attempted in this paper.

Scale Economies of Banking in India

Most of the studies referred to above are based on data from U.S. banking industry. Literature on scale and/ or scope economies of Indian banks are very few. Rangarajan & Mamipally (1972) studied economies of scale in Indian banking by regressing total operating costs of banks on size of deposit and other control variables like deposit-mix, number and spread of branches etc. and derived the shape of marginal and average cost curves. Using the data for the period 1967-69, this study found that the marginal cost curve reached its minimum at the deposit size of Rs. 300 crore which was taken as the least-cost size of the banks. The authors acknowledged major shortcoming of the study as its exclusive reliance on deposits as indicator of banks' output. Ray & Sanyal (1995) conducted an econometric investigation of scale efficiency in Indian commercial banking based on the data for the year 1989-90. They fitted a TL function as also a hybrid TL function and minflex Laurent's approximation to cost data in the single equation framework as well as in the framework of a system of equations (which included cost share equations). The study concluded that substantial scale economies exist among the sample banks and it would be more cost effective to expand output at existing branches than to expand output through opening of new branches. The study was, however, based on a sample of only 16 nationalised banks which constrained the authors to make several compromises such as, aggregation of different output indicators into a single index, dropping of capital price variable from the cost equation etc., thus making the results somewhat circumspect. The authors considered number of branches as an output variable whereas in all other studies the same was considered as a control variable. This specification is quite confusing when used to measure the scope economies of banking.

SECTION IV

Methodology of the Present Study

For reasons discussed in Section III, this study has preferred the cost function approach to measure the scale economies of banks in India.[4] Data on output and costs for the banks included in the study were culled out from the Balance Sheets and Profit & Loss Accounts. Balance Sheets provide information on different components of assets and liabilities in value terms but they do not provide information on number of deposit and loan accounts serviced by the banks. Therefore, 'intermediation' approach was used to define banks' output instead of 'production' approach. Accordingly, total advances and total investments (in value terms) were taken as output indicators and labour, fixed capital and purchased funds (deposits plus borrowings) were taken as inputs. Consistent with the intermediation approach, operating costs included expenses on labour and fixed capital as also interest expenses (on deposits and borrowings). Price of labour was determined by the ratio of establishment expenses to the total number of employees (irrespective of their grades)[5]. Price of capital was determined by the ratio of the sum of expenditure on rent, repairs and depreciation to the total value of assets.[6] Price of the purchased fund was determined by the ratio of total interest expenses to the outstanding deposits and borrowings as on the balance sheet date. Apart from the output variables and the input prices, the number of branches was included as a control variable in the cost function.

A Translog model was fitted to the cost function as follows:

$$\ln C = a_0 + \Sigma a_i{*}\ln y_i + \Sigma b_j{*}\ln P_j + 1/2\ \Sigma\Sigma c_{ir}{*}\ln y_i{*}\ln y_r + 1/2\ \Sigma\Sigma d_{js}{*}\ln P_j{*}\ln P_s + \Sigma\Sigma f_{ij}{*}\ln y_i{*}\ln P_j + g_0{*}\ln B + \Sigma g_i{*}\ln y_i{*}\ln B + \Sigma h_j{*}\ln P_h{*}\ln B + k/2{*}\ln B{*}\ln B. \quad ...(1)$$

where, C is total operating cost including interest expenses,

Y_i's are the output indicators; i = 1, 2,

P_j's are the input prices; j = 1,2,3,

and B is number of branches.

Symmetry condition required

$$c_{ir} = c_{ri} \text{ for all } i,r \text{ and } d_{js} = d_{sj} \text{ for all } j,s. \quad ...(2)$$

Further, linear homogeneity of the cost function in input prices imposed the following conditions on the parameters:

$$\Sigma\ b_j = 1; \quad ...(3a)$$

$$\Sigma\ d_{js} = 0 \text{ for } j = 1,2,3; \quad ...(3b)$$

$$\Sigma\ f_{ij} = 0 \text{ for } i = 1,2 \quad ...(3c)$$

$$\Sigma\ h_j = 0 \quad ...(3d)$$

All the independent variables were normalised with respect to their means before taking logarithms.

The cost function was augmented by the input share equations as follows:

By Shephard's lemma, factor demand equation for input j is

$$X_j = \delta C/\delta P_j \quad ...(4)$$

So that $\delta \ln C/\delta \ln P_j = P_j{*}X_j/C$, the share of jth input (S_j) in the cost.

But, $\delta \ln C/\delta \ln P_j = b_j + \Sigma d_{js}{*}\ln P_s + \Sigma f_{ij}{*}\ln y_i + h_j{*}\ln B.$ ...(5)

Thus,

$$S_j = b_j + \Sigma d_{js}{*}\ln P_s + \Sigma f_{ij}{*}\ln y_i + h_j{*}\ln B, \text{ for } j=1,2,3 \quad ...(6)$$

This together with the cost function formed the system of equations to be solved.

However, as $\Sigma S_j = 1$, one of the input share equations, viz., that of the capital, was dropped and the remaining 3 equations in (1) and (6) were simultaneously solved through Seemingly Unrelated Regression (SUR) technique.

After obtaining the parameter estimates as above, Ray Scale Economies (RSCE) were measured as elasticity of cost with respect to output keeping product mix constant.

$$RSCE = \Sigma \delta \ln C/\delta \ln y_i = \Sigma a_i + \Sigma\Sigma c_{ir}{*}\ln y_r + \Sigma\Sigma f_{ij}{*}\ln P_j + \Sigma g_i{*}\ln B \quad ...(7)$$

RSCE<1 implies economies of scale while RSCE>1 implies diseconomies of scale. RSCE=1 means there is no economy of scale.

RSCE for the whole sample was evaluated at the overall means of each variable which by construction equals 1. Therefore, RSCE for the whole sample was Σa_i. To see how scale economies change over the various ranges of output, RSCEs were also evaluated at different data points.[7]

RSCE as defined above, keeps the number of branches fixed as output expands. Thus, it can be considered as a measure of scale economy when output expands from the existing branches (labelled as 'plant' level scale economy and denoted by $RSCE_p$). However, as argued in the literature, banks (firms) normally operate through multiple branches (plants) and output expansion can take place by opening new branches rather than by expanding the output in existing branches. For measuring the scale economies when the number of branches are allowed to vary along with the output, following the approach of Noulas *et al.*, branch variable was dropped from the cost function at (1) as well as from the equation (7). This measure is lebelled as 'firm' level scale economy and denoted by $RSCE_f$.

Following Berger *et al.* (1987), Expansion Path Scale Economies (EPSCE), which is defined as elasticity of incremental cost with respect to incremental output along the expansion path (which may have changing product mix) was evaluated through:

$$EPSCE(Q^A, Q^B) = \Sigma\left[\frac{Q_i^B - Q_i^A}{Q_i^B} * \frac{C(Q^B)}{C(Q^B) - C(Q^A)} * \frac{\delta \ln C(Q^B)}{\delta \ln Q_i}\right] \quad ...(8)$$

where $Q^A = \{Q_1^A, Q_2^A\}$ and $Q^B=\{Q_1^B, Q_2^B\}$ are the output bundles on expansion path AB and $C(Q^A)$ and $C(Q^B)$ are the costs associated with the above output, obtained from equation (1). $EPSCE(Q^A,Q^B)<1$ indicates scale economy on segment AB, while $EPSCE(Q^A, Q^B)>1$ indicates diseconomies.

As in the case of RSCE, EPSCEs were also measured at 'plant' and 'firm' levels by including and excluding the 'branch' variable in the cost function (1). They are denoted by $EPSCE_p$ and $EPSCE_F$ respectively.

SECTION V
EMPIRICAL RESULTS FOR INDIA

Estimation of the Cost Function

Translog cost model described in equation (1), together with the input share equations given in (6) fitted the data well as can be seen by the high R^2 value and low standard error (Table-4). There was no evidence of heteroskedasticity of the errors.[8] The parameter estimates are given in Table-5. All output and price coefficients were positive and statistically significant implying positive cost elasticities and input shares. The branch coefficient was positive and statistically significant.

TABLE 4

Goodness of Fit of the Cost Function and Share Equations under Alternative Models

	With Branch Variable	Without Branch Variable
1. Cost Function		
R^2	0.9978	0.9869
D-W Statistic	2.04	1.97
Mean of Dependent Variable	14.2802	14.2802
Std. Error of Regression	0.0794	0.195
2. Share Equation for Labour		
R^2	0.891	0.398
D-W Statistic	1.87	1.54
Mean of Dependent Variable	0.1965	0.1965
Std. Error of Regression	0.0303	0.0728
3. Share Equation for Borrowings		
R^2	0.8921	0.4492
D-W Statistic	1.93	1.56
Mean of Dependent Variable	0.7511	0.7511
Std. Error of Regression	0.0343	0.0757

For measuring the scale economies at the firm or bank level, the system of equations constituting (1) and (6) was reestimated after dropping the branch variable. The model omitting the 'branch' variable reported slightly lower R^2 and higher standard error for the cost equation. The estimation of the share equations turned out to be more imprecise. Some interaction terms had reverse signs but all output and price coefficients were positive (Table-5).

TABLE 5

Parameter Estimates of the Cost Function for Alternative Models

Parameter	With Branch Variable		Without Branch Variable	
	Estimate	Std. Error	Estimate	Std. Error
a_0	15.643**	0.127	15.554**	0.027
a_1	0.419**	0.042	0.368**	0.086
a_2	0.519**	0.044	0.636**	0.083
b_1	0.270**	0.006	0.195**	0.013
b_2	0.060**	0.006	0.064**	0.008
b_3	0.670**	0.007	0.741**	0.011
c_{11}	0.112	0.071	-0.125	0.126
c_{12}	-0.055	0.066	0.164	0.114
c_{22}	0.044	0.071	-0.178	0.108
d_{11}	0.092**	0.013	-0.052*	0.02
d_{12}	0.023**	0.008	0.042**	0.012
d_{13}	-0.115**	0.011	0.010	0.014
d_{22}	0.056**	0.008	0.042**	0.011
d_{23}	-0.079**	0.007	-0.084**	0.01
d_{33}	0.195**	0.012	0.074**	0.015
f_{11}	-0.064**	0.009	-0.080**	0.023
f_{12}	-0.016	0.01	-0.008	0.015
f_{13}	0.080**	0.011	0.088**	0.02
f_{21}	0.008	0.01	0.082**	0.021
f_{22}	0.008	0.01	0.006	0.014
f_{23}	-0.015	0.011	-0.088**	0.019
g_0	0.056*	0.023		
g_1	-0.013	0.013		
g_2	-0.001	0.013		
h_1	0.061**	0.004		
h_2	0.003	0.003		
h_3	-0.065**	0.004		
k	-0.005	0.011		

*: Significantly different from zero at 5% level.

**: Significantly different from zero at 1% level.

The Translog cost function represents a very general production structure which is non-homothetic and has no restriction on elasticities of substitution. However, by imposing restrictions on the values of certain parameters, TL cost function nests more simplified models like homogeneous or homothetic production structure as also production structure with unitary elasticities of substitution. Validity of such restrictions can be tested statistically through likelihood ratio (LR) tests.[9]

Restrictions on parameters which reduce the production structure underlying a TL cost function homogenous in outputs are,

$$\Sigma c_{ir} = 0;\ r = 1,2$$

$$\Sigma f_{ij} = 0;\ j = 1,2,3$$

$$\text{and} \quad \Sigma g_i = 0. \qquad \text{...(9)}$$

However, the validity of such restrictions was rejected as the LR test statistic at 933.7 far exceeded the critical value of 11.1 for Chi-square distribution with 5 d.f.[10] at 5% level of significance.

Homotheticity is tested through separability of the variable cost function in the outputs and all other variables. For the TL function at (1), the testable restrictions for homotheticity are

$$f_{ij} = 0;\ i = 1,\ 2 \text{ and } j = 1,\ 2,\ 3.$$

$$\text{and} \quad g_i = 0;\ i = 1,2. \qquad \text{...(10)}$$

The LR test statistic in this case was 205.9 and was also rejected at 5 per cent level of significance (Critical value of Chi-square distribution with 6 d.f.[11] = 12.6). This implied that a valid aggregation of banks' outputs into a single index is not possible and the cost function representing the banking firms must take explicit account of the multi-product nature of banks' output.

Ray Scale Economies (RSCE)

Based on the parameter estimates of the cost function, the ray scale economies (RSCE) were calculated for the whole sample as well as at different data points using the formula at (7). RSCE for the whole sample was evaluated at the sample mean value of each independent variable. RSCE for the whole sample at 'plant' level i.e. when output expands at the existing branches, was estimated at 0.9384 with a standard error of 0.0208. Thus, $RSCE_p$ for the whole sample was found to be significantly less than 1[12]. This means that a bank whose output is at the respective averages of the whole sample, will find it cost efficient to increase its scale of operation (equi-proportionate increase in both the outputs) provided it can handle the increased business without increasing the number of branches. RSCE for the whole sample at 'firm' level i.e. when output expands through opening of new branches, was however, estimated at 1.0047 with a standard error of 0.0188. Thus, $RSCE_F$ for the whole sample was found to be not significantly different from 1[13]. This means that an average sized bank will not have any cost benefit from equi-proportionate increase in its output if the number of branches also increase alongwith the output.

As TL cost function can have varying scale economies at different output sizes, RSCEs were also evaluated at different data points. Data points chosen in this study were the averages (geometric mean) of output and other variables of banks in 5 size groups detailed in Section II. To neutralise the effect of input price changes on the cost elasticities, input prices were kept constant at the overall mean (G.M.) of all banks.

Table 6 shows that at the 'plant' level, significant economies of scale exists among the commercial banks in India in the first four size classes i.e. with deposit size upto Rs. 7,000 crore. RSCE for the largest deposit size class was, however, not significantly less than 1. This means that all private sector banks (Indian and foreign) as also the small and medium sized public sector banks will find it cost efficient to increase their scale of operation (equi-proportionate increase in advances and investments) with the help of the existing number of branches.

The picture changes substantially if one looks at the scale economy figures at the 'firm' level. Here the economies of scale operate only upto the second size class i.e. for deposits upto Rs. 2000 crores which include small and medium sized private sector (Indian and foreign) banks. At higher deposit size classes, the scale economy measures are not significantly different from 1. This implies that the cost efficiency which some banks could enjoy from increasing the scale of operation would be lost if the number of branches also increase commensurately with the increase in the output. However, this mode of output expansion will be cost efficient for the very small sized banks. This result also suggests that there exists unutilised capacity at the branch level in a large segment of the banks in India.

Expansion Path Scale Economies (EPSCE)

EPSCE which is defined as the elasticity of cost with respect to output when the output mix changes along the expansion path was estimated through equation (8). The expansion path chosen for this purpose were the mean (geometric) output levels of 5 bank size-groups referred to earlier. Under the condition that output expansion takes place at the existing branches, EPSCE for the first three size classes (i.e. banks with deposits upto Rs. 4,000 crore) were significantly lower than 1 while for the size-group 4 i.e. banks with deposits Rs. 4,001-7,000 crore, EPSCE was not significantly different from 1 (Table 6). Thus if banks expand their output from existing branches but alter their output mix in the process of this expansion, then banks from the first 3 size-groups, which comprise the private sector banks (Indian and foreign) and small public sector banks, will gain in terms of cost efficiency. However, in this process of output expansion, if new branches are opened to handle the increased output, banks in none of the size-groups will gain in terms of cost efficiency as EPSCE measures for none of the size groups at 'firm' level was found to be significantly different from 1.

TABLE 6

Scale Economy Estimates by Size Class

Deposit size class (in Rs. crore)	$RSCE_p$	$EPSCE_p$	$RSCE_F$	$EPSCE_F$
Upto 500	0.8599** (0.0128)	0.9284** (0.0083)	0.9316** (0.0216)	0.9899 (0.0095)
501-2000	0.9156** (0.0112)	0.9355** (0.0106)	0.969* (0.0162)	0.9972 (0.0076)
2001-4000	0.9424** (0.0135)	0.9006** (0.0252)	0.9888 (0.0153)	0.9978 (0.0083)
4001-7000	0.9478** (0.0188)	0.9688 (0.0305)	1.0015 (0.0176)	1.0210 (0.0143)
More than 7000	0.9783 (0.0265)	-	1.0292 (0.0258)	-
Whole Sample	0.9384** (0.0208)	-	1.0047 (0.0188)	-

*: Significantly lower than 1 at 5% level.

**: Significantly lower than 1 at 1% level.

SECTION VI

SUMMARY AND CONCLUSIONS

Based on the accounting data of 73 scheduled commercial banks for the year 1994-95, it was observed that a translog function adequately represented the cost behaviour of the banks in India. The feasibility of explaining the costs through a homogeneous or a homothetic production structure was statistically rejected.

Based on the estimated parameters of the cost function, the study measured scale economies at different output ranges for the banks in India. Two modes of output expansion viz., constant output-mix and changing output-mix were considered. Under each mode, the effect of output expansion from the existing branches as also through opening of new branches was studied. It is observed that most of the banks in India will gain in cost efficiency if they expand their business from the existing branches and keep the output-mix unaltered. However, with constant output-mix, if new branches are opened to handle the increased business, only the small and medium sized private sector banks will gain in cost efficiency. The scope for increased cost efficiency was found to be narrow in the case of changing output-mix. In this case, private sector banks of all sizes and the small public sector banks will stand to benefit from output expansion from the existing branches. However, with addition of branches alongwith output, the study found no evidence of scale economies in the banks of any size-group. The findings of the study therefore are:

(i) there exists scale economies in the Indian banking industry;

(ii) expansion of output at existing branches is more cost efficient than expansion through new branches; and

(iii) greater cost efficiencies are gained through equi-proportionate expansion of output levels rather than their non-proportional expansion.

One policy implication of the results found in the study is that with increased competition and the need to minimise the cost, a number of banks, notably those in the private sector, may find that they are not operating at the optimum size. This raises the issue of regrouping and merger among the banks with a view to reaping the benefits of scale economy.

The objective of cost minimisation under perfect competition presupposes that firms are price takers and therefore can not alter the revenue structure. In actual practice, this may not be so as individual banks may be able to exercise a fair degree of control on the prices they charge on their financial products. The existence of several imperfections, particularly the information imperfection, and service differentiation are some of the factors contributing to the asymmetric price structure of the banking industry.

With the greater degree of financial liberalisation, the banking industry in India would have to cope up with the increasing pressures of competition in future. Indeed, the competitive forces are going to be further strengthened with greater degree of openness in the external capital account and growing trade in financial services. In this milieu, optimising the size of the firm will be of critical importance. The results of this study showed that while there are unrealised potential of scale economies in the case of a large number of banks which can expand their output without expanding their branch network, there are also opportunities for a smaller number of banks which can increase their cost efficiency by expanding the scale of operation through increased branch network.

Notes

1. A fundamental result of duality theory is, provided that certain regularity conditions are satisfied, there exist cost and production functions which are dual to each other. The regularity conditions on the cost function in multiproduct case are that it be non-negative, real valued, non-decreasing, strictly positive for non-zero output and linearly homogeneous and concave in input prices for each output. In such a case, the structure of production can be studied empirically using either a production function or a cost function - the choice is made on statistical grounds. Panzar and Willig (1977) has further shown that when outputs are produced in cost efficient manner, degree of scale economies is the same, whether it is measured using the transformation function or the cost function. As the specification that input levels are endogenous and the output levels are exogenous is more plausible in the case of banking industry, almost all the studies used the cost function approach to measure the scale economies. Further, the duality conditions are generally derived in a deterministic framework. The correspondence of these conditions to the stochastic frameworks could be an area of study.
2. This measure is also known as 'plant' or 'branch' level scale economy.
3. This measure is also known as 'firm' or 'bank' level scale economy.
4. Some doubts may be expressed about the reasonableness of the underlying assumption in this case that banks in India, especially the 27 nationalised banks, produce their outputs in a cost efficient manner. It may, however, be mentioned that while some social objectives were behind nationalisation of the banks, it has been subsequently realised that normal profit maximisation/cost minimisation objective can not be altogether ignored, which formed the very basis of financial sector liberalisation. Thus it may be assumed that over a period of last few years, even the nationalised banks are moving towards the objective of cost minimisation.
5. Arguing that banks vary in composition of their employees, in terms of officers, clerks and subordinates staff, Keshari and Paul (1994) converted the employees data into homogeneous units of subordinate staff using the ratio of 1/3:1/2:1 for officers, clerks and subordinate staff, respectively.
6. One could use the book value of premises, furniture and fixture in the denominator. However, as rented premises are used for performing a significant portion of the banking business in India, book values of the premises shown in the Balance Sheet are very low. Use of number of branches in the denominator has the limitation in that the cost of maintaining branches located in different areas (viz., rural, semi-urban, urban and metropolitan area) can be very much different. Thus, it was assumed that use of fixed assets is proportional to the total assets maintained.
7. Statistical significance of difference of RSCE values from 1 was tested using the ANALYZ procedure of TSP.
8. Heteroskedasticity of the errors was tested by regressing squares of the residuals on size parameters like deposits, advances, total assets etc., separately. In none of the cases, the regression coefficients were found to be significantly different from zero.
9. It has been shown that estimation through Zellner's SUR procedure are asymptotically equivalent to MLE and therefore, variance-covariance matrix obtained in the final iteration can be reasonably used to perform LR tests.
10. The actual number of additional restrictions are 5 in view of equation 3(c).
11. The actual number of additional restrictions are 6 in view of equation 3(c).
12. Significance of the scale economy measure is tested through H_0 : $RSCE_p = 1$ vs. H_1 : $RSCE_p < 1$, the test statistic for which is (RSCEP-1)/ s.e. ($RSCE_p$) and it follows t-distribution with 52 d.f. under H_0. Critical value for the one-sided test at 5% level of significance is -1.6747.
13. The test in this case is exactly similar to that for $RSCE_p$ described above but the test statistic follows t-distribution with 58 d.f., critical value for which at 5% level of significance is -1.6715.

References

Benston G.J., G.A. Hanweck and D.B. Humphrey (1982): Scale Economies in Banking: a Restructuring and Reassessment", *Journal of Money, Credit and Banking*, 14, Part-I, pp. 435-456.

Berger A.N. and D.B. Humphrey (1991): "The Dominance of Inefficiencies Over Scale and Product Mix Economies in Banking", *Journal of Monetary Economics*, 28, pp. 117-148.

Berger A.N., G.A. Hanweck and D.B. Humphrey (1987): "Competitive Viability in Banking", *Journal of Monetary Economics*, 20, pp. 501-520.

Christensen L.R. and W.H. Greene (1976): "Economies of Scale in U.S. Electric Power Generation", *Journal of Political Economy*, 84, pp. 655-676.

Christensen L.R., D.W. Jorgenson and L.J. Lau (1973): "Transcendental Logarithmic Production Frontiers", *The Review of Economics and Statistics*, 55, pp. 28-45.

Clark J.A. (1988): "Economies of Scale and Scope at Depository Financial Institutions: a Review of Literature", *Economic Review, Federal Reserve Bank of Kansas City*, Sept./Oct. 1988, pp. 16-33.

Gilligan T. and M. Smirlock (1984): "An Empirical Study of the Joint Production and Scale Economies in Commercial Banking", *Journal of Banking and Finance*, 8, pp. 67-76.

Gilligan T., M. Smirlock and W. Marshall (1984): "Scale and Scope Economies in Multiproduct Banking Firm", *Journal of Monetary Economics*, 13, pp. 393-405.

Glass J.C. and D.G. Mckillop (1992): "An Empirical Analysis of Scale and Scope Economies and Technical Change in an Irish Multiproduct Banking Firm", *Journal of Banking Finance*, 16, pp. 423-437.

Humphrey D.B. (1995): "Cost and Scale Economies in Banking Intermediation" in R. Aspinwall and R. Eisenbers (eds.), *Handbook of Banking Strategy*, Wiley, U.S.A.

Hunter W.C. and S.G. Timme (1986): "Technical Change, Organisational Form and the Structures of Bank Production", *Journal of Money, Credit and Banking*, 18, pp. 152-166.

Hunter W.C., S.G. Timme and W.K. Yang (1990): "An Examination of Cost Subadditivity and Multiproduct Production in Large U.S. Banks", *Journal of Money, Credit and Banking*, 22, pp. 504-525.

Keshari P.K. and M. Thomas Paul (1994): "Relative Efficiency of Foreign and Domestic Banks", *Economic and Political Weekly*, Feb. 26, pp. M. 31-36.

Kim H.Y. (1986): "Economies of Scale and Economies of Scope in Multiproduct Financial Institutions: Further Evidence from Credit Unions", *Journal of Money, Credit and Banking*, 18, pp. 220-26.

McAllister P.H. and D. McManus (1993): "Resolving the Scale Efficiency Puzzle in Banking", *Journal of Banking and Finance,* 17, pp. 389-405.

Murray J.D. and R.H. White (1983): "Economies of Scale and Economies of Scope in Multiproduct Financial Institutions: A Study of British Columbia Credit Unions", *Journal of Finance*, 38, June, pp. 887-901.

Noulas A.G., S.C. Ray and S.M. Miller (1990): "Returns to Scale and Input Substitution for Large U.S. Banks", *Journal of Money, Credit and Banking*, 22, pp. 94-108.

Panzar J.C. and R.D. Willig (1977): "Economies of Scale in Multi-Output Production:, *Quarterly Journal of Economics*, Vol. XCI, pp. 481-493.

Rangarajan C. and P. Mamipally (1972): "Economies of Scale in Banking", *Technical Studies Prepared for the Banking Commission*, Reserve Bank of India, Vol.II.

Ray Indrajit and S. Sanyal (1995): "Scale Efficiency in Indian Commercial Banking: An Econometric Investigation", *Prajnan*, 23 (No. 4), pp. 459-486.

20

Technical, Allocative and Scale Efficiency of Public Sector Banks in India

Abhiman Das

THE banking system plays a crucial role in mobilising savings and allocating them to the users with the objective of reducing risks for the provider of funds while trying to maximise returns. The process of financial intermediation supports increasing capital accumulation through institutional savings and investments and fosters economic growth. Therefore, the gains of the real sector economy depend on how efficiently the financial sector performs the function of financial intermediation (Rangarajan, 1997). The prime focus of the development of Indian banking system has basically been confined to ensure timely and adequate credit support for the viable and productive sectors of the economy. Indeed, nationalisation of major banks in 1969 was a historic step in recognition of the potential of the banking system to promote broader economic objectives viz. growth, regional balance and diffusion of economic power. Since nationalisation, Indian banking industry has made an impressive progress, especially in extending geographical spread and functional reach. Since 1969, the number of commercial bank branches has increased over seven-fold, to a little over 64,000 in 1996. In 1969, deposits amounted to 13 per cent of GDP and advances to 10 per cent. By 1996, deposits had risen to about 43 per cent and advances to 26 per cent. While these developments reflect growth of the banking system, it is necessary to see whether the system has been efficient or not. Many observers believe that nationalisation has led to a myriad of restrictions and social obligations affecting the productivity and profitability of banks. Several committees [Luther Committee (1977), Goiporia Committee (1991) and Narasimham Committee (1991)] set up to examine the efficiency and productivity of the banking system *inter alia* envisaged the need for deregulation, competitiveness, strengthening of capital base and improving customer services. From there to move over to a more comprehensive financial sector reform effective in 1992 was only a logical step. As a result, banks are required to move towards efficient assets-liability management (ALM) to achieve a high degree of competition and efficiency as against safety and stability. There are many studies pertaining to performance of banks in respect of productivity, profitability and efficiency of Indian banks [(Divatia and Venkatachalam (1978), Angadi (1987), Swami and Subrahmanyam (1993) and Sarker and Das (1996)]. None of these studies, however, examined the fundamental issue on how far a bank can increase its ouput by simply increasing its efficiency through optimal deployment of resources.

A distinction is often made in the literature between technical efficiency and allocative efficiency of a firm; while the former reflects producers, ability to reduce all variable inputs to produce same level of output or to expand all variable outputs for given inputs, the latter reflects the ability of producers to select the 'right' input-output vector in the light of prevailing input and output prices. As the optimisation is implicit in the problem, operations research (OR) techniques greatly help in finding an appropriate solution to the problem. Considerable research has been done by optimising the cost structure of banks [Benston (1965), Berger *et al.* (1987), Mester (1987)]. Yet most of these studies used cross-sectional data and focused on estimating cost functions and measuring economies of scale [Clark (1988)] with the implicit assumption that firms operate on efficient frontier. There are very few studies which explicitly allow for inefficiency in banking firms without the assumption that banking firms are cost minimisers i.e. they operate efficiently. In fact, investigation of

The author is thankful to Dr. R.B. Barman, Officer-in-Charge and Shri V.S. Santhanam, Director, DESACS for their invaluable academic help to finalise this study.

inefficiencies in banking units has received very limited attention. Rangan *et al.* (1988), Aly *et al.* (1990) derived several efficiency measures for the US banking industry using cross sectional data and provided some insights into the measures of efficiency with legal environment under which the US banks operate.

Beginning with 1992, several changes have taken place in the operations and structure of the banking industry (Das, 1996). The increased opportunities for banks provided by the deregulation have expanded their portfolios, but at the same time introduced new uncertainties and risks. Competition has increased considerably within and outside depository institutions. Against this backdrop this study has the following objectives:-

(a) To examine the efficiency of Indian banking firms over a time path starting from the period of nationalisation at 1969 using longitudinal data; decomposition of overall efficiency into allocative efficiency and technical efficiency; and decomposition of technical efficiency into pure technical efficiency and scale efficiency.

(b) To examine the response of Indian banking firms to the deregulations since 1992 by examining the change (if any) in the economic efficiency of banking firms using pre- and post regulation data.

The remainder of the paper is organised as follows: the nonparametric methodology used in this study is introduced in section I. Some issues pertinent to the specification of bank costs, inputs and outputs are discussed in section II; data and empirical results are provided in section III. A summary and conclusions feature in section IV.

SECTION I

METHODOLOGY

The works of Farrell (1957, 1962) and Fare *et al.* (1985) have resulted in the development of a nonparametric approach to measuring efficiency. This method has been applied to the analysis of banking industry in the works of Aly *et al.* (1990), Rangan *et al.* (1988), Ferrier and Lovell (1990), and Grabowski *et al.* (1994). The nonparametric methodology, like any other methodology, has its advantages and disadvantages. The major advantage of this technique is that it does not require *a priori* restrictive functional form of production function as well as cost function. In that respect this method is more robust in nature. However, this method, a nonparametric one, does not take into consideration the random effects in measuring efficiencies. This implies that the extent of inefficiency in each year is likely to be overstated. However, as long as the overstatement is similar in nature for each of the years it should not affect the conclusions drawn with respect to changes in efficiency over time. Stochasticity of Farrell efficiency measures has been a part of recent theoretical research (Sengupta, 1996).

Consider a firm employing only two factors of production to produce a single output, under conditions of constant returns to scale.

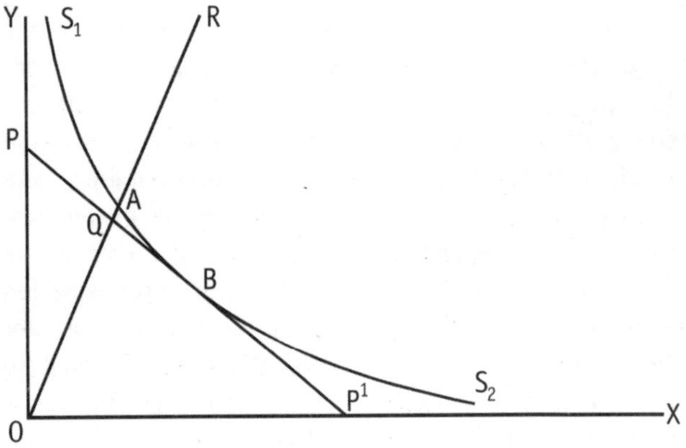

Suppose the efficient production function is known i.e. the output that a perfectly efficient firm could obtain from any given combination of inputs is given. The assumption of constant return permits all the information to be presented in a simple isoquant. Consider figure 1, where S_1S_2 represents an isoquant of the upper level set L(u) of the production technology. A production technology transforms inputs $\underline{x} = (x_1, ...x_n)$, $x_i \geq 0$ for all i-1(1)n, into outputs $\underline{u} = (u_1,....u_m)$, $u_j \geq 0$ for all j = 1(1)m. Given the technology and input prices, efficient operation in the sense of cost minimisation occurs at the point B on the isoquant, a point where the slope of the isocost line (PP^1) is equal to the slope of the tangent of the isoquant. A firm is said to be overall efficient, if it is a cost minimising firm on the isoquant. Symbolically, the overall efficiency of a firm is denoted (following Fare, *et al.*, 1985) by O ($\underline{u}$, $\underline{p}$, $\underline{x}$), where $\underline{u}$ refers to outputs, $\underline{p}$ refers to input prices and $\underline{x}$ refers to inputs. Thus, R is not an overall efficient firm. The degree of overall efficiency (OE) of R is defined by OQ/OR. A firm operating on the isoquant is only an efficient firm but may not be overall efficient. Thus, A is an efficient firm and R is not an efficient firm.

The point A represents an efficient firm using the two factors in the same ratio as R. It produces the same output as R using only a fraction OA/OR as much of each factor. In other words, it can be thought of as producing OR/OA times as much output from the same inputs. Technical efficiency (TE) of the firm R is defined as (Farrell, 1957), $K(\underline{u}, \underline{x}) = OA/OR$. Any firm operating on isoquant has value $K(\underline{u}, \underline{x}) = 1$ i.e. it is technically efficient. $K(\underline{u}, \underline{x})$ has the properties that a measure of efficiency obviously needs. It takes the value unity (100 per cent) for a perfectly efficient firm and will become indefinitely small if the amounts of inputs per unit of ouput become indefinitely large.

However, one also needs a measure of the extent to which a firm uses the various factors of production in the best proportions, in view of their prices. In figure 1, A and B both represent 100 per cent technical efficient firm but the cost of production at B will only be a fraction OQ/OA of those at A. This ratio is defined as allocative efficiency $[A(\underline{u}, \underline{p}, \underline{x})]$ or price efficiency (AE). Further, if the observed firm were to change the proportions of its inputs until they were the same as those represented by B, while keeping technical efficiency constant, its cost would be reduced by a factor OQ/OA, as long as factor prices did not change. It is observed that

$$O(\underline{u}, \underline{p}, \underline{x}) = K(\underline{u}, \underline{x}) * A(\underline{u}, \underline{p}, \underline{x}) \text{ since}$$

$$OQ/OR = OA/OR * OQ/OA \quad \ldots(1)$$

The technical efficiency $K(\underline{u}, \underline{x})$ is further decomposed into measures of scale $S(\underline{u}, \underline{x})$ and pure technical efficiency $[P(\underline{u}, \underline{x})]$. With respect to the former, if a firm is not at the optimal long-run scale of operation i.e. constant return to scale, the firm can hypothetically produce its current level of output with fewer inputs if constant return to scale is attained.

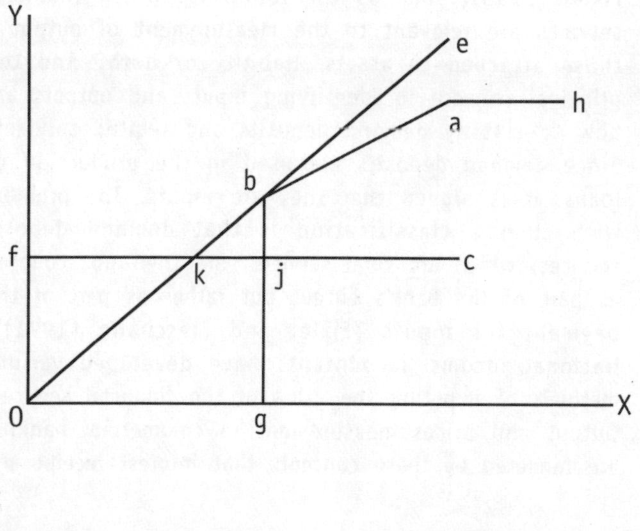

This is represented in figure 2. For one input and one output case, the constant return to scale production frontier is represented by oe. Three observations, c, b, a are labeled in the figure. If constant return to scale is assumed, then technical efficiency corresponds to the point c=fk/fc, which is OA/OR for two factors of production.

In order to measure scale efficiency $S(\underline{u}, \underline{x})$, the constant return to scale assumption is dropped and a variable return to scale production frontier is developed as represented by gbah. The pure technical efficiency $P(\underline{u}, \underline{x})$ (PTE), is defined in respect of variable return to scale frontier. For observation c, $P(\underline{u}, \underline{x})$ is defined as $P(\underline{u}, \underline{x}) = fj/fc$. From the measures of $K(\underline{u}, \underline{x})$ and $P(\underline{u}, \underline{x})$, a measure of scale efficiency (SE) is defined as

$$S(\underline{u}, \underline{x}) = K(\underline{u}, \underline{x})/P(\underline{u}, \underline{x}) = fk/fc * fc/fj = fk/fj < 1 \quad \ldots(2)$$

This measures the proportional reduction in input usage that is achieved if the firm is operating at constant returns to scale. For constant returns to scale the $S(\underline{u}, \underline{x}) = 1$ and all values less than 1 reflected scale inefficiency.

Here, a nonparametric linear programming approach is used to calculate various efficiency measures. Instead of estimating cost and production functions using statistical techniques (which in general assumes a functional form of production and cost function), a linear technology is derived from the observed inputs and outputs. And then we use LP techniques to calculate the efficiency measures for each individual firm. In other words, we judge the efficiency of each firm relative to the best practice technology determined from all of the firms i.e. the reference technology is constructed by taking a convex combination of the observed inputs and outputs.

Suppose that the input matrix N^{pxn} and output matrix M^{pxm} are given for p homogeneous firms. Then best production technology is given by

$$L(u) = \{x : u \leq zM, zN \leq x, z \in R^+\}, u \in R^+.$$

In simple terms it means that any firm cannot produce output greater than the best combination of output with fewer inputs than the best input combination. L(u) satisfies the following properties as assumed by Farrell (1957) viz. (a) constant return to scale : i.e. $L(\theta u) = \theta L(u)$, $\theta > 0$ and (b) strong disposability i.e. at least same output can be obtained using more input than the earlier i.e. if $y \in L(u)$ and $x \geq y$, then $x \in L(u)$.

In order to calculate overall efficiency $O(\underline{u}, \underline{p}, \underline{x})$, we need to determine the cost minimising input combination relative to given input prices. Given the input price vector $\underline{p} = (p_1 \ldots p_n)$, the minimum cost is determined from

$$Q(u, p) = \min_{\underline{x}} \{p^1x : x \in L(u)\}$$

$$\text{i.e. } \min_{\underline{z}, \underline{x}} p^1\underline{x}, \text{ subject to } u \leq zM,\ x \geq zN;\ z \in R^+.$$

Thus given this $Q(\underline{u}, \underline{p})$, the overall efficiency measure is obtained as $O(\underline{u}, \underline{x}, \underline{p}) = Q(u,p)/p^*x$ = (minimum cost)/(actual cost), which corresponds to OQ/OR.

A measure of technical efficiency is calculated by solving a second linear programming problem stated as

$$K(\underline{u}, \underline{x}) = \min \{\lambda: \lambda\underline{x} \in L(u)\} \text{ i.e.}$$

$$\min_{\underline{z}} \lambda, \text{ subject to } u \leq zM,\ \lambda x \geq zN;\ z \in R^+.$$

In this problem λ is a scalar. The λ parameter is used to determine the amount by which observed inputs can be proportionately decreased if they are utilized efficiently, which is equivalent to OA/OR.

As illustrated in figure 2, if the measure of scale efficiency $S(\underline{u}, \underline{x})$ is to be calculated, then a variable returns to scale frontier is to be developed and a pure technical efficiency $P(\underline{u}, \underline{x})$ measure is to be derived. It can be shown that any input set satisfying variable return to scale and strong disposability can be represented as

$$L_1(u) = \{x: u \leq zM,\ zN \leq x,\ \Sigma zi = 1,\ z \in R^+\}.$$

For multiple input and multiple output case, pure technical efficiency is calculated by solving a third LP problem stated as follows:

$$P(\underline{u}, \underline{x}) = \text{Min. } \{\theta: \theta x \in L_1(u)\} \text{ i.e.}$$

$$\min_{\underline{z}} \theta, \text{ subject to } u \leq zM,\ zN \leq \theta x,\ \Sigma zi = 1,\ z \in R^+.$$

Once $P(u, x)$ is calculated, scale efficiency $S(u, x)$ can be easily calculated from the identity given in equation (2).

SECTION II

Specification of Bank Cost, Outputs and Inputs

The proper estimation of bank costs depends on appropriate definition and certain assumptions regarding the measurement of variables. However, the banking literature is divided on the issue of bank cost and it is not clear which variables provide good proxy measures of economic values, such as, the proxy measure of total cost. Several authors have argued in favour of the concept that interest expenses has to be excluded from the total cost. The reason behind this is that interest costs are purely financial and hence not pertinent in measuring efficiency. Others have argued that excluding interest costs disregards the process of financial intermediation by which deposits are transformed into loans. Considerable disagreement exists in banking on the definition of banks output and inputs also [Benston *et al.* (1982)]. Cost and output measurement are especially difficult because many of the financial services are jointly produced and prices are typically assigned to a bundle of financial services. In general, two alternative approaches have been evolved in banking studies: (a) the 'intermediation approach' and (b) the 'production approach'. The first approach views banks as intermediators of financial services. The outputs are measured in rupees, and total costs are defined to include both interest expenses and total production costs. In contrast, in the latter approach, banks are viewed as producers of loans and deposit accounts services using available inputs. Under the production approach, the total costs are exclusive of interest expenses, and the outputs are measured by the number of accounts services as opposed to rupee values.

However, in a large part of the banking literature it is found that the 'intermediation approach' has larger appeal than the 'production approach'. One reason for this could be the non availability of published data on number of accounts serviced for different financial instruments. Aly, *et al.* (1990), Grabowski, *et al.* (1994) etc. used the intermediation approach to identify bank output and costs. But they have used demand deposits as output of banking firms. Here some crucial issues were raised by a number of writers [Sealy and Lindley (1977); Fixler (1993)] such as the following: which financial services are relevant to the measurement of output - those attached to assets, liability or both? And the principal concern in identifying inputs and outputs are how to classify demand deposits and related services. Since demand deposits are used in the production of loans, it is argued that they are inputs. The problem with such a classification is that demand deposit services, which are final services, are then not counted as part of the bank's output but rather as part of the payment for inputs [Fixler and Zieschang (1991)]. National income accountants have developed various methods of imputing the value of the financial services. Output and prices measurement in commercial banking are hindered by these concepts that interest receipt and interest paid do not emanate from the payment for productive services. But the remuneration for intermediation is partly based on interest rate and interest rates are essential component of financial services. However, as interest earned is not over the own funds, but as a part of intermediation, mere interest earned cannot be treated as output. Thus, based on value added, imputed services approach of national accounting techniques, the following outputs are defined (a) u_1: Margin = total interest earned - total interest paid and (a) u_2: commission, exchange, brokerage, etc. It is important to note that while the first variable essentially reflects financial intermediation, the second variable is specifically for the services provided by the banks.

Total cost is taken as the sum of expenditure on labour and expenditure incurred for loanable funds by the bank in the production of output and services. The inputs used in the calculation of various efficiency measures are: labour (x_1) and loanable funds (x_2) i.e. deposits plus borrowings. Labour is measured by the number of employees as given in the published annual reports at the end of the financial year. P_1, the price of labour was derived by taking total establishment expenses divided by the total number of employees. P_2, price of funds, was derived by taking the sum of interest expenses on loanable funds divided by total funds.

SECTION III

DATA AND EMPIRICAL ANALYSIS

This study examines efficiency of all public sector banks in India which operate under the same regulatory framework and has equal social obligations. This enables one to compare the performance of banks across time points. Public sector banks account for more than eighty per cent of banking business. Data for price, input and output of banks are basically taken from published annual accounts of banks which are collected from several IBA publications and various issues of 'Statistical Tables Relating to Banks in India'. For a historical perspective of the development of Indian banking since nationalisation, 1969 was taken as the base year of comparison. But due to non availability of bank-wise data on those parameters, the year 1970 is taken as the base year. Subsequent data points are chosen for the year 1978, 1984, 1990 and 1996 respectively, depending on the availability of data. The years 1990 and 1996 are chosen to examine the changes in efficiency measures to assess the impact of deregulation of the financial sector. Table 1 presents sample statistics for cost, inputs and outputs of public sector banks for the years 1970, 1978, 1984, 1990 and 1996 respectively.

TABLE 1

Sample Statistics$ for 1970, 1978, 1984, 1990 and 1996

Variable	*1970*	*1978*	*1984*	*1990*	*1996*
C					
Sample Size	22	28	28	28	27
Mean	1614	7612	26013	66221	155450
Std dev	2036	10659	37066	92845	210994
Minimum	229	1237	3904	10613	26957
Maximum	9818	58128	202366	506249	1157756
U_1					
Sample size	22	28	28	28	27
Mean	705	2093	7240	16055	56680
Std dev	860	2497	8782	21139	87373
Minimum	89	382	1336	3421	9226
Maximum	4173	13612	47978	116214	473265
U_2					
Sample size	22	28	28	28	27
Mean	263	993	2285	5831	16295
Std dev	430	2009	5196	10688	32195
Minimum	27	170	349	923	2947
Maximum	2118	11095	28826	59512	176221
X_1					
Sample size	22	28	28	28	27
Mean	25591	103076	302471	741697	1548890
Std dev	31679	138532	413415	1014624	2012381
Minimum	3351	13985	41384	130736	252936
Maximum	150644	749363	2251128	5506219	10905520
X_2					
Sample size	22	28	28	28	27
Mean	8748	22374	35269	30898	33259
Std dev	10978	30206	45928	39341	42556
Minimum	1689	3668	7842	6450	6752
Maximum	55869	167829	255777	219299	233000

$ All variables except X_2 are measured in lakhs of Rs.

C = Cost; U_1 = Margin = Interest earned - interest paid; U_2 = Commission, exchange and brokerage; X_1 = Funds = Deposits + borrowings; X_2 = Labour = Total number of employees.

TABLE 2

Summary Statistics of Several Efficiency Measures@

	Mean	*Std Dev*	*Minimum*	*Maximum*
Year = 1970				
OE	0.8296	0.1145	0.5973	1.0000
TE	0.8566	0.1166	0.5981	1.0000
AE	0.9689	0.0302	0.8960	1.0000
PTE	0.8864	0.1190	0.5981	1.0000
SE	0.9681	0.0540	0.8410	1.0000
Year = 1978				
OE	0.8095	0.1050	0.6162	1.0000
TE	0.8833	0.0941	0.6282	1.0000
AE	0.9173	0.0717	0.7423	1.0000
PTE	0.9077	0.0970	0.6282	1.0000
SE	0.9741	0.0351	0.8776	1.0000
Year = 1984				
OE	0.8031	0.1172	0.6567	1.0000
TE	0.8503	0.0941	0.6836	1.0000
AE	0.9433	0.0710	0.7787	1.0000
PTE	0.8552	0.0990	0.6836	1.0000
SE	0.9950	0.0198	0.8980	1.0000
Year = 1990				
OE	0.8128	0.1236	0.5766	1.0000
TE	0.8918	0.1050	0.6541	1.0000
AE	0.9103	0.0727	0.7358	1.0000
PTE	0.9004	0.1074	0.6541	1.0000
SE	0.9912	0.0260	0.8803	1.0000
Year = 1996				
OE	0.7600	0.2016	0.2861	1.0000
TE	0.7770	0.1995	0.3676	1.0000
AE	0.9749	0.0465	0.7783	1.0000
PTE	0.8035	0.1993	0.3676	1.0000
SE	0.9676	0.0555	0.8100	1.0000

@ See appendix for exact calculation of efficiency measures

OE = Overall Efficiency, TE = Technical Efficiency,

AE = Allocative Efficiency, PTE = Pure Technical Efficiency,

SE = Scale Efficiency

Table 2 presents summary statistics for the values of the various efficiency measures for the years under view. The results indicate that from 1970 to 1978, the overall efficiency and allocative efficiency measures declined. But during this period, the technical efficiency of banks improved due to improvement in pure technical efficiency. The overall efficiency remained almost unchanged during 1978 to 1990. While the technical efficiency declined in 1984 and improved in 1990, the allocative efficiency improved in 1984 and declined in 1990. During this period, the scale efficiency was almost constant at 0.99. Therefore, the fluctuation in technical efficiency during this period was due to pure technical efficiency only. The overall efficiency declined during 1990 to 1996 due to a noticeable decline in the technical efficiency although the allocative efficiency improved by 6 points. The decline in the technical efficiency was in respect of both the pure technical efficiency and scale efficiency.

It must be recognised that the efficiency measures calculated in this study are relative in nature. A bank's performance is not judged relative to some absolute standard, but relative to other banks in the sample. The best production technology is derived by taking the best combination of the characteristics of these variables of the sample and it is confined to public sector banks only. Therefore, high values of the efficiency measures for a bank mean that the bank is relatively efficient within the group. The main sources of inefficiency can be determined by comparing the relative sizes of various measures. In the five years under study, on an average, public sector banks were more allocatively efficient than technically efficient. Thus, inefficiency in public sector banks may, to a greater extent, be attributed to underutilisation or wasting of inputs rather than choosing the incorrect input combination. Further, looking at the components of technical efficiency, scale and pure technical, it can be seen that pure technical was the main source of technical inefficiency. That is, banks in this sample were losing very little output due to scale inefficiency. Instead, much of the lost output was the result of underutilisation or wasting of resources. Wasting resources may be in the form of labour inputs, because most of the public sector banks are in general over staffed.

In order to determine whether the average efficiency measures (Table 3 and Appendix) in the years under examination are significantly different, two nonparametric testing procedures were conducted viz. median test and wilcoxon test [See, Lehmann (1975)]. The median test compares the two sample distributions of efficiency on the basis of their central tendency, as measured by the median. Wilcoxon test, on the other hand, compares the entire structures of the distributions, not just the central tendency.

It can be seen that, from 1970 to 1996 though the overall efficiency measure declined, it was not statistically different from 1970 to 1996. In fact, the overall efficiency of public sector banks never changed significantly ever since nationalisation (See, Appendix). From 1970 to 1990, the allocative efficiency has declined significantly. The effect of deregulation on the efficiency of banks can be judged by comparing the efficiency measure between 1990 and 1996 (Table 3). During this period, the overall efficiency has moved down from 81 per cent to 76 per cent. This result may give an erroneous idea that deregulation has a negative impact. A disaggregated analysis of efficiency measure, given in the following subsections, would explain the outcome in a structured way. The allocative efficiency, on the other hand, improved significantly during this period. This is a direct effect of deregulation where banks are able to choose more efficiently the best combination of inputs in terms of their prices. In contrast to this, the scale efficiency of public sector banks declined significantly during this period.

TABLE 3

Summary of Tests of the Different Efficiency Measures@

	Between 1970 & 1990		*Between 1970 & 1996*		*Between 1990 & 1996*	
Efficiency Measure	*Median Test*	*Wilcoxon Test*	*Median Test*	*Wilcoxon Test*	*Median Test*	*Wilcoxon Test*
	χ^2 (Prob>χ^2)	χ^2 (Prob>χ^2)	χ^2 (Prob>χ^2)	χ^2 (Prob>χ^2)	χ^2 (Prob>χ^2)	χ^2 (Prob>χ^2)
OE	0.999 (1.000)	0.153 (0.696)	0.195 (0.659)	0.856 (0.355)	0.159 (0.690)	0.512 (0.471)
TE	1.273 (0.259)	1.371 (0.246)	0.016 (0.898)	1.236 (0.266)	1.453 (0.228)	3.864 (0.049)
AE	7.955 (0.005)	11.973 (0.001)	2.491 (0.114)	3.061 (0.080)	17.146 (0.001)	17.658 (0.001)
PTE	0.318 (0.572)	0.127 (0.722)	0.485 (0.486)	1.482 (0.224)	1.453 (0.228)	2.448 (0.118)
SE	2.812 (0.139)	2.930 (0.087)	0.966 (0.326)	0.146 (0.702)	5.624 (0.018)	4.748 (0.029)

@ : Tests of significance of the difference of efficiency measures between 1970 and 1978, 1970 and 1984, 1978 and 1984, 1978 and 1990, 1978 and 1996 and 1984 and 1990 and 1984 and 1996 are presented in appendix.

Disaggregated Analysis: Bank-wise efficiency measures are presented in Table 4. It is observed that while the State Bank group, in general, improved in overall efficiency, nationalised banks registered a gradual decline over the time path since nationalisation and this is more pronounced after 1990. A few nationalised banks performed so poorly during this period that the overall industry score came down. These banks are the Indian Bank, the United Bank of India, the Andhra Bank and the Punjab & Sind Bank. The United Bank of India is the only bank whose performance has declined continuously and consistently after nationalisation. The reason for very poor performance of these banks is purely technical. Under prudential accounting norms, which were introduced in 1992, assets that have two consecutive quarterly defaults in interest accrual cannot be taken into account for showing income. Till 1992, under mercantile accounting practices, the interest accrued on these assets was treated as income generating. This shift in accounting on actual realisation basis compressed public sector banks' income, and more specifically it reduced banks' operating margins. The expected growth in the operating margin was not in tandem with the growth in deposits. Deposits were underutilised and the margin has got reduced considerably for those banks which had sizable non-performing assets. There exists a significant degree of asset-liability mismatch also. As a result, the technical efficiency of these banks has come down heavily after deregulation. This was so in the cases of the Indian Bank, the Punjab & Sind Bank and the Punjab National Bank. The Punjab National Bank, a middle-high level overall-efficient bank in 1990, performed poorly in 1996 due to depreciation provided on securities marked to market. These were practically acid tests of public sector banks' abilities to cope up with the challenge of a system that is increasingly being aligned to global norms of banking practice. Thus deregulation may have had its biggest impact on efficiency by forcing inefficient banks to change the composition of the assets portfolio to a sustainable standard. In contrast, there are many banks which have shown marked improvement during this period. Except the State Bank of Patiala and the State Bank of Travancore, all banks in the State Bank group turned out to be very efficient in 1996. The State Bank of Bikaner and Jaipur and the State Bank of Hyderabad maintained good track record consistently. Among the nationalised banks, the Oriental Bank of Commerce, the Bank of Baroda and the Corporation Bank improved their efficiency significantly. These banks are well managed and aggressive public sector banks. Two of them have already entered the capital market to raise fresh equity to widen their capital base so that they can expand their credit portfolio to obtain a healthy operating margin.

If we look into the variations in several efficiency measures (Table 5 and 6), we observe that the Bank of Baroda, from 1990 to 1996, improved its overall efficiency by 26 per cent, followed by the Oriental Bank of Commerce by 15 per cent. Almost all banks, including the Indian Bank and the United Bank of India, improved their allocative efficiency during this time. Therefore, the public sector banks have become more efficient in dealing with the distribution of mobilised funds among competing demands. This is certainly a positive impact

TABLE 4

Bank-wise Efficiency Measures of Public Sector Banks

Bank Name	*1970*			*1978*			*1984*			*1990*			*1996*		
	OE	*TE*	*AE*	*OE*	*TE*	*AE*	*OE*	*TE*	*AE*	*OE*	*TE*	*AE*	*OE*	*TE*	*AE*
State Bank Group															
State Bank of Bikaner & Jaipur	1.00	1.00	1.00	1.00	1.00	1.00	0.93	0.96	0.97	0.94	0.96	0.98	1.00	1.00	1.00
State Bank of Hyderabad	0.93	1.00	0.93	0.86	0.89	0.97	1.00	1.00	1.00	1.00	1.00	1.00	1.00	1.00	1.00
State Bank of Indore	0.68	0.70	0.98	0.90	0.95	0.95	0.96	0.98	0.99	0.96	1.00	0.97	1.00	1.00	1.00
State Bank of India	0.87	0.96	0.91	0.90	1.00	0.90	1.00	1.00	1.00	0.93	1.00	0.93	0.95	1.00	0.95
State Bank of Saurashtra	0.82	0.84	0.98	0.93	0.93	1.00	1.00	1.00	1.00	0.98	1.00	0.98	0.92	0.96	0.95
State Bank of Mysore	0.87	0.88	0.99	0.86	0.88	0.98	0.93	0.93	1.00	1.00	1.00	1.00	0.89	0.89	1.00
State Bank of Travancore	0.73	0.76	0.96	0.62	0.63	0.98	0.85	0.86	0.99	0.82	0.84	0.98	0.83	0.87	0.96
State Bank of Patiala	0.60	0.60	1.00	0.68	0.76	0.89	0.71	0.74	0.95	0.94	0.97	0.96	0.70	0.71	0.99
Mean	0.81	0.84	0.97	0.84	0.88	0.96	0.92	0.93	0.99	0.95	0.97	0.98	0.91	0.93	0.98
Standard Deviation	0.13	0.15	0.03	0.13	0.13	0.04	0.10	0.09	0.02	0.06	0.06	0.02	0.10	0.10	0.02
Coefficient of Variation (%)	16.46	17.4	3.42	15.23	14.4	4.44	10.84	9.83	1.86	6.11	5.70	2.33	11.50	11.08	2.40
Nationalised Bank Group															
Oriental Bank of Commerce				0.95	1.00	0.95	0.83	0.84	0.99	0.84	0.97	0.87	0.99	1.00	0.99
Bank of Baroda	0.81	0.82	0.98	0.76	0.95	0.80	0.72	0.90	0.80	0.71	0.95	0.75	0.98	1.00	0.98
Corporation Bank				0.66	0.68	0.97	0.76	0.76	1.00	0.89	0.93	0.95	0.97	0.99	0.98
Dena Bank	0.94	0.95	0.99	0.85	0.90	0.94	0.83	0.83	1.00	0.90	0.95	0.94	0.88	0.88	1.00
Bank of Maharashtra	0.69	0.69	0.99	0.71	0.79	0.89	0.69	0.69	1.00	0.79	0.85	0.93	0.86	0.88	0.99
Canara Bank	0.78	0.79	0.99	0.88	0.94	0.94	0.78	0.79	0.98	0.86	1.00	0.86	0.83	0.83	1.00
Union Bank of India	0.78	0.80	0.97	0.86	0.90	0.96	0.77	0.84	0.92	0.82	0.89	0.92	0.83	0.83	1.00
Syndicate Bank	0.81	0.83	0.98	0.83	0.88	0.95	0.75	0.79	0.95	0.85	0.88	0.96	0.73	0.75	0.98
Central Bank of India	0.99	1.00	0.99	0.76	0.79	0.95	0.74	0.82	0.90	0.73	0.84	0.87	0.72	0.72	1.00
Bank of India	0.74	0.83	0.90	0.69	0.93	0.74	0.67	0.81	0.83	0.62	0.84	0.74	0.71	0.80	0.89
Allahabad Bank	1.00	1.00	1.00	0.93	1.00	0.93	0.68	0.68	1.00	0.62	0.73	0.86	0.65	0.66	0.99
United Commercial Bank	0.89	0.93	0.95	0.75	0.85	0.89	1.00	1.00	1.00	0.58	0.65	0.88	0.63	0.67	0.94
Punjab National Bank	0.95	1.00	0.95	0.72	0.84	0.86	0.69	0.74	0.93	0.76	0.85	0.89	0.61	0.61	1.00
Vijaya Bank				1.00	1.00	1.00	0.86	0.90	0.95	0.92	1.00	0.92	0.59	0.59	1.00
Indian Overseas Bank	0.71	0.77	0.92	0.74	0.93	0.79	0.68	0.88	0.78	0.73	0.80	0.91	0.54	0.54	0.99
Punjab & Sind Bank				0.84	0.87	0.97	0.79	0.83	0.95	0.73	0.79	0.92	0.53	0.53	1.00
Andhra Bank				0.70	0.91	0.76	0.66	0.75	0.87	0.78	0.86	0.90	0.51	0.51	1.00
United Bank of India	0.91	0.93	0.99	0.75	0.87	0.87	0.70	0.86	0.81	0.62	0.68	0.91	0.38	0.38	0.99
Indian Bank	0.76	0.79	0.97	0.78	0.88	0.89	0.67	0.79	0.85	0.74	1.00	0.74	0.29	0.37	0.78
New Bank of India				0.75	0.79	0.96	0.84	0.84	1.00	0.72	0.74	0.96			
Mean	0.84	0.87	0.97	0.80	0.89	0.90	0.76	0.82	0.93	0.76	0.86	0.88	0.70	0.71	0.97
Standard Deviation	0.10	0.10	0.03	0.09	0.08	0.08	0.09	0.07	0.08	0.10	0.11	0.07	0.20	0.20	0.05
Coefficient of Variation (%)	12.46	11.5	3.04	11.71	9.16	8.40	11.33	9.13	8.26	13.15	12.24	7.68	28.66	27.62	5.55
Public Sector Banks															
Mean	0.83	0.86	0.97	0.81	0.88	0.92	0.80	0.85	0.94	0.81	0.89	0.91	0.76	0.78	0.98
Standard Deviation	0.11	0.12	0.03	0.10	0.09	0.07	0.12	0.09	0.07	0.12	0.11	0.07	0.20	0.20	0.05
Coefficient of Variation (%)	13.70	13.5	3.10	12.89	10.6	7.87	14.55	11.1	7.51	15.15	11.88	7.87	26.49	25.68	4.79

OE = Overall Efficiency TE = Technical Efficiency AE = Allocative Efficiency of deregulation. In 1996, the Canara Bank is the only bank which registered a noticeable departure from the optimal long-run scale of operation (constant returns to scale) i.e. the bank can produce its current level of output with fewer inputs if constant returns to scale is attained.

TABLE 5

Variations in Efficiency Measures in 1996 over 1990

Bank Name	*OE*	*TE*	*AE*	*PTE*	*SE*
Bank of Baroda	26.39	5.26	22.43	5.26	0.00
Oriental Bank of Commerce	15.24	3.36	12.32	3.36	0.00
Bank of India	9.77	-3.90	15.84	-4.71	1.03
Corporation Bank	8.40	6.19	2.53	6.19	0.00
Bank of Maharashtra	7.04	2.58	5.29	9.73	-7.51
State Bank of Bikaner & Jaipur	5.83	4.27	1.63	4.08	0.20
United Commercial Bank	5.11	1.51	5.65	8.03	-8.88
State Bank of Indore	3.76	0.43	3.34	0.43	0.00
Allahabad Bank	2.90	-6.82	13.18	-5.36	-2.16
State Bank of India	1.85	0.00	1.85	0.00	0.00
State Bank of Travancore	1.27	3.32	-2.28	-0.37	4.44
Union Bank of India	0.68	-6.02	7.51	-9.82	3.75
State Bank of Hyderabad	0.00	0.00	0.00	0.00	0.00
Central Bank of India	-0.65	-11.41	12.86	-3.06	-10.37
Dena Bank	-1.99	-7.09	5.34	-5.62	-1.72
Canara Bank	-3.07	-16.72	13.58	0.00	-16.72
State Bank of Saurashtra	-6.06	-3.73	-2.51	-3.73	0.00
State Bank of Mysore	-10.96	-10.56	-0.45	-7.36	-3.45
Syndicate Bank	-11.57	-13.30	1.68	-16.22	1.17
Punjab National Bank	-14.83	-24.52	11.29	-14.18	-14.59
Indian Overseas Bank	-18.96	-26.11	8.64	-25.84	-0.50
Punjab & Sind Bank	-19.46	-25.83	7.98	-25.83	0.00
State Bank of Patiala	-23.53	-26.06	2.25	-25.94	-0.17
United Bank of India	-23.91	-29.80	8.41	-28.18	-4.05
Andhra Bank	-27.26	-35.53	9.56	-34.05	-2.83
Vijaya Bank	-33.23	-41.25	7.96	-41.06	-0.32
Indian Bank	-45.02	-63.24	4.20	-63.24	0.00

The public sector banks are grouped in respect of overall efficiency over the time path after nationalisation and are presented in Table 7. It is clear that in 1970 the only bank in the low category was the State Bank of Patiala. In other words, all nationalised banks at the time of nationalisation were at least medium level efficient. The United Bank of India is a unique example of sliding down the path from very high level efficiency in 1970 to very low level in 1996. The Allahabad Bank was also not far behind than the United Bank of India. These two banks have almost similar level labour inputs. Most of the State Banks were on the top and some of them were even 100 per cent efficient. There were some banks namely Union Bank of India and the Canara Bank which maintained their high overall efficiency from 1970 to 1996. On the average, one-third of public sector banks were consistently rated in the very high group. It is quite likely that banks like the Bank of Baroda and the Oriental Bank of Commerce, have achieved improvement in efficiency as a result of deregulation. On the other hand, it is not necessarily true that some banks like the Indian Bank, the United Bank of India regressed as a result of competition. Though the overall efficiency of nationalised banks declined after nationalisation, it does not imply that nationalisation had negative bearing on the performance of these banks. Nonetheless, the contamination of the credit portfolio of these banks over a period of 26 years was partly due to pressure of 'social banking', the management of which posed a serious strain on the banking system. The basic problems of these banks lie in the areas of asset quality, management and congestion of labour. Therefore, these banks have to search a turnaround strategy for their survival and global presence in the near future.

TABLE 6

Variations in Efficiency Measures in 1996 Over 1970

Bank Name	*OE*	*TE*	*AE*	*PTE*	*SE*
State Bank of Indore	32.12	30.47	2.37	30.47	0.00
Bank of Maharashtra	17.37	18.27	-0.91	25.64	-7.76
Bank of Baroda	17.21	17.73	-0.14	16.18	1.84
State Bank of Patiala	10.56	11.42	-1.18	11.54	-0.16
State Bank of Travancore	10.51	10.89	0.11	7.20	4.43
State Bank of Saurashtra	9.49	12.61	-3.01	12.61	0.00
State Bank of India	7.50	4.07	3.79	0.00	4.07
State Bank of Hyderabad	6.81	0.00	6.81	0.00	0.00
Union Bank of India	5.19	2.72	3.07	-9.50	12.66
Canara Bank	4.56	4.21	0.46	6.19	-1.00
State Bank of Mysore	2.02	1.87	0.18	5.07	-3.45
State Bank of Bikaner & Jaipur	0.00	0.00	0.00	0.00	0.00
Bank of India	-2.62	-2.76	-0.18	-3.57	1.02
Dena Bank	-6.08	-6.67	0.60	-5.65	-1.25
Syndicate Bank	-7.69	-8.00	0.19	-14.59	5.09
Indian Overseas Bank	-17.05	-22.47	6.83	-27.03	5.44
Central Bank of India	-26.68	-27.80	1.10	-19.45	-10.36
Punjab National Bank	-34.49	-39.12	4.54	-24.84	-18.99
Allahabad Bank	-34.61	-33.75	-1.29	-32.29	-2.15
Indian Bank	-47.40	-41.84	-18.87	-46.76	5.89
United Bank of India	-53.03	-54.21	0.96	-56.10	-0.39

TABLE 7

Classification of Banks in Respect of Overall Efficiency

Overall Efficiency	*1996*	*1990*	*1970*
Very High (90% to 100%)	State Bank of Hyderabad State Bank of Bikaner & Jaipur State Bank of Indore State Bank of India State Bank of Saurashtra Oriental Bank of Commerce Bank of Baroda Corporation Bank	State Bank of Hyderabad State Bank of Mysore State Bank of Saurashtra State Bank of Indore State Bank of Bikaner & Jaipur State Bank of Patiala Dena Bank	State Bank of Bikaner & Jaipur State Bank of Hyderabad Allahabad Bank Central Bank of India Dena Bank Bank of Baroda Punjab National Bank United Bank of India
High (75% to 90%)	State Bank of Mysore State Bank of Travancore Dena Bank Canara Bank Union Bank of India Bank of Maharashtra	State Bank of Travancore Corporation Bank Oriental Bank of Commerce Canara Bank Union Bank of India Syndicate Bank Andhra Bank Vijaya Bank	State Bank of India State Bank of Mysore State Bank of Saurashtra United Commercial Bank Canara Bank Union Bank of India Syndicate Bank Indian Bank
Medium (60% to 75%)	State Bank of Patiala Syndicate Bank Central Bank of India Bank of India Punjab National Bank Allahabad Bank United Commercial Bank	Bank of Baroda Central Bank of India Punjab National Bank Indian Overseas Bank Punjab & Sind Bank Indian Bank Bank of India Allahabad Bank United Bank of India United Commercial Bank	State Bank of Travancore State Bank of Indore Bank of Maharashtra Bank of India Indian Overseas Bank
Low (50% to 60%)	Indian Overseas Bank Punjab & Sind Bank Andhra Bank Vijaya Bank		State Bank of Patiala
Very low (less than 50%)	United Bank of India Indian Bank		

SECTION IV

Summary and Conclusions

The purpose of the paper is to examine the change in efficiency measures of public sector banks in India over the time path after nationalisation and compare the efficiency of the banks prior to deregulation with the efficiency after deregulation. A nonparametric frontier methodology has been utilised to derive several efficiency measures for public sector banks in India for the years 1970, 1978, 1984, 1990 and 1996.

The results indicate that, in general, the State Bank of India and its Associates are more efficient than the nationalised banks. Though the overall efficiency has declined in the post deregulation period, it is not a statistically significant change. Most of the public sector banks improved their allocative efficiency significantly in the deregulation period. Finally, inefficiency that existed in these banks was more the result of technical rather than allocative efficiency. Public sector banks in 1996 had the scope of producing 1.3 (100/77) times as much output from the same inputs.

One point, however, is worth noting. Deregulation is not the only change to affect the efficiency of a bank. There are many factors in the economy which influence and shape the performance of a bank favourably or unfavourably depending on the banks' risk exposure.

In conclusion, it may be noted that while the results of this study are not very conclusive, they are interesting in that they hold a promise of change. The financial sector is going through a transition phase by restructuring and reorienting business activities. The banks are trying to clean up their asset portfolio by making provision for non-performing assets and modernising delivery of services through computerisation and redeployment of manpower. This study provides an early assessment of the changing performance in the recent period which augurs well in terms of allocative efficiency as well as overall efficiency with the exception of two outliers.

References

Aly Y. Hassan, Richard Grabowski, Carl Pasurka and Nanda Rangan (1990): "Technical, Scale and Allocative Efficiencies in US Banking: An Empirical Investigation", *The Review of Economics and Statistics*, Vol. 72, May, pp. 211-218.

Angadi, V.B. (1987): "Integrated Approach to Study Banks' Profitability", *Prajnan*, Vol. XVI, No. 4, October-December, pp. 523-538.

Benston, G.J. (1965): "Branch Banking and Economies of Scale", *The Journal of Finance*, May, Vol. 20, pp. 312-331.

Benston, G.J. Hanweck, G.A. and Humphrey, D.B. (1982): "Scale Economies in Banking: A Restructuring and Reassessment", *Journal of Money, Credit and Banking*, Vol. 14, November, pp. 435-456.

Berger, A.N., Hanweck, G.A., and Humphrey, D.B. (1987): "Competitive Viability in Banking: Scale, Scope and Product Mix Economies", *Journal of Monetary Economics*, Vol.20, pp. 501-523.

Clark, J. (1988): "The Economies of Scale and Scope of Depository Financial Institutions: A Review of Literature", *Economic Review*, Federal Reserve Bank of Kansas City, pp. 16-33.

Das, Abhiman (1996): "Structural Changes and Asset-Liability Mismatch of Scheduled Commercial Banks in India", *Reserve Bank of India Occasional Papers*, Vol.17, No. 4, pp. 303-329.

Divatia, V.V. and Venkatachalam, T.R. (1978): "Operational Efficiency and Profitability of Public Sector Banks", *Reserve Bank of India Occasional Papers*, Vol.3, No. 1, June, pp. 1-17.

Fare, R., S. Grosskopf and J. Logan (1985): "The Relative Performance of Publicly-owned and Privately-owned Electric Utilities", *Journal of Public Economics*, Vol.26, pp. 89-106.

Farrell, M.J. (1957): "The Measurement of Productive Efficiency", *Journal of the Royal Statistical Society*, Series A, General 120, Part 3, pp. 253-281.

Farrell, M.J. and M. Fieldhouse (1962): "Estimating Efficient Production Functions Under Increasing Returns to Scale", *Journal of the Royal Statistical Society*, Series A, General 125, Part 2, pp. 252-267.

Ferrier, G. and Knox Lovell, C.A. (1990): "Measuring Cost Efficiency in Banking: Econometric and Linear Programming Evidence", *Journal of Econometrics*, Vol.46, pp. 229-245.

Fixler, D.J. and Zieschang, K.D. (1991): "Measuring the nominal value of financial services in the national income accounts", *Economic Inquiry*, Vol. 29 pp. 53-68.

Fixler, D.J. (1993): "Measuring Financial Services Output and Prices in Commercial Banking", *Applied Economies*, Vol.25, pp. 985-993.

Goiporia Committee (1991): *Report of the Committee on Customer Service*, Reserve Bank of India, December.

Grabowski R., Rangan N. and Rezvanian R. (1994): "The Effect of Deregulation on the Efficiency of US Banking Firms", *Journal of Economics and Business*, Vol.46, pp. 39-54.

Lehmann, E.L. (1975): *Nonparametrics: Statistical Methods based on Ranks, San Francisco:* Holden-Day.

Luther Committee (1977): *Report of the Productivity, Efficiency and Profitability Committee on Banking*, Reserve Bank of India, June.

Mester, L.J. (1987): "A Multiproduct Cost Study of Savings and Loans", *Journal of Finance*, Vol.42, June, pp. 423-444.

Narasimham Committee (1991): *Report of the Committee on Financial System*, Reserve Bank of India, November.

Rangan Nanda, Hassan Y. Aly, Carl Pasurka and Richard Grabowski (1988): "The Technical Efficiency of US Banks", *Economics Letters*, vol.28, pp. 169-175.

Rangarajan, C. (1997): "Banking Sector Reforms: Rationale and Relevance", SICOM Silver Jubilee Lecture, *Reserve Bank of India Bulletin*, Vol.L1, No.1, January, pp. 41-51.

Sarker, P.C. and Abhiman Das (1977): "Development of Composite Index of Banking Efficiency: Indian Experience", Unpublished Paper, Reserve Bank of India.

Sealy, C.W, and Lindley, J. (1977): "Inputs, Outputs and a Theory of Production and Cost at Depository Financial Institutions", *Journal of Finance*, Vol.32, pp. 1252-1266.

Sengupta, J.K. (1996): "Systematic Measures of Dynamic Farrell Efficiency", *Applied Economics Letters*, Vol.3, pp. 91-94.

Swami, S.B. and Subrahmanyam, G. (1993): "Comparative Performance of Public Sector Banks in India", *Prajnan*, Vol.XXII, No.2, July-September, pp. 185-195.

APPENDIX

Calculation of efficiency measures: Suppose that the input matrix N^{pxn} and output matrix M^{pxm} are given for p homogeneous firms. The linear programming problem to calculate minimum cost for the kth firm for given prices of inputs (p_1, p_2, ...p_n) is given by:

Minimise $p_1x_1 + p_2x_2 + \ldots\ldots + p_nX_n$, subject to x,z

$$z_1u_{11} + z_2u_{21} + \ldots\ldots + z_pu_{p1} \geq u_{k1}$$

$$z_1u_{12} + z_2u_{22} + \ldots\ldots + z_pu_{p2} \geq u_{k2}$$

$$\ldots\ldots\ldots\ldots\ldots\ldots\ldots\ldots$$

$$z_1u_{1m} + z_2u_{2m} + \ldots\ldots + z_pu_{pm} \geq u_{km}$$

$$x_1 \geq z_1x_{11} + z_2x_{21} + \ldots\ldots + z_px_{p1}$$

$$x_2 \geq z_1x_{12} + z_2x_{22} + \ldots\ldots + z_px_{p2}$$

$$\ldots\ldots\ldots\ldots\ldots\ldots\ldots\ldots$$

$$x_n \geq z_1x_{1n} + z_2x_{2n} + \ldots\ldots + z_px_{pn}$$

$$x_1 \geq 0,\ x_2 \geq 0,\ \ldots\ldots\ x_n \geq 0$$

$$z_1 \geq 0,\ z_2 \geq 0,\ \ldots\ldots\ z_n \geq 0$$

Other linear programming problem can be formulated in the similar fashion.

SUMMARY OF THE TESTS@ OF DIFFERENCE OF EFFICIENCY MEASURES

Years	*OE*	*TE*	*AE*	*PTE*	*SE*
1970 & 78	NS	NS	$**	NS	NS
1970 & 84	NS	NS	NS	NS	$**
1978 & 84	NS	$*	NS	$*	$**
1978 & 90	NS	NS	NS	NS	$**
1978 & 96	NS	NS	$**	NS	NS
1984 & 90	NS	$*	$*	$*	NS
1984 & 96	NS	NS	NS	NS	$**

@ : NS: Not significant.

$* : Significant at 5% level.

$** : Significant at 1% level

Comments / Media Reviews....

"This book is undoubtedly a work of encyclopædic proportions, which only a master of the subject will dare to undertake. ...Vasudevan's tantalising voyage through the theory and practice of central banking is a path-breaking and salutary effort. It deserves to be a manual for the modern central banker and those outside who wish to unravel the traditional mystique of monetary or economic policies...."

— ***A.S. Jayawardena***
Governor, Central Bank of Sri Lanka

"Excellent piece of work ...Your vast erudition on the subject of central banking and monetary issues is clearly evident in this book. The book should be a required reading for central bankers and indeed for all those interested in studying issues of monetary management and financial stability..."

— ***M. Narasimham***
Chairman, Administrative Staff College of India
(In his congratulatory letter to the author)

"In the preface, Vasudevan says modestly that his book is intended to be a reference volume for advanced students in universities and officer staff of central bank, especially in what he calls the emerging market economies (EMEs). He has, in fact, done much more, and with consummate skill. Virtually all aspects of central banking are covered in this book so systematically and fairly that it may well turn out to be an indispensable guide-book for both advisers and policy-makers in monetary authorities as well as finance ministries..."

— ***Economic and Political Weekly (EPW)***
Book Reviewed by Dr. K.S. Krishnaswami (Ex-Dy. Governor, RBI)

"Dr. A. Vasudevan has rendered a signal service to all those interested in economic and financial development by writing this comprehensive book. While admittedly, the work is a well-conceived attempt at presenting a reference book for advanced students, it has turned out to be a cross between a textbook and an encyclopaedic reference book. ...The book includes a comprehensive and competent summary of East Asian crisis and the need for a new global financial architecture. ...Dr. Vasudevan's book opens a window on what goes on – and what should go on – in the corridors of central banks."

— ***Business Line***
Book Reviewed by Dr. S. Venkitaramanan (Former Governor, RBI)

"This book is a comprehensive analysis of modern central banking and brings into focus the changing role and content of central banking over the last two decades..."

— ***The Hindu***
Book Reviewed by Dr. T.K. Velayudham
(Former Principal, Bankers' Training College, Mumbai and Ex-Advisor, RBI)

" '...Central banking for such economies [EMEs) has to be dynamic and interactive.' It is this thought that made him write a work of encyclopaedic proportions — which only someone like Vasudevan could do."

— ***Business Standard***
Book Reviewed by Dr. K.V. Krishnamurthy (CMD, Bank of India)

"The information provided and the examples illustrated in the book will be very educative and useful for the professionals, academicians and the students associated with finance and banking. Further, I will recommend the book in particular for the executives of Central Banks of developing countries"

— ***Bank Quest (The Journal of Indian Institute of Bankers)***
Book Reviewed by Dr. Amitabha Ghosh (Former Dy. Governor, RBI)